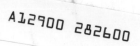

Readings in Rhetoric

Readings in Rhetoric

Compiled and Edited by

LIONEL CROCKER
Department of Speech
Denison University
Granville, Ohio

and

PAUL A. CARMACK
Associate Professor of Speech
Ohio State University
Columbus, Ohio

CHARLES C THOMAS • **PUBLISHER**
Springfield • *Illinois* • *U. S. A.*

Published and Distributed Throughout the World by
CHARLES C THOMAS • PUBLISHER
BANNERSTONE HOUSE
301-327 East Lawrence Avenue, Springfield, Illinois, U.S.A.
NATCHEZ PLANTATION HOUSE
735 North Atlantic Boulevard, Fort Lauderdale, Florida, U.S.A.

*With THOMAS BOOKS careful attention is given to all details of
manufacturing and design. It is the Publisher's desire to present books
that are satisfactory as to their physical qualities and artistic possibilities
and appropriate for their particular use. THOMAS BOOKS will be true
to those laws of quality that assure a good name and good will.*

Printed in the United States of America
H-2

Dedicated to
The Founders of
The National Association of
Academic Teachers of Public Speaking
1914

I. M. Cochran

Loren Gates

J. S. Gaylord

H. B. Gislason

H. B. Gough

Binney Gunnison

C. D. Hardy

J. L. Lardner

G. N. Merry

J. M. O'Neill

J. M. Phelps

F. M. Rarig

L. R. Sarett

B. C. Van Wye

J. A. Winans

I. L. Winter

C. H. Woolbert

PREFACE

MORTIMER ADLER, Director of the Institute of Philosophical Research, has sifted the great ideas of the ages and has reduced them to one hundred and two. Rhetoric is one of these great ideas that can not be dispensed with.

Rhetoric has occupied the attention of man ever since he has been able to communicate with his fellows by language. Rhetoric in these essays is concerned almost exclusively with the handling of ideas orally. When man has sought to persuade, to report, to convince, to impress, to advocate, to entertain, to clear up misunderstandings, he has used rhetoric.

The pages of rhetorical history bear the names of individuals who have made significant contributions to the fund of knowledge of how to use the spoken word effectively. This compendium of essays is focused on such contributors as Corax, Plato, Aristotle, Cicero, Quintilian, Campbell, Blair, Whately, and others. In addition to the essays of interpretation of these rhetoricians, there are a few articles which deal with periods of rhetorical influence. Students of public speaking who are interested in the history of their subject will find in this collection a convenient storehouse of enlightenment and comment.

Can anyone doubt that this is the age of the spoken word? What with radio and television, the movies and dictating equipment, telephones and public address systems, one is surrounded night and day by the human voice. This vocal activity has spurred an intense interest in the theory of how to handle ideas orally. Fifty years ago a collection of essays such as this would have been impossible because the interest of the academic world was largely on the effects of the written word. In fact, Lane Cooper sensed this mounting pressure and in translating Aristotle's *Rhetoric* in 1932 wrote, "But the persons I have kept in mind are the undergraduate and the graduate student of public speaking in America, and the large body of teachers of this subject who have not studied Rhetoric in its sources and otherwise lack a classical background."[1]

In 1964, the Speech Association of America celebrates its fiftieth anniversary of its separation as a discipline from Departments of English and its founding as an organization. The development of undergraduate and graduate programs in speech during this time has been nothing short of phenomenal. Franklin H. Knower in his article, "The Communication Explosion and the Study of Speech,"[2] emphasizes the growth of the study of speech by these statistics: "The average rate of increase for all subject matters over this period in the number of Master's degrees is 137 per cent and of doctorate degrees is 178 per cent. The increase for the field of physics over this period for the master's and the doctorate degrees are 110 per cent and 180 per cent, for Sociology they are 114 per cent and 188 per cent, for English they are 130 per cent and 204 per cent. The number of master's degrees in Speech over this ten year period increased 216 per cent and the number of doctorate degrees increased 500 per cent. Of all specific disciplines granting a fairly substantial number of doctorate degrees, Speech made by far the greatest advance in ratio of degrees to our level of ten years ago. To the extent that doctorate degrees in Speech are an index of growth, Speech can be said to be the most rapidly growing discipline in American universities today."

This growth has been accompanied by a searching of the past for useable ideas in the field of rhetoric and public address. A good example of this attempt to make adequate tools available is this collection of essays. For years these materials were mimeographed and put in the hands of students. We trust that this volume will meet a need. We realize that no anthology can please everyone. We should liked to have included more but space forbids. One can be sure that as time goes on and the interest in the spoken word increases more collections such as this will be made available to the student.

---

[1]Lane Cooper: *The Rhetoric of Aristotle.* New York, Appleton, Century-Crofts, Inc., 1932, p. viii.
[2]*Central States Speech Journal,* Volume *XIV,* Number 4.

ACKNOWLEDGMENTS

THE LATE PAUL A. CARMACK and I wish to thank the many individuals and organizations who have permitted us to draw upon their studies. Our debt to the Speech Association of America, to the Western Speech Association, and the Southern Speech Association for the use of essays from their several publications is heavy indeed. In addition to the blanket permissions from these organizations, we have sought and obtained permissions from each author or authorized representative.

We wish especially to thank: Helen Friend Wagner for articles by her husband Russell H. Wagner, Mrs. E. Lloyd Boutilier for an article by her father James A. Winans, John L. Heller for "Ancient Rhetoric in the Modern College," and Allyn and Bacon for "Two Ideals of Composition" by Fred Newton Scott.

The source of each article is given in the Table of Contents.

L.C.
P.A.C.

TABLE OF CONTENTS

*Abbreviations: QJS, *Quarterly Journal of Speech;* SM, *Speech Monographs;*
WS, *Western Speech;* SSJ, *Southern Speech Journal.*

Readings in Rhetoric

WHAT TEACHERS OF SPEECH MAY LEARN FROM THE THEORY AND PRACTICE OF THE GREEKS*

PAUL SHOREY

University of Chicago†

IT IS NOT EASY to speak on any topic of classical antiquity in these days without wasting time on what should be superfluous apologies. The new education has prepared a class of readers for Wells' *Outline of History* who are ready to swallow blindly his pronouncement that the literature of Rome counts for nothing in our culture and the literature of Greece for much less than it is the interest of the pedants who teach it to claim. I shall take it for granted that this audience does not require a warning against this poisoning of the wells of history and that, though most of you may be too busy to give much time to the study of the classics you all have a notion of the right perspective and truth of the matter, which is quite simple. The ancients did not have the science and the scientific industrialism which the modern world has developed in the past hundred and fifty years. They did have, through a continuous civilization of a thousand years, a literature, a literary culture and an education the equal of our own. This culture, apart from its intrinsic beauty, is historically the chief source of ours. These elementary truisms suffice to make the Greek and Roman classics, whether in the original or in translation, and in spite of all temporary ebbs and flow of fashion far more significant for any genuinely liberal modern education than ever can be the prehistoric anthropologies, the

---

*Read at the Convention of the National Association of Teachers of Speech, 1921.
†The location listed for the authors throughout the book will be the author's location at the time the article was published.

psychologies, and the sociologies which students, recalcitrant to the labor of mastering either science or classics, prefer to substitute for them.

The quickest way to convert a sceptic about the civilization of the Greeks is to bring him face to face with Greek architecture and sculpture. These speak a universal language. But the material of the subject on which you have asked me to speak is perhaps next in effectiveness and universality of appeal to the sincere student. The theory of the ancient rhetoricians and "teachers of speech" could with the aid of a very few technical terms be adequately reproduced in English, provided it were translated and summarized by really competent interpreters. Even as it is, a patient reader can learn a great deal from the "education of the orator" of the judicious Quintilian, which John Stuart Mill often commended as a compendium of the experience and good sense of the ancient world in this matter. If you do not shy and start away at the first diversity of ancient life that strikes you as quaint or odd, but read patiently on, you will find that there are few modern text-books so good and so full of meat. The corpus of Greek rhetoricians published in the nine volumes of Walz and less fully in the three volumes of the Teubner text has never been translated as a whole and the terminological refinements of Hermogenes on "ideas" and the scholiasts on Hermogenes, and the technicalities of the series of nonentities and anonymities who composed arts of rhetoric, Progymnasmata and treatises on figures, would hardly repay the labor of a translation, which would be a *tour de force*. The Loeb series will probably give us the excellent criticisms of the Greek orators and historians by Dionysius of Halicarnassus, and it would be well if it also included the so-called rhetoric to Alexander which, if not, as Jebb pronounces it, the best practical treatise on rhetoric which has come down to us, is at any rate needed for the full understanding of the relation between the philosophic rhetoric of Aristotle and the environment in which it took shape. Meanwhile the best of the Greek doctrine is already available to the English reader in Sandys' edition of Jebb's almost infallible translation of *Aristotle's Rhetoric* and in Roberts' useful editions, with translation, of Demetrius on Style, Longinus on the Sublime, and the Three Literary Letters of Dionysius of Halicarnassus. These translations and the specimens of Hermogenes and other late writers in Jebb's

Attic Orators illustrate the difficulty and yet the possibility of a practically sufficient rendering of the language of the Greek rhetoricians. The difficulty lies in the fact that the Greek vocabulary of rhetoric and literary criticism is richer and more discriminating not only than the English but than the French and English combined and that it is not yet correctly recorded in any lexicon.* Yet the successes of Jebb and Roberts when at their best prove that it is entirely possible for a scholar who fully understands the originals to translate or paraphrase them, with transliteration perhaps of a few of the technical terms in such wise that the English reader would lose little.

That is, of course, not quite true of the masterpieces of ancient oratory. But it is more nearly true, I think, than it is of the other two chief divisions of classical literature, poetry and philosophy. A modern reader may enjoy the story of the Odyssey, the tragic poignancy of the Agamemnon, but he loses what Germany will never know that she misses in Shakespeare, the poetry. There is, and probably can be, no translation that makes it safe for the English-reading professor of philosophy to debate nice points in the philosophy of Plato and Aristotle. But though oratory, too, loses something in translation, it need not lose so much. There are probably no entirely adequate translations of Demosthenes and Cicero. But for a skilful translator, who had the courage to aim at equivalents rather than school-boy literalness, there would be no inherent and insuperable obstacle to the reproduction of almost any effect of ancient oratory without misrepresentation of the thought. If I had half an hour to spare, I would engage myself with all the defects of elocution that would be painfully apparent to your expert ears to translate to you from the open text passages from Demosthenes *On the Crown,* or the speeches in Livy that would make you directly feel, and not merely perfunctorily acknowledge, the equivalence of the mature ancient oratory to the best in that kind of the modern world.

We estimated the life of the ancient culture at a thousand years. I could for our present purpose plausibly add five hundred years to that estimate and appeal to Homer. The Homeric poems describe different styles of oratory, and show a conscious interest in the subject. Glad-

---

*Cf. Ernesti: *Lexicon Technologiae;* Prof. La Rue Van Hook's Chicago dissertation, The Metaphorical Terminology of Greek Rhetoric and Literary Criticism; and the glossaries in Roberts' Dionysius of Halicarnassus, Demetrius, and Longinus.

stone once said that Achilles' reply to Agamemnon's envoys in the ninth
book of the Iliad was the greatest speech in the world. A witty popular
lecturer amuses himself by assuring his audience that Homer's literary
art must be and is as childish and immature a thing as is his science of
medicine. Who shall adjudicate? With ten minutes to spare I would
undertake, the bare text of Homer in hand, to convince nine-tenths of
you that Professor Leacock's statement was an outrageous absurdity
and Gladstone's, at the worst, a pardonable exaggeration.

But Homer tells us nothing of the education of Achilles except that
he learned the healing art from the centaur, whom Pope styles, "sage
Cheiron, sire of pharmacy." The continuous history of ancient rhetoric
and oratory began with the Attic orators nearly five hundred years
after Homer. Democracy, the ancients said, gave birth to oratory in
the revolutions of Sicily and Athens. Men studied the art of speech because their lives and their fortunes depended on it, in the popular assemblies and the popular courts. And the new professors of the art of
speech, often identical with the so-called Sophists, met a deeply-felt
need and were the objects of a cult by ambitious and enthusiastic youth
which is satirically depicted in Plato's *Protagoras and Gorgias*. I pass
over the anecdotes, which you have doubtless read in Jebb's *Attic
Orators,* by far the best book on the subject, though Blass' ponderous
Attische Beredsamkeit retains its value for specialists and J. F. Dobson,
The Greek Orators, London, 1919, is a readable resumé for the hurried
reader.* This Attic oratory covers about a hundred years, from the
speeches of Pericles and Cleon and Hermocrates reported by Thucydides[1] in a tortured style of his own, which no orator ever used and
no audience ever could have understood, to the finished eloquence of
Demosthenes. And from this Attic oratory and from the later Greek
criticism and study of it, and its Roman imitation by Cicero, all the
artistic oratory and nearly all the philosophy of rhetoric and prose style
of the European world are ultimately derived.

What was it like? Even the roughest answer to that question requires
us to distinguish between kinds and periods. The Greek rhetors, like

---

*Useful also are the sketches in Sandys' introduction to Cicero's *Brutus and Wil-
kins' De Oratore,* vol. i., and Cope's elaborate introduction to his edition of
Aristotle's *Rhetoric.*

Cf. The Speeches of Thucydides, in Jebb's *Essays and Studies,* and Shorey in
Trans Amer. Phil. Ass., 1893, pp. 66-88.

Webster, according to Rufus Choate's eulogy, thought different styles appropriate in the court room, before a deliberative political assembly, and in a Fourth of July or epideictic oration. The real Greek oratory is the mature and flexible oratory of Demosthenes and his contemporaries. The early orators interest mainly the student of the evolution of prose style. Some of them, in their first strivings towards mastery of expression, were quaintly stiff and formal, as Antiphon. Others, under the influence of the Sicilian rhetoric, experimented with the florid, antithetic, jingling style of sophomoric ornament, which they called the Gorgian figures, which has at other times been variously known as, *stile culto,* gongorism, or euphuism, and which Miss Amy Lowell dignifies by the name of polyphonic prose, and innocently imagines to be original with herself or her French models. The good sense of the ancients soon laughed polyphonic prose out of court, literally out of court. For Lysias, the model of Attic purity and simplicity, never employs it in his forensic orations, though he toys with it frequently in his perhaps spurious funeral or Fourth of July oration. Plato uses it, half in earnest, half in jest, somewhat in the manner of Ruskin, in his *Menexenus* and in passages of elaborate description or heightened feeling. But parody is never far off, and in the speech of Agathon in the Symposium [197 C] he lets himself go, out Heroding Herod, outgorgonizing Gorgias, outamying Amy to this result:

> "Love brings: to mortals peace, to wind-vexed ocean calm, and to the tired couch sweet slumber's balm. He alienates hostility and conciliates civility bringing us together in such reunions as this, in festivals, dances, and sacrifices, leader and guide. To mildness impelling all wildness repelling, donor of kindness, disowner of unkindness, gracious to the good beheld by the wise, admired by the gods, desired by the hapless and acquired by the happy, of wantonness, daintiness, luxury, grace, desire, and yearning the sire, regardful of the good, regardless of bad, in labor, in terror, in yearning, in learning, guide, consoler, supporter and saviour best, of all gods and men the glory, the leader fairest and rarest whom every man should follow fairly fair hymns reciting wherein delighting he casts his spell on the hearts of gods and men alike."

Demosthenes never made obtrusive use of this florid ornamentation. And all the sober critics of later antiquity deprecated its abuse, and

restricted its use within the narrowest limits. Nevertheless florid ornament is an instinct of human nature on a certain level of culture. And
during the eight hundred years after Demosthenes it was often revived
from the so-called Asian rhetoric, which Cicero contrasts with the
soberer teaching of the Rhodian school, to the conceits of the Latin
declaimers reported in the entertaining book of the elder Seneca, the
extravagances of the radical wing of the so-called new Sophistic, or
Greek revival under the Roman empire, and the elaborate ingenuities
of the style of Apuleius, which Walter Pater makes the text of an
apology for his own style in *Marius the Epicurean.*

The text-books of later antiquity that transmitted the classical heritage of the Middle Ages were largely composed in one or more of these
florid, jingling, antithetic, euphuistic, and mannered styles. And the
Renaissance combined this tradition of the Middle Ages in fine writing
with its own renewed study of the theory of Greek rhetoric, and the
practise of the Gorgian figures in Isocrates in the style which in England took the name of Euphuism, and which is parodied in Shakespeare's *Love's Labor Lost.*

The history which I have thus sketched is detailed in Norden's chaotic but instructive book, *die Antike Kunstprosa.* Norden traces the
origins of the flamboyant style back to philosophers and poets who
preceded the Silician rhetors, and, as is the way of philologers when
they exaggerate a thesis, he assumes that all modern euphuisms are
directly traceable to these sources, whereas they are often, of course,
merely the expression of the sophomoric taste of the natural man. Even
at the height of the fashion of Euphuism sensible Renaissance critics
judged it as the more rational critics of antiquity had done. Our histories do further injustice to some of the practitioners of Euphuism in
the older English literature by failing to recognize the strict limits
within which most of them confined it. They adopted the distinction
of the ancients that polyphonic prose, though unsuitable for business
uses, was appropriate for set-pieces, epideictic displays, and compliments. Very sober writers, otherwise, employ it in complimentary dedications of their books to King James or other noble patrons; and to
quote these specimens, as is usually done, without noting this distinction is to convey a false impression of their prevailing good sense.

Having followed this historical digression to its conclusion, we return to our question, What is Greek oratory, the real Greek oratory of Demosthenes, like? De Quincey says that Greek oratory is emotional, illogical, irrelevant to a degree that a modern jury or deliberative assembly would not tolerate. But De Quincey loved a paradox; the statement is the reverse of the truth. Greek lawyers and politicians were no more scrupulous than others of their kind, in the means they used to carry their point. But Greek oratory, and Demosthenes in particular, is more, not less, rational and consequently argumentative than the oratory of the modern world. The first impression made by Demosthenes on the untrained modern reader is disappointment at the absence of eloquence. He does not satisfy the expectation of readers habituated to the exuberant rhetoric of the Ciceronian tradition that descends through Burke and Webster. There is nothing in Demosthenes remotely resembling Prentiss' "He who taught the eagle of our country, while yet unfledged, to plume his young wing and mate his talons with the lion's strength;" or the peroration of Webster's reply to Hayne; or Ingersoll's "plumed knight"; or Garfield's "the coming fight is our Thermopylæ"; or Proctor Knott's "zenith city of the unsalted seas"; or Bryan's "cross of gold"; or Roosevelt's "we stand at Armageddon." Charles Sumner was our scholar in politics, yet there is no better example of what Demosthenes was not than the overloaded outburst in his Kansas-Nebraska speech:

> "It has already drawn to its bosom a population of freemen larger than Athens crowded within her historic gates when her sons under Miltiades won liberty for mankind on the field of Marathon; more than Sparta contained when she ruled Greece and sent forth her devoted children, quickened by a mother's benediction, to return with their shields or on them; more than Rome gathered on her seven hills when under her kings she commenced that sovreign sway which afterward embraced the whole earth; more than London held when on the fields of Cressy and Agincourt the English banner was carried victoriously over the chivalrous hosts of France."

That is not unlike the style of some of the later and more degenerate Greek rhetoricians. Sumner read Greek, but he had not mastered the first principles of Greek art, *meden agan*.

And strangely enough the best illustration I could give you of what

Demosthenes *is* like would be Lincoln, who knew no Greek, but who was educated, not by electives in sociology and anthropology, but on Shakespeare and Blackstone, *Euclid,* the *Bible* and the *Constitution of the United States.* I would not overstrain the parallel. Lincoln of course produced no such body of finished oratory as has come down to us from Demosthenes. He never underwent Demosthenes' long and severe discipline in the art of rhetoric and the practise of speaking. But he is far more like Demosthenes than is Charles Sumner or any other American orator whom I could name. He is free alike from the old-fashioned florid southern oratory and from the quaint mixture of Bowery slang and sophomoric declamation that too often passes for eloquence in Congress today. He does not strain after epigram and conceit, indulge in cheap classical allusions or mix his metaphors. His Gettysburg speech shows, I think, that he had read Pericles' funeral oration in Thucydides. It may be that he had looked through a translation of Demosthenes, for he must have associated with many statesmen, who, like Mr. Bryan, had read Demosthenes *On the Crown* at college and didn't care who knew it. At any rate he affords the best modern illustration of the prevailing seriousness of the Demosthenic logic, suffused with, but not overmastered by emotion. He has the Demosthenic power of crowding an opponent into a corner, forcing him to a definite issue by a swift succession of inevitable and unanswerable questions. And he resembles Demosthenes also in the incomparable effectiveness of the sudden flashes of passionate eloquence introduced at just the apt place, and confined to the right measure. There have been many vain attempts to translate Demosthenes' oath taken by those who fell at Marathon, belauded by critics from Longinus *On the Sublime* to the present day. But there is perhaps no better way to realize its effect than to reread the much simpler and slighter, but similar surprise that thrilled the audience to thunderous applause in Lincoln's Kansas-Nebraska speech: the battle of freedom, he said, "is to be fought out on principle. Slavery is a violation of the eternal right. We have temporized with it from the necessities of our conditions. *But as sure as God reigns and school-children read,* that black, foul lie can never be consecrated into God's hallowed truth." Rufus Choate, apologizing for the scream of the American eagle, says that higher laws than those of taste determine the consciousness of nations: "There is an eloquence of an expiring nation, such as seems to sadden the glorious speech of Demosthenes . . . and there is an eloquence of a state beginning to ascend to the first class of power . . . and conscious of itself. It is to no purpose that they tell you it is bad taste." These words were spoken in 1853 before Lincoln became prominent. The resemblance of Lincoln's logic to Demosthenes' may be partly due to his practise in debate and partly to the fact that, like Demosthenes, he lived in and for and with one great patriotic idea, which he mastered in all its details and applications. The miracle of Lincoln's Greek sense of measure and his self-emancipation from the florid taste for which Choate half-apologizes in himself and Webster I cannot explain. We may say it was his genius, and we may fancy that it was the saddening and sobering effect of the fratricidal conflict, whose imminence haunted his dreams.

But we must not press this analogy to the point of forgetting that Demosthenes was what Lincoln was not, the inheritor of an elaborate culture, the severely-trained and conscious master of all the arts of speech and rhetoric. He is too great an artist to display his art obtrusively. The unsophisticated reader feels it only in the secure frame work of the logic, the lucid disposition of the whole, the relief of argument by narration and of both by touches of eloquence, denunciation, and if not humor an *ethos* that had the effect of humor, in the union of dignity, vigor, naturalness, and purity in the vocabulary, the escape from monotony by apt variation of phrases, by rhetorical question, irony, apostrophe, figures of speech, figures of thought and tropes, the rhythms, carefully calculated not to irritate the ear by harshness, or tease it by long successions of short syllables, or disgust it by too soft and facile and obviously poetical cadences.

All these things and the qualities, good and bad, of Lysias, Isocrates, and the other Attic orators, were analyzed, classified, and technically named by the contemporaries of Demosthenes and still more by those later Greek schools of rhetoric which taught, imitated, and commented on his orations for seven hundred years. This, together with the Philo sophic rhetoric that began with Plato, which was carried on by Aristotle and the Stoics,[1] and was more or less blended with the other in the writings of Cicero and Quintilian, constitutes a huge body of

---

[1] *Striller de Stoicorum Studiis Rhetoricis.*

rhetorical theory and literary criticism which it would be useless for me to attempt to summarize here. It is still being actively and critically studied by philological specialists in Germany and America.[2] The main outlines of the doctrine are summed up in Volkmann's *Rhetorik der Griechen und Römer* and for style more especially in Gerber's *Die Sprache als Kunst*. Much of it, like much in modern handbooks of rhetoric, is trivial and hair-splitting, multiplying terminology for terminology's sake. And some of the treatises collected in Walz are only less silly than medieval scholasticism or twentieth century educational psychology. But there is hardly an idea of distinction of modern rhetoric and literary criticism of prose style that cannot be found somewhere in the mass.

For seven centuries all educated ancients knew something of this body of doctrine, and many had made a special study of it. Most educated men at the Renaissance knew something of it, cither at first hand, or from translations and paraphrases in the vernacular. Today it is forgotten by all but specialists. Yet if we are to study and analyze oratorical expression and prose style at all, there is much both in its substance and its terminology that would save us from intellectual confusion and futile logomachy.*

It is easy to ridicule the subtlety which having made necessary distinctions goes on to make unnecessary ones. A notable passage of Plato's *Phædrus* (266-67) set the fashion of this satire and reads almost like a prophecy of the prodiorthosis, epidiorthosis, amphidiorthosis, the epanalepsis, anadiplosis, and epanaphora, the pareklasis and the paradiegesis of the later rhetoricians. But all the terms which the Greek language so readily coins have some meaning, and many become indispensable categories of the thought, permanent additions to the vocabulary of anyone who has once learned their application. Thesis and hypothesis, ethos and pathos, peribole, ongkos, emphasis in its true meaning, kakozelia, the "fond affection" of Puttenham, deinotes, gor-

---

[2]Cf. Shorey: Classical Studies in America, *Trans. Amer. Phil. Ass., 50*:48 and 54. The Drerup series there mentioned now includes nine studies.

*Saintsbury: *History of Criticism*, I, 87-108, gives a general notion of the matter in readable form. But he cannot be trusted in details or in the translation of rhetorical terminology. E.g.; the specimen passage from Hermogenes on p. 100 is completely misunderstood, though it is fairly well explained in Volkmann, p. 259. Cf. also Saintsbury, p. 25 with Shorey: Phusis, Melete, Episteme, *Trans. Amer. Phil. Ass., 40*:185.

gotes, semnotes and the rest. The higher culture of the Renaissance, as I have said, retained this doctrine in memory for a century. Now it is as completely forgotten as the logic of the schoolmen. We can dispense perhaps with the distinction between aition, synechon, and krinomenon or that between a hyperthetic and a parenthetic hyperbaton or an epanaphoric and an antistrophic comma. We can be content not to discriminate diegesis and aphegesis, epicheireme and enthymeme, energeia and enargeia. We need not blush if we cannot define an epembolic hypostrophe or decide offhand whether Demosthenes' apostrophe to Aeschines is to be classified as an example of "method" or "schema." But some tincture of this learning is still needed for the intelligence of our own literature. A letter of Tennyson shows him composing his earlier poems with a view to effects which he describes in the terminology of Dionysius of Halicarnassus. And though an eminent scholar speaks of Shakespeare's presumed "ignorance of all the figures catalogued by Puttenham," the fact is that Sakespeare had evidently studied them in some Elizabethan handbook and consciously endeavored to realize their suggestions in his own writing. To take the most obvious example, I wonder what proportion of those engaged in teaching literature today are quite clear in their minds about the difference between the ancient and the present-day use of the expression, "figures of speech," or could sharply distinguish a figure of speech from a figure of thought and from a trope. Yet Shakespeare who had small Latin and less Greek, knew. When Polonius says, " 'Tis true 'tis pity, and pity 'tis 'tis true, a foolish figure but farewell it, for I will use no art," he employs figure in the correct ancient sense. And when Hamlet says, "the Mouse-trap. Marry, how Tropically," he is aware of the difference between a figure of speech and a trope. Even so widely-read a critic as Mr. Gosse apparently is not. He calls Sir Thomas Browne's "tropically" "one of his odd turns of phrase" with no hint that to Browne it wasn't odd at all—but elementary education.

After the Attic orators the next and only other age of real political oratory was the century of Cicero. But through the seven or eight hundred years remaining of ancient civilization the oratory of the courtroom and the declamation of the schools were assiduously practised. And there are always opportunities in every civilization for the epideictic oratory of compliment and display and the due celebration

of functions and occasions.* Throughout these centuries the higher
education, the high-school and college education so to speak, of the
Greek or Roman gentleman, centered in the study of either of rhetoric
or of philosophy, or, more rarely, of both in combination. The link
between these two competing systems of education was the treatment
of the theory of rhetoric by the philosophers. This began with Plato,
or with the sophists whom Plato satirized. Plato's dialogues on rhetoric,
the Gorgias and the Phaedrus, either as wholes or in extracts, were always read or lectured on in the rhetorical as well as in the philosophical
schools. Cicero, for example, read them with his professors at Athens,
[De Or. I. 11] and their influence is to be felt in nearly everything he
wrote. Quintilian [II. 15, 24] complained that those who hastily read
only a few extracts did injustice to Plato. History repeats itself in our
schools of education today. The Gorgias is a bitter assault upon the
rhetoric of the politician, the lawyer, and the professional teacher,
from the point of view of the absolute, philosophical, and ethical ideal.
Gorgias accepts the definition of rhetoric as the art of persuasion and
pleads that it is no more reasonable to blame its teachers for the occasional misuse of this faculty than it would be to complain of the
teachers of boxing because an unruly boy had boxed his father's ears.
Socrates denies that rhetoric is an art or science at all. It is only a trick
of flattery, like Sicilian cooking, or the imitation of the hues of health
and exercise by lip-stick and rouge. The persuasion that it effects, is
opinion, not knowledge. It is taught and practised at Athens, not as
an indispensable means of the social control of the multitude, for their
own good, but as an instrument of selfish profit, and of advancement
in the courtroom and the assembly.

The questions thus started were debated throughout antiquity and
are still, under other forms, discussed today. I myself can hardly resist
the temptation to digress and preach from the text that our own teaching of rhetoric is too much concerned with the success of the speaker
and too little with the edification of the audience. It is more interested
in the "psychology" of "putting it over" and "getting it across" than
in the training of the habits of logical analysis and suspense of judgment that would enable an audience to resist such hypnotization. Yet

---

*Cf. Dr. Theodore C. Burgess: *Epideictic Literature,* University of Chicago Studies
in Classical Philology, vol. III.

the greatest service which high school and college education could render to America today would be, not to multiply the number of fluent, plausible, and self-confident speakers, but to create in every audience a resisting minority that cannot be stampeded by plausible sophistry and emotional volubility. But that would be a digression, and I have no moral authority to enforce my preaching, so I return to history.

The practical sense of Aristotle, disregarding Platonic idealism, accepted Gorgias' plea that the abuse of rhetoric does not discredit the use. He added the consideration nobly developed in Milton's *Areopagitica* and still used to justify partisan advocacy in the courtroom, that truth and right are inherently stronger than wrong, and will, in the end, gain more by the development of the arts of persuasion. The quibble that a science or art must achieve its end and that the orator does not always, in fact, persuade, he met by the distinction that the end of rhetoric is not to persuade, which may be impossible in a given case, but to speak persuasively. Quintilian, four hundred years later, discussing the various definitions of rhetoric, has a sentence which would be enigmatic without reference to this distinction. He says, eliptically and cryptically, "some have abstracted from the outcome." That is my translation of 2. 15. 2: *quidam recesserunt ab eventu.* I had the curiosity to look the passage up in the new Loeb translation by Professor Butler. It is there rendered: "some on the other hand pay no attention to results."

The specific question started in Plato's Gorgias, whether rhetoric is an art or a trick, was discussed with an excess of ingenuity in the later Peripatetic and Epicurean schools. Echoes of these debates have also come down to us through an Epicurean essay, fragments of which have been rescued from the charred rolls of Herculaneum, and somewhat conjecturally translated, or paraphrased by Dr. H. M. Hubbell of Yale in the Transactions of the Connecticut Academy for September, 1920. The Epicurean view seems to have been that the study of ornamental and epideictic style may be in a sense an art, but that there is no rhetorical science of political persuasion for the government and good of mankind.

Plato's *Phædrus* will seem to the hasty reader an incongruous confusion of the two themes, Platonic Love and rhetoric. We cannot delay for that. The discussion of rhetoric and the theory of style are associated with the critical comparison of two sample speeches of Lysias and Socrates on Platonic Love. Very amusing and not without a significance for today is Plato's satire of the tautologies and the superfluous terminologies of contemporary rhetoric. But he himself, somewhat scornfully, outlines a program for a rhetoric of the future which if based on psychology and dialectic might be an art of science. Such a rhetoric would analyze and classify ideas, on the one hand, and types of mind and temperament on the other. It would then proceed; such and such a mind is accessible to, easily persuaded by such and such arguments for such and such reasons. That would be the teachable theory and science of rhetoric. But practical success as an orator requires in addition natural gifts and long practise.* The acquisition and mastery of a style is no light task. It is hardly worth while to undertake that labour to curry favor with your fellow-slaves, but only to please the gods. In other words, the higher function of the art of speech is to write philosophic masterpieces, not to convince Athenian juries. The greatest masters of all the arts of style have often affected this disdain for their cunning. Plato says that no elaborate prose style can dispense with an element of jest and unreality. Renan speaks of his own talent as almost a sin before the altar of the higher intellect. And Ruskin alludes with playful disparagement to his youthful knack of putting his words together prettily.

Though Aristotle rarely neglects an opportunity to contradict his old teacher, he evidently wrote with a card-catalogue of Plato's notable passages on his desk. The main body of the *Rhetoric,* the first two books, is a working out of Plato's idea that if rhetoric is to be more than a rule of thumb it must be a combination of logic and ethical psychology. The book is accessible in many translations, and Jebb's summary of it in the article "Rhetoric" in the *Encyclopædia Britannica* is better than any that there is time for here. All the rhetorics that stress chiefly the logic of persuasion are derived from this. Much of what Aristotle has to say runs parallel to one of his neglected, but most significant, logical works, the *Topics.* Topic for us, means a subject, a theme. It also means for us, as it did for Cicero, and the later Greeks

*Cf. Shorey: *Phusis, Melete and Episteme.*

and Romans, a commonplace, which an orator may prepare and use as needed, a declamation against luxury or profiteers or rolled stockings.

But for Aristotle it further meant a typical form or method of argument. It is not really, as some of the ancients already said, any more possible to classify arguments exhaustively and definitively than it is figures or tropes or etymologies or jokes or associations of ideas, or dreams, or a university library by the Dewey system. But the Aristotelian and Spencerian type of mind will always be tempted to try. Observing for twenty or thirty years the philosophic, the forensic, the political debates of fourth-century Athens, Aristotle could not be happy till he had reduced this immense chaotic experience to order, and found a fit pigeon-hole and label for every type of argument and oratorical device that he had collected in his *zettel*. He did not of course succeed. Even to understand his classification requires close attention and some historical knowledge of Athenian life and politics.* And after the system is understood, every ingenious thinker will be ready with a better classification of his own. Nevertheless, it is the most original and stimulating part of the Rhetoric. It made a great impression on Cicero, who never quite understood it, but relished the idea of a provision of commonplaces and a bundle of tricks which would never leave an orator in the lurch. Cicero's own work, entitled *Topica,* is a very superficial and inaccurate sketch, scribbled, so at least he affirms, from memory and far from books, at the solicitation of a friend.

The third book of *Aristotle's Rhetoric,* by hypercriticism thought spurious[1] deals with what is most prominent in modern rhetoric, style (diction, and delivery), vocabulary, metaphor, and other ornaments, false taste, rhythm, the adaptation of style to the three kinds of oratory, forensic, deliberative and epideictic, the ordering of the parts or subdivisions of a discourse or speech and the tone appropriate to each, and similar themes. The *Poetics* goes over some of the same ground from the point of view of poetry. From the two derive all European theories and criticisms of style. The history of the *Poetics* does not concern us, further than to fix its relation to the oratorical tradition. The Roman empire, like the British, educated its future rulers, not in the

*On the meaning of "topic" cf. Grete's *Aristotle,* vol. I and Jebb's translation of the *Rhetoric,* pp. 12 and 142.
[1]Cf. however, Hendrickson, in *A. J. P., xxvi*:251.

college of commerce and politics, but by the reading of old poetry and the practise of new verse composition. Mr. H. G. Wells would say that that was the reason why the Roman and the British empires were such egregious failures. At any rate that was in fact their education. But in the Roman scheme the poetry was preparatory and subordinate to the study and practice of oratory. They, if I may so express it, reversing our practice, put Virgil in the third year of the high school and Cicero in the fourth. The object of the poetry was to develop the linguistic sense, impart general culture, quicken the imagination, and especially to enlarge the vocabulary. When that was accomplished, the professor of classics turned the boy over to the more serious ministrations of the professors of speech. The consequence of this was, that the literary criticism of antiquity is predominantly the criticism of prose, and especially of oratorical style. Not exclusively of course. Aristotle's *Poetics,* Horace's *Arts Poetica,* and Longinus' *On the Sublime* represent another line of criticism well worth studying. But Cicero and Dionysius of Halicarnassus and Quintilian, Hermogenes and the great mass of the Greek rhetoricians, considered style chiefly from the standpoint of oratory, and Quintilian's survey of the history of literature (Book x) estimates poets by their contribution to the formation of the taste, the logic, and the vocabulary of the orator.

To return a moment to the *Rhetoric of Aristotle* as a whole, it of course had other sources than Aristotle's card-catalogue of Plato. The fourth century successors of the Sophists developed a considerable literature of rhetoric, the results of which Aristotle, before composing his own *Rhetoric,* characteristically collected or had his students collect in a compilation called the *Synagoge of the Arts* (art of rhetoric, that is). The work is lost, but its fragments have been collected by industrious Germans.* Aristotle also, as the numerous quotations and anecdotes in his *Rhetoric* show, drew much from his observation of the actual practise of the Athens of his day.[1] The chief influence here, besides Plato, was Isocrates, who for fifty years conducted a rival school to the Platonic Academy and the Aristotelian Lyceum. Isocrates after a few experiments in youth, did not speak in public himself, but com-

---

*Cf. especially Spengel's *Artium Scriptores,* a repertory of texts and anecdotes exploited by all later writers. Navarre's *La Rhetorique Grecque avant Aristote,* Paris, 1900, is readable.

posed in the form of orations, treatises and pamphlets on problems of the day, political, social and educational. He read these essays or had them read to his pupils, and encouraged them to discuss, analyze, criticize, and imitate these performances. He maintained that this was a better and more practical education that the "mental discipline" which the dialectics, the metaphysics, the mathematics and the astronomy of the rival school supplied. Isocrates was also what we call a "stylist." In epideictic pieces he made a moderate but unmistakable use of the Gorgian figures, the antitheses, the balancings and the jingles of polyphonic prose.* And this was perhaps the most conspicuous feature of his influence on certain minds, and at certain periods. But his own mature judgment would have attached more importance to his care in the choice and discrimination of vocabulary, the flow and harmony of the rhythm, the avoidance of hiatus, of harsh combinations of consonants, and the inelegant repetition of the same syllable in such collocations as "an antagonist," or "in ineptitude." He is, through Cicero and Burke, the chief source of the smooth, rounded, grammatically impeccable, unelliptical long sentence in periodic style which the present generation finds so intolerably pompous, hollow, and monotonous. Isocrates was much relished also as a moralist by the scholars of the Renaissance.* The recent revival of interest in him is, I must be permitted to say, since it is true, in part German and radical propaganda. The radicals like to oppose him to what they fancy was the metaphysics of the absolute and the dogmatism of preaching in Plato. The Germans and their accomplices or dupes in England and America set the fashion of using his flattery of King Philip to disparage the futile patriotism of Demothenes, whose eloquence only fostered the illusion that an undisciplined democracy could resist the mighty Beamtenstaat of the North. This idea is now being widely inculcated in America by Mr.

---

[1]He set the fashion of illustrating the principles of rhetoric by quotation from the literature. This constitutes a large part of the charm of Longinus and lends a kind of interest to the silliest treatises of the most degenerate of the later rhetoricians. The rhetorics of Apsines and Hermogenes are almost analytic commentaries on the orations of Demosthenes. The *Rhetoric to Alexander* and the so-called *Auctor ad Herennium* (in Cicero's works) represent the opposite practice, the uses of examples invented by the writer.

*Cf. the Chicago dissertation of John F. Hollingsworth on: Antithesis in the Attic Orators.

*Cf. Shorey: Isocrates, in Hasting's *Encyclopaedia of Religion and Ethics.*

H. G. Wells and in textbooks of Greek History, manufactured by
professors who, like the present speaker, hold a German degree and
unlike him, were made or remade in Germany. Professor Goodwin's
edition of the oration *On the Crown* is the indicated antidote. And so
long as that kind of propaganda continues, I acknowledge no impropriety in answering it and exposing it whenever an audience grants
me a hearing.

The two and a half centuries that followed the death of Demosthenes and Aristotle witnessed the extinction of genuine political oratory, the expansion of the schools of rhetoric and the declamation of
the schools both as an end in itself and as a preparation for the bar,—
and lastly the elaboration of the technique and terminology of what
became the common body of Græco-Roman rhetoric.

True political eloquence is the child of liberty, as the history of British, American, French, and German oratory would suffice to show. It
can flourish only where the votes of parliaments and people determine
the destinies of states. After the death of Cicero Greek and Roman
critics both recognized this truth, which the Greeks could not be expected clearly to forsee at the death of Demosthenes. Many besides
Quintilian wrote treatises on the cause of the decline and corruption
of eloquence and found the dominant cause in the loss of the old political freedom. Tacitus' *Dialogue on Orators* has an eloquent peroration
on this theme. And there is a fine passage to the same effect in Longinus
On the Sublime.

The declamation of the schools supplies the material of a facetious
or ironical chapter in nearly all recent histories of Greek and Roman
literature.* It could be made—I have sometimes myself made it—the
theme of a more entertaining lecture than this. But I think that the
summary I am attempting will be more profitable. The beginnings
could easily be traced back to the Sophists who preceded Aristotle, and
to that school of Isocrates, from which Cicero said as from the Trojan
horse a line of princes of eloquence emerged. But later tradition attributed to Demetrius of Phalerum, who ruled Athens circ. 317-310 B. C.
shortly after the death of Demosthenes, the institution of the practise
of formal declamation on imaginary and scholastic themes. Another

---

*Cf. Simcox: *Latin Lit.* 1, VIII, p. 433ff, "The Declaimers;" Summers: *Silver
Age of Latin Literature,* pp. 3-15.

tradition told of the foundation of the rhetorical school of Rhodes by Aeschines who went into exile after his defeat by Demosthenes. His chief stock-intrade and texts were his own oration *Against Ctesiphon* and Demosthenes' *On the Crown.* When his audience admired the latter, he said, "You should have heard the brute recite it himself." Whatever its origin the practise of declamation became a conspicuous feature of ancient education, culture, literature, and social life for 700 years. Cicero for many years declaimed daily in both Greek and Latin, and at the height of his youthful reputation visited Greece, Rhodes, and Asia Minor for several months' study in the schools; which is as if Webster after the reply to Hayne or Mr. Bryan after the *Cross of Gold* had taken up a course in the study of rhetoric at a German university.

One Latin and one Greek book are the two chief sources of modern facetiousness on the topic. The Latin book is the volume of the elder Seneca on *Suasories and Controversies,* from which Ben Johnson's *Discoveries* copies entire paragraphs without acknowledgement. A suasory was a speech advising Sulla to resign the dictatorship, or Hannibal to retire from the gates of Rome, or Wilson not to go to Paris. As an instrument of education it was not so silly as it sounds. For to write a good suasory you had to get up all the circumstances and think yourself into the life and character of your personage. A controversy was a debate for and against some proposition of ethical casuistry or real or fancied law embodied in an imaginary case. The writing and declaiming of suasories and controversis was the crown and consummation of the education in rhetoric which began with the reading of the poets and the writing of innumerable daily themes in the forms of fables, narrations, descriptions, moral anecdotes and other exercises, many text-books of which have come down to us under the title of Progymnasmata, or propædeutic exercitations.* In the school the students declaimed to one another and to the teacher, whom the satirist Juvenal commiserates when he must listen to a numerous class as it slays the bloody tyrant. The teacher also declaimed specimens of his own eloquence to the class, who were expected to applaud. There were open days on which fond parents could attend to hear young hopeful declaim. There were public exhibitions to which the orator invited his

---

*Saintsbury: *History of Criticism,* vol. 1, p. 89ff, is fairly full on these.

friends as the new poets did to their recitations. In short the pursuit of amateur literature by culture-chasers under the Roman Empire anticipated and surpassed the achievements of our old-fashioned American women's clubs before social service and the ballot diverted them from the idea of nemesis in Greek tragedy to the league of nations and the milk supply of Kalamazoo. The Greek side of the movement is known to us from Philostratus' *Lives of the Sophists* nearly 200 years later than Seneca's book. The Sophists mean now, not the old targets of Socratic irony, but the so-called "new" Sophists, or teachers of rhetoric, itinerant lecturers and practioners of *ex tempore* declamation in all the foremost cities of the Roman empire, from Asia Minor to the Scottish wall. Philostratus recounts the lives of a large number of these gentry, relates many anecdotes about them, and gives brief specimens of their eloquence, their conceits and their "epigrams."

The relative advantage of *ex tempore* and prepared speaking were debated in antiquity as they are today. There is an amazingly modern essay on the subject by one Alcidamas, a contemporary of Isocrates and Plato. The more sober ancients recognized the fact which sentimentalism and vanity vainly try to hide, that nearly all the best oratory of the world has been written and memorized. They esteem memorizing one of the most difficult and important divisions of the whole art of oratory, and their precepts and suggestions on the subject have left very little for the modern pseudo-science of psychology to add. One of the best, but by accident least-known, of all the doctoral dissertations which I have guided is the treatise of Miss Hazel Louise Brown, *Extemporary Speech in Antiquity,* which is full of information that some clever person will sometimes plagiarize with inpunity. It runs through the whole history of ancient oratory and collects the evidence that the ancients memorized their speeches, adding many illustrations in proof of the fact that this is also the actual, though concealed, practise of most modern orators. The genuinely *ex tempore* speaker is always liable to such accidents as befell ex-president Taft, as his lecture is reported in the Rice Institute Pamphlet (VII, 2, April, 1920, p. 77); "Just read," he cried, "how Queen Elizabeth lived; cold palaces, buggy-beds, —everything that we now regard as indispensable to the reasonable comforts and cleanliness of modern life!" In antiquity the artistic school naïvely admitted that the object of memorizing was to produce an illusion of improvisation. Quintilian laments that if the later arrival of a distinguished visitor constrains you to repeat a memorized declamation it is very difficult to lie. For you can hardly help repeating it in the same words. Philostratus tells the story of a professor who by calling on his friends in the audience would always procure the proposal to him of a theme for *ex tempore* declamation on which he was already prepared. A malicious rival took his speech down by short hand and the next time he extemporized it read the manuscript in competition like a prompter. But though some virtuosos practised improvisation, and all strove for the appearance of it, the artistic school affected to disdain this crude volubility. No one, said Quintilian, can extort my admiration for mere fluency and a flux of words, a thing in which any two quarreling women superabound. The ancients perceived as clearly as we do the defects of an education based merely on this artificial rhetoric. They anticipated most modern satire of culture-chasing and amateur literature, and there is little that Shaw, Wells, Dewey, and their imitators can say in denunciation of the alleged divorce of the school from "life" that could not be matched in the fulminations of some classical critic. The reason why boys are made so stupid at school is that they learn nothing there that concerns real life, says Petronius Arbiter. The Ohio school superintendent who uses the word "life" forty-six times in seven pages in his first chapter would say amen to that.

Much of the ancient criticism is more special. It expresses the practical lawyer's distrust of the unreality of mind engendered by the practise of irresponsible declamation. The topics treated were often hair-splitting, casuistical, romantic, fanciful. And in the development of such questions Quintilian observes we always interpret in our own favor every point not explicitly against us in the statement of the case. Moreover, the declaimer seeking the applause of student or of a dilettante audience was tempted to substitute conceits, epigrams, or flights of fine writing for serious argument on the theme. Quintilian, Seneca, and Philostratus give examples of the so-called epigrams which would match the choicest specimens of twentieth century smartness. "Our up-to-date style," Quintilian caustically remarks, "does not really achieve many epigrams. But it gets everything off as if it were an epigram."

The unreality of the closet orator exhibited itself in other ways. He

abused the figures of rhetoric he had learned at school and soared
into eloquence inopportunely. "Why," exclaimed one of these novices,
apostrophizing his opponent in court, "Why are you turning the stern
gaze of those truculent eyes upon me?" "Well, in fact I wasn't," interrupted his hard-boiled adversary; but since you will have it so, here
goes." And he made a horrible face at the youth which convulsed
the jury and spoiled the speech.

That kind of criticism requires only common sense. The poet Martial
has an epigram on a young lawyer who would practise the Charles
Sumner style of oratory in the municipal court.

> 'Tis not for murder, arson, or assault
>   I've brought this action, but three goats I own
> Which now are missing by my neighbor's fault.
>   That is the thing the judge wants to be shown.
> But you of Cannae and the furious
>   Wars waged with perjured Carthage and the name
> Of dire Mithridates, Mucius,
>   Of Marius and Sulla, still declaim,
> With fervent gestures and stentorian throat.
> Now Postumus, say a word about my goat.

And yet with time I would be willing to maintain the thesis that
despite the overweighting of the literary side, it was not a bad education. Generalized and qualified it remained the basis of French education until quite recently. It was not so good for many purposes as a
severe discipline in mathematics and the real sciences,—not perhaps
so good as a sound study of language and a critical interpretation of
great literature. But it was more effective and a better education than
that which now muddles the undergraduate mind under the elective
system in the preposterous predominance of the pseudo-sciences psychological, sociological, prehistorical, and anthropological in all their
multitudinous ramifications and pretended applications. However that
may be, its significance for the history of culture can hardly be over-
estimated. To this is due the oratorical quality of Roman literature
which De Quincey brings out so well in his essay on rhetoric. Livy is,
as Taine's brilliant monograph shows, essentially an orator. There are
good critics who enjoy the speeches in his history more than they do
the orations of Cicero. Virgil is almost as much of an orator as a poet.
Many of the finest passages of Juvenal's fierce satires are obvious motives of declamation borrowed from the schools. Ovid distinguished

himself in the schools and two of the finest speeches in the world—the contention of Ajax and Odysseus for the arms of Achilles in his *Metamorphoses*—are really but familiar themes of the declaimers reproduced in hexameter verse.

But it is time to turn back and finish our historical survey. The third feature of the interval between Demosthenes and Cicero was the development of the technical theory of rhetoric. As in the parallel case of the evolution of logic, there was not really much to add to the fundamental ideas of Plato and Aristotle. But the ingenuity of the later schools and especially of the Stoics elaborated and refined unweariedly in definitions, distinctions, classifications, terminology, and practical precepts, and in so doing hit upon many interesting minor ideas of education, psychology, the logic of debate, and the literary criticism of style. The detail of this is infinite and would swamp us here. The literature is lost, and we have to reconstruct the doctrine from Cicero's quotations and the Greek writers of the first four Christian centuries. While style and diction were not neglected, attention seems first to have been concentrated by the Stoics on the logic of forensic argument. In the decline of political eloquence the oratory of the court room absorbed their interest. A certain Hermagoras won great fame by his theory and classification of what was called the *status* or in Greek the *stasis* of a case or question. It has been the theme of many erudite German dissertations—some of them partly right, many of them largely wrong.* The best brief notion that I can give of it is that it closely resembles the logic of the old English doctrine of the determination of an issue by successive pleadings. It was an attempt to classify and name all possible sorts of debatable questions by the issue on which they turned, and like all would-be exhaustive categories it was foredoomed to failure. Quintilian handles it gingerly merely to show that he is not wholly ignorant, and dismisses it with disdain as mere Greek pedantry. There were similar attempts at exhaustive and final classification of all figures of speech, tropes, and ornaments of style. They are interesting enough for any one who has time to study them—which the editors of Liddell and Scott's Greek lexicon have obviously not done—but they are mentioned here only as a warning to all prospective authors of analyses of literature and new systems of re-

---

*Cf. Thiele: *Hermagoras.*

forming rhetorical and critical terminology. The Greeks have been
there before.

For practical and cultural purposes the essence of it all is in Cicero's
rhetorical works. Cicero has suffered in the estimate of the fastidious
by his ambition to be the Roman Demosthenes and Plato, with neither
of whom he or anybody else can sustain the comparison. Too docile
American pupils have sometimes followed his Prussian detractors in
sneering at Cicero's unavailing opposition to the imperious autocratic
genius of Cæsar. And, as we have already seen, the Ciceronean amplitude and flowery fluency of style are now out of fashion. None the less
Cicero remains in Matthew Arnold's words the first man of letters of
the ancient world, or to phrase it more ambitiously, he is the central
figure in the history of European culture.* In addition to all his original achievements in oratory and statesmanship, it is he who mainly
transmitted to the Middle Age, the Renascence, and the Eighteenth
Century the knowledge of what constituted Graeco-Roman culture for
1000 years—the philosophy in his philosophical works, the rhetoric in
his *De Oratore*, his *Brutus, or History of Roman Oratory*, his *Orator,
or Ideal of the Perfect Order*. They are not Platonic dialogues. There
is no dramatic rendering of the cut and thrust of real debate. That
would ruffle senatorial dignity, and the grave Romans left such logo-
machies to Greek levity. But when they retired from the wealth and
the smoke of Rome and the roar of the insane forum to their luxurious
villas overlooking the Campagna or the Bay of Naples, they discoursed,
or Cicero loved to fancy that they did, in reminiscences of their studies
at the university of Athens or of the lectures that they had dropped
in to hear in the intervals of Eastern campaigns and diplomatic missions. It is a pretty if idealized picture of the culture of the Roman
nobility, resembling that which Matthew Arnold sketches in his essay
on translating Homer, of the culture of the eighteenth century nobility
of England.

Cicero's senators, after an interchange of stately compliments and
a few remarks on Roman and world politics, agree to discuss some
large subject of their Greek studies. They will discuss it, not as Greek-
lings and Sophists, but as Romans, statesmen, lawyers, and men of the

---

*Cf. Zeilinski's: *Cicero im Wandel der Jahrhunderte,* and the readable summary
of it by A. C. Clark in *English Literature and the Classics,* Oxford, 1912.

world. Each of the speakers is assigned a topic or aspect of the general subject, which he presents in what is probably Cicero's imitation of the best recent Greek book he had read, or lectures he had heard. But Cicero imitates freely, introduces much from his own reading of Plato and Aristotle, something perhaps of the conversation of Greek philosophers who had been inmates of his household, and adds his own reflections and many illustrations from Roman history and literature. The *De Oratore* is the best of these compositions. For here Cicero can speak out of a richer personal experience than fell to the lot of any Greek theorist. Whatever slips a specialist may detect in the verification of the quotations or in the accuracy of the translations of Greek technical terms, there can be no doubt that Cicero had a life-long familiarity with the principles of Greek rhetorical theory. He did not seem to cram them up for his book. And so he writes with a freedom, a sweep, a mastery that make his treatment much more interesting than any professorial text-book could be. The discussion takes the form of a debate on the old rhetorical question: Is the orator a tricky specialist—master of an art of knack of words, or must he be a broadly and philosophically educated man? But a much more definite significance is given to the problem by the fact that the speakers are Roman senators who can draw their arguments and illustrations from a long experience in the practise of the Roman law. At times we seem to be listening to English statesmen, recalling the parliament of Burke and Fox, at times to American lawyers telling stories of cases in which Choate was pitted against Webster. In the frame work and interstices of this debate Cicero contrives to insinuate a sensible and readable account of the main body of Greek rhetorical doctrine in which the technicalities are rapidly and sometimes contemptuously summarized, while the interesting ideas or practically helpful suggestions are brought into the foreground. The book has been well-edited and is accessible in translations. It is the best introduction to the more detailed and prosaic work of Quintilian, and to the more special study of the Greek sources.

Here I must break off rather than come to an end. You would not in any case wish me to recite to you the names of the countless Greek rhetoricians who continued to rewrite every form and type of rhetorical treatise in the next four or five, nay ten or twelve centuries. Still less

to enumerate all the hair-splitting refinements of their definitions, divisions, classifications, and terminologies. With more time I might have
tried to entertain you with the dry humor of some of the precepts of
Quintilian's caustic common sense:

Don't try to write better than you can.

Dress is not the chief requisite in an orator, but it is the most
conspicuous.

When you have to strain your voice, put the strain on your ribs,
not in your head.

What these modern stylists call punch is really intoxication.

To register emotion is not a figure.

A man can pretend to be a philosopher and get away with it, but
you can't simulate eloquence; you have to deliver the goods.

But have I answered the question, what is there in it for you as
students and practical teachers of the theory and "art of speech"? I
might repeat that somewhere in this vast body of ancient rhetorical
literature you will find at least a hint of every useful idea that modern
study of the subject has suggested, and that in the four or five best of
these old books, these ideas are presented with a directness, simplicity,
lucidity, and above all an immunity from the infections and pretensions
of pseudo-science that few ambitious modern text-books attain. But
you may reverse the argument and say that all that these ancients have
to teach can also be found somewhere in the best literature, French and
English, of today if one knows where to look for it. That is true, and it
is not easy in the present temper of the world to prove to anybody
who is not already convinced, the necessity of the value of anything
that used to be called culture, of any knowledge of the past, or for
that matter of any study of theory except perhaps engineering, or indeed of any higher education. You can become a millionaire or a
senator without any of these things. And animal spirits, vivacity,
fluency, magnetism and a good voice will make a very effective popular
orator of a man who has never heard a philosopher or opened a book
of rhetoric and literary criticism.

I am tempted to fall back on vague generalities, on the old-fashioned
notion that a specialist ought to have at least enough intellectual
curiosity to study the history of his own specialty; or on Cicero's saying that not to know about anything that happened before you were

born is to remain always a child. But this again would carry weight only with those already persuaded. Having spent all my life in studying the literature and thought of the past and trying to link it with the thought and literature of the present in the larger unity of the human spirit,[*] I should feel baffled and helpless in the face of an uncompromising and implacable modernism that cares only for those things whereof the memory of a flapper runneth not to the contrary.

Our query is in another form the old problem, what is the value of history? The most obvious answer would be its direct explicit lessons and their immediate application to the problems of today. But those who have reflected most profoundly, felt most nobly and spoken most eloquently about history would not put it in that way. The too-hasty and overconfident exploitation of historical analogies for immediate use in political life, is the mark of the fanatic and the sciolist. History may be philosophy teaching by example, but the lessons are often obscure and the interpretation doubtful. What is not doubtful is that some acquaintance with the great human story and the intelligence of the unity of the human spirit can be won only in this way, and once won will enlarge the vision, deepen the sympathies, quicken the imagination, make supple the intelligence, and so help us to become better scholars, better teachers, and better men.

---

*Cf. Shorey: The Unity of the Human Spirit, in *Representative Phi Beta Kappa Orations,* Boston, 1915.

ANCIENT RHETORIC IN THE
MODERN COLLEGE COURSE IN SPEECH

JOHN L. HELLER

Allegheny College

In a recent note, Tacitus on Changes of Style in Public Speaking *(The Classical Weekly, 28:*112) Professor Henry C. Montgomery raises a point which, it seems to me, calls for further discussion. With the observation of Tacitus *(Dialogus De Oratoribus,* I) on the disregard in which the earlier masters of oratory were then held he aptly compares the modern distaste for formal oratory and all things connected with it. "Even the nomenclature has changed," Professor Montgomery says. He calls to witness the fact that fifty years ago the members of a College faculty who were entrusted with the instruction of youth in the accurate and effective use of language were known as Instructors in Rhetoric or Oratory, whereas to-day the corresponding teachers are styled Professors of Speech.

This is, indeed, an undeniable fact. On the other hand, I believe that an examination of the *material* actually taught in the modern classes in Speech would reveal that in many respects it is very much the same as it was, not only fifty years ago in collegiate courses in Rhetoric, but also in the days of Quintilian or Cicero or Aristotle. Moreover, there still are institutions, such as the Jesuit Schools, in which the study of Rhetoric (not Speech) is proudly and thoroughly based on ancient precept and practice[1a]. The truth of the matter is, not that *even* the nomenclature has changed, but rather that, while

---

[1a]See the excellent books of the Rev. Francis P. Donnelly, S. J.: *Persuasive Speech,* New York, Kenedy, 1931, and *Principles of Jesuit Education in Practice,* New York, Kenedy, 1934.

names have changed, the thing itself is still the same. Let me quote from Professor Baldwin:[2]

The only art of composition that concerns the mass of mankind, and is therefore universal in both educational practise and critical theory, is the art of effective communication by speaking and writing. This is what the ancients and most moderns call rhetoric . . .

A convenient illustration is furnished by the outline for the "organization of material" for written and oral speeches which is taught to the Freshmen at Allegheny College, under the direction of Professor Anderson.[3] This is, in very brief form, as follows:

A. Introduction: 1) To secure good-will; 2) To secure attention; 3) To prepare audience; 4) To suggest speech purpose.

B. Body. This is subdivided, by means of parallel columns, into 1) Outline, 2) Illustrations, Examples, etc., 3) Facts, Authority, etc.

C. Conclusion: 1) To round out thought; 2) To summarize; 3) To appeal to basic wants.

Now, this can be demonstrated to be very similar to the order of the parts *(dispositio)* of a speech as laid down by the ancient rhetoricians. In the following discussion I have attempted to summarize and reduce to conformity the directions concerning this topic that are given in five ancient treatises: 1) the *Ars Rhetorica* of Aristotle, 2) the *Rhetorica ad Herennium* by an unknown Roman teacher of about 85 B. C., 3) the early handbook of Cicero, *De Inventione,* 4) Cicero's later sketch, *Partitiones Oratoriae,* and 5) the *Institutio Oratoria* of Quintilian.

Aristotle (3,13,4) says that the necessary parts of every speech are the statement of the case ($\pi\rho o\theta\epsilon\sigma\iota s$) and the proof ($\pi\iota\sigma\tau\iota s$), although in some speeches he admits a four-fold division, prefixing to these two an introduction ($\pi\rho oo\iota\mu\iota o\nu$) and adding a conclusion ($\epsilon\pi\iota\lambda o\gamma o s$). Without attempting to point out here more than a surface resemblance between the two, I remark that the modern three-fold division ap-

---

[2]Charles S. Baldwin: *Ancient Rhetoric and Poetic,* 6, New York, Macmillan, 1924. <For a review, by Professor George C. Fiske, of this work see *The Classical Weekly, 19:*62-63. C. K.>.

[3]*The Manual in Oral and Written English,* prepared by Professor Hurst B. Anderson, consists chiefly of duplicates of this outline, with directions for its use. Copies of the *Manual* may be procured from the Allegheny College Book Store, Meadville, Pennsylvania.

pears to omit the προθεσις of Aristotle. A closer inspection, to be undertaken below, will show that the προθεσις is not really omitted, but is included by Professor Anderson (see note 3, above) as the fourth subhead of his Introduction. This is not in itself particularly striking. An examination of what the Latin handbooks on rhetoric have to say under the topic of *dispositio* is more illuminating.

The *Auctor ad Herennium* (1,4) asserts that there are six main parts of a speech: *exordium, narratio, divisio, confirmatio, confutatio, conclusio.* Cicero, in his youthful treatise *De Inventione* (1,19), lays down the same six divisions (with a slight change in nomenclature, be it noted): *exordium, narratio, partitio, confirmatio, reprehensio, conclusio.* Quintilian (3,9,1) reduces them to five: *prooemium, narratio, probatio, refutatio, peroratio.* He shows, with much justice, that the method of the *partitio* (enumeration of points to be covered) might be followed in any part of the speech, and that therefore the *partitio* is not to be regarded as a complete division in itself. If it may further be assumed that the *confirmatio and the refutatio* of the Romans, when they are taken together, are merely two parts of Aristotle's general heading πιστις,[4] then there is general agreement that there are only four essential parts of a speech: *exordium* or *prooemium, narratio, confirmatio, conclusio.* This is exactly the position assumed by Cicero in his later manual, *Partitiones Oratoriae.*[5] The Roman rhetoricians agree with Aristotle, assuming that *narratio* is the same as προθεσις and Aristotle (I invert the chronology) agrees with Professor Anderson's outline.

The only point that remains to be settled is the equivalence of the Roman *narratio* with the προθεσις of Aristotle. *Narratio* is a translation of διηγησις, which, Aristotle admitted (3,13,3), was generally

---

[4] Aristotle (3,13,4) mentions refutation as a part of the proofs: τὰ ὁϱλ τὸνπϱὸs ἀντίδικον τῶν πίστεών ἐστι. The *Auctor ad Herennium* gives no separate treatment to *confirmatio* and *confutatio*, but discusses them together. He shows clearly (1,18) that he regards them as the main body of the speech: Tota spes vincendi ratioque persuadendi posita est in confirmatione et in confutatione. Nam cum adiumenta nostra exposuerimus contrariaque dissolverimus, absolute nimirum munus oratorium confecerimus.

[5] He names them thus (4): *principium, narratio, confirmatio, peroratio.* He explains his synthesis (33): C.—Nempe ea sequuntur quae ad faciendam fidem pertinent. P.—Ita est: quae quidem in confirmationem et in reprehensionem dividuntur.

accepted in his time as a full part of the division. He objected
to it as a term on the grounds that a full and detailed 'rehearsal'
(διηγσις) of antecedent events was proper only to forensic speeches
(λογοι δικανικοι, genus iudiciale), and that his own term πρoθεσις,
'statement of the facts', was applicable also to epideictic and demonstrative speeches.[6] But the problem is, once more, merely a matter of
nomenclature, for the Romans recognized clearly enough that *narratio*
was essentially a statement of the facts of the case, and that actual
narration was not to be used in all types of speeches.[7]

The most interesting part of the evidence, however, is to be found
in a comparison of Roman theory with Professor Anderson's outline
for the Conclusion and especially for the Introduction. On the purpose of the *exordium* there is universal agreement. This is well stated
by Quintilian (4,1,5) : "The reason for a beginning is merely to induce the audience to be more ready to hear us in the rest of the speech.
This can best be done by three things, as almost all authorities agree—
if we render the audience *well-disposed, attentive, tractable*."[8] Now,
these three aims of the *exordium* are exactly the first three points in
Professor Anderson's Introduction, where they are given in Quintilian's
order: 1) To secure good-will, 2) To secure attention, 3) To prepare
the audience. The first two points require no comment. The third is
explained by the *Auctor ad Herennium* (1,7): "We shall be able to

---

[6] See John H. Freese: *The "Art" of Rhetoric of Aristotle*, 424, note (The Loeb
Classical Library, 1926).

[7] The *Auctor ad Herennium* (1,17) thus defines *narratio:* Primum [per narra-
tionem] debemus aperire quid nobis conveniat cum adversariis, quid in contro-
versia sit. The text cited in the preceding sentence is that of Wilhelm Freidrich,
M. Tulli Ciceronis Opera Rhetorica, 1 (Leipzig, Teubner, 1893). Quintilian says
(4,2,1): Maxime naturale est et fieri frequentissime debet, ut, praeparato per
haec quae supra dicta sunt iudice, res, de qua pronuntiaturus est, indicetur. Haec
est narratio.

[8] *Benivolum, attentum, docilem.* Cicero: *De Inventione* 1, 20, agrees with this
completely; in *Partitiones Oratoriae*, 28, he varies the form of his expression and
the order: *ut amice ut intelligenter, ut attente audiatur.* The *Auctor ad Herennium*, 1,6 uses the same words in a different order: *ut attentos, ut dociles, ut
benivolos auditores habere possimus.*

[9] *Dociles auditores habere poterimus, si summam causae [breviter] exponemus.*
Again I cite Friedrich's text (see note 7, above). The meaning of the term *docilis*
is explained with admirable lucidity and scholarship by the Rev. Francis P. Donnelly, S. J.: A Function of the Classical Exordium, *The Classical Weekly*, 5:
204-207.

render the audience tractable, if we briefly give the substance of the case."[9]

But Professor Anderson's Introduction has a fourth subhead: To suggest speech purpose. This, it is now possible to show, is nothing more than the *narratio* of the Romans or the πρόθεσις of Aristotle. Quintilian (4,2,1, cited in note 7, above) defines *narratio* simply as the statement to the *iudex* of the points on which he must come to a decision, i.e., the points which the speaker will attempt to prove. This should come immediately after the *iudex* has been put in the proper frame of mind by the Introduction. Indeed, Quintilian himself has some doubt as to whether the *narratio* is not better included as a subhead under the *prooemium,* and discusses this question at some length (4,2,24-30).

I come now to the Conclusion. Professor Anderson's outline recognizes three functions of the Conclusion: 1) To round out thought, 2) To summarize, 3) To appeal to basic wants. The lore of the Roman rhetoricians is somewhat different here. They all recognize the need of a summary *(enumeratio)*. All (except Cicero, in *Partitiones Oratoriae,* 52) put it first. Cicero, however, follows Aristotle (3,19,1) in reserving the summary for the very end. The other function of the Conclusion was to arouse the emotions *(affectus).*[10] No reader of ancient oratory can fail to feel the stress laid by the orators upon an appeal to the emotions. Except for Cicero's later treatise, all the Roman manuals make this the final and most emphatic point. The first two of these even distinguish appeal to two separate emotions, anger or indignation, and pity.[11] This is surely the purpose of Professor Anderson's category, "appeal to basic wants."

The problem of the first point, however, is impossible to solve in terms of the ancient rhetoricians. "To round out thought" is not the ancient *amplificatio (Rhetorica ad Herennium,* 2,47; Cicero, *Partitiones Oratoriae,* 52), which is rather a stronger statement of certain facts for the sake of arousing indignation. Nor is it the αὔξησις of

---

[10]Quintilian, 6,1,1, 9. Aristotle (3,19,1, 3) states this clearly: εἰς τὰ πάθη τὸν ἀκροατὴν καταστῆσαι.

[11]See *Rhetorica ad Herennium,* 2,47-50, and, for a clearer statement, Cicero, *De Inventione* 1,100, *Indignatio est oratio per quam conficitur ut in aliquem hominem magnum odium aut in rem gravis offensio concitetur,* and 106, *Conquestio est oratio auditorum misericordiam captans.*

Aristotle (3,19,1; 2,18,4-2; 19,27), exaggeration for the sake of intellectual conviction, not emotion. Perhaps we may best assume that, just as the formal beginning (to suggest speech purpose) of the main body of the speech was included as the last point in the Introduction, so, in the first point of the Conclusion, we have a formal close to the argument, bringing all its points to a full stop.[12]

It is thus evident that, except for a few minor alterations, the directions given to the college freshman today for the arrangement of his speeches are exactly the same, both in general and in particular, as the lore on the same points to be found in the classical rhetoricians. Now, this similarity is not to be attributed to any conscious imitation of the ancients on the part of the moderns,[13] but rather, I suspect, to two things. First, college courses in rhetoric fifty years ago would have been based very closely on the work of the classical rhetoricians. Their lore would have become a part of the modern tradition of rhetoric.[14] Secondly, modern emphasis on the practice of speaking[15] would have rediscovered certain principles grasped long ago by the ancients, and thus the modern (but traditional) theory might be modified where it became too rigid. In either case, we should recognize that, while the nomenclature of modern rhetoric may be altered, the matter itself is still the same.

However, there has indeed been a change in nomenclature, testifying, no doubt, to the desire on the part of modern educators to get away from the connotation of such exceedingly classical words as

---

[12]Professor Anderson (see note 3, above), to whom my thanks are due for his helpful criticisms, confirms my interpretation here. In his Outline, he would stress the functional rather than the categorical aspect. Hence it might often happen that the speaker would be obliged to omit or to combine various points, or to change their order. Accordingly, the first function of the Conclusion, before a detailed summary is begun, is to intimate in general terms that the end has actually been reached, in other words, "to round out the thought."

[13]Indeed, Professor Anderson assures me that this is not the case with his Outline, although he also expresses his admiration for such a work as the *Institutes of Quintilian*.

[14]Charles S. Baldwin: *College Composition*, 135, New York, Longmans, 1928, does, indeed, cite the traditional parts of an argumentative speech, giving the Latin names, according to Quintilian, in a note. Francis P. Donnelly: *Persuasive Speech* (see note 1a, above), naturally devotes much space (73-199) to the parts of the speech and a discussion of each part.

[15]Compare the words of the *Auctor ad Herennium* (1,1): *si te unum illud monuerimus, artem sine adsiduitate dicendi non multum iuvare. . . .*

rhetoric or oratory. Insofar as the teaching of those subjects fifty years ago tended to become traditional, unimaginative, cut-and-dried, it was bound to create a reaction against the classical sources from which it drew its substance. This is a great pity, for modern teachers of speech might still find much to learn from the ancients, themselves no mean practitioners in the art of speaking. One should always remember that, at a time when facilities for the distribution of the written word were so infinitely more restricted than they are at present, there was a correspondingly greater emphasis on the use of the spoken word and likewise a greater effectiveness in that use. Insofar also as the vast increase in the numbers of those seeking an advanced education brought about a diminution in the amount of formal knowledge of language which the students might be expected to possess, it was natural and necessary that some practical effort be made to close the gap between the old theoretical course in rhetoric or logic, based on *written* composition, and the earnest desire of students clamoring for a mastery of the principles of good usage, for practice in public speaking, and for an elementary knowledge of rhetorical theory. If classical rhetoric refused to demean itself to that level, to be concerned with matters of grammar and diction, then a new Department of Speech must take its place. Its program and its nomenclature were designed to avoid the forbidding aspects of a classicism too remote from the needs of the students or too difficult for their interests. But, at the same time, its theory and many parts of its actual material were bound to remain pretty much what they have always been.

I should say that the moral of all this is to be found in the words of the *Auctor ad Herennium* (1,1): *nam illi, ne parum multa scisse viderentur, ea conquisiverunt quae nihil attinebant, ut ars difficilior cognitu putaretur.*[16] Surely it is worth while to preserve a conscious sense of the tradition behind all modern knowledge, but all teachers, and especially teachers of the Classics, should realize that their tradition

---

[16]The reader will be glad to learn that in the latest anthology of Latin prose and verse for use in College courses portions of the *Rhetorica ad Herennium* have happily been rescued from the oblivion to which they are usually consigned. See Professor Dean P. Lockwood: *A Survey of Classical Roman Literature,* 1,152-160, New York, Prentice-Hall, 1934. Professor Lockwood likewise calls attention to this sentence in his Preface, xii.

should not be allowed to become static, and thus remote from the present, but must adapt itself, must, in a word, be alive.

CORAX AND PROBABILITY

BROMLEY SMITH

Bucknell University

ANALYSIS

"To oon kakon kakou Korakos" wrote a punning scholiast[1] centuries ago. *"Mali corvi malum ovum"* echoed a Latin commentator, as he handed on the story. Both were expressing an opinion that Tisias, a pupil of Corax of Syracuse, was a bad egg because laid by a bad crow *(korax)*. The occasion which caused these humorous remarks was a lawsuit in a Greek court between the pupil and his master. Corax is said to have demanded pay for his lessons in rhetoric, arguing as follows, "You must pay me if you win the case, because that proves the worth of my lessons. You must pay me also, if you lose the case, for the court will issue a decree against you. Either by our stipulation or by judgment of the court you fail. What's the use of going on with the case?" To this Tisias replied, "I will pay you nothing, because if I lose the case, your instruction has been worthless; whereas if I win, the court will absolve me from the claim." The judges, unable to solve the dilemma, probably postponed their decision in the usual way, while they cracked the bad egg joke already related, at the expense of both parties.[2]

Being now pleasantly introduced to the litigious authors of the first text-books on art—in this case, rhetorical art—, we are about to become more intimately acquainted with them. Both happened to be

---

[1]Prolegomena to Hermogenes, in Walz's *Rhetores Graeci*. Syidas, quoted by Hamilton.

[2]Syidas, quoted by Hamilton: *Logic*, Lecture XXIII. A similar story is related of Protagoras and his pupil Euathlus by Aulus Gellius, c. 10.

Sicilian Greeks in those marvelous days when a real Marathon was run, when Xerxes lashed the Hellespont—days when:

> *"A king sate on the rocky brow*
> *Which looks o'er sea-born Salamis,*
> *And ships, by thousands, lay below,*
> *And men in nations;—all were his!*
> *He counted them at break of day—*
> *And when the sun set, where were they?"*

Those were the days when the great despotism, symbolized by the huge cables that bound Europe to Asia, was broken; and with it innumerable small tyrannies in the Grecian world. Marathon and Salamis meant more than the defeat of Asiatic despots; they meant the establishment of democracy among the Hellenic peoples. This was true not only on the continent, but also on the island of Sicily. Hard by old Aetna great Gelo ruled with an iron hand—he who became so inflated with his own importance that he signified his willingness to aid Sparta, Athens, and Corinth in the struggle with Persia, provided that he be made generalissimo of all the forces.[3] Thereon was boss of Agrigentum; while Thrasydaeus held the reins in Himera.[4] Hiero patronized Pindar, Simonides, and Aeschylus. Phalaris moulded a hollow brazen calf that he might gloat over the cries of victims as they roasted within.[5] Panaetius took the seat of authority in Leontini. Cleander and Anaxilaus left their names as leaders in Gela and Rhegium. Thrasybulus had been advised by Periander "to cut off the tops of the tallest ears of corn, meaning that he must always put out of the way the citizens who overtop the rest."[6] Evidently he followed the advice of his fellow tyrant, for Diodorus tells us that during the eleven months of his tyranny he put to death many citizens, banished others by false accusation, and seized their property. By so doing he aroused such indignation that a revolution began which overthrew not only Thrasybulus, but also the other tyrants of the island. Universal freedom having been acclaimed, governments more or less democratic were set up everywhere (B. B. 467).[7]

---

[3] Ilerodotus: *VII*, 161, 162.

[4] Ousted in 472 B.C.

[5] Diodorus: *IX*, 20.

[6] Aristotle: *Politics, V*, 10, 13.

[7] Diodorus: *XI*, 67, 5; 68, 5. *Tás de allás poleís tás tyrannounmenás é phrourás echousás eleutheurósantes apokatestásan tais polesi tás demokratiác.*

What was Demos to do with his newly acquired independence? For one thing he began to talk; he could not help it, for as Democritus once remarked, "The sign of liberty is freedom of speech." For a while he probably talked in order to experience the pleasure of hearing himself talk, but soon he betook himself to the ecclesia and the court room. Liberty of speech brought with it responsibility, the responsibility of making laws and interpreting them. At this point Demos made a discovery—even as he did in the time of the French Revolution; even as the Germans and the Russians are now doing—that the order which seems to prevail under the dominion of a single will, gives way to apparent chaos when the many attempt, without experience, to rule themselves. Politics, law-making and court-room procedure always mean a divergence of ideas. Out of the innumerable disputes in Sicily after the revolutions, rhetoric was born—proof of which fact will now be given.

Mention was just made of court-room procedure, because one of the questions that bothered the Trinacrians was the ownership of the land. Of course, the original Sikels were not considered as having any title—they were serfs bound to the soil. The descendants of the Greek colonizer, however, on returning from the banishment, to which they had been sent by the tyrants, naturally recalled the days when their fathers owned the estates and held the offices, conditions which gave their claims the precedence, at least in their own minds. Opposed to them, however, were the favorites of the former tyrants, men to whom the estates had been given, sometimes a whole generation before the revolutions. Then came Demos, loudly declaring that the land was his because he tilled it and because, just at that moment he controlled the legislature, the courts, and the army. In fine, the old oligarchs and the concessionaires of the late tyrants found themselves face to face with the possessors of the soil. Very similar are the conditions today in Mexico, where the former peons have taken possession of the land held by the descendants of the conquistadores of by the friends of Juarez, Diaz, and Co., heads of pseudo-republican administrations that succeeded the Spanish dominion. Naturally the haciendados will carry their cases into court as soon as the political wheel turns. So also, Ivan Ivanovitch and Hans of Deutschland-uber-alles will soon be reaping a harvest of lawsuits when the junkers and titled heads recover their breath. Nowadays, of course, the rival claimants will hire lawyers who will attempt to find precedents for the enlightenment of the judges, forgetting, it may be, that revolutions often overthrow precedents as they establish society of a new basis. In the days of Sicilian upheaval, however, there were no lawyers, but each free man according to the Greek custom pleaded his own case.[8] It soon became evident that the best speakers, those who won applause and verdicts, possessed something which was lacking in their opponents. What was that something? A study of the speeches made in the courts and of those delivered in the assembly, when laws were being considered or when some prominent citizens was about to be handed an olive leaf,[9] led to the discovery that the ability to organize or marshal material was helpful and that the skilful, persuasive handling of winged words was necessary. The man who made the discovery, who wrote the first treatise on the art of the orator *(rhetorike techne)*—the first text-book on art of any kind—, and who began to give lessons in public speaking[10] according to a system, was Corax of Syracuse.

Concerning the man we know nothing. He was born, he died, yet his name remains as the founder of rhetoric.[11] We must content ourselves with an examination of the contents of the treatise, first, however, running briefly over the evidence that he really wrote such a work. As in the cases of Protagoras[11] and Prodicus[12] our knowledge of the text, because no fragment of the original has survived, must be gleaned from stray references by various authors. Curiously enough, what information they do give is generally connected with his pupil,

---

[8]Thycydides: *VII,* 55. "The Sicilians were the only cities which the Athenians had encountered similar in character to their own." *Id.:* VIII, 96. "The Syracusans who are most like the Athenians fought best against them." Jowett, tr.

[9]Diodorus Siculus: *XI,* 86. In Athens the oyster shell was used when voting banishment, whence ostracism *(ostreon,* oyster) ; in Syracuse, the olive leaf was used, whence petalism *(petalon,* leaf).

[10]Scholiast on Hermogenes: Tisias was a pupil of Corax. *"Mathétés tou Korakos."*

[11]It is sometimes stated that Erupedocles made the first observations or rules concerning rhetoric. Diogenes Laertius: *VIII,* 57. Aristotle in *The Sophist* remarks: *proton Empedoklea rhétorikén heurein.* Quintilian states (*III,* 1) : *Primus movisse aliqua circa Rhetoricen Empedocles, dicitur.* But we are absolutely ignorant of anything that the philosopher may have written on rhetoric.

[12]See the rhetorical study on Protagoras: The Father of Debate in the *Quart. J. Speech Ed.,* March 1918.

[13]Prodicus of Ceos: The Sire Of Synonymy, in *Quart. J. Speech Ed.,* April 1920.

Tisias. Both Greek and Latin writers seem fond of coupling their names, altho one is occasionally mentioned without the other. For instance, Cicero in his *Brutus* refers to both, as follows: "Aristotle, therefore, informs us that the tyrants were expelled from Sicily, and private property, after a long interval of servitude, was secured by the administration of justice, the Sicilians, Corax and Tisias, (for this people in general were very quick and acute, and had a natural turn for disquisition), first attempted to write precepts on the art of speaking. Before them, he says, no one spoke by prescribed method, conformably to rules of art, tho many discoursed sensibly, and generally from written notes."[14] As this remark of Aristotle occurs nowhere in his extent writings it is surmised that Cicero probably had in hand the lost *Synagoge technon,* wherein an account was given of the systems of Greek rhetoric.[15] In another place Cicero remarked that "no writer on the art of rhetoric was even moderately eloquent, going back as far as Corax and Tisias who appeared to be the inventors and first authors of rhetorical science."[16] Some years later Quintilian, having apparently been over the same ground, bears witness: "The first who laid down rules for rhetoric were two Sicilians, Corax and Tisias."[17]

So much for the evidence of authorship in which the two are mentioned together; another phase occurs in which each is mentioned without the other. The *Rhetoric to Alexander,* which was probably an early work of Aristotle's, speaks of two works, one by himself and another by Corax.[18] If Aristotle wrote the book, he forgot it when he penned the *Sophistical Elenchi,* for therein he overlooks Corax, as he mentions those "who discovered principles rhetorical made but little

[14]Cicero: *Brutus,* 12.

[15]That Cicero had read the lost work is known from his statement in *De Oratoriae,* II, 38: "I have read the book in which he explains the rhetorical systems of all who went before him, as those in which he gives us some notions of his own on the art." Again, in *De Inventione,* II, 2: "Aristotle indeed has collected together all the ancient writers on the art, from the first writer on the subject and inventor of it, Tisias, and has compiled with great perspicuity the precepts of each of them, mentioned them by name, after having sought them out with exceeding care."

[16]Cicero: *De Oratoriae,* I, 20.

[17]Quintilian: *Institutio Oratoria,* III, 1: *Artium autem scriptores antiquissimi Corax et Tisias Siculi;* II, 17: *doctores artis sero jam et circi Tisiam et Coraca primum repertos.*

[18]*Rhetoric ad. Alexander,* 1, 17.

progress, but men who are now celebrated (receiving, as it were, by succession from any who promoted art by parts) have increased it: Tisias after the first authors, but Thrasymacus after Tisias, Theodorus after him and many others, and brought together many particulars, wherefore it is no wonder that the art has a certain multitude of precepts." What has become of Corax? Note the expression "Tisias after the first." The first was probably Corax, for Aristotle specifically mentions him in his *Rhetoric* (II:24:11) as we shall presently note therein, but omits Tisias.

The same trick is played by Plato in the *Phaedrus,* for he draws from Socrates these words: "I cannot help feeling that this is a wonderfully mysterious art which Tisias has discovered, or whoever the gentleman was, or whatever his name or country may have been, who was the discoverer."[19]

Enough has been said on the question of authorship. For those who may be curious as to the details of individual, or joint, authorship, the researches and opinions of Verrall[20] and Hamberger,[21] both of whom have thoroughly thrashed out that phase, are valuable. There seems to be no doubt, in spite of the fact that his name does not always appear, that Corax composed a treatise on rhetoric, which was probably the first.

What was in that treatise? Here again we must be content with scanty gleanings. In the first place we learn from the *Prolegomena ad Hermogenem* that Corax defined rhetoric. He called it the art of persuasion *(peithous demiourgos).*[22] The definition indicates that at a very early date men had discovered the value of pleasant, agreeable, delightful speech. They had observed the effect of honeyed words, uttered by some sweet-voiced Nestor, advocating, urging, counselling, advising, recommending. Those who could speak fitly, prudent words were heard with rapt attention by their fellows. They had their way in the hearts and minds of men. To discover the secret of the enchanters, to set it down in a book, to reduce to rules the methods of the successful orators, became the task of the rhetoricians. Quite generally they agreed on the function of their profession. Apollodorus, for

---

[19]Plato: *Phaedrus,* 273, C. "Whoever the gentleman was"—was probably Corax.
[20]Korax and Tisias, *Journal. of Phil., IX,* 1881.
[21]Hamberger: *Die Rednerische Disposition.* Paderborn, 1914.
[22]Walz: *Rhetores Gracei, IV,* 19.

instance, said that "the first and supreme object of judicial pleading is to *persuade* the judges, and to lead him to whatever opinion the speaker may wish." Patrocles called it the "power of finding whatever is persuasive in speaking." Ariston agrees, for he defines it as "the science of discovering and expressing what ought to be said on political affairs, in language adapted to *persuade* the people." Cornelius Celsus is of the opinion that it is used when the orator wishes "to speak *persuasively* on doubtful and political matters."[22a] Pass on to Aristotle, who regarded "rhetoric as the faculty of discovering or finding in any question presented that which is adapted to produce *persuasion,* or the possible means of *persuasion.*"[23]

Agreeing apparently with the ancients, a modern authority or two may be cited. Whately, for instance, says "the province of rhetoric . . . in the narrowed sense would be limited to *'persuasive speaking.'* " Sir Richard Jebb calls it "the art of using language in such a way as to produce a desired impression upon the hearer or reader. The object is strictly persuasion, rather than intellectual approval or conviction."[24] The *New English Dictionary* defines rhetoric as "the art of using language so as to *persuade* or influence others." With such an array of authorities in practical agreement on the definition, Corax is certainly in the best of company. The honor of defining the subject that he taught is not, however, the only honor that must be conferred upon the ancient Sicilian.

The second crown due Corax must be awarded because he named the parts of a discourse. Strange as it may seem, men had delivered speeches for hundreds, perhaps thousands of years, but no one had analyzed those speeches. Corax listened to the pleas in the courts, to the addresses in the forum with the mind of a philosopher. He perceived that the majority of those harangues might have five divisions: the *prooimion* (proem, exordium, or introduction), the *diegesis* (narration), the *agon* (struggle, argument, proof), the *parekbasis* (digression, subsidiary remarks), and finally the *epilogos* (peroration, or conclusion).[25] There is some dispute, however, as to the number of

---

[22a]These authorities are quoted from De Quincey's *Essays on Style, Rhetoric, and Language,* P. 140. Edited by F. N. Scott.

[23]Arist: *Rhet.,* I, 2.

[24]Jebb: Rhetoric, in *Encyclopedia Brittanica.*

[25]Walz: *Rhetoric Graec.,* IV, p. 12.

these divisions ascribed to Corax. For instance, Doxopatros and an unknown writer attribute to him only a tripartite division—exordiu, argument, and peroration.[26] Further, after a careful study of all available sources Hamberger came to the conclusion that Cicero, Sopatros, Troilos, and others had drawn from a common reservoir, namely, Aristotle's lost work; and that the treatise credited Corax with seven divisions: *prooimion, prokataskeue, prokatastasis, katastasis, agones, parekthesis, epilogos.*[27] A little study of these terms, however, will make it evident that the first three are equivalents, practically synonyms, and that *katastasis* is so nearly akin to *diegesis* that the number after all is really five. If Aristotle ever did mention in his lost *Synagoge technon* that Corax divided speeches into seven parts, he took great pains to state in his own *Rhetoric* that "a speech has two parts. It is necessary first to state the case *(prothesis)* and then to prove it *(pistis)* . . . It appears than that the only indispensable parts of a speech are the statement of the case and the proof. These are the only proper characteristic parts; but if more are added, they must not exceed four, vis: exordium, exposition, proof, and peroration."[28] Whatever then may have been the number of divisions in that first treatise it is safe to say that Corax, after listening to the pleas in the courts and to the arguments in the legislatures, conceived that out of the mass of complicated details, out of the evidence direct, documentary, and circumstantial, a logical order could be made which would probably apply in most cases. No one has been able to procure a better *dispositio* than the quintuplex, altho many attempts have been made, from the dual division of Aristotle centuries ago to that suggested by Winans in his recent work on *Public Speaking.*[29] Accordingly, a teacher who places before his pupils the model arrangement of five parts for orations and debates is paying a tribute to the old Sicilian rhetorician.

There were probably other features of merit in the first treatise be-

---

[26]Walz: *Rhetoric Graec,* IV, p. 13.

[27]Hamberger: *Die Rednerische Disposition,* p. 38.

[28]Aristotle: *Rhetoric,* III, 13.

[29]The suggested outline of Winans, p. 452, is adapted especially to debate: I. The Approach. 1. Exordium, 2. Explanation, 3. Elimination of irrelevant matter, 4. Concessions, 5. Common Ground, 6. Issues, 7. Partition of Proposition. II. Discussion. III. Conclusion. Note how minutely The Approach is divided, while no analysis is made of the Discussion.

sides the definition of rhetoric and the dispositio, but, unfortunately, only one of them has survived. This surviving part is, however, so original, so fundamental, so far-reaching that the fame of Corax would rest secure had he given nothing else to science and to letters. In the beginning of this paragraph I used the word *probably,* having in mind that the surviving relic of the first treatise on rhetoric dealt with the principle or topic or probability. Indeed, it was Aristotle who remarked the rhetorical system of Corax was composed of this topic, and then placed it among his fallacies. In order to make clear his contention he gave an illustration: "If the defendant is not liable to the charge brought against, as, for instance, if a feeble person were to be tried for assault and battery, he defends himself upon the ground that it is improbable (that he a weak man should attack a strong one). Or if he be liable, as for instance, if he be a strong man against whom the charge is brought, he argues that it is improbable, on the ground that it was sure to seem probable; and therefore knowing that he would be exposed to the suspicion he was less likely to bring upon himself an almost certain punishment."[30] To Aristotle this stock story from the rhetorics of the schools furnished evidence of faulty logic; he did not seem to grasp its real significance in human action. Before him there was a problem of assault in which the argument in one case would be that the probability of guilt was absolute *(eikos haplos)* and in the other case was particular or relative *(eikos ti).* He saw that it might be possible for a scheming attorney to present a particular probability so adroitly that it would defeat an absolute probability. Such a procedure he regarded as immoral. "This in fact," he said, "is the meaning of converting the worse argument into the better."[31]

Plato, likewise, in the *Phædrus,* failed to see the real bearing of Corax' principle, for he caused Socrates to relate with gusto the same story with variations, ascribing it however to Tisias. "If a weak, but courageous man, is brought to trial for having knocked down and robbed of his clothes, or purse, a strong and cowardly one, neither accuser nor accused is to tell the truth to the judges, but the coward is to say that the other had assistance when he knocked him down;

---

[30]Artistotle: *Rhetoric,* II, 24. Welldon, tr.
[31]See the defense of Protagoras, in *W.J.S.,* Ed. March 1918, who maintained that every subject had two sides opposite and contradictory.

while the brave man must first prove the fact of his being alone, and then appealing to his favorite probable, exclaim, 'Why, how could a man like myself have ever thought of attacking a man like that?' But the other, you may be sure, is not to plead his own cowardice, but rather essay some fresh falsehood, which will, perhaps, supply the adversary with the means of refuting the accusation. And so, whatever be the matter on hand, this, Tisias says, is the style of pleading warranted by art."[32] For this art Socrates had nothing but scorn. He apparently never discovered that his attacks should have been directed at men instead of at rhetoric. "For men," he says, "intending to be competent speakers, there is not the slightest occasion at all to do with the truth, about actions just or good . . . Whatever you say, it is the *probable* that you must chiefly aim at, and pay no regard at all to the true."[33]

Having thus paid his respects to the schools of rhetoric, at least to the lessons taught in them, Plato then trips himself neatly, for he defines the thing he is condemning. "The *probable*," he says, "means that which accords with the opinion of the many," and "this vaunted *probability* of yours only made itself felt in the minds of the many by virtue of its resemblance to the truth."[34] On account of these definitions one might concede that Plato was not really attacking probability itself, but the misuse of it by tricky speakers, by the shyster lawyers of his day; for he must have known, as Aristotle should have known, that direct, unimpeachable evidence (that is, absolute probability) is difficult to obtain, and that most audiences and juries are swayed by the particular probabilities of a case. Indeed, Aristotle himself bears witness to the importance in human affairs of probabilities, for he devoted a portion of his Organon—the *Topics*—"to discover a method by which to syllogize about every proposed problem from probabilities."[35] He defines his term as follows: "Probabilities are those things which appear to all, or to most men, or to the wise, and to these either to all or the greater

[32]Plato: *Phaedrus*, 273. Wright, tr.
 Similar stories of altercations between young and old, strong and weak, rich and poor, violent and mild, are mentioned in *Rhetoric ad. Alexander*, 36, evidently stock cases for use in schools.
[33]*Phaedrus*, 272. Jowett, tr.
[34]*Phaedrus*, 273.
[35]Aristotle: *Topics*, I, 1.

number, or to such as are especially renowned and illustrious."[36] Again, he defines it in the Rhetoric as "something that usually happens, altho the definition must not be stated, as it sometimes is, without qualification, but something that usually happens in such matters as are indeterminate."[37] If he had allowed that definition to stand on its own feet, he would never have condemned Corax for giving the world a false system of rhetoric.

Why did Aristotle run off at a tangent in his condemnation of the Sicilian? Perhaps he was at the time he wrote those lines in the throes of logical parturition. A casual reading of his *Rhetoric* will reveal the fact that a goodly portion of the immortal work is applied logic. In the application of logic to public address he employed probabilities in spite of his opinion that they are fallacious and immoral. That is to say, in theory he was opposed to the use of probabilities, but in actual practice he found it necessary to use them and to give instruction concerning them. For instance, he says "the orator must employ his speech in upsetting an opposite hypothesis."[38] To obtain skill in this he must practise on common topics (koinois topoi), such as that of possibility and impossibility. One of these is the topic tending to show that a thing either has or has not occurred, a kind which is used especially in judicial oratory. The evidence used is that of likelihood (probability), as, "if it was a person's intention to do a thing, it may be argued that he did it, as there is always a probability that the intention was carried out."[39] It would seem that Aristotle is giving rules for using what he condemned. No matter how antagonistic he may have been in theory, in practice he was compelled to use the method of Corax. From this it may be seen that the Sicilian had given to speakers and writers of all ages a permanent principle, a practical method of handling the affairs of life. It was nothing new to any man, for all had used it every day, but Corax had the honor to be the first to set it down in a book. That principle or method which he called probability I shall now attempt to explain.

---

[36] Aristotle: *Topics,* I, 3.

[37] Aristotle: *Rhetoric,* I, 2. Consult also the *Prior Analytics,* II, 27, on the use of *eikos, semeion,* and *tekmerion.* Cope's Introduction, 160-163, has an excellent exposition of these terms.

[38] Aristotle: *Rhetoric,* II, 18.

[39] Aristotle: *Rhetoric,* II, 19, 20. *eikos gar ton mellonta kai poiésai.*

To explain and interpret probability one must plunge into the "boundless deep" of human experience, there to struggle feebly with the mighty waves. Already the definitions of the term according to Aristotle and Plato have been given. Other philosophers, ancient and modern, have exercised their wits in giving it a meaning. No one has done better than Locke in his *Essay on Human Understanding,* wherein he says that probability is nothing but the appearance of such an agreement or disagreement, by the intervention of proofs, whose connection is not constant and immutable, or at least is not perceived to be so, but is, or appears for the most part to be so, and is enough to induce the mind to judge the proposition to be true or false, rather than the contrary. . . . Probability is likeliness to be true; the first notation of the word signifying such a proposition for which there be arguments or proofs to make it pass, or be received for true. . . . The entertainment the mind gives this sort of proposition is called belief, assent, or opinion, which is admitting or receiving any proposition for true, upon arguments or proofs that are found to persuade us to believe it as true, without certain knowledge that it is so. . . . The grounds of probability are first, the conformity of anything with our own knowledge, observation and experience. Secondly, the testimony of others, touching their observation and experience.[40]

An application of the definition to the illustration given by Aristotle will make clear that the plea of the feeble man in the assault case was probable, for it had the appearance of "likeliness" to the truth, as founded upon the experiences of men—that is, the weak seldom attack the strong. This position is not a universal, because the opposition could argue that the weak man might have committed the assault, because he would reason that the jury would not suspect him on account of his weakness. Likewise the plea of the strong man would have a likelihood of winning credence; but there could be counter probability that he committed an assault because he was by nature a bully. It will be seen then that the jury in deciding cases would not be guided by unimpeachable evidence, that is, by Aristotle's absolute probability or certainty, but by their own "previous observation, experience, and by the testimony of others." That, at least, is the way juries do nowadays, and they probably acted in the same way in the days of Aristotle and

---

[40]Locke: *Essay on Human Understanding.* Bk. IV, ch. 15.

Plato. Corax then was only applying common sense when he wrote about probability. He knew that when men were at loggerheads absolute truth could seldom be found; but that the probabilities of the case decided the issue. If he were alive in our day, he might have the pleasure of reading that the Supreme Court of the United States has been so uncertain of the truth that they settled cases by a 5 to 4 vote.

Why a five to four vote? Why not make the decision unanimous? There are many reasons. The observations and experiences of men differ. They come to different conclusions because their early environments, education, family beliefs, temperaments, even physical health prevent them from seeing the same things in the same way. Some are radicals, others conservative; some are cowardly, others brave; some look for what they think is right, others for what is expedient. Hence the voting is unanimous only in clear-cut cases, those with unmistakable absolute probability as "common observation in like cases and particular testimonies in that particular instance favor or contradict it."[41] An English jury, hearing that a man had slipped and fallen while walking on ice, would unanimously agree that such an accident might happen, for it would be within their own observation and experience; but the king of Siam when told by the Dutch ambassador "that the water in Holland would sometimes be so hard that men walked upon it, and that it would bear an elephant if he were there,"[42] was of the opinion that the ambassador was a liar. Such a phenomenon being contrary to the king's experiences, he would not have believed it though sworn to by a dozen ambassadors. If the Dutchman wanted to make this story probable, he would have to show his majesty an icicle or a film of ice, whereupon the mind of the king would have made an inductive leap from scanty evidence to a universal. Yet in doing so he might have fallen into the grave danger that Aristotle may have had in mind when he condemned particular probabilities. Errors may be made because the evidence is insufficient for certainty. Certainty, the universal, his logical mind demanded. Often he fell into error by accepting the testimony of too few particulars. Sometimes when he thought he had the whole truth because based on some observation, as when he wrote that "the back of the head is empty and hollow . . .

---

[41]Locke: *IV*, 16, 9.
[42]Locke: *IV*, 15, 5.

the brain is without blood . . . it is naturally cold to the touch. . . . Man is the only animal with ears that cannot move them. . . . Man is the only ambidexterous animal. . . . Longlived persons have one or more lines which extend through the whole hand, short lived persons have two lines not extending through the whole hand."[43] There are many other cases dealing with physical phenomena in which Aristotle erroneously employs universals. They are simply indications of a tendency among all men, even philosophers, to generalize from too few particulars. Modern scientists, having a greater knowledge of the universe than the ancients, would probably employ qualifying phrases, for they have come to know by long experience that many things which seem certain for a time are afterward found to be false, even with the evidence furnished by the senses. If this be true of trained scientists, how much more so will it be of those whose powers of observation have not been trained?

A personal illustration may not be out of place. Some months ago while making a call on a neighbor I happened to glance toward the window. I saw streaks extending downward, saw a paper whirled by the wind, heard a pattering sound, and smelled moisture. I knew then of a certainty that rain was falling, for three senses had furnished their data. Imagine my astonishment, when I left the house a few moments later, at finding the sun shining, the sidewalk dry, and the street dusty. Nonplussed I returned to the same position to repeat the observations. They were the same; yet a closer scrutiny developed the streaks into wire netting, the patter into the frying of meat in an adjoining room, and the odor of moisture into the vapor of a recent scrubbing of the floor. If now the evidence furnished by the senses cannot be trusted, cannot give certainty, belongs in a large measure to the realm of probabilities, what shall we say of the inferences of the mind from intangible material?

At this point we are forced to say that altho we are seldom sure of certainty, nevertheless we act as though we were sure, both in regard to tangible and to intangible things. We act in this way, dependent on probabilities, living in the sphere of particular probability as tho it was absolute. Shall we cease from action until we are sure that everything is certain? Long ago Cicero answered that question, for he wrote,

---

[43]Aristotle: *The History of Animals*, I, 13, 3; I, 9, 10; II, 1, 3.

"the wise man is often guided by what is *probable,* not being comprehended, nor perceived, nor assented to, but only likely; and unless a
man acts on such circumstances there is an end to the whole of life.
For what must happen? Has the wise man when he embarks on board
ship a positive comprehension and perception in his mind that he will
have a successful voyage? How can he? But suppose he goes from this
place to Puteoli, thirty furlongs, in a seaworthy vessel, with a good
pilot, and in fine weather like this, appears *probable (probabile videa-
tur)* that he will arrive safe. According to the appearances of this kind
then he will make up his mind to act or not to act."[44]

The illustration just used is found in the Academics, a work in which
Cicero refers many times to Carneades. His interest in the distinguished
Academician was two-fold, Carneades being an excellent orator was
well as an eminent philosopher. His powerful voice and acute mind
caused pupils to quit their own schools in order to listen to his lectures.[45] So effective was he that the Greeks sent him on an embassy
to Rome. While there he incurred the wrath of Cato the Censor by
haranguing one day in praise of justice and the next day proving it to
be an odious institution. Thereby the philosopher was simply putting
into practice the pedagogy or Protagoras and Corax: that every question has two sides and that there are probabilities on each side. To
Cato's simple mind such teaching was dangerous to morals, hence he
persuaded the senate to send Carneades back to Greece without delay.
There he continued his heretical doctrines, for he taught that the
imagination, the understanding that the senses deceive so frequently
that they cannot be regarded as the infalliable judges of truth. For the
guidance of life only probabilities are attainable. These probabilities
are the common agreements in man's sensations and experiences, which
represent in some degree the truth. Carneades then began an analysis,
distinguishing three degrees of probability:[46] first, that which is probable in itself.[47] This is the kind termed by Locke "matter-of-fact" . . .
"the argument from the nature of things themselves," as fire arms,
iron sinks in water—things not controverted by anybody.[48] Second,

---

[44]Cicero: *Academics,* II, 31.
[45]Diogenes Laertius: Carneades, in *Vit. Phil.*
[46]Article on Carneades, in *Encyclopedia Brittanica.*
[47]Sextus Empiricus: *Adv. Math.,* VII, 171.
[48]Locke: *IV,* 16.

that which is probable and uncontradicted *(aperispastos)*, literally "not pulled aside," not distracted when compared with others.[49] This is the condition when the testimony of many reliable witnesses agrees; as, for instance, that men prefer their private advantage to the public good, that it is agreed by all historians concerning Tiberius that he did so and so.[50] Third, that which is probable, uncontradicted and thoroughly investigated and confirmed, as well in its several parts as in the relations to the subject out of which it arose, and without any circumstances being discovered which might militate against probability.[51] Accordingly, the highest degree of probability is possessed by an idea which after being analyzed in itself and tested in all possible combinations with others, appears to be wholly devoid of improbability.[52]

This attempt of Carneades to classify probabilities is of little value except as showing the philosophic mind at work on the problems of life, hunting vainly for a solution. Locke saw this when he wrote that "circumstances, reports, different qualifications tempers, designs, oversights, etc., of the reporters make it impossible to reduce to precise rules the various degrees wherein men give their assent. This only may be said, in fine, that as the arguments and proofs, pro and con, upon due examination, nicely weighing every particular circumstance, shall to any one appear upon the whole matter, in a greater or less degree, to preponderate on either side; so they are fitted to produce in the mind such different entertainment as we call 'belief, conjecture, guess, doubt, wavering, distrust, disbelief, etc.' "[53]

From the quotation just given one can easily see that Locke did not follow the lead of Carneades: probabilities were to him incapable of classification. Both of these men were philosophers and both were interested in the theological problems of their day. Others also, especially since the Renaissance, were interested in theology who, in attempting to solve its problems, seized on probabilities and the possibility of classifying them. Forgotten then was Corax and the application of his principle to the ownership of land, the guilt of criminals, and the policies of state, as the clergy lost themselves in the bogs

---

[49] Sextus Empiricus: *Adv. Math.*, VII, 176, sqq.
[50] Locke: *IV*, 16.
[51] Sextus Empiricus: *Adv. Math.*, VII, 184.
[52] Ritter: *Hist. of Phil.*, III, 618.
[53] Locke: *IV*, 16, 9.

of casuistry. They began by asking themselves for definitions of sin. Were there two kinds, venial and mortal; that is, pardonable and unpardonable? What were the boundaries between the two? Could the priest forgive sin? In the attempt to define sins and to adjudicate penalties and pardons the learned fathers descended the spirals of Inferno until they stood in the very presence of Satan himself. On the downward path they invented direction of intention, mental reservation, and Probabilism.

We must digress for a moment, in the interest of future clergymen, to see the bearing of Corax's teaching in the realm of religion. There arose a school of thinkers in the church who were called Probabilistae, men who maintained that a certain degree of probability as to the lawfulness of an action was enough to secure against sin. This certain degree could be furnished by a single very grave doctor who having made a special study of the subject could give a good and sufficient reason.[54] Whenever there was morality a man might adopt the opinion in favor of liberty with absolute certainty that he was justified in doing so, even though there was greater probability on the opposite side.[55] Of course, such cases there would always be two sides and consequently those who were fond of ecclesiastical disputation would find themselves in clover. It was utterly impossible for men to agree when they attempted to systematize morality. For instance, a discussion arose as to whether it was sufficient to love God once in one's life (Vasquez), or thrice (Henriques), or once every three years (Coninch), or once every year (Mendoza). As indicated by the authorship in the parentheses, each view had its supporters, whereupon Escobar held that a confessor was morally bound to give absolution on any of these terms. Thus with probability on its side a soul might in nearly every case squeeze its way into Paradise.

Against this doctrine of Probability the Sorbonne, in 1620, protested, but without effect. The world seemed to be waiting for the *Provincial Letters* of Blaise Pascal, a work in which he impaled the learned doctors both by direct lunge and by skilful riposte. His attack was just as much needed as was that of Plato against the Bad Sophists of his day. Pascal showed that the doctrine of Probabilism always made

---

[54] Pascal: *Provincial Letters,* V.
[55] G. H. Joyce, S. J.: Probabilism, in *Encyclopedia of Religion and Ethics.*

it possible for a sinner to find an authority who would decide in his favor. The system had all the advantages referred to in the old saying: "When one god presses hard, another brings relief." As an example of this, note the working out of the doctrine of Probabilism in a case of assassination. Here was a crime which was so heinous that the perpetrator was denied sanctuary in the church. How could he escape damnation? How could he secure absolution for his crime? The probability of innocence was established by interpreting the word assassin as follows: "Are assassins unworthy of sanctuary in churches? Yes, by the bull of Gregory XIV, they are. But by the word assassin we understand those that have received money to murder one; and accordingly, such as kill without taking any reward for the deed, but merely to oblige their friends, do not come under the category of assassins."[55a] By such monstrous perversions of Probabilism it was possible to legalize theft, assault, rape and murder.

There were those who saw this flaw and sought a way of escape. They began a hedging process by pleading for Probabiliorism. According to this principle of morals a man was bound in the presence of several alternatives to choose the one which had the greatest likelihood of being right; this is, there being several opinions, he should be guided by the reasons and the scholars militating in favor of the more probable opinion.[56] Then there arose a faction called the Aequiprobabilistae who took a middle ground, that in a balance of opinion the less safe opinion might be lawfully followed, provided it be as probable, or nearly as probable as its opposite.[57] Besides these systems were two others differing *toto coelo:* Laxism and Rigorism. Of these, the Laxists maintained that it was justifiable to follow any probability, however slight, in favor of liberty. They were somewhat akin to the Latitudinarians of the English church. On the other hand the Rigorists maintained that in doubtful cases the strictest course is always to be followed.

In order to illustrate these grades of ecclesiastical probability I draw from Viscount St. Cyres.[58] "Suppose, for instance, that some casuists held it wrong to dance on Sunday, while others held it perfect lawful.

[55a]Pascal's *Letters,* VI.

[56]*Encyclopedia of Religion and Ethics.* Also *Catholic Encyclopedia.*

[57]*New English Dictionary.*

[58]*Encyclopedia Brittanica, XVI:* 679.

There were four ways of answering the question. Strict moralists—called rigorists, or 'tutiorists'—maintained that the austerer opinion ought always to be followed; dancing on Sunday was certainly wrong if any good authorities had declared it to be so. Probabiliorists maintained that the more general opinion ought to prevail, irrespectively of whether it was the stricter or the laxer; dancing on Sunday was perfectly lawful if the majority of casuists approved it. Probabiliorists argued that any opinion might be followed, if it could show good authority on its side, even if there was still better authority against it; dancing on Sunday must be innocent if it could show a fair sprinkling of eminent names in its favor. The fourth and last school—the 'laxists' —carried the principle one step further and held that a practice must be held unobjectionable if it could prove that any one 'grave Doctor' had defended it; even if dancing on Sunday had hitherto lain under the ban of the church, a single casuist could legitimate it by one stroke of his pen. Liguori's great achievement lay in steering a middle course between the various extremes. The gist of his system, which is known as 'equiprobabilism,' is that the more indulgent opinion may always be followed, whenever the authorities in its favor are as good, or nearly as good, as those on the other side. In this way he claimed that he had secured liberty in its rights without allowing it to degenerate into licence. However much they might personally disapprove, zealous priests could not forbid their parishioners to dance on Sunday, if the practice had won widespread toleration; on the other hand, they could not relax the usual discipline of the church on the strength of a few unguarded opinions of too indulgent casuists."

Such then was the peculiar phase which the doctrine of probability assumed in the Roman church. As an attempt to systematize morality it was a dismal failure; yet there was a modicum of good in the procedure, for it represented a sincere effort to help the clergy in the confessional as they dealt with the sins of men.

While the Jesuits of the continent were wrestling with probabilities in morals, Bishop Butler of England was laboring over his great work on *The Analogy of Religion, Natural and Revealed,* a work which when published profoundly influenced the thinking of millions. The modest bishop protested that he did not profess to give an absolute demonstration that the Holy Scriptures were the word of God, so much as *probable* proof. This probable evidence he thought varied from the highest moral certainty to the lowest presumption. That which chiefly constitutes probability is expressed in the word likely, i.e., like some truth or true event. Again, probable evidence in its vary nature affords but an imperfect kind of information; and it is to be considered as relative only to beings of limited capacities. For nothing which is the possible object of knowledge, whether past, present, or future, can be probable to an infinite intelligence; since it is in itself, certainly true, or certainly false. But to us, *probability is the very guide of life.* The decision in a case rests on the weight of evidence, for there are many probabilities, which cannot be confuted, i.e., shown to be no probabilities, and yet may be overbalanced by greater probabilities on the other side. Thus did the keen minded Bishop speak in the introduction to his immortal work. He then proceeded to draw from analogies the proofs of future life, revelation, miracles, and other theological propositions, holding that the weight of probability lies with the affirmative.[59] Students of Argumentation who may be interested in Theology will find *The Analogy* a splendid supplement to their text-books. They will see the doctrine of Corax applied in a manner far different from what the originator had ever dreamed.

Every question having two sides, however, as Protagoras had long ago written, there would naturally arise an opposition to Bishop Butler. This opposition also arose in England, where the philosopher Hume went over the ground carefully and came to the conclusion that the probabilities were all negative. His course of reasoning runs as follows: "We are determined by custom to transfer the past to the future, in our inferences; where the past has been entirely regular and uniform, we expect the event with the greatest assurance, and leave no room for any contrary supposition. But where different effects have been found to follow from causes, which to appearances are exactly similar, all these various effects must occur to the mind in transferring the past to the future, and enter our consideration, when we determine the probability of an event.[60] Applying his reasoning to miracles he concluded that they are not in accord with the regularity and uniformity of nature, and that "no testimony for any kind of a miracle has ever

---

[59] Hume's *Analogy.* I have used largely his own words.
[60] Of Probability. Hume's *Essays,* Sec. VI.

amounted to a probability."[61] Of course, such an attitude brought
upon the head of Hume the anathemas of all believers in the miracu-
lous. A curious result in clerical circles has been the tendency to *interpret* supernatural occurrences, to use them as stories from which
helpful conclusions may be drawn, rather than admit their improbability, or cast them in toto from the Canon of Holy Scripture. By thus
approaching Hume's position the clergy have rendered miracles more
acceptable.

A moment ago Butler's expression, "probability is the very guide of
life," was used. Strange to say in that statement the orthodox bishop
finds himself in agreement with Voltaire, the free-thinker. The sceptical, some say atheistical, Frenchman once wrote an "Essay on Probabilities in Judicial Proceedings," in which he used these words:

> "*Presque tout la vie humaine roule sur des probabilités. Tout
> ce qui n'est pas demontré aux yeux, ou reconnu pour vrai par
> les parties évidemment intéressés à la nier, n'est tout au plus que
> probable. . . . L'incertitude étant presque toujours le partage
> de l'homme, vous détermineriez trèsrarement, si vous attendiez
> une démonstration. Cependant il faut prendre un parti: et il ne
> faut pas le prendre au hasard. Il est donc nécessaire à notre nature
> faible, aveugle, toujours sujette à l'erreur, d'étudier les probabilités
> avec autant de soin, que nous apprenons l'arithmétique et la
> géométrie.*"[62]

Inasmuch as Voltaire was discussing judicial inquiries it may not
be out of place to use his remark as a transition to the next phase of
the subject: the application of probabilitfies in law . . . In so doing
we return, after wandering in the fields of philosophy and theology,
to the original sphere. We enter the court, behold the jury, and listen
to the impassioned pleas of the opposing attorneys. At once we are
struck by the uncertainties of the suits. Seldom is there a clearly proved
case. Most of the legal disputes seem to have strong probabilities on
each side. This circumstance so attracted the keen mind of Corax that
it lead him to base his work upon it. In making the effort he furnished
the starting point for innumerable discussions and treatises on proof

---

[61] Of Miracles. Hume's *Essays,* Sec. X.
[62] Voltaire: *Works,* XXVI, p. 457. Quoted by Gladstone in an article on Probability as the Guide of Conduct in the *Nineteenth Century,* 5:908.

and evidence, inference and demonstration, testimony and conjecture, fact, hearsay and opinion. All of these have become more or less crystallized in law and in judicial decisions; but, first, they had to pass thru the classrooms and courts of antiquity, thru that stage which caused condemnation by Plato and Aristotle. Traces of their feelings toward probabilities, toward questions having two sides, are manifest to this day in the attitude of many people toward the legal profession, the lawyer being looked upon as a man of questionable morality because he is ready to defend either side of a case for pay. Now the period of transition, we might almost say of misunderstanding, in ancient days may be called, for want of a better term, the era of the sophists. What happened during that period has very fortunately for the student of Rhetoric been reproduced by the logographer Antiphon. In the famous *Tetralogies* he reveals the classroom methods and court procedure of the generations immediately following the enunciation of probabilities by Corax. No better type forms for brief in argumentation and debate are used by modern teachers than those exercises of the first speech writer, changing the subjects, of course, from murder cases to modern problems, except in moot courts.

Suppose we enter the school of Antiphon while a class is debating the question: Resolved that an Athenian citizen has committed murder. The Affirmative opens with a warning that the defendant's cunning is so great as to make it difficult to prove a case against him. The defendant is, however, probably guilty of deliberate murder, for

I. The facts of the case exclude any other supposition. Thieves, for instance, would *probably* have robbed the deceased, but he was not plundered; the time and place show that the act was *probably* not the result of a drunken brawl; and it was not *probable* that he was killed by mistake, for the man's slave was also attacked, injured and slain.

II. The general *probabilities* point to the defendant as the murderer, for he had the motives of revenge on account of past defeats and the fear of losing a pending lawsuit.

III. The dying slave *probably* told the truth when he testified that he recognized the defendant, for dying men have no good reason for lying.

The Negative then being called maintains that the defendant is *probably* innocent, for

I. It is not *probable* that so cunning a man as the affirmative mentioned would commit a murder, knowing that he would be suspected.

II. The thieves were *probably* frightened away before robbing the victim.

III. The murdered man was *probably* slain where, and when, he was because he was a witness of some brawl.

IV. Some other enemy *probably* did the killing, because he would know that suspicion would be sure to fall on the defendant.

V. The slave's evidence is *probably* untrustworthy, for in his terror he could easily be mistaken.

VI. The defendant would *probably* not run the risk of detection by being present in person.

VII. He would probably *reason* that the loss of the suit would be a small thing compared with the loss of his life.

VIII. The defendant appeals to his services to the state.

In rebuttal the Affirmative notes:

I. It is *probable* that there would be witnesses to show that thieves were frightened away.

II. It is *probable* that no other committed the murder, for those less in danger would have less motive.

III. It is *probable* that the defendant was alone, for he would not then run the risk of betrayal by an accomplice.

IV. He would *probably* reason that he could not win the lawsuit, but he might escape trial for murder.

V. Those with less motive would *probably* be likewise deterred.

VI. His services to the state show his wealth and not his innocence.

The Negative in refutation avers:

I. It is *probable* that the passersby who frightened the robbers would themselves be afraid of being found with two dead bodies.

II. As the slave was not tortured and knew he was going to die, he would *probably* give the answer his owners wanted.

III. Conclusion: the defendant can prove an alibi, for his slaves can testify that he did not leave his house on the night of the murder. Wherefore he did not commit the crime.[63]

---

[63]Good digests of the *Tetralogies* may be found in Jebb's *Attic Orators,* I, 48 sqq.; Jevons' *History of Greek Literature,* p. 374; and Müller and Donaldson's *History of the Literature of Ancient Greece,* II, 106.

It is rather amusing to note the triumph of the negative, as the trump card of an alibi is slipped from its sleeve. In modern practice, all the cards are supposed to be laid on the table, except in college debates. Lest the reader think that this is a mere classroom exercise, I need only to refer to an actual case—Antiphon's Murder of Herodes—in which the very same methods are used.

Such treatment of causes developed the sophistry which produced the raw material out of which Aristotle created his rhetorical and logical treatises. But before the analyst appeared, the philosopher Plato had already condemned the sophists and their rhetoric. They seemed to him plausible, fallacious reasoners who puzzled inquirers after truth and weakened faith in the current religion. Curiously enough while he was condemning these teachers of eloquence, philosophy and politics, he was himself producing the greatest sophist of all—the renowned Socrates. He did not seem to understand that those who discussed the conduct of life were moral teachers, that those who lectured on methods of handling evidence were educating the future leaders of the state; that men who gave the youth practice in weighing probabilities, imaginary and real, were developing good citizens. It is only fair to say that Plato's antagonism diminished as he grew to maturity and began to comprehend the real actions of the human mind. This is revealed very plainly in *The Sophist,* wherein he describes the "minister of the art of intellectual purification, the teacher who cross-examines and refutes his pupils until he has freed them from self-conceit, and forced them to think for themselves."[64] A splendid picture indeed of Corax in his Syracusan classroom!

The students of that classroom were forced to think for themselves, and probably wanted to, because each man expected to become his own lawyer. They knew that they could not secure the necessary experience by reciting passages of Homer, but by the keen conflict of man face to face with his fellow. They perceived that law suits occurred between clients whose views were diametrically opposite. Each client or his attorney seemed to be bound to present the case in the most probable manner. There is no "ipse dixit" in the court room as there often has been in the pulpit. Nowhere is this better shown than in Erskine's Defense of Lord Gordon. Did the defendant, in the language

---

[64]Plato: *The Sophist,* 230.

of the indictment, "maliciously and traitorously compass, imagine and intend to raise and levy war and rebellion against the King?" His guilt must be determined according to law, not upon "conjectural presumptions or inferences, or strains of wit; but upon plain and direct proof . . . or the King, Lords, and Commons," said Lord Coke, "did not use the word *probably,* for the common argument might have served; but *provably,* which signifies the highest force of demonstration." The evidence of guilt was improbable for it consisted of "a few broken, interrupted, disjointed words, without context or connection—uttered by the speaker in agitation and heat—heard by those who relate them to you, in the midst of tumult and confusion—and even those words, mutilated as they are, in direct opposition to, and inconsistent with repeated and earnest declarations delivered at the very same time and on the same occasion, related to you by a much larger number of persons, and absolutely incompatible with the whole tenor of his conduct." In a similar manner Webster, defending the Kenistons against a charge of assault and robbery, said "There is no end to the series of *improbabilities* growing out of the prosecutor's story." . . . If the jury are satisfied that there is the highest *improbability* that these persons could have had any previous knowledge of Goodridge, or been concerned in any previous concert to rob him; if . . .; if . . .; if. . .; it will be for the jury to say whether they can pronounce them guilty." These cases are only typical of the thousands tried every year in courts, wherein the jury or the judge must decide by the probabilities.

Having drifted into the court room we will try to find a channel thru which to guide our craft. We note that two beacons light the way to decisions: one being positive proof, the other being proof circumstantial. For instance, how carefully the *Constitution* provides that "No warrant (for searches and seizures) shall issue, but upon *probable* cause, supported by oath and affirmation, and particularly describing the place to be searched, and the persons or things to be seized." In this use of the word probable it would seem that the original meaning, *probus,* is used. Curiously enough from the same root come provable and probable. If the positive proof is lacking, then circumstantial evidence must be used, of which there may be presumptions violent and presumptions probable; that is, "those arising from such circumstances as usually attend the fact."[65] At this point the rocks in the channel begin to obstruct the way; wherefore we must call for the assistance of some legal lights. Judge McGowen speaks thus: "It seems to us that there is a difference between probability and proof. The object of both words is to express a particular effect of evidence, but proof is the stronger expression. All the dictionaries give different definitions of probability. That of Worcester is 'Likelihood of the occurrence of an event in the doctrine of chance, or the quotient obtained by dividing the number of favorable chances by the whole number of chances;' and one in Webster is 'Likelihood, appearance of truth, that state of a case or question of fact which results from superior evidence of preponderation of argument on one side, inclining the mind to receive it as the truth, but having room to doubt.' 'Demonstration produces certain knowledge, proof produces belief, and probability opinion.' "[66] "Probable cause is the existence of such facts and circumstances as would excite the belief in a reasonable mind, acting on the facts within the knowledge of the prosecutor, that the person charged was guilty of the crime for which he was prosecuted."[67] Probable cause is such a state of facts, as would lead a man of ordinary caution and prudence, acting conscientiously, impartially, reasonably and without prejudice, upon facts within the party's knowledge, to believe, or entertain an honest and strong suspicion that the person accused is guilty.[68] Probable cause means not *prima facie* evidence, or such evidence as in the absence of exculpatory proof would justify condemnation, it means reasonable grounds of presumption that the charge is or may be well founded.[69]

From these definitions by eminent authorities one may perceive a substantial agreement with the original idea of Corax: likelihood of truth must always be present in order to be convincing.

> *"Lest men suspect your tale untrue,*
> *Keep Probability in view."*

Indeed, there is no way to escape from such a condition, for direct

---

[65]Blackstone's *Commentaries*, III, § 371. Good illustrations may be found in the foot notes of Sharwood's Edition.

[66]*American and English Encyclopedia of Law*, Vol. 19.

[67]*American and English Encyclopedia of Law*, Vol. 14.

[68]Hilliard on *Torts*, ch. 12, § 18.

[69]Malicious Prosecution, in *American and English Encyclopedia of Law*, Vol. 14.

first hand evidence, unimpeachable, is generally very difficult to secure. Shakespeare, with his marvelous insight into human action, understood this, for Antony presented such plausible evidence of the deeds of Caesar that the mob was persuaded that he "was not ambitious." Barbantio believed that Othello had won his daughter probably by charms and drugs. How did Cleopatra die?

> *Caesar: If she had swallow'd poison, 'twould*
> *appear by external swelling; but she looks like*
> *sleep,*
> *As she would catch another Antony*
> *In her strong toil of grace.*
> *Dolabella: Here, on her breast,*
> *There is a vent of blood, and something blown;*
> *The like is on her arm.*
> *Guard: This is an aspic's trail; and these fig leaves*
> *Have slime upon them, such as the aspic leaves*
> *Upon the caves of Nile.*
> *Caesar: Most probable,*
> *That so she died; for her physician tells me*
> *She hath pursued conclusions infinite*
> *Of easy ways to die.*[70]

Again the master speaks from the depths of some awful experience concerning the death of Gloster:

> *"See, his face, black and full of blood;*
> *His eyeballs farther out than when he lived,*
> *Staring full ghastly like a strangled man:*
> *His hair unrear'd, his nostrils stretch'd with struggling;*
> *His hands abroad, displayed, as one that grasp'd*
> *And tugg'd for life, and was by strength subdued.*
> *Look, on the sheets, his hair, you see, is sticking;*
> *His well-proportion'd beard made rough and rugged,*
> *Like to the summer's corn by the tempest lodged.*
> *It cannot be, but he was murder'd here:*
> *The least of all these signs were probable."*[71]

If probable signs are evidence in law, what might be said of them in other lines? Any scholar who has delved into the mysteries of textual criticism knows that he is soon in a maze of probabilities as to the exact words of the original manuscript. He must apply commonsense, must wish, sift, even guess, as he meets errors of emendation, transposition, omission, insertion, substitution, confusion of letters, and

---

[70] *Antony and Cleopatra*, V, 2, 356.
[71] *Henry VI*, Part II, Act III, 2, 178.

contractions.[72] Let him invade the realm of Sociology; he will soon be entangled in the problem of unionism, immigration, penology, pauperism, and divorce. Touching the field of Economics he will no longer wonder why it has been called the "dismal science," especially when he listens to the learned authorities discussing the probabilities of reducing the high cost of living. Politics will give him the nightmare if he tries to solve the problems of suffrage, finance, or civil service. What are the probabilities concerning the origin of man? Did he evolve, or was he created, by divine fiat, from the dust of the earth? Whence came the various races if all had a common progenitor? The teacher of mathematics finds whole text-books on Probabilities, dealing among other things with the flipping of coins and statistics of birth and death. Insurance of all kinds is based on probabilities determined by actuarial experience.[73] Note how a prospect must balance between the absolute and unrequited loss of the premium, if his house does not burn down, and the gain he will derive if the less probable contingency of a fire should be his lot. Drop into the stock market in order to watch the attempts to predict the trend of securities. All writers on stocks and bonds invariably use the word probable. How guarded they are in stating that there will probably be a good yield of corn, on account of the snow fall; that it is very probable that the demand will be great for sugar on account of the scarcity; that it is extremely probable that high prices will continue for another year. These predictions are often made after consulting "Old Probabilities," as the weather man is facetiously called, because everyone knows the possibility of flarebacks after the prognostications. It would seem that all that is exact in science has been attained by way of probabilities, from the discovery of a planet to the finding of a new element.[74]

All of these scientific phenomena have a mathematical background or are subject to experimentation, but when one enters the court room and presents a case to the jury, mathematics and experiment are of little value, for the conditions are wondrously intricate, not only on account of the fallibility of human beings but because the heart of man is "deceitful above all things, and desperately wicked." Laplace, author

---

[72]Linday's Introduction to *Latin Textual Emendation* gives an excellent presentation of the difficulties met in reaching the original text of Plantus.

[73]De Morgan: Logic of chance. *Quart. Rev., 64*:285.

[74]Jevons: The Theory of Probability, Ch. X, in *The Principles of Science*.

of a profound work on Probability, realized the fact else he could not have written, *"Tant de passions, d'interests divers et de circonstances compliquent les questions relatives a ces objets, qu'elles sont presque toujours insolubles."* Because human actions are so frequently insoluble, they cannot be reduced to formulae, hence we are forced to adopt the method of Corax. Like the wily Ulysses who sailed past the home of the rhetorician years ago, we steer carefully between the Scylla of our doubts and the Charybdis of our fears, piloted by probabilities. How often the frail bark of life has been cast on the rocks or swallowed in the whirlpool on account of some slight error in judgment. Life is a die with a thousand sides, who knows which side will rise?

> *"He that toss'd you down into the Field,*
> *He knows about it all—HE knows—HE knows!"*

Having now reached the end of our tether, it would not be out of place to tie the frayed ends of the discussion. In what way could this be better done than by uniting Corax' definition of rhetoric to his principle of probability? Rhetoric is the art of persuasion. Persuasion is to be attained by presenting matter with such a likeliness to truth that it will be accepted and, if necessary, acted upon. Could any pedagogical principle be sounder? Yet strangely enough the principle has been well nigh forgotten. No modern texts on rhetoric mention it, altho they beat the bush in all directions, striving to drive out the game. They contain pages on persuasion, showing how audiences may be won by a modest bearing, by a pleasant smile, by conciliatory remarks, by silvery tongue and graceful gesture, by sounding phrase and brilliant climax. Primarily they seem to agree that persuasion is largely emotional. Likewise, they agree that conviction deals with the understanding. Rules are given to hammer these wedges into the mind. Yet the great rhetorical principle which might act as the sledge is hardly mentioned. The writers on rhetoric have apparently forgotten Corax' probability. Only here and there does one catch a glimpse of the word. Foster, for instance, states that evidence may prove possibility, probability, or actuality. No matter how strong your evidence may be on a really debatable proposition, it seldom proves more than a high degree of probability.[75] In some texts the word is used in connection with the argument from Cause to Effect under

---

[75]Foster: *Argumentation and Debating*, p. 77.

the term Antecedent Probability, losing sight of the fact that arguments from Sign and from Example are also dependent upon probability.

Now, it might be possible to show that the foundation of rhetoric lies, after all, in making things appear true. Dimly do the writers perceive this when they use the words plausible, verisimilitude, or verisemblance, striving thereby to indicate probability. They resort to antonyms, such as unlikely, inconceivable, incredible, unnatural, and unreal, to indicate improbability. It would seem that a whole test might be based upon the system of Corax. According to such a system, narration must be treated so that events will happen in a probable manner. Descriptions must represent objects with a semblance to actuality. Argumentation must try to make audiences accept something as probable which they do not at the outset admit. They will at least be willing to admit that the preponderance of probabilities is on one side or the other. Exposition must state facts so clearly that the listener believes he understands them. In order to accomplish these purposes rules for the choice of words have been given—generally summed up in the expression, the right word in the right place; rules for the formation of sentences; rules for sincerity; vision, and beauty; rules for plots, situations and characterizations; rules for unity, coherence, and emphasis. All of these are valuable, for they help to persuade the mind that the ideas presented are probable.

Thus we have made our stumbling way over the infinite complex of human activities, following the trail of the ancient rhetorician. Instead of being a crow that "hatched out young birds in a nest to fly forth disagreeable and troublesome bawlers," as Cicero asserted, Corax gave to the world in his pedagogy the great principle that "probability is the guide of life." Strange it is that the paradox of Agathon becomes true:

> *"It may be one would call it probable*
> *That many things improbable occur."*

PLATO'S VIEW OF RHETORIC

EDWIN BLACK
University of Pittsburgh

Whether Plato had a consistent view of rhetoric and, if he did, what that view was have been subjects of considerable debate among commentators and critics of the dialogues. The interpretive controversy of twenty-three centuries has so encrusted his ideas that, though we seldom seem to see them in the same way, it must be even more seldom that we really see them at all. Of course, Plato is difficult to understand. He is complicated, variegated, audacious, and sometimes paradoxical. The apparent elusiveness of his view of rhetoric, alone, has engendered a vast accumulation of commentary, with few of the commentators in substantial agreement on the defining characteristics of that view. Indeed, the only uniformity which crystallizes from this diversity of interpretation is the judgment that Plato disapproved of rhetoric, and was, in fact, rhetoric's most effective historical opponent.[1]

Fortunately, we still have the dialogues, their durability so manifestly established that they could not be impaired by one more fresh look. The object of the present investigation is to attempt that fresh look.

It is inevitable that any expositor will approach a work from a certain point of view. His frame of reference may be subconscious and unsystematized, but it will assuredly be present, shaping the bias of his interpretation by influencing the direction of his attention, selectively sharpening some and dulling others of his sensibilities, and molding the nuances of his judgment in a thousand imperceptible ways. The critical presuppositions of this study can be simply and dogmatic-

[1] See, e.g., Everett Lee Hunt: Plato and Aristotle on Rhetoric and Rhetoricians, *Studies in Rhetoric and Public Speaking in Honor of James Albert Winans,* New York, 1925, esp. pp. 18-42. In this volume, see pp. 100-158.

ally put. They are that Plato was both a subtle and disciplined thinker and a subtle and disciplined writer, that he would not have allowed patent inconsistency or contradiction into the constantly revised body of his work,[2] and that the dialogues, as speculative inquiries, must explain and justify themselves independent of any circumstances impinging on their composition.[3]

Such are the premises from which the present examination of Plato's view of rhetoric will proceed. The dialogues in which the view itself receives its most elaborate and methodical treatment are the *Gorgias* and the *Phædrus*. Plato's treatment of rhetoric is not confined exclusively to these two dialogues; on the contrary, his consideration of rhetoric bears relations with philosophical subjects treated throughout his extant writings. But these relations will develop and clarify as we explore the main body of Platonic rhetoric expounded in the *Gorgias* and the *Phædrus*. The former is generally considered to have been the earlier written of the two and hence invites our scrutiny first.

The diversity of interpretations which have been placed on the *Gorgias* amply evidences its perplexity for Plato's literary interpreters.[4] It is curious that these interpreters, all excellently equipped for study in classical philology, and all having reference to exactly the same document, cannot agree on its meaning. The cause of the confusion does not seem to lie in any obscurity of statement in the dialogue. Rather, we discover what troubles the commentators the moment we compare the *Gorgias* with the *Phædrus:* the former, satirical, contentious, and refutative, the latter emerging with a constructive, affirmative judgment expressed through the most majestic poetry. The contrast is both striking and discomfiting. Have we here irreconcil-

---

[2] If the dialogues themselves are not evidence enough of a systematic perfection of literary and philosophical technique, we have also the testimony of Dionysius of Halicarnassus that Plato "curred and combed the locks of his dialogues" to the end of his days.

[3] Some commentators undertake to "understand" the dialogues in terms of events which are thought to have affected Plato. See: Theodor Gomperz: *Greek Thinkers. A History of Ancient Philosophy*, II, trans. by Laurie Magnus, London, 1867; William Hepworth Thompson: *The Gorgias of Plato*, London, 1894, esp. pp. xiv-xvii. Such psychologizing is fascinating to read, but of limited utility in the interpretation of the dialogues. Likewise, Richard Weaver's "reading" of the *Phaedrus* in The Phaedrus and the Nature of Rhetoric, in *The Ethics of Rhetoric*, Chicago, 1953, is an interesting performance, but is so deficient in evidence as to be irrelevant to the study of Plato.

ably views of rhetoric expressed by the same author? The dilemma solicits resolution, and the commentators have responded by maintaining either that Plato changed his mind or that Plato did not mean by "rhetoric" in the *Gorgias* what he meant by "rhetoric" in the *Phœdrus*. The first position tacitly assumes that our author admitted a patent and obvious contradiction into his literature; the second position tacitly assumes that our author was inconsistent or, at the least, careless about his use of language. Since I hold that one should not

---

⁴Thompson, after quoting Olympiodorus approvingly, paraphrases him: "The aim of the Gorgias is to discuss the principles which conduce to political well-being. It [the preceding paraphrastic sentence] explains, at least to a considerable extent, the later as well as the earlier discussions; whereas if we assume that the main end of the dialogue is to bring the art of rhetoric and its professors into discredit, we can assign no significant motive for the importance assigned to a character like Callicles, who heartily despises the profession of a Sophist and hates the schools and their pedantry." Pp. xii-xiii.

Thompson asserts that the *Gorgias* was "the public vindication" of the conviction, held by a Plato disillusioned by the execution of Socrates, that "it was hopeless to amend the laws and practices of the Greek communities by any of the ordinary and constitutional means." P. xxx.

Herman Bonitz's interpretation of the *Gorgias* is summed up in the statement, *"Schwerlich kann dann noch ein Zweifel sein, dass die mit Kallikles verhandelte Frage: 'ist Philosophie im Platonische Sinne, oder ist politische Rhetorik in ihrem damaligen thatssächlichen Zustande eine würdige Lebensaufgabe?' den Kern und Zweck des ganzen Dialogs bezeichnet."* *Platonische Studien,* Vienna, 1858, p. 33.

Bonitz's position is, in its general characteristics, shared by E. M. Cope: *Plato's Gorgias,* 2nd ed. London, 1883. See esp. Cope's introduction; and Werner Jaeger: *Paideia: The Ideals of Greek Culture,* III, trans. by Gilbert Highet, Oxford, 1954, p. 50. Both Cope and Jaeger take the references to "rhetoric" in the *Gorgias* to refer to all the activities of Athenian society associated with oratory, especially the practices of the courts, the aspirations of the young, and the popular systems of education.

Gomperz interprets the *Gorgias* as a literary counterattack against Polycrates, who was supposed to have written a lampoon of Socrates after the latter's execution. II, p. 343.

Eduard Zeller interprets the *Gorgias* as containing a wholesale condemnation of rhetoric as an instrument of Sophistical ethics. *Plato and the Older Academy,* trans. by Sarah Frances Alleyne and Alfred Goodwin, London, 1876, p. 190. This condemnation is unqualified in Zeller's view, although when, in the same book, Zeller deals with the treatment of rhetoric in the *Phaedrus,* p. 515, he does not seem even to recognize a logical difficulty in his interpretation, nor does he attempt to resolve the question of how Plato can be read as unqualifiedly condemning rhetoric in one place and writing of it constructively in another.

Walter Pater argues that Plato opposed rhetoric, and opposed it because it represented to him the abhorrent Heraclitean metaphysics. *Plato and Platonism,* London, 1920, esp. chap. 4.

adopt either of these assumptions in interpreting Plato except only as a last resort, after every more generous alternative has been vainly tested, I shall tentatively reject these possibilities.

One other difficulty, besides the apparent difference in the moral attitude toward rhetoric expressed in the *Gorgias* and in the *Phædrus*, plagues the commentators. This other difficulty relates to the internal structure of each of the two dialogues, and presents itself to us in the form of two questions: "What is the theme of the *Gorgias?*" and "What is the theme of the *Phædrus?*" If the *Gorgias* is concerned with ethics, why is so sizeable a portion of it devoted to the subject of rhetoric? If the *Phædrus* is concerned with rhetoric, why is so much of the dialogue taken up with a consideration of love? Of course, these questions, and those who ask them, presuppose that a literary work must have a single theme. One might reply to these questions by denying the assumption and asserting that in the *Gorgias* and the *Phædrus* we have two dialogues with multiple themes. I shall not adopt this position at this stage of the analysis. The search for a single theme in a literary work can provide fruitful insights into the work. But the point is worth making that, after all, there is no binding fiat of literary activity nor any logical necessity demanding that a piece of writing, even a great piece of writing, and especially a dialectical inquiry, must have one and only one paraphrasable theme. The suggestion, once made, need not be pursued. It is enough to note for the present that determining the themes of the two dialogues is one of the major difficulties which commentators have found.

All major modern commentators on Plato's view of rhetoric, with the exceptions of Walter Pater, Paul Shorey, and possibly Werner Jæger, design their interpretations of the *Gorgias* or the *Phædrus* to deal with one or both of the difficulties mentioned. Troubled by the apparent inconsistency of the *Gorgias* and *Phædrus,* they infer a change of heart and mind, and a concomitant modification of doctrine, by Plato. Or, troubled by an inability to assign a single theme to one or both of the dialogues, they redefine and expand the meanings of key terms to make the work fit themes which they wish to assign to it. Now, it follows that if these two difficulties can be resolved with more parsimony of assumption and with stricter adherence to the texts of the dialogues than has heretofore been the case, then the interpreta-

tions of the commentators will have been circumvented, for the problems which these interpretations were designed to resolve will have
evaporated. Further, if these two difficulties are to be resolved, their
resolution would involve a clear and accurate explication of Plato's
view of rhetoric, which is the object of this inquiry. With these observations before us, we might begin the investigation of the *Gorgias* by
determining what the term "rhetoric" means there.

The crucial passages in the *Gorgias* which deal directly with the
definition of "rhetoric" occur in what might be called the first act,
i.e., the conversation between Socrates and Gorgias. Pressed for a
definition of "rhetoric," Gorgias defines this term as meaning the art
of that kind of persuasion which is exercised before public assemblies
and is concerned with the just and the unjust. Having elicited this
definition, Socrates goes on to force from Gorgias the admission that
sometimes rhetoric is used for unjust purposes. Since Gorgias contends
that the rhetorician has knowledge of the just and unjust, or, at least,
must have such knowledge before Gorgias will call him a "rhetorician,"
Socrates claims to have discerned a contradiction in Gorgias's position.
It has been alleged by some commentators, Cope and Shorey among
them,[5] that Socrates is made to argue sophistically in this portion of
the dialogue. The main objection is that Socrates is incorrect in assuming that if a person knew the just and unjust, then he could not act
but justly. As a matter of fact, there are strong reasons which Plato
might have adduced to support this assumption.[6]

Suppose the case of a man who enjoyed committing murder and
who committed murder at every opportunity; yet, every time someone
asked the man if he knew that murder was wrong, he said that he did.
Suppose further that this man made no claims of acting under duress
or compulsion, but chose to commit murder freely and soberly. Should
we not conclude, in the presence of such evidence, that he did not
really "believe" or "know" that murder was wrong? In assuming, as
he did, that the rhetorician who knows the nature of justice and in-

---

[5]Cope: pp. xlii-xliii; Paul Shorey: The Unity of Plato's Thought, in *The Decen-
nial Publications of the University of Chicago*, First Series, VI, Chicago, 1904,
p. 23.

[6]The assumption was evidently considered too obvious to require explanation. Cf.
the concept of *phronesis* in Aristotle's *Nichomachean Ethics*, esp. Book VI,
chap. 12.

justice will actually be just, Plato took the position that to understand a moral rule necessarily involves obeying it, since part of understanding the rule would be understanding its obligatory quality, i.e., understanding that it is a *rule*.

To dismiss the exchange between Gorgias and Socrates as a "conscious dialetical sport," as does Shorey,[7] is to ignore an important moral insight which Plato presented. Put in simpler terms, Plato's analysis of the Gorgian definition of "rhetoric" might run as follows:

If a person (the rhetorician) claims knowledge of the just, then it follows *as a necessary condition of having such knowledge* that the person will be just. What if Gorgias had refused to concede the point, and had instead contended that the rhetorician does not necessarily know the just? In that case, Socrates could rightly claim that such a person could not possibly use rhetoric because, since part of the definition of rhetoric is that it is persuasion about the just and unjust, such a person could not know what rhetoric was and hence could not use it. So Gorgias is obliged to concede that, according to his definition of rhetoric, the rhetorician must have knowledge of the just and unjust. As a result of the arguments in the dialogue, we can see that Gorgias's definition implicatively claimed a moral feature for rhetoric which in fact rhetoric does not have. A logical consequence of the Gorgian definition is that there can be no such thing as morally bad rhetoric, or rhetoric which is unjust. Plato knew, as we know, that there is morally bad and unjust rhetorical discourse. It therefore follows that the Gorgian definition is false.

We must bear in mind that the definitions which Plato sought by the dialetical process were neither stipulative nor lexical definitions. They were what Richard Robinson calls "real definitions."[8] That is to say, when Plato sought a definition, he was not satisfied with a stipulation about how a term was to be used or with a report about how it was generally used; he sought, rather, a description of the nature of the thing designated by the term. Looked at in this way, we can understand how Plato could call a definition "false" in the sense that the definiendum was inaccurately described, while a lexical definition might be false only in an entirely different sense, and a stipulative definition could not be false at all.

---

[7]*Loc. cit.*

[8]Richard Robinson: *Definition,* Oxford, 1950, pp. 7, 8, 161, 162.

It will assist our consideration of the *Gorgias* to amplify Plato's dialectical procedure. It is a procedure which is described in the *Phædrus, Philebus, Cratylus, Sophist, Politicus,* and *Laws*.[9] Cornford gives the following account:

> The expert in Dialectic will guide and control the course of philosophical discussion by his knowledge of how to "divide by Kinds," not confusing one form with another. He will discern clearly the hierarchy of Forms which constitutes reality and make out its articulate structure, with which the texture of philosophic discourse must correspond, if it is to express truth. The method is that method of Collection and Division which was announced in the *Phaedrus* and has been illustrated in the *Sophist*. Finally, to discern this structure clearly is the same thing as "to know how to distinguish in what ways the several Kinds can or can not combine." In other words, the science will yield the knowledge needed to guide us to true affirmative and negative statements about the Forms, of which the whole texture of philosophic discourse should consist . . .[10]

> The meanings of common names and verbs are the Forms. Statements are not propositional forms but actual significant statements, existing while we utter them. The science of Dialectic does not study formal symbolic patterns to which our statements conform, nor yet these statements themselves. Nor does it study our thoughts or ways of reasoning, apart from the objects we think about. It is not "Logic" if Logic means the science either of *logoi* or *logismoi*. What it does study is the structure of the real world of Forms. Its technique of Collection and Division operates on that structure.[11]

> . . . Dialectic is not Formal Logic, but the study of the structure of reality—in fact Ontology, for the Forms are the realities.[12]

> The goal of Dialectic is not to establish propositions ascribing a predicate to all the individuals in a class. The objective is the definition of indivisible species—a Form—by genus and specific

---

[9]*Phaedrus* (section nos.) 265, 266, 270D; *Philebus,* 16-18; *Cratylus,* 424C; *Sophist,* 226C, 235C, 253 ff; *Politicus,* 285A ff; *Laws,* 894AA, 936D, 965C.
[10]Francis Macdonald Cornford: *Plato's Theory of Knowledge,* London, 1935, pp. 263-264.
[11]*Ibid.,* p. 265.
[12]*Ibid.,* p. 266.

differences. What we define is not "all men" but the unique Form "Man."[13]

These cullings from Cornford's exposition should serve to clarify not only Plato's *modus operandi* in all the dialogues, but as well the way in which he deals with the Gorgian definition of rhetoric. When Plato sought the meaning of "rhetoric," he was seeking a series of true propositions about an existential class.

What does all of this imply for our analysis of the *Gorgias*? Primarily that all we have a right to infer from the first conversation between Socrates and Gorgias is that Gorgias's description of "rhetoric" has been overthrown. *Rhetoric in general has not been attacked.* Indeed, up to this point in the dialogue,[14] Plato has not written a single line about rhetoric, the Form. Plato's concern has been with Gorgias's description of rhetoric, and nothing else. Why has Plato given so much space to overthrowing a definition which he has put into the mouth of Gorgias? Of course, we cannot be certain of all his reasons, though we can be reasonably sure that they are not reducible to "conscious dialectical sport." The probability, suggested in somewhat different contexts by Cope, Bonitz, and Jaeger,[15] is that what Plato represents as Gorgias's view of rhetoric was widely held by influential and respected Sophists; it was a view with sufficient currency and respectability to seem to Plato to merit careful examination.

It is in the portion of the dialogue with Polus that Socrates is made to formulate the famous argument that rhetoric is not an art but is merely a knack like cookery, a counterfeit of a part of politics. This passage, like the one discussed above, has been widely interpreted as a wholesale condemnation of rhetoric. Such an interpretation is unwarranted by the text. We have, for example, within the passage itself clear indications that the "rhetoric" being dismissed as a knack is not *all* rhetoric. We find Socrates hesitating about making accusations against rhetoric with the comment, "I fear it may be somewhat rude to say the truth; for on Gorgias' account I am reluctant to speak out for fear he should suppose that I am satirizing his professional pursuits. At the same time whether this *is* the kind of rhetoric that Gorgias

---

[13]*Ibid.,* p. 269.
[14]*Gorgias,* 461.
[15]*Loc. cit.*

practises, I really don't know."[16] It is perfectly clear that Plato conceives of a rhetoric that is not open to this analysis since he suggests here that Gorgias might practice another kind of rhetoric. Later in the same dialogue, in the conversation between Socrates and Callicles, Socrates says, "So then it is to this [justice] that the genuine orator,[17] the man of science and virtue will have regard in applying to men's souls whatever words he addresses to them, and will conform all his actions; and if he give any gift he will give it, or if he take aught away he will take it, with his mind always fixed upon this, how to implant justice in the souls of his citizens and eradicate injustice, to engender self-control and extirpate self-indulgence, to engender all other virtue and remove all vice."[18]

It is impossible to maintain that Plato intended the *Gorgias* to be a total condemnation of all rhetoric as a "knack" and a "counterfeit of politics" when, in that very dialogue, he already sketches out some of the conditions of a rhetoric which would deserve the name of art. Obviously, the passage in which rhetoric is called a knack has been misinterpreted. The "rhetoric" referred to in the passage must be that which Gorgias has attempted to define. Plato's attack is limited only to a particular practice of rhetoric, and it is clear enough from the *Gorgias* alone that the attack was legitimate, deserved, and, given the Platonic theory of Forms, logically valid.

When we add to the evidence already adduced from the *Gorgias* the passage in the *Laws*[19] in which Plato, with a clear opportunity to condemn rhetoric as unscientific, waives the question of whether rhetoric is an art or a knack, and the passages in the *Phædrus*[20] which lay down the conditions for rhetoric to be an art, we are bound to the conclusion that Plato did not intend his condemnation to apply to *all* rhetoric. At the risk of being repetitious I shall reiterate that all we have a right to infer from the text of the *Gorgias* is that Plato opposed only a particular view of rhetoric unsuccessfully defended in the dialogue by

---

[16]*Gorgias,* 462D. Unless otherwise indicated all quotations are from Cope's translation.

[17]The phrase is rendered, "true and scientific rhetor," by Paul Shorey: *What Plato Said,* Chicago, 1933, p. 503.

[18]*Gorgias,* 504C.

[19]*Laws,* 938A.

[20]E.g., *Phaedrus,* 263B.

Gorgias, Polus, and Callicles, and probably actually defended by leading Sophists and rhetoricians of Plato's time.

At this point the question might arise, if Plato wished to oppose
the Gorgian view of rhetoric, why did he attack its definition rather
than its practice? The answer to this question must be, as previously
indicated, stated in terms of the objectives and methods of dialectic.
Plato sought to know the true Form. In the *Gorgias* and the *Phædrus*
he was seeking the Form of rhetoric. That was his objective. His
method, too, has been mentioned. A Ross has described it: "Plato has
in the *Phædrus* described dialectic as consisting in a joint use of collection and division. Of these operations, the first seems to be merely
preliminary to the second. In the attempt to reach the definition of a
specific term the first stage—the 'collection'—is the tentative choice of
a wide genus under which the term to be defined seems to fall."[21]

With the dialectical procedure in mind we can understand why
Plato approaches the subject of rhetoric in quite the way that he does
in the *Gorgias* and also why that dialogue is a unified literary work
with a single theme. Plato's attack was on the Gorgian view of rhetoric
(which was probably a general Sophistical view of rhetoric). The attack focussed on the Gorgian definition, though "definition" in the
distinctively Platonic sense. This definition could be expected to have
two parts: the collection and the division. The *Gorgias* is a refutation
of both parts of the Gorgian definition. We find in the first two parts
of the dialogue, where Gorgias and then Polus are Socrates' prime antagonists, that Socrates aims to overthrow the "collective" definition.
The burden of Socrates' argument in these sections is to establish that
rhetoric does not belong to the genus, art-concerned-with-justice. The
introduction of Callicles does not represent a change in theme; rather,
it represents a shift in focus to the "divisive" definition. Against Callicles, Socrates might describe his own position thus:

"But even if we grant for the sake of argument this 'collective'
definition which I have just refuted, I shall now demonstrate that
even your 'divisive' definition is false."

This is what Socrates proceeds to do. The animus of the argument
against Callicles is that Callicles' analysis of justice is wrong. Why did
Plato trouble to refute a definition represented by Callicles in the dia-

---

[21]W. David Ross: *Plato's Theory of Ideas,* Oxford, 1951, pp. 116-117.

logue? While the question is not central to the present study, the prob-
ability is that Callicles' views were widely and influentially held in
Plato's time, just as we know them to be held in our own time. We
can further infer that, if the present view of the thematic unity of the
Gorgias is correct, the opinions represented by Gorgias, Polus, and
Callicles were probably held as a coherent theory by the people whom
Plato intended to refute when he wrote the *Gorgias*.[22]

Before proceeding to a consideration of the *Phædrus,* it might be
well briefly to review. I have attempted to demonstrate the following
points:

1. The *Gorgias* is a thematically unified dialogue having for its single
main theme the refutation of the Gorgian definition of rhetoric.

2. The *Gorgias* is concerned with ethical questions because the definition being subjected to dialectical inquiry claims a moral characteristic for the definiendum; however, there are no issues raised in the
Gorgias which are not demonstrably pertinent to the definition of
"rhetoric" presented by Gorgias early in the dialogue.

3. The *Gorgias* is fundamentally a refutative rather than a constructive dialogue, as are other of the "Socratic" dialogues, i.e., dialogues
written early in Plato's career, as the *Gorgias* evidently was.

4. Plato cannot be interpreted as having pronounced a general condemnation of rhetoric.

With these points clear, I shall proceed to propose that the *Phaedrus*
is the constructive complement of the *Gorgias* and that the two dialogues taken together constitute a consistent view of rhetoric. A. E.
Taylor pronounces the judgment with which my proposal is consistent:

> In taking leave of the *Phaedrus,* we may note that while it sup-
> plements the *Gorgias* in its conclusions about the value of "style," it
> modifies nothing that was said in the earlier dialogue. The moral
> condemnation pronounced on the use of eloquent speech to pervert
> facts and produce false impressions remains the same. So does the
> verdict that the sort of thing professional teachers from Tisias to
> Thrasymachus profess to expound is not a science but a mere
> "trick" or "knack" (and therefore cannot be conveyed, as they pro-
> fess to convey it, by "lessons"). In adding that a thorough knowl-
> edge of a subject-matter and a sound knowledge of the psychology

---

[22]The important thing is that we not strain credulity by attributing to a philosophical genius reasons that are ill-defined, trivial, or plain silly.

of the public addressed furnished a really scientific basis for a
worthy and effective style, Plato is saying nothing inconsistent with
the results of the *Gorgias*. There is thus no sufficient ground for
thinking that the teaching of the *Phaedrus* represents a later development" from the more "Socratic" position of the *Gorgias*.[23]

Since there is considerably less disagreement among students of Plato
and among expert commentators about the interpretation of the
Phædrus, there is no need for a detailed examination of that dialogue
here. Plato turns the collective and divisive resources of dialectic on
"real" rhetoric, and his examination is clearly reported in the *Phaedrus*.
The collective definition is: ["Must not the art of rhetoric, taken as a
whole, be a kind of influencing of the mind by means of words, not
only in courts of law and other public gatherings, but in private places
also?"[24] And further on: "The function of oratory is in fact to influence men's souls."[25]]

Plato's divisive definition is explicated by his setting forth the
conditions necessary to make speech-writing an art:

> The conditions to be fulfilled are these: first, you must know
> the truth about the subject that you speak or write about: that is
> to say, you must be able to isolate it in definition, and having so
> defined it you must next understand how to divide it into kinds,
> until you reach the limit of division; secondly, you must have a
> corresponding discernment of the nature of the soul, discover the
> type of speech appropriate to each nature, and order and arrange
> your discourse accordingly, addressing a variegated soul in a
> variegated style that ranges over the whole gamut of tones, and a
> simple soul in a simple style. All this must be done if you are to
> become competent, within human limits, as a scientific practitioner
> of speech, whether you propose to expound or to persuade.[26]

In sum, Plato conceived a true art of rhetoric to be a consolidation
of dialectic with psychogogia—applicable to all discourse, public and

---

[23]A. B. Taylor: *Plato, the Man and his Work,* New York, 1929, p. 319.

[24]*Phaedrus,* 261Z. Unless otherwise indicated, all quotations from the *Phaedrus*
will be from R. Hackforth: *Plato's Phaedrus,* Cambridge, England, 1952.

[25]*Phaedrus,* 271C. The more famous rendering of this passage, "Oratory is the art
of enchanting the soul . . . ," is by Benjamin Jowett: *The Dialogues of Plato,*
New York, 1937, I.

[26]*Phaedrus,* 277BC.

private,[27] persuasive and expository, which aims to influence men's souls. Dialectic was Plato's general scientific method; rhetoric is a special psychological application of it.[28] This definition of rhetoric is in one sense narrower, in another broader than the definition which Plato overthrew in the *Gorgias*. It is narrower in the sense that he does not admit the nature of justice and injustice to be a part of the "art" of rhetoric, but places it rather in the "art" of statesmanship. It is a broader definition in that Plato does assign to the art of rhetoric a specific province of its own, and a province which is not, as with the earlier Sophists, confined to forensic and deliberative oratory, but extends to all discourse which influences men. Plato's position here is fully consonant with that of the *Gorgias;* indeed, the treatments of rhetoric in the two dialogues supplement one another.

The question of the thematic unity of the *Phædrus* too has puzzled commentators. It is evident from the dialogue itself that its main subject is rhetoric; on this point, there is virtually unanimous agreement. But the three speeches on love in the dialogue, occupying as they do such a large proportion of space and reaching, in the third speech, such a luminous intensity of poetic eloquence and philosophical insight, have suggested to some readers a formal defect in the dialogue's structure.[29] The speeches fasten the reader's attention on themselves; Socrates' second speech is the climax of the drama: all converse in the dialogue builds up to and then down from that section. How can we account for the unity of the dialogue? I believe that we can account for the speeches by observing that they operate on at least seven different levels of meaning, at least five of which are directly and clearly pertinent to a consideration of rhetoric. By my reference to "levels of meaning," I indicate only that there are at least seven different ways in which these speeches might legitimately be understood by a reader:

1. The three speeches are investigations of love, and are intended to convey Plato's ideas on that subject. As such they are not directly and clearly pertinent to a consideration of rhetoric, though they still have great value taken exclusively in this non-rhetorical sense.

2. The speeches, culminating in Socrates' second speech, are intended

---

[27]*Cf.: Sophist,* 222C.
[28]See Shorey: *What Plato Said,* p. 52.
[29]See, e.g., Shorey: p. 198.

to express Plato's counterpart of Sophistical education. It is clear that Socrates' second speech focuses on and advocates the development of the intellectual and moral qualities of the beloved by the lover. It would not be inaccurate to characterize Plato's ideal lover as a philosophical tutor; certainly he is given a primarily educative function with respect to the beloved. Since, in the *Gorgias,* Plato attacked some of the pretensions of rhetorical education as conducted by the Sophists, we might expect a more constructive treatment of education in the *Phædrus.*[30] Even so, the speeches, read in this way, cannot be said to have an unqualifiedly clear and direct relevance to the subject of rhetoric. The remaining five "readings," however, do have such relevance.

3. The three speeches can be taken as specimens of rhetoric. In this way they serve a function to the theme of the dialogue so obvious that few commentators have even troubled to remark it directly. The speeches represent different kinds of persuasion, each superior to its predecessor, and the third represents the apogee of rhetorical discourse. The first speech, besides being subject to all the criticisms which Socrates makes of it, appeals exclusively to the prudential self-interest of the auditor. It is devoid of dialectic, and its disorder is evidence of its lack of adaptability to any possible person.[31] The second speech argues from grounds of definition and moral self-interest. It is better than the first because at least it is a kind of dialectic, though it is not "true" dialectic, as Socrates' later critique of it observes. The third speech is the perfection of the technique: the consummate amalgam of dialectic and psychogogia.

In exemplifying dialectic in a speech, Plato would not encounter any unusual literary problems. All of his dialogues illustrate dialectic in one way or another. But the exemplification of psychogogia certainly must have been a perplexing literary problem to Plato, a problem which he brilliantly resolved by choosing love as the subject of the speeches. Plato could not very well have exemplified the psychogogic aspect of rhetoric *only* by having Socrates' speeches adapted to

[30]This interpretation is obliquely suggested by W. C. Helmbold and W. B. Holther: The Unity of the Phaedrus, *University of California Publications in Classical Philology, XIV,* No. 9, Berkeley and Los Angeles, 1952.

[31]Plato insisted that principles of organization be based on human psychology. See *Phaedrus,* 277C.

Phædrus. If Plato had done only that, his exemplification might not have been clearly made, and he uncharacteristically would have limited the applicability of his paradigm to the dramatic situation created in the dialogue. Plato's resolution of the problem is to have Socrates discourse directly on the soul, which the subject of love enables him to do. Since the theory of the soul presented in the speech is itself the product of dialectic, the speech becomes an explicit consolidation of dialectic and psychogogia and, as such, a paradigm of Platonic rhetoric in a philosophical as well as a literary sense.

4. The three speeches can be taken as considerations of a particular type of rhetoric: courtship. As such, the speeches can be interpreted as dealing with the objectives of the suitor and, implicatively, with the objectives available to rhetors in general. Plato rejects personal pleasure and reciprocal pleasure as worthy objectives, finally endorsing the love of wisdom as the aim worthy of fulfillment. Considered in this way, the third speech can be taken as a synecdoche of the doctrine developed in the *Gorgias* that the true orator and statesman aims at the moral improvement of his audience. This reading would reveal that the speeches in the *Phædrus* contain paradigms within paradigms, i.e., the speeches *qua* speeches are paradigms of artistic form, and their content are also paradigmatic.

5. The three speeches can be taken as Plato's advice to audiences. In a view of rhetoric so concerned as Plato's with the sorts of things rhetors ought to say, we should rather expect a concomitant treatment of what audiences ought to attend to. The speeches of the Phædrus can be read as functioning that way. We must not neglect the care with which the character of Phædrus is drawn in the dialogue. He is neither a witless foil for Socrates' ironies nor the representative of an antagonistic philosophical idea. Phaedrus is a lover of discourse, a young man who is impressionable, an auditor. Several times in the dialogue Socrates insinuates that the Lysian speech was composed to influence Phædrus and that Socrates' own speeches have the same objective.[32] The three speeches, taken together, constitute a symposium on the subject of whether one ought to yield to the lover or the non-lover. Since, as was observed in the fourth "reading" above, the wooing of the lover would be a type of rhetoric in Plato's schematism, we

---

[32]E.g., *Phaedrus,* 237B and 257.

might suppose him to have wished his readers to generalize from the particular case, wooing, to the general Form, rhetoric. Since these speeches are addressed to Phædrus, we might be expected to take him as the paradigm of audiences. Once the generalization is made, it becomes evident that the speeches deal with what sorts of arguments one should be influenced by, and to what sorts of speakers one ought to listen. In this light, too, the speeches would be taken as a restatement of the *Gorgias's* doctrine about the proper objective of oratory, with the emphasis falling on the moral implications which this doctrine has for audiences.

6. The speeches can be taken as poetic discussions of the moral attitude which the speaker takes toward his speech. More than once in the dialogue Socrates describes Phædrus and himself as "lovers of discourse." They would therefore belong to the genus "lover" according to the prescriptions of Platonic dialectic, and whatever is true of that genus would be true also of them with respect to discourse. Accordingly, the third speech would be read as saying that the true lover of discourse will strive to enhance the moral quality of the object of his love; his discourse.

It may seem odd to the modern reader to encounter the concept of a "love" of discourse, but we know from Plato's writings and from a multitude of other sources in antiquity that the Greeks did take a deep and studied pleasure in rhetorical discourse. Plato, then, was setting down the conditions for the expression of that love, holding, in effect, that the lover of discourse will imbue his discourse with moral elevation.

7. The three speeches can be taken as a consideration of benign and malign forms of "madness" or inspiration, with the third speech exemplifying poetic inspiration in form and erotic inspiration in content. Plato recognized the existence of four types of benign madness, two of which are discussed and exemplified in these speeches.[33] The relationship between poetic madness and Platonic rhetoric will be briefly examined below.

These seven readings of the speeches may well not exhaust the possibilities, but the levels of possible interpretation are numerous

---

[33]For a fuller discussion of this subject see Ivan M. Linforth: Telestic Madness in Plato, *University of California Publications in Classical Philology, XIII,* Berkeley and Los Angeles, 1950.

enough to reveal the plurality of function of the speeches. Since Plato
was a conscious literary artist, I believe that we must take this
ambiguity as deliberate. Considering the fact that this ambiguity
enables Plato to write on one level about an apparently disparate
subject while, at other levels, still to maintain a unitary theme in the
dialogue, we must judge that his ambiguity is actually a *tour de force*.
I hope at least to have established that the speeches in the *Phædrus*
represent a violation of the dialogue's thematic unity only when they
are read in a single way of several possible ways. The general inference
which can be drawn is that there is no lack of thematic unity in either
the *Gorgias* or the *Phædrus*, nor are the positions taken in those two
dialogues anything but fully consistent and logically complementary
to one another.

Plato is not so directly concerned with rhetoric in dialogues other
than the two we have been considering, but even so, some of the
darker corners of Platonic rhetoric are illuminated by his insights in
other areas. This is especially true of his seminal contributions in the
area of epistemology.

One recurrent distinction which Plato makes between knowledge or
intelligence and true belief is particularly noteworthy for its relevance
to rhetorical theory. The pertinent section in the *Timæus* is:

> If intelligence and true belief are two different kinds, then
> these things—Forms that we cannot perceive but only think of—
> certainly exist in themselves; but if, as some hold, true belief in
> no way differs from intelligence, then all things we perceive
> through the bodily senses must be taken as the most certain reality.
> Now we must affirm that they are two different things, for they
> are distinct in origin and unlike in nature. The one is produced in
> us by instruction, the other by persuasion; the one can always give
> a true account of itself, the other can give none; the one cannot
> be shaken by persuasion, whereas the other can be won over; and
> true belief, we must allow, is shared by all mankind, intelligence
> only by the gods and a small number of men.[34]

We find a restatement of this position in the *Theætetus*,[35] and
though the context in that dialogue is different, the important point is

---

[34]*Timaeus*, 51DE. Translation from Francis Macdonald Cornford: *Plato's Cosmology*, London, 1937.
[35]*Theaetetus*, 201A.

that Plato did draw a distinction between knowledge and conviction, and based this distinction on the method by which each was attained. Plato looked upon knowledge, the object of instruction, as accompanied by an unshakeable certitude which conviction, the object of persuasion, lacked. This deficiency of certitude was not affected by the truth-value of the conviction. "True belief," by which Plato meant a state of having been persuaded to accept a proposition that was in fact true, was still, despite its truth, more tenuously held than knowledge (*episteme*) or intelligence (*noesis*), i.e., rational intuition.[36]

To Plato, belief or conviction *(pistis)* was one of four possible states of mind in an hierarchy of mental states.[37] The lowest of these states of mind is imagining (*eikasia*), which Cornford describes as, "the wholly unenlightened state of mind which takes sensible appearances and current moral notions at their face value—the condition of the unreleased prisoners in the Cave allegory . . . who see only images of images."[38]

Above imagining is belief which, when true, is a sufficient guide to action, but which can be shaken by persuasion and is the objective of persuasion. Higher on the scale is thinking (*dianoia*) characteristic of mathematical procedure. It is reasoning from premise to conclusion in which the premises are taken axiomatically. The highest state of mind is intelligence or knowledge, in which the premises themselves are examined and the ultimate principle on which they depend is apprehended.

In the third speech of the *Phœdrus* and in the *Meno*,[39] Plato discussed an unusual mental phenomenon which he called "madness" or inspiration, by which one, possessing only true belief, utters profound truth. It is clear in these passages that Plato did not consider the profoundest insights to be exclusively the product of intelligence or knowledge. The poet, the statesman, and the orator might have moments of vivid revelation by which audiences can be inspired, but the source of this revelation is not in any state of mind. Rather, it is divinely inspired.[40] Its capacity to persuade is due to the epidemic quality of

---

[36]Cornford: *The Republic of Plato*, Oxford, 1941, p. 223.

[37]*Republic,* 6.509 ff.

[38]Cornford: *Republic,* p. 222.

[39]*Meno,* 98B ff.

[40]This notion is developed in the *Ion.*

divine madness. Such inspirations have nothing to do with art. They are the gifts of the gods, and cannot be further explained.[41]

In these considerations we have perhaps the only instance in the formal history of rhetorical theory of a sustained investigation of the epistemological character of rhetoric, and of the relative strength with which any persuasively induced belief will endure measured against a broad psychological scale. Plato's conclusion was that no matter how fervent our conviction that a proposition is true, that conviction will always be less secure than the knowledge even of a more trivial proposition. The method by which a belief has come to be held makes all the difference.

Given the observation that belief or conviction is inferior to knowledge in certitude and persistence, and given also Plato's deep commitment to the pursuit and cultivation of knowledge, the question arises: What place, if any, would rhetorical persuasion have in Plato's doctrine of politics? What place could rhetoric have when the state itself is designed to serve philisophical ends, when its leaders are carefully selected and arduously trained philosophers, and its economy, educational system, family pattern, artistic enterprise —all of its institutions, including even the most personal and intimate —are arranged to serve the interests of abstract Justice? Where is there room for the flexibility of argument, the contingency of decision, and the inconstancy of commitment, all so characteristic of rhetorical activity, when the fabric of society is woven after the pattern of certain, immutable, universal Truth? Plato answers these questions, and defines with precision the place of rhetoric in the Platonic commonwealth.

In considering the social utility of rhetoric, Plato's emphasis falls on the function of persuasion as a means of social control. As such, its utility to the state is obvious, and Plato has not neglected it. Despite the ideological differences between the *Republic* and the *Laws,* a congruous view of the function of rhetoric is maintained. Its place is defined in the *Politicus,* where rhetoric is made subordinate to the art of statemanship; but even though in a subordinated capacity, rhetorical persuasion is considered by Plato as the only means of social control besides coercion which the statesman can exercise.[42]

---

[41]See Hackforth: pp. 60-62.
[42]*Politicus,* 304.

In the *Republic,* Plato not only holds that rhetoric should be used by the Guardians, but explicity condones the use even of willful deception in the best interests of the community.[43] The state is to be organized and governed after metaphysical principles, yet metaphysical knowledge cannot be apprehended by unmetaphysical minds. Hence, it is justifiable to simplify complex truths and to present them appealingly.

In the "second best state," rhetoric occupies the same place and discharges the same function as in the *Republic.* Here too, it is a means of social control to be used by the Legislator,[44] who may use even a benevolent lie to persuade.[45] Since Plato considered freedom of expression inimical to the best interests of the community, his condoning of deception is not general, but is always confined to the governing class. The *Laws* explicitly bans unrestricted forensic advocacy and shyster lawyers from the state,[46] but nowhere in his political writings do we find a general banishment of rhetoric.

In addition to social control, Plato attributes an educational value to rhetoric. Moral and metaphysical truths are to be rhetorically disseminated, not alone for the maintenance of political order, but so that they will be believed for their own sakes as well.[47] Young men who are without philosophy, and so are not yet equipped to attain true knowledge, would be attracted to the study of philosophy by "persuasion."[48]

It may not be apparent that Plato did not despise rhetoric, but only the excesses of the Sophists. He was far from blind to the practical need for social order and to the limitations of the popular mind, and he gave to rhetoric some functions for which, even today, no apologies need be offered. Certainly Plato was repelled by the Gorgian view of rhetoric: by the pretensions of its claims, the flaccidity of its formulation, and the easy virtue of its practice. But he was far too good a writer and clear a thinker to overstate his case or to extend it unreasonably.

It is undeniable that Plato's preoccupation with the moral character of rhetoric in his critique colored his positive formulations of rhetorical theory, so that he gives us not an account of rhetoric, but an account of

---

[43]*Republic,* 3:388, 413, 459.
[44]*Laws,* 4:720-722; 10.885D.
[45]*Laws,* 2:663 ff.
[46]*Laws,* 11:937E.
[47]*Laws,* 2:664.
[48]*Euthydemus,* 274ff.

a "true art" of rhetoric, not an account of the general social functions of rhetoric, but an account of its utility to the Ideal State. That there were actually theories and practices of rhetoric which did not fit his mold, no author has observed more brilliantly than he. But these other theories and practices were not "true" arts of rhetoric; they were "false" arts, knacks only. Plato did not deny their reality; what he denied was their moral efficacy.

From our perspective in history, we are able to confront the irony that Plato, the arch-enemy of the Sophists, was actually closer to them in his rhetorical theory than was his successor, Aristotle. Plato's repudiation of Sophistical rhetoric was neither so complete nor so thorough as his student's, for, though Plato rejected and refuted with finality the particular moral interpretation of rhetoric which the Sophists propounded, he did not reject the attempt to suffuse an investigation of rhetoric with a moral concern. It is on this very point that his great disciple parted from him.

Still, we must regard it as an open question whether Aristotle surpassed him by that particular departure. Can it be denied that so fearsomely potent a force as rhetoric participates in moral values? Is it the case that any instrument which affects human life is not subject to moral assessment? Aristotle affirmed the moral neutrality of rhetoric; Plato's answer to both these questions was an emphatic negative. When, in recent history, we find the clamorous spirit of fanaticism at large in the world, sustained by rhetorical discourse; when we contemplate the undiminished and undiminishing potentiality for savagery latent in all men, waiting to be triggered by suasive language; and when we observe the Sophists of our time, rationally discredited but thriving still, we may begin to suspect that, after all, Plato was even wiser than we had thought.

THE RHETORIC OF ARISTOTLE*

LANE COOPER

Cornell University

IT IS A PLEASURE to be here, to see so many friends, and others who, as I hope, will be friendly when this address is over. According to ancient rule, I fancy, and surely according to modern democratic example, a speaker can afford to be more personal in his remarks when he is invited to speak to an audience because it would contain more than a sprinkling of his former pupils and some well-nigh lifelong friends. And I am going to talk about a lifelong friend of mine who is a friend of yours well-known to most of you, a friend to all of us whether we all realize it, or some do not. This friend to all writers and speakers, and all teachers of speech and writing, is Aristotle, author of an *Art of Poetry* and a *Rhetoric* which have had a deal of influence throughout the ages; so much influence, in fact, that every student of discourse is sure to be a debtor to these treatises of Aristotle whether the student is aware of it or never has read either of the works. No one can be a reader of books, and not read some one who has profited by reading Aristotle. Accordingly, his influence is pervasive.

Again, no one is likely to advance beyond the point which Aristotle reached in studying the arts of poetry and eloquence unless he has gone with Aristotle as far as the *Rhetoric* and *Poetics* will take him. Of course, we may as well admit at once, and once for all, that there are spiritual realms where Aristotle is not comfortable at home; where Plato, for example, is more at home; and yet higher realms, since the birth of Christianity, where pagans generally are not at home and comfortable. And one may say, of course, that Aristotle's theory does not

*Presented at the Eastern Public Speaking Conference, Atlantic City, April, 1934.

fully explain the pagan art of Aeschylus or Sophocles, or the eloquence of Plato. That is true. No theory of art ever fully accounted for any work that is but partly the result of art and partly results from inspiration. But Aristotle on the arts of poetry and eloquence comes nearer to explaining ancient tragedy and Attic eloquence than to accounting for the Bible, the Greek and Latin hymns of the Church, and the *Commedia* of Dante. Even with respect to these, however, to Dante, for example, nobody is likely to go far in studying eloquence and structure if he is unwilling to see how far the ancient Greek will carry us. And Dante knew that. If I am not mistaken, the most important commentary on *Inferno, Purgatorio,* and *Paradiso* that is now in preparation is the one Mr. W. S. Howell has in hand. This commentary is a systematic research into Dante's theory of eloquence and his practice of the Aristotelian rhetoric. Mr. Howell's unpublished work has helped me more, and helped my students more, than any other recent thing on Dante. And it shows that Dante used the *Rhetoric* of Aristotle, consciously, with great effect. In a capital instance it shows that no other inquiries into the nature of composition are so practically helpful, so useful when you directly apply them to a literary masterpiece. At all events, that is our considered judgment with respect to Dante's masterpiece. For Dante, Aristotle is in Limbo, without suffering, but without hope; but even in the *Paradiso,* which incidentally is much indebted to Aristotle's treatise *On the Heavens,* even in a realm of Christian poetry where the spirit of Aristotle would not find itself at home, in comfort, and where modern pagans find themselves, to say the least, uneasy, there the *Rhetoric* of Aristotle is the surest guide to Dante's method and aim in constructing the speeches of the persons he represents. And so we must go on saying, until some one else believes us, that while Aristotle probably did not give the final utterance on poetic art and spoken prose, and no one ever will succeed in giving it, nevertheless the individual student is not likely to come nearer to that final utterance than Aristotle did unless he patiently goes with Aristotle as far as Aristotle will guide him. If the student goes as far as that, he will have nothing to unlearn, and will have a head full of real knowledge about literary art. One fine quality in Aristotle is his excellent perspective, so that those who go to school to him become less likely to mistake the trivial for the important. Another is his wonderful fertility in germinal thoughts. The number of interesting remarks on human nature in the *Rhetoric* is amazing. Take the one, for instance, on the reason why the ordinary person in his ordinary mood—I am not quoting—is not afraid of death. Or turn to the *Poetics*. Ross, editor of the great Oxford translation of Aristotle's works, has not in his time been mainly interested in the side of Aristotle's thought to which the *Poetics* belongs, and hence may count for an impartial witness; and it is Ross who thinks that it contains "a greater number of pregnant ideas on art than any other book."

It is easy to see that my friends and I, a considerable element in the gathering of people here, are enthusiastic about Aristotle, though not enthusiastic without measure or reason. Some of them probably used to think me highly enthusiastic about the *Poetics*, at a time when I knew far too little about the *Rhetoric* to understand the *Poetics* as fully as one ought. And some may now consider me lukewarm about the *Rhetoric* since I have, quite recently, turned to Plato, and have been translating his dialogue *Phædrus;* I am trying to do for it and possibly other things of Plato what was done for Aristotle in the version of the *Rhetoric,* which Messrs. Appleton were good enough to publish. But, in the history of my friends and me, the work on Plato is all one with that on Aristotle, save for this, a point which may be brought out in a species of confession. The point is mentioned, not because the story is of something that happened to one person, but because many persons, among them persons in this audience, must have had the like experience. Further, I may dwell upon the following bit of personal history because it should promote my special aim for today. That aim is to make those who have read the *Rhetoric* of Aristotle read it more, along with the *Phædrus* of Plato, and to make those who are not yet friendly with it as friendly as may be.

Well then, the bit of personal experience is this. When I somewhat unexpectedly took up the teaching of English, as they call it, over thirty years ago, I found experimentally that young people could be thoroughly interested in the better novels like Scott's *Bride of Lammermoor,* or George Eliot's *Romola,* or Hawthorne's shorter stories of New England, along with Homer's *Odyssey,* if the teacher helped himself and his pupils with concepts that may be discovered in the works of Aristotle, but at the time I did not know enough about the

Rhetoric. I found that our Freshmen could examine any first-rate specimen of imaginative fiction to advantage when you introduced those Freshmen to the principles of imaginative structure that one may read in Aristotle's work on poetry, if you didn't lay undue stress on the source from which the principles were drawn. There are still some people, since the time of Bruno and Francis Bacon, who do not like the name of Aristotle; and traditional scholarly prejudices somehow find their way into the undergraduate mind. At all events, you could dodge the prejudice by letting the ideas of Aristotle pass for any one's ideas, even your own. Being principles, not rules, they worked quite well irrespective of their source. When tested by examples they seemed to have validity, made the Freshmen think their instructor more original than he was, and, what is very important, gave the pupil faith in his teacher, and *vice versa.* The source, however, could not long be hid. Very soon, and very often, the truth about the source came out, and a strange matter began to be talked of. There was a teacher, and there were students, before long actually graduate students, who believed that Aristotle's *Art of Poetry* was something more than a mere historical document to be looked at with a cooler eye than an entomologist turns upon a bug. The honest entomologist, I fancy, does not think himself superior to the bug or other work of nature he is studying. But you know there are a good many persons who think themselves superior to Aristotle, and if they are right it is a hopeful sign in our times, for long and careful study has convinced me that Aristotle, while altogether human, and not incapable of mistakes, was a very intelligent person, with the uncanny habit of being right at least nine times out of ten. He is above all right where the study of human relations is concerned, for this is a study in which the Greeks from Homer down to Aristotle and Menander excelled the department of noble name at Yale. Because Aristotle is, so to speak, invariably right in studying human relations, the loving scholarship which the Italian and French Renaissance lavished upon his *Rhetoric* and *Poetics* was just, while the envy of Giordano Bruno and of Francis Bacon provides the model which our day must undertake not to follow. Read Bacon's envious notes on the *Rhetoric,* and blush at his ingratitude when he was so heavily indebted to this work, the ingratitude of Bacon, that head without a heart.

But let us be more precise in our confession. My error with regard to the *Poetics* and the *Rhetoric* lay where any one can guard against it, once it is pointed out. The error lay in sometimes paying more attention to a commentary than I paid to the work on which the comments have been written. Let us keep calling it an error rather than a fault. Students of a modern literature who feel the need of learning about Greek ideas, about the background of culture that endures, necessarily go to the books on ancient history and literature that pass for reputable scholarly helps. Such a reputable book is the one I am about to mention, and I have no doubt that with regard to it the views of some of you have undergone the change that mine have undergone, while perhaps some of you continue to think as well of it as I once did. It is the well-known work called *Aristotle's Theory of Poetry and Fine Art,* by the late Samuel Henry Butcher. For many years it has held the field as, for our time, the standard commentary on the *Poetics* of Aristotle to be had in English. Even among classical scholars outside the circle of those who specialize in the study of Aristotle, the far superior work of Bywater has not made the right headway against Butcher. Let us add that the volume of Butcher remains a stimulating book. For myself, I still refer my classes to it, but every year now with increasing caution. What is wrong with it? Well, for example, Butcher has an essay, his Chapter 8, entitled The Ideal Tragic Hero, supposedly interpreting what Aristotle says of tragic character, and full of lively reference to Shakespeare, Schiller, and Corneille, to ancient and modern tragedy in general. But the word "hero," the Greek word ηρως, does not occur in Aristotle's *Poetics;* in fact, it does not occur in the singular number throughout Aristotle's extant writings; and the emphasis Butcher lays upon one agent in an action where several agents are required obscures the real demand of Aristotle with regard to tragic character. What Aristotle says of *ethos* in a tragedy applies to all the agents that engage in the action of a play; and he says specifically that having one |man| for the story does not produce a unity of action. You could have perfect unity of action in the tale of the fifty daughters of Danaus running from wedlock with the fifty sons of King Aegyptus. In various ways, and in the long run, Butcher does not put the emphasis where Aristotle puts it, or where we need it. The Briton is an honorable man, no doubt the soul of honor in his usual relations, who does

not realize his own sophistication, and is all unknowingly infected with
the modern love of paradox. Aristotle is a subtle, I will not say "slip-
pery" Greek, who on occasion will force a poor example to illustrate
a principle that is sound, is absolutely free from the Greek Sophistical
tradition, and is untainted by the Sophist's love of paradox.

I shall give one other illustration of false emphasis in Butcher, but
take the opportunity first to speak of a most admirable edition of the
Poetics which has just appeared in Germany, by Alfred Gudeman.
Gudeman's text of the *Poetics* and his commentary are far and away
the best so far, so good, I think, that they will never really be improved
upon unless a new and better manuscript than we now possess for the
Poetics is discovered in papyrus.

The second point of emphasis I wish to raise concerns the *Rhetoric*.
Butcher says of the *Poetics,* quoting Goethe, that "it needs some insight
into Aristotle's general philosophy to understand what he says about
the drama; that otherwise he confuses our studies." The statements are
given in the words of Butcher, The first is true, and would be equally
true of any author you please. The more you know about the rest of an
author's works, the better you can interpret any one of them. But the
implication that in order to read Aristotle's *Poetics* with intelligence
you need first to know his *Physics* and *Metaphysics,* for example, is
nonsense. The assertion that without a knowledge of his *Physics* or
Metaphysics the study of his *Poetics* is confusing is absolutely false.
The knowing how that the ablest of the British students of this *Art of
Poetry* in our time was Bywater, who properly links the *Rhetoric*
with the *Poetics,* and says of the latter:

> The book taken as it is, with perhaps an occasional sidelight
> from some of his other works, is intelligible enough; after a brief
> introduction he gives us in outline all that he has to say on the
> subject immediately before him, the technique of the Drama and
> the Epic. He tells one in fact how to construct a good play and a
> good epic, just as in the *Rhetoric* he tells one how to make a good
> speech. And in doing this he has succeeded in formulating once for
> all the great first principles of dramatic art, the canons of dra-
> matic logic which even the most adventurous of modern dramatists
> can only at his peril forget or set at naught.

Fortunately, when Bywater's great edition appeared I could recognize the superiority of a master hand to the somewhat amateurish Butcher. My version of the *Poetics* aimed simply to make clear the meaning of it to a Sophomore or Junior student, say, more especially by expanding the curt memoranda of examples in the text and by adding more examples. I trusted Bywater, though not uncritically, and let the text and translation of Butcher alone. His smooth English somehow glides over the Greek, and does not come to grips with it. Yet thanks to him I did once use the word "hero," which Aristotle does not use, thus: "The Unity of a Plot does not consist, as some, as some suppose, in having one man as the hero." I believe that word is the only one I deplore in my amplified version of Aristotle's *Poetics*. And you observe that it is after all not so bad, perhaps good enough, in effect, because of Aristotle's saving "as some suppose." Some still suppose it. The thing I really deplore is this. It is a sin not of commission but of omission. I did not betimes go at the *Rhetoric* of Aristotle as a self-respecting teacher of literature should, and as Aristotle says you should in order to understand the *Poetics*. Butcher says, if you wish to know this book, study Aristotle's philosophy; he nowhere shows the slightest interest in Aristotle's *Rhetoric as a* substantial help with the *Poetics,* or as a help in studying literature. If Butcher had told my generation, "By all means read the *Rhetoric*," we would have read it. Aristotle, we thought, wasn't always right, but Butcher was. How many of this audience in their time have felt that way? Let us give more heed to Aristotle and to those who interpret him as one who is superior to them than we give to the clever critics who think they rise superior to him.

Now, as compared with Butcher, what does Aristotle say? In effect he says: An epic poem or a tragedy is all made up of speeches. A poet therefore must be able to compose a speech, in fact a number of speeches, for each and every kind of person which the plot or action may demand. By extension we could say with Aristotle: the writer of a comedy, as Aristophanes, or of a dialogue, as Plato, or of a novel, as George Eliot, is all the while composing speeches for the characters. That is precisely what the author has to do after he has made an outline of his plot or structure, and settled on his *dramatis personae,* and sits down with his pencil or his stylus in his hand, and takes up the actual business of composing his drama, or Platonic dialogue, or novel.

He has to write just one speech after another. By way of preparation, therefore, let the poet, or the writer of dramatic dialogue in general, study Aristotle's *Rhetoric*. That, in brief, is what Aristotle thinks ought to be done. Because he treats the art of writing speeches, and treats it fully, in this work, therefore Aristotle deals cursorily with this matter in the *Poetics*, where he devotes to it but a few important sentences. These sentences lead directly to the *Rhetoric*, which thus to the student of the *Poetics* becomes, as it were, one great chapter of the latter work, a section bulkier than the *Poetics* as this stands. The advice of Aristotle is correct. If the poet, novelist, writer of short stories, is composing speeches all the time, he ought to study Rhetoric, and Aristotle's *Rhetoric* is a good one. My friends and I believe it is the best. And we have much the same advice for any one who really wishes to see how Dante goes about his task in the *Commedia*.

So for a number of years, and thanks to Butcher, I failed to understand the bearing of the *Rhetoric* as a whole on the *Poetics*. I thought that the part of Aristotle's *Rhetoric* that concerned my students and me was the third book, the one on Diction and Arrangement, but especially his remarks on Diction. And I put Welldon's rendering of the twelve chapters on Diction into a book called *Theories of Style*, a quarter of a century since. Then gradually my own pupils taught me better, Drummond first and chiefly, and later Caplan among others. And finally, as some of the audience know, I was converted, and tried to do an English version of the *Rhetoric* that would help my students of poetics, and would meet the need of public speakers, too. So it comes about that I am here to-day, urging every one who cares for literature not to neglect the *Art of Poetry*, and to read, and keep rereading Aristotle's *Rhetoric*. Of course, I should like to have you read my version. If you don't like that, then read the excellent translation by Rhys Roberts; it is better than any other version that has been made in England. However, Roberts did not specially intend his version for the kind of student we meet in American classes, and I specially did. I tried to keep in mind the kind of student Herrick said he taught in Iowa, that kind I was at Rutgers, the kind of undergraduate I have met in Ithaca, New York, Urbana, Illinois, and elsewhere. I hoped the book would find a use in larger classes than I think have used it, and believe that any one who tries it there will find, not my translation, but Aristotle's *Rhetoric*, the best book for written composition and as a practical guide to public speakers that ever was put forth.

This belief is not unusual. Others have shared it. A century or more ago, Bishop Copleston said of Aristotle and the *Rhetoric*:

> If ever an author labored more than another, in an age of sophistry and dogmatism, to establish the empire of common sense and reason, it was Aristotle. . . . It is unfortunate for the fame of Aristotle that he should be known chiefly as the author of the Logical Treatises. The Treatise on Rhetoric is a magazine of intellectual riches. Under an arrangement the most accurate perhaps and the most luminous ever marked out, the diversified elements of thought, of feeling, and of taste, are presented in due order to the reader's mind. Nothing is arbitrary, nothing gratuitous. Long experience with mankind, attentive observation of human nature in public and in private life, the political history of past times, and the occurrences of his own age, furnished him with the materials of this great work. In the course of the inquiry, nothing is left untouched on which Rhetoric in all its branches, has any bearing. His principles are the result of extensive original induction. He sought them, if ever man did seek them, in the living pattern of the human heart. All the recesses and windings of that hidden region he has explored; all its caprices and affections, whatever tends to excite, to ruffle, to amuse, to gratify, or to offend it, have been carefully examined. The reason of these phenomena is demonstrated, the method of creating them is explained. The Third Book contains a body of rules for good writing, traced to those natural principles out of which they all grow, and illustrated by examples which his own intimate acquaintance with the best poets and orators of Greece readily supplied. The whole is a textbook of human feeling; a storehouse of taste; an exemplar of condensed and accurate, but uniformly clear and candid, reasoning.

Voltaire said of the treatise and its author:

> I do not believe there is a single refinement of the art that escaped him. . . . Nothing better proves the great sense and good taste of Aristotle than his having given each thing its place.

The late Rhys Roberts said:

> As in the *Politics*, . . . so here, he takes all due account of pre-

vious efforts and experience. . . . His repeated references either to
"the present-day writers on rhetoric" generally, or to specified
teachers and theorists, are enough to show that he has faithfully
reviewed the rhetorical field of his own and previous days. And in
the light of current shortcomings he lays down the true philosophical principles of rhetoric, considered as a branch of the science of
man, and writes a treatise which has never been superseded, and is
never likely to be superseded. The *Rhetoric* has been described as
an "isolated" work. Its true distinction is that it does not stand
alone without predecessors or successors, but that it stands apart
and pre-eminent even where the predecessors and successors are so
numerous; it is the most philosophical (or, scientific) work ever
produced on the subject.

Ernest Havet said:

> My task is completed if I have made the reader see that this
> Rhetoric, the oldest of all, nevertheless is the one that has aged the
> least, the one that to-day remains the most useful, because it is
> based upon principles higher and more universal than any other.

Cardinal Newman was heavily indebted to the *Rhetoric* in his theory
of composition, in his actual writings of the longer sort, and in his
sermons. In his *Idea of a University,* having just quoted from the
ancient treatise, he thus begins Part 5 of Discourse V:

> Do not suppose that in thus appealing to the ancients I am throw-
> ing back the world two thousand years, and fettering philosophy
> with the reasonings of paganism. While the world lasts will
> Aristotle's doctrine on these matters last, for he is the oracle of
> nature and of truth. While we are men, we cannot help, to a great
> extent, being Aristotelians, for the great Master does but analyze
> the thoughts, feelings, views, and opinions of human kind. He has
> told us the meaning of our own words and ideas, before we were
> born. In many subject-matters, to think correctly is to think like
> Aristotle; and we are his disciples whether we will or no, though
> we may not know it.

Finally, let us attend to what the best-known schoolmaster of recent
times, Arnold of Rugby, had to say of his school and of his hopeful
Matthew who was about to leave it:

We have been reading some of the *Rhetoric* in the Sixth Form
this half-year, and its immense value struck me again so forcibly
that I could not consent to send my son to a University where
he would lose it altogether.[1]

---

[1]Apart from the quotation from Cardinal Newman, the source of which is indi-
cated above, these passages which have just been cited, beginning with that from
Copleston, can be most easily found in my translation, *The Rhetoric of Aristotle,*
New York, 1932, pp. xi-xiii.

PLATO AND ARISTOTLE ON
RHETORIC AND RHETORICIANS

EVERETT LEE HUNT

Swarthmore College

T HE art of rhetoric offered to the Athenian of the fifth century B.C.
a method of higher education and, beyond that, a way of life. Plato
attacked both. He gave rhetoric a conspicuous place in his dialogues
because it represented in Athenian life that which he most disliked.
His pictures of the rhetoricians are so broadly satirical that at times
they become caricatures; but his literary power and philosophical
originality have so impressed themselves upon succeeding ages that the
sophists and rhetoricians of Athens have become symbolical of false
pretense of knowledge, overweening conceit, fallacious argument, cultivation of style for its own sake, demagoguery, corruption of youth
through a scepticism which professed complete indifference to truth,
and, in general, a ready substitution of appearance for reality.

We have the more readily accepted Plato's account because these
faults have never been absent from cultivation. If the sophists and
rhetoricians of Plato's dialogues had not existed, it would have been
necessary to invent them. The qualities they typify are so universal
that certain collective names for them have become a necessity for
thought. Even Grote, the great defender of the historical sophists, when
he desires to point out the fallacies of the Platonic Socrates, finds it
convenient to accuse Plato of "sophistry."[1] These qualities are not only
objectively ever present, but we attribute them readily to any persons or
arguments when for any reason our approval has not been won. An
argument which we do not accept is sophistical, and the person who

---

[1] George Grote: *Plato,* London, 1888, III, 63.

represents it a sophist. An appeal to the feelings of men which does not happen to warm our own hearts is rhetorical, and its author a rhetorician. It was so in Plato's time, and it was no more safe then than now to take the words "sophistry" and "rhetoric" at their face value.

When we ask, who were the sophists, what did they teach, and what is the connection between sophistry and rhetoric, we have asked questions involving great historical and philosophical dispute. Generations of historians of philosophy, accepting Plato's account, have made the sophists the scapegoats for all intellectual—and, at times, moral—delinquencies. It is to Hegel that the sophists owe their rehabilitation in modern times.[1] G. H. Lewes, five years before Grote published his famous defense of the sophists, characterized them as professors of rhetoric,[2] and pointed out the bias which had caused their unfair treatment at the hands of Plato. Grote's classic treatment of the sophists in his *History of Greece*[3] was termed by Henry Sidgwick "a historical discovery of the highest order." "Before it was written," says Professor Sidgwick, "the facts were all there, but the learned world could not draw the right inference." In two vigorous essays he defends Grote and makes some significant contributions to the controversy.[4] John Stuart Mill, in an extended review of Grote's *Plato*, defends his interpretation in almost all points, and furnishes many additional arguments in defense of the sophists.[5] E. M. Cope, in his essays on the sophistic rhetoric, rejects many of Grote's conclusions.[6] Zeller is not inclined to look upon the sophists with favor.[7] Chaignet, in his history of rhetoric, accepts the conventional contrast between Plato and the sophists.[8] Jowett, Plato's translator, accepts many of Grote's conclusions, but

[1]G. W. Hegel: *Lectures on Philosophy*, 2d ed., 1840, tr. E. S. Haldane, London, 1892.
[2]G. H. Lewes: *Biographical History of Philosophy*, London, 1857, pp. 87 ff.
[3]Grote: *History of Greece*, London, 1851, VIII, 67.
[4]H. Sidgwick: The Sophists, *Lectures on the Philosophy of Kant and other Philosophical Lectures and Essays*, London, 1905.
[5]J. S. Mill: Grote's *Plato*, *Dissertations and Discussions*, New York, 1874, IV.
[6]E. M. Cope: The Sophistic Rhetoric, *Journal of Classical and Sacred Philology*, II:129-69, 1855, III:34-80, 253-88, 1856.
[7]E. Zeller: *Pre-Socratic Philosophy*, tr. S. F. Alleyne, London, 1881, II, sect. iii. For still other points of view, see A. W. Benn: *The Greek Philosophers*, London, 1882, ch. 2. Also Sir A. Grant: *The Ethics of Aristotle*, London, 1874, I, 103-54.
[8]A. E. Chaignet: *La Rhetorique et son Historie*, Paris, 1888, pp. 43, 44.

rejects others.[1] Gomperz, in his *Greek Thinkers,* written fifty years
after Grote's history was published, says of his own contemporaries
among historians of philosophy:

> They still begin by handsomely acknowledging the ambiguity
> of the word "sophist," and the injustice done to the bearers of
> that name in the fifth century B.C. by the ugly sense in which
> the term came to be used, and they admit that restitution is due.
> But the debt is forgotten before it is paid; the debtor reverts to
> the old familiar usage, and speaks of the sophists once more as if
> they were really mere intellectual acrobats, unscrupulous tor-
> mentors of language, or the authors of pernicious teachings. The
> spirit may be willing, but the reason is helpless against the force
> of inveterate habits of thought. Verily the sophists were born
> under an evil star. Their one short hour of triumphant success
> was paid for by centuries of obloquy. Two invincible foes were
> banded against them—the caprice of language, and the genius
> of a great writer, if not the greatest writer of all times.[2]

The itinerant sophists founded no schools, and most of their works
have been lost. The evidence in the case is therefore of the kind which
makes endless arguments possible. A few conclusions may, however,
be stated as generally agreed upon. The term sophist originally had no
unfavorable connotation, and was applied to any man who was thought
to be learned. Thus the seven sages of Greece, universally honored,
were at times called sophists.[3] In the time of Plato the word carried
with it something of reproach, but it was not a definitely understood
term. Rival teachers employed it against each other. Thus Isocrates
regarded speculative thinkers (Plato among them) as sophists, because
he thought their speculations fruitless. He also attacked as sophists
other teachers of rhetoric whose instruction he regarded as unintelli-
gent, and whose promises to their pupils he thought impossible of ful-
filment.[4] The general public used the term with almost no discrimina-

[1]Introduction to his translation of Plato's *Sophist.*
[2]Theodore Gomperz: *Greek Thinkers,* tr. L. Magnus, New York, 1901, I, 422.
[3]For citations illustrating the various uses of the word "sophist" by Greek writers,
see Gomperz: *op. cit.,* I, 579.
[4]Isocrates: *Antidosis, Against the Sophists.* For translations of selected passages see
Jebb: *Attic Orators,* London, 1893, II, 124-47. See also W. H. Thompson: On the
Philosophy of Isocrates and his Relation to the Socratic Schools, in his edition of
Plato's *Phaedrus,* London, 1868.

tion, and Aristophanes seized upon Socrates as the sophist who could be most effectively lampooned.

As to what they taught, it has been established that such terms as a sophistic mind, a sophistic morality, a sophistic scepticism, and others implying a common basis of doctrine, are quite without justification. Their common characteristics were that they were professional teachers, that they accepted fees, and that rhetoric was a large element in the teaching of virtually all of them. The general emphasis upon rhetoric does not mean that, as scholars, all the sophists found their intellectual interests centered in rhetoric. But rhetoric was the one subject with which they could be sure to make a living. The conditions which made rhetorical training a universal necessity in Athens have been frequently set forth. The sophist who was a master of rhetoric had a number of possibilities before him. He could win power and repute by the delivery of eulogistic orations at public funerals, or deliberative addresses at times of political crises. He could appear at games, or upon occasions of his own making, with what we sometimes call occasional, or literary, addresses, expounding Homer or other works of Greek literature. He could write speeches for clients who were to appear in court. He was not allowed to appear in person as an advocate unless he could show that he had a direct connection with the case, but the profession of logographer was profitable. Finally, he was more certain of pupils in rhetoric than in any other subject.[1] It is not strange, then, that with a wide range of individual interests, the sophists, with varying emphasis, should unite upon rhetoric as the indispensable part of their stock in trade.

The claim to impart virtue has at times been held to be the distinguishing mark of the sophist, and the attempt has been made to divide the sophists from the rhetoricians upon this basis. This cannot be done, for the two activities of making men virtuous and making them eloquent were inextricably intermingled. Hegel has pointed out what he regards as an essential difference between the sophists and modern professors.[2] The professor makes no pretension to making men good or wise; he only presents to students his organized knowledge, realizing that knowledge comes but wisdom lingers. The sophists, on

---

[1]See O. T. Navarre: *Essai sur la Rhétorique Grecque avant Aristote,* Paris, 1900.
[2]Hegel: *op. cit.,* I, 352.

the other hand, laid claim to some actual effect from their teachings; they made men wise. This was at least in part due to the dominance of rhetoric. Aristotle might lecture upon the theoretical aspects of rhetoric—a procedure which seems to have been productive of little eloquence—but the prime purpose of the teaching of rhetoric was practical. Certain sophists made the payment of their fees dependent upon some proof that they had actually given to a pupil the ability to persuade an audience. With such a background, it is natural that the teaching of ethics as abstract knowledge would seem about as futile as the teaching of an abstract rhetoric. A man who taught ethics taught it practically, with injunctions and exhortations, and he expected practical consequences to follow. But one of the consequences always looked for was that the pupil should become such a person as to be persuasive when speaking in a public assembly. Ethics thus was often absorbed in rhetoric. The failures of many pupils to become either good or persuasive gave rise, then as now, to cynical reflections upon the futility of education, and there were many arguments as to whether virtue or rhetoric could be taught. In these arguments there were two extreme positions. Some inclined to believe that if you teach a man to be virtuous, he will naturally be eloquent, and rhetorical instruction is unnecessary. Other sophists believed it quite impossible to teach virtue, but by constant attention to becoming a persuasive speaker, virtue would be unconsciously acquired. The controversy over the relation of virtue to eloquence runs through the history of rhetoric, and may be viewed as a technical question in that field. The attitude of sophists toward the teaching of virtue, then, cannot distinguish the sophists from the rhetoricians, and for the purposes of our study the two terms may be used almost synonymously—the word sophist, perhaps, being somewhat more inclusive.

The way in which the sophists combined their own intellectual interests with the teaching of rhetoric may best be made clear by a brief study of the four principal figures: Prodicus, Hippias, Protagoras, and Gorgias. Since these are the men most often referred to by Plato, it is also desirable to have some historical knowledge of them with which to correct the impressions given by the Platonic pictures.

Protagoras and Gorgias were older than Prodicus and Hippias, but they lived longer and matured later. They were therefore more affected by the movement away from the natural sciences, and as humanists devoted a larger portion of their energies to definitely rhetorical instruction.

Prodicus of Ceos has been called the earliest of the pessimists.[1] He was frail of body, but with a powerful voice he moved his audiences by descriptions of the different ages of man from birth to second childhood and death. He would depict death as "a stony-hearted creditor, wringing pledges one by one from his tardy debtor, first his hearing, then his sight, and next the free movement of his limbs."[2] His pessimism had none of the usual consequences—passive resignation, retreat from the world, or a great desire to seek pleasures while they might be found. To face death courageously was a virtue, and he taught his disciples that while we are, death is not; when death is, we are not. Life, while it lasted, was to be lived vigorously. His most famous lecture, *The Choice of Hercules,* has been preserved by Xenophon,[3] who tells us that Socrates quoted it with approval; through many centuries it has had a great effect in exalting the ideals of labor, hardihood, and simplicity. It was not in popular religion that Prodicus found his sustaining faith, for his speculations upon the origin of religion have the point of view of the modern critical historian. He accounted for the divinities of the various nations by pointing out that they deified the objects most useful to them—sun, moon, rivers, fruits of the field, and heroic men.

The more technical instruction of Prodicus was devoted to a study of language. He sought to collect and compare words of similar meaning. He desired to reduce the ambiguities in the arguments of the Greeks, and to aid in the development of literary style. He attempted to clarify ideas by insisting upon accuracy in the use of words, believing, with Hobbes, that "the light of human minds is perspicuous words."

The lectures of Prodicus were well known in all the cities of Greece, and commanded large sums in all places except Sparta, where foreign

---

[1]For Prodicus, see the following: Philostratus: *Lives of the Sophists,* tr. W. C. Wright, New York, 1922, pp. 37-9; F. Welcker: Prodikos von Keos, Vorgänger des Sokrates, *Rheinisches Museum für Philologie,* III, 1833, 1-39; Gomperz: *op. cit.,* I, 425-30; Benn: *op. cit.,* I, 77-81; Bromley Smith: Prodicus of Ceos, *Quarterly Journal of Speech Education,* VI, ii, 1920, 51.

[2]Pseudo-Platonic *Axiochus,* 360, D. Cited by Gomperz: *op. cit.,* I, 428.

[3]Xenophon's *Memorabilia,* tr. E. C. Marchant, New York, 1923, II, ch. 1.

teachers were discouraged by a law against the payment of fees. Nevertheless he was welcomed there. He served his native island frequently as ambassador, and in the discharge of his civic duties displayed the qualities which in his lectures he urged upon youth.

Prodicus, then, was the rhetor rather than the teacher of rhetoric; and his chief contributions to the thought of his time were made as philosopher and grammarian.

Hippias of Elis, whom Plato especially disliked, is chiefly remembered for his versatility.[1] As an orator he was known throughout Greece. He recited certain well-known compositions of his in which figures of the Iliad are compared upon the basis of their virtues, or old men give advice to aspiring youths. He was rewarded by being made a freeman of many cities, and it is especially significant that his lectures on history and ethics were also acceptable to the conservative Spartans. He never gave himself to the routine of perfecting his students in rhetoric, but was occupied with innumerable pursuits. He was a mathematician of considerable note; he wrote on theories of sculpture and painting, on phonetics, rhythm, and music; he developed a system that enabled him to perform surprising feats of memory in his old age; he was an ambassador for his native city, Elis; he attempted most of the prevailing forms of literature; and he prided himself upon his facility in mastering all the arts and crafts.

The antithesis between nature and convention seems to have originated with Hippias. He observed the variety and changeability of the laws of the Greek democracies, and felt that only laws possessing the universality and permanence of the laws of nature should be really sacred and binding. To give validity to the laws of men, the laws of all states should be compared, and the universal elements in them selected as the "natural" laws for the governing of nations. In believing that all men were by nature equal, Hippias was perhaps the originator of the doctrine of natural rights. When the distinction between nature and convention has been clearly made, one may, of course, espouse either. Hippias was one of the first preachers of a return to nature. This suggests a reason for his efforts to achieve so wide a versatility. The return to nature is only possible when each person is relatively self-

[1]For Hippias, see Philostratus: *op. cit.*, p. 35; Gomperz: *op. cit.*, I, 431-4; Benn: *op. cit.*, I, 81-5.

sufficient, and self-sufficiency was a favorite doctrine with Hippias. He doubtless believed, as have men of other ages, that the development of personality gained by the consciousness of being equal to any situation more than offsets the dissipation of energy and efficiency incurred by the performance of all sorts of tasks; but one motive was clearly that of independence, and the development of the sort of ingenuity that enables a Robinson Crusoe to exist. Such a man would live by his work as well as by his wits. Rhetoric would not be the chief means of obtaining what he desired, and it is not surprising that rhetoric should be relatively less important to those who would be governed by nature than to those who saw in convention the power that offers the best government.

Hippias was more than a popular orator preaching to the cities of Greece. In his thought we have the beginnings of the cosmopolitanism of the later Cynics, the self-sufficiency of the Stoics, the belief in natural rights, and the ideal of versatility as a means of developing the whole man.

Protagoras of Abdera accepted the distinction of Hippias between nature and convention; but he had no sympathy for the return to nature.[1] In the variety and changeability of the laws of men lay the great hope of progress. He therefore turned away from the natural sciences and devoted himself to the "humanities." He, too, was a man of great versatility; he invented a porter's pad; as a friend of Pericles, he was given the task of framing the laws for the colony at Thurium. As a teacher, his instruction was chiefly intended to offer a training for public life. He included within his curriculum oratory and its auxiliary arts, educational theory, jurisprudence, politics, and ethics. In his teaching of public speaking he insisted upon the value of practical exercises. He declared that there were two sides to every proposition, and that a speaker should be able to set forth the arguments on either side. His practice of having his students argue upon both sides of certain general themes may have been responsible for the charge against him, recorded by Aristotle, that he made the worse appear the better reason.

---

[1]For Protagoras, see the following: Philostratus: *op. cit.*, pp. 33-5; Diogenes Laertius: *Lives of the Philosophers*, tr. C. D. Yonge, London, 1853, bk. ix, ch. 8; Hegel: *op. cit.*, I, 372-8; Gomperz: *op. cit.*, I, 438-75; Benn: *op. cit.*, I, 85-95; E. Barker: *Greek Political Theory*, London, 1918, pp. 60-4; Bromley Smith: Protagoras of Abdera, *Quarterly Journal of Speech Education, IV*, 1918, 196.

But as this was a standing reproach against philosophers as well as rhetoricians, and as we have no evidence which impeaches his moral character, we may believe that this charge applied no more to his teaching than to all instruction in the art of reasoning.

In addition to the training in debate, Protagoras practiced his pupils in the development of what were called commonplaces. Speeches were made which praised or blamed certain human qualities, such as patriotism, friendship, courage, cupidity. These speeches had no reference to a concrete situation, but they equipped the pupils with a stock of thoughts and phrases for use when a real occasion demanded ready utterance. The debates developed keenness and dexterity; the commonplaces gave the speakers a certain copiousness and elegance.

Grammar was also given attention, and Protagoras is recognized as the first to introduce the subject into his curriculum. It has been remarked that the level attained by Greek literature before Protagoras write his book *On Correct Speech* seems to indicate that a mastery of language may be acquired quite independently of conscious rules. But the desire of Protagoras to introduce order and consistency in the tenses of the verb, moods of predication, and genders of substantives, was in harmony with the intellectual tendencies of the times, and shows him to have been by no means totally absorbed in the practical business of advising youth how to get on in the world.

The ethical theory of Protagoras was set forth in the lost work, *On the Incorrect Actions of Mankind*. In his seventieth year he read publicly, at the house of Euripides, his work, *On the Gods*. Only the first sentence has been preserved.

> In respect to the gods, I am unable to know either that they are or that they are not, for there are many obstacles to such knowledge, above all the obscurity of the matter, and the life of man, in that it is so short.[1]

Whether Protagoras meant to assail the belief in the gods, or whether he meant merely to point out that in the nature of the case we could not have *knowledge* of them, we do not know. At any rate, his scepticism so alarmed certain of his contemporaries that his book was publicly burned, and he was exiled.

---

[1]Diogenes Laertius: *IX,* 51.

The philosophical doctrine for which Protagoras is chiefly known, and for which he was vigorously assailed by Plato, is summarized in the dictum that man is the measure of all things. Since we have only the first sentence of the work in which this doctrine was developed, it is not strange that scholars are far apart in their interpretation of the meaning of Protagoras; but they are generally agreed that the Platonic interpretation of it in the *Theœtetus* is quite unfair. Few interpreters now consider it to involve the degree of relativity and subjectivism with which Protagoras and the sophists generally have been burdened. Gomperz points out that a man who preached that anything was true which any one believed to be so, would not be the man to suffer for a denial of the possibility of knowledge of the gods. Professor F. C. Schiller, in his *Studies in Humanism,* devotes two dialogues to Protagoras; one explaining his humanism, and the other defending his scepticism. In his introduction to the volume Professor Schiller says:

> Our only hope of understanding knowledge, our only chance of keeping philosophy alive by nourishing it with the realities of life, lies in going back from Plato to Protagorus, and ceasing to misunderstand the great teacher who discovered the measure of man's universe.[1]

But this is not the place to discuss the philosophical aspects of the teachings of Protagoras; it is only desired to make it clear that there are grounds for regarding him as did Hegel.

> [He was] not merely a teacher of culture, but likewise a deep and solid thinker, a philosopher who reflected on fundamental questions of an altogether universal kind.[2]

Gorgias of Leontini,[3] who first appeared in Athens as the head of an embassy petitioning for aid against the aggressions of Syracuse upon Sicilian cities, is known as the founder of the art of prose. Chiefly

---

[1] Schiller: *Studies in Humanism,* London, 1907, p. xiv.
[2] Hegel: *op. cit.,* I, 373.
[3] For Gorgias, see the following: Philostratus: *op. cit.,* pp. 29-33; Diodorus Siculus: bk. xii, ch. 7; *The Historical Library of Diodorus the Sicilian,* tr. George Booth, London, 1814, I, 465-6; F. Blass: *Attische Beredsamkeit,* Leipzig, 1864, I, ch. 2; Navarre: *op. cit.,* ch. 3; W. H. Thompson's introduction to his edition of Plato's *Gorgias,* London, 1871; Hegel: *op. cit.,* I, 378-84; Gomperz: *op. cit.,* I, 476-94; Benn: *op. cit.,* I, 95-100; Bromley Smith: Gorgias: A Study of Oratorical Style, *Quarterly Journal of Speech Education, VII,* 1921, 335.

interested in oratory of the epideictic type, he employed what is termed the "grand" style. The resources of the poets, whose works were so successful in holding the attention of Greek audiences, were turned to the purposes of the orator. Gorgias was interested in style for style's sake; his foreign accent and distinguished air delighted the Athenians; and throughout his career he sought to persuade by pleasing. The extravagances and artificialities of his style have often been pointed to as the source of the euphuism of the seventeenth century, and of the stylistic eccentricities of other periods of decadence.

It cannot be said, however, that the oratory of Gorgias was devoid of ideas. In common with other itinerant teachers, he preached Pan-Hellenism in all the cities of Greece. In his Olympian oration he urged the Greeks to cease their internal rivalries, and to turn their spears against the barbarians. In the Athenian funeral oration he warned his hearers that victories over their fellow Greeks called for dirges of lament. As a teacher of oratory, Gorgias was condemned by Aristotle for placing too much emphasis upon memorization and declamation.[1] Little is known concerning his pedagogical method, but there is no reason to suppose that it differed markedly from the custom of having the pupils declaim speeches written by themselves and by the master, drill in topics of amplification and depreciation, and practise upon commonplaces and disputations. Although an epideictic speaker would be constantly praising virtue and censuring vice, and in so doing could hardly avoid entertaining certain ethical theories, Gorgias never announced himself as a teacher of virtue. He agreed with Isocrates that one who tried to become persuasive in discoursing about justice and virtue and expediency would probably become as virtuous as mere knowledge could make him.

As a philosopher, Gorgias engaged in controversy with the Eleatic school. All we know of his book *On Nature or Not-Being,* is its three-fold thesis that "Being does not exist, if it did exist it would not be cognizable, and if it were cognizable, the cognition would not be communicable."[2] We cannot here enter upon metaphysical questions; but the conventional construction put upon this thesis is that it goes beyond Protagoras, and is the ultimate of sophistical scepticism, that it

---

[1] Aristotle: *Sophistici Elenchi,* tr. Edward Poste, London, 1866, ch. 34.
[2] As translated in Gomperz: *op. cit.,* I, 482.

is a nihilism which makes all knowledge impossible, that it makes immediate plausibility the sole standard of the critical judgment, and that rhetoric was the chief of all subjects for Gorgias because the one certainty of life was that the man who could persuade others to do his will was, temporarily at least, the possessor of great power. This interpretation is not justified either by an examination of the philosophical disputes of the time, or by a study of the life of Gorgias himself. The Eleatic school, following Parmenides and Melissus, was quite willing to doubt all evidence of the senses, and yet to trust implicity in *a priori* reasoning about Absolute Being. The protest of Gorgias against this was quite in harmony with the growing modesty of the scientific endeavor of the times, which was beginning to see the necessity of increasing knowledge bit by bit, and to question the claim of the philosophers to a higher knowledge. Had Gorgias, in denying the tenets of the Eleatics, meant that he believed scientific truth to be unattainable, it is not likely that he would have written upon physics, nor that a statue would have appeared upon the tomb of Isocrates representing Gorgias as directing the attention of his pupil to a globe. The attack of Gorgias upon the contradictions of his predecessors in philosophy does not show that he abandoned all search for truth. Socrates attacked his philosophical predecessors in a similar manner, he abandoned all inquiry in natural science, and he had as little confidence in the attributes of being as Gorgias; yet he is not accused of denying the validity of established scientific truth, or of abandoning all belief in the possibility of knowledge. The account of Gorgias offered by many historians of philosophy is a *reductio ad absurdum* rather than an interpretation.

Although we think of Gorgias chiefly as an orator and a teacher of oratory, and as a creator of a style which is now looked upon unfavorably, he was too active a participant in the philosophical controversies of his time for us to dismiss him as intellectually insignificant. Since we have lost his philosophical works, we cannot prove that he made a constructive contribution to the thought of his time, but his attack upon an absolutistic philosophy was something, and the evidence certainly does not warrant the supposition that he was guilty of meaningless absurdities, or that his teaching was necessarily immoral in its implications.

Numerous other rhetoricians might be mentioned—Polus and

Thrasymachus especially—but our information concerning them is scanty, and the four we have dealt with are the most significant when we consider their prominence as rhetoricians, their contribution to the thought of the time, and the attention they received from Plato.

One is inevitably led to ask why such men as these have suffered so greatly in the estimation of posterity. Why has Plato's opinion been accepted uncritically and its perversions further distorted by later commentators? In addition to what has already been suggested—that we need the terminology of the attack upon the Athenian sophists to describe an ever present sophistry—there is the fact that Athenian hostility to the sophists has often been taken as a confirmation of Plato's account. This is to forget that Athenian public opinion distrusted the sophists for reasons similar to those which led it to execute Socrates, and that the disagreement between Plato and the Athenian public was profound. The activities which gave these teachers their influence with the Athenians were just the ones which led Plato to condemn them; while many aspects of their thought which led to popular disfavor were the ones which Plato would have regarded with approval. We may learn much about the sophists by contrasting the typical Athenian criticism of them with that of Plato.

In accounting for the disfavor with which the Athenians looked upon the sophists it must not be forgotten that a complementary picture

---

[1]G. H. Lewes has shown why the relationship between the solitary thinker and the public speaker tends to remain constant. "The Sophists were wealthy; the Sophists were powerful; the Sophists were dazzling, rhetorical, and not profound. Interrogate human nature—above all, the nature of philosophers—and ask what will be the sentiment entertained respecting the Sophists by their rivals. Ask the solitary thinker what is his opinion of the showy, powerful, but shallow rhetorician who usurps the attention of the world. The man of convictions has at all times a superb contempt for the man of mere oratorical or dialectical display. The thinker knows that the world is ruled by Thought: yet he finds Expression gaining the world's attention. He knows that he has within him thoughts pregnant with human welfare; yet he sees the giddy multitude intoxicated with the enthusiasm excited by some plausible fallacy, clothed in enchanting language. He sees through the fallacy, but cannot make others as clear-sighted. His warning is unheeded; his wisdom is spurned; his ambition is frustrated; the popular Idol is carried onward in triumph. The neglected thinker would not be human if he bore this with equanimity. He does not. He is loud and angry in lamenting the fate of a world that can be so led; loud and angry in his contempt of one who could so lead it. Should he become a critic or historian of his age, what exactness ought we to expect in his account of the popular idol?" Op. cit., p. 88.

of their power and influence could quite as easily be drawn, and that both are necessary to a true estimate of their position in Athenian life. The sophists exerted a much greater influence upon their times than Plato, and the element of jealousy should not be entirely overlooked in considering his attitude toward them.[1] But the conservative elements of the city, of whom Aristophanes was a prominent representative, charged the sophists with corrupting the youth. Plato dissented from this charge in the case of Socrates, and defended the sophists generally from it, asserting that the real corrupter of youth in Athens was public opinion, which the sophists only reflected.[1] John Stuart Mill, who had reasons for analyzing the motives of those who are overzealous in protecting the young, has stated the case most clearly:

> When the charge of corrupting youth comes to be particularized, it always resolves itself into making them think themselves wiser than the laws, and fail in proper respect to their fathers and seniors. And this is a true charge; only it ought to fall, not only on seniors. And this is a true charge; only it ought to fall, not on the Sophists, but on intellectual culture generally. Whatever encourages young men to think for themselves, does lead them to criticize the laws of their country—does shake their faith in the infallibility of their fathers and elders, and make them think their own speculations preferable. It is beyond doubt that the teaching of Socrates, and of Plato after him, produced these effects in extraordinary degree. Accordingly, we learn from Xenophon that the youths of rich families who frequented Socrates, did so, for the most part, against the severe disapprobation of their relatives. In every age and state of society, fathers and elder citizens have been suspicious and jealous of all freedom of thought and all intellectual cultivation (not strictly professional) in their sons and juniors, unless they can get it controlled by some civil or ecclesiastical authority in which they have confidence. But it had not occurred to Athenian legislators to have an established Sophistical Church, or State Universities. The teaching of the Sophists was all on the voluntary principle; and the dislike of it was of the same nature with the outcry against "godless colleges," or the objection of most of our higher and middle classes to any schools but denominational ones. They disapproved of any teaching and unless they could be certain that all their own opinions would be taught. It mattered

---

[1]*Republic,* VI, 492.

not that the instructors taught no heresy; the mere fact that they
accustomed the mind to ask questions, and require other reasons
than use and wont, sufficed at Athens, as it does in other places,
to make the teaching dangerous in the eyes of self-satisfied respectability. Accordingly, respectability, as Plato himself tells us, looked
with at least as evil an eye on Philosophers as on Sophists.[2]

This explanation of Mill's is more applicable to the ethical and
philosophical, than to the rhetorical, aspects of the sophists' teaching.
To be sure, the rhetoricians professed to be able to speak upon either
side of any case, and to impart this ability to their pupils; this was the
cause of a certain distrust analogous to that with which lawyers are
sometimes viewed today. But when lawyers turn public orators, they
are the most vigorous and platitudinous upholders of the *status quo.*
So the sophists, as public orators, illustrated and reënforced the received dogmas of Athenian society. Their speeches were acceptable to
the most conservative. Even their teaching of the art of speaking upon
either side of any case did not rest so much upon a willingness to attack prevalent morality and customs as it did upon the cultivation of
an ability to make either side of the case *appear* to be consistent with
common standards of right and justice. Rhetoric as the art of persuasion must always appeal to the people upon the basis of whatever
beliefs they may happen to have. It is not likely, then, that it was the
rhetoric of the sophists which led to the charge that they broke down
religion and corrupted youth. It was rather that they concerned themselves enough with philosophy to incur something of the distrust with
which speculative thought has always been viewed. In all the disputes
between the earlier schools of philosophy there was one point upon
which they were agreed; namely, that the popular beliefs and explanations of phenomena were entirely wrong. For them, as for modern
philosophers, the incarnation of ignorance was "the man in the street."
Their arrogance and their contempt for the public naturally roused
resentment. Their lofty pretensions were contrasted with their apparent
practical helplessness, and the story of Thales falling into a well while
gazing at the stars is typical of the popular attitude toward philosophers. The popular distrust of the sophists was not so much that, as

---

[2]*Op. cit.,* IV, 262.

rhetoricians, they were different from Socrates and Plato, but that, as philosophers, they were so much like them.

There was a certain aspect of the rhetorical teaching which caused a portion of the public to dislike the popular teachers. After the downfall of the Thirty in Athens, it was evident that democracy was the order of the day. Members of the aristocracy could retain their power in the state only by developing their ability to persuade an audience. Teachers of rhetoric, in such a situation, were indispensable. But the fees charged by the sophists placed their instruction beyond the reach of many, who naturally resented what seemed an unfair advantage possessed by those more adequately trained for public life.

The fees of the sophists seem to have been a cause of universal reproach, but the feeling was too complex to be explained simply. There was, of course, the aristocratic bias of Athenian life. Physicians were the only wage-earners who suffered no loss of social standing. Sculptors were artisans rather than artists because their work was a method of gaining a livelihood. Plato, the man of wealth and family, was for once in agreement with the popular prejudice, and he attacked the sophists both for the insignificance of their petty fees, and for the large fortunes that they made.[1] The acceptance of fees marked a certain institutionalizing and mechanizing of higher education, which was disliked. The philosopher whose chief occupation was the pursuit of truth might impart his wisdom to such persons and at such times as suited him, without seriously interrupting his own thinking. He probably found a certain number of disciples a stimulus. But the introduction of fees and the acceptance of responsibility for practical training in public speaking made the teacher seem to be a servant of the pupil. He became a professional educator, and as such insisted disagreeably upon the importance of education. As philosophers, the sophists could probably have retained the measure of freedom and leisure that Plato demanded, even while accepting pay for their work. But as teachers of rhetoric they tended to become submerged in the routine of schoolmastering.

As philosophers, the sophists incurred a different sort of penalty for their fee-taking. Then, as now, certain activities of what may perhaps be termed men's higher natures were especially removed from thoughts

---

[1]*Apology,* 20; *Cratylus,* 384 and 391.

of gain. We do not like to think that popular preachers are making money; we deplore the commercialized theatre, and the novel written only to sell. These activities, we believe, should be ends in themselves. It is not difficult to understand why the spectacle of foreign teachers coming to Athens to teach virtue for a price should have roused a resentment somewhat distinct from that of those who disliked the teaching of rhetoric.

Turning to Plato, we have already noted that he shared the general dislike of fee-taking; but we should consider also those aspects of his thought which led him to dislike any persons who accepted Athenian life and institutions and participated actively in public affairs. Mill has pointed out:

> Plato, if he returned to life, would be to the full as contemptuous of our statesmen, lawyers, clergy, authors, and all others who lay claim to mental superiority as he ever was of the corresponding classes at Athens.[1]

This would be true because Plato would find that our life bears a much closer resemblance to the Athens he knew, than to his *Republic*. We may cite the *Republic* and the *Laws* as a sufficient evidence of Plato's discontent with the sorry scheme of things entire. He was not a reformer who could be contented with a gradual evolution in the direction of his ideals; nor did it disturb him that his Republic was not an earthly city; he was satisfied to believe that its pattern was laid up in the heavens. Scholars are becoming increasingly conscious, however, that his gaze was not exclusively heavenward as he wrote the *Republic*. He knew what he disliked in Athens, and his utopia owes at least as much to his dislikes as to his desires. Had the sophists and rhetoricians been the only objects of his scorn he might not have been driven to writing the *Republic*. But the politics, poetry, art, education, and religion of Athens were all wrong—so wrong that it was easier to paint a utopia than seriously to attempt the reformation of Athens. We may say in the beginning, then, that Plato's condemnation of rhetoric and rhetoricians is merely a small part of his condemnation of all contemporary civilization. We may note in passing, that rhetoric has its uses even for those who attack it; and that Plato's contrast between

---

[1] *Op. cit.*, IV, 245.

the rhetorician's world of appearance and the philosopher's world of reality was drawn with consummate rhetorical skill.

The supreme remedy for the ills of civilization, Plato believed, lay in the government of philosopher-kings. But until philosophers were kings, and could govern autocratically by their wisdom, without the necessity for persuading the multitude, they were to remain aloof from public affairs.

> The lords of philosophy have never, from their youth upwards, known their way to the Agora, or the dicastery, or the council, or any other political assembly; they neither see nor hear the laws or votes of the State written or spoken; the eagerness of political societies in the attainment of offices,—clubs, banquets, and revels, and singing maidens, do not even enter into their dreams.[1]

In Plato's ideal realm, there was no place for rhetoric as a political agency. Large questions of policy were to be settled by the philosophers. Administration of routine affairs was to be in the hands of experts. There would be no litigation, for there would be no laws. Laws were as absurd and useless for philosopher-kings as decrees of the public assembly would be for pilots and physicians, whose actions were governed by their own arts. Later in life Plato despaired of finding philosophers, even in utopia, who could be trusted to govern without laws, or of inducing people to have confidence in them, even if they could be found, and his *Laws* is a concession to that feeling. But even in his later utopia there was no freedom of utterance, without which, of course, the development of rhetoric would be an impossibility. With the dogmatism of age upon him, he laid down laws which were to be permanent. The games of children,[2] the restrictions upon foreign travel,[3] the denial of freedom of speech, and the enforcement of ethical and theological dogmas,[4] were all designed to protect the city against changes of any sort. The use of rhetoric in administering and interpreting the laws was also carefully guarded against.[5]

Although rhetoric had no place in the courts or political assemblies

---

[1] *Theaetetus*, 173. Jowett's translation.
[2] *Laws*, VII, 798.
[3] *Laws*, XII, 950.
[4] *Laws*, II, 662.
[5] *Laws*, XI, 938.

of Plato's ideal realms, its scope in another field was to be greatly increased. All the literature and art of the Greeks was to be examined
with a single eye to its effect upon the morals of the citizens. Truth and
beauty were subordinated to goodness—to goodness as Plato conceived
it. Whenever the attempt is made to govern the ideals of a people
by censoring art in the interests of a dogmatic morality, all art tends
to become rhetorical. To say that rhetoric was banished from the Republic, then, is not quite true. It was driven out the door only to fly
in at the window. The unsympathetic interpreter of Plato would say
that literature became part of the educator's rhetoric, with Plato as
chief educator and chief rhetorician; a better Platonist, however, would
hold that literature and education became philosophy, with Plato as
chief philosopher.

One source of rhetoric and rhetoricians in any democracy is the con-
tinual and restless striving of the people to better their individual conditions. They perpetually seek to become what they are not, and in
doing this they strive to bend the wills of others to their own ends.
This state of affairs Plato avoided, in his *Republic,* by having a fixed
and settled order of society, an order of experts, in which every man
did his own work, and no man attempted the work of another. In this
way ambitious, self-seeking demagoguery was to be eliminated.

There is no indication in the *Republic,* that even under philosopher-
kings, with a scheme of education devised by Plato himself, and with
art and literature revised in the interest of morals, the mass of the
people were expected to rise to greater heights than a certain efficiency
in minding their own routines. It is not particularly strange, then, that
Plato had a great contempt for the people of Athens, who lived under
a government so little influenced by Platonism. Plato adhered to the
philosophic tradition in regarding public opinion as always wrong both
because it was public and because it was merely opinion. Plato despised
mere opinion almost as much as he did the public. He was never tired
of contrasting the knowledge of the philosopher, who had attained real
knowledge by dialectical investigation, and by contemplation of Ideas,
with that shadow knowledge called opinion.[1] Sometimes, of course,
opinion would turn out to be right. And right opinion had a certain
value as a guide to action in practical affairs; but even right opinion

---

[1] See especially *Republic,* VI, 509 ff.

fell far short of philosophic knowledge. Plato never believed that probability was the guide of life. Education, for him, was a process of keeping the mass of people at their tasks with as few opinions as might be, and of enabling the few whose intelligence would permit, to attain philosophic knowledge. Those who knew, were to abandon the pleasures of knowing, at stated intervals, and govern those who did not know. Thus opinion was largely to be eliminated from the State. The education given by the sophists and rhetoricians, on the other hand, was for the purpose of enabling a man to get on in a world of conjecture. Isocrates (whom we have not discussed, because, though he receives passing mention, he is hardly a figure in the Platonic pictures of contemporary rhetoricians) stated as his philosophy of education:

> It is impossible to attain absolute knowledge of what we ought or ought not to do; but the wise man is he who can make a successful guess as a general rule, and philosophers are those who study to attain this practical wisdom.[1]

Akin to this is the educational aim of Protagoras—given us by Plato, but probably quite acceptable to Protagoras:

> If a young man comes to me he will learn prudence in affairs private as well as public, he will learn to order his own house in the best manner, and he will be best able to speak and act in affairs of state.[2]

The education given by the sophists varied with individual teachers, but in general it aimed to enable the pupils to become leaders of men in a democracy. It was practical in the sense in which all training for public affairs is practical; and it sought to enable the individual to use existing institutions rather than to overthrow them. The perversions of such education—half-knowledge, propaganda, demagoguery, philistinism, worship of the appearance of success—are probably even more prevalent now than then. Whether they are worse than the perversions of Platonism is too large a question to be argued here. But whether for good or ill, the conception of the aims and purposes of the American liberal college as set forth by the most distinguished

---

[1] *Antidosis,* tr. J. F. Dobson, in his *Greek Orators,* New York, 1920, p. 142.
[2] *Protagoras,* 318.

modern educators, is much closer to Isocrates and Protagoras than to Plato.

It is evident, from Plato's literary activities as an idealistic reformer and creator of utopias, from his conception of the philosopher as the true governor of mankind, and from his social, political, and educational philosophy, that he would have differed profoundly from the sophists and rhetoricians, even had all of them possessed the highest character and wisdom.

It will be convenient to discuss Plato's treatment of rhetoric and rhetoricians under four heads: the pictures he has given us of the individual rhetoricians, his general indictment of rhetoric in Athens, his suggestions for the creation of a nobler and better rhetoric, and his later attack upon the eristical rhetoricians who imitated the argumentative methods of Socrates.

The Platonic pictures of the sophists are scattered throughout the dialogues; but the most extended and vivid characterizations of them are in the *Protagoras,* the *Hippias Major* and *Hippias Minor,* the *Gorgias,* and the *Euthydemus.* Plato constantly contrasts them with the ironical Socrates. Socrates affects a great humility, the sophists are conceited and self-confident; Socrates is skilled in closely reasoned argument, the sophists are helpless in his hands; Socrates defines his terms, but the sophists, accustomed to haranguing uncritical audiences, use their terms with all the looseness and inaccuracy of common conversation.

Protagoras is pictured at the head of a group of admiring listeners, pleased at an opportunity to lecture in the presence of rival sophists.[1] Although the reader feels that in the discussion with Socrates common sense is with Protagoras, he cannot but be amused at the spectacle of the eloquent, deep-voiced orator unable to defend even a sound argument against the dialectical attack of Socrates. Protagoras, with his popular lectures and his conventional morality, was too powerful a figure to please Plato, who was somewhat neglected in the Academy.

Hippias seems to have incurred the most vigorous enmity of Plato.[2]

---

[1]For the Platonic treatment of Protagoras, see the dialogue of that name, and also *Cratylus,* 386; *Euthydemus,* 286; *Theaetetus,* 152-78; *Meno,* 91; *Republic,* 600; *Phaedrus,* 267.

[2]See *Hippias Major* and *Hippias Minor.* Only *Hippias Minor* is admitted into the Platonic canon by Jowett. Grote held to the genuineness of the *Hippias Major,* and gives an exposition of it in his *Plato.*

In the *Hippias Minor* Socrates exposes the fallacies in the popular lecture on Homer that Hippias was accustomed to give before approving audiences. In the picture of Hippias at the Olympic games in garments, rings, and accoutrements of his own make, there is no suggestion that he was attempting to reenforce his favorite doctrine of self-sufficiency; the Platonic view is that Hippias was insufferably conceited over his versatility.

The references to Prodicus are scattered and incidental. He is described as a "taker to pieces of words,"[3] as "drawing useless distinctions about names,"[4] and as beginning his instruction with "initiation into the correct use of terms."[5] In the *Cratylus* there is a satirical reference to the relationship between the fees of Prodicus and the amount of knowledge imparted.[6]

Gorgias is portrayed in the dialogue bearing his name[1] as professing to be able to answer any questions which may be asked him, and as being so familiar with all possible subjects of discussion that for many years he has heard no new question. He indulges in oratorical praise of the art of rhetoric, and is shown to be quite incapable of dialectical argument.

Polus,[2] a young pupil of Gorgias, Callicles,[3] a practical politician rather than a professional rhetorician, and Thrasymachus,[4] the spokesman for doctrines that Plato wished to discredit, are described as being much like the better-known sophists.

Euthydemus and Dionysodorus, who belong to a later group of sophists, are caricatured in the *Euthydemus* with a dramatic vivacity and comic force which almost equals the *Clouds* of Aristophanes. They are characterized as "a new importation of sophists," who "will give lessons in speaking and pleading, and in writing speeches."[5] This occupation is new to them, for they were previously teachers of the art

---

[3]*Laches*, 197.
[4]*Charmides*, 163.
[5]*Euthydemus*, 277.
[6]*Cratylus*, 384.
[1]Other characterizations of Gorgias are found in *Meno*, 70; *Phaedrus*, 267; and *Symposium*, 198.
[2]*Gorgias*, 466 ff.
[3]*Gorgias*, 481 ff.
[4]*Republic*, I.
[5]*Euthydemus*, 272.

of fighting in armor. They also profess to be teachers of virtue.

Although there are no formal charges made against any individual sophists in any of the dialogues, Plato has used all his literary resources to add to the effectiveness of his philosophical attack upon them.

There is in the *Gorgias* a deeper purpose than an exhibition of the deficiencies of the predominant rhetorical technique. Plato here gives us a contrast between the true and the false life. The philosophic import of the dialogue has led some commentators to believe that the treatment of rhetoric is only incidental, or that rhetoric is used merely as introductory to the higher themes of philosophy. But Plato, for all his idealism, took as the point of departure for his reforms the weaknesses which he thought he saw in Athens, and rhetoric is, after all, a chief subject of the dialogue. Rhetoric, as philosophy, was a way of life. Rhetoric dealt not only with form and style; it also treated the matter and policy of public speaking. It offered something of a philosophy to the orator. It was almost indistinguishable from political science, and to the general public the orator was the statesman.

> If there was anything which could pretend to dispute with philosophy the position of a master knowledge, or put forward a rival claim for the guidance of life and affairs, it was this art of rhetoric, which professed to train men for politics, and to make them able to act as well as speak efficiently. The teacher of philosophy had thus to be vindicated against the teacher of rhetoric; the philosophical statesman had also to be vindicated against the orator-statesmen of actual Athenian politics.[1]

In contrasting the philosopher and the rhetorician, Plato at times gives the impression of being on the defensive. This is not merely because rhetoric is more popular, but also because he had felt the reproaches of his friends for his inactivity in Athenian affairs. He was keenly conscious of the criticism of the philosopher which he put into the mouth of Callicles:

> He [the philosopher] creeps into the corner for the rest of his life, and talks in a whisper with three or four admiring youths, but never speaks out like a freeman in a satisfactory manner.[2]

One way to establish the supremacy of philosophy was to show that

---

[1] E. Barker: *op. cit.,* p. 133.
[2] *Gorgias,* 485.

the claims of rhetoric as "the art of becoming great in the city,"[3] were not to be taken seriously. There must be an appeal to higher values. The belief that might makes right, the trust in things that are seen, must be replaced with a desire for the goods of the soul. The ignorance, prejudice, and selfishness of the rhetorician must be exposed; the most popular of arts must be shown to be no art at all when subjected to the scrutiny of a philosophical mind. The *Gorgias,* then, undertakes to refute the claims made for rhetoric by Gorgias, Polus, and Callicles. Socrates defeats each one in turn, so that we really have three dialogues in one, each antagonist advancing a somewhat different claim for rhetoric.

Gorgias, in the beginning, praises rhetoric for the power and influence it confers. He also defends it from the oft-repeated charge that it is frequently used wrongfully and works mischief in the state. But the definition of rhetoric is what Socrates seeks, and Gorgias appears to be as devoid of abstract ideas with which to frame a definition as the other rhetoricians. The art of formal logic did not yet exist, and Socrates presses Gorgias with various analogies and ambiguities which both appear to mistake for valid arguments. Logic and rhetoric have not yet been clearly conceived as universal arts or sciences which admit of application to any subject matter; and it is not strange that Gorgias was unable to furnish the clear conception that Socrates sought. Socrates, then, had no great difficulty in establishing his own definition, that *rhetoric is the art of persuading an ignorant multitude about the justice or injustice of a matter, without imparting any real instruction.* Rhetoric is most powerful with the ignorant many, because the rhetorician, as rhetorician, does not really know what he is talking about, he only appears to know; and the appearance is persuasive only with the ignorant. Plato here limits rhetoric to the discussion of matters concerning justice. He probably chose to discuss the forensic rather than the deliberative or epideictic rhetoric because the contemporary rhetoricians devoted most of their attention to it.

Socrates also compels Gorgias to admit that *rhetoricians do not really know their business,* for they do not teach their pupils about justice and injustice (an essential part of rhetoric, by the definition previously established). The actions of the pupils show that they have never

[3]*Gorgias,* 513.

learned to know justice—any rhetorician must admit that his pupils often act unjustly. Two things are to be noted about this argument. Gorgias and Socrates have different ideas of what it means to know justice. Gorgias means by it a sufficient practical knowledge of men and affairs to know what is conventionally moral in any given case. Socrates, on the other hand, means abstract, philosophical knowledge of the nature of justice. There is also underlying the argument the "vicious intellectualism" of Socrates. The Platonic Gorgias fails to object to the Socratic thesis that if students of rhetoric knew the nature of justice, they would never commit an injustice. To Gorgias the teaching of justice was not a heavy responsibility, because the just or unjust actions of his pupils did not depend upon any ethical theories taught by him. The just rhetorician was just because he sought to live in a manner which his common sense told him would win the approval of his fellow men, and not because he had been taught to be virtuous.[1] It is difficult to believe that the real Gorgias would have been so easily entrapped by the argument that the injustices committed by pupils of the rhetoricians proved the ignorance of the teachers.

Polus indignantly attempts to rescue his master, but he also falls an easy victim to the Socratic dialectic. Since both Gorgias and Polus have been more apt at praising rhetoric than at defining it, Socrates proceeds to attack their claims and to establish the point that *rhetoric is not of much use in the world*. There are four arguments to substantiate this: 1) Rhetoric is not an art; 2) Rhetoric does not confer power; 3) Rhetoric as a protection against suffering wrong is of little importance; and 4) Rhetoric as a means of escaping a deserved punishment is not to be commended. The philosophy developed in support of these points loses little of its significance when separated from its immediate purpose of refuting the claims of rhetoric; but the unity of the dialogue is not perceived until it is understood that the philosophical theses are part of a consistent argumentative plan.

Rhetoric was not an art, Plato believed, because it did not rest on universal principles. It was really only a knack, a routine, or experience. Aiming at persuasion, it cared only for appearance. It did not aim at justice, but only at a semblance of justice. By an art, Plato meant more nearly what we should call a science, that is, a body

---
[1] See *Meno*, 95.

of knowledge organized on universally valid principles. The dispute as to whether or not rhetoric was an art was of great practical significance to the rhetoricians. If it was not an art and rested upon no principles, then the attempt to teach it must be futile. There has always been considerable scepticism as to the possibility of teaching rhetoric profitably. Its rules have often been multiplied in order to have something more to teach. Plato, in common with other writers of genius, was fond of minimizing the importance of technique, just as teachers as a class are fond of overemphasizing it.

Aside from the immediately practical effect upon the teaching of the subject, it was injurious to the prestige of rhetoric to deny it a scientific character. As Gomperz observes of the age:

> All the business of mankind, from cooking a dinner to painting
> a picture, from going a walk to waging a war, was guided by rules
> and, wherever possible, reduced to principles.[1]

Plato's charge that rhetoric was not an art, then, was somewhat analogous to the denial of a place among the sciences to sociology or psychology. Such a charge, even if unaccompanied by any implications concerning the doubtful morality of persuading ignorant multitudes, was enough to injure the subject.

In denying that rhetoric is an art, Plato gives it a place among the pseudo-arts. In the hierarchy of arts and pseudo-arts, the higher arts aim at the production, real or apparent, of permanent conditions; the lower, at the removal, real or apparent, of temporary derangements. Sophistry is distinguished from rhetoric and placed above it. Sophistry is an imitation of the statesman's art, which is higher than the art of the pleader, because the pleader only remedies miscarriages of justice, while the statesman has the opportunity to create permanent institutions which give society an organization based upon justice. We probably agree today in paying more honor to the statesman than to the trial lawyer. In the *Gorgias,* the sophist is the sham statesman; the rhetorician is the pleader who "makes the worse appear the better reason," and forgets justice in the winning of his case.

The second argument against rhetoric in the dialogue with Polus

---

[1]*Op. cit.,* I, 386.

is that rhetoric, in spite of appearances, does not really confer power. People who do not know, in the philosophical sense (and Plato believed that very few could know anything in the philosophical sense), what is really good for them, have no power, for they are unable to do what they will. When they do evil, they are not doing what they will, for no one really wills to do evil; he only makes a mistake in the art of measuring. The Socratic belief that no man errs voluntarily is again the basis of the argument. The minor premise, that rhetoricians have not the philosophical insight to know what is really good for them, Plato believes may safely be assumed.

The third and fourth assertions about rhetoric which Socrates established against Polus gain significance when considered in relation to the conditions of Athenian court procedure. With a jury of five hundred—somewhat predisposed to convict any wealthy man, since his goods would be at the disposal of the state—innocent persons were liable to be convicted on the flimsiest of charges. The size of the jury made oratory a much more important matter than evidence. This would make it quite as possible for the guilty to escape punishment, as for an innocent man to suffer at the hands of his enemies. Any practical-minded person would therefore conclude that rhetoric was of great importance to the innocent as a protection against injury, and to the guilty as a means of avoiding a just penalty. Socrates, however, denies both of these claims, and advances his famous paradoxes in support of his argument. Rhetoric is not of great importance as a protection against suffering wrong; the really important thing is to keep oneself from doing wrong, for doing wrong is a greater evil than suffering wrong. The dialectic by which Socrates establishes this is hardly as noble as the conclusion which he reaches, but Polus is not able to offer any effective opposition. Again, rhetoric as a means of escaping punishment is of no great service, for the man who is punished for his injustice is happier than he who is not punished. This Socratic thesis is a matter of feeling and belief rather than of logical proof, but against Polus it was not difficult to establish dialectically. If it is honorable to inflict punishment on a guilty person, then it must be honorable to receive it. Punishment, as a deliverance of the soul from evil, should be welcomed by the guilty as a medicine.

When Polus seems to be hopelessly defeated, Callicles takes up the argument. In the discussion with him the argument turns more directly to the contract of philosophy and rhetoric as ways of life. In the words of Socrates:

> We are arguing about the way of human life; and what question can be more serious than this to a man who has any sense at all: whether he should follow after that way of life to which you exhort me, and truly fulfill what you call the manly part of speaking in the assembly, and cultivating rhetoric, and engaging in public affairs, after your manner; or whether he should pursue the life of philosophy, and in what this differs from the other.[1]

Callicles vigorously attacks philosophy, upholds rhetoric, and offers in its support the doctrine that might makes right, that justice is but an artificial convention invented by the many weak to protect themselves against the few strong, that the law of nature decrees that the strong should take what they can get, and that in a society full of conventions, rhetoric offers the strong man the means of getting what he wants. The Socratic argument in reply to this passes into the realm of ethics, and deals with the self-seeker as such, rather than merely with the rhetorician.

Socrates is disposed to admit that there might conceivably be a true and noble art of rhetoric. The true rhetorician would attempt to improve the people, rather than to please them. He would attempt this, not only for the moral benefit of the people, but also because any process which does not improve souls is not really an art; it is an ignoble flattery. Among such flatteries are music, poetry, drama, and painting. They may occasionally improve the people, but for the most part they are to be viewed with distrust.

Although there might be a noble rhetoric, and true rhetoricians, none such have ever existed. All statesmen and rhetoricians of the past, even the best, such as Themistocles, Cimon, Miltiades, and Pericles, have failed to make the citizens any better.[1] The proof of this is that the citizens treated these men very ungratefully and unjustly,

---

[1] *Gorgias*, 500.

[1] Aelius Aristides, a sophist of the second century A.D., replied to the charges made against rhetoric in the *Gorgias*. One of his discourses is devoted to a defense of the four statesmen here attacked. For a discussion of this see André Boulanger: *Aelius Aristide et la sophstique dans la province d'Asie au II*e *siecle de nôtre ère,* Paris, 1923.

which they would not have done if they had been taught justice by the statesmen. The professional teachers of rhetoric, even though the teaching of justice should be a part of the instruction in rhetoric, dare not trust their own pupils to treat them justly, for they exact a fee instead of leaving it to the pupil's sense of honor.

Socrates is further offended at the pretentiousness of rhetoric and rhetoricians. If rhetoric occasionally saves a life in courts of law, there are other life-saving arts which are equally important, and much more modest. A swimmer may save many lives, but he is not likely to boast that he practices the greatest of the arts. Or a pilot, if swimming seems to be a contemptible example, is also a great lifesaver. But he keeps his modesty. If he has any philosophy in him, he knows that some of the lives he has saved were probably not worth saving; but a rhetorician never seems to indulge himself in such sobering reflections.

Rhetoric destroys the integrity of a man's soul, for it involves conformity to the ways of the multitude. The philosopher, on the other hand, sees further:

> The noble and the good may possibly be something different from saving and being saved, and that he who is truly a man ought not to care about living a certain time; he knows, as women say, that none can escape the day of destiny, and therefore he is not fond of life; he leaves all that with God, and considers in what way he can best spend his appointed term.[2]

The dialogue closes with a myth of the after-world, in which the judgment that bestows rewards and punishments is not based upon appearances, as are the judgments won by the rhetoricians, but upon the true nature of the soul. The myth sums up the whole argument of the dialogue. The fundamental contrast is between appearances and reality; the rhetorician deals with appearances, the philosopher with reality.

In the *Gorgias,* the rhetoricians appear to be men bent upon getting on in the world. They seem to believe that an unjust man who escapes punishment, and practises his injustice on such a large scale that he is conspicuously successful, is a man to be envied and imitated. It is easy for us, made familiar with the doctrine that injustice is an

---

[2] *Gorgias,* 512.

evil, through the teachings of Plato, of the Stoics, and of Christianity, and accustomed at least to pay lip-service to it as a truism, to suppose that Plato was upholding the traditional righteousnss against a peculiarly corrupt set of public teachers, the sophists and rhetoricians. It should be remembered, however, that public opinion in Athens was not with Plato. Instead of regarding the Gorgias and Polus and Callicles as especially corrupt, we should regard Plato as the reforming philosopher, attacking public opinion through its prominent representatives. That Plato himself took this view is shown by his remark in the *Republic* that the youth are not corrupted by individual sophists, but by the public.[1]

It is also worthy of note that this attack upon rhetoric is itself a rhetorical triumph. The rhetoricians are ridiculed for their inability to reason closely, and to defend themselves against the dialectic of Socrates; but the triumph of the Platonic Socrates is not a triumph of logic over oratory. John Stuart Mill has put this clearly:

> This great dialogue, full of just thoughts and fine observations on human nature, is, in mere argument, one of the weakest of Plato's works. It is not by its logic, but by its ηθος that it produces its effects; not by instructing the understanding, but by working on the feelings and imagination. Nor is this strange; for the disinterested love of virtue is an affair of feeling. It is impossible to prove to any one Plato's thesis, that justice is supreme happiness, unless he can be made to feel it as such. The external inducements which recommend it he may be taught to appreciate; the favorable regards and good offices of other people, and the rewards of another life. These considerations, however, though Plato has recourse to them in other places, are not available in the *Gorgias*. . . . It is the picture of the moral hero, still *tenax propositi* against the hostility and contempt of the world, which makes the splendor and power of the *Gorgias*. The Socrates of the dialogue makes us *feel* all other evils to be more tolerable than injustice in the soul, not by proving it, but by the sympathy he calls forth with his own intense feeling of it. He inspires heroism because he shows himself a hero. And his failures in logic do not prevent the step marked by the *Gorgias* from being one of the greatest ever made in moral culture.[1]

---

[1] *Republic*, 493.
[1] *Op. cit.*, IV, 291, 292.

The *Phaedrus,* which has been described as a dramatized treatise on rhetoric, contains three speeches upon the general subject of love; one of which Plato introduces as the work of Lysias, a noted rhetorician of the day, and two of which are put into the mouth of Socrates. It is in a comparison of these speeches that Plato's ideas about rhetoric are expressed. At the close of the final speech upon love, delivered by Socrates, Phædrus expresses his admiring approval; he fears that Lysias, whose speech he had just read to Socrates, could not produce anything as good;[2] indeed, he had already been reproached for his speech writing. Socrates remarks that it is not writing speeches, but writing them badly, that is disgraceful. This opens the way for a discussion of the entire practice of speaking and writing.

Socrates enunciates as the first rule of good speaking:

> The mind of the speaker should know the truth of what he is going to say. . . . There never is nor ever will be a real art of speaking which is unconnected with the truth.[3]

This rule of Socrates is contrasted with the prevalent conception of rhetoric. Rhetoric is usually considered to be an "art of enchanting the mind by arguments"; it has no concern with the nature of truth or justice, but only with opinions about them. Rhetoric draws its persuasive power, not from truth, but from harmony with public opinion. This conception of rhetoric, however, Plato thinks inadequate. The objection here is not, as is often stated, from high moral motives. In the *Gorgias* and elsewhere it is stated that the genuine rhetorician must be a true and just man. And from many sources we know how Plato abhorred the "lie in the soul." But here the ground is simple expediency. The art of persuasion is the art of winning the mind by resemblances. The speaker goes by degrees from that which is accepted to that which he wishes accepted, proceeding from one resemblance to another. If the difference between two resemblances is small, there is an excellent opportunity for making the audience believe that one is the other.

This rule that "the mind of the speaker should know the truth of

---

[2] Plato had no doubt that a philosopher could easily outdo a rhetorician at his own art. He wrote the *Menexenus* in order to satirize the conventional funeral oration and to show how easily a philosopher could dash off such a speech.
[3] *Phaedrus,* 259.

what he is going to say" and not "catch at appearances," may seem to be a commonplace. But it is not mere faithfulness to fact that Plato has in mind; it is that Truth which only philosophers know. All others dwell in a darkened cave.[1] The moving figures they behold are not realities; they are shadows, phantoms. Only the philosopher has ascended into the clear light of day. Only he has beheld Ideas in their Absolute form. Only he it is who is able to see "unity and plurality in nature." Hence the exclamation of Socrates:

> Come out, children of my soul, and convince Phædrus, who is the father of similar beauties, that he will never be able to speak about anything unless he be trained in philosophy.[2]

These Platonic conceptions are not new to Phædrus, and no time is wasted in explaining them. Having secured acceptance of the first rule of good speaking, Socrates proceeds to lay down two corollaries. First, rhetoric has greater power in discussions where men disagree and are most likely to be deceived. The rhetorician ought therefore to have in mind a clear distinction between debatable and non-debatable subjects. Secondly, particulars must be carefully observed, so that they may be properly classified. In other words, careful definitions must be drawn, and mere matters of opinion separated from matters of scientific knowledge.

A lack of any definition of the subject of love is the first criticism of the speech of Lysias. This is particularly reprehensible as love is used in two different senses. Socrates, however, was careful in both speeches to start from a definition of the love he was treating. Again, there is no principle of order in the speech of Lysias. He is accused of beginning at the end, and his topics follow one another in a random fashion.

> I cannot help fancying that he wrote off freely just what came into his head. . . . Every discourse ought to be a living creature, having its own body and head and feet; there ought to be a middle, beginning, and end, which are in a manner agreeable to one another and to the whole.[1]

---

[1] *Republic,* VII, 515.
[2] *Phaedrus,* 261.
[1] *Phaedrus,* 264.

From this study of the speeches on love, two fundamental principles of composition emerge:

> First, the comprehension of scattered particulars in one idea; the speaker defines his several notions in order that he may make his meaning clear. . . . Secondly, there is the faculty of division according to the natural ideas or members, not breaking any part as a bad carver might.[2]

But these processes of generalization and division, which the speech of the famous rhetorician failed to employ, are principles that Socrates has hitherto held to belong to dialectic, and not to rhetoric.

> I am a great lover of these processes of division and generalization; they help me to speak and think. And if I find any man who is able to see unity and plurality in nature, him I follow, and walk in his steps as if he were a god. And those who have this art, I have hitherto been in the habit of calling dialecticians.[3]

Phædrus acknowledges that these principles rightly belong to the dialecticians, but persists in inquiring about the principles of rhetoric; he mentions a number of prominent rhetoricians together with some characteristic elements of their systems. Socrates admits that in addition to the really fundamental principles of composition to be found in dialectic, there may be in rhetoric some "niceties of the art." Theodorus, Evenus, Tisias, Gorgias, Prodicus, Hippias, Polus, Protagoras, and the other rhetoricians spend much time upon proems, statements of fact, witnesses, proofs, probabilities, confirmations, superconfirmations, refutations, diplasiology, gnomology, and other technicialities. These theories and practices of the rhetoricians, however, are not really principles of the art of rhetoric. They are mere preliminaries, as the tuning of strings is preliminary to playing upon an instrument. But no one would call the tuning of strings the art of music. The contemporary rhetoricians have no more real claim to be practitioners of the art than a man who knows a few drugs, but does not know how to use them, could claim to be a physician. Since all these teachings of the rhetoricians are not true principles of the art, and are altogether useless except when used in conjunction

---

[2]*Phaedrus,* 265.
[3]*Phaedrus,* 266.

with the principles of dialectic, Socrates proceeds to give what might be called an outline of a true art of rhetoric.

> Oratory is the art of enchanting the soul, and therefore he who would be an orator has to learn the differences of human souls— they are of so many and of such a nature, and from them come the differences between man and man. He will then proceed to divide speeches into their several different classes. Such and such persons, he will say, are affected by this or that kind of speech in this or that way, and he will tell you why; he must have a theoretical notion of them first, and then he must see them in action, and be able to follow them with all his senses about him, or he will never get beyond the precepts of his masters. But when he is able to say what persons are persuaded by what arguments and recognize the individual about whom he used to theorize as actually present to himself, This is he and this is the sort of man who ought to have that argument applied to him in order to convince him of this; when he has attained the knowledge of all this, and knows also when he should speak and when he should abstain from speaking, when he should make use of pithy sayings, pathetic appeals, aggravated effects, and all the other figures of speech, when, I say, he knows the times and seasons of all these things, then, and not until then, is he perfect and a consummate master of his art.[1]

Such an outline of rhetoric, Socrates feels, may be discouraging to the young Phædrus. The road to the mastery of such an art is obviously long and hard. The sophists, on the other hand, are represented by Plato as offering promises to impart culture quickly and easily.[2] Here, then, is an opportunity for Socrates to compare the true way of mastering the art of rhetoric with the sophistic short cut. The rhetoricians succeed in imparting a certain skill in making plausible speeches because they content themselves with creating an appearance of probability. They teach that "in speaking the orator should run after probability and say good-by to truth."[3] The teaching of Tisias on the topic of probability, which enabled a man quickly to make a case either for the defense or the prosecution, regardless of

---

[1] *Phaedrus*, 271.
[2] For a later, satirical development of this idea, see Lucian: The Rhetorician's Vade Mecum, *Works of Lucian*, tr. H. W. and F. G. Fowler, Oxford, 1905, III.
[3] *Phaedrus*, 273.

the evidence, is cited as typical of the rhetoricians. To show the superiority of the true rhetoric over such trickery, Socrates repeats his former statement:

> Probability is engendered in the minds of the many by the likeness of the truth, and he who knows the truth will always know best how to discover the resemblance of the truth.[1]

The rhetoric of Tisias, then, is deficient in two respects. First, it is not even effective, for it is not quick at perceiving likenesses of truth; and secondly, such a rhetorician is as likely to deceive himself as his audience. Further, the true rhetorician masters his art after much labor:

> Not for the sake of speaking and acting before men, but in order that he may be able to say what is acceptable to God and in all things to act acceptably to Him so far as in him lies.[2]

Rhetoric, then, like all the arts, is to be an instrument of righteousness. After stating that enough has been said of the true and false art of rhetoric, Socrates feels that something remains to be said of the propriety and impropriety of writing. He proceeds to speak of writing, but only to condemn the practice.[3] Concerning the invention of letters

---

[1]*Phaedrus,* 273.

[2]*Phaedrus,* 273.

[3]Scholars have commented variously and at length on this attitude of Plato toward the art of writing. Schleiermacher (*Introduction to the Dialogues of Plato,* tr. William Dobson, London, 1836, p. 67) argues from this attitude that the *Phaedrus* was written in Plato's early youth. Such contempt for writing, he thinks, is inconceivable in a man who has already written very much. Lutoslawski (*Origin and Growth of Plato's Logic,* London, 1897, ch. 6) insists that Plato did not despise writing in general, but only bad writing, and the cult of mere literary erudition which substitutes opinion for knowledge, and leads men to put all their attention on the form, making it impossible to have a clear view of general ideas. Lutoslawski has an ingenious explanation of the passages which at the close of so wonderful a piece of writing seem to condemn writing. In Plato's time, and in his own opinion, oral teaching stood very much higher than written handbooks. Plato was very proud of his own eloquence. The purpose of these passages, therefore, is to raise the reader's expectation to the highest pitch by announcing that this beautiful sample of written eloquence is nothing compared with his oral teaching.

A different view is taken by S. H. Butcher in an essay entitled "The Written and Spoken Word" (*Some Aspects of the Greek Genius,* London, 1893). He cites the *Phaedrus* in asserting that the Greek dislike for writing was general. In proof of this thesis he offers arguments which may be summarized as follows: (1)

he cites a myth in which the prophecy is made that the art of writing will create forgetfulness and a pretense of wisdom. Contrasted with this futility of writing is "an intelligent writing which is graven in the soul of him who has learned, and can defend itself, and knows when to speak and when to be silent."[1] This expression of opinion about writing concludes Plato's theory of rhetoric as found in the *Phædrus*.

That these suggestions of Plato for the organization of rhetoric into a scientific body of knowledge may be more clearly in mind when we come to contrast the *Phædrus* with Aristotle's *Rhetoric*, we shall here summarize them.

    1. "The first rule of good speaking is that the mind of the speaker should know the truth of what he is going to say." This cannot be interpreted as an injunction to speak the truth at all times. It is rather to *know* the truth in order (a) to be persuasive by presenting to the audience something which at least resembles truth, and (b) to avoid being oneself deceived by probabilities. In order to know the truth, the rhetorician must be a philosopher.

    2. The rhetorician must define his terms, and see clearly what subjects are debatable and what are not. He must also be able to classify particulars under a general head, or to break up universals into particulars. The rhetorician, then, must be a logician.

    3. Principles of order and arrangement must be introduced. "Every discourse ought to be a living creature, having its own body and head and feet; there ought to be a middle, beginning, and end, which are in a manner agreeable to one another and to the whole."

    4. The nature of the soul must be shown, and after having

---

The Greeks gave a very cold reception to the discovery of letters; for centuries they employed it, not as a vehicle of thought, but almost wholly for memorial purposes, such as registering treaties and commercial contracts, preserving the names of Olympic victors, and fixing boundaries. (2) They shrank from formulæ; unvarying rules petrified action. To reduce laws to writing was to kill the spirit and exalt the letter. (3) Writing was inartistic, as the letters conveyed no images. (4) The Greeks had a high conception of the dignity of knowledge. True knowledge is not among the marketable wares, that can be carried about in a portable shape in books, and emptied from them into the mind of the learner. True knowledge is a hard-won possession, personable and inalienable. "Much learning does not teach wisdom," was a saying of Heraclitus, and even Aristotle declared that "much learning produces confusion."

For a further account of Plato's aversion to writing see Grote's *Plato*, I, 358.
[1]*Phaedrus*, 276.

"arranged men and speeches, and their modes and affections in
different classes, and fitted them into one another, he will point
out the connection between them—he will show why one is naturally persuaded by a particular form of argument, and another
not." In other words, the rhetorician must be a psychologist.

5.   The rhetorician must "speak of the instruments by which
the soul acts or is affected in any way." Here we have the division
under which comes practically all of rhetoric when viewed more
narrowly and technically. The "instruments" by which rhetoric
affects the soul are style and delivery. Plato believed style to be
acquired, however, as Pericles acquired it, by "much discussion and
lofty contemplation of nature."

6.   The art of writing will not be highly regarded; nor will
continuous and uninterrupted discourse be regarded as equal to
cross-examination as a means of instruction. This is Plato's way of
saying that any method of attempting to persuade multitudes must
suffer from the very fact that it is a multitude which is addressed,
and that the best of rhetoric is unequal to philosophic discussion.

7.   The rhetorician will have such a high moral purpose in all
his work that he will ever be chiefly concerned about saying that
which is "acceptable to God." Rhetoric, then, is not an instrument
for the determination of scientific truth, nor for mere persuasion
regardless of the cause; it is an instrument for making the will of
God prevail. The perfect rhetorician, as a philosopher, knows the
will of God.

De Quincey says that rhetoric has, in general, two connotations:
one of ostentatious ornament, and the other of fallacious argument.
That part of Plato's attack upon rhetoric which we have considered,
largely concerns itself with rhetoric as "ostentatious ornament"
(although the two aspects can seldom be completely separated).
And it was this attack which led Plato to the constructive theory of
the *Phædrus*. But there was a later assult upon the sophists which
concerned rhetoric as an art of fallacious argument.[1] The sophists
of Plato's earlier dialogues are declaimers and rhetoricians who can
overwhelm opponents with long speeches, but they are tyros in the

---

[1]Henry Sidgwick in his essays on the sophists was the first to point out this distinction. See his *Lectures on the Philosophy of Kant and other Philosophical Lectures
and Essays*. For a discussion of Sidgwick's essays, see Sir A. Grant: *The Ethics of
Aristotle*, Essay 2.

art of argumentation. In the *Euthydemus, Sophist,* and *Statesman,* Plato caricatures the imitators of Socrates, who practise argumentation by question and answer, but who resemble Socrates as the wolf does the dog.

The *Euthydemus* is the earliest known attempt to exhibit a variety of fallacies. In it Plato desired to make clear the distinction between truly philosophical argumentation and that eristical disputation which served no purpose except to display a certain type of cleverness. A young man, Cleinias, is cross-examined by two sophistical teachers of argument, Euthydemus and Dionysodorus. They conduct their examination in a spirit of horse-play, and soon have the youth hopelessly confused. Socrates then rebukes them, and offers to examine Cleinias in a truly philosophical fashion. His kindly questions (much more kindly here than in other dialogues, but they serve Plato's purpose in emphasizing the contrast), which lead Cleinias to the conclusion that wisdom is the only good, and ignorance the only evil, are an example of the way in which a philosopher conducts an argument— for the enlightenment, and not the confusion, of youth.

Having distinguished the philosopher from the sophistical teachers of fallacious argument, Plato in an epilogue contrasts the philosopher and the orator-statesman. Here Plato is probably thinking of Isocrates and his "philosophy," which was a mixture of rhetoric and politics. Philosopher-politicians and speech writers, Socrates is made to say, imagine themselves to be a superior sort; they think they have a certain amount of philosophy, and a certain amount of political insight; thus they keep out of the way of all risks and conflicts and reap the fruit of their wisdom. Socrates asserts, however, that philosophy and political action tend to such different ends that one who participates in both achieves little in either. The Isocratean ideal of the orator-statesman, which had so great an influence upon Cicero, was objectionable to Plato for at least three reasons. In the first place, the true statesman was a philosopher rather than an orator; he ruled arbitrarily through his wisdom rather than through persuasion. Secondly, if the statesman was forced to stoop to the use of oratory, it was to be clearly understood that oratory was a subordinate instrument. The ideal of the orator-statesman only helped to confuse the superior art of politics with rhetoric. Thirdly, the orator-statesman falsely imagined that the ideas which he used in the persuasion of the public constituted his philosophy; whereas in reality he was so tied to particulars in all his speaking and thinking that he never approached the wisdom of the true philosopher.

In the *Euthydemus,* then, we have pictured a later development of the older sophists. Imitators of Socrates had appeared who taught the art of argumentation for pay: Isocrates had enlarged and dignified the instruction of the rhetoricians by allying it more closely with pan-Hellenic politics, and had become much more popular and successful than Plato. Plato insists that true philosophy is a different sort of thing, and indulges in caricature and satire to make it evident.

In the *Sophist,* we have an abstract and methodical discussion of that which is dramatically pictured in the *Euthydemus.* Plato planned a trilogy of dialogues, the *Sophist,* the *Statesman,* and the *Philosopher,* in which the man of the world and the man of wisdom should be contrasted. The *Philosopher* was never written, but from the *Sophist* and the *Statesman* we get the Platonic discussion of the false art of argumentation known as eristic.

The sophist, in the dialogue of that name, is discovered by a preliminary study of the angler, which suggests a method of search, and also furnishes an implied analogy, for the sophist is found to be a fisher of men who finally destroys them. By a series of homely figures the sophist is revealed in his various aspects. He is 1) a paid hunter after youth and wealth, 2) a retail merchant or trader in the goods of the soul, 3) he himself manufactures the learned wares which he sells, 4) he is a hero of dispute, having distinctly the character of a disputant, 5) he is a purger of souls who clears away notions obstructive to knowledge. In the last-named characteristic, Plato seems about to admit that the sophist serves a great educational purpose, for he has previously admitted that "refutation is the greatest and chiefest purification." But the sophist, as the supposed minister of refutation, is related to the real purger of souls as "a wolf, who is the fiercest of animals, is to the dog, who is the gentlest."[1] Here Plato does not seem to see that a given logical procedure is as a method essentially the same, whether used by a sophist or a philosopher. For Plato, even the logical nature of cross-examination seems to be changed by the *moral*

---

[1]*Sophist,* 231.

nature of the examiner. No sophist ever employed greater fallacies than the Socrates of the Platonic dialogues; yet fallacies in the arguments of a philosopher seemed somehow elevated by their moral purpose. Aristotle followed Plato in this error. Probably no fallacy is more persistent than the judgment of logical method by the standard of moral purpose.

The eristical sophists, as the rhetorical, profess a knowledge which they do not have. They profess that the art of disputation is a power of disputing about all things. Plato puts the sophists in the position of teaching that a mastery of form gives also a mastery of substance. The sophists delight in the discovery that a certain facility in logical method, accompanied by entire unscrupulousness, can make almost any proposition appear to be plausible. With no standard of consistency looking farther than the immediate discussion, method can so arrange any small group of facts, or alleged facts, that any thesis may be made to appear tenable. The sophists *seem* to teach young men to argue about all things because "they make young men believe in their own supreme and universal wisdom." They are enabled to do this by their readiness in offering "conjectural or apparent knowledge of all things," as a substitute for truth. They are like painters who profess "by one art to make all things."[1] What the sophist makes is a resemblance, but it is easy to deceive the less intelligent children, by showing his pictures at a distance, into believing that he has the absolute power of making what he likes. In the same way there is an imitative art of reasoning, and by the use of this art, the sophist passes himself off as a philosopher. There are two types of these imitators: the popular orator, who makes long speeches to the multitude and who appears to be a statesman, and the sophist, who teaches argumentation and pretends to be a philosopher.

The *Statesman* is an attempt, by the same method of division used in the *Sophist,* to discover the true statesman. Here we have an introductory analogy concerning the weaver. As the weaver has the auxiliary arts of the fuller, the carder, and the maker of the warp and woof, so the statesman has the auxiliary arts of the rhetorician, the general, and the judge. There is always the danger, however, that the rhetorician may be mistaken for the statesman. Poli-

---

[1] *Sophist,* 233, 234.

tics is the science that tells us when to persuade, and of what; rhetoric merely tells how to persuade. If the rhetoric be a noble rhetoric, however, and does really persuade men to love justice, it may be regarded as a useful instrument in our second-best state, where persuasion is an unfortunate necessity in government. Rhetoric, however, should never lose its instrumental character, and should never aspire to be more than one of the several subordinate arts which the statesman weaves together into the whole which is the state.

In these two dialogues, then, the *Sophist* and the *Statesman,* we are warned against the rhetorician, who appears in different guises. In the *Sophist,* he appears as the dialectician who purges the soul of false knowledge, but he is really an eristical disputant. In the *Statesman,* he appears as the persuader of the public who is quick to sieze power as a demagogue unless he be kept strictly under the direction of the true statesman.

To summarize briefly our whole discussion of Plato: we have shown that his treatment of rhetoric is based upon his feelings toward certain rhetoricians, and upon his dislike of the rhetorical tendency of all Athenian life. Plato never viewed rhetoric abstractly, as an art of composition, as an instrument that might be used or abused; he always considered it a false impulse in human thought. He therefore attacked in published dialogues the more prominent contemporary teachers and the art they professed to teach. The evidence seems to show that the sophists of the earlier attacks were intellectually respectable, and that they made significant contributions to the thought of their time. At the conclusion of his earlier attacks (if we may trust the attempts to arrange Plato's dialogues in approximately chronogical order) Plato offers an outline of a reconstructed rhetoric. Here, too, he shows his inability to conceive of rhetoric as a tool; the ideal rhetoric sketched in the *Phaedrus* is as far from the possibilities of mankind as his Republic was from Athens. In later life, a new generation of teachers that patterned its methods after Socrates, aroused the wrath of Plato, and he wrote other dialogues to distinguish the false art of argumentation from the dialectical processes of the true philosopher.

In turning to Aristotle,[1] we shall be chiefly interested in his relation

---

[1] For translations of Aristotle's *Rhetoric,* see those by Welldon, London, 1886; Jebb, Cambridge, 1909; and Roberts, in *The Works of Aristotle,* vol. XI, Oxford, 1924. Citations of the *Rhetoric* in this study are taken from Roberts.

to Plato. To explain the relation of any one of Aristotle's treatises to Plato is, according to Sir Alexander Grant, almost a sufficient account of what it contains. Familiarity with the Platonic dialogues and their Athenian background, makes it possible to proceed more rapidly with the systematic work of Aristotle upon any particular subject under investigation. It is not our purpose here to present an exposition of the *Rhetoric*,[a] and the preceding discussion should make it possible to condense the account of Aristotle, although his contribution to rhetoric is greater than that of Plato or the sophists.

It is obvious that as Plato's pupil, Aristotle must have had his attention called to those aspects of Athenian life which interested his master. As a reader of Plato's dialogues, Aristotle found a wealth of concretely pictured material ready for classification into various compartments of knowledge. Aside from the magnificent gesture of the *Phœdrus*, Plato apparently gave little constructive thought to rhetoric. He did not teach its practice, nor lecture upon its theory. Aristotle, however, during the first period of residence at Athens, and while still a pupil of Plato at the Academy, opened a school of rhetoric in competition with Isocrates. We have here an instance of the way in which rhetoric in Athens, as in other times and places, has offered men whose minds could not be confined to a single field, an opportunity to establish themselves as teachers and thinkers. The works upon rhetoric which have been lost were probably composed during this earlier period. There seem to be adequate grounds for attributing three such works to Aristotle: a history of rhetoric, a dialogue upon the subject, named for Gryllus, a son of Xenophon, and the *Theodectea*, mainly devoted to style, composition, and arrangement, and which probably contained in greater detail the subject matter of the third book of the extant *Rhetoric*.[1] It is not known when the *Rhetoric* was composed, but it was not published until Aristotle's second period of residence and teaching in Athens (336 B.C. is the most generally accepted date of publication). It is believed that the third book, which deals with style and arrangement, was not written until some time after the first two

---

[a]For expositions of the *Rhetoric*, see E. M. Cope: *An Introduction to Aristotle's Rhetoric*, London, 1867; Gomperz: *op. cit.*, IV; Zeller: *Aristotle and the Earlier Peripatetics*, London, 1897; and Baldwin: *Ancient Rhetoric and Poetic*, New York, 1924.

[1]See Cope's *Introduction to Aristotle's Rhetoric*, section entitled "Aristotle's Lost Works on Rhetoric."

books. The *Poetics* was written before the third book of the *Rhetoric*,
but probably after the earlier books. From this it is sometimes inferred
that Aristotle's interest in style as a part of rhetoric was of late
development. This is hardly consistent with his earlier treatment of
the subject in the *Theodectea*. A more probable explanation of the
greater interest which Aristotle seems to have felt in the subject of
proofs and their sources is that this part of rhetoric represented most
distinctly his own contribution to the subject. In writing of style and
arrangement he was dealing with questions already fully treated by
many writers, for most of whom he had little regard. In the first two
books, however, he was organizing a new unity out of material drawn
from logic, psychology, ethics, and politics. It may have been an
additional source of pleasure to him to be able to draw from his own
treatment of these special fields such material as was needed to give
rhetoric a more philosophical character. It is significant that Aristotle,
having taught rhetoric in his early youth, and having waged war with
both preceding and contemporary rhetoricians, should, in his age,
after having surveyed all the fields of knowledge, return to the treatment of the same subject. It seems to be one of the ironies of history
that that portion of rhetoric which was most particularly his own,
and which owed most to his previous work in other fields, should be
forever slipping back into its component parts of logic, psychology,
ethics, and politics; and that style and arrangement, regarded by both
himself and Plato as mere preliminaries to the art, rather than the art
itself, should fix more permanently the character of rhetoric.

While Aristotle agreed with Plato in his contempt for the unscientific nature of the instruction given by other teachers of rhetoric,[1]
and in applying the term sophist to false pretenders to knowledge,[2]
his approach to rhetoric was affected by certain philosophical and
temperamental divergences from Plato. It is an oft-quoted remark
of Friedrich Schlegel's that every man is born either a Platonist or
an Aristotelian. This is generally interpreted to mean that the tribe
of Platonists are poets and mystics, seeking a truth above the truth
of scientific knowledge, while the Aristotelians rely upon methodical

---

[1] See the concluding section of the *Sophistici Elenchi;* also the first chapter of the
Rhetoric.
[2] *Sophistici Elenchi,* ch. 1; and ch. 1 of the *Rhetoric.*

experience and classified observations. It cannot be said that Aristotle paid greater attention than Plato to the facts of experience in the creation of a philosophical rhetoric, for he constructed the entire art from the general principles of dialectic, psychology, and ethics, referring to any existing examples of eloquence only most casually for the sake of illustration. But it is, perhaps, a safe generalization to say that Plato sought to reform life, while Aristotle was more interested in reorganizing theory about life. For this reason Aristotle's *Rhetoric* is largely detached from both morality and pedagogy. It is neither a manual of rules nor a collection of injunctions. It is an unmoral and scientific analysis of the means of persuasion.

We have seen that Plato was predisposed to feel a contempt for rhetoric and rhetoricians by certain of his political ideas—his belief in a government of philosophers, administered by experts; his desire for a permanent stratification of society, free from attempts of men to rise out of their class; and his profound contempt for public opinion. Aristotle had no enthusiasm for what has been called Plato's "pedantocracy." He realized that expert knowledge and professional training have their limitations, and that in political matters the judgment of the people may be superior to that of those who have special knowledge.[1] Although Aristotle shared Plato's belief that a laborer could hardly possess a virtue which should entitle him to citizenship, he never expected ranks and classes to be permanently fixed, as in the *Republic*. In the *Politics* he suggests that final power should rest with the multitude, which, of course, would make rhetoric a universal political instrument. And Aristotle's attitude toward public opinion— the common sense of the majority—is distinctly different from that of Plato. This is most marked, perhaps, in his *Ethics*,[2] although it is difficult to distinguish ethical from political thinking in the speculation of the period. But one impulse which set Plato to writing was his intense dissatisfaction with the empirical and prudential morality of his countrymen. The constant contrast in his dialogues is between

---

[1] *Politics,* 1282.

[2] For the contribution of public opinion to Aristotle's *Ethics,* see Burnet's introduction to his edition of the work, London, 1900. See also L. H. G. Greenwood's essay, Dialectic Method in the Sixth Book, in his edition of the sixth book of the *Ethics,* Cambridge, 1909. Sir A. Grant's *Ethics of Aristotle* is also useful in this connection.

unreflective, chaotic public opinion, and reasoned, philosophic knowledge. He did not care to organize public opinion, subject it to definitions, and extract from it its modicum of truth. The mind must not
only reason about the good; it must contemplate the Idea of the Good
in the heavens above until conformed to it. Aristotle attacked the
Platonic doctrine of ideas, separated ethics from metaphysics, and took
as his guiding principle a practical good, happiness. In discussing
happiness, Aristotle did not limit himself to the doctrines of the
philosophers; he often accepted generally received opinions, and
where he rejected them he at least paid them the honor of refutation.
The lists and divisions of goods presented in the *Ethics* were largely
derived from current Athenian discussion, and many ideas which
Aristotle accepts as authoritative were common property. In the
Topics,[3] when he discusses the uses of dialectic, he explicitly recognizes
value of a wide acquaintance with public opinion. There was little
danger that a Socrates, discoursing freely in the market place with
any one he chanced upon, would be unfamiliar with the beliefs of
"the man in the street." But the growth of schools, the habit of
scientific study, and the production of written compositions tended to
make of the philosopher a man apart. Aristotle recognized the
dangerous effect of this upon the public influence of the learned; he
recommended the practice of dialectical discussion as a means of
keeping in touch with the opinions of men. He himself drew up a
collection of current proverbs. Even his more scientific works have been
criticized for his willingness to accept common opinion where accurate
observation was called for. We may say, then, that Aristotle approached the subject of rhetoric with a belief in its necessity as a
political instrument, and a conviction that both the trained thinker
and the multitude would benefit by making a common stock of their
wisdom for the guidance of the state.

   The effect of these philosophical divergences upon the treatment
of rhetoric becomes clearly evident when we compare the Platonic
discussion between Gorgias and Socrates on the nature and functions
of rhetoric with the statements upon the same subject in the early
part of Aristotle's *Rhetoric*. Aristotle states clearly what Gorgias
seemed to be groping for, and unmistakably sides with Gorgias

---

[3]See Grote's *Aristotle,* London, 1872, for an exposition of the *Topics.*

against Plato in practically all controverted points. In the *Gorgias,* Socrates asserts that teachers of rhetoric know nothing of justice, and that the art of rhetoric is inimical to justice. Aristotle in the first chapter of the *Rhetoric,* expresses his belief that rhetoric makes for the prevalence of truth and righteousness.

> Rhetoric is useful because things that are true and things that are just have a natural tendency to prevail over their opposites, so that if the decisions of judges are not what they ought to be, the defeat must be due to the speakers themselves, and they must be blamed accordingly. . . . Further, we must be able to employ persuasion, just as strict reasoning can be employed, on opposite sides of a question, not in order that we may in practice employ it both ways (for we must not make people believe what is wrong), but in order that we may see clearly what the facts are, and that, if another man argues unfairly, we may on our part be able to confute him. No other of the arts draws opposite conclusions: dialectic and rhetoric alone do this. Both these arts draw opposite conclusions impartially. Nevertheless, the underlying facts do not lend themselves equally well to the contrary views. No; things that are true and things that are better are, by their nature, practically always easier to believe in.[1]

It is worthy of note that Aristotle, although he does remark parenthetically that the rhetorician should not make people believe what is wrong, does not base his faith in the benefits of rhetoric upon the moral training of the rhetorician, but rather upon the nature of things. Rhetorical effectiveness does not add equally to the strength of a just and an unjust cause. To use an imperfect analogy, we may say, perhaps, that skilful presentation of a just cause strengthens its appeal geometrically, while an unjust cause is aided only arithmetically. The inherent superiority of just and true things is thus increased by the universal use of rhetoric. This is a broader and sounder view than Plato was able to take. As a reformer Plato had no patience with the evils which inevitably accompany all good things. Aristotle is quite cognizant of the evils of rhetoric, but is content that the good shall, on the whole, outweigh it.

And if it be objected that one who uses such power of speech

---

[1] *Rhetoric,* 1355a.

unjustly might do great harm, that is a charge which may be made
in common against all good things except virtue, and above all
against the things that are most useful, as strength, health, wealth,
generalship.[2]

In the *Gorgias,* Socrates establishes the point that the power of
rhetoric is only an apparent power, because it rests upon the ignorance
of the multitude addressed. The persuasion of the ignorant many is
a rather unseemly occupation for a philosopher. As to the essentially
popular function of rhetoric, Aristotle agrees, but without conde-
scension.

> Moreover, before some audiences not even the possession of the
> exactest knowledge will make it easy for what we say to produce
> conviction. For argument based on knowledge implies instruction,
> and there are people whom one cannot instruct. Here, then, we
> must use, as our modes of persuasion and argument, notions pos-
> sessed by everybody, as we observed in the *Topics* when dealing
> with the way to handle a popular audience.[3]

The Platonic Socrates argued against Gorgias and Polus that the
persuasion of multitudes was not properly an art at all, but only a
knack or routine or experience. The first claim that Aristotle makes
for rhetoric is that it may properly be considered as an art.

> All men attempt to discuss statements and to maintain them, to
> defend themselves and attack others. Ordinary people do this at
> random or through practice and from acquired habit. Both ways
> being possible, the subject can plainly be handled systematically,
> for it is possible to inquire the reason why some speakers succeed
> through practice and others spontaneously; and every one will at
> once agree that such an inquiry is the function of an art.[1]

One of the Platonic reasons for refusing to admit that rhetoric
was properly an art was the difficulty of discovering its proper subject-
matter. Gorgias is exhibited to us as struggling with this question,
and as insisting that persuasive discourse is the proper subject matter
of rhetoric; but when Socrates presses him with analogies from the
other arts, and asks him if instruction in music and geometry and

---

[2]*Rhetoric,* 1355b.
[3]*Rhetoric,* 1355a.
[1]*Rhetoric,* 1354a.

arithmetic is not persuasive discourse, Gorgias is unable to make a satisfactory statement. This interested Aristotle; it led him to distinguish between rhetoric and the special sciences, but it did not lead him to deny that rhetoric was a discipline in itself.

> Rhetoric may be defined as the faculty of observing in any given case the available means of persuasion. This is not the function of any other art. Every other subject can instruct or persuade about its own particular subject-matter; for instance, medicine about what is healthy and unhealthy, geometry about the properties of magnitudes, arithmetic about numbers, and the same is true of the other arts and sciences. But rhetoric we look upon as the power of observing the means of persuasion on almost any subject presented to us; and that is why we say that, in its technical character, it is not concerned with any special or definite class of subjects. . . . The duty of rhetoric is to deal with such matters as we deliberate on without arts or systems to guide us, in the hearing of persons who cannot take in at a glance a complicated argument, or follow a long chain of reasoning. . . . But the more we try to make either dialectic or rhetoric not, what they really are, practical faculties, but sciences, the more we shall inadvertently be destroying their true nature; for we shall be refashioning them and shall be passing into the region of sciences dealing with definite subjects rather than simply with words and forms of reasoning.[2]

The argumentative purpose of the Socratic thesis in the *Gorgias*, that it is better to suffer wrong than to do it, was to disparage the claim made for rhetoric that it was useful for purposes of defense. Aristotle agrees that a man may well be eulogized for choosing to suffer wrong rather than to do it.[3] Such a choice, however, is a *moral* problem for the individual, and is quite irrelevant to a consideration of the uses of any art—rhetoric or boxing or generalship. Aristotle insists that the use of speech and reason as a method of protection against injustice is distinctively human.[1]

It is not surprising that Aristotle, as a writer on rhetoric, should disagree with the passionately hostile treatment of his subject in the *Gorgias*. Most writers who have compared the *Rhetoric* with Plato's

---

[2] *Rhetoric,* 1355b, 1357a, 1359b.
[3] *Rhetoric,* 1364b.
[1] *Rhetoric,* 1355b.

sketch in the *Phaedrus,* content themselves with indicating the similarities of the two works.[2] Aristotle's indebtedness to Plato is pointed
out, and it is suggested that Plato, in lectures or conversation, may
have given Aristotle a pretty complete outline for his work. When we
consider the specific suggestions of the *Phædrus* for a philosophical
rhetoric, however, the differences between the Platonic and the
Aristotelian conception of the subject are at least as manifest as the
likenesses.

Taking up first the relationship of rhetoric to Truth, we note a wide
divergence. Plato held that the rhetorician must know the Truth,
because probability was engendered by a likeness to Truth. Here Plato
seems hardly consistent with himself, for a public so depraved as Plato
felt all multitudes to be, would never care so much for a resemblance
to Truth, as for a probability based upon a consonance with its own
interests and tastes. Such a probability, however, could not, according
to Plato, form the basis for any art.

For Aristotle, however, probability forms the very groundwork
of rhetoric. Rhetoric is frankly an art of appearances. Its function is to
enable a man to see quickly what are the available means of persuasion
on either side of any proposition. The whole plan of the *Rhetoric* bears
out this conclusion. Consider first the topics, or commonplaces, or, as
Roberts translates the term, lines of argument. The topics, according
to some critics, represent Aristotle's determined effort to classify the
essentially unclassifiable.[3] Aristotle himself seems hardly clear in his
own mind whether the topics were to be regarded as premises or
methods of argument, whether they were indicative or imperative. At
any rate, they were collections of brief statements with which the
rhetorician was to be familiar in order to call to mind immediately all
the available arguments for either side of the case. If, for example, a

---

[2]See Lutoslawski: *Origin and Growth of Plato's Logic,* p. 344. Also Gomperz:
op. cit., IV, 421. W. H. Thompson, in the introduction to his edition of the
Phaedrus, London, 1868, compares it with the *Rhetoric,* and emphasizes the likenesses of the two works. E. M. Cope recognizes the fundamental difference between
Plato and Aristotle on the matter of probability. See the introduction to his edition of the *Gorgias,* London, 1883.

[3]For discussions of the topics, see Grote's *Aristotle;* Edward Poste's essays in his
translations of Aristotle's *Posterior Analytics,* Oxford, 1850, and *Sophistici Elenchi;*
and Copes *Introduction to Aristotle's Rhetoric.* See also Hoyt H. Hudson: Can
We Modernize the Theory of Invention? *Quarterly Journal of Speech Education,*
VII:325, 1921.

written law is adverse to one's case, one can impugn its authority by an appeal to a higher and more universal law. On the other hand, if the law favors one's case, it can be urged that the attempt to be wiser than the law increases the bad habit of disobeying authority. It is noteworthy that as aids to invention the topics were not axioms, propositions universally true, but were often less than half-truths. For almost any Aristotelian topic, which was to serve as a reminder of or a basis for an argument, another topic could be found which would serve equally well for a contrary argument. The topics, then, constituted a sort of rhetoricians' first aid. They were to assist him in producing immediately, and perhaps without any special knowledge of the subject, a plausible argument upon either side of a debatable proposition.

Additional evidence of the merely contingent and probable nature of rhetoric, as opposed to the Platonic conception, is to be seen in the distinct method of reasoning which Aristotle elaborated for popular persuasion. Realizing, with Plato, that a general audience cannot be *instructed* by close reasoning, but must be *persuaded* by an easier procedure, he substitutes in rhetoric the enthymeme for the syllogism, and the example for the more careful induction of scientific reasoning. The enthymeme was a rhetorical syllogism; that is, a syllogism drawn, not from universal principles belonging to a particular science, but from probabilities in the sphere of human affairs. In proceeding hastily with a subject before an audience, it would usually happen that one of the three members of the formal syllogism would be omitted. Whether or not the essential distinction between the enthymeme and the syllogism is in the merely probable nature of the premises or in the suppression of one of the parts,[1] the enthymeme is to be regarded as the principal method of popular presentation of thought. For the persuasive use of examples (less conclusive but more persuasive than a logical induction) Aristotle offers the astute advice, "If you put examples first, you must use many; if at the end, even one is enough."[1]

A study of the topics, of enthymemes and examples, makes it evident that the rhetorical *processes* of invention and logical formula-

---

[1] On this controverted point, see Cope's *Introduction to Aristotle's Rhetoric,* p. 103 and note. See also De Quincey's essay on Rhetoric.
[1] *Rhetoric,* 1394a.

tion were designed for quick plausibility. Turning from processes to *content*, this impression is heightened. For each of the three branches of rhetoric—deliberative, epideictic, and forensic—an outline of the usual subject-matter treated by the speaker is offered. A student of each of the special sciences represented would probably say that Aristotle has given us as the subject-matter of deliberative rhetoric a superficial political science; for epideictic rhetoric a conventional ethics; and for forensic rhetoric a very loose and inexact criminal jurisprudence.

The subjects suggested as the content of deliberative speeches are all much more fully treated in the *Politics.* The *Rhetoric* takes from the *Politics* a brief sketch of political matters upon which speakers must be persuasive. The rhetorician should be familiar with the various forms of government—democracy, oligarchy, aristocracy, monarchy—not that he shall determine which is best, or shall speak as a political philosopher, but in order that he may gain persuasiveness by being able to adapt himself to the political beliefs of his audience. It is, of course, perfectly possible for the student of rhetoric to be a political scientist, as Aristotle himself was, but as a rhetorician his task is to use whatever political commonplaces are most likely to win approval. That Aristotle was fully conscious of the differences between his scientific and his rhetorical treatment of the same subject, is indicated by the statement with which he concludes his section on the forms of government in the *Rhetoric:*

> We have also briefly considered the means and methods by which we shall gain a good knowledge of the moral qualities and institutions peculiar to the various forms of government—only, however, to the extent demanded by the present occasion; a detailed account of the subject has been given in the *Politics.*[2]

The epideictic speaker, as his function is to praise or blame, finds that his subject-matter lies largely in the field of ethics. We have in the *Rhetoric,* therefore, a summary view of the needed ethical material—happiness, goods, virtue and vice, wrong-doing and injustice, pleasure, equity, laws, and friendship. These subjects are given a much fuller exposition in the *Ethics,* and some of the rhetorical definitions,

---

[2]*Rhetoric,* 1366a.

notably that of pleasure, are there repudiated. While neither ethics nor politics were exact sciences in Aristotle's eyes, and while he repeatedly insisted that the exactness of the physical sciences should not be expected in them, he nevertheless put forth a much greater effort in those fields than in rhetoric to arrive at conceptions that would bear searching criticism. The ethical conceptions of the *Rhetoric* are the conceptions of the man in the street   current popular notions that would supply the most plausible premises for persuasive speeches.

Aristotle remarks in the opening of the *Rhetoric* that forensic oratory, more than political, is given to unscrupulous practices. But the oratorical jurisprudence which he offers as the material of the forensic speaker would not go far to elevate the argumentation of the courtroom. This section of the rhetoric most clearly indicates that Aristotle's was a scientific and not a moral earnestness; the dialectician is here in the ascendant.

> In dealing with the evidence of witnesses, the following are useful arguments. If you have no witnesses on your side, you will argue that the judges must decide from what is probable; that this is meant by "giving a verdict in accordance with one's honest opinion;" that probabilities cannot be bribed to mislead the court; and that probabilities are never convicted of perjury. If you *have* witnesses, and the other man has not, you will argue that probabilities cannot be put on their trial, and that we could do without the evidence of witnesses altogether if we need do no more than balance the pleas advanced on either side. . . . So, clearly, we need never be at a loss for useful evidence.[1]

The entire section on forensic rhetoric recognizes that each pleader's loyalty is to his case, and that as a skilful rhetorician he must be quick to discern all the persuasive possibilities of any situation. Aristotle professed a dislike for the business, but once engaged in the classification of arguments he is concerned with rhetorical effectiveness and not with moral justifiability.

The explicit statement which shows that Aristotle regarded rhetoric as an instrument of persuasion quite detached from the moral nature of the rhetorician, occurs in the third book, in connection with the discussion of delivery.

---

[1] *Rhetoric,* 1376a.

Besides, delivery is—very properly—not regarded as an elevated subject of inquiry. Still, *the whole business of rhetoric being concerned with appearances,* we must pay attention to the subject of delivery, unworthy though it is, because we cannot do without it.[1]

Turning now from the general problem of the relationship of the *Rhetoric* to Platonic Truth, we take up the second of Plato's suggestions in the *Phaedrus,* that the rhetorician must be a dialectician, a man who can distinguish between particulars and universals, who can define his terms, and who can distinguish debatable from undebatable questions. With this Aristotle seems to be in agreement. He opens his *Rhetoric* by declaring that it is the counterpart of dialectic. Elsewhere he refers to rhetoric as parallel to, an offshoot or branch of, dialectic.[2] He also says that the master of dialectic will be the true master of rhetoric. But it is impossible to make clear the relation between dialectic and rhetoric without explaining the Platonic contrast between the two, and the great advance made by Aristotle in relating both of them to demonstrative science.

After all, the sum and substance of Plato's suggestions for rhetoric is that rhetoric, if it is really to be an art, must coincide with philosophy. When Plato said that the rhetorician must be a dialectician, he meant that he must be a philosopher. So far as he differs from the philosopher, he is an impostor; so far as he coincides with him, his art of rhetoric is superseded. But Aristotle gave to the term dialectic such a different significance that it is another thing entirely to say that the rhetorician should be a dialectician. For Plato, dialectic was the whole process of rational analysis by which the soul was led into the knowledge of Ideas. It had both a positive and a negative aspect. In the earlier dialogues the negative function was most prominent, and the principal contribution which the Socratic dialectic made to the wisdom of those who underwent his cross-examination was to disabuse them of their false knowledge. As Plato developed his own doctrine of Ideas, dialectic became the instrument of awakening by which the soul recollected the eternal Ideas which it had known in a preexistént state. Dialectic became a means of positive instruction, as well as of

---

[1] *Rhetoric,* 1404a. See the translation of this passage by C. S. Baldwin in his *Ancient Rhetoric and Poetic,* p. 23. Professor Baldwin denies that Aristotle had a "philosophic contempt" for delivery.

[2] *Rhetoric,* 1355 and 1356.

refutation. As Plato grew old and became more dogmatic in exposition, he found the dialectical form somewhat inconvenient, but he did not develop a new form for didactic procedure. The teachings implanted by dialectic represented reasoned and tested conclusions, carrying with them the certainty of philosophical knowledge, as opposed to the superficial opinions which constituted the material of rhetoric, and which persuaded without giving any real instruction. In Plato's later life, mathematical reasoning came to represent the type of demonstrated knowledge, but at the time of the attacks upon the sophists and rhetoricians, certainty and exactitude were to be found through the dialectical process.

Aristotle had even more clearly in mind the antithesis between opinion or common sense, and scientific knowledge or real instruction. He had, however, no sympathy with the Platonic doctrine of Ideas, and was free from any sense of a mystical significance for dialectic. Observing the didactic elements of the Platonic dialectic, he perfected the syllogism as the instrument of scientific knowledge and teaching. In the two books of the *Analytica Priora* he developed the functions and varieties of the syllogism and suggested that it could be applied both to scientific demonstration and to the process of argumentation in the realm of opinion. There is, however, such a difference of matter and purpose in scientific and nonscientific discussion that the use of the syllogism in the one and in the other is to be governed by a distinct body of theory. The *Analytica Posteriora* develops the use of the syllogism for demonstrative reasoning, and the *Topica,* together with the *Sophistici Elenchi,* for dialectic. The material for the *Topica* and the *Sophistici Elenchi*—which is really the last book of the *Topica*—is drawn from that type of argumentation pilloried by Plato in the *Euthydemus, Sophist,* and *Statesman.* Aristotle in his classification of fallacies cites the *Euthydemus* frequently. Plato drew a vivid picture of the fallacious disputers and excited the feelings of the reader against such arguments without really analyzing the fallacies. But Aristotle, in the *Sophistici Elenchi,* analyzed and classified fallacies with the purpose of enabling the reader to use them more skilfully. That type of disputation which Plato made a variety of false rhetoric, the very antithesis of true dialectic, is for Aristotle an integral part of dialectic. Thus it is evident that Aristotle has allowed dialectic to descend into that realm of opinion inhabited by sophists and rhetoricians. Where Plato had been chiefly impressed by the contrast between rhetoric and dialectic, Aristotle noticed the similarities. The realm of opinion, which Plato had regarded as unworthy the attention of the philosopher, is thus accorded by Aristotle two distinct disciplines, dialectic and rhetoric. There are differences between the two, but the more fundamental contrast is between rhetoric and dialectic on the one hand, and scientific reasoning, on the other.[1]

Scientific procedure, for Aristotle, starts with universal or necessary principles and proceeds to universal and necessary conclusions. Both dialectic and rhetoric, however, take as their premises current popular opinions, or perhaps the opinions of dissenters. Any probable or plausible assertion will serve. The fundamental principles of a science cannot be proved within the bounds of that science; they are therefore assumed. The only way of questioning them is in dialectical debate. A few fundamental principles, as axioms, are common to all or to several of the sciences; but by far the larger part of the principles employed are special to the sciences concerned. As against this, rhetoric and dialectic are not limited to the propositions of any particular field. They may regard the ultimate assumptions of any science as mere probabilities and discuss them as such. In dialectic, the number of special propositions, corresponding to scientific laws peculiar to one field, is small. On the other hand, the number of general propositions, called topics (corresponding to the comparatively few axioms of science), is large. In science, again we do not have matter to be settled by debate, but rather by impartial investigation. Dialectic and rhetoric can argue as easily upon one side of the question as another. They may employ any material conceded by an opponent. They may be indifferent to the truth of a conclusion if the form and method have been accurately followed.

From all this it is evident that as contrasted with scientific knowledge, dialectic and rhetoric are much alike. There are certain differences, however, which Aristotle regarded as sufficiently fundamental

---

[1]For the relations of science, dialectic and rhetoric, see Cope's *Introduction to Aristotle's Rhetoric,* p. 67; Poste's introduction to his translation of Aristotle's *Analytica Posteriora;* Appendix D in his translation of the *Sophistici Elenchi;* and Grote's *Aristotle.*

to justify their treatment as separate disciplines. The most obvious difference, and one which accounts for several others, is that dialectic is an argument conducted by two speakers with a small audience of interested listeners who will see that the argument is fairly conducted. Such a method of argument is best fitted for speculative questions, although it can be applied to anything. It will be concerned with logical processes and not with the feelings of an audience. It is aimed not so much at persuading the opponent as at defeating him by involving him in contradictions. The method of reasoning employed is the syllogistic or inductive, the only difference from genuinely scientific reasoning being that the materials are taken from the realm of the merely probable. Rhetoric, on the other hand, because of the fact that one speaker is continuously addressing a large audience of untrained hearers, cannot use the form of scientific reasoning. In place of the syllogism and induction it uses the enthymeme and example. Since the feelings of the hearers will probably be more influential than the logic of the speaker, rhetoric must include an account of the emotions and characters of men. While rhetoric is not necessary to the dialectician, the rhetorician will be better for a thorough knowledge of dialectic.

One additional contrast between rhetoric and dialectic is of significance. Theoretically, Aristotle regarded rhetoric and dialectic as applicable to the same range of subjects. Theoretically, anything could be discussed by either method. But practically, as we see when we compare the topics of the *Topics* and the *Rhetoric*,[1] rhetorical discussion is limited to human actions and characters. The subject-matter of rhetoric is for practical purposes limited to ethics and politics. There is a mention of the popular exposition of scientific subjects as one of the uses of rhetoric, but the system as Aristotle develops it, is much more limited than the system of dialectical argument.

Analytics (logic), dialectic, and rhetoric form the organon of thought and expression for the ancient world. Aristotle, as much indebted to the Platonic dialogues, perhaps, as to his own observations of Athenian life, observed scientific thought, systematized it,

---

[1] For a comparison of the *Rhetoric* with the *Topics,* and with all the other works of Aristotle with which it comes in contact, see C. A. Brandis: Über Aristoteles' rhetorik und die griechischen ausleger derselben, in Schneidewin's *Philologus,* IV, 1849, I.

and gave us logic; observing the sport dear to all Athenians—argumentation by question and answer———and systematizing it, he gave us dialectic; observing and systematizing the art of persuading crowds, he gave us rhetoric. Thus, although Aristotle agrees with Plato that the rhetorician should also be a dialectician, it is evident that the dictum has a very different meaning for the two writers.

Another suggestion in the *Phædrus* concerned order and arrangement. This suggestion is developed by Aristotle in the second half of the third book of the *Rhetoric*. He attacks as unnecessarily complex the numerous divisions of the contemporary rhetoricians, and treats arrangement under the heads of Proem, Narrative, Proofs, and Epilogue. As our purpose is to compare Aristotle with Plato, rather than to give an exposition of his *Rhetoric,* we need observe only that this Platonic suggestion is carried out by Aristotle, although he was probably much more indebted to other rhetoricians than to Plato for his discussion of arrangement.

The Platonic requirement that the nature of the soul must be shown, and arguments adapted to the different kinds of people addressed by the speaker, is the basis of the oft-repeated assertion that the *Rhetoric* is an expanded *Phædrus.* There are two reasons for this. In the first place, that part of the second book of the *Rhetoric* which treats of the emotions and characters of men is the part which has the greatest interest and significance for the modern reader.[1] Secondly, it is, perhaps, the most distinct addition Aristotle

---

[1]Gomperz, in his *Greek Thinkers,* IV, 435, seems to feel that those sections of the *Rhetoric* which are genuinely a part of the subject are of relatively little significance for a philosopher, while the parts for which he professes admiration are really out of place in rhetoric. Referring to the treatment of the emotions and characters of men, he says: "It is surprising to find this subject, which seems to belong much more properly to psychology or descriptive ethics, imported into a work on rhetoric, and there treated with an exhaustiveness that goes far beyond the end in view. That which moved Aristotle to this procedure was probably, in the first place, the Platonic ideal of the art as set forth in the *Phaedrus;* and secondly, the wish, cherished no less warmly by him than by his master, to separate the new exposition of rhetoric as widely as possible from the old empirical methods and routine wisdom. It so comes about that we have before us foundations of much greater strength and depth than is justified by the superstructure which rests upon them. We shall, perhaps, be not far wrong in conjecturing that Aristotle was glad of the opportunity to raise the tone of that initiation into rhetorical fencing tricks which practical considerations forced upon him. Another cause operating in the same direction may have been a recollection of the fact that at

made to the work of his predecessors in the field. But even here, where Aristotle has apparently carried out the suggestions of his master most brilliantly, it must be observed that his treatment is only a popular and inexact discussion of the external manifestations of character and emotions, and not the sort of treatment he would have given the doctrine of the affections, had he developed it in his *De Anima*. It is also to be noted that while the classification of the emotions is as complete as the rhetorician would desire, Aristotle did not share Plato's notion that a true art of rhetoric would enable a speaker to adapt himself to each of the persons of an audience as the dialectician adjusts himself to one deuteragonist. He expressly disclaims such a belief.

> The theory of rhetoric is concerned not with what seems probable to a given individual like Socrates or Hippias, but with what seems probable to men of a given type.[1]

Nor does Aristotle suppose that even the best of rhetoricians will always succeed with his audience. The function of rhetoric is not simply to succeed in persuading, but rather to discover the means of coming as near such success as the circumstances of each particular case allow.[2]

Style and delivery, Plato stated, were necessary preliminaries to the art of rhetoric. An elevated style, however, was to be attained, not by technique, but by contemplation of lofty subjects. Aristotle seems to have shared his master's feeling that style and delivery should be subordinate matters, as spectacle was the least artistic element of the drama. His classifying mind, however, was much better able than Plato's to resist the tendency to place all subjects in a hierarchial order of moral dignity and to slight all the lower orders. He dismisses delivery briefly with the explanation that not enough is yet known about it to treat it scientifically; but he does regard both delivery and diction as means of persuasive discourse.

the beginning of the work he had been unwilling to allow emotional effects any place at all in oratory. Now that he felt constrained to descend from that ideal height, he preferred to do so in such a manner that the subject proscribed at first might appear in strictly scientific garb, not as merely auxiliary to rhetorical success."

[1]*Rhetoric,* 1356b.
[2]*Rhetoric,* 1355b.

Plato's dislike for writing, which in our day would so limit the province of rhetoric, does not seem to have disturbed Aristotle. He wrote several times as much as Plato, and upon subjects which Plato would probably have regarded as unsuitable for literary presentation. It is only on the heights of learning that truth and beauty are always compatible, and for the most part Plato kept to the heights. Aristotle saw his own writing, not as moral truth to be graven on the soul of a reader, but as an instrument by which his thought was systematized and preserved. Had he agreed with the Socrates of the *Phædrus,* he would not have devoted twelve chapters of the *Rhetoric* to style.

In comparing Aristotle with Plato, we have seen that the *Rhetoric* discusses most of the questions of rhetorical theory raised by Plato in the *Gorgias;* it agrees with the rhetoricians that rhetoric is an art, that the universality of its applications does not mean that it has no subject matter of its own, that the evils arising from rhetoric are no greater than the evils that arise from the abuse of all good things, that truth and righteousness are, on the whole, more prevalent because of a general knowledge of rhetoric, and that the persuasion of multitudes of relatively ignorant people, instead of being merely a vulgar task, fit only for demagogues, is a necessary part of education and government in a stable society.

A contrast of the *Rhetoric* with the *Phædrus* makes it evident that even here Aristotle is closer to the rhetoricians than to Plato. Rhetoric *is* an art of appearance; and this fact neither prevents it from being an art, nor from serving the ends of truth and righteousness. Rhetoric, instead of being a sham dialectic, is the *counterpart* of dialectic, a dialectic fundamentally different from the Platonic conception of it. The analysis of the emotions, which seems to follow Plato, is, after all, of a loose, inexact, and external character, as Aristotle thought was suitable for rhetoric. Aristotle agreed with Plato that the rhetorician should be virtuous and intelligent, that he should be a keen logician, that he should understand the ordering and arranging of material, and that he should know many things beyond the principles of rhetoric. They were also agreed that contemporary rhetoricians fell far short of these ideals. But the fact that Aristotle and Plato agreed upon the deficiencies of Athenian rhetoricians seems to have blinded us to the equally significant fact that Aristotle's rhetorical theory bears more resemblance to that of Protagoras and Gorgias than to that of Plato.

The significance of a study of rhetoric in Athens is not entirely historical. However indifferent we may be to Protagoras and Gorgias, we live in a world of journalists, publicists, advertisers, politicians, diplomats, propagandists, reformers, educators, salesmen, preachers, lecturers, and popularizers. When in Platonic mood we condemn them all as sophists and rhetoricians. And the Platonic attitude is supported by the growth of specialization and "research." To large classes of specialists the rest of mankind is made up of ignorant laymen. These scholars and experts share Plato's contempt for the masses; they apparently are as blind as he to the limitations of the academic mind; they dwell so securely in the well-mapped areas of knowledge that they decline to venture into the uncharted realms of opinion and probability. The modern sophists may justly be reproached for their habit of offering mere opinion when knowledge is obtainable; but it may be questioned whether theirs is a greater error than the specialists' habit of mistaking knowledge for wisdom. In the problem of the relation of Plato to Protagoras, of philosopher to sophist and rhetorician, are involved the issues which we debate when we discuss the aims of a liberal education, the desirability of government by experts, the relation of a university to the state, the duty of a scholar in a democracy, the function of public opinion in a popular government, the difference between a conventional and a rational morality, to say nothing of more speculative questions.

We cannot agree with Bishop Welldon's statement that Aristotle's *Rhetoric* is "a solitary instance of a book which not only begins a science, but completes it," but we do not regard the *Rhetoric* as of merely historical interest. It is the one treatment of the subject which raises clearly the problem of the relation of rhetoric to psychology, ethics, politics, jurisprudence, and literary criticism. If we have made any progress in these subjects since Aristotle, in so far his *Rhetoric* may be inadequate for modern needs. But for a sense of proportion and a grasp of relations, we do well to acquaint ourselves with the survey of the subject made by the great classifier of knowledge.

TWO IDEALS OF COMPOSITION TEACHING*

FRED NEWTON SCOTT

University of Michigan

THAT THE VALUE of teaching depends largely upon the teacher's ideals will, I suppose, be readily granted. Other things being equal, the teacher who holds before himself and puts into daily practice a high and noble and true ideal of his calling is a far better teacher and a far greater influence for good than the teacher who clings to a low and sordid and false ideal. All teachers know this truism, and with few exceptions endeavor to profit by it. Unfortunately, however, the ideals which are implicit in methods of teaching and in text-books are not always easily apprehended. They may be so buried in details or disguised by conventions that the teacher, unless he has unusual powers of analysis, fails to see the drift of what he is insidiously influenced to do. With the best intentions in the world he may actually be guilty, in his daily practice, of following an unworthy and vicious ideal, to the detriment both of himself and of his pupils.

I wish, therefore, to raise the question whether the ideal of composition teaching which prevails at the present time, which appears in our text-books and school-room methods, is on the whole the best ideal that has been discovered. If it is, we may congratulate ourselves and go on our way rejoicing. If it is not, then our plain duty is to abandon it for a higher ideal as quickly as we can.

Looking over the history of composition teaching for the past 2400 years, we may distinguish two principal aims which have guided most teachers of the subject. I shall term them the ideal of success

---

*Read before the Indiana Association of Teachers of English, November 11, 1911. Published in the *Proceedings of the Association,* 1911.

and the ideal of social service. Both originated among the Greeks within a few years of one another.

The first, the ideal of success, was the invention of one Korax, a native of Sicily who flourished in the fifth century B.C. On the fall of the Greek tyrants, when the redistribution of holdings of land filled the courts with a mass of petty litigation, Korax made the interesting discovery that the man who selected the materials for his argument according to certain principles and who arranged his plea in an orderly way, stood a much better chance of winning his suit than the man who presented his facts and arguments just as they happened to come into his head. He therefore wrote what he called an art of rhetoric, or as it may better be described, an art of Greek composition, composed of simple suggestions for the selection and arrangement of topics in forensic speeches. The purpose of the new art was to teach the unprofessional man how to persuade. It described for him the arts and devices of speech. It enumerated the tricks and subterfuges by which judges could be blinded and juries moved to tears.

Its aim was success, and only that. Whether the speaker's cause was right or wrong, whether justice was being promoted or defeated, was no business of the teacher. Having put into the hands of the pleader the keen knife of persuasion, his task was ended. What the pupil did with his weapon after he got possession of it was a matter of no consequence to him.

The new art proved highly attractive. Followers of Korax sprang up in Sicily, and developed the master's ideal in a variety of ways. In course of time the system, carried over to Athens by the orator Gorgias, became all the rage in Greek society. So rapidly and effectually did it displace other subjects of study that before long it came to be, in a sense, the basis of all Greek education. Meanwhile two significant things occurred. In the first place, Greek composition became the plaything of the orators, and a popular mode of amusement among the cultured Athenians. People gathered at private houses to hear speeches read or recited, or delivered impromptu, just as nowadays they go to parlor concerts or private theatricals. A nice appreciation was acquired of words and phrases and rhythms. The ideal of composition was still success, but it was success not only in persuading but in producing an effect of wonder, amusement, and delight. Rhetoric, in other words, was cultivated for rhetoric's sake. In the second place, the subject attracted the attention of the two greatest philosophers of antiquity—Aristotle and Plato. Both speculated upon the art, but with widely different results.

Upon Aristotle the system of Korax and the practice of the orators had a profound effect. Although he criticized the preceding teachers of composition, he nevertheless in the end adopted the fundamental principle of Korax, that the sole aim of prose composition is success in persuading. Having assumed so much, he was compelled by force of logic to concede the employment of tricks and subterfuges for selfish ends, and to lay stress upon the value of speech for its own sake.

The outcome of his speculation was that monumental treatise, *The Rhetoric*. Its influence upon the teaching of composition has been extraordinary. For more than 2000 years it has shaped the methods and aims of teachers in all civilized countries. Adapted in a hundred different ways by succeeding Greek and Roman rhetoricians, its principles and points of view came on down through the middle ages to the renaissance, penetrated like a subtle essence manuals and textbooks, and established themselves in the systems of the schools, in the practice of the courts, in the public and private organs of communication. It is today the prevailing influence. Literally our teaching of composition and our attitude toward composition are still controlled, whether we know it or not, by the ingenious thought of the Sicilian Korax, as elaborated by the powerful mind of Aristotle.

But the system of Korax attracted the attention also of the other great philosopher of antiquity, Plato, and at his hands received very different treatment. I can perhaps best indicate Plato's attitude by a quotation. In one of his dialogues, the *Phædrus,* two characters, Phædrus and Socrates, converse upon the teaching of rhetoric and composition. Says Socrates: "They say that . . . he who would be a skilful rhetorician has no need of truth—for that in courts of law men literally care nothing about truth, but only about conviction; and this is based on probability,[1] to which he who would be a skilful orator should give his whole attention. And they say also that there are cases in which the actual facts ought to be withheld and only the probabilities should be told either in accusation or defence, and

---

[1] Perhaps better translated plausibility.

that always in speaking the orator should run after probability, and say good-bye to the truth. And the observance of this principle throughout a speech furnishes the whole art."

To this Phædrus replies: "This is what the professors of rhetoric do actually say, Socrates, for I remember that although we have touched upon this matter but slightly, the point is all-important with them."

And Socrates continues: "I dare say that you are familiar with Tisias. Does he not define probability to be that which the many think?"

PHÆDRUS: "Certainly he does."

SOCRATES: "I believe he has a clever and ingenious case of this sort: He supposes a feeble and valiant man to have assaulted a strong and cowardly one, and to have robbed him of his coat or of something or other; he is brought into court, and then Tisias says that both parties should tell lies: the coward should say that he was assaulted by more men than one; the other should prove that they were alone, and should use this argument: 'How could a man like me have assaulted a man like him?' The other will not like to confess his own cowardice, and will therefore invent some other lie which his adversary will thus gain an opportunity of refuting. These and others like them are the precepts of the doctors of the art."

And elsewhere Socrates sums the whole matter up by saying: "Rhetoric is of two sorts; one which is mere flattery and disgraceful declamation; the other which is noble and aims at the training and improvement of the souls of the citizens."

In this criticism of the school of Korax, and especially in the distinction between the true rhetoric and the false, Plato laid the foundations of a rhetorical system which in ideals and methods is at the other pole from that of Aristotle. For the tricks and "flattery" of the latter, he substitutes strict adherence to the truth; for the ideal of success at any cost he substitutes the ideal of self-sacrificing devotion to the interest of the community. To say only what we believe to be true and what we think will be helpful to our fellow-men, is the end and aim, according to Plato, of instruction in this noble art. By this ideal he would test not only speeches in the courts and in the legislative assemblies, but all forms of composition, both spoken and written.

Such was the lofty and beautiful conception of Plato. Unfortunately, it was not destined to prevail. The Aristotelian system carried the day, and the thought of Plato has virtually lain submerged for 2200 years.

I wish now to raise the question which I asked at the beginning, whether the teachers of the present day are not following the lower ideal, whether they are not instilling into their pupils motives drawn from the false theory of rhetoric rather than from the true.

A few illustrations will make the distinction clearer. Picking out at random the other day a popular book on composition, I ran through its pages and noted the ideals that were presented to its readers as motives for using good English. They were as follows: Good English marks the gentleman; good English will help you to obtain a position as a stenographer; a command of English will enable you to win a lawsuit, to carry an election, to write a successful novel, to become a highly-paid editor or newspaper correspondent. All these, it will be seen, are instances in which the ideal held up before the learner is that of success.

It is not that these aims are in themselves harmful; the danger lies in making them primary instead of subordinate; in elevating into great leading principles what should properly be regarded only as corollaries; in substituting a low and temporary ideal for a high and abiding one.

To take a more specific illustration. Everyone has doubtless read the article by Professor Lounsbury in the November number of *Harper's Magazine* entitled "Compulsory Composition in Colleges;" but it may not have occurred to everyone to ask what is the ideal of composition teaching which the author has assumed to prevail in this article and then endeavor to state what is implied or expressed in them.

"There are certain results, largely mechanical in their nature, which can be achieved in the class room. For the attainment of these the business of instruction can hardly be commenced too early or carried on too thoroughly. The child can be trained to master certain matters which are essential to all correct speaking and writing. He can be made to avoid, at any rate to recognize, certain common improprieties and vulgarities of expression. He can be taught the leading facts of declension and conjugation. He can be shown how to construct simple sentences which are not characterized by a virulent hostility to the ordinary rules of grammar. It is possible to go farther and make clear to the most immature mind how the arrangement of words in the sentence can cause or cure ambiguity of meaning. It is desirable also to impart a knowledge not of what grammar requires, but merely convention, such, for example, as the capitalization of words as practiced in English. Again it is well for the pupil to learn some of the various systems of punctuation in vogue, if at the same time care be taken not to give him the conviction that the particular punctuation he is taught to use has been somehow divinely inspired."

In another place Professor Lounsbury speaks of that felicity of expression which it is the aim of the writer to attain, and of "the first law of writing," which is readableness. Contrasting two compositions, one dull and the other readable, he says, "The difference between the two pieces is due to the presence in the one and to the absence in the other of a trace of that alchemical power of style which in its perfection can transmute the bare matter of common thought and incident into the gold of literary achievement." Summing the whole matter up, he names knowledge of the subject, clearness of statement, power, and beauty of expression as the four constituent elements which enter into the composition of the perfect style.

To this statement of the qualities of good composition most teachers would, I suppose, give their assent. And yet taken in themselves, regarded as fundamental, what do they amount to? Young people are to study composition—if it can be studied—in order that they may acquire an irresponsible power, or that they may be successful in literature, or that they may cultivate a finer sense of literary values than their fellows. How this power is to be used, what is the object of this literary achievement, wherein is the gain in cultivating a greater sensibility—to these questions there is in this article not even the suggestion of an answer.

The sleight-of-hand performer, the professional gambler, even the adroit pickpocket or confidence man, might lay down the same requirements. Any one of these characters might protest that his art demanded great knowledge of human nature, extreme deftness in manipulation, and a delicate sense for the artistic side of his profession which differentiated him from other men.

In other words, as long as we hold to the ideal of mere success or achievement of the individual writer, composition has no solid foundation. It may be nothing more than a system of verbal tricks to hold the reader's attention or to titillate his literary palate. If this is the sort of composition that is being taught in the college, then, from the Platonic point of view, Professor Lounsbury is quite right in holding it up to ridicule.

Let me illustrate my point again by an example from the work of a popular writer of short stories. I am sorry to be personal, but in cases of this kind it is necessary to cite chapter and verse. I refer, then, to the story entitled "The Married Lovers" which appeared in the December number of the *Cosmopolitan Magazine*. Tested by the ideals of Korax and Aristotle, it is a good story. That is to say, the language is well-chosen, the characters are vigorously drawn, the technique is skilful, the narrative has power, in the cant of the day, to "grip the reader." It accomplishes what the writer intended it should accomplish. He sold the story; the story helped to sell the magazine. As a piece of literary workmanship, it is eminently successful.

And yet, judged by the higher ideal, this story is, in my opinion, a rank failure—more than that, it is rotten to the core. I do not say this on the ground of ethics. I will not say that from the moral viewpoint the story is suggestive, or poisonously alluring, or corrupting to the young, or confusing to the moral sense, or that it tends to break down the distinctions between right and wrong. I put all these things aside. What I do say is that judged by the lofty ideal of Plato, this writer has yet to learn the one great requisite of English composition. He has yet to learn—or he has forgotten—that mastery of the mother-tongue carries with it the obligation to use this great instrument for the training and instruction of the souls of the citizens. A man who has not learned this has need to go back to the primary school and begin his composition work over again. No command of verbs and adjectives, no resources of description and characterization will avail him. He must first acquire this one thing needful.

If a student in an elementary course had submitted that story to me as one of his themes, I should have handed it back to him with the remark that he was deficient in English composition and not fit to enter the course, and I should have followed it up by saying that to use the English language for such low and sordid ends was little less than criminal.

Let us be frank about these matters. To me most of the stories which appear in the popular magazines seem the work of men who are either ignorant of this fundamental principle of good writing or for the sake of gain have deliberately turned their backs upon it. When I come upon such abominations, the work of writers of distinguished talent, I feel like asking who were their teachers. Why did not someone burn into the minds of these men when they were learning to write, such a conviction of the purpose of composition that they would not dare thus to misuse or degrade their mother-tongue?

To some, no doubt, this ideal of Plato, as I have interpreted it, will seem absurd and Quixotic. It runs counter, they will say, to all the currents of this age, whose god is success and whose temple is the market-place. So be it. But for my part I have faith that in the end the nobler principle will prevail. There are two reasons for this hope. In the first place, the Platonic view is more nearly akin to the deepest and most abiding characteristic of the Anglo-Saxon race—their insistence that the things by which they live shall be genuine and real, not formal and superficial. And in the second place, this ancient doctrine is for us only an application to one phase of human activity of the fundamental principle of Christianity—that man can save himself only by giving what is best in him to his fellow-men. Some day this truth will come home to our speakers and writers. Then we shall have less insincerity in our courts, less eroticism in our magazines, less bombast and fustian in our legislative halls, less yellow in our newspapers.

Whether that time shall come slowly or swiftly depends in large part upon the teachers of composition in our schools and colleges. The responsibility rests upon them. They can train up writers and speakers whose sole ambition is success, or they can train up writers and speakers eager to use their talents in the service of their fellows. To teachers who are beginning their work I would say: Here is where the path divides. Choose ye this day.

Let me say in conclusion that there is one gain from adherence to the better ideal that can hardly be over-estimated. It is the power to give new life and meaning to what in your teaching may have become stale and commonplace, and to dignify what through familiarity may have become mean.

I fear that under the spell of the old ideal, teachers of composition are sometimes ashamed of their work and sometimes weary of it. It seems to them perhaps less dignified than the teaching of English literature or of Latin. They speak of it, or allow others to speak of it, as drudgery, or at best as work that has less scope and "uplift" than some other subjects in the cirriculum.

This is a most unfortunate frame of mind. It cannot fail, if it is indulged, to do harm to the teacher and to the cause of English generally. To such teachers the ideal of the true rhetoric will come, I hope, as a stimulus and an inspiration.

I like to recall in connection with this aspect of my theme, the words of Dr. Samuel Johnson when he was trying to dispose of Thrale's brewery: "We are not here," he said, "to sell a parcel of boilers and vats, but the potentiality of growing rich beyond the dreams of avarice." In the same spirit, I would say to teachers of composition who are depressed by the seeming drudgery of their daily routine and who perhaps long to escape into what seems a more attractive field: Lift up your hearts. We are not here to drill pupils in spelling, punctuation, and grammar, but to bestow upon them the potentiality of service to thousands and perhaps millions of their fellow country-men—to develop in them the power to move humanity to noble deeds by the communication of the truth. If there is in the teaching pro-fession a higher and more stimulating function than that, I do not know what it is.

THE RHETORICAL THEORY OF ISOCRATES

RUSSELL H. WAGNER

Davidson College

IN THE STUDY of rhetorical theory and practice today, students now and then come upon this memorable passage in Plato's *Phædrus:*

> PHÆDRUS: But there is a friend of yours who ought not to be forgotten.
> SOCRATES: Who is that?
> PHÆDRUS: Isocrates, the fair.
> SOCRATES: Isocrates is still young, Phædrus, but I think he has a genius which soars above the orations of Lysias, and he has a character of a finer mould. My impression of him is that he will marvelously improve as he grows older, and that all former rhetoricians will be as children in comparison with him. And I believe he will not be satisfied with this, but that some divine impulse will lead him on to things higher still. For there is an element of philosophy in his nature.

However little the prophecy may mean, because of our doubts as to the real opinions of Plato concerning Isocrates, there can be no question that the real work of Isocrates merits an even greater compliment. Perhaps no one of the great rhetoricians of the past has exerted so great an influence upon the succeeding ages of oratory; and perhaps none has been so much underestimated.

Isocrates was born in 436 B.C. He early began his studies, was trained by Protagoras, Prodicus, Gorgias and Theramenes, and was influenced to some extent by Socrates. He was ten years a logographer, or writer of forensic orations. In 390 B.C. he began to teach rhetoric, forsaking the law courts for instruction in a higher type of writing and speaking. From this time until his death forty-eight years later he was continuously engaged in teaching and writing.

This, perhaps, was the most successful school of rhetoric ever known. Among its most celebrated graduates it numbered the states-men Timotheus and Leodames; the orators Lycurgus, Hypereides, and Isaeus; the historians Androtian, Ephoros, and Theopompos; the nephew and successor of Plato—Speusippos. Even Aristotle may have been a pupil at one time.[1] Cicero says that this was the school in which the eloquence of all Greece was trained and perfected, and forty-one illustrious pupils are mentioned as foremost among the accomplished writers and debaters of the intellectual ages.[2] Even Mahaffey, contemptuous of Isocrates as he is usually, admits that Cicero "used him as a model—as indeed did Demosthenes, and through these two orators he has moulded all the prose of modern Europe."[3] At a famous panegyrical contest in which many celebrated orators participated, not one but had been a pupil of the school of Isocrates. Learners came from every quarter of the world, attracted by the fame of that great teacher. The most eminent men of the day, statesmen, generals, philosophers, were frequenters of the school where they discussed public affairs with the orator and statesman Isocrates.

Small wonder that the success of Isocrates caused a great deal of pique among the other teachers of his day. The sophists and Platonists, rhetoricians and philosophers, all attempted to discredit him. The fact that he had more pupils than all the philosophers combined was put down in his disfavor.[4] Aristotle himself, while a young man, charged the school with inadequacy, with lack of theory and applicability. Not even the scholarly Aristotle was justified in his criticisms, however; according to ancient commentators Isocrates came in for too large a share of the attack made by the youthful Aristotle who was dissatisfied with the forms of learning he found in existence.[5]

Undoubtedly the lack of definitely stated theory in Isocrates'

[1] Grote: *History of Greece*, Vol. viii.
[2] *Brutus*, VIII; *De Oratore*, II, xxii.
[3] Mahaffey: *Hist. Clas. Greek Lit.*, Vol. ii, Pt. ii, Chapt., i, p. 29.
[4] *Antidosis*, p. 318.
[5] Grote: *Hist. of Gr.*, Vol. viii, p. 35.

school provoked the writing of the *Rhetoric* by Aristotle.[6] The failure of Isocrates to consider "invention" gave rise to the first and second books; but the third, written after Aristotle had had considerable experience in the teaching of rhetoric and had become convinced of the "depraved nature" of the audience of the day, adopted a very conciliatory attitude toward Isocrates and followed his theories closely. Several authorities have suggested that the mature Aristotle came to a compromise with his former master. We note with Cope that he quotes no rhetorician so often in the third book.[7]

The two ideals of Plato and Isocrates were of course diametrically opposite. Political science and rhetoric were considered almost one and the same by Isocrates; and political science an antecedent for oratory by Plato. Some time after the death of Isocrates, philosophy triumphed and rhetoric was reduced to a study of style and technique of argumentation.[8]

The fortunes of the magnificent school of Isocrates suffered eclipse in the second and third centuries B.C. The broader view of rhetoric had to await its full appreciation in the first century B.C. in "a movement reflected in more than one author of the period." "The principles of education expressed by Isocrates became the natural rallying point for those dissatisfied with both the philosophical sect and the rhetorical schools. To the statement of this Isocratean ideal of education, long obscured by the predominance of philosophy, Cicero addressed himself in *De Oratore*."[9]

Great as was Isocrates' influence on his time and his immediate pupils, his best influence was not comtemporary, but of permanent and of lasting value in other lands and succeeding ages—a real test of value. "The best representative of Isocrates in his influence on the development of oratory is Cicero. Cicero was intellectually stronger than Isocrates; he had the power for real contest; living force and passion——. But as a stylist he is inferior to Isocrates. The brilliancy of Isocrates had come to Cicero thru the school of Rhodes."[10]

To what extent Cicero was the oratorical descendent of Isoc-

[6]*Ibid.*
[7]Intro., *Aris. Rhet.*
[8]Hubbell: *Infl. Isoc.,* p. 11.
[9]Hubbell: *Clas. Phil.,* Vol. XI.
[10]Jebb: Vol. II.

rates is, of course, a question. The ideal of the Isocratean school—
the orator-statesman—was unquestionably set up in Rome; and the
influence of this school upon Cicero, Quintilian, Tacitus, Dionysius
and Aristides is certain. In Cicero's own words we find Isocrates
called "the Father of Eloquence,"[11] which probably caused Milton
to speak of him in a later day as "the old man eloquent." Many
times does Cicero admit his obligation to Isocrates; he says definitely
in one place that he has used "all the fragrant essences of Isocrates
and all the little stores of his disciples."[12]

Isocrates may be regarded merely as a stylist; as such his style
became incorporated in the works of the chief orators, writers and
historians and was handed down for centuries; so that it has been
computed with admitted accuracy that the school of Isocrates lasted
over nine hundred years. He may be regarded also, as he considers
himself, a teacher of something more than rhetoric, of a complete
philosophy of life;[13] as such his influence on liberal education has
lasted until this day. But it is as a practical teacher of rhetoric that
we have still much to learn from him.

Ancient rhetoric texts are proverbially dull. A modern commentator[14] candidly states that Aristotle's *Rhetoric* is the driest book
in the world. Even the scholarly Dobree sighed with relief to have
finished translating the works of Isocrates.[15] Fortunate may we be,
then that Isocrates left no *Art of Rhetoric* to a modern world; for
the text of that name, concerning the authorship of which many
ancient writers were in doubt, ascribing it to Isocrates in the main,
is not extant. And yet the student of rhetorical theory would find his
task much easier were he able to turn to this book. As it is we can
glean only here and there in his orations and letters the principles
and methods of this famous teacher.

In the first place, we may do well to inquire into the purpose
of Isocrates in establishing his school. We can easily imagine that the
singular state of oratory at this time would be repellant to such a man
as Isocrates. Unfitted by nature for the delivery of speeches, compelled

[11]Cicero: *De Oratore*, II, iii.
[12]Jebb: Vol. ii.
   [13] bell: *Influ. Isoc.*
[14]Monroe: *Cyc. of Ed.*
[15]Thompson: Edition of Plato's *Phaedrus*, Appen., p. 171.

to exist as a professional writer of speeches, Isocrates undoubtedly must have chafed under these restrictions. Imagine a plaintiff or defendant in our own courts reciting an argument which his lawyer had written out for him, and a judge, jury, and assembled court gravely listening to an argument written for some farmer or artisan, the like of which they heard yesterday and might hear tomorrow.

Turning from the logographer's field, then, the young Isocrates saw his chosen field crowded with sophists and eristics. The former professed to be able to impart universal knowledge, virtue, and justice for about one-third the fee Isocrates was compelled to charge.[16] Equally faulty was their system of rhetoric; they selected paradoxical themes for their subjects, as: that the lot of beggars was more enviable than that of the rest of mankind; or uttered encomia upon the most trival subjects, as; "Humble Bees," "Salt," "Mice," "Pots and Pebbles."[17] Their system, Aristotle says, was to have their pupils commit to memory first speeches then dialogues. This method was quick but inartistic and barren of results. It was as if a shoemaker, instead of making his apprentices acquainted with the processes of his art, should content himself with showing them several pairs of shoes.[18] Justly, then, did Isocrates censure these teachers of practical rhetoric for their extravagant claims and obvious inefficiency. The eristics Isocrates also attacked for their quibbling and their failure to teach anything practical.[19]

We need not be surprised, then, to find Isocrates' school characterized by thoroughness of methods, seriousness of purpose, largeness of views and permanent results. The keynote of the school was the practical application of the loftiest principles. To this end Isocrates was the first to require his students to present entrance credits. He expected them to have a previous knowledge at least of mathematics and the sciences.[20] To complete his course the student was required to exhibit, first, capacity, or natural ability, which included three interesting qualifications—intellect, voice, and nerve. (Perhaps Isocrates' own lack of the last two made him

[16]Freese: Intro., p. 15.
[17]*Ibid*, p. 12.
[18]Aristotle, quoted by Jebb: Vol. ii, p. 46.
[19]Against the Sophists.
[20]Monroe: *Cyc. of Ed.*

poignantly aware of their need.) In the second place the student must have training or study. Last, he must have had experience.[21] In addition to all this, revolutionary as it was in his day, Isocrates required his students to remain in his instruction from three to four years.[22] This was far longer than any other rhetor of the day thought of keeping his pupils. As a result Isocrates' school became a respected and efficient educational center. In spite of the length of its curriculum, it did not weary its pupils; when graduates were about to depart, they took leave often with tears.[23]

Isocrates' own testimony of his school states that its purpose is to make practical "philosophers" of its students. He did not mean "philosopher" as we understand it today, as we shall see later. At any rate he contended that his system was effectual, or scientific, for all his students bore the stamp of a common method. He claimed that his school possessed three easily recognized marks: first, it was practical, because it avoided barren subtilties; second, it was rational, for it rested on the development of the whole intelligence and not on technicalities—a liberal education in all lines, not a highly specialized, one-sided affair; third, it was comprehensive, for it was not limited to any professional routine—it brought its pupils into contact with all the professions and duties of life.[24]

The plan of Isocrates' school provided that each student must first have sat under a series of lectures of "technical expositions" by the master, in which the theory of writing, speaking and "culture" was expounded. The abstract rules were then applied to actual composition.[25] Here an important phase of Isocratean training manifests itself. The themes on which his students wrote were carefully selected with a view to keeping ideas of Greece above all others. The student was early impressed with the great advantages Athens offered him, whether he was from Syracuse, from Sparta, or from the shores of the Euxine. He was told that the greatest prizes in the world lay at the feet of the successful student at Athens, for he would inherit political power or literary fame. Again, here were the

---

[21]*Antidosis.*
[22]Walden: pp. 21, 32.
[23]Thompson, p. 177, note.
[24]*Antidosis.*
[25]Jebb: Vol. II, pp. 43-53.

most numerous and most varied fields of exercise. Finally, Athens offered the most valuable experience and the greatest results of using these opportunities of any city in the world.[26] He selected to this end the most dignified and serious subjects, avoiding mythical and heroic themes, and directed all his efforts and those of his pupils to what was likely to prove of service to the Hellenic world, as: "national unity;" "mutual coöperation against the Persians." "My endeavor has been," he says, "according to the best of my ability to give good counsel to the city, the Hellenes, and the most distinguished of mankind."[27]

The high standards set in topics continued in the development of subject matter. Diction and style were stressed but a special emphasis was put on "matter."[28] Content had mattered little before this; to Isocrates it was all-important. When the speech was written, it was subjected to the most careful criticism and revision. It is clear that Isocrates stood alone in the stress he laid and the critical pains he bestowed on the work done by his pupils. Ancient writers said that "he taught not merely by technical precept, but also by practice under the eye of a master."[29] We are also told that Isocrates taught his subject, not as a cut and dried system, but as a philosophy, which was adapted to the aptitude and ability of each individual student.[30] To the student who had successfully passed these stages, was open the last degree of training, which was the first in all the other schools of the day; to the finished and gifted pupil, the use of selections of "examples" was offered as a means of perfection. Finally there was added hard work or actual practice under actual speaking conditions in Athens while the pupil was still under the wing of the master.[31] Small wonder that this school attained such a remarkable degree of efficiency!

There are many vexing questions to decide, when we turn from Isocrates the trainer, to Isocrates the educational theorist. How closely the great teacher united theory and practice, we do not know. It is unquestionably true that we have allowed Isocrates the stylist to obscure Isocrates the teacher; and it is probably more

[26] *Antidosis.*
[27] Quoted by Freese, p. 15.
[28] Monroe: *Cyc. of Ed.*
[29] Jebb: Vol. II, p. 46.
[30] Walden: pp. 31, 32.
[31] Jebb: Vol. II, p. 46.

true that the teacher or trainer may always obscure the expositor
of educational theory. True it is, and to his credit be it, that
Isocrates continued the encyclopædic education of the sophists of
the fifth century.[32] It is also true that his rhetorical instruction
was by no means merely rhetoric. That inborn philosophy of which
the Platonic Socrates spoke still showed itself.[33] Not only did Isocrates
turn the attention of his classes to the political life of Greece and to the
highest topics and modes of expression, but he went further; he claimed
that his course was in itself an excellent training for character.
Although he did not believe in a philosophic basis for morals, he
asserted that his pupils would be distinguished for their nobility of
character. He said that virtue could not be taught, but that the
philosopher would be virtuous.[34] It is obvious that he expected, then,
to train his students to become not only orators but philosophers.

Isocrates' use of the term "philosophy" has resulted, as Jebb
says,[35] in the most serious prejudice against him that exists. Isocrates
himself says that it is the art of conjecturing what should be done;
that it is a theory of culture; that what gymnastics is for the body
philosophy is for the mind. As far as he taught and practiced and
understood it Isocrates was no doubt right in asserting his claim to be
a philosopher; it was in his vanity and pride of success that he yielded
to a human weakness and excluded from its realm all other professors,
not even excepting Plato.[36] The whole difficulty is in the understanding
of the word "philosophy." This word had come into Athenian use
just before the time of Socrates. Until long after the time of Isocrates
it was commonly used in the sense of "literary taste and study—culture
generally" and not in the sense of philosophy as Plato and later
writers used it or in the modern way.[37] It is always as a "method of
culture" that Isocrates uses the term, and so is never in conflict with
the Socratic idea.[38]

It is, then, as a school where students are trained by "philosophy"

---

[32]Hubbell: *Influence of Isoc.,* p. 11.
[33]Jebb: Art. on Isoc., in *Enc. Brit.*
[34]*Antidosis.*
[35]Jemm: Art. on Isoc., in *Enc. Brit.*
[36]Thompson: p. 176.
[37]Jebb: Art. on Isoc., in *Enc. Brit.*
[38]Thompson.

how to act in life, that Isocrates wished his establishment to be distinguished. He thought it was the function of the mind to deliberate both about one's own affairs and the affairs of the state; the body would then be brought under the direction, if not the subjection, of the mind.[39] "Take thought for every thing which concerns your life, but especially cultivate your reasoning powers; for a sound mind in a man's body is the greatest thing in the smallest compass."[40] His school, then, provided the best training for life in all its forms, so that his students became orators, generals, kings, and in private life showed their training by virtue and refinement. "In modern terms he provided training in oratory, statesmanship, and ethics,"[41] and established the ideal that each person should unite in himself the three persons of orator, statesman, and philosopher.

It is this phase of his work, more than any other, that raised the standards of Isocrates' school and made his the method followed in training the great orators of Greece and Rome and "in almost identical terms is of course also characteristic of the rennaissance."[42] "Like the sophists against whom he inveighs he professed to prepare young men for the duties of public life, but unlike them he attained his object, rather by educating the mind and character of his pupils, *than by supplying them with* a mass of ready-made material. The means of this preparation was the study of rhetoric and eloquence, or, in a word, oratory."[43] It was as if Isocrates made the dictum of a later day—"No impression without expression" read "No education without a basis of true oratory."

The "philosophy" of Isocrates meant, then, a liberal education with the further qualifications that it include, first, a thoroughly aroused and intense patriotism of the highest type, which would be satisfied not with voting merely, but with acting, doing, talking, planning for the best interest of the state; second, a personal philosophy of life closely akin to the Stoic idea. It is the latter idea that Isocrates stresses when he says: "Whom then do I call educated, since I refuse that name to those who have learned only certain trades,

[39]Hubbell: *Influence of Isoc.,* p. 11.
[40]To Demonicus ("ch. Mens sana in corpore sano").
[41]Hubbell.
[42]Monroe: *Sys. of Ed.*
[43]Walden: p. 31, 32.

or certain sciences, or have had only certain faculties developed? First,
those who manage well the daily affairs of life as they arise, and
those whose judgment is accurate and rarely errs when aiming at the
expedient. Then those who associate in dignified and honorable fashion
with all whom they come in contact, bearing easily and good naturedly
what is unpleasant or offensive in others, and softening as much as
possible their own asperities of manner. Further, those who never
become the slaves of passion, and who by misfortunes are not unduly
cast down—bearing themselves in their presence manfully and in a
manner worthy of our common nature. Fourthly, and most important
of all, those who are incorrupted by good fortune and do not lose
their heads and become arrogant, but, retaining control of themselves
as intelligent beings, rejoice not less at the goods they have acquired at
their birth by their own natures and intelligence than in the benefits
that have been cast in their way by chance. Those whose souls are in
permanent and harmonious accord, not with one of these things,
but with all of them, these I say are wise and perfect men, possessed
of all the virtues. This is my opinion with regard to educated men."[44]

The moral side of the question is even more important. "Now
all who compose those hortatory discourses addressed to their friends
essay indeed an honorable task, yet do not devote their attention to
the noblest branch of philosophy; but those who instruct the young
not in the means whereby they may cultivate oratorical skill but
whereby they may show themselves to be of naturally good moral
character, benefit their hearers more than the other class of teachers,
inasmuch as the latter stimulate the mind to discourse alone, while
the former set right the conduct of their pupils."[45]

As to the best methods for accomplishing this ideal, Isocrates
has this to say: "If you love learning, you will attain too much
learning. What you know, preserve by exercise, and what you have
not learnt, add to your knowledge; for it is just as disgraceful to
hear useful discourse without gaining instruction from it as it is to
refuse some good gift when offered you by your friends. Spend
the leisure time of your life in cultivating a ready ear for conversation;
for by this you will be able to learn easily what others have acquired

[44] *Panath,* p. 30; ff.
[45] *To Demonicus,* 3, 4.

with difficulty. Consider that there are many precepts that are better than much wealth; for wealth speedily fails, but precepts abide with a man forever; wisdom is the only possession which is immortal. Do not hesitate to go a long ways to visit those who profess to give useful instruction; for it would be disgraceful if, while merchants crossed such great seas for the sake of increasing the property they possess, young men should not even undergo journeys by land in order to improve their understanding."[46]

"Try to be in your body a lover of toil and in your soul a lover of wisdom, that with the one you may be able to execute your resolves and with the other to forsee what is expedient. Whenever you propose a question, turn it over in your mind beforehand; for with many the tongue outruns the understanding. Choose two moments only for speaking, the one when you know the subject well, the other when it is necessary to speak about it. These are the only occasions when speech is better than silence; on all others it is better to be silent than to speak."[47]

"By the aid of their example [the gods] you ought to seek after true nobility, and not merely to abide by what I have said, but also to become acquainted with the best work of the poets and to study all the useful precepts of the sophists. For just as the bee settling on all blossoms and sipping what is best of each, so ought those who strive after education to have some knowledge of everything and to collect what is profitable from every side. For it is only with difficulty even by this diligence that a man will overcome the defects of nature."[48] "Whenever you wish to master any subject, pursue it both by practice and theory; for philosophy will show you the theory, while exercising yourself upon actual facts will make you able to deal with events."[49]

Isocrates was a thorough-going believer in the relationship of politics and oratory. He believed that "All the blessings of human society have proceeded from persuasion. In all other qualities man is inferior to many animals. But once the powers of persuasion were given us,

---

[46]*To Demonicus,* p. 7.

[47]*Ibid,* p. 12.

[48]*Ibid,* p. 15.

[49]*To Nicocles,* pp. 26, 27.

*Note—The seven wise men of Greece are meant here—Solon, etc.

we cease to live like brutes and formed a society, founded cities, established laws, invented arts. Speech has aided man in nearly everything he has devised. It is this which has established our laws, defining what is just and unjust, honourable and base, without which society would be impossible. It is by this we convict the guilty and protect the good. . . . In short all men of great executive ability have had oratorical ability as part of their equipment."[50] "She [Athens] saw besides that men who have received a very liberal education from the very first, are not to be known by courage or wealth or such advantages, but are most clearly recognized by their speech, and that this is the surest token which is manifested of the education of each one of us and that those who make good use of language are not only influential in their own states but are also held in honor among other people."[51]

The value of this ideal is not easy to point out, for the elements of thoroughness and permanency in Isocrates' methods as a whole may have succeeded despite and not because of this theory. That the combination of orator-statesman was the Ciceronian ideal and was inherited from Isocrates seems well established.[52] Cicero, Tacitus, and Quintilian all agree that the orator is the educated man who puts his intelligence and his learning to practical uses; they agree that the orator as a type is higher than the philosopher because it includes him; they agree that the orator should have a command of the whole realm of knowledge; they agree that the orator should be a good man.[53] Isocrates' ideal of liberal education, of which rhetoric or oratory, seems to have borne abundant fruit. "We see in Isocrates' attitude toward his subject, again a partial explanation of the great vogue which rhetoric had in the curriculum of the Greeks later. Rhetoric correctly taught not only formed the accomplished orator or advocate, but educated the taste, the judgment, and the character."[54] Leaving the realm of the orator-statesman, let us observe the effect of this idea upon the educational theory of his day and succeeding periods.

---

[50]*Ibid.*
[51]*Panegyricus.*
[52]Hubbell: *Influence of Isoc.*
[53]Monroe: *Cyc. of Ed.*
[54]Walden: pp. 31, 32.

We need no longer wonder that for half a century Isocrates' school in Athens was a gathering point and center of attraction for those who wished to be educated in the "higher genteel learning" of the day.[55] "Young men could learn more from Isocrates than the graces of style; nor would his success have been so great if his skill had been confined to the art of expression."[56] It is evident that a genuine contribution to education was made by the first real school of rhetoric.

When we compare this school with the schools of philosophy we note certain important differences. First, Isocrates devoted less attention to the form of government. Other schools were landed corporations and had a regular succession to the headship. "The school of Isocrates was an assemblage of students drawn together by the name of one man and acknowledging no other bond of union except a common admiration for their master and a common desire to profit."[57] In this way the student was free to put in his time on actual work instead of consuming it in useless bickerings over elections of officers and teachers. Second, the teaching was less speculative on one hand and less technical on the other than in the schools of philosophy. It was the form of training providing a broad and liberal culture.[58]

It is preeminently the element of permanency which best characterizes the school of Isocrates. This is true for several reasons. In the first place, it was because of his ability to grasp and illumine complex subjects, so as to treat them with unified effort and yet in intricate detail.[59] This is what Hermogenes praises as the "distinctness" of Isocrates. "This faculty sets an example useful beyond the sphere of Rhetoric. It helped to show historians how large masses of material might be written into a form at once clear and interesting."[60] In the second place, the element of permanency may be laid to the fact that the Isocratean method answered more nearly to the genuinely Greek conception of education—a preparation for active life in the service of the state on the basis of the development of the individual. "This widening of the bounds of knowledge and the transforming of

[55]*Ibid.*
[56]Jebb: Art. on Isoc., in *Ency. Brit.*
[57]Walden: p. 33.
[58]*Ibid.*
[59]Jebb: Art. on Isoc., in *Ency. Brit.*
[60]Jebb: Vol. II, quoting Curtius, *Hist. of Gr.,* Vol. V, p. 175.

education was Isocrates' greatest service."[61] "In his school he did a service peculiarly valuable to that age by raising the tone and widening the circle of popular education, by bringing high aims and large sympathies into the preparation for active life and by making good citizens of many who perhaps would not have aspired to become philosophers."[62] In the third place, there was a clear-cut, definite aim on Isocrates' part to produce work which should be respected—he says it boldly—"in all times and in all companies." This rule—to be thorough, to aim at solid results—intended first for writers, was not less needed in that age than in the present day. It gave a tremendous impetus to literary genius; for the first time historians began to produce scholarly work. It was a benefit to an age intellectually poor in all but speculative interests.[63] It was even more beneficial to the young students studying oratory and rhetoric.

The transforming of education from the speculative to the practical training for life opened the way for a tremendous expansion of oratory. It made that subject one of the regular studies of the Greek youth. "The influence of the man and his teaching survived and effected strongly the subsequent course of rhetorical education."[64] Among the Romans oratory reached a much higher plane than among the Greeks; as we have seen, the Isocratean ideal was set up early in Rome and continued until the fall of the Empire. That the Isocratean ideal became the ancient standard, we can see by examining Monroe's definition: "By rhetoric, the ancients, indeed, mean oratory. Their ideal in the training of rhetoric was to inculcate habits of public effectiveness, of persuasiveness on the platform, indeed, but also in the moving of men in all communal affairs. . . . Thus focused rhetoric filled at once a distinct and large place in the ancient scheme of education and thus focussed it has held its place for centuries."[65]

Teachers of speech may find much of interest in studying Isocratean methods. In the revival of classical rhetoric we shall do well to consider the importance of Isocrates upon the whole field. Professor Baldwin has pointed out that the main ideas of modern rhetorical

---

[61]Walden: p. 33.
[62]Jebb: Vol. xi, p. 35.
[63]Jebb: Vol. ii, pp. 47, 48.
[64]Walden: p. 33.
[65]Monroe: *Cyc. of Ed.*

discussion, including the making of rhetoric the organon of all studies, are all ideas of classical rhetoric.[66] It follows, then, that the modern tendency toward a more liberal culture, and the greater emphasis upon content, theme, and thoroughness are identical with the aims and purposes of the *Father of Eloquence.*

ISOCRATES

BIBLIOGRAPHY

Antidosis, and Against the Sophists, from Jebb's *Attic Orators,* Vol. ii.

Baldwin, C. S.: Article on Rhetoric, in Monroe's *Cyclopedia of Education.*

Capes: *University Life in Ancient Athens.*

Cope, E. M.: *Introduction to Aristotle's Rhetoric.*

Croiset: *An Abridged History of Greek Literature,* translated by G. F. Heffelbower. Chapter on Greek Oratory.

DeQuincey: *Essay on Greek Orators.*

Dobson, J. F.: *The Greek Orators.* Chapter on Isocrates.

Freese, J. H.,: *Orations of Socrates,* Vol. i.

Grote: *History of Greece,* Vol. viii.

Hubbell, H. M.: Article in *Classical Philology,* Vol. xi.

Hubbell, H. M.: *Influence of Isocrates on Cicero, Dionysius, and Aristides.*

Jebb, R. C.: Articles on Isocrates, and Rhetoric in *Encyclopedia Brittanica.*

Jebb, R. C.: *Attic Orators,* Vol. ii.

Mahaffey: *History of Classical Greek Literature,* Vol. ii, part ii, chapt. i.

Mahaffey: *Old Greek Education.*

Monroe, Paul: *Cyclopedia of Education.* Articles on Isocrates, and Rhetorical Schools.

Shorey, Paul: *Encyclopedia of Religion and Ethics.* Article on Isocrates.

Thompson: Edition of Plato's *Phaedrus,* appendix ii.

Walden, J. W. H.: *Universities of Ancient Greece.*

---

[66]C. S. Baldwin: in Monroe's *Cyc. of Ed.*

SOME PLATONIC INFLUENCES IN THE RHETORICAL WORKS OF CICERO

WILLIAM M. SATTLER

University of Michigan

IN HIS LAST strictly rhetorical treatise Cicero says: " I confess that whatever ability I possess as an orator comes, not from the workshops of the rhetoricians, but from the spacious grounds of the Academy."[1] The unequivocal eulogy of the Platonic Academy which Cicero here expresses may be considered as an hypothesis subject to examination. The object of this study is to discover in what respects, and to what degree, Cicero's testimony in the *Orator* can be accepted.

It is certainly fair to say that the statement above exaggerates the influence of the Academy upon Cicero's rhetoric and oratory, and undervalues that of his non-Academic rhetorical and philosophical training. Moreover, in this instance Cicero fails to give recognition to other significant sources from which he fashioned considerable portions of his theory of rhetoric. These sources, exclusive of Cicero's independent instruction in law and rhetoric, are at least three: 1. the writings of Aristotle and Theophrastus and the practices of the Peripatetic school,[2] 2. the teachings of the Stoic philosophers in the

---

[1] *Orator*, trans. H. M. Hubbell, London, 1939, 3, 12; also Otto Jahn and Wilhelm Kroll: *M. Tullii Ciceronis Orator*, Berlin, 1913, 11-12.

[2] Friedrich Solmsen: The Aristotelian Tradition in Ancient Rhetoric, *American Journal of Philology*, 62, January 1941 and April 1941; also, Aristotle and Cicero on the Orator's Playing upon the Feelings, *Classical Philogy*, 33, October 1938.

[3] George Thiele: *Hermagoras: Ein Beitrag zur Geschichte der Rhetorik*, Strassburg, 1893.

fields of rhetoric, dialectic, and ethics,[3] and 3. the educational and rhetorical principles of Isocrates and the Isocratean tradition.[4]

When Cicero indicates that eloquence issues directly from the Academy, he is thinking primarily of the program of studies and tenets of the Academy of his time, namely, the New Academy. This is not to say that Cicero fails to honor Plato's first school, but rather that the New Academy is Cicero's conception of a proper interpretation of the Platonic tradition. It is therefore important to consider the problem of the influence of Plato from two points of view: 1) the direction which Cicero's thought takes under the influence of the Middle and New Academy as distinguished from the original Academy, and 2) the materials which Cicero takes directly from the dialogues of Plato.

Plato's distrust of a rhetoric of persuasion is well known.[5] In addition to the dialogues which are largely concerned with a critique of rhetoric, Platonic opposition to persuasion is evident in those passages in the *Republic,* Bk. VII, which deal with the curricular studies. Here Plato suggests, as he elsewhere explicitly states, that rhetoric is a form of knowledge which must be classified as *ignorance* or *opinion*. Rhetoric is thus distinguished from disciplines designed to produce *philosophic* knowledge. With this point in mind, as well as the Platonic arguments against sophists and rhetoricians, one is hardly prepared to discover that rhetoric was later accepted as a part of the curriculum in the Academy.

Philo of Larissa, who was president of the Academy during Cicero's youth, formally introduced rhetorical instruction in his school. Philo visited Rome in 88 B.C. and Cicero indicates that he followed the lectures of Philo with much enthusiasm.[6] "Philo, as we remember, for we often heard him lecture, made a practice of teaching the rules of the rhetorician at one time, and those of the philosophers at another."[7]

[4]Russell H. Wagner: The Rhetorical Theory of Isocrates, *QJS,* 8:323-34, 1922; also Harry M. Hubbell: The Influence of Isocrates on Cicero, Dionysius and Aristides, *Classical Weekly,* 9:79, 1915.

[5]Everett Lee Hunt: Plato and Aristotle on Rhetoric and Rhetoricians, *Studies in Rhetoric and Public Speaking in Honor of James A. Winans,* New York, 1925, 3-60.

[6]*Brutus,* trans. G. L. Hendrickson, London, 1939, 89; also *De Oratore,* trans. E. W. Sutton and H. Rackham, London, 1942, iii, 28, 110.

[7]*Tusculan Disputations,* trans. J. E. King, London, 1927, ii, 3, 9.

It will be recalled in this connection that the union of philosophy and eloquence is one of Cicero's favorite doctrines. In the *Tusculan Disputations* Cicero himself follows the method of Philo: "Accordingly, after spending the morning in rhetorical exercises, we went in the afternoon, as on the day before, down to the Academy, and there a [philosophical] discussion took place."[8]

The action of Philo and his New Academy in teaching both rhetoric and philosophy appears to be the result of the influence of the system of logic and dialectical practices of the Middle Academy. Under Arcesilaus *(c.* 315-240 B.C.) and Carneades *(c.* 213-129 B.C.) the Academy adopted a philosophy of skepticism. This in turn, as will be indicated shortly, led to a logic of probabilities which was suited to the purposes of rhetoric.

An explanation of the change of emphasis in the Academy can be discovered in the writings of Cicero. The reports of Cicero, our best and most complete authority in this matter, show that Arcesilaus abstracted from the Platonic dialogues those passages which emphasize the fallibility of mental and sensory judgment.[9] With these passages as his evidence, Arcesilaus framed his arguments in refutation of the Stoic tenet that the syllogism was an instrument for attaining certainty or truth.[10] He argued, for example, that arguments of equal validity could be marshalled *for* and *against* any statement. The broad skeptical view of Arcesilaus was modified by Carneades to mean that if arguments on a given problem were weighed, a balance of probability could be reached. He distinguished degrees of probability which were used by the Academy to carry on further opposition to the Stoic dogma that every proposition is either true or false.[11]

The two Middle Academy philosophers were both competent theorists in the principles of dialectical reasoning and also persuasive and skillful in public address. Cicero repeatedly refers to the rhetorical proficiency of these leaders of the Academy, particularly of Carneades,

---

[8]*Ibid.,* ii. 3. 10; see also Willhelm Kroll: *Die Kultur der Ciceronischen Zeit,* Leipzig, 1933, II, 133.

[9]*De Oratore,* iii, 18, 67.

[10]*Posterior Academics,* trans. J. S. Reid, London, 1880, i, 14; also Diogenes Laertius: *Lives of Eminent Philosophers,* trans. R. D. Hicks, London, 1925, iv, 6, 28.

[11]*De Fato,* trans. H. Rackham, London, 1942, 16, 38; also Diogenes Laertius: iv, 9, 62.

and makes a special point of the fact that they are famous for eloquence as well as philosophy.[12] "Even the rhetoricians," says Diogenes Laertius, "would dismiss their classes and repair to Carneades to hear him lecture."[13]

The theory of knowledge advanced by the Middle and New Academy is of course only a partial representation of Platonic doctrines. The point is, however, that the leaders of these schools, and Cicero as a member of the New Academy, argued that a logic of probabilities more nearly reflected Plato's views than did the dogmatic certitude of the Stoics. Cicero was much impressed with the Platonic dialogues of investigation in which Socrates shows hesitancy in reaching any given conclusion. Furthermore, Plato makes no claim for blind consistency: thus he argues against *probability* in the *Gorgias* but *nevertheless* gives his plan of *resemblances* (resemblance to the truth) in the *Phædrus*. "With Plato," says Lane Cooper, "it is safer to look for system in the individual work."[14] In this regard Paul Shorey states: "Plato's very fairness of mind and literary cleverness could be used to prove him a skeptic . . . he states the case of the doctrine he repudiates so plausibly as to disconcert his own adherents."[15] Finally, it should be noted that in the *Phædrus*, 263, Plato directly assigns the word *doubtful* to the class of subject matter with which rhetoric deals, distinguishing the rhetorical from subjects about which men do not *waver*. While this theory of knowledge is generally perpetuated by Cicero, as it is to even a greater extent by Aristotle also, Cicero fails clearly to identify the Aristotelian enthymeme as the instrument of rhetorical proof.[16] His doctrine of the probable nature of conclusions stems more directly from the indecision of Socrates and the skepticism of Arcesilaus and Carneades, and, of course, from Greek rhetorical tradition as well.

It is of more than passing interest to note that the principle of probability of the New Academy is expressed in all the rhetorical works of Cicero. Even in the *De Inventione* which reflects Stoic in-

---

[12]*De Oratore,* i, 11, 47; ii, 39, 161; iii, 18, 68; iii, 21, 80; also *Orator,* 16, 51.

[13]Diogenes Laertius: iv, 9, 63.

[14]Lane Cooper: *Plato,* Oxford, 1938, xix.

[15]Paul Shorey: *Platonism, Ancient and Modern,* Berkeley, 1938, ii.

[16]James H. McBurney: The Place of the Enthymeme in Rhetorical Theory, *Speech Monographs,* 3:68, 1936.

fluence, Cicero shows that tentative conclusions rather than dogmatic pronouncements are characteristic of his school. Thus he reports that he is willing to change his mind when he is taught better;[17] again, in the *Orator* he says: "I have never found anything more substantial to hold to or use in forming my opinions than what seemed most like the truth."[18]

The latter observation which is made in the closing section of the *Orator* possibly suggests Plato's principle of *resemblances to the truth* as expressed in the *Phædrus*. Apart from a few highly suspect references concerning a correlation between *probable conclusions* and the worldly copy of *essential truth*, the Platonic theory of Ideas is not utilized in Cicero's system of logical proof. Cicero was accustomed to weigh evidence on the basis of likelihood of occurrence, and in such matters was not disposed to ponder the unchanging truths of Plato.

It is clear that the skeptical elements of the Platonic dialogues as reflected in the teachings of the above mentioned Academies exerted a positive influence on Cicero's writings. The dictum of the New Academy that certainty was not within the reach of man was well suited to the demands of oratory. The Academy is thus advanced by Cicero as an authority in support of the presumptive proofs of rhetoric.

Cicero also makes many direct references to the dialogues of Plato which are largely independent of the influence of the Middle and New Academy. In his writings, rhetorical and philosophical, he shows that he is familiar with more than ten of the Platonic dialogues,[19] including, of course, the *Gorgias* and *Phædrus*.[20]

While it is here impossible, and perhaps unfruitful, to document all Platonic references in the rhetorical works of Cicero, it is believed that the materials which follow are nevertheless both reasonably complete and of primary rhetorical interest.

1. The dialogue form which is so often used by ancient writers as a substitute for strictly expository writing is followed by Cicero in the *Brutus* and *De Oratore* as well as in many of the philosophical compilations. The guidance offered by Plato in this matter has usually been

---

[17]*De Inventione*, trans. C. D. Yonge, London, 1879, ii, 3.
[18]*Orator*, 71, 238.
[19]See for example J. E. Sandys: Cicero's *Orator*, Cambridge, 1885, 12.
[20]See especially, *De Oratore*, i, 11, 47; *Orator*, 13, 41.

recognized as of considerable importance. In the writings of Cicero there are many instances (see *De Oratore*, i, 7, 28) in which he tells us that he wishes to imitate Socratic dialectic. But the fact is that Cicero's dialogues are modeled after Aristotle's exoteric works. *In Ad Familiares* (i, 9) Cicero states that the *De Oratore* was an attempt to emulate the dialogue pattern of Aristotle; again, in *Ad Atticum* (xiii, 19) much the same point of view is expressed. Based upon Cicero's reports and the fragments of the Aristotelian dialogues which remain,[21] the Aristotelian scientific discussion dispenses with the conversational give and take of the typical Platonic dialogues. Moreover, Cicero describes the Aristotelian dialogue as one in which "the conversation is so put forward as to leave him [Aristotle] the principal part" (*Ad Atticum*, xiii, 19). Cicero follows this practice in most of his dialogues, although the *De Oratore* the assumed historical setting requires the use of characters other than himself.

2. Cicero in the *Orator* argues that the Platonic theory of Ideas has a significant relationship to rhetoric (see 7; 10; 100; 237). Here he associates the universal truths of Plato with his doctrine of the perfect or ideal orator. The Platonic transcendental universals, which incidentally were repudiated by Aristotle and Plato's immediate successors alike, are transformed by Cicero to mean simply a variable ideal. Although Cicero indicates that Platonic *Forms* are eternal and unchanging, he concludes the *Orator* by saying that conceptions of the perfect orator might differ. He says, for example, that Brutus might have opinions different from his own and that even his personal conception of perfection might change.[22] In Cicero's earlier rhetorical works the correlation between perfect eloquence and the Platonic *Idea* is not clearly drawn, although some probable references to this conception are discernible in the *De Oratore* (see iii, 16; 21; 85).

3. By insisting upon the learning offered through philosophy (logic, physics, ethics), Cicero frees rhetoric at least in part from the Platonic charge that the rhetorician is deficient in *wisdom*. He consistently recommends studies in dialectics, ethics, and at times, natural philosophy. Although Cicero was highly skeptical of natural philosophy, he

---

[21]Werner Jaeger: *Aristotle, Fundamentals of His Development*, trans. R. Robinson, Oxford, 1934, 28.

[22]Cicero translated the *Timaeus* in 45 B.C. It is believed that this Platonic work prompted Cicero to give exemplification to the theory of Ideas.

mentions the point made by Plato in the *Phædrus* (270) that Pericles was an effective speaker because he studied under Anaxagoras (see *De Oratore*, iii, 138; *Orator*, 4, 15; *Brutus*, 10, 44). While it is well known that Cicero emphasizes training in all areas of knowledge in his later writings, little or no thought is given to the matter in his earliest rhetorical treatise. We find, however, that this same doctrine is also present, with less emphasis to be sure, in the opening chapters of the first book of the *De Inventione*.[23]

4. The union of philosophy and eloquence is of course the Ciceronian ideal. Cicero directly quotes from the *Phædrus* (279) the language Plato used in praise of Isocrates (*Orator*, 13, 42). Perhaps it should be added that Plato's words in this passage permit of more than one interpretation and that he also expresses a contradictory position. In the *Euthydemus* (304-5) for example, he refers to *philosopher-politicians,* and this reference may well be to Isocrates, as being deficient in both of these fields of endeavor. The fact nevertheless remains that Cicero literally interprets the commendation given by Plato in the *Phædrus* to support the union of the philosopher, statesman, and orator; or in other words, the Isocratean ideal of education.

5. In Cicero's later works he makes some statements concerning the divisions of the speech which suggest that he is taking into account the Platonic critique. Plato in *Phædrus* (266) speaks disparagingly of the divisions of the speech as mere *niceties* of the art of rhetoric.[24] The *De Inventione* makes use of the divisions of the speech as a frame of reference almost exclusively, and we can therefore be certain that Cicero was well schooled in the rhetoric which places primary attention upon matters of arrangement. The position of Cicero in the *De Oratore* is modified: here he says that "prefaces, perorations and similar trumpery" are secondary in importance to the philosophical learning of the orator (i, 86; i, 143; iii, 122). In other words, Cicero shows the inadequacy of rhetorical instruction narrowly conceived in the sense of formal rules of arrangement. It is hazardous to say that Cicero's attitude regarding the divisions of the speech is the direct result of his reading of the *Phædrus*. The remarks of Aristotle on this point and

---

[23]Pauly-Wissowa, M. Tullius Cicero, *Real-Encyclopädie der classischen Altertumswissenschaft,* Stuttgart, 1939, 1094.

[24]Cf.: Aristotle, *Rhetoric,* i, 1, 1354b.

the Peripatetic tradition are probably of greater importance. But since it is quite certain that Cicero was aware of Plato's opposition to the formal rules of rhetoric, it is probable that this knowledge had some bearing upon the statements made in the *De Oratore*.

Among the materials reported in this section, the theory of Ideas is obviously a direct Platonic influence. In other matters, however, the Platonic writings may not always be the dominant force which prompted Cicero to develop a given point of view. But it is nevertheless apparent that Cicero makes use of the testimony of Plato whenever possible to confirm a doctrine or a principle of rhetoric.

In a negative, although still in a direct, sense the writings and influence of Plato made it necessary for Cicero to defend rhetoric from the attacks of the philosophical schools. The post-Socratic schools (Cyrenaic, Cynic, Megarian) perpetuated the divorce between eloquence and philosophy (*De Oratore*, iii, 60-64). In Cicero's own day the Epicureans, who were second only to the Stoics in popularity, repeated some of the Platonic arguments. The Stoics advanced the syllogism as the instrument for attaining certainty, and the Epicureans, in a similar although opposite form, referred to the enthymeme as "mere padding used to evoke applause."[25] The Academy itself changed its former favorable attitude towards rhetoric when Antiochus assumed the leadership. Cicero studied philosophy under Antiochus at Athens, but it was necessary for him to pursue the further study of rhetoric under a specialized teacher.

Cicero's constructive answer to the critique of the *Gorgias* is his reestablishment of principles relating to the concept of the philosopher-orator-statesman. In addition to his own reasoning showing the superiority of one who can both *think* and *speak*, Cicero follows the tradition of Isocrates, the authority of Aristotle and the Peripatetic school, and the doctrines of the Middle and New Academy. Plato himself who recorded the original distinction between philosophy and eloquence and whose works exercised so powerful an influence was actually considered by Cicero as a witness in support of the Ciceronian position. To conclude his argument upholding the union of philosophy and eloquence, Cicero says that he regards Plato as the most eminent example of one who combines wisdom and skill in persuasion.

---

[25]Philodemus: *Rhetorica*, trans. H. M. Hubbell, New Haven, 1920, 4, 328; 7, 339.

The evidence cited in this paper should not be interpreted to mean that Plato, or even the two later Academies, exerted the dominant influence upon Cicero in his theory of rhetoric. The actual body and substance of his rhetorical teachings stem largely from Isocrates, Aristotle, and Stoic writings.

Cicero makes his references to the Middle and New Academy, and to Plato, to support principles which in most instances had their inception elsewhere. As a matter of fact, the methods of reasoning and proof used by Arcesilaus and Carneades appear to be likely products of the dialectics of Aristotle. But during the earlier years of Cicero's life, the New Academy was the only philosophical school which vigorously championed the teaching of practical public speaking. The Peripatetic school had a rhetorical tradition from the time of Aristotle, but in Cicero's age this school had little influence. Cicero was, of course, highly pleased with the record of the Peripatetic school; the Academy, however, had a rhetorical tradition of a more recent date.

It is impossible here to restate in full the inadequacies which Cicero discovered in the Epicurean and Stoic conceptions of rhetoric. Briefly stated, neither the Epicurean approval of epideictic speaking nor the Stoic instruction in logical analysis and reasoning provided the bases for a complete theory of rhetoric.

In the field of philosophy Cicero is singled out as the greatest of the Roman eclectics. Much the same is the case with his rhetorical writings. He frankly reports that he is not devoted to "one fixed leader." (*De Inventione,* ii, 2); he seeks and uses such materials as are "most fully akin to the orator" (*De Oratore,* iii, 17, 64). In this sense one can perhaps understand why Cicero regarded himself as a Platonist, although he is not always faithful to the details of Platonic thought.

The central doctrine of the New Academy can best be summarized in Cicero's words when he says: "I shall explain what you wish as best I can, not however as if I were the Pythian Apollo, making statements to be regarded as certain and unalterable," (*Tusc. Disp.,* i, 17). Certainly "the spacious grounds of the Academy" to which Cicero refers in the *Orator* is the proper philosophical school to which a rhetorician should claim allegiance. And what is more, this choice apparently provided Cicero with the authority to select the aspects of Platonic writings which suited his purpose.

QUINTILIAN'S MESSAGE*

J. P. RYAN

Grinnell College

A FEW YEARS AGO Herbert Hoover translated from the Latin, and privately published, Agricola's *De Re Metallica*—a treatise on mining engineering and smelting. To Hoover this was a labor of love, not a practical contribution to his profession. His interest in the book was born out of his desire for professional continuity and his pedagogical curiosity. Hoover was well aware that his beloved treatise in mediaeval Latin was neither great as "literature of knowledge," nor as "literature of power."

Into these two classes all mediaeval Latin literature may be grouped. As these were the divisions first used by DeQuincey for all literature, so the same classification might well be applied to ancient Latin literature—"the literature of knowledge," and "the literature of power."

The contributions in ancient Latin to "the literature of power" are so large and so substantial that the world is unwilling to forget them. The works of Virgil, and Horace, Cicero and Lucretius will be cherished and read as long as human nature remains what it is.

But the contributions of ancient Latin that deal with "the literature of power" are destined to exercise an ever narrowing circle of influence. Many Latin books on the natural and social sciences, because of the changed conditions of our life, and the increase of our body of knowledge are bound to pass away and be forgotten. Books on bridge-

*The Presidential address at the annual convention of the National Association of Teachers of Speech, Chicago, December 27, 1928.

building or cooking, theology or chariot-racing, psychology or education, though they may hold the interest of the special student, can make little appeal to the modern mind unless those books contain some fundamental truths which give them a perennial freshness.

And it is because there are so many fundamental truths on education and on rhetoric found in Quintilian's *Institutio Oratoria* that I have chosen him and his book as the subject of my address.

This author can not rigidly be classed as a writer of "the literature of power," nor of "the literature of knowledge." His one book might well be placed in either class. To the lovers of "the literature of power" the *Institutio* has long been cherished as a permanent contribution to the growth and education of the human spirit; while to the present-day teacher of rhetoric, here is a textbook which some of them are unwilling to forget, and none of them can afford to neglect. The *Institutio Oratoria,* written by Marcus Fabius Quintilianus in the first century is a treatise on rhetoric so complete and so fundamental that any modern teacher could use it as a textbook in his classes today.

My purpose in this address is neither to deal with the history of this book, nor with the story of its influence from the time it was first discovered in the monastery of St. Gall in 1415 by Poggio Bracciolini to the present, nor to give a summary of its contents. There is here no attempt at scholarship in exegesis or exposition. My modest purpose is to tell the story of his life and work in such a way as to make you feel its perennial freshness; and to comment upon some of his dicta about rhetoric so as to lead you to think that there may be something of permanence in his message.

My first point, then, is the modernity of the man and his book. But, before we pass into even a cursory examination of his *magnum opus* it is well to orient ourselves on the period, and the writer.

The golden age of Latin literature had passed. Both the literature and the empire were slowly but steadily declining. But that fall was stopped for a time by the great influx of fresh blood from one of the provinces. There came from Spain to Rome a group of young men: Seneca, Lucan, Martial, Quintilian, and others, who not only wrote their names large in the history of the imperial city, but were all of one mind in setting themselves to stem the tide of popular taste, so artificial and so fantastic, which found expression in what we are

wont to call silver Latin. Quintilian, then, is placed in the silver age
of Latin literature.

And the story of his life is easily set, and more easily remembered.
At a time when there were so many little religious squabbles going on
in one of the eastern provinces of the Roman empire, in another
province, over on the western border, in Spain, there was peace,
prosperity and progress. Spain was furnishing to Rome not only the
products of trade, but the sinews of war, of state, and the pith of
culture.

About the very same year that Jesus was being crucified in Jerusa-
lem, a babe was born in the little town of Calagurris in northern Spain.
This babe was Quintilian. As a boy, he was sent down to the city
for his education. How long he stayed in Rome we know not. But in
Rome, all the records agree, he studied with the leading teachers
of the city, chiefly with Palaemon, and with Afer. Whether he took
the grand tour of visiting other university cities about the Mediter-
ranean we do not know.

We know that he returned to his native city and set up as a teacher
of rhetoric, and practitioner of law. These professions, at that time,
were combined. He was successful and attracted the attention of the
provincial governor,—one Galba. Later, about sixty-eight, when the
Roman senate elected Galba emperor, Quintilian and a great group
of young Spaniards, were brought back to Rome in Galba's retinue.

In Rome, Quintilian was appointed the first professor of Latin
Rhetoric. His salary of 100,000 sesterces was paid from the imperial
treasury. This translated in the language of today, or rather guessed
at, in our values has been estimated to be about $10,000. For the
next twenty years he continued as the most successful and most popular
professor of rhetoric in the city. Emperors and dynasties changed, but
Quintilian seemed to be as popular and strong with the incoming
party as with the outgoing powers. At the end of twenty years he
retired as professor emeritus. And in the quiet of his little villa a few
miles from Rome he devoted his leisure to the composition of his
memorable work. After about two years he published his *Institutio
Oratoria*. The book achieved the same great success which marked
everything else he attempted. If ever the word successful could be
applied to a professor it could be given to Quintilian. Many pro-

fessors deserve success, but only a few win it. Not so with Quintilian, he deserved and won success. Throughout all his public life and works from the day he left his Spanish hills till he passed away in his Roman villa his life was one *marche de triomphe.*

The minor note of sadness is found in his private life. Grief, pain, and disappointment met him many times along the road. His wife and one child died. His home was broken up. All his hopes and love were centered upon his only remaining son. In an eloquent preface to one of his books he tells that his love for this son, who with the emperor's two boys he was tutoring, was the motive-power of his writing. But at the age of nine this boy died. Quintilian was alone. Then it was that his Stoic philosophy stood him in good stead. He finished the book and lived to a ripe old age. He died some time during the last few years of the first century, the possessor of wide lands, of consular rank, full of years, honor, and wisdom.

Now we may turn to an examination of his book. The title, *Institutio Oratoria,* is really a military term and means "the setting-up exercises," or as it is generally translated, *The Training of an Orator.* But the title is too narrow for the contents.

The contents of the book go beyond technical training, and penetrate to the roots of fundamental problems in education. Many of these problems are as unsolved today as in days of the first century. But because Quintilian throws some light upon their solution his book has a permanent appeal. And, in the second place, its appeal is due to the fact that Quintilian does not attempt to give any "setting-up exercise," or special training in speaking, but outlines the education and training of an orator from the day of his birth to his death.

And in reading this account of the education of an individual from his birth to his death there are rich rewards for careful perusal. Here are many cross references, and questions in scholarship worthy of attention. But we pass over to consider the modernity of his message and the permanency of his dicta on rhetoric.

A representative from a department of education might tell you what Quintilian has to say upon such problems as:

1) The value of the public school over the private.
2) The question of home study versus classroom study.
3) The value of kindergarten training.

4) The importance of employing the best teachers in the lower grades.
5) The importance of careful training in the beginning of the subject.
6) The place of memory in intelligence and intelligence testing.
7) The question of reformed or phonetic spelling.
8) Good usage as a standard of pronunciation.
9) The problem of extra and wide reading.
10) The elective versus the required courses.

Such a list might well be taken as the program of round-table discussions in a present day convention of teachers of education. Or to some it might suggest a series of topics set for graduate study. But to everyone it must demonstrate the surprising modernity of this man.

If ever there was a professor of public speaking who in a certain sense could be called modern, Quintilian was the man. But in all this modernity there is one ultra modern note that you will not find in him. That is the note of "Wisdom while you wait," the *multum in parvo,* or much-in-a-few-minutes-a-day; or "the complete course in public speaking in twenty lessons." Quintilian's favorite dictum was that the training of an effective speaker is not a matter of twenty easy lessons but a lifetime's work in the liberal arts.

I would not have you think that this old Roman, with his scanty knowledge of the social sciences, and less of the physical and natural sciences, is a complete or competent guide in the complicated and difficult life of our day. But I would have you think that any teacher, like Quintilian, who strives to collect the best knowledge of his day upon his field of study, and is forever trying to get to the bottom of his problems brings to his teaching a perennial freshness; and that is what I mean by being modern.

Now we may take up the second point, or the permanency of his dicta. In discussing this point I propose to speak briefly about his dicta on the product, or the speaker. What kind of speaker is the teacher of rhetoric trying to produce? And secondly, what are his dicta upon the process, or the teaching technique? What pedagogical methods will best produce the effective speaker? Finally there should be a word about his dicta on the practitioner, or the professor. What are the characteristics of the ideal professor of public speaking?

At every step Quintilian turns the attention to the ideal. With

him it is not what can be done, but what should be done. Again
and again when he was told that his system was not practical his
reply was, "I do not claim that these studies will make the perfect
orator, . . . they will tend towards perfection." The hope of his
permanency, therefore, is in the height of his ideal. Just as the
Christian religion is the best religion yet developed on this earth,
because it gives to man an unrealizable ideal, so the teachings of
Quintilian give to the teachers of rhetoric ideals which may become
permanent contributions in their professional lives.

In speaking first about his dicta upon the product we must not
confuse in our mind the ideal of the product of our department with
the ideal of the product of the course in rhetoric. Today the department of speech is based in science. And speech is treated both as a
science, and as an art. Speech is not only the great means of social
adjustment and control, but one of the most important factors in the
making of an individual personality, as well as the commonest means
of the expressions of that personality. The great field of science, and
the equally great field of education for the rectification and development of the individual personality, were not sensed by Quintilian. So
in thinking of the product it is unfair to think of the ideal of the product of a department in our highly organized, and perhaps foolishly
departmentalized curriculum, as if we were thinking of the product
of a course in public address.

It is, moreover, unwise to judge the men and methods of a past
period by the standards of the present. We talk about Quintilian's
ideas of the product of his course rather to clarify our own ideas of
our own product than to prove his ideas wrong, ours right, or his
ideas sound, and our similar.

First he speaks of the product of his training. What constitutes an
effective speaker? He paints the picture thus, "The man who is a
true citizen, fit for the administration of public and private business,
capable of guiding cities by his counsels, establishing them by his laws,
and reforming them by his judgments, such a man is an orator."

Of course, this is nothing more than a revival of Cicero's concept
of the "good man." This idea is today carried on in our phrases of
"the educated man," or the "the cultivated man." To Cicero's concept
Quintilian added the ability to speak well, and so Quintilian's phrase

is, "a good man skilled in speaking." Such a description is one characterization of an educated man, and as such a characterization was most appropriate when rhetoric was the center and integrating subject of the whole curriculum. But today, when Oratory as a fine art is dead, and the orator as a professional man has passed away, this description, or this ideal, hardly applies.

In another place he states an ideal of the product which may at least challenge the thought of our day. He says, "The perfect orator is a man who has consummate ability in speaking, highly trained intellectual powers, and is accomplished in all the fields of learning." If we could agree upon what constitutes "consummate ability in speaking" and what it means to be "accomplished" in the fields of learning, we might have a working ideal.

But there is, in another place, a statement descriptive of the effective speaker upon which we may agree. In discussing the purpose of his teaching, he argued that its purpose was to produce first, a thinker, and second, a speaker. The product therefore, of rhetoric as Quintilian sees it, is a man who is "a thinker of the best thoughts and a speaker of the best words to fit those thoughts."

In his discussion of teaching technique and teaching methods, Quintilian's dictum was that success in teaching rests equally upon a progressive and profound knowledge of the subject matter, as well as upon the use of the best teaching methods. And the best methods are those that meet the age, and advancement of the pupils. Though he was known as the teacher of many methods, he is the advocate of none.

To attempt to give the hundreds of hints on teaching, or how to conduct a recitation in rhetoric, which are scattered through his book is out of the question. Let it suffice to say that in the main he followed three steps in teaching rhetoric: First, study of models; second, extensive reading; third, extempore speaking. Of the last he says, "The richest fruit of all our study, the most ample recompense of all our labor is the faculty of extempore speaking."

Probably the most important item in his teaching technique was the use of the Declamation. About this all his methods centered. The Declamation was an exercise for the learner. Now it was the method of teaching technique, or of style, or an attitude of mind. But always it was an exercise, a means to an end. Though it had been misused, and though it had been developed as an end in itself, a vehicle of fancy, and a means of show, yet Quintilian maintained that it was the center and core of teaching rhetoric.

If someone is looking for a topic upon which to write a doctor's thesis, here it is—The Declamation. The declamation is the father of the modern case-method of teaching law and business, and the mother of the "Etude" in the fine arts. To unravel this thread in the history of oratory, to tell of its uses and abuses in the different periods, and of its meaning, and place and importance in our own day is a task well worth the doing. I would not disparage the splendid work now being done in some of our graduate schools on the history of oratorical criticism, and on rhetorical analysis nor the excellent researches in the laboratory, and the studies in speech science; but I would most earnestly plead the great need for more graduate work in the pedagogy of our subject.

And here we pass to Quintilian's third dictum, on the ideal teacher. What are the characteristics of the ideal professor of rhetoric?

Let me read, from the second chapter of the second book, what the master *ipse dixit*.

> As soon as the boy has made sufficient progress in his studies he should be placed under the professor of rhetoric.—What of the teacher?—Our first task is to make sure that the teacher is of good character. For the purity of the teacher's character should preserve those of tender years from corruption, while its authority should keep the bolder spirits from breaking out into license. Nor is it sufficient that he should merely set an example of the highest personal self-control. He must be able to govern his pupils by the strictness of his discipline.
>
> The teacher, therefore, should adopt a parental attitude to his pupils and regard himself as the representative of those who have committed their children to his charge. Let him be free from vice himself and refuse to tolerate it in others. Let him be strict but not austere, genial but not too familiar; for austerity will make him unpopular, while familiarity breeds contempt. Let his discourse continually turn on what is good and honorable; the more he admonishes the less he will have to punish. He must control his temper, without however shutting his eyes to faults requiring cor-

rection. He must be ready to answer questions, and to put them unasked to those who sit silent in class. In praising the recitations of his pupils he must be neither grudging nor over generous. The former will give the pupil a distaste for work while the latter will produce a complacent self-satisfaction. In correcting faults he must avoid sarcasm, and above all abuse, for teachers whose rebukes seem to imply a positive dislike for the student, discourage industry. The professor must daily speak something that is worth taking home, for the living voice is more potent than the written word.

These are a few of the strokes by which he paints the picture of the ideal professor, but these few are enough to block out the portrait.

Fellow teachers, in the half hour that we have communed together I have tried to have you think that this ancient teacher of rhetoric, because of the modernity of his message, and the permanency of his dicta is no stranger to us.

And if he were to come into this convention he would find many principles with which he was perfectly familiar, and many persons with whom he could fraternize.

To those plodding patiently in their graduate studies, cordial would be his greeting. He knew what it meant to do research in both the older Latin writers, and the still older Greek authors. He knew what it costs to carry on research without the concomitant neglect of the students.

Cordial, too, would be his greeting to those whose primary interest is teaching. The daily drudgery of the classroom may bear heavily, but it yields the most durable satisfactions of life. And no other subject in the curriculum can furnish more difficult teaching opportunities, or yield richer educational values, because the primary purpose in teaching rhetoric is not so much the acquisition of a body of knowledge as the development of the student's personality. The body of knowledge may change and grow, but the great anomaly of education is that though personality is ever changing yet it is ever permanent. There is a permanency in a personality as there is an inevitability in the progress of the human spirit. Man must go forward; and go free. Speaking has been and is one of the greatest means of securing a truer and freer individual development, as well as one of the ways of attaining a juster and a better social solidarity. There can be no progress save in the individual and by the individual.

And very cordial and gracious would be his greetings to those who are interested in the relation of speech and personality. After all, speaking is nothing more than passing truth through a personality. And well he knew about speaking as a factor in the formation and expression of personality. But he would go deeper and say that speaking is a virtue. And hence all of the rhetorical qualities: clearness, force, elegance, coherence, etc., are sourced in the spiritual side of man's personality.

And to all, his greetings would be: carry on the great work of Rhetoric. For a man speaking is, or should be, functioning at his highest point of efficiency. Let each man, therefore, speak the truth as he sees it. But let the truth be spoken. Or as one of the American poets put it:

> *"Get but the truth once uttered; and 'tis like*
> *A star, new born that drops into its place,*
> *And which once circling in its placid round*
> *Not all the tumult of the earth can shake."*

And our answering message is: Quintilian, you will not be forgotten, you cannot be neglected; because your search for truth was so deep and penetrating, because your vision of truth so clear and broad, and your hope and faith in human intelligence, and the spiritual qualities of man were so firm and undimmed.

Man is the one animal, escaping the weary treadmill of existence by his intelligence, that goes ever on and on in his search for truth, with an ever growing faith in that intelligence—till the truth shall set him free.

SAINT AUGUSTINE AND THE
DEBATE ABOUT A CHRISTIAN RHETORIC

JAMES J. MURPHY

Princeton University

T HE IMPORTANCE of Saint Augustine's *De Doctrina Christiana* to rhetorical history has long been recognized. Charles Sears Baldwin asserts the book "begins rhetoric anew" after centuries of sophistry.[1] Sister Therese Sullivan applauds it for returning to the *doctrina sana* of Cicero as a base for Christian preaching.[2] More recent studies find in the work "a Christian theory of literature"[3] or a foundation of medieval preaching theory.[4] Its influence is clearly visible, being copied or quoted by such writers as Rhabanus Maurus in the ninth century, Alain de Lille in the twelfth, Humbert of Romans in the thirteenth, and Robert of Basevorn in the fourteenth.[5]

Since Augustine's attitude toward the Second Sophistic is so clearly

---

[1]Charles S. Baldwin: *Medieval Rhetoric and Poetic,* New York, 1928, p. 51.

[2]S. Aurelii Augustini: *De Doctrina Christiana liber quartus,* trans. Sister Therese Sullivan, Catholic University Patristic Studies, Vol. 23; Washington, D.C., 1930, p. 8.

[3]Bernard Huppé: *Doctrine and Poetry: Augustine's Influence on Old English Poetry,* New York, 1959, p. v.

[4]Dorothea Roth: *Die mittelalterliche Predigttheorie und das Manuale Curatorum des Johann Ulrich Surgant,* Basel, 1956.

[5]Rhabanus Maurus: *De clericorum institutione,* J. P. Migne, *Patrologia Latina* [*PL*] CVII, col. 294-420; Alain de Lille: *Summa de arte praedicatoria* [*PL*] CCX, col. 110-98; Humbert of Romans: *Treatise on Preaching,* trans. Dominican Students, Westminister, Md., 1951; Robert de Basevorn: *Forma praedicandi,* in Th.-M. Charland, *Artes praedicandi,* Publications de l'Institut d'études médiévales d'Ottawa; Paris, 1936. This last work has been translated by Leopold Krul, O.S.B.: M.A. Thesis, Cornell University, 1950.

expressed,[6] there has been some tendency to regard his work as a mere attempt to rescue rhetoric from the taint of the sophistic. Indeed his firm espousal of a union between meaning and expression marks his rejection of the sophistic, as Baldwin has pointed out.

Nevertheless the attention paid to his later influence and to his rejection of the Second Sophistic may obscure Saint Augustine's role in providing an answer to a Christian dilemma of the fourth century. A brief survey of the Church's position during this period may illustrate the nature of the dilemma, and of Augustine's solution of it.

The Emperor Theodosius formally abolished paganism by decree in A.D. 342, seventeen years after the first ecumenical council at Nicea had outlined twenty canons for the government of the Church. With the exception of such lapses as that under Julian, the fourth century was marked by such gains that the converter of Saint Augustine, Ambrose of Milan (340-397), could refer to his age as Christian times, *christiana tempora*. As one historian says:

> Until the peace of the Church, the hostility of the public powers had weighed heavily on the life of the Christian community. On the day when it had definitely been removed we see the church coming forth, as it were, from a long winter, consolidating and developing her ranks, discussing her hierarchal powers, defining the lines of her doctrines, drawing up the formulae of her faith, regulating her worship, surrounding the holy places with public marks of veneration, providing holy retreats for souls desirous of perfection, and giving to the Latin half of the Church a more faithful version of the Bible. All these fruits are the harvest of the fourth century.[7]

The century was therefore one for many decisions. During the lifetime of Augustine, for instance, the Church faced the heresies of Manichæans, Pelagians, Donatists, and Priscillianists. But besides the problems of defining Christian doctrines in reply to heretical attacks, the Christian community faced another problem of almost equal

---

[6]*E.g., De Doctrina Christiana* IV.v.7 and IV.xxviii.61, *De catechizandis rudibus* 9, and *Confessions* IX.ii.4. Note also the careful discussion of the utility of pleasure in *De Doctrina* IV.xxv.55-58, where pleasure is made to serve the purpose of persuasion.

[7]M. Paul Lejay, quoted in Pierre DeLabriolle: *The History and Literature of Christianity from Tertullian to Boethius,* New York, 1924, p. 231.

magnitude—the problem of defining the intellectual base for a culture which would permit the Church to perform its duty of leading men to salvation. This was a matter of the greatest moment, for upon its success depended the training of future apologists to defend doctrine against heresy, the formation of future poets to carry the Word of God to the people through literature, and the very education of the people themselves.

The basic issue was whether the Church should adopt in toto the contemporary culture which Rome had taken over from Greece. The fate of rhetoric, as a part of the Greco-Roman culture, was involved not only in the debate over the larger issue, but in more limited controversies about its own merits. Indeed, the contrast between *Verbum* (Word of God) and *verbum* (word of man) was stressed from the very beginnings of the Church,[8] long before the broader cultural issue was joined.

Ecclesiastical leaders of the fourth century continued the debate begun more than a century earlier when the conversion of many writers, poets, orators, and other public figures had at last given the Church a corps of well-equipped apologists. From the first, some individuals reacted violently to their former pagan culture; Lactantius speaks of pagan literature as "sweets which contain poison;"[9] Arnobius, converted in his old age, tried to show his new fervor by writing a book which among other things tried to show that even the old grammar was no longer necessary:

> Or how is the truth of a statement diminished if an error is made in number or case, in preposition, particle, or conjunction?[10]

Cyprian, who had been a teacher of rhetoric at Carthage when he

---

[8] St. Paul, for instance said: "And my speech and my preaching was not in the persuasive words of human wisdom, but in the showing of the Spirit and the Power" (I Cor. 2:3-4). Virtually every early Christian writer stresses the difference between *sapientia huius saeculi* and *sapientia spiritualis*. John of Antioch, for instance, declares in his sermon *On the Heroes of the Faith:* "But the Cross wrought persuasion by means of unlearned men; yea, it persuaded even the whole world."

[9] Lactantius: *Divinae institutiones* (*Corpus Scriptorum Ecclesiasticorum Latinorum*) CSEL, XIX, 400.4.

[10] Arnobius: *Adversus nationes*, CSEL, IV, I.59. Arnobius helped make a watchword of a phrase of Saint Paul: "The wisdom of man is foolishness before God" (I Cor. 3:19).

was converted, renounced profane letters completely and for the rest of his life never again quoted a pagan poet, rhetorician, or orator.[11]

Titian rails against literature in general and rhetoric in particular:

> You have invented rhetoric for injustice and calumny . . . you have invented poetry to sing of battles, the loves of the gods, of everything which corrupts the spirit.[12]

Justin warns against venerating unduly words (i.e., literature) which are not from God.[13] Clement of Alexandria points out that this revulsion against the old order was not limited to the intellectual classes: "The common herd fear Greek philosophy just as children fear goblins."[14]

Tertullian directs an attack against Greek philosophy and other pagan writings. "Where is there any likeness between the Christian and the philosopher?" he asks in his defense of pure faith, and terms philosophers "patriarchs of heresy." In a famous passage in his *De præscriptione hæerecticorum* he outlines the problem as many of his contemporaries saw it:

> What indeed has Athens to do with Jerusalem? What concord is there between the Academy and the church? What between heretics and Christians?[15]

The necessity for education posed a dilemma to Tertullian, who realized that it would be foolhardy to espouse ignorance, but who declared also that it was not licit for Christians to teach literature because it dealt with false gods.[16]

---

[11]Gustave Bardy: L'église et l'enseignment pendant les trois premiers siecles, *Revue des sciences religieuses, XII,* 1932, 1-28. The awful magnitude of this renunciation may easily be overlooked by a modern reader who does not recall the pervasiveness of teaching through *imitatio* in Roman schools.

[12]Titian: *Oratio,* 1-3, quoted in Gustave Combès: *Saint Augustin et la culture classique,* Paris, 1927, p. 88.

[13]*Ibid.*

[14]Labriolle: p. 17.

[15]Tertullian: *De praescriptione, PL* II, col. 20a-b, 7. Centuries later Gregory the Great, reproving a clerk who taught classical literature to his classes, expressed a similar view: "The same mouth singeth not the praises of Jove and the praises of Christ." R. L. Poole: *Illustrations in the History of Medieval Thought,* London, 1884, p. 8.

[16]For a survey of Tertullian's views on these related subjects, see Gerard L. Ellspermann: *The Attitude of the Early Christian Latin Writers toward Pagan Literature and Learning,* Catholic University of America Patristic Studies, Vol. 82, Washington, D.C., 1949, pp. 23-42.

Similar remarks may be found in the writings of Justin Martyr, Clement of Alexandria, Synesius of Cyrene, and the historian Socrates. As Labriolle observes: "There emerges, therefore, the fact that we can state that during the first centuries of the Empire there is hardly a Christian writer in whose case there does not intrude or show itself more or less sincerely, more or less diplomatically, a hostility in some regard to the different forms of pagan learning."[17] Nor was this antipathy short-lived, for even while Augustine was engaged in writing the first books of *De Doctrina,* the fourth Council of Carthage (398) forbade bishops to read *libros gentilium* unless necessary.

From the Christian point of view there were many reasons for such attitudes. Even if Rome had not been the Rome of persecutions with their awful memories, its literature was studded with man-like gods parading what some Christian writers saw as a virtual gallery of sins. What is the use of decrees against sin, Augustine asks, when the adulteries of even Jove are portrayed by actors, painters, writers, reciters, and singers?[18] Referring in scathing tones to the fables of the pagan gods, Minucius Felix points out that men even study how to improve on such tales, "especially in the works of the poets, who have had such fatal influence in injuring the cause of truth." He adds that Plato was wise to exclude Homer from his ideal republic, for giving the gods a place in the affairs of men, and then asks: "Why should I mention Mars and Venus caught in adultery, or Jupiter's passion for Ganymedes, hallowed in Heaven? Such stories are but precedents and sanctions for men's vices."[19] At best, secular education would divert the attention of the devout toward earthly things rather than spiritual matters. And since heretics often used logical argument to attack the doctrines of the Church, there was a corresponding tendency to fall back upon fideism (e.g., Tertullian: *regula fidei*) and decry reasoning itself. Hilary of Poitiers, for instance, states that truth is impervious to "marvelous devices of perverted ingenuity" in Arian logic."[20]

---

[17]Labriolle: p. 18.

[18]Augustine: *Epistle* XCI, in *Select Letters of Saint Augustine,* trans. James H. Baxter, Loeb Classical Library, London, 1930, p. 159.

[19]Minucius Felix: *Octavius,* trans. Gerald H. Rendall, Loeb Classical Library, London, 1953, xxiv, 2, 7.

[20]Hilarius: *De trinitate, PL* X, vii, 1.

Another aspect of Greco-Roman culture which drew fire was the rhetorical excess of the Second Sophistic. Moreover, the rhetorician Fronto had been an early opponent of the Church, Minucius Felix notes. Although attacks upon rhetoric had an ancient tradition, the Christian writer often say in rhetoric of his time the taint of a worldly, pagan culture which could lead men away from God. It is in this light that Gregory Naziensus reproves Gregory of Nyssa for abandoning Christian books to take up the trade of rhetorician.[21] Augustine himself was, in a certain sense, converted from rhetoric to Christianity.

"Our writers do not waste their time in polishing periods," declares Basil of Cæsarea, "we prefer clarity of expression to mere euphony." And again, "The school of God does not recognize the laws of the encomium," nor does it deal in "sophistic vanities."[22]

The most extreme Christian viewpoint seemed to be that rhetorical forms might be dispensed with altogether. In the middle of the third century Cyprian had posed the problem as follows:

> In courts of law, in public meetings, in political discussions, a full eloquence may be the pride of vocal ambition, but in speaking of the Lord God, a pure simplicity of expression *(vocis pura sinceritas non eloquentiae)* which is convincing depends upon the substance of the argument rather than upon the forcefulness of eloquence.[23]

Both Ambrose and Jerome decry rhetorical excesses in their fellow preachers, calling for adherence to Paul's advice. The Donatist Cresconium went so far as to quote Proverbs 10:19 as proof that eloquence was sinful; although this drew a sharp reply from Augustine,[24] the incident may serve as an illustration of the temper of the times.

This is not to say, of course, that opinion was completely aligned in one direction. A true debate took place among the leaders of the Church as official persecution faded into the background and the

---

[21]A. S. Pease: The Attitude of Jerome toward Pagan Literature, *Transactions and Proceedings of the American Philological Association,* L:150-167, 1919.

[22]Cf. James Campbell: *The Influence of the Second Sophistic on the Style of the Sermons of Saint Basil the Great,* Patristic Studies, Vol. 2, Washington, D.C., 1922.

[23]Cyprian: *Ad Donatus,* 2, quoted in Ellspermann: p. 51.

[24]Augustine: *Contra Cresconium et donatistam libri, IIII, CSEL,* LII, I, i, 2.

exigencies of ecclesiastical organization forced new decisions upon its leaders. Some of the most vehement opponents of pagan literature, admitted the necessity of education, while others (like Saint Cyprian) resolutely turned their backs upon the old order.

Saint Basil and Saint Ambrose, for example, illustrate the mixed feelings of the Fathers of the Church as they faced a cultural dilemma. Basil recommends gathering roses among the thorns of pagan literature, on one hand, yet warns students not to abandon themselves to their pagan professors' ideas as they would their course to a navigator on a ship.[25] He also feels constrained to defend the Bible even though it is written in "a barbarian tongue." This points up still another cultural problem for the educated ecclesiastic of the fourth century, the apparently unliterary style of the Scriptures. Basil concludes that "although their style is unlearned, their content is true and they are the thoughts to which we give utterance."[26]

Ambrose also has mixed feelings. Although he emphasizes the distinction between *sapientia sæculi* and *sapientia spiritualis,* he recognizes the need for training of preachers and condemns not rhetoric itself but its sophistic abuses. His defense of the Scriptures is based on his approval of their simple style in contrast with the "showy" language of philosophers and orators. Saint Luke, he asserts, excells, in *stilus historicus.* Nevertheless he admits that rhetorical ornament may sometimes be useful and indeed, sometimes occurs in the Scriptures themselves.[27]

His ingenious solution to the problem of pagan philosophy, on the other hand, was one which did not win general approval. The pagans, Ambrose states, originally got their wisdom from Scriptures; Plato went to Egypt to "know the deeds of Moses, the oracles of the law, the worthy sayings of the prophets."[28] As Laistner observes, this was an attractive way out of a dilemma—one which even attracted Augustine for a time—but one which could not long withstand further

---

[25]Combés: p. 97. For a survey of Basil's reactions to pagan culture, cf. Sister Mary M. Fox: *The Life and Times of Saint Basil the Great as Revealed in His Works,* Patristic Studies, Vol. 57, Washington, D.C., 1939.

[26]Basil: *Epistle,* CCCIX, quoted in Fox, p. 89.

[27]Ellspermann: pp. 120-123.

[28]*Ibid.,* p. 114. The idea was of course not original with Ambrose, having antecedents in pre-Christian Alexandrian thought. Cassiodorus repeated it for the later middle ages.

inquiry.[29] Ambrose was sufficiently impressed with Roman learning, however, that he modeled his instruction book for priests upon Cicero's *De officiis*.[30] Hilary of Poitiers condemns Arian verbal display, yet prays for a good style in his own sermons. Honor, he says, is given to the word of God by one who speaks with beauty of expression.

But Saint Jerome, contemporary and friend of Augustine, may perhaps illustrate best the inner conflict faced by many Christian leaders in the fourth century. In his famous letter of advice to the virgin Eustochium, he warns:

> What communion hath light with darkness? What concord hath Christ with Belial? What has Horace to do with the Psalter, Vergil with the Gospels and Cicero with the Apostle [Paul]? . . . we ought not to drink the cup of Christ and the cup of devils at the same time.[31]

Later in the same epistle he relates a dream which came to him after he had been wrestling with the question of whether a Christian could legitimately enjoy the Greek and Roman classics:

> Miserable man that I am! I was fasting and then I began to read Cicero; after many nights spent in watching, after many tears, which the remembrance of my faults of not so long ago drew forth from the depths of my heart, I took Plautus in my hands. If by chance, on recollecting myself, I started reading the Prophets, their unadorned style awoke in me feelings of revulsion. My eyes, blinded, no longer saw the light, and it was not on my eyes that I laid the blame, it was on heaven.
>
> While the old serpent thus misused me, a violent fever penetrated the marrow of my worn-out body towards the middle of Lent, without any respite, in an incredible manner, it so consumed my poor members that I had scarcely any flesh on my bones. Already people were thinking of my funeral. My body felt quite frozen; a remnant of vital heat no longer palpitated save in the lukewarmness of my poor breast.
>
> Suddenly I felt myself ravished away in ecstacy and transported before the tribunal of the Judge. Such a dazzling light emanated

---

[29]Max W. Laistner: The Christian Attitude to Pagan Literature, *History*, XX, 1935, 49-54.

[30]Ambrose: *De officiis ministrorum, PL XVI*, col. 23-184.

[31]Jerome: *Epistle* XXII, *CSEL*, LIV, translated in Ellspermann, pp. 159-60.

from those present that, crouched on the ground, I dared not lift up my eyes. On being asked my profession, I replied, "I am a Christian." Whereupon He who presided, thundered: "Thou dost lie—thou art not a Christian, but a Ciceronian. Where thy treasure is, there is thy heart also."

Then Jerome relates that he swore an oath in his dream: "Lord, if it ever happens to me to possess or read profane books, I shall have denied Thee." From the moment the dreamer betook himself "to the reading of the divine books with as much passion as I had formerly given to reading the books of men."[32]

Interpretations of this dream have been many and varied, and it is generally wise to refrain from taking too literally a work designed to point up a moral. Nevertheless, Pease points out, Jerome did refrain from using classical quotations in his works for about fifteen years following the time at which the dream is supposed to have occurred. The very fact that Jerome felt it necessary to reply to Rufinus in A.D. 402 may be another indication of the state of the times, and possibly of his contemporaries' views of his so-called oath.[33]

His basic dilemma reveals itself elsewhere too. At one point he is concerned because heathen sources are used to attack the doctrine of resurrection of the body, and enjoins Christians to "lay aside the weapons of the heathens" in their replies; it is better to have a just unlearnedness than an evil wisdom.[34] In another place:

> We do not wish for the field of rhetorical eloquence, nor the snares of dialecticians, nor do we seek the subtleties of Aristotle, but the very words of Scripture must be set down.[35]

He refers often to his desire for a simple, clear style which will avoid "pomp . . . structures of words," yet he was a student of the famous

---

[32]The translation follows that of Labriolle, pp. 11-12.
[33]A. S. Pease: The Attitude of Jerome toward Pagan Literature, *TPAPA*, L, 1919, 150 167. Rufinus had accused Jerome of teaching the classics and of having a monk copy Cicero.
[34]Ellspermann: p. 157.
[35]Jerome: *Liber contra Helvidium de perpetua virginitate Mariae*, xii, quoted in Sister M. Jamesetta Kelly: *Life and Times as Revealed in the Writings of St. Jerome Exclusive of His Letters*, Patristic Studies, Vol. 52, Washington, D.C., 1944, p. 59.

grammarian Donatus and in later life recommended Demosthenes and Cicero to his students as models.[36]

Jerome employs the figure of the "captive woman" at one point to illustrate his desire to take from the old what was useful for the new order. The figure occurs in Deuteronomy 21:10-13.

> If thou go to fight against thy enemies, and the Lord thy God deliver them to thy hand, and thou lead them away captives, and seest in the number of the captives a beautiful woman, and lovest her, and wilt have her to wife, thou shalt bring her into thy house: and she shall shave her hair, and pare her nails and shall put off the raiment, wherein she was taken: and shall remain in thy house, and mourn for her father and her mother one month: and after that thou shalt go unto her, and shalt sleep with her, and she shall be thy wife.[37]

The captive woman, of course, is secular wisdom, to be purged of its falsities and dangers. The metaphor clarifies the desire of Jerome, but does not specify what is to be sheared away and what is to be kept whole.

In the case at hand—the matter of the worth of rhetoric—his feelings are ambivalent. "Saint Jerome's attitude toward rhetoric," concludes Ellspermann, "cannot be summed up in one bald statement. In the texts considered there is indeed unfeigned favor of the rhetorical art, but there are also sentiments of mixed approval and disapproval, and even of evident disapproval."[38]

Even so, it might be argued at this point that the bulk of these Christian statements might be attributed to a reluctance to acknowledge publicly the worth of the Roman cultural heritage, while at the same time taking advantage of it. The Church Fathers were trained in Roman rhetorical schools, and many had actually taught rhetoric themselves. It might be expected that they would readily avail themselves of their training.

---

[36]Jerome: *Epistle*, LVIII, *CSEL*, LIV, quoted in Ellspermann, p. 147. Interestingly enough, he also recommends Lysias and the Gracchi. The rest of the list (*e.g.*, for poetry, Homer, Virgil, Menander, and Terence) is reminiscent of the typical Roman grammar school curriculum.

[37]Cf. *De Doctrina* II. xl.60-xlii.63, where Augustine compares useful pagan learning to the gold and silver which the Israelites took away from Egypt in the Exodus.

[38]Ellspermann: p. 167.

Nevertheless, two factors must be appreciated. The first is that the few citations offered above could be multiplied many times, the abundance of Christian comment offering clear indication that this issue was one of real concern up to and including the fourth century.[39]

A second point is that, despite the rhetorical training of the major ecclesiastical orators, the fourth century marks a high point of popularity for the simple "homily" style of preaching. Students of such preachers as Chrysostom and Basil have generally concluded that their sermons show less of the contemporary sophistic than might ordinarily be expected from men of their educational background. Coupled with the many utterances denouncing the sophistic, the comparative simplicity of the homilies might be seen as further indication of the dilemma of the times.[40] The reader's attention is directed, for example, to Chrysostom's first homily on the Statues: the sermon has no proper beginning or end, and might satisfactorily be ended at any point without damaging the speaker's point; the use of figures is comparatively restrained, and there is virtually no repetition for emphasis.

Whatever the modern critic may decide about the intrinsic merit of the homily form of the fourth century, its very appearance in a highly sophisticated age might well argue a deliberate choice on the part of preachers. It was an age, after all, when the same man who delivered the eulogy for the archsophist Prohæresius could castigate a friend for forsaking Christian books for the rhetorician's trade.[41] It was an age also in which former teachers of rhetoric—Jerome,

---

[39]For other discussions, see Laistner: *Christianity and Pagan Culture in the Later Roman Empire*, Ithaca, New York, 1951, pp. 49-73; Franz Maier: *Augustin und das antike Rom.*, Stuttgart, 1955, especially pp. 17-36 and 206-214; E. K. Rand: *Founders of the Middle Ages*, New York, 1957 reprint, pp. 1-134; and Labriolle: pp. 6-32.

[40]Thomas E. Ameringer: *The Stylistic Influence of the Second Sophistic on the Panegyrical Sermons of St. John Chrysostom*, Patristic Studies, Vol. 6, Washington, D.C., 1921; Sister M. Albania Burns: *St. John Chrysostom's Homilies on the Statues: A Study of Rhetorical Qualities and Form*, Patristic Studies, Vol. 22, Washington, D.C., 1930; and Campbell: *op. cit.* Sample homilies are printed in a number of anthologies, including those of Guy Lee, David Brewer, and Mabel Platz.

[41]Gregory Naziensus. For a revealing biography of the notorious Prohaeresius, perhaps the best single exemplar of the Second Sophistic, see Philostratus and Eunapius: *Lives of the Sophists*, trans. Wilmer C. Wright, Loeb Classical Library, London, 1922.

Basil, and Augustine, among others—felt that they must decide whether their former profession deserved a place in the new order.

The resolution of this question was demanded at a critical period in the history of Western culture, for the barbarian erosion of the Roman Empire was already well under way. Alaric swept into Rome itself in 410, and Augustine's episcopal seat of Hippo was under Vandal seige as he lay on his deathbed in 430. The homogeneous Roman culture had already begun to suffer from the questionings of the new Christian element within it, and at the same time it faced annihilation from without. From the Christian point of view, it was an age of selection, a time to examine the *sapientia sæculi* to extract from a thousand-year-old heritage whatever would aid in the work of the Lord. The decisions made would influence Western culture for another thousand years.

The historian is often tempted into a feeling of inevitability about events, a feeling that since events took a certain turn they could have taken no other. But it has been noted that some of the most influential Christians were at least undecided about the role of rhetoric and indeed about Roman culture in many aspects. When it is recalled that Greco-Roman culture was largely transmitted to the early Middle Ages through the very narrow funnel of the encyclopedists like Isidore and Cassiodorus, it might well be wondered what might have occurred if a spokesman as influential as Augustine had denied rhetoric a place in Christian culture.[42]

It was perhaps inevitable that Augustine's opinions would have a strong influence on the future development of rhetoric—if for no other reason than his general influence in a number of fields which gave added weight to his rhetorical ideas. Moreover, the *De Doctrina* provided the basic statement of a Christian homiletic until the emergence of the highly-formalized "thematic" or "University Style" sermon about the beginning of the thirteenth century.[43] In the light of

---

[42]Portions of the following have appeared in *Western Speech, XXII*, 24-29, 1958.

[43]To the best of this writer's knowledge, the texts of the sermons preached at the University of Paris during the academic year 1230-31 provide the earliest evidence of a new sermon mode. See the Latin texts in M. M. Davy: *Les sermons universitaires parisiens de 1230-31: contribution a l'histoire de la prédication médiévale,* Paris, 1931. The earliest extant manuals of the new style are of an even later date. Cf. Ray C. Petry: *No Uncertain Sound: Sermons that Shaped the Pulpit Tradition,* Philadelpha, 1948, pp. 4 ff.

these factors, then it would seem useful not only to identify Augustine's contribution to the debate, but to determine his own assessment of the problems presented in it.

Augustine composed the four books of *De Doctrina Christiana*[44] between 396 and 426, the first of three books being completed almost a quarter of a century before he decided to resume work on the volume by adding Book Four. His goal was a treatise which would give the preacher both the substance and the form for sermons:

> There are two things necessary to the treatment of the Scriptures: a way of discovering *(modus inveniendi)* those things which are to be understood, and a way of expressing to others *(modus proferendi)* what we have learned.[45]

The first three books deal with the *materia* of the sermons—that is, with the ways in which the words of Scripture may be understood. Book One deals with signs of realities, Book Two with words as conventional signs, and Book Three with the problem of ambiguity. Throughout the three books he is concerned with the uses of words, and points out that the preacher needs a knowledge of language to equip himself with the tools of understanding. Thus he treats both ambiguities growing out of words used literally, and ambiguities deriving from words used figuratively.

It is plain throughout that he intends the student of this subject to master the ordinary things taught in the schools. Although Augustine severely limits the number of things which a student might profitably learn from the profane culture, he is equally quick to point out that the young should pursue "those human institutions helpful to social intercourse in the necessary pursuits of life."[46]

But it is the fourth book which contains an outspoken plea for the use of *eloquentia* in Christian oratory, making the volume what has

---

[44]*S. Aurelii Augustini de doctrina christiana libros quattor,* edidit H. J. Vogels, Florilegium Patristicum, Fasciculus XXIV, Bonnae, 1930. For an easily available translation, see *Saint Augustine on Christian Doctrine,* trans. D. W. Robertson, Library of Liberal Arts, No. 80, New York, 1958. The fourth book is edited with translation and commentary by Sister Therese Sullivan in Patristic Studies, Vol. 23. Charles S. Baldwin supplies a brief summary of Book Four in his *Medieval Rhetoric and Poetic,* chap. ii.

[45]*De Doctrina,* II, i, 1.

[46]*Ibid.,* II, xxxix, 58. In the same book he refers to "rules of eloquence" as desirable, II, xxxvi, 54.

been called "the first manual of Christian rhetoric." His basic principle is presented in an *a fortiori* argument early in the book:

> But a man who has merely an empty flow of eloquence ought the more to be guarded against as he is the more pleasing to those in his audience in those matters which have no expedience, and, as his audience hears him speak with fluency, it judges likewise that he speaks with truth. This view, indeed, did not escape even those who considered rhetorical training necessary, for they hold that wisdom without eloquence is of small avail to a country but that eloquence without wisdom is generally a great hindrance, and never a help. If, therefore, those who have given us the rules of oratory, in the very books in which they have treated this subject are forced through the urgency of truth to make this concession, ignorant as they are of the true, the supernal wisdom which comes down from the Father of Lights, how much more so are we, the ministers and children of this wisdom, under obligation to hold no other opinion?[47]

In an effort to combat the point of view represented by such writers as Cyprian and Cresconium, he restates the point in another place:

> For since through the art of rhetoric both truth and falsehood are pleaded, who would be so bold as to say that against falsehood, truth as regards its own defenders ought to stand unarmed, so that, forsooth, those who attempt to plead false causes know from the beginning how to make their audience well-disposed, attentive, and docile . . . so that the one, moving and impelling the minds of the audience to error by the force of its oratory, now strikes them with terror, now saddens them, now enlivens them, now ardently arouses them; but the other, in the cause of truth, is sluggish and cold and falls asleep! Who is so foolish to be thus wise?[48]

Augustine takes his stand, therefore, in the great debate about the use to which the new Christian society is to put the *sapientia mundi*. He declares that the art of eloquence should be put into active service, and not rejected out of hand because it is tainted with paganism. To

---

[47]*Ibid.*, IV, v, 8. The reference to "wisdom. . . . eloquence" is to the opening passage of Cicero's *De inventione*.

[48]*De Doctrina*, IV, 2, 3. The *officia* of the *exordium* of a speech in Roman rhetorical theory was to render the audience "attentive, docile, and well-disposed." Cf. *Rhetorica ad Herennium*, I, iv, 6 and *De inventione*, I, xv, 20.

those who might reply that rhetoric is the tool of the wicked, he responds with the Aristotelian dictum that the art can serve both truth and falsehood:

> Since, therefore, there has been placed equally at our disposal the power of eloquence, which is so efficacious in pleading either for the erroneous cause or the right, why is it not zealously acquired by the good, so as to do service for the truth?[49]

Still another concern to ecclesiastical authorities in the fourth century was the matter of examples to be used in literary education. Almost every writer from Paul to Jerome had warned of the dangers inherent in sending Christians to school which taught through *imitatio* of Homer and Virgil. Augustine's proposal is to look at the Scriptures themselves for examples of style, and the bulk of Book Four is taken up with an attempt to demonstrate how this could be done. Indeed, Augustine postulates the existence of a new type of eloquence:

> Thus there is a kind of eloquence fitting for men most worthy of the highest authority and clearly inspired by God. Our authors speak with an eloquence of this kind, nor does any other kind become them.[50]

Since Ciceronian rhetorical doctrine insisted that three levels of style must be employed, however, Augustine is careful to show that all three levels exist in the Scripture.

It should be noted also that Augustine is unwilling to relegate rhetoric to the position of a mere preliminary study. Instead he wishes to use it in the active service of the ministry. Jerome and Ambrose were apparently somewhat willing to accord rhetoric a place in primary education, but were unsure of the extent to which it should be allowed elsewhere. Augustine insists upon the homiletic

---

[49]*De Doctrina*, IV, iii, 3. He expresses the same idea elsewhere: *ibid.*, II, xxvi, 54, and *Contra Cresconium*, I, i, 2.

[50]*De Doctrina*, IV, vi, 9. Sections xviii through xxvi of Book Four provide numerous examples, especially from Saint Paul. It is interesting to note that when Saint Bede wished to provide examples of the tropes and schemes of the Latin Grammarian Donatus, he was able to produce 122 Scriptural passages to illustrate them. Bede, *Liber de scematibus et tropis*, in Carolus Halm, ed.: *Rhetores Minores Latini*, Lipsiae, 1863, pp. 607-18.

utility of the subject, whether its study followed *præcepta* or *imitatio*.[51]

Moreover, it will be recalled, he begins the *De Doctrina* with the statement that the *modus inveniendi,* or means of discovery, is distinct from the *modus proferendi,* or means of expression. The structure of the whole work therefore becomes an argument for the necessity of studying the "means of expression" with the same care given to the study of the Scriptures themselves. The disproportionate amount of space accorded each of the two subjects is due to the fact that he is in a sense creating the first, while merely arguing for the use of the second. It is for this reason that he begins Book Four with the statement that he does not intend to supply the rules of rhetoric which can be found elsewhere. Book Four is intended as a *ratio eloquentiæ Christianæ.*

It would therefore seem to be misleading to imply, as do Baldwin and Sister Therese Sullivan, that Augustine intended the fourth book of *De Doctrina* as a mere rejection of the Second Sophistic. Certainly his attitude toward the "empty eloquence" of the sophistic is clear enough, but this was an attitude which was shared after all by every one of his Christian contemporaries and thus one which needed little proof.

Instead it might be more nearly accurate to say that he saw the dangers of an opposite rhetorical heresy. The sin of the sophist is that he denies the necessity of subject matter and believes that *forma* alone is desirable. An opposite vice, one to which historians of rhetoric have never given a name, depends upon the belief that the man possessed of truth will *ipso facto* be able to communicate the truth to others. It is a dependence upon *materia* alone. Its chief proponent in ancient times was the young Plato, and it would seem fair to label it the "Platonic rhetorical heresy" just as we apply the term "sophistry" to its opposite theory. This is not to say that the ecclesiastical writers of the fourth century looked to the *Gorgias* and *Protagoras* for a theory

---

[51]Roman rhetorical training followed three major methods: the teaching of rules *(praecepta),* the imitation of models *(imitatio),* and free composition on a theme *(declamatio).* Augustine in Book Four seems to favor *imitatio* as a method of acquiring eloquence (cf. IV, iii, 4-5), but it must be noted that earlier he recommends study of *praecepta* (II, xxxix, 58). For a comment on Augustine's possible larger uneasiness later about his recommendation, cf. Laistner: The Christian Attitude to Pagan Literature, *History,* XX, 1935, 51.

of communication, but rather that their reactions to the pagan culture of Rome led many of them to take up a somewhat similar attitude toward the rhetoric which was a part of that culture. Augustine apparently recognized a danger in this aspect of the cultural debate of his times, and used the *De Doctrina* to urge a union of both matter and form in Christian preaching.

Only if one views the book as a part of the great debate of the fourth century, therefore, does its historical importance emerge clearly. The reader is struck by the author's insistence upon the folly of abandoning a useful tool to the enemy.For this is a book written, not for enemies, but for other Christians. It can only be his own fellows in the Church whom he describes as "dull and cold" (*lenti fridique*) when they try to speak as if the mere utterance of God's Word would by itself move the minds of men. Augustine appreciates the role of God's grace in preaching, but he warns that the preacher must do his work well too.[52]

The *De Doctrina Christiana* emerges, consequently, as a book written as a rebuttal to those who would deprive the Church of a useful tool in the work of winning souls. Significantly, the debate ends with its appearance. Marie Comeau states the conclusion well:

Il était indispensable qu' Augustin abordât dans ce traité la question de la légitimité de la rhétorique, question constamment agitée depuis Platon, et que le christianisme présentait sous un jour nouveau. Il semble avoir dit le dernier mot sur le problème.[53]

---

[52]*De Doctrina,* IV, xv and IV, xxx. For an analysis of an earlier treatment of the same problem, see Jean Daniélou: *Origen,* trans. Walter Mitchell New York, 1955, pp. 102 ff.

[53]Marie Comeau: *La rhétorique de Saint Augustin d'apres les Tractatus in Joannem,* Paris, 1930, p. xv.

RHETORIC AND THE LITERATURE OF THE ENGLISH MIDDLE AGES

DONALD LEMEN CLARK

Columbia University

MEDIEVALISTS are habituated to meeting the most abstract and abstruse concepts under the guise of allegory. They will have no difficulty in recognizing that allegories of rhetoric may be, not only picturesque, but accurate representations of what the Middle Ages conceived rhetoric to be. Hence the opening of this discussion, in an effort to teach delightfully, will present some allegories of Lady Rhetoric. The unadorned exposition of doctrine will follow.

The allegory of Lady Rhetoric owes its popularity to the fifth century treatise of Martianus Capella, whose *Marriage of Philology and Mercury* combines a compend of the Seven Liberal Arts with allegorical descriptions of the Seven Learned Ladies. Martianus describes Rhetorica as "a woman of loftiest stature and great assurance, with countenance of radiant splendor . . . Helmeted and crowned with royal majesty, she held ready for defense or for attack weapons that gleamed with the flash of lightning. Beneath her armor, her vesture glittered with the various light of all *figuraé*, all *schemata;* and she was cinctured with most precious *colores* for jewels."[1]

A thousand years later Rhetorica is recognizable as the same lady in a woodcut from the medieval encyclopaedia *Margarita Philosophica* (1503).[2] But she reflects an even more accurate and full statement of

---

[1] Martianus Capella: *De nuptiis Philologiae et Mercurii et de septem artibus liberalibus libri novem,* ed. Adolph Dick, Leipzig, 1925. The description of Rhetorica, as translated, is from C. S. Baldwin, *Medieval Rhetoric and Poetic,* New York, 1928, pp. 93-94.

[2] G. Reisch: *Margarita Philosophica,* Freiburg, 1503; Strasburg, 1504.

traditional Greco-Roman rhetoric. By the sword and the lily which extend from her mouth she represents allegorically the two traditional functions of rhetoric: to attack and defend by verbal arguments and to embelish speech with verbal adornment. The beauty of her gown and the ringlets of her coiffure represent beauty of style. The words embroidered on the hem of her robe designate the *colores* or figures of speech, and the enthymemes and *exempla*, types of deductive and inductive argument. Her gown is embraced by the Zone of Justice.

In the picture Rhetorica is surrounded by human figures identified by name. At the top Aristotle represents natural philosophy; Justinian, the use of rhetoric in support of law; Seneca, moral philosophy; Sallust, history. Less to be expected is Virgil, crowned with laurel and holding in extended hands a book marked *Pœsis*. His presence on the lily side of Lady Rhetoric symbolizes the influence of the embellished style of rhetoric on the style of poetry. In the foreground Cicero is clearly shown defending Milo in a court of law, and the Senatus Populusque Romanus figures forth the scene of deliberative rhetoric.

The combative aspect of rhetoric as a verbal weapon for attack or defense is emphasized in a sculptured relief of Lady Rhetoric on the campanile at Florence. She is armed with sword and shield, but is unadorned by the embellishments furnished by the hairdresser or dressmaker. In her functional plainness she is an unusual allegory. In most medieval allegories Lady Rhetoric is shown to represent little but embellishment of style. Characteristic is the *Court of Sapyence,* formerly attributed to Lydgate, and *The Pastime of Pleasure* by Stephen Hawes.[3]

I had hoped that the allegory would help me to fulfill the first duty which rhetoric imposes on a speaker: the duty of defining his terms. This I believe the allegory does, whether we accept the habitual Roman definition of rhetoric as the *ars bene dicendi*, the art of effective public speech, or the more philosophical Aristotelian defini-

---

[3]H. N. MacCracken, ed.: *The Minor Poems of John Lydgate,* Early English Text Society, extra series, CVII, London & N. Y., 1911 (for 1910). Stephen Hawes: *The Pastime of Pleasure,* ed. W. E. Mead, E.E.T.S., CXVI, Oxford, 1928 (for 1927). I discuss rhetoric as aureate language in *Rhetoric and Poetry in the Renaissance,* New York, 1922, pp. 47-55.

tion, the art of discovering all available means to persuasion in any
subject.

The picture also helps me to fulfill the second duty of a rhetorician
—that of analysis. One mode of analysis depends on what the speaker
wants to accomplish in a given speech situation. He may have to deal
with a situation growing out of a trial in court, a debate in a
deliberative assembly, an occasion to be adorned. In a trial he practices
what is variously termed forensic or judicial rhetoric. He endeavors to
prove that Milo should be acquitted of a charge of murder. He is
debating the justice or injustice of a past action. In the realm of
imaginative literature, the owl and the nightingale debate the good
or bad effects of their past actions and present influence. The body
and the soul debate the question, Who was to blame for the disaster
they both find themselves in after death? The speakers are presented
as well trained in forensic rhetoric.

If the speaker urges someone to do or not do something, he is
practising deliberative rhetoric and will endeavor to show that the
line of conduct recommended for the future is or is not possible,
honorable, and expedient. Naturally enough, perhaps, one of the
oldest themes for deliberation in the ancient schools of rhetoric was:
Should a man marry? Chaucer, in *The Merchant's Tale,* shows his
familiarity when he gives an account of the deliberations of January,
Justinus, and Placebo. It is just to marry, possible, expedient as
bringing many comforts; it is fitting as showing a disposition not
savage. A great deal of the imaginative literature of the Middle Ages,
as of all periods, is concerned with urging a course of action. The lady
should love the poet. The reader should love Truth. Rhetoric is at
hand to help.

If, however, the speaker is adorning an occasion, such as a funeral,
the visit of an ambassador, or a saint's day, he will lavish encomium
on the person whom he celebrates. Or he may vituperate an evil person,
such as a political opponent or heretic. He will be practicing what
Aristotle called epideictic and the Romans demonstrative rhetoric.
The whole corpus of anti-feministic literature in the Middle Ages
utilized the traditional topics of rhetorical vituperation. Likewise the
literature of praise, saints' lives, hymns, panegyrics of princes utilized
the topics of encomium. St. Basil alone warned that only true virtues

were to be praised in lives of saints and martyrs. He well knew that in secular panegyric all good things were rhetorically attributed to the hero whether he possessed them or not.[4]

Thus far I have dealt with the first of the arts a speaker must learn to use in all speech situations—*inventio,* rhetorical invention, the art of exploring the issues to discover what arguments can be used for or against the probability of a proposition. Modern critics sometimes deplore that the Middle Ages did not have Aristotle's *Rhetorica,* Cicero's complete *De oratore,* more of Quintilian. But they did have Cicero's *De inventione* and the *Rhetorica Ad Herennium,* attributed to Cicero until the fifteenth century. When a medieval writer speaks of Tully in rhetorical contexts, he is speaking of these works. They are not so philosophical as Aristotle, nor so charming as *De oratore,* but no more practical guides to rhetorical precept could be wished for. Medieval speakers and writers did have access to many manuscripts of these works (over 100 of *Ad Herennium* survive)[5] and made good use of them.

The second art the speaker or writer could learn from rhetoric is the art of arranging or disposing his matter in such a sequence as to lead his audience to understand and believe. In part this art of *dispositio* dealt with the parts of a speech. First is an *exordium* which aims to make the hearer attentive, friendly, and docile. This is followed by a *narratio,* a statement of facts colored in the speaker's favor. The body of the speech is the *confirmatio* and *refutatio,* the marshalling or arguments in support and in rebuttal. Finally the *peroratio,* which recapitulates and drives home.

When the official business of secular and ecclesiastical princes, and especially of the papal curia, made written communication more useful and frequent than oral, the art of the oration was easily adapted to the art of the formal Latin epistle or *dictamen.* Thus in his *Flores Rhetorici* of the eleventh century Alberico of Montecassino is thinking of *dictamen* when he says, "The writer will

---

[4]*In Gordium,* 142D-143A. Quoted in J. M. Campbell: *The Influence of the second sophistic on the style of the sermons of St. Basil the Great,* Washington, D.C., 1922, p. 147.

[5]*Ad C. Herennium: de ratione dicendi* with an English translation by Harry Caplan, The Loeb Classical Library, Harvard Univ. Press, 1954, p. xxxv. This annotated edition will be a great help to students of medieval rhetoric.

design his proem to render the mind of the reader attentive, friendly, and docile."[6] The epistle, to be sure, also has a salutation which Alberico hopes will be adapted to the person addressed, to the circumstances, and to the writer's intention. The Latin epistle, of course, had been a literary form in antiquity as it continued to be in the Renaissance. John of Salisbury was only one of the accomplished letter writers of the Middle Ages. I am claiming as literature, of course, quite a variety of literary kinds, prose compositions as well as poems, Latin as well as vernacular, which benefited from the inherited precepts of ancient *inventio* and *dispositio*. Medieval rhetoric was a respectable intellectual discipline. Romantic critics can and do deplore the tendency of this rhetoric to encourage an argumentative and disputatious tendency in imaginative literature. Scholastic logic encouraged the same tendency. Both encouraged a temper of didacticism. The Middle Ages believed that poetry as well as philosophy was founded on *doctrina*.

But students of medieval literature have not forgotten Virgil with his book of poetry on the lily side of Lady Rhetoric in the allegorical woodcut. These students might believe that Virgil has wandered into this allegory from another allegory which should be devoted to poetry. But in the scheme of the Seven Liberal Arts in ancient and medieval education there was no separate place for poetry, whether interpreted narrowly as verse or in the broadest Aristotelian terms as fiction, either narrative or dramatic. St. Thomas Aquinas and Roger Bacon made poetry a part of logic. This makes sense if we take logic, as John of Salisbury did, to be the art of the *logos,* the word, all verbal communication.[7] In ancient and medieval schools of grammar poetry was taught as a sanction for linguistic purity and for stylistic appropriateness and beauty. This is illustrated by Priscian whose precepts of grammar are exemplified by excerpts from the best Latin literature. Grammar-school boys also wrote verses to help them understand the metrics of ancient poetry. That poetry is closely related to rhetoric is pointed out by Aristotle. Both are closest in their literary style as distinguished from their matter. The school of the orator Gorgias, he said, learned

---

[6]Alberici Casinensis: *Flores Rhetorici,* ed. D. M. Inguanez and H. M. Willard, Montecassino, 1938. *Prologus,* II, 1.
[7]*Metalogicon,* I, 10.

stylistic embellishment from the poets. Later literary history shows that the poets, in turn, learned stylistic embellishment from rhetoric. From the rhetoricated prose of the second sophistic and from the sophisticated verse of Ovid, throughout the Middle Ages to mid-seventeenth century, poets devoted what to modern taste was as excessive attention to embellishment of style. The principal sources of embellishment were such tropes as metaphor, irony, and insinuation; such verbal patterns, *schemata,* as alliteration, assonance, antithesis, balance, and parallelism. These and many more departures from plain statement we lump together as figures of speech.[8] In antiquity and in the Middle Ages they were frequently referred to metaphorically as *colores* in the picture of Lady Rhetoric or as *flores* as in the *Flores Rhetorici* of Alberico. Some puritans in antiquity and later considered them flowers of evil, but most people loved them. They occupy as much as half of the *Rhetorica Ad Herennium.* When I was studying the medieval contributions to the vogue of aureate language in my *Rhetoric and Poetry in the Renaissance* (1922), the most portentous work I had access to was the *Poetria* of John of Garlandia.[9] This work, a combination of *Ars Dictaminis* and a treatise on style, was characterized by the same preoccupation with beauteous language that I found in *The Castle of Sapyence,* then ascribed to Lydgate, and in Hawes' *Pastime of Pleasure.* But since Faral's valued editions with commentaries of the Arts Poétiques of the twelfth and thirteenth centuries (1923),[10] medieval rhetoric has almost become synonymous with the arts of stylistic embellishment which the authors of the treatises, especially Geoffrey of Vinsauf, Matthieu of Vendôme, and Evrard l'Allemand, had learned from *Ad Herennium,* as Faral has pointed out in detail. Since his publication of the sources there has been a whole school of critical books and articles on Chaucer's rhetoric, which have made good use of his collection, beginning with Manly,

---

[8]D. L. Clark: *Rhetoric in Greco-Roman Education,* New York, 1957, pp. 25-26; 83-107.

[9]*Poetria magister Johannis anglici de arte prosayca metrica et rithmica,* ed. G. Mari, *Romanische Forschungen,* 1902, XIII, 883 ff.

[10]Edmond Faral: *Les Arts Poétiques du XIIe et du XIIIe Siècles,* Paris, 1923.

Chaucer and the Rhetoricians (1926).[11] The discussion of medieval rhetoric as beauteous language has continued and gives a very full treatment of what Virgil in the woodcut had learned about the flowers of rhetoric. I need not recapitulate the well-known story, but I must add that most medieval poets probably learned more about the embellished style from *Ad Herennium* and other school books than from their later reading of the poets writing poetry about poetry. Geoffrey of Vinsauf belongs on the library shelf with Horace, Vida, and Boileau, not in the school room.

What has received less attention than it deserves is the influence on poets of their grammar school training in boyhood. To this problem I shall now turn—still using allegory when possible. Let me describe Lady Grammar as she appears in another woodcut from the *Margarita Philosophica*. She stands before the Tower of Knowledge with a child standing at her feet. In one hand she holds a hornbook which shows the letters of the alphabet. In her other hand she holds the key to unlock the door of the narrow gate to the Tower. She is not so pretty as Lady Rhetoric, nor so elaborately dressed. But she seems kind. Much kinder than Lady Grammar carved on the portico of Chartres Cathedral, with a switch in her hand threatening a child who cowers at her knee. In the woodcut the ground floor of the Tower is occupied by a schoolmaster labeled Donatus, who had been teaching elementary grammar to boys from the time of St. Jerome. On the floor above sits Priscian, prepared to teach more advanced grammar. Of him more anon. On the next floor above sits Tully (Cicero) whose labels indicate that he teaches both rhetoric and poetry. He is the Tully who was assumed to have written *Ad Herennium* as well as *De inventione*. His joint function here is quite as significant as the presence of Virgil at the knee of Lady Rhetoric in the other allegory. Rhetoric taught the poets.

---

[11]J. M. Manly: Chaucer and the Rhetoricians, *Wharton Lecture on English Poetry,* XVII, 1926; C. S. Baldwin: Cicero on Parnassus, *PMLA,* XLII, March 1927, 106-12; Traugott Maunin: *Der Einfluss der mittelalterlichen Rhetorik auf Chaucer's Dichtung,* Bonn diss., 1929; Marie P. Hamilton: Notes on Chaucer and the Rhetoricians, *PMLA,* XLVII, June 1932, 403-09; Florence E. Teager: Chaucer's Eagle and the Rhetorical Colors, *PMLA,* XLVII, June 1932, 410-18; Benjamin S. Harrison: Medieval Rhetoric in the *Book of the Duchesse, PMLA,* XLIX, June 1934, 428-42; Helge Kökeritz: Rhetorical Word-Play in Chaucer, *PMLA,* LXIX, September 1954, 937.

As I have already said, the ancient grammar school and such teachers as Priscian taught a great deal of literature as well as what we think of as grammar. So in his thirteenth-century allegorical poem, *The Battle of the Seven Arts,* Henri d'Andeli shows Lady Grammar leading the cohorts of the Latin authors, as models for imitation, against the *Artes,* or textbooks, devoted to teaching the precepts of the arts. Priscian fights in her army.[12] But teachers of grammar also taught elementary exercises in rhetoric. My thesis is that the practises of the ancient grammar schools in this respect continued in medieval schools, although the stream was undoubtedly reduced to a trickle between Ausonius and Alcuin. In the north the stream may well have dried up for a while. But certainly the very best traditions were flourishing in the school of Chartres as described by John of Salisbury in the *Metalogicon.*[13] I have not enough evidence to prove that elementary exercises in rhetoric were taught much earlier than the twelfth century, but I wish to present at least some arguments in support of my conjecture. One of these arguments is derived from the works of Priscian of Cæsarea, a school-master in Constantinople, who, in the early sixth century wrote a most complete grammar of the Latin language, to help Greeks, it seems, to learn the language of the West. Consequently this grammar became an invaluable aid in teaching Latin to the assorted tribes of barbarians who had destroyed western civilization and were in process of becoming Christianized and civilized. They had to learn Latin if they were to become priests who could read the Scriptures and participate in the liturgy. The responsibility for teaching passed early from the monasteries to the cathedral grammar schools. Lecturers on Priscian were, as Richard Hunt has shown, preparing young men to teach young men to teach boys in *parvis scholis,* which prepared for the grammar schools.[14] Priscian's own works show what the master of a grammar school was expected to teach. In addition to his *Institutionum grammaticarum libri xviii* Priscian wrote on Roman numerals, a treatise on the meters of Terence, and an explication of the text of twelve lines of Virgil, as a model per-

---

[12]Henri d'Andeli: *La Bataille des VII Ars,* edited and translated with introduction and notes by L. J. Paetow, Berkeley, 1914.

[13]*Metalogicon,* ed. and trans. by D. D. McGarry, Berkeley, 1955, I, 17-24.

[14]Richard Hunt: Studies in Priscian in the Eleventh and Twelfth Centuries, *Medieval and Renaissance Studies,* I, 1943; and II, 1950.

haps, for the new critics.[15] Most important for my argument, he published a close translation of the elementary exercises in rhetoric, or *progymnasmata*, attributed to Hermogenes, a second-century schoolmaster of Tarsus.[16] Priscian's version was, I believe, accessible to most medieval schools in England. Aldhelm, who died in 709, is the first to note Priscian's arrival in Britain.[17] It seems more than probable that Theodore of Tarsus, when he went to England as Archbishop in 667, had the elementary exercises in rhetoric in his baggage, not only Priscian's Latin version, but the Greek of Hermogenes of Tarsus as well, which probably had contributed to making his own school days miserable. In England he and Abbot Hadrian instructed their scholars in Latin and Greek.

Hertz states that in the neighborhood of 1000 manuscripts survive.[18] In their present condition some of these do not include the elementary exercises in rhetoric, which traditionally appear as the final treatise in Priscian's *Opera*. Worn out with use, perhaps. The oldest manuscript is Paris 7530, written in the eighth century.[19] It includes the rhetorical exercises as do all thirteen printings of Priscian from 1470 to 1500.

By 1542, Priscian's Hermogenes was superseded as a manual for speaking and writing themes by Latin translations of Aphthonius, who was teaching in Antioch in the fourth century. His precepts are almost identical with those of Priscian's Hermogenes, but he won the textbook market in the sixteenth and seventeenth centuries because he included

---

[15]Priscian: *Opera*, ed. by Martin Hertz in Vol. III of H. Keil, *Grammatici latini*, Leipzig, 1870-1880. Keil himself edited the *Praeexercitamina*.

[16]*Praeexercitamina Prisciani grammatici ex Hermogene versa*, in K. Halm: *Rhetores latini minores*, Leipzig, 1863, pp. 551-560. In his *Praef.*, xiii-xiv, he says his text is better than Keil's. The best modern treatment of Priscian is R. Helm's article *Priscianus*, in Pauly-Wissowa-Kroll, *Realencyclopädie der classischen Altertumswissenschaft (Neue Bearbeitung)*, XXII, 1954, 2327-2346.

[17]Aldhelm used a good bit of Priscian in his own treatise on grammar and metrics. Max Manitius: *Geschichte der Lateinischen Literatur des Mittelalters*, München, 1911, I, 137. For Aldhelm's and Theodore's contribution to the Medieval grammar schools see A. F. Leach: *The Schools of Medieval England*, New York, 1915, pp. 31-45.

[18]Martin Hertz: *Gram. Lat.* III, *Praef.* ix. Hilda Buttenwieser considers Hertz's estimate an exaggeration. She counts about 370 MSS which were transcribed before the Fourteenth Century. "Popular Authors of the Middle Ages," *Speculum*, XVII, January 1942, p. 53.

[19]*Praef.* to Priscian's minor works.

model themes.[20] A very good idea of what the elementary exercises taught can be gained by Baldwin's translation from Hermogenes[21] and from Nadeau's translation of Aphthonius.[22] Priscian's Latin version differs somewhat from Hermogenes in that he introduces examples from Roman writers not mentioned in the Greek.

Priscian's own view of the value of the elementary exercises in rhetoric is contained in his dedicatory epistle to Symmachus, who was consul in 485 and was in Constantinople some time during his consulship. The exercises, he writes, give youths practice in all kinds of rhetoric, "nec non etiam de praeexercitamentis rhetoricis, quae Graeci progymnasmata vocant, quoniam diligentius ea sophistae iuniores, quos sequimur, aptioribus divisionibus ad exercendas iuvenes ad omne rhetoricae genus exposuisse creduntur."[23] All our manuscripts are descended from a transcript by Priscian's pupil the calligrapher Theodorus, made in 526-527. Keil, who edited the text, says the oldest and best MS is Paris 7530, written in the eighth century. In this MS the elementary excersises in rhetoric open, "Incip. praeexercitamina prisciani grammatici de fabula."[24]

But let me briefly describe the exercises as they were available to English schoolboys from the late seventh century in Priscian. As the *incipit* states the first exercise is *fabula*.

PRAEEXERCITAMINA PRISCIANI

1. Fabula was a retelling of fictitious stories by the younger boys— stories they were familiar with from their reading of the poets. These paraphrases might be either expanded or condensed.

2. Narratio was slightly more advanced. The boys might retell historical as well as legendary and fictitious stories, based on their reading. *Ad Herennium* recommends both of these as elementary exercises.[25] Chaucer was only one medieval poet given to retelling, shortening, or expanding old tales.

---

[20]D. L. Clark: The Rise and Fall of Progymnasmata in Sixteenth and Seventeenth Century Grammar Schools, *SM*, XIX, November 1952, 259.

[21]*Medieval Rhetoric and Poetic*, pp. 23-38.

[22]R. Nadeau: The Progymnasmata of Aphthonius in Translation, *SM*, XIX, November 1952, 265, ff.

[23]*Gram. Lat.* III, 405, 1.

[24]Keil: *Praef.* to Priscian's minor works.

[25]I, 12-13.

3. Usus is the name Priscian gives to the exercise known to the Greeks as *chreia*. It drills the boys in a set pattern for dilating on such a theme as "Isocrates said that the root of education is bitter but its fruit is sweet." The pattern was: first praise the sayer, then paraphrase the saying, cite a contrast, give an illustration, cite an example, quote an authority, urge the hearer to follow what was said. *Ad Herennium,* the earliest surviving textbook to describe the exercise, called it *expolitio.*[26] As *expolitio* it was explained among the figures of amplification by Geoffrey of Vinsauf.[27] As *expolitio* or as *usus* the exercise encouraged many medieval poets to stop their story in order to expatiate, amplify, dilate, pile it on, and inflate.

4. Sententia, or proverb, was essentially more practice in dilating on a theme and taught the use of the same topics. The pattern was: praise the author of the proverb, paraphrase the proverb, give a reason, cite a contrast, make a comparison, give an example, quote an authority, end with a hortatory conclusion.[28]

5. Refutatio, as the exercise was developed, included *confirmatio.* The boys were taught to subject such legends as that of Arion and the dolphin to destructive analysis by alleging that the legend is obscure, incredible, impossible, inconsistent, unfitting, inexpedient. The stories were drawn from the poets the boys were reading. Unlike medieval schoolboys ancient schoolboys were not taught to accept the legends when interpreted allegorically.

6. Locus Communis, as an exercise, is not the same as the use of the word *commonplace* to describe *loci* or places where arguments may be discovered. It is called commonplace, says Priscian, because it deals with the common or general, not the individual. As an exercise it is an amplification of a thing admitted. It does not investigate whether anyone has robbed a temple, for instance. That is admitted. But it enlarges on the viciousness of all temple robbers. The theme is to follow this pattern: analyze the contrary, describe the deed itself, quote a proverb, make a comparison, make a defamatory surmise of the past life of the criminal, repudiate pity by

[26]IV, 54-58.

[27]*Poetria Nova,* 11.1245-1251. Faral, 235.

[28]Priscian on *Sententia* was taken over by Lorich in his expanded Latin Aphthonius (1546) and served as a model for Milton's *Prolusion on Early Rising.* D. L. Clark: *John Milton at St. Paul's School,* New York, 1948, pp. 234-237.

drawing on the final topics of equity, justice, expediency, possibility, and propriety, and by description of the crime. Chaucer's Pardoner or his sources, the Parson or any preacher, is adept in using commonplaces against any or all of the seven deadly sins and the sinners who practice them. The exercise of *locus communis* is planned to make them adept.

7. Laus, including its opposite, vituperation, is familiar to us as encomium or panegyric. I have already mentioned praise and dispraise as functions of demonstrative or epideictic rhetoric. Priscian is exceedingly full. He teaches how to praise men, cities, animals, virtues. If you praise a man you praise his race, city, and family; his education; the nature of his soul and body; his achievements in war and peace; the manner of his end; his children. Then draw comparisons. Each of these heads has, of course, subheads. *Ad Herennium* follows closely the topics of the elementary exercise, but properly deals with praise and dispraise as something to use in mature rhetoric dealing with actual cases, usually as part of the *narratio* of a speech.[29]

8. Comparatio, Priscian points out, has already been included under *commonplace* and *laus*. But other writers include it as a separate exercise, so he includes it. Sometimes one compares two men, praising one and dispraising the other, or praising both in differing degrees.

9. Allocutio is the name Priscian gives to an exercise that the Greeks called *prosopopoeia* and we might call impersonation. *Ad Herennium* calls it *conformatio* as do the *Arts Poétiques*.[30] The students are set to compose speeches appropriate to real or imagined characters under given situations: What words Andromache might speak to Hector. Priscian calls the exercise *conformatio* when we invent a speaker who was not there as well as words for him to speak, as Cicero has the Republic speak an invective against Catiline. Let the diction be appropriate to the person supposed to be speaking.

The characters and situations were drawn from literature the boys were reading. And as Quintilian remarked, the exercise would be especially useful for a boy who, when he grew up, would be a poet or historian.[31] The effect of the exercise would be to make the speech

---

[29]III, 13-15.
[30]Faral, p. 54.
[31]III, viii, 49.

appropriate to the speaker and the situation, but it would encourage the poet to write set speeches rather than dialog in imitation of conversation.

10. Descriptio is an exercise in "bringing before one's eyes what is to be shown." the description, or ecphrasis, may be of people, actions, times, places, seasons, alone or in combination. Priscian illustrates with a line and a half from Virgil. As the exercise was unrelated to a context, it encouraged the composition of detached set pieces of decoration, frequently on a stock subject, which could be and were inserted in longer works. Chaucer's long description of Lady Blanche is characteristic, and closely parallels Geoffrey of Vinsauf's model description of a beautiful woman in *Poetria Nova*.[32] But the bad habit of the set description, or "purple patch," was much older than Horace's ridicule of it.

11. Positio is Priscian's word for what the ancients and the moderns call *thesis*. The thesis was the first exercise to require the boys to argue both sides of a matter still in doubt. It occupies the field of general debate, not referring to any particular person. The *positio* or *thesis* debates, Should a man marry? not, Should a particular man marry? The topics are justice, expediency, possibility, propriety. Thus: It is just to marry and make the contribution to life of life itself; it is expedient as bringing many comforts; it is possible; it is fitting as showing a disposition not savage. I have already pointed out Chaucer's use of these arguments.

12. Legislatio is an exercise in speaking for or against a law, not a real law in an actual situation but a fancied or perhaps an archaic law not associated with any attendant circumstances. The example is, Should governmental positions be put on sale? Arguments are drawn from the following places: Is it manifest, just, legal, expedient, possible, proper? Priscian's Hermogenes includes the exercise because others do, although it really constitutes a separate study.

Priscian's elementary exercises were the only ones available to the Latin West until the sixteenth century. But other textbook writers appropriated the exercises of Priscian and helped to give them added currency. As Engelhardt points out, "Priscian uses the very terms

---

[32]Chaucer: *Blanche,* 11.816-1040. Geoffrey, 11.563-597.

which Geoffrey of Vinsauf later applied to dilation and abbreviation: *latius, breviter, producere.*[33]

The first two exercises, *fabula* and *narratio,* taught how to condense and abbreviate a story through paraphrase. The paraphrase at times might be longer than the original, but the emphasis was on brevity demanded by all rhetoricians in the *narratio* of a speech. All the other exercises taught the art of expatiating on a theme by the use of the *loci* or *topoi,* the places of argument, including definition, genus and species, cause and effect, contrast, similarity, consistency, conjunction, repugnancy, time (present, past, and future), magnitude (greater or less), paraphrase, example, and testimony of authorities. It was the art of exaggerating, piling up, dilating, expanding, iterating. It sought the *copia verborum* and the *copia rerum* which Erasmus learned from the rhetoric of the Middle Ages and taught to the sixteenth century. When applied to narrative, prose or poetry, this art seeking amplitude envelops the narrative in superabundance.[34]

Whether Chaucer learned this rhetorical art from Geoffrey of Vinsauf, *Ad Herennium,* or Priscian, or carried it over from his sources, he does, as Manly demonstrated, follow the formulas for amplification by means of description, digression, piling up examples, prosopopoeia, paraphrase, and circumlocution. For abbreviation he uses asyndeton and condensed versions of *fabula,* and his favorite, *occultatio* (paralipsis), the refusal to describe or narrate. He does, to be sure, use these artificial devices for abbreviation or elaboration in the high style, appropriate to the Monk, not in the low style of the Miller.

Kemp Malone has pointed out that "our study of the art of the Beowulf poet needs to take into account the parallelism of parts and other structural features."[35] G. J. Engelhardt considers these and other rhetorical features in his article, "Beowulf: a Study in Dilation." He suggests that the Beowulf poet may well have been introduced to the rhetorical devices of amplification and dilation through the Latin version of the *progymnasmata,* as Priscian was available. He then points out that the structure and development of Beowulf proceed topically, not narratively, by: contrast, cause and effect, opposites,

---

[33]George John Engelhardt: Mediaeval Vestiges in the Rhetoric of Erasmus, PMLA, LXII, June 1948, 739 ff.

[34]*Op. cit.*

[35]Coming Back from the Mere, PMLA, LXIX, December 1954, 1292.

comparison, differences, similarities, and adjuncts. In describing persons the poet uses the *loci* taught by the elementary exercise of *laus*: race, city, family, education, nature of his soul and body, achievements in war and peace, manner of his end, his children. Moreover the events in Beowulf are not given in time order, but are woven forward and backward.[36]

So I conclude with the suggestion that all boys who grew up to be writers went to school to learn to read and write, and that they were drilled in rhetoric, not only by *De inventione* and *Ad Herennium*, but by the elementary exercises of Priscian. Rhetoric was not the only influence on Medieval literature in England, but it was one of them. Rhetoric did teach the poets, as well as the prose writers, to find arguments and to use an embellished and copious style, as the allegories attest.

---

[36]PMLA, LXX, September 1955, 825.

THOMAS WILSON'S CONTRIBUTIONS TO RHETORIC

RUSSELL H. WAGNER

Cornell University

W ILSON's *Arte of Rhetorique* (1553) has received attention from scholars because it is the first complete work in English on the subject. Cox, in his *Arte or Crafte of Rhethoryke* (1531), aimed to treat invention alone. Sherry's *Treatise of Tropes and Schemes* (1550), is confined to figurative language. A lesser reason for interest in Wilson is the fact that his *Rhetorique* was popular in its day; it was published eight times between 1553 and 1585. Another is Wilson's own prominence, for he was not only the author of the first *Logic,* and the first translator of Demosthenes in English, but also Secretary of State under Elizabeth.

These facts, however, only raise the question: "How significant, if significant at all, is Wilson's *Rhetorique?*" The answer, to be complete, would be not only difficult but long. But if we pose a narrower question: "What distinctive contributions to rhetorical theory, especially to the theory of public address, did Wilson make?" we may be able to suggest some answers to the larger query.

By contributions, let us understand not absolutely original ideas, of which there are few in any age, and very few in such a period as Wilson's. Let us understand principles from whatever source derived, but which bear, in formulation, those marks of originality we ourselves accept today—selection, assimilation, change in concept, in application, or in emphasis. If we can also observe the persistence of these concepts among later writers, we may reinforce our answer.

The first and the most important contribution of all has already been mentioned—the completeness of Wilson's treatise. Wilson was the first to re-assemble, in English, the lost, strayed, or stolen doctrines of rhetoric. For some centuries before Wilson wrote, the possessions of rhetoric had been absorbed, for the most part, by sister arts or sciences, or lost entirely. *Inventio* had been recaptured by logic, *dispositio* figured little except in arts of preaching, *elocutio* was partially enveloped by grammar and poetics. *Memoria* and *pronuntiatio* had almost completely disappeared. Cox, in his truncated work, attempted to interpret *inventio* as a rhetorical doctrine to school children. But Sherry's *Tropes and Schemes,* also a school text-book, reveals the more typical sixteenth century conception of rhetoric.

Exceptions can be found, of course. Trapezuntius and Cæsarius, for example, treat all the departments of rhetoric, though more in the manner of mediaeval writers who are bent on preserving antique doctrine than as functional contributors to the needs of a new age. The supposed exception of Talæus is a doubtful one, for, until after Wilson's *Rhetorique* appeared, Talæus' *Rhetoric* contained nothing of invention or disposition. Erasmus would be by far the greatest exception, were it not for the fact that his re-discoveries and contributions are not made under the title of rhetoric, but are sparkled through other works, philological and homiletic, and are, even taken as a whole, an incomplete reconstruction. Moreover, Erasmus, like Talæus and Trapezuntius, wrote in Latin.

Thus, it was Wilson's task to re-assemble, under the head of rhetoric, all the scattered principles which in ancient times had been thought indispensable to the complete art of the orator. He added to this task another, that of making his rhetoric useful to men in his time by writing it in their native language and by adapting it to their needs. Moreover, he wrote his book for the use of all—not merely school boys but, as he says, "For all such as are studious of eloquence"—for men of affairs and of state, for lawyers and preachers. Croll, in his *Introduction to Lyly's Euphues,* observes that Wilson's book "was too advanced for use in schools or even in colleges."[1] It appears, therefore, that Wilson's is the first rhetoric since Quintilian's to give a full and unified treatment of the best of the classical doctrines and to make them useful in the world of practical affairs.

---

[1]Croll, M. W.: *Introduction to Lyly's Euphues,* 1916, p. lxiii.

The concept underlying this complete treatment of his subject is in itself important. Wilson conceives rhetoric as the art of discourse. First, it is art, or method—principles derived from observation of effective speakers, principles for use in real situations. It is not a faculty, nor a science of speaking well, nor a set of static, artificial conventions, but a pragmatic, dynamic body of principles. Thus he imprints upon our subject the hand of Cicero, the orator-statesman-philosopher of the *De Oratore,* not that of Hermagoras or of Aphthonius or of Mosellanus. That imprint it has borne ever since.

Moreover, it is oral discourse, mainly and typically. Rhetoric is recalled from its close association with grammar, poetics, school composition, and letter writing, to its ancient position as, first of all, the art of the orator. It is true that in his first sentence Wilson defines rhetoric very generally—"the art of setting forth matter at large, by utterance of words." We may believe that "utterance" here covers written and spoken language, and we note that written persuasion receives much attention, mainly under the head of deliberative oratory, but also in other sections. But the second sentence begins: "An Orator must be able to speak fully . . ." And the orator is mentioned continuously thereafter. Nor is "orator" to Wilson merely a conventional term for any user of rhetoric, for example, a writer of rhetorical prose or verse, as we find it in some works of the time. The lawyer and the preacher—these are the orators meant, and their problems are much in Wilson's mind. They are reflected, for instance, in the frequent references to methods of keeping audiences awake and sympathetic with the speaker; and the sections on memory and delivery, which conclude the book, have meaning only for the speaker. Rhetoric, then, though it ministers to the needs of writers, is to Wilson, as to the Greeks, the art of the speaker; and so it has remained, consistently in British thought, less so in American.

At this point it is proper to ask why a work so thoroughly conceived as the art of the speaker, and devoting itself so consistently, with one exception, to the problems of speech-making, should be so continuously misrepresented by scholars generally? From Warton to Mair, literary historians and critics have regarded Wilson's *Rhetorique* as a book on style, mainly the style of written prose. Thus Warton, in 1778, called it "The first book or system of criticism in our language,"[2] and

---

[2] Warton, Thomas: *The History of English Poetry* (1778), London, 1870, p. 841.

commentators generally have chiefly regarded it as an antiquarian curiosity in the field of literary history. There is more than one reason for this mistaken view. Wilson's famous blast against "ink horn terms" has linked his work with the study of written composition. The style of the book seems difficult and archaic; the type and spelling of available editions magnify these impressions. Mair frankly confesses that for him the principles set forth make "no more cheerful reading" than in other writers.[3] In sum, we may conjecture that the misrepresentation has arisen from sheer failure to read the whole work with more than perfunctory attention. The fact remains, however, that our first rhetoric in English is a treatise dealing almost wholly with the art of public oral address.

Two or three special doctrines of Wilson's may be selected to exhibit the nature of his contributions to that art. The first concerns the importance of winning attention. On this Wilson is emphatic. Early in the book Wilson says that not only must the orator, early in his speech, "utter his mind in plain words, such as are usually received, and tell it orderly, without going about the bush,"[4] but that he must speak so that "the ears may find much delight . . . for except men find delight, they will not long abide; delight them and win them; weary them and you lose them forever . . . therefore even these ancient preachers, must now and then play the fools in the pulpit . . . or else they are like sometimes to preach to the bare walls . . ."[5] Later, under disposition, he begins by offering the usual classical advice on the best methods of "entrance" or exordium, but goes on to stress such other methods of capturing attention early as novelty ("strange news"), humor ("foolish tales"), the desirability of getting on common ground, oblique, tactful, methods of securing favorable consideration, arousing curiosity, and anticipation.

Closely associated with the unique stress on getting attention, is the even greater emphasis on holding attention. One can hardly exaggerate the importance of this theme in Wilson's book. The very first sentences make rhetoric the art of amplifying—"of speaking largely." There is no doubt that Wilson was more impressed by

[3]Mair, G. H.: *Wilson's Arte of Rhetorique*, Oxford, 1909, p. xxii.
[4]*Ibid.*, p. 2.
[5]*Ibid.*, p. 116.

Cicero's and Quintilian's praise of amplification as the peculiar and distinctive and highest quality of oratory, than by any other one precept in ancient rhetoric. "Among all the figures of Rhetoric," he says, "there is no one that so much helpeth forward an oration . . . as amplification."[6] Erasmus had taken the same view in *De Copia and Ecclesiastes,* and in both books had heavily emphasized amplification. Wilson with even more reason gave it stress in his English Rhetoric for English speakers. For this was the outstanding need of the age— skill in expressing ideas in a language which was just coming into general use—not alone skill in elaborating and enlarging the bare statement, but skill in intensifying, making more striking and effective what one had to say. The result is that throughout his work Wilson takes as his objective "copie"—amplification by examples, by sententious utterances, by variety of expression, by figurative language; to amplification he devotes almost one-fifth of the book, not counting topics closely related though not actually subordinated to this subject; emotional proof itself is made a sub-category of amplification; and Wilson's own style demonstrates what he seeks to teach.

Wilson, therefore, makes getting and holding attention the essential principle of effective oral discourse, and, with emotional proof, into which it rapidly fuses, the grand principle of persuasion. This concept and emphasis, differing from that of all his predecessors, is, of course, largely conditioned by the peculiar needs of the times. And whether right or wrong, whether Wilson has been directly influential or not, the principle persists in rhetorical theory today.

I have elsewhere[7] pointed out the lack of logical and ethical proof in Wilson's *Rhetorique.* In the main, Wilson's distinctions between logic and rhetoric, as those between rhetoric and poetic, and grammar, are so carefully made as to deserve special notice: far more than any previous writer in English, and more than almost all sixteenth century writers in any language, he restored and to some extent improved on the boundaries and lines of demarcation. In this one respect, however, his judgment may be questioned. His omission of ethical proof, whether influential or not, is probably to be deplored. His omission of logical proof—the apparatus of reasoning—which may have resulted from the

---

[6]*Ibid.,* pp. 3, 4.
[7]*Quarterly Journal of Speech, XV*:140.

well established hold with logic had on that topic—is less easily condemned. Modern theorists have long debated the subject, but the
tendency has been, as in Wilson, to leave the logic of proof to logic,
or to the applied logic of argumentation.

To an even greater extent, Wilson's emphasis on emotional proof
marked a new departure and established a modern trend. Though
emotional proof is nominally subordinated to amplification, it tends
to become the chief method of securing and holding attention, and
its image is visible in almost every page of the treatise. The methods
of delighting and moving to pity early in the book are made the
guiding principles of securing attention. Most of the long treatment of
amplification consists of suggestions on arousing varied emotions. And
throughout the rest of the work, the methods of appealing to the
feelings are liberally interspersed. This concentration on emotional
proof is unique in rhetorical theory up to this time. Nor is Wilson
reflecting contemporary practice, for, as Sir Thomas Elyot says, in
respect of forensic eloquence at least, "the sterynge of the affections of
the mynde in this realme was neuer used . . ."[8] And this conception
of persuasion and of oral discourse generally, as, essentially, the
securing of the desired emotional response, has wide acceptance with
us today.

The most famous contribution of Wilson—his strongly expressed
preference for plain, English words as opposed to "ink horn terms"—
strange, Latinate, Italianate, or Gallic importations—should not fail
to remind us of another signal contribution in the field of style: in
an age when rhetoric itself, quite generally, and *elocutio,* almost
without exception, meant adornment and beautifying by figurative
terms, Wilson recalled style to its former status by insisting on plainness,
aptness, and sound composition, as indispensable qualities to be
achieved *before* attention should be paid to the heightening of style
by use of figurative language.

There is significance too in Wilson's conception of composition. To
the ancients, *compositio* had meant word-combination for the sake
of rhythm and modulation; it had included no concepts of composition
in the large, as Baldwin justly observes.[9] But Wilson, under the head

---

[8]Croft, H. H. S., ed.: *The Boke Named the Gouernour,* 1531, by Sir Thomas
Elyot, London, 1883, I, 149.
[9]Baldwin, C. S.: *Ancient Rhetoric and Poetic,* New York, 1924, p. 67.

of composition, gives only brief treatment to the subject of word-joining, and proceeds to discuss such stylistic faults as prolixity, obscurity, crabbedness, pedantry, lack of variety and especially lack of good order and coherence generally. For example, he says, "Some burden their talk with needless copie, and will seem plentiful when they should be short . . . And some use so many interpositions, both in their talk and in their writings, that they make their sayings as dark as hell." Here we have, in embryonic form, a statement of those broad and pervasive qualities of style with which we have become so familiar—unity, coherence and emphasis,—with clearness and brevity added for good measure. This may be the first statement of the principles of composition, in English, as we conceive them today.

Enough has been said of the novelty in Wilson's presentation of rhetorical doctrine to lay the ghost conjured up by Hallam in 1843 and re-evoked by Jebb, Saintsbury, and others: "Wilson embodied rules chiefly from Aristotle, with help from Cicero and Quintilian."[10] In re-uniting, selecting, and adapting the classical principles of public address, Wilson restored the body and, to some extent, reformed the concepts of rhetorical theory. In recalling rhetoric from the museum to the market-place, he not only re-established the ancient conception of rhetoric as the art of the speaker, but, because of his own self-imposed purpose of adapting old doctrines to new times and new needs, he effected far reaching changes which have greatly influenced the theories of public address we hold today.

[10]Hallam, Henry: *Introduction to the Literature of Europe,* London, 1843, II, 209.

ORATORY AND POETRY IN
FENELON'S LITERARY THEORY

WILBUR SAMUEL HOWELL

Princeton University

Fenelon is believed to have written his famous *Dialogues on Eloquence* in the year 1679.[1] At that time he was twenty-eight years old, and his career as priest of the parish of Saint-Sulpice in Paris had just been terminated by his appointment as Superior of the "New Catholics," an institution designed to strengthen the orthodoxy of young women newly converted from Protestantism to Catholicism. Thirty-five years later, his life almost at an end, he composed his *Letter to M. Dacier, Permanent Secretary of the French Academy, on the Occupations of the Academy.* Between these two epochs in his literary career, he distinguished himself in various ways: he served for ten years as preceptor of Louis XIV's grandson, heir presumptive of the throne of France; he became a member of the French Academy and wrote his best-known work, *The Adventures of Telemachus;* he was named Archbishop of Cambrai; and he identified himself with the doctrine of Quietism as advocated by Madame Guyon. This doctrine, with its emphasis upon the annihilation of self and the passivity of the soul as the conditions necessary to achieve a mystical union between man and God, cast a shadow across the last two decades of Fénelon's life. His support of Madame Guyon when she fell from favor at court led to the termination of his productive friendship with

---

[1] C. Revillout: Un problème de chronologie littéraire et philologique: date présumable des 'dialogues' de Fénelon 'sur l'éloquence,' *Revue des Langues Romanes,* XXXIII, 1889, 5-30, 194-216. See also E. Carcassonne: *État présent des travaux sur Fénelon,* Paris, 1939, p. 109.

the great preacher Bossuet, and caused such other misfortunes as his dismissal from his preceptorship in the royal household and the condemnation of one of his works by Pope Innocent XII. These events occurred during the last three or four years of the seventeenth century. Thereafter Fénelon lived at Cambrai and devoted himself to his duties as Archbishop and his pursuits as writer.

His *Letter to the Academy* was first published at Paris in 1716, the year after his death, and it achieved immediate recognition in intellectual circles. At Amsterdam in 1717 it was printed in company with the *Dialogues on Eloquence,* which up to that moment had lain in manuscript.[2] Upon these two works Fénelon's reputation in the field of aesthetics and rhetorical theory pretty largely depends.[3] At no place in the whole body of his writings is oratory analyzed with the care and brilliance that he bestows upon it in the *Dialogues,* where he also has things to say about historical and philosophical composition, poetry, music, dancing, painting, and architecture. The *Letter to the Academy* is concerned with much the same subject matter. It begins by recommending that the Academy complete its dictionary of the French language. It then proposes a grammar and a rhetoric as projects of immediate concern. Next it furnishes a detailed plan for treatises on poetics, tragedy, comedy, and historical writing. It concludes with a contribution to the controversy between ancients and moderns, and with an indication that Fénelon had not lost his earlier preference for Greek architecture as against Gothic.

The *Letter to the Academy* has received more praise than have the *Dialogues,* no doubt because the predominance of aesthetic interests in the former turned out to be more congenial to subsequent taste than did the predominance of rhetorical interests in the latter. But it should be emphasized that Fénelon himself did not in either of these works take the part of the aesthetic interests against the rhetorical. He makes no invidious assumptions about the superiority of poetry to oratory. Nor does he give more care to one than to the other, as if they were of unequal value and deserved unequal kinds of intellectual effort from the theorist who chose to write upon both. He does not see them as so

---

[2] A. Cherel: *Fénelon au XVIIIe Siècle en France (1715-1820),* Paris, 1917, p. 269.
[3] For an enumeration of other works by Fénelon on these subjects, see Carcassonne: *op. cit.,* pp. 73-74.

disparate in quality that oratory has to be patronized for claiming a persuasive function and a concern for a practical method, whereas poetry has to be exalted for its capacity to give delight by means veiled in the higher mysteries of genius. He does not account for the differences between the oration and the poem by postulating that they stand in relation to each other in the kingdom of letters as commoner stands to aristocrat in the monarchy of the Bourbons. The fact is, Fénelon sees oratory and poetry as instruments of similar value in human affairs. But he is aware that there are differences between them, and he devotes productive attention to the formulation of these differences.

In this essay I should like to state what Fénelon's conception of these differences is. I shall not attempt to handle my subject in terms of everything Fénelon had to say upon all matters pertaining to critical and aesthetic theory. My discussion instead will be limited to his analysis of oratory and poetry in the *Dialogues* and the *Letter to the Academy*.[4] These two works, as I have already indicated, represent in concentrated form the essential principles of this aspect of his thinking. This aspect is worthy of attention for three reasons. First, it illustrates a specific application of the views of Plato, Cicero, and St. Augustine to the problems of the seventeenth century. Secondly, it raises issues similar to those involved in the modern question of the relations between propaganda and art. Thirdly, it indicates the frustrations that attend even the most promising distinctions between the rhetorical and the poetic branches of literature.

The basic principle in Fénelon's conception of the relations between oratory and poetry is that these two arts, in common with all the others, are persuasive in function. By this he means that the various arts cannot be logically grouped to one side or the other of a dividing line between that which gives pleasure and that which influences thought and action. His belief is that, if there seems to be a class of artistic works devoted wholly to the giving of pleasure, the critic should deal with it, not as something fundamentally unpersuasive, but as a case of concealed persuasion. He insists, in short, that all works of art

---

[4]For other studies bearing upon Fénelon's theory of aesthetics, criticism, and rhetoric, see F. Brun: *Fénelon critique d'art*, Meulan, 1899; P. Bastier: *Fénelon. Critique d'art*, Paris, 1903; G. Landolf: *Esthétique de Fénelon*, Zurich, 1914; E. B. O. Borgerhoff: *The Freedom of French Classicism*, Princeton, 1950, pp. 220-234.

act to influence the conduct of mankind, pleasure being an intermediate aim, a way station on the road to ultimate persuasiveness.

This view is applied to oratory early in the *Dialogues on Eloquence.*
One of the spokesmen, who is called *A,* and whose importance suggests
that he expresses Fénelon's own ideas, demands of another spokesman,
B, the definition of eloquence. *B* replies that eloquence is the art of
speaking well. *A* wonders whether men speak simply to speak well,
whether talk has no design except that of achieving the status of refinement. This observation leads *B* to declare that men speak in order
to please and in order to persuade. Thus are two rival aims of oratory
brought into focus, the former being no doubt intended by Fénelon
to represent the prevailing conception of rhetoric as derived from the
teachings of Peter Ramus,[5] while the latter is the conception of Fénelon
himself. What *A* says in reply to *B* is not only a denial that these two
aims are in any final sense mutually exclusive, but also a fresh approach
to the pleasure-persuasion dichotomy in artistic theory. *A* remarks at
once that a careful distinction should be made between "to please"
and "to persuade." Then he states how orators proceed in practice:

> They speak to persuade—that is what they always do. They also
> speak to please—that is merely what they too often do. But when
> they seek to please, they have another, a more distant, aim, which is
> nevertheless the principal one. The good man seeks to please only
> that he may urge justice and the other virtues by making them
> attractive. He who seeks his own interest, his reputation, his for-
> tune, dreams of pleasing only that he may gain the bow and
> esteem of men able to satisfy his greed or his ambition. Thus, even
> his case can be reduced like that of the good man to persuasion
> as the single aim which a speaker has; for the self-interested man
> wishes to please in order to flatter, and he flatters in order to incul-
> cate that which suits his interest.[6]

---

[5]See below, sec. V. The relation between Fénelon's *Dialogues on Eloquence* and
the dialectical and rhetorical doctrines of Peter Ramus is discussed at some length
in the present author's *Fénelon's Dialogues on Eloquence A Translation with an
Introduction and Notes,* Princeton: Princeton University Press, 1951. A brief
summary of that relation appears in the concluding section of this paper.

[6]*Oeuvres de Fénélon,* ed. J. -E. -A. Gosselin and A. -P. -P. Caron, Versailles and
Paris, 1820-1830, XXI, 9. All quotations from the *Dialogues on Eloquence* and
the *Letter to the Academy* in this paper are referred to this edition, the translations being by the present author.

Later in the *Dialogues, A* reverts once more to the thesis that pleasure is an effect to be striven for only because it lies athwart the road
to persuasion. He demands of *C,* Fénelon's third character, whether
anything in a discourse can have any function except that of influencing the hearer. *C* replies that certain things in discourse will contribute
to the hearer's pleasure. *A* observes:

> Let us distinguish, if you will. That which serves to please in order
> to persuade is good. Solid and well-expounded proofs are unques-
> tionably pleasing; the lively and natural movements of the speaker
> have much charm; faithful and animated portraitures enchant.
> Thus the three things which we make essential to eloquence give
> pleasure; but they are not limited to this effect. It is a question of
> knowing whether we shall approve of thoughts and expressions
> which have no purpose but to please, and which cannot in any
> way have a more substantial purpose. These I call conceits. Of
> course, you are always to keep well in mind, if you will, that I
> praise in discourse all the pleasing traits which minister to persua-
> sion; and that I reject only those wherein the author, full of self-
> admiration, has sought to exhibit himself and to amuse the listeners
> with his wit, rather than to absorb them utterly in his subject.[7]

Oratory in Fénelon's scheme is not the only art that has persuasion
as its principal function and pleasure as an intermediate effect. He
puts poetry and the other fine arts in the same class. In the *Dialogues*
C observes: "But if true orators are poets, it seems to me that poets
are also orators, because poetry is by rights persuasive." And *A* replies:
"Unquestionably they both have the same end."[8] These statements are
made in connection with Fénelon's attempt to differentiate poetry
from oratory, and later we shall see what that differentiation amounts
to. Just now, however, we need perhaps only to notice that, whatever
differences he has in mind, he insists at least upon the complete identity
of these two arts in respect to persuasiveness. In the *Letter to the Academy* he attributes the same function to the other fine arts, emphasizing
again that pleasure is an auxiliary effect:

---

[7]*Ibid.,* p. 50. Lines 26-27 read, "je ne rejette que celles où l'orateur. . . ." The
first Paris edition of the *Dialogues,* Paris, 1718, p. 102, lines 13-14, reads, however, "je ne rejette que celles où l'Auteur. . . ." At this particular point the
translation follows the first Paris edition, which is ordinarily regarded as the most
authoritative of the texts of the *Dialogues.*
[8]*Ibid.,* p. 49.

Plato does not permit in his republic any music with the effem-
inate pitch of the Lydian style. The Lacedaemonians excluded from
their republic all the highly complicated instruments which were
able to weaken the spirit. Harmony which goes only so far as to
flatter the ear is merely an amusement of weak and idle folk. It is
unworthy of a well-governed republic. It is good only so far as the
sounds of it agree with the sense of the words, and the words of it
inspire virtuous sentiments. Painting, sculpture, and the other fine
arts, ought to have the same end. Without question eloquence
ought to enter into the same design. Pleasure ought to be mingled
in it only to form a counterbalance against evil passions and to
make virtue attractive.[9]

The words just quoted echo a passage in the *Dialogues* upon the
subservience of pleasure to persuasiveness in ancient art. In the course
of a panegyric upon the serious intent of the art of the early Greeks
and Hebrews, *A* remarks:

All the arts which consist in melodious sounds, or in movements
of the body, or in the use of language—in a word, music, dancing,
eloquence, poetry—were devised only to express the passions and
to inspire them in the very act of expressing them. By such means
as these, mankind wished to impress great thoughts upon the
human soul and to bring to men lively and striking pictures of
the beauty of virtue and the ugliness of evil. Thus all these arts
appeared to be for pleasure, but were in reality among the ancients
a part of their deepest striving for morality and religion.[10]

Thus does Fénelon admit pleasure and persuasion into artistic theory
without making these effects mutually exclusive or using them as keys
to the difference between the fine and the practical arts. He recognizes,
however, that throughout the entire domain of art, practical as well as
fine, pleasure may receive more emphasis than persuasion, even though
when this happens the effect must still be counted persuasive in the
final analysis. In fact, one of his critical principles is that pathologies
in the world of art appear as the product of a persuasive intention
which is limited on the one hand to the promotion of the artist's personal fortunes and on the other to the excessive exploitation of the
spectator's fondness for pleasure. This principle receives some develop-

---

[9]*Ibid.,* pp. 176-177.
[10]*Ibid.,* p. 18.

ment in the *Dialogues* and the *Letter to the Academy*. I should like to examine it now in order to show that it underlies Fénelon's distinction between health and disease in art rather than his distinction between the poetical and the rhetorical branches of literature.

Interpreted in the broadest sense, Fénelon's view of good and bad art, whether oratorical or poetic, stresses the concern of the artist for the interests of mankind as opposed to the interests of himself. If someone were to object that this principle belongs more to the realm of morality than to aesthetics, Fénelon would doubtless answer by denying the desirability or possibility of separating these two realms. Indeed, this phase of his critical thinking derives special support from the theological doctrine of Quietism, which, as I indicated earlier, strives for the annihilation of self as one condition of spiritual perfection. Good art in Fénelon's sense of the term is that which inspires men in the quest for wisdom, good laws, justice, and individual betterment, whereas bad art inspires men to favor their flatterers, to follow their private inclinations, to give rewards on the basis of something less than merit, or to seek personal power, wealth, reputation, at no matter what expense. It is in this latter kind of art where pleasure tends to be the most visible of the possible effects, seeming at times to be the artist's only aim, and at other times to be the aim which but partly masks his desire for personal advancement.

Many passages in the *Dialogues* and the *Letter to the Academy* illustrate this principle. For example, when *A* is mentioning the degeneracy which followed the period of Athenian rule in ancient Greece, he characterizes it as one wherein "pleasure, which ought only to be the means to inculcate wisdom, usurped the place of wisdom herself."[11] Thus is the concept of social decadence linked with the concept of art as mere diversion. The same spokesman had earlier borrowed the Socratic manner and the Platonic doctrine to get *B* to consent to banish from the ideal republic "any of the sciences or any of the arts which serve only for pleasure, for amusement, and for curiosity."[12] And why are they to be banished? Because, as *B* finally concedes, they are not merely indifferent to the struggle between good and evil, but actually are on the side of evil. His words are:

---

[11]*Ibid.*, p. 19.
[12]*Ibid.*, p. 16.

If anything can assist the cause of virtue, the identification of virtue with pleasure can do so. On the contrary, when you separate them, you strongly invite men to abandon virtue. Besides, everything that pleases without instructing beguiles and softens merely.[13]

But the principle is not developed only in terms of abstract moral precepts. It is made highly concrete in its application to oratory. *A's* unfavorable opinion of Isocrates, a recurrent theme of the *Dialogues,* shows that orator to typify an art devoted, not to national ends, but to self-exhibition, with ostentatious ornaments the artist's means, and amusement his principal, almost his only goal.[14] Again, a concern for his own fortune, as distinguished from the fate of the Roman republic, is alleged by the same spokesman to be a visible blemish in the works of the youthful Cicero.[15] *A* also remarks that a selfish concern vitiates Pliny's eulogy of Trajan.[16] And in the course of constructing his own theory of oratory, he lays great stress upon the necessity for complete disinterestedness on the part of a speaker both as a matter of good morality and good oratorical strategy.[17]

The issue of preoccupation with self as opposed to preoccupation with the interests of mankind has the same application to poetry as to oratory. *A* cites the *Aeneid* as being open to the charge, if one cared to press it, of showing somewhat more interest in flattering Augustus and his family, and thus in advancing Virgil's own fortune, than in giving the Roman people an unmixed image of their national destiny.[18] This charge against Virgil *A* does not regard seriously. On the contrary, he emphasizes in the same breath that the *Aeneid* is an example of high poetic excellence. But the charge, as a possible line of attack upon Virgil, embodies a precise principle by which criticism may separate good poetry from bad, and that principle is given a general formulation by Fénelon himself in the following words from the *Letter to the Academy*:

Just in the same degree as one ought to despise bad poets, so ought

---

[13]*Ibid.,* pp. 19-20.
[14]*Ibid.,* pp. 10-13, 74-76.
[15]*Ibid.,* pp. 45-46.
[16]*Ibid.,* p. 25.
[17]*Ibid.,* pp. 27-41.
[18]*Ibid.,* p. 26.

one to admire and cherish a great poet, who does not make
poetry into a play of wit to attract unto himself a vainglory, but
uses it to transport men in favor of wisdom, virtue, and religion.[19]

Fénelon's distinction between good and bad art rests upon the teachings of Plato and St. Augustine. He leaves no doubt upon this score,
not only because he probably thought it simple honesty to acknowledge
his philosophic debts, but also perhaps to suggest that his theory cut
across the boundaries between paganism and Christianity, and thus
could not be called merely parochial. At any rate, he has *A* emphasize
that one does not have to be a Christian to believe in the self-forget-
fulness of the artist as the precondition of great art, inasmuch as Socrates and Plato had taken the same position.[20] *A* documents this statement with a lengthy analysis of Plato's *Gorgias* and a shorter reference
to the *Phœdrus*.[21] As for St. Augustine, who figures preponderantly in
the Third Dialogue by virtue of his authority in the field of sacred rhetoric, he too is used to support Fénelon's view that the aesthetic stature
of a work of art is determined by the stature of its selflessness of purpose. In a passage in the First Dialogue made up of borrowings from
two separate chapters of St. Augustine's *De Doctrina Christiana, A*
declares:

> For what do a man's beautiful speeches serve, if fine as they are
> they contribute no benefit whatever to the public? Words are
> made for men, as St. Augustine says, and not men for words.[22]

Thus far we have seen that Fénelon does not use the distinction between pleasure and persuasiveness as a means of separating poetry from
oratory. He uses it instead to show that there is a kind of bad art
devoted seemingly to pleasure but actually to the inculcation of attitudes which suit the artist's material interests. He sees poetry and oratory as alike persuasive in their healthy forms. He sees pleasure as
normally common to both in the sense that this effect accompanies
persuasion. He sees good oratory and good poetry as kinds of discourse which contribute primarily, and in the first instance, to the

---

[19]*Ibid.*, p. 186.
[20]*Ibid.*, p. 30.
[21]*Ibid.*, pp. 30-37.
[22]*Ibid.*, p. 23. See *De Doctrina Christiana,* 4. 10. 24, and 4. 28. 61.

public benefit. What, then, is his distinction between the rhetorical and the poetic branches of literature?

His answer to this question is that oratory is almost poetry. This is the simplest way to state his distinction. This is also the way he himself follows when he comes in the *Dialogues* to the problem of maintaining on the one hand that poetry as well as oratory is persuasive and on the other that the well-established habit of thinking these two arts to be somehow different must receive attention in criticism. Let us hear what he says on this matter.

The conversation in the Second Dialogue has paused upon the question of the difference between the genuine and the false ornament of style. *A* has been insisting that persuasion is the end of oratory, and that oratory deserves to be called eloquence only when it really succeeds in persuading men to virtue. Now persuasion, *A* explains, requires that discourse prove something and excite strong feelings towards what it proves.[23] To prove, he goes on, is to convince the auditor that a proposition is true. The method by which this is done is characterized by exactness, dryness, bareness; by an adherence to the forms of good argument; by a sense of order similar to that followed in geometry; and by a speculativeness similar to that found in metaphysics.[24] To excite strong feelings is to be forced to do two things beyond proof: to portray and to strike. "To portray is not only to describe things," remarks *A*, "but to represent their surrounding features in so lively and so concrete a way that the listener imagines himself almost seeing them."[25] The term "to strike" is defined later, after *A* has identified it with "movement" as distinguished from "proof" and "portraiture."[26] "Movement" turns out to be not only the stylistic variation of the speech, as the speaker's linguistic patterns move in accordance with his inner patterns of thought and emotion, but also the physical swing of speaking, as the speaker's voice and body respond to his mind and will.[27]

Of these three elements in persuasive discourse or eloquence, portraiture is of central importance in persuasion; and it is thus a common

---

[23]*Ibid.*, pp. 42, 44, 47.

[24]*Ibid.*, pp. 43-44.

[25]*Ibid.*, p. 47.

[26]*Ibid.*, p. 50.

[27]*Ibid.*, pp. 51-61.

feature of the oration and the poem. *A* sees a difference in degree, however, between the portraiture produced by the orator and that produced by the poet. Upon this difference in degree he founds his distinction between the two arts. To illustrate portraiture at its best, he points to Virgil's account of the death of Dido. Then he says:

> I have given you an example drawn from a poet, in order to make you better understand the matter; for portraiture is still more lively and stronger among the poets than among the orators. Poetry differs from simple eloquence only in this: that she paints with ecstasy and with bolder strokes. Prose has its paintings, albeit more moderated. Without them one cannot heat the imagination of a listener or arouse his passions.[28]

Versification, *A* proceeds at once to remark, has nothing to do with the question of distinguishing the poetical from the non-poetical discourse. In either form, genuine effectiveness is the product of portraiture. "If one does not have this genius to portray," insists Fénelon's chief spokesman, "Never can one impress things upon the soul of the listener—all is dry, flat, boring."[29] A moment later the whole matter is summed up in this exchange between *A* and *C:*

> *A:* The entire difference [between oratory and poetry] consists in that which I have set forth to you. Over and above orators, poets have ecstasy, and this makes them still more elevated, more lively, and more daring in their utterances. You will remember what I told you yesterday from Cicero?
> *C:* What! Is it . . . ?
> *A:* That the orator ought almost to have the diction of the poet. That "almost" tells the whole story.[30]

Thus poetry and oratory in Fénelon's basic view turn out to have persuasion as their end and portraiture as a common means, the distinction between them being that portraiture in poetry has about it an ecstasy, a heat of genius, not found in oratory. In short, as I suggested before, oratory is almost but not quite poetry. Fénelon himself points out in the passage last quoted that the "almost" comes from Cicero. To be more precise, it comes from *De Oratore* 1. 28. 128, where ora-

---

[28]*Ibid.,* p. 48.
[29]*Ibid.,* p. 49.
[30]*Ibid.,* pp. 49-50.

tory, comprehensively defined, is said to demand not only a dialectician's acuteness, a philosopher's knowledge, a lawyer's memory, a tragedian's voice, and an accomplished actor's gesture, but also a diction almost that of the poet.

We might in passing note the relations established by Fénelon among the other traditional kinds of discourse. He strongly intimates that philosophical discourse or learned writing in the field of the scientific disciplines differs from oratory as proof isolated from portraiture and movement differs from proof combined with these things.[31] He also says in effect that historical writing differs from poetry as a moderated and impartial portrait of events and personalities differs from a bolder, more inspired, portrait.[32] But it is only against the background of his concept of eloquence that these distinctions have their full meaning. According to that concept, any discourse which actually succeeds in improving men deserves alone to be called eloquent; and no discourse can have that effect without portraiture. Hence poetry, which is in essence inspired portraiture, becomes eloquent when it acts to make men more perfect. Hence history, which is moderated and impartial portraiture, becomes eloquent when it produces the selfsame result. Hence oratory, which combines proof and movement with a portraiture almost poetic, becomes eloquent when it achieves no different goal. Of the four conventional types of discourse, only philosophy, which has no concern with image-making as a necessity of its own style, fails to achieve the full stature of eloquence. But its emphasis upon conviction as effect and proof as means gives it a primary concern for truth; and thus, when it succeeds in presenting things as they are, it induces knowledge, which is not least among the preconditions of virtue.

Three aspects of Fénelon's theory of the relations between oratory and poetry call for attention by way of conclusion.

First of all, his insistence upon the persuasiveness of oratory is in line not only with the best classical and modern emphasis but also with the tendency of the late seventeenth century to abandon the rhetorical teachings of Peter Ramus. At the time when Fénelon wrote the *Dialogues on Eloquence,* the influence of Ramus upon logical and rhe-

---

[31]*Ibid.,* pp. 43-46.
[32]*Ibid.,* pp. 47-48, 228-229, 232-233.

torical theory in France (and in England) was still pronounced, despite the fact that Ramus had died as long before as 1572. One of Ramus' key doctrines was that one art could not claim any function or subject matter belonging to another art. Accordingly, if logic professed to offer to writers and speakers the theory of invention and arrangement, and thus to provide the means of convincing audiences, rhetoric must abandon these subjects and confine herself to other aspects of composition. As a consequence of this doctrine, Ramus' colleague, Talaeus, created a rhetoric limited to style and delivery, and copiously elaborated in terms of all the figures of speech and all the ornamental contrivances of style. This sort of rhetoric, with its emphasis upon antithesis, paradox, word-play, conceit, and epigram, came to have the reputation of being exclusively devoted to amusement. Against the theory that men spoke only to give pleasure, and that they used as means only the conceits of style, Fénelon leveled his heaviest guns. To some extent he also leveled his guns against Ramus' theory that a work on rhetoric could include nothing pertaining to logic or the other liberal arts, although Fénelon's contemporary, Antoine Arnauld, had effectively attacked this aspect of Ramus' doctrine in the famous *Port Royal Logic,* published seventeen years before Fénelon wrote the *Dialogues.* In Fénelon's emphasis that oratory is primarily an instrument of persuasion, and that the orator is an honored partner of logician and historian in the enterprise of learning and communication, we see a wholesome restoration of Ciceronian doctrine as well as an imaginative anticipation of modern interests.

The same reminiscence of a classical attitude, the same foretaste of a modern conviction, is visible in a second aspect of Fénelon's theory of the relations between oratory and poetry. This aspect emerges in his insistence that delight is the intermediate and contributory, persuasiveness the ultimate, object of both of these arts. So far as poetical theory is concerned, Fénelon is here suggesting the impossibility of divorcing expression from communication or aesthetics from rhetoric and logic. He is assuming instead that man's response to a work of art springs from a complex of adjustments, some of which are aesthetic, others, intellectual. He sees no point in treating such a response as if one could unerringly separate its pleasurable from its intellectual phases. No doubt he felt that knowledge of either phase by itself would not be the same as knowledge of both phases in all their complicated interactions. At any rate, at one point in the *Dialogues* he has *C* observe: "As for myself, I wish to know whether things are true before I find them beautiful."[33] If this statement seems to give priority to logic above aesthetics in an act of literary evaluation, Fénelon might have explained his real intention by saying that, in an age which gave the latter more emphasis than the former, counterexaggeration was the approved way to restore the balance between the two.

The third aspect of Fénelon's distinction between oratory and poetry involves a complication which I did not mention earlier for fear of emphasizing it more than our author does. This complication appears both before and after the passages in which he says that poetry differs from oratory only in the superior vividness of its portraiture. There is no doubt that he is convinced of the validity of this major difference; but he seems to realize that it does not completely exhaust the subject. Thus he introduces two terms which suggest that poetical and oratorical portraiture differ not so much in degree as in kind. These two terms are "imitation" and "fiction." In the *Dialogues,* as *A* is comparing a historian's portrait of the death of Dido with that in the *Aeneid,* he says of the latter: "There one sees the power of imitation and of portraiture."[34] Later, after he has dismissed versification from the list of qualities that poetry must have, *A* remarks: "In the last analysis, poetry is nothing but a lively fiction which portrays nature."[35] In the *Letter to the Academy,* speaking in his own person, Fénelon declares: "Poetry is without doubt an imitation and a portraiture."[36] These passages make it clear that, although Fénelon is insisting upon portraiture as an element in poetry, he half doubts whether oratorical and poetic portraiture differ only in degree, and in his hesitancy he resorts to the terms "imitation" and "fiction," perhaps to satisfy his subconscious realization that poetry, at least in its epic, dramatic, and narrative forms, portrays situations different from those handled in oratory and history. Had he gone on to show that portraiture in poetry is usually the lifelike representation of an imagined situation, whereas portraiture in oratory and history is usually the lifelike representation

---

[33] *Ibid.,* p. 7.
[34] *Ibid.,* p. 48.
[35] *Ibid.,* p. 49.
[36] *Ibid.,* p. 198.

of a real situation, he would have been able to preserve his emphasis upon portraiture as an essential characteristic of these three literary forms, and at the same time to preserve his emphasis upon fiction and imitation as the distinguishing conditions of portraiture in poetry.

Without some recognition of the difference between actual and imagined situations, it is hard to see how Fénelon's account of the difference between oratory and poetry can explain distinctions taken for granted by the literary critic on the one hand and the rhetorical and historical critic on the other. The literary critic, speaking of portraiture in a play, a novel, or a narrative poem, uses as a matter of course the machinery of oppositions between the romantic and realistic, the naturalistic and symbolic, the allegorical and non-allegorical, the classical and Gothic, to indicate changing fashions in poetic portraiture. The theory that oratory and history differ from poetry only as the moderated portrait differs from the inspired appears to suggest that the same machinery and the same fashions apply to rhetorical and historical criticism. But do they? Except in a pejorative sense, is there a romantic as opposed to a realistic oratory or history? Is there a school of symbolist and another school of naturalist orators and historians? Hardly. And this answer suggests that some concepts applicable to poetry are not applicable to oratory and history, despite Fénelon's apparent indication to the contrary in the basic phase of his distinction between the oration and the poem.

JOHN WARD AND HIS RHETORIC

DOUGLAS EHNINGER

University of Florida

I. INTRODUCTION

WHEN JOHN WARD died in October 1758, he left among his papers "a fair copy" of a manuscript bearing the title *A System of Oratory.*[1] This treatise, a careful revision of the lectures on rhetoric which for thirty-eight years he had delivered at Gresham College in London, is briefly summarized in studies by Sandford, Harding, and Guthrie.[2] It has not, however, been made the subject for extended investigation, nor has anyone inquired closely concerning its author. By assembling data, much of which is now widely scattered and in certain instances not easily available, I shall in this paper attempt to formulate a somewhat more complete picture of the man and his rhetoric.

II. THE MAN

A. Early Life and Education

John Ward was born at London in April, 1679, the son of a dis-

---

[1]Published under the same title in two volumes (London, 1759). References to the *System* are to lecture and page.

[2]Sandford, William P.: *English Theories of Public Address, 1530-1828,* Columbus, Ohio, 1938, pp. 107-10. Harding, Harold F.: English Rhetorical Theory, 1750-1800, Ph.D. Dissertation, Cornell University, 1937, pp. 40-8 and ff. Guthrie, Warren A.: The Development of Rhetorical Theory in America, 1635-1850, *SM, XIV*:44-7, 1947. Ward's treatment of ethical proof is analyzed in Sattler, William M.: Conceptions of *Ethos in Rhetoric,* Ph.D. Dissertation, Northwestern University, 1941, p. 301 ff., and his treatment of pathetic proof in Lee, Irving J.: A Study of Emotional Appeal in Rhetorical Theory, With Special Reference to Invention, Arrangement, and Style, Ph.D. Dissertation, Northwestern University, 1939, p. 214 ff.

senting clergyman of the same name, and one of the younger of a family of fourteen children.[3] Denied an extensive formal education because of religious restrictions and limited financial means, he early found employment as a clerk in the Navy Office. Here, however, the routine proved little to his liking, and it was soon evident that deep interests in literature and history inclined him toward a life of scholarship.[4]

During leisure hours Ward prosecuted with great "eagerness" and "diligence" a private course of studies under John Ker, master of a nonconformist academy at Bethnal Green.[5] If, as may be supposed, he followed more or less closely the syllabus prescribed for students regularly enrolled at the academy, his training was heavily classical, but also included an introduction to modern writers, and especially to the great French and Dutch scholars of the seventeenth century.[6]

It was very probably under Ker's direction that Ward first gave serious attention to the rhetorical treatises of Vossius, Cicero, and Aristotle, as well as to those works in history and moral philosophy which helped to shape his views on the function of oratory. It is also probable that he profited in less tangible ways from his association with

---

[3] J. T.: Sketch of the Life and Writings of Dr. Ward, *Universal Theological Magazine and Impartial Review,* I:232-3, 1804; Chalmers, Alexander: *The General Biographical Dictionary,* London, 1812-7, XXXI, 123; Nichols, John: *Literary Anecdotes of the Eighteenth Century,* London, 1812-6, V, 517-8.

[4] Nichols: *op. cit.,* V, 518.

[5] Chalmers: *op. cit.,* XXXI, 124.

[6] From a letter published by Samuel Palmer, who had been one of Ker's pupils, we have, fortunately, a rather complete list of the books used at Bethnal Green. For logic Heereboord was read; for metaphysics, Fromenius' *Synopsis,* with additional work in Baronius, Suarez, and Colbert. Heereboord again constituted the textbook in ethics; More, Cicero's *De Officiis,* Epictetus, Arian, Simplicius, Pufendorf, and the *Proverbs* of Solomon also being recommended. Natural philosophy was read principally from Le Clerc, though Aristotle, Descartes, Colbert, and Stair received some attention. In addition, pupils were encouraged to do considerable browsing in the Greek and Roman historians, orators, and poets, in the Greek testament, and in works on geography and practical divinity. During the last year of the four year course time was set apart to introduce rhetoric, Vossius' *Elementa* and *Constitutio,* Aristotle, and the *De Oratore* being read. See Palmer, Samuel: *A Defence of the Dissenters' Education in Their Private Academies* . . ., London, 1703. The greater portion of this letter is quoted in McLachlan, Herbert: *English Education Under the Test Acts.* Being the History of Nonconformist Academies, 1662-1820, Manchester, 1931, pp. 87-94.

Ker, who was both a skilled tutor and a liberal in theology and pedagogy.[7]

Ward's reading under Ker appears to have terminated in the summer of 1710. At that time he resigned from the Navy Office and opened a children's school in Tenter Alley, Moorfields. This school, which he kept for exactly a decade, not only provided the young scholar with a more agreeable mode of earning a living but supplied valuable classroom experience which he later put to use in editing grammar school textbooks.[8]

Continued studies were stimulated by Ward's election in 1712 to a society of young "gentlemen, divines, and lawyers" who for many years met regularly to discuss their researches in civil, natural, and international law, and to read together such works as the *Corpus Juris Civilis*, Grotius' *De Jure Belli ac Pacis*, Pufendorf's *De Officio Hominis et Civis*, and Cicero's *De Officiis*.[9]

B. The Gresham Professorship

On September 1, 1720 Ward, then forty-one years old, was appointed Professor of Rhetoric at Gresham College, a position which he held for the remainder of his life and in which he developed the lectures comprising the *System*.[10]

Gresham College was not of the common cut of eighteenth-century academic institutions. Founded through a bequest in the will of the fabulously wealthy Elizabethan merchant-statesman, Sir Thomas Gresham, it served as a sort of adult education center "for the gratuitous instruction of all who chose to come and attend the lectures."[11] After a brilliant beginning, in which for many years the institution attained "to much of the usefulness contemplated by the founder,"[12] and gained added lustre as the home of the Royal Society, it was by 1720

---

[7]See McLachlan: *op. cit.*, pp. 85-6.

[8]Nichols: *op. cit.*, V, 510.

[9]*Ibid.*, J. T., *op. cit.*, p. 233.

[10]*Ibid.*, V, 519. He delivered his inaugural oration on October 28. *Ibid.*

[11]On the founding and early history of Gresham College see especially Burgon, William: *The Life and Times of Sir Thomas Gresham,* London, 1839, II, 436-40 and ff.; Ward, John: *The Lives of the Professors of Gresham College,* London, 1740, Preface.

[12]Anon.: *Life of Gresham,* London, 1844, p. 222.

in a state of scholarly decadence and acute financial embarrassment.[13] Criticized as early as 1647 for their laxness and incompetence,[14] the Gresham professors were after 1700 often completely unqualified, and in a number of instances were "broken down tradesmen, or connexions, or dependents" of the trustees.[15]

It may, in fact, be this general decadence of the college which explains Ward's election to its faculty. By 1720 he had gained only limited recognition as a scholar, and of his few published works only one bore even remotely on the subject of rhetoric.[16] Certainly candidates with superior qualifications would have been reluctant to present themselves for a professorship in an institution which was held in contempt by the public and in which the remuneration was not only small but exceedingly irregular.[17]

We can only speculate as to whether Ward was more punctilious than some of his colleagues in discharging his academic duties. He was by nature conscientious and industrious: and his lectures most carefully written and edited, underwent several revisions. On the other hand, he found abundant time to hold positions of responsibility in learned societies, to carry on a heavy correspondence, and to write extensively about matters other than rhetoric. It is almost certainly to these extra-curricular pursuits rather than to his work as a rhetorician that he owed the very considerable reputation which he enjoyed among his contemporaries.

C. Scholarly and Literary Activities

Three years after his appointment to the Gresham professorship Ward was elected (November 30, 1723) a member of the Royal

---

[13]Ward: *Lives of the Professors,* pp. xvi-xviii; Maitland, George: *The History of London,* London, 1739, II, 803-13.

[14]See the anonymous quarto tract of eight pages, *Sir Thomas Gresham, His Ghost,* London, 1647, and the pamphlet *An Account of the Rise, Foundation, Progress, and Present State of Gresham College . . .,* London, 1707. Cf. Burgon: *op. cit.,* II, Appendix XXX, 525-6.

[15]Anon.: *Life of Gresham,* p. 225.

[16]*De Ordine, Sive de Venusta et Eleganti tum Vocabulorum, tum Membrorum Sententiae Collocatione,* 1712.

[17]Salaries of the Gresham professors were in arrears in 1701, 1706, 1719, and 1730, being eight years behind at the last date. Burgon: *op. cit.,* II, Appendix XXX, 521; Maitland: *op. cit.,* II, 813; *Notes and Queries,* CLIX, 1930, 272.

Society, then under the distinguished presidency of Sir Isaac Newton.[18] This was followed a little over a decade later (February 1735) by induction into the Society of Antiquaries, and, during the same year, into the Society for the Encouragement of Learning.[19] As time passed Ward's status in these bodies grew. Frequently a member of the Committee of the Society for the Encouragement of Learning, he was in 1747 made a Director of the Society of Antiquaries and in 1753 its Vice President. A year earlier (1752) he had been chosen Vice President of the Royal Society.[20]

The papers communicated by Ward to the Royal and Antiquarian Societies number nearly thirty.[21] For the most part, they deal with British antiquities, though occasionally with Roman archeology or ancient social customs. Ward's particular forte as an antiquarian appears to have been the deciphering and dating of inscriptions. To this task he brought a thorough knowledge of the classical languages and cultures, and while some of his assumptions may strike the reader as naive, nearly all of the essays make careful use of the available evidence and are closely reasoned.[21]

Though in themselves numerous, these papers represent but a fraction of Ward's writings. In addition to a long catalogue of minor works,[22] and of prefaces,[23] and translations,[24] he produced, besides the

---

[18]Nichols: *op. cit.*, V, 519.

[19]*Ibid.*, V, 521 and II, 90; Chalmers: *op. cit.*, XXXI, 125.

[20]Nangle, Benjamin C.: *The Monthly Review, First Series, 1749-1789*. Indexes of Contributors and Articles, Oxford, 1934, pp. 45-6.

[21]See *Philosophical Transactions*, XXXVI-XLIX, 1730-56, and *Vetusta Monumenta*, I, 1717 ff. Additional papers, probably unpublished, are indexed in Church, A. H.: *The Royal Society. Some Account of the "Classified Papers" in the Archives. With an Index of Authors*, Oxford, 1907.

[22]In all I have noted more than forty original works by Ward—exclusive of reviews—and this list is obviously not complete. Typical of his lesser efforts are "De Asse et Partibus Ejus Commentarius" (1719), reprinted in *Monumenta Vetustatis Kempiana*, 1720; "Essay on Peutinger's Table So Far as It Relates to Britain," in John Horsley's *Britannia Romana*, 1732; "De Vasis et Lucernis, et Amuletis, de Annulis et Fibulis," in Robert Ainsworth's *Monumenti*, 1729; *Collections Relating to the British Museum*, 1753-8.

[23]Among the many prefaces and dedications which came from Ward's pen special interest attaches to the Latin letter addressed to Dr. William Wishart, Principal of the University of Edinburgh, and printed (1751) in his edition of *De Animi Tranquillitate*. It was very probably as a result of this letter that Edinburgh in the same year conferred upon Ward the degree Doctor of Laws. Chalmers: *op. cit.*, XXXI, 126.

System, four books of major importance. *The Lives of the Professors of Gresham College* (1740), a folio volume of 518 pages, beautifully printed and illustrated by Ward's friend George Vertue, contains an authoritative sketch of the life of Sir Thomas Gresham and brief accounts of all of the professors who had been associated with the institution since its founding. It is clearly the result of extensive research into original sources. *Four Essays Upon the English Language* (1758) has separate discussions of orthography, syllabication, the use of articles, and the formation of verbs. *Dissertations Upon Several Passages of the Sacred Scriptures,* published posthumously in 1761 (a second volume, the contents "selected according to the instructions which Ward left in a paper, entitled 'Dissertations, vol. ii,' " appearing in 1774[25]), is a careful, if pedantic, attempt to explain certain vague, contradictory, and curious scriptural passages.

As an editor Ward is chiefly to be remembered for his revision of the Lily-Colet Latin *Grammar.* Prepared at the request of the booksellers who were patentees for publishing that work,[26] Ward's edition first appeared in 1732, and was reprinted at least four times before the end of the century (1760, 1767, 1770, and 1792).[27] Working from the famous 1542 text. Ward purged the *Grammar* of numerous errors which had crept into it over the space of two hundred years, and gave, as Chalmers tells us, "a very correct edition."[28] In the Preface he included an essay on the history of the *Grammar* which is still admired by scholars. Flynn calling it "one of the principal sources for our knowledge of the early history" of the book[29] and Baldwin, "the best and most complete account of [its] formation."[30]

---

[24]Works translated by Ward from English into Latin include the eighth edition of Mead's *Discourse on the Plague* (1723); three introductory letters in Buckley's edition of *De Thou's History* (1728); and the *Life* of Dr. Johnson prefixed to Benson's edition of that author's version of the *Psalms* (1741).

[25]J. T.: *op. cit.,* p. 235.

[26]Chalmers: *op. cit.,* XXXI, 125.

[27]*The British Museum Catalogue of Printed Books.* Entry "Ward, John."

[28]*Op. cit.,* XXXI, 125.

[29]Flynn, Vincent Joseph: *The Grammatical Writings of William Lily, ?1468-?1523.* Separate from the *Papers* of the Bibliographical Society of America, XXXVII (1943), 30.

[30]Baldwin, T. W.: *William Shakespeare's Small Latine & Lesse Grecke,* Urbana, Illinois, 1944, II, Appendix II, 693.

Ward's edition of the *Grammar* was used as a textbook at Bristol Academy

Also deserving of special comment is Ward's edition of Vossius' *Elementa Rhetorica* and the introductory essay, "De Ratio Interpungendi," which he prepared for it.[31] Except for the *System* this work represents his only major excursion into the field of rhetorical theory. Since it appeared a short time after he assumed the Gresham professorship it may have been intended for use in connection with his lectures.

As a reviewer Ward was particularly active. On the basis of strong circumstantial evidence Nangle has identified him as the author of no less than sixty full-length reviews and three shorter notices which appeared in the pages of that famous nonconformist journal, the *Monthly Review*, between July, 1749 and September, 1757.[32]

The books reviewed by Ward for the *Monthly* cover a broad range of subjects—music, philosophy, oratory, history, science, law, commerce, and religion. For the most part, however, he handled historical, philosophical, and religious works, writing at greatest length and most learnedly about those dealing with antiquarian researches.

In view of the sparsity of biographical data and the impersonal nature of most of his correspondence, Ward's reviews are the chief source of what little we know concerning his opinions on literature, politics, and religion. Fortunately, they also furnish additional insight into his character, for one need not read far to be convinced that, whatever Ward's limitations, narrow mindedness and pettiness were not among them. Not only does he habitually treat with eminent fairness views incompatible with his own, but on one occasion goes so far as to decry the caustic nature of certain attacks made on Conyers Middleton, a scholar with whom he himself had once carried on a brief but sharp controversy.[33] Only in speaking of religion does Ward sometimes show intolerance: but even here the most vitriolic anti-Catholic language is tempered by a genuine abhorrence of religious

---

about 1770 (McLachlan, *op. cit.*, p. 95) and is recommended in *A Letter to His Grace the Lord Archbishop of Canterbury, Containing a Proposal for the Improvement of Latin Schools* (London, 1748).

[31]London, 1724.

[32]Nangle: *op. cit.*, pp. 45-6.

[33]Ward, John: Account of Some of Dr. Middleton's Opponents, *Monthly Review*, III:16-25, 1750.

strife and a conviction that in the good society freedom of worship must be guaranteed.[34]

Everywhere evident are an intimate knowledge of ancient languages and cultures, and a veneration for all things classical. At the same time, it is apparent that Ward was more than a novice in the fields of modern philosophy and literature. Sufficiently acquainted with Pope to be sensitive to his faults as well as his virtues, he also knew a good deal of Locke, and had read Hutcheson, Bolingbroke, Berkeley, Condillac, and Warburton.[35]

D. Friends and Correspondents

Either through correspondence or personal acquaintance Ward had more than passing contact with numerous leaders in the fields of religion, science, and medicine, as well as with scholars and critics. Numbered among his closer associates were Dr. Richard Mead, Thomas Secker, Archbishop of Canterbury, the Reverend Samuel Chandler, John Arbuthnot, Dr. John Friend, the Reverend John Lewis of Margate, John Loveday of Magdelan College, the Reverend Francis Wise, Dr. William Warren of Trinity, Dr. Andrew Ducarel, E. M. DaCosta, author of the *Natural History of Fossils,* Dr. Francis Drake, historian of York, and Thomas Hollis.[36] Many of the letters which passed between Ward and these men have been preserved and give strong evidence of the respect uniformly accorded him by his contemporaries.[37]

E. Later Years and Death

Upon the establishment of the British Museum Ward was elected (December 11, 1753) a trustee of that institution. Though in his middle seventies he entered upon the duties of this office with en-

---

[34]See, for example, *Monthly Review, III*:214, 1750 and *XVI*:5:210, 1757.

[35]*Ibid., III*:22, 1750; *XV*:43-52, 106-11, 1756; *XVI*:227-8, 238-42, 1757.

[36]On Ward's association with Mead, Friend, and Arbuthnot see especially Macmichael, William: *The Gold-Headed Cane,* New York, 1926, p. 81 ff.

[37]Nichols, John: *Illustrations of the Literary History of the Eighteenth Century,* London, 1817-58, II, 123-4; III, 577-8; IV, 165-6, 169, 189-90, 190-1, 441, 618-9, 619-20, 683-4, 685, 686; V, 257, 262, 599-600. Ellis, Sir Henry: *Original Letters of Eminent Literary Men of the Sixteenth, Seventeenth, and Eighteenth Centuries,* London, 1843, pp. 363-4, 368-71, 371-2, 379-80, 389-94.

thusiasm, giving, in fact, so much of his time to the affairs of the Museum—especially to drawing up rules for its government—that his own writing was seriously neglected.[38]

On Tuesday, October 17, 1758, "having gone well to bed . . . he waked between three and four in the morning with a complaint of coldness in the head, and soon after expired."[39] He was buried seven days later in the nonconformist cemetery at Bunhill Fields.[40] As one of his two executors Ward named a certain John Ward, bookseller in Cornhill opposite the Royal Exchange—"a very distant, if any relation."[41] It was he who, in the following year, had the *System* printed for sale in his shop.

Determined that young nonconformists should receive educational opportunities he had been denied, Ward provided in his will for a trust, the income from which enabled students designed for the dissenting ministry or for tutorships in dissenting academies to spend four years at a Scottish university.[42] At a later date funds derived from the trust were also used to finance students through English academies.[43]

Following Ward's death his old friend Andrew Ducarel persuaded Dr. Thomas Birch to prepare a suitable memorial in the form of a brief biography.[44] This work, corrected by Loveday and with a preface by Dr. Matthew Maty is titled *An Account of the Life of John Ward* . . . (1766). Although unavailable, it is evidently the principal source upon which later biographers drew.

III. THE BOOK

A. Introduction

The *System* consists of two volumes totaling 863 pages, and is among the longest of the major English rhetorics. Following out his announced plan of restating, with appropriate illustrations, the prin-

---

[38]Chalmers: *op. cit.*, XXXI, 126; Nangle: *op. cit.*, pp. 45-6.

[39]Nichols: *Literary Anecdotes*, V, 523.

[40]*Ibid.*

[41]*Ibid.*, p. 524.

[42]McLachlan: *op. cit.*, p. 30 and Appendix 1, 305.

[43]*Ibid.* On the Ward Foundation see also letter signed E. J. in *Universal Theological Magazine and Impartial Review*, I:301, 1804.

[44]Nichols: *Illustrations of Literature*, III, 646-9; IV, 632-3.

ciples and methods of the classical rhetoric, Ward treats in fifty-four separate discourses the history and nature of eloquence,[45] four of the traditional "parts" of rhetoric—invention, disposition, elocution, and delivery[46]—and, under the general head "Of other helps to Oratory," discusses the elements of a sound rhetorical education. Prefacing the whole is an Inaugural Oration, "De Use et Praestantia Artis Dicendi," "Spoken in Latin, before the Commencement of the LECTURES, according to the usual Custom."

B. Rhetoric and Logic

Of prime significance in any analysis of the *System* is the fact that in his second and third lectures Ward establishes the independence of rhetoric from logic by delineating three fundamental differences between these disciplines. First, logic employs a "short and concise way of reasoning" which stands in marked contrast with the "fluency and copiousness of oratory"; second, logic finds its end in a "knowledge of the truth" while rhetoric goes further and attempts to apply "truth," through ethical and pathetic as well as logical appeals, in order to induce belief and action; third, the propositions of logic are arranged only with a view to making evident the conclusion they imply, but in rhetoric arrangement "consults the pleasure and entertainment of [the] hearers, as well as their instruction."[47] Because of these differences rhetoric must necessarily have systems of invention and disposition peculiar to itself. Though these will, of course, be similar to their counterparts in logic, they cannot, for the reasons shown, be identical.

C. Invention

Having thus proved that invention and disposition are legitimate "parts" of rhetoric, Ward defines the first as "the discovery of such things as are proper to persuade," at the same time reminding us that in order to effect persuasion we must prove or illustrate the proposition

---

[45]*System*, I, 15.

[46]Memory is treated as a subdivision of delivery. See Lecture LI, 378-92 and especially 381-2.

[47]*System*, II, 25; III, 31-3. Cf. *Institutio*, II, 20-7; *Partitiones Oratoriae*, XXIII, 79, etc.

advanced, conciliate the audience, and arouse their passions.[48] In more technical language, there is a point-to-point relationship between the provinces of *pistis*, *ethos*, and *pathos* and the ends *docere*, *conciliare*, and *movere*. Each of the modes of persuasion supplies one of the necessary ingredients of the total persuasive process.[49]

Keeping within the framework of this typically Ciceronian analysis,[50] Ward develops an inventional system which gives in most major respects a faithful, albeit somewhat simplified, picture of the classical *inventio*. His discussion of "general arguments" is drawn principally from Cicero's *Topica*,[51] his treatment of the "more particular places" for judicial and epideictic speaking, from *Institutio*.[52] Although the source of the material on "deliberation" is not entirely evident, it is related, probably through an intervening source, to the analysis of this genre found in *Partitiones, De Inventione, and Institutio*.[53] Under the head of *pathos* Ward reproduces more or less servilely, but with excellent illustrations, Aristotle's classic description of the passions.[54] Ethical appeal he treats after the fashion of Quintilian, though placing a somewhat greater emphasis on artistic means for assuming the appropriate character or appearance.[55]

Ward's only important deviation from classical inventional doctrine is his tendency to bring "selection" and "judgment" under the head of invention.[56] Minor departures are the confusion of "external topics" with "quasi-states," the failure to distinguish between *quaestio* and "state," the distortion of the classical view that "necessity" hold first

---

[48]*Ibid.*, IV, 44. For a detailed analysis of Ward's inventional doctrine see Ehninger, Douglas: Selected Theories of *Inventio* in English Rhetoric, 1759-1828, Ph.D. Dissertation, The Ohio State University, 1949, pp. 81-137.

[49]*Ibid.*, IV-XI *passim*.

[50]*Orator*, XXI, 69; *De Oratore*, II, 27, 115 ff.

[51]Cf. *System*, IV-V; *Topica*, III-XVIII. See also *Partitiones Oratoriae*, II, 7 and *De Oratore*, II, 39, 164-7.

[52]Cf. *System*, IX, 123-39; *Institutio*, VII. Also *System*, VII, 92-106; *Institutio*, III, 7. See *De Inventione*, II, 4-51.

[53]Cf. *System*, VIII, 119; *Partitiones Oratoriae*, XXV. Also *System*, VIII, 111; *Institutio*, III, 8, 28-9; *De Inventione*, II, 51-8.

[54]Cf. *System*, XI; *Rhetorica*, 1378a-1388b.

[55]Cf. especially *System*, X, 140-54; *Institutio*, VI, 2, 8-25.

[56]In the major classical tracts these functions were assigned to disposition. See Wagner, Russell: The Meaning of *Dispositio*, in *Studies in Speech and Drama in Honor of Alexander M. Drummond*, Ithaca, New York, 1944, pp. 285-94.

place among topics for deliberation, and the failure to recognize that "places" for epideictic speaking are sources of proof as well as devices for elaborating praise or blame. It is evident, however, that all of these result from an imperfect grasp of ancient theory rather than from deliberate attempts to modify it.[57]

D. Disposition

Shorn of the functions of "selection" and "judgment," Ward's *dispositio*, while retaining the general structure and also much of the content given to this department by the classical writers, tends to be reduced to little more than the mechanical art of arranging previously evaluated "proofs." His remarks on the Introduction and Narration are derived from *Partitiones* and *Institutio*,[58] those on the Proposition, from *De Inventione* and *Institutio*,[59] while the treatment of Confirmation is, by his own admission, based on "the Greek writers."[60]

While correctly placing the analysis of syllogism-enthymeme and induction-example under the head of disposition, Ward misses entirely the Aristotelian distinction between these modes.[61] Enthymeme he defines as a rhetorical syllogism from which one premise has been omitted as "sufficiently manifest";[62] by "induction" he understands the argument from generalization;[63] "example," on the other hand, is a "comparison of two single facts," or that "which is brought either to prove or illustrate some general assertion."[64]

Of particular interest in Ward's discussion of Confirmation is his assertion that all forms of reasoning ("argumentation") may be reduced to syllogistic form.[65] Though not unknown in logic, no other

---

[57]These deviations and their effect on Ward's inventional doctrine are discussed in Ehninger: *op. cit.,* 97-8, (note), 98-100, 107-9, 114-9.

[58]Cf. *System,* XII, 179-91, XIII, 192-207; *Partitiones Oratoriae,* VIII, 27-33; *Institutio,* IV, 1-2.

[59]Cf. *System,* XIV, 208-22; *De Inventione,* I, 13-4; *Institutio,* IV, 4-5.

[60]*System,* XV, 224. The Influence of *Partitiones Oratoriae,* XIII is, however, also discernible.

[61]*Ibid.,* XV-XVI. For a definitive interpretation of the Aristotelian enthymeme see McBurney, James H.: The Place of the Enthymeme in Rhetorical Theory, *SM,* III, 1936, 51-68.

[62]*Ibid.,* XV, 231.

[63]*Ibid.,* XVI, 238.

[64]*Ibid.,* XVI, 242.

[65]*Ibid.,* XV, 231-7; XVI, 249-50.

important English rhetorician until Whately, some seventy years later, was to designate syllogism as the universal category of inference.[66]

"Amplification," which is discussed under the rubric of disposition rather than invention, Ward treats in characteristic Ciceronian fashion. With a single exception, the "places" for amplification which he lists correspond exactly with the standard catalogue of "places" for logical proof.[67]

E. Elocution

Although strong in his insistence that elocution is but one of four co-equal "parts" of the science of rhetoric, Ward devotes nearly half of the *System* to this subject. Out of a total of 863 pages, 330 deal with it directly and forty-nine more are given over to exemplifying the various levels of style as they are found in epistles, dialogues, historical writings, and orations.[68] Moreover, it is significant to note that of this very considerable amount of space roughly one-third is allotted to a discussion of "the right use of tropes and figures." Ward describes and illustrates at length no less than twelve tropes and thirty-seven figures, taking occasion in almost every instance to dwell upon the beauty and usefulness of the device in question.

In an effort to give his discussion a naturalistic basis, Ward, influenced no doubt by Quintilian, advances the principle that "Nature and art are not opposite to each other, and different in kind, but only in degree, as art is nature improved."[69] The precepts of art, springing out of nature, serve to perfect it by giving artistically planned discourse "the nearest resemblance to nature."[69]

Applying this principle to figures and tropes, he asserts that they are verbal expressions of fundamental relationships existing among phenomena. Certain tropes—synecdoche, metonymy, metaphor, and irony—are "primary" in the sense that they express these relationships directly; others are "secondary" in that they are derived from and referable to one or more of the "primary" types. All, however, are

[66]Whately, Richard: *Elements of Rhetoric*. Reprinted from the Seventh . . . Edition, Louisville, 1854, pp. 71-2. See also Whately, Richard: *Elements of Logic*, Boston, 1845, pp. 43-4, 48, 52, 61, 214.

[67]*System*, XIX, 292-301.

[68]See Lectures XX-XLVI.

[69]*System*, XXII, 337. Cf. *Institutio*, IX, 4.3-10.

ultimately grounded in the nature of things, and if man is to describe accurately, let alone eloquently, the world about him, they must enter into discourse.[70]

Adducing an abundance of telling examples, Ward shows how the proper use of "properties and ornaments" may produce the various levels of style.[71] To some extent, he implies, the process is purely a mechanical one. Given the proper number of ornaments, and the appropriate kind of periods, a particular style results almost automatically. At the same time, he recognizes that inborn talent and aptitude play a part, and recommends that every speaker employ that manner to which his own genius seems most naturally inclined.[72]

On the principle that "the greatest fund of jests lies in the language, that is, in tropes and verbal figures," Ward treats "wit" under the general head of elocution rather than in its usual place under invention.[73] His analysis, though both naive and sketchy, derives some interest from the fact that he eschews the ancients and draws upon Locke as his chief source.

F. Delivery

Despite the fact Ward's discussion of delivery is predicated upon a strongly naturalistic philosophy, it tends at more than one point to degenerate into a sterile repetition of mechanical rules and principles.

At the outset he lays down the blanket rule that since "the perfection of art consists in its nearest resemblance to nature," the more "natural" pronunciation is, the more "moving" it will be.[74] On the same page, however, he not only recognizes that "art . . . if well managed, will assist and improve nature," but even goes so far as to suggest that under certain circumstances "the force of it [is] so great and powerful, that where it is wholly counterfeit [as, for example, in

---

[70]*Ibid.*, XXV, 387; XXIX, 17, etc.

[71]*Ibid.*, XXXVI, 140-5; XLVI, 304-5.

[72]*Ibid.*, XLVI, 312.

[73]*Ibid.*, XI, 201.

[74]*Ibid.*, XLVII, 319-20. Following Quintilian (XI, 3, 154), Ward relates "natural" delivery to the "good man" theory, pointing out that "a person of this character will make the cause he espouses his own, and the more sensibly he is touched with it himself, his action will be the more natural, and by that means the more easily affect others in the same manner." *Ibid.*

the theatre], it will for the time work the same effect, as if it were founded in truth."

A similar confusion is evident in the analysis of voice. While Ward professes to base his remarks on an observation of "what nature does, when free and unconstrained," the beauty and music of speech are declared to result from a conscious tempering of the voice between various extremes, and an *a priori* standard of graveness and decency is imposed on vocal delivery.[75]

As to the mode of delivery, Ward, condemning the practice of reading speeches from manuscript, advocates that orators "consider well the subject, on which they are to speak, range all the parts of it in a proper order in their mind, and prepare the figures and cheif [sic] expressions they design to use," but that they also "leave room to add what may occasionally be suggested from present circumstances, when they come to speak."[76] This method, proposed on the authority of Quintilian, results, he believes, in a more natural, fluent, and vehement delivery than may be achieved either by reading or word-for-word memorization.[77]

A final matter of interest under this department is Ward's view that memory is a subdivision of pronunciation. Apparently overlooking the uses this faculty may have in building up a wide background of knowledge, he declares that its chief value is to enable the orator to bear in mind the substance of his remarks, thus making it unnecessary for him to speak from manuscript, a practice which impairs eye contact and therefore detracts from the effectiveness of natural delivery.[78]

G. The Elements of a Rhetorical Education

We have no direct information concerning Ward's own teaching methods. However, our knowledge of the general purpose of Gresham College and of the instructional practices commonly followed there leads us to suppose that he confined his activities principally to the reading of the lectures embodied in the *System*. At the same time, he recognized that attendance at lectures was not in itself sufficient to

---

[75]*Ibid.*, XLVIII, 321-2, 329, etc.
[76]*Ibid.*, LI, 383. Cf. *Institutio*, X, 7.30-2.
[77]*Ibid.*
[78]*Ibid.*, LI, 380-1 Cf. *Orator*, XVII, 54, etc.

form an orator. This is made evident in the closing pages of the treatise where, under the broad title "Of other helps to Oratory,"[79] he presents a thoughtful and well-rounded philosophy of rhetorical education.[79]

Taking exception to Crassus' view that the orator must be a universal scholar,[80] Ward recommends that he center his attention in certain relatively restricted areas.[81] In addition, he lays major emphasis upon the use of imitation.[82] Admitting that when abused it has definite evils, he stoutly maintains that properly conceived and employed, it plays a crucial role in training the public speaker. Citing Seneca, Ward compares the imitative process to the action of the stomach, pointing out that as in digestion various kinds of foods are transformed into a single substance, so should that which we imitate appear no longer to belong to the model, but be wholly one's own.[83] Thus conceived imitation enables the orator to make full use of past achievements without curbing his own creative genius. As additional steps in training Ward recommends extensive use of written exercises and wide reading in the poets, historians, philosophers, and orators.[84]

H. Sources and Originality

A complete catalogue of Ward's sources would include nearly all of the major writers of antiquity—dramatists, scientists, and men of letters, as well as rhetoricians. The great majority of his borrowings are, however, from Quintilian and Cicero. From the first of these authors he derives not only the general philosophy of the *System,* but also much of its basic framework; from the second comes the bulk of his illustrative material. Quintilian, whose *Institutio* he calls "the most perfect [work] of its kind," is cited some 135 times; Cicero's orations alone are either directly quoted or referred to more than 250 times. In addition, at some point or other during the course of his lectures, Ward mentions practically everything Cicero wrote, the references characteristically being accompanied by unqualified praise.

---

[79]Lecture LII.
[80]*De Oratore,* I, 46 ff., etc.
[81]See *System,* LII, 393-407.
[82]He devotes two entire lectures to the subject, LIII and LIV.
[83]*System,* LIV, 432-3. Ward's reference is to Epistle 85.
[84]*Ibid.,* LII, 397-407.

Drawn preponderantly from Roman rather than from Greek writers, Ward's rhetoric has a distinctly Latin flavor. There are, in fact, in the entire treatise only four noteworthy borrowings from Greek theorists: 1. the discussion of the "passions"—derived from Aristotle;[85] 2. the description of the characteristics of young, mature, and old men—also taken from Aristotle;[86] 3. the analysis of the "sublime"—described by Monk as Longinus "in Bolevian dress";[87] and 4. the adoption of the four-fold Greek system for classifying the forms of inference.[88] Though Hermogenes, Demetrius, Phalereus, Dionysius, Isocrates, and Plato are each mentioned one or more times and Demosthenes quoted in some dozen instances, none of these writers may be said to have had an important influence on Ward's thinking.

Of modern writers Ward refers most frequently to Vossius, citing not only the ponderous *Constitutio* but many of his other works as well.[89] Other moderns mentioned by Ward include—besides Locke and Pope whom I have already named—Milton, Newton, Erasmus, Chaucer, Addison, and Fénelon. While the manifest points of contact with Fénelon are few, it seems indisputable that Ward derived from him the significant paragraph in which the basic plan of the *System* is set forth, this prospectus being little more than a loose translation of a passage in the Archbishop's *Lettre Ecrite a l'Académie Française.*[90]

A fact almost certain to strike the investigator of Ward's sources is that in composing the *System* he drew little or nothing from those fields outside rhetoric in which we know he was expert. No important

---

[85]Cf. *System*, XI, 159 ff; *Rhetorica*, 1378b-1388b.

[86]Cf. *System*, X, 151-3; *Rhetorica*, 1388b-1390b.

[87]Monk, Samuel H.: *The Sublime: A Study of Critical Theories in XVIII-Century England*, New York, 1935, p. 107. See *System*, XXXIX.

[88]*System*, XXV, 224.

[89]While generally following Vossius' doctrines, Ward rejects his division of rhetoric into two parts, invention and disposition. See *System*, III, 39; cf. Vossius' *Logices et Rhetorices Natura et Constitutione*, 1658, XVII.

[90]Cf. *System*, I, 15; Lettre sur les Occupations de l'Académie Française. *Oeuvres de Fénelon*, Paris, 1844, p. 400.

In addition to the modern writers mentioned above, Ward apparently was acquainted with the works of the Jesuit rhetoricians. In his lectures on delivery he cites Louis Cresol four times, the references probably being to that author's *Theatrum Veterum Rhetorum* (Paris, 1620). Upon another occasion, this time in his discussion of imitation, he gives as a source the abbreviated reference "Causs." The context of the remark thus attributed suggests that it is drawn from Nicolas Caussin's *De Eloquentia Sacra et Humana*, La Fleche, 1619.

rhetorical work of the eighteenth century, or perhaps of any century, shows less responsiveness to neighboring subject-areas or current developments in thought. None reflects less its political and social environments.

Lastly, the fashion in which Ward used his sources deserves comment. Having found in one of his favorite reference works a discussion suited to his needs, he more frequently than not proceeds, with a typical eighteenth-century disregard for literary ethics, to appropriate it almost bodily. In many instances his borrowings fall little short of plagiarism; and in almost no case—except perhaps in the discussion of rhetorical training—are they supplemented by original contributions or reworked into a new integration.

I. Contemporary Reception and Influence

Within a year of its publication the *System* had been reviewed in the two leading critical journals of the time, the *Critical Review* and the *Monthly Review,* and had also been duly noted in the book lists of the *Gentleman's Magazine* and the *London Magazine.*[91]

Interestingly enough, the *Critical* and the *Monthly* did not agree in their evaluations of the work. The *Monthly,* to which Ward himself had contributed for so many years, assigned the *System* to its outstanding reviewer, William Rose,[92] and used his eight-page essay as the lead in its June, 1759 issue.

Rose was sceptical of the part which "systems" of rhetoric play in training orators. Of the book itself, however, he spoke with unqualified praise, calling it completely worthy of its "learned and judicious author," and asserting that Ward had reproduced "in a very clear, distinct, and accurate manner . . . the most important and useful observations that are to be met with in treatises upon oratory." It is, he said in summary, "written with more exactness and judgment than any modern system we are acquainted with."[93]

The *Critical,* on the other hand, was distinctly cool. Its anonymous reviewer not only echoed in the strongest language Rose's doubts concerning the efficacy of rhetorical "systems," but was particularly

[91]*Critical Review, VII*:367-9, 1759; *Monthly Review, XX*:481-8, 1759; *Gentleman's Magazine, XXIX*:183, 1759; *London Magazine, XXVIII*:224, 1759.
[92]See Nangle: *op. cit.,* p. 37.
[93]*Monthly Review, XX*:482, 488, 1759.

caustic in commenting on the style of the work and on its failure to adapt ancient doctrine to modern needs. In addition, he felt that it was needlessly repetitious.[94]

In reading these reviews the divergent religious and political biases of the two journals must, of course, be kept in mind.[95] At the same time, it should be noted that the *Monthly* did not uniformly praise Ward's efforts, speaking unfavorably both of the *Four Essays Upon the English Language* and of the *Dissertations Upon Several Passages of the Sacred Scriptures*.[96] In the face of this evidence it appears correct to assume that, although the *Critical's* reviewer may have had ulterior motives in condemning the *System*, Rose in the *Monthly* expressed his honest judgment concerning the book.

As a textbook the *System* had a much greater vogue in America than in England. After considerable research I am able to report with certainty but a single instance of its use as a textbook in an English school or academy. This was at the famous nonconformist establishment of Hoxton where at least through 1769, and probably beyond 1784, it was studied in the course on rhetoric offered by Andrew Kippis.[97] In America, on the other hand, as Guthrie has shown, Ward's

---

[94]*Critical Review, VII*:386,9, 1759.

[95]Not only was Ralph Griffiths, who founded and for many years edited the *Monthly*, himself a dissenter, but he largely staffed the magazine with co-religionists. The *Critical*, on the other hand, was "established under Tory and Church patronage" for the specific purpose of maintaining "principles in opposition to those of the *Monthly*." Graham, Walter: *English Literary Periodicals*, New York, 1930, p. 213.

[96]*Monthly Review, XIX*:335-42, 1758; *XXV*:80, 1761.

[97]McLachlan: *op. cit.*, p. 123 and Appendix I, 305.

Though the *System* is listed in the catalogue of books belonging to Warrington Academy in 1775, the probability is that it never formed part of the regular course of instruction at that institution, since little or no rhetorical training appears to have been included in the curriculum until 1762 when Joseph Priestley began to develop his own course of lectures on the subject. See Parker, Irene: *Dissenting Academies in England*, Cambridge, 1914, Appendix IV, 154-9; Rutt, John T.: *Life and Correspondence of Joseph Priestley*, London, 1831 2, I, 53 4; Bright, H. A.: Historical Sketch of Warrington Academy, *Christian Reformer*, *XVII*:733, 1861.

A set of shorthand notes on Ward's lectures and the history of eloquence which Kippis appended to them—transcribed in 1764 by one William Wood— is preserved in Unitarian College Library, Manchester. There is no direct evidence, however, that the *System* was there used as a textbook. See McLachlan: *op. cit.*, Appendix I, 284-5.

treatise, along with the standard Latin works, pretty well dominated the college field until 1780.[98]

Generally speaking, the *System* exerted little influence on subsequent writers. Joseph Priestley is the single important English rhetorician of the eighteenth century to acknowledge Ward as a source. In the short but revealing Preface to his *Course of Lectures on Oratory and Criticism* (1777) he says he has borrowed from Ward a number of the examples used in that work. As Harding has observed, he also is apparently indebted to the *System* for the titles of certain of his lectures.[99] Even so, Ward's treatise may hardly be regarded as one of Priestley's major sources.[100]

Only on a minor work of the period did the *System* leave more than a passing impress. In his *Rhetorical Grammar* (1785), John Walker appropriates material from Burgh, Priestley, Blair, Gibbons, and Steele, as well as from Ward. Ward, together with Priestley, provides him with most of his remarks on invention, being at some points quoted verbatim and at others under the thinnest disguise. Since, even with its obvious deficiencies, the *Rhetorical Grammar* continued in popularity well beyond 1800, it constituted a channel through which Ward's influence was for a time transmitted and preserved.[101]

An interesting negative reaction to Ward's doctrines may be found in Thomas Gibbon's *Rhetoric,* a figure book published in 1767. Expressing dissatisfaction with the way both Ward and Blackwall *(Introduction to the Classics,* 1718) had treated tropes and figures, Gibbons sets out to improve upon their works by deriving his examples almost exclusively from the scriptures rather than from classical writers.

So far as I know, the only twentieth-century textbook which draws in any significant way upon the *System* is O'Neill, Laycock, and Scales' *Argumentation and Debate.* Here Ward is quoted four times,

[98]Guthrie: *op. cit.,* p. 45. On Ward in America see also Fritz, Charles A.: The Content of the Teaching of Speech in the American College Before 1850: With Special Reference to Its Influence on Current Theories, Ph.D. Dissertation, The School of Education of New York University, 1928, Appendix, Plate I. Snow, Lewis F.: *The College Curriculum in the United States,* New York, 1907, p. 91. Bronson, Walter C.: *The History of Brown University, 1764-1914,* Providence, 1914, p. 102.

[99]Harding: *op. cit.,* p. 176.

[100]An analysis of Priestley's sources is given in Ehninger: *op. cit.,* pp. 223-5.

[101]Harding: *op. cit.,* pp. 184, 189, 286. Sandford: *op. cit.,* p. 110.

and his phrase "the stress of the controversy" is given considerable prominence in the discussion of "analysis."[102] Thonsen and Baird, and other writers occasionally refer to him in passing.[103]

A handful of present-day scholars have commented on the *System* or offered critical appraisals of it. Harding, while recognizing that the work has definite weaknesses, calls it "the best synthesis of ancient rhetorical theory to be found in English."[104] Guthrie emphasizes Ward's contribution in declaring the independence of rhetoric from logic, pointing out that his "justification of the inclusion of invention and disposition [in that science] gives a clear picture of the shift which [had] taken place in English rhetorical thought since the days of Dugard and Smith."[105] Sandford, though somewhat less specific, expresses an essentially similar judgment.[106] Lee and Sattler content themselves with remarking that the work clearly falls within the classical tradition.[107] The only distinctly dissonant note is struck by the critic Monk who in his previously cited monograph, *The Sublime: A Study of Critical Theories in XVIII-Century England* writes:

> The fact that [Ward's lectures] were published and sold bears witness to the interest of the age in rhetoric and to the apparently infinite capacity of the eighteenth-century reader to endure repetition, for Ward says nothing that had not been said before.[108]

IV. SUMMARY AND INFERENCES

A. The Man

John Ward was evidently a figure of considerable importance in the intellectual life of his age, and enjoyed the respect of his most distinguished contemporaries. Unusual industry, coupled with wide interests, a thorough knowledge of the classical languages and literature, and an infinite capacity for the minutiae of historical and

---

[102]O'Neill, James, M., Laycock, Craven and Scales, R. L.: *Argumentation and Debate,* New York, 1917, pp. 50, 189, 330, 348.

[103]Thonssen, Lester and Baird, A. Craig: *Speech Criticism,* New York, 1948, pp. 205, 206, 357, 385.

[104]Harding, Harold F.: Quintilian's Witnesses, *SM, I*:12, 1934.

[105]Guthrie: *op. cit.,* p. 45.

[106]Sanford: *op. cit.,* p. 109.

[107]Lee: *loc. cit.;* Sattler: *loc. cit.*

[108]Monk: *op. cit.,* p. 107.

literary research gained for him some measure of fame as philologist, antiquarian, grammarian, rhetorician, reviewer, student of religion, and also as editor and translator.

At the same time Ward had definite limitations as a scholar, and especially as a rhetorical theorist:

1. He was not a creative, nor even a penetrating thinker. His writings, not only on rhetoric but on all subjects, while carefully conceived and elegantly polished, are at best pedestrian restatements of ideas advanced by others.

2. He was a dilettante, more remarkable for the range of his learning than for his mastery of any single discipline. Not only did the very breadth of his interests spread him dangerously thin, but he further dissipated his energies in "hack projects" undertaken either at the request of friends or for the sake of the remuneration involved.

3. He was, in two quite different senses of the word, a pedant. Drawing his materials almost exclusively from books rather than from first-hand observations and experiences, he also was frequently guilty of amassing citations and dwelling upon the esoteric, less for the purpose of substantiating a point than to display his own erudition.

4. He was led by inclination—a preference reinforced by his training under Ker—to regard the authors of classical antiquity with a veneration bordering upon idolatry. This persistent bias, while not completely closing his mind, certainly narrowed his perspective and warped his judgment.

5. He had little formal training in the intricacies of rhetorical theory, and, so far as one may judge, no abiding interest in the subject. The *System* itself and an edition of Vossius are his only major writings in the field, while, on the other hand, he produced a large number of books and articles in areas outside of rhetoric.

6. Though Ward knew the writings of some of the great eighteenth-century epistemologists and was for more than thirty years closely associated in the Royal Society with men who were laying the foundations of modern science, he apparently failed to see the significant implications their thought might have for the science of rhetoric.

B. The General Character of the System

As one might expect from a knowledge of Ward's interests and training, the *System* is, not only in spirit but also in structure, essentially classical. Of prime importance, of course, is Ward's recognition that rhetoric is a self-contained discipline, independent from logic and possessing its own methods for devising and disposing "proofs." Hardly less significant, however, is the fact that, with the exception of memory, he assigns all of its traditional "parts" positions theoretically equal in dignity and importance.

Admittedly, one may find in the work a number of deviations from ancient theory. The placing of memory under the rubric of delivery not only narrows the classical conception of this department as embracing "the speaker's whole command of his material,"[109] but actually reduces it to the role of a mechanical means for securing audience contact. Style, on the other hand, is extended to include advice on the writings of epistles, dialogues, and history, and is treated in a fashion which brings it into close proximity with the general philosophy of the belletristic school. Furthermore, as has been observed, syllogism is declared to be the universal category of inference, tropes are described as expressions of fundamental relationships among phenomena, and Crassus' ideal of the orator as universal scholar is modified.

Yet, while these and similar deviations deserve recognition, the fact remains that even when viewed in sum they do not seriously disturb the dominately classical tone and framework of the treatise. Adhering, by and large, to his announced purpose of restating, with appropriate illustrations, the principles of the ancient theorists. Ward may be said to have given us the most comprehensive overview of their doctrines ever put into English.

C. Evaluation

Taken out of the stream of rhetorical history and looked at in isolation the *System* displays both marked strengths and marked weaknesses:

1. The work as a whole, and especially those portions of it dealing with the highly technical problems of invention and arrangement, is sprinkled with erroneous interpretations of classical doctrine.

2. More serious than these, either individually or collectively, how-

---

[109]Baldwin, Charles Sears: *Ancient Rhetoric and Poetics,* New York, 1924, p. 67.

ever, is Ward's obvious failure to delve beneath the surface of the principles he rehearses. As a result, he gives us what is at best a watered-down and schematic picture of doctrines that are by nature vibrant and stimulating. Moveover, the rich epistemological and ethical foundations of the classical rhetoric are largely absent.

3. As Harding has observed, the *System* lacks that close integration among the various departments of rhetoric which is so important a feature of the best classical tracts.[110] Our examination of the text and its sources has demonstrated that the work is essentially a series of more or less independent disquisitions lifted, in some cases almost bodily from easily identifiable sources, and set down with little regard for the coherence of the whole. Whatever organic unity it possesses is, therefore, derived more from the natural cohesiveness of classical doctrine than from Ward's own efforts at synthesis.

On the side of strengths, one cannot fail to discern the skill with which Ward illustrates rhetorical principles. As even a casual reading of the *System* will show, he combines a keen sense of the pertinent with a sure knowledge of the sort of examples which will best enable students to understand a particular doctrine. Moreover, it should be mentioned that, in addition to its notable wealth of illustrative material, the *System* has a number of other features which especially recommend it as a textbook. Among these are its well calculated motivation, its frequent internal summaries, and its extensive documentation.

Nor, as a matter of fact, is this at variance with what we might expect from our knowledge of Ward's equipment as a rhetorician. For just as his shallowness as a thinker and the relatively sketchy attention he gave to rhetoric may, in large measure, account for the work's errors and its general lack of penetration, so may his experience as a schoolmaster explain its aptness in illustration and its useful pedagogical aids.

D. The Place of the System in Rhetorical History

Despite the implications found in certain earlier studies,[111] Ward's decision to base his treatise upon the writings of the ancients was in

---

[110]Harding:*op. cit.,* pp. 49-50.
[111]Guthrie: *op. cit.,* p. 45, etc.

no sense revolutionary. By as early as 1660 the English rhetoric of exornation had fairly run its course, and after 1700 the so-called "reversion to classicism" constantly gained momentum.[112] Thus, when considered in the light of preceding treatises, the historical importance of the *System* lies not so much in the originality of its purpose and plan as in the fact that, whatever its limitations, it is superior both in scope and thoroughness to earlier works in the reversionist movement. More specifically, it is significant because it is the expression *par excellence,* and in that sense the culmination, of the unadulterated classicism at which that movement aimed.

What, however, is to be said when we alter the focus of our inquiry and, instead of considering the *System* in the light of preceding treatises, view it in terms of subsequent rhetorical history? Here the crucial fact appears to be that, though it enjoyed popularity as a textbook in the colleges of colonial America, it exerted practically no influence on later writers. How is this to be explained and evaluated?

The answer is that the *System* culminates the reversionist movement chronologically as well as logically. It is not only the ultimate expression in English of classical rhetorical doctrine, but it is the last of the major English rhetorics to be based almost exclusively upon ancient tracts. After Ward rhetorical theory began to move in new directions, Campbell, for example, drew heavily upon the "common sense philosophy" of Thomas Reid; Priestley, upon the associationism of David Hartley; and Blair constructed a rhetoric out of the critical doctrine of "original genius." While retaining important elements of the classical analysis, each of these men altered it to a greater or lesser extent. In so doing they took rhetoric out of the intellectual vacuum in which Ward had kept it, and brought it into line with contemporary developments in psychology, epistemology, and literary criticism.

Putting this analysis into more general terms, one may suggest that the great weakness of the *System* lies not so much in its shallow and frequently erroneous interpretation of classical doctrine as in the fact that, with its gaze fixed constantly upon the ancients, it fails to adapt rhetoric to the thought of the age and to the needs of the men for whom it was written. As a result, it not only loses intellectual stature but fails to meet the pragmatic test of maximum usefulness.

---

[112]Sandford: *op. cit.,* p. 92; Ehninger: *op. cit.,* pp. 9-13.

On the other hand, the work clearly has historical importance, and in a very real fashion contributed to the development of modern rhetorical theory. For, though later writers may have departed from classicism, unless the full scope of the classical rhetoric had been firmly established they hardly could have advanced beyond it. It was Ward's ultimate contribution—and one for which he was eminently fitted—to sweep away once and for all the last vestiges of the Ramean apostasy, and thus help pave the way for the great creative rhetorics of the eighteenth century.

JOHN LAWSON'S
LECTURES CONCERNING ORATORY

RAY E. KEESEY

University of Delaware

THE FIRST EDITION of John Lawson's *Lectures Concerning Oratory* was published in Dublin in 1758, almost two hundred years ago. During this period brief mention of the *Lectures* has occasionally appeared in the writings of scholars of rhetorical theory, but no comprehensive study of the Lectures has been undertaken previous to the present investigation.[1]

Some of the comments that have appeared are inaccurate with respect to the sources, influence, content, and publication data of the *Lectures*. The purpose of this article is to examine the rhetorical theory presented in the *Lectures* and to assign this work its proper place in the stream of rhetorical tradition. Invention, disposition, style, and delivery provide the main headings for this study. These, together with memory, constitute the five departments of rhetoric first outlined by Cicero in *De Oratore*. Lawson's treatment of memory, however, is brief and insignificant, and because of this it is omitted from the present consideration.

I. INVENTION

The theory of invention outlined in the *Lectures* is the Aristotelian concept of invention as the discovery of all available means of persuasion.[2]

---

[1]This article is based on the author's Ph.D. Dissertation, The Rhetorical Theory of John Lawson, Ohio State University, 1950, directed by Professor H. F. Harding.

[2]Lawson's discussion of invention is found in Lectures 7, 8, 10, 11, 19, 20, and 21.

Under the heading of invention Lawson includes consideration of the choice of a subject for a speech, division of the subject into appropriate parts, and discovery of the effective developmental details needed to support these parts. He is aware of the sources of persuasion inherent in disposition, style, and delivery in the proper management of those arguments discovered by the speaker during his "mature Consideration of a Subject."[3]

The act of discovering (invention), cannot be separated, except in theory, from the selection, adaptation, and arrangement (disposition), the form of expression (style), and the manner of presenting (delivery) the available means of persuasion. Each of these has its function in the inventive process.

Logical proof, or the "Reasoning Part," Lawson advises his students to regard as "the most important of all, and accordingly take care to be most exact herein."[4] He recommends that the speaker inform his audience of the general plan for speaking, and that internal summaries be added whenever needed to assist the listener's memory and comprehension.[5] Development of the subject of logical proof in the *Lectures* is, however, superficial in comparison with that found in the *Rhetoric*. Lawson limits himself to a consideration of enthymemes, examples, commonplaces, and a brief discussion of the function of logic in arrangement.

He explains the enthymeme of Aristotle's invention as a syllogism with one premise missing. He fails to show that the distinguishing characteristic of the enthymeme is the subject matter with which it deals, as McBurney clearly points out.[6] The example, as discussed by Lawson, consists only of those from history, from experience, omitting reference to the fictitious example, the "invented parallel" of Aristotle.[7] And the advice he gives his students on the value of collecting and using commonplaces is in general terms only. He omits significant

---

[3]*Lectures,* p. 135. (Pagination based on the 1758 first edition.)

[4]*Ibid.,* p. 386.

[5]*Ibid.,* pp. 382-83.

[6]J. H. McBurney: The Place of the Enthymeme in Rhetorical Theory, *SM,* 3:58, 1936. Cope, however, in one place offers a defence of the same approach taken by Lawson—that the essential difference between the enthymeme and the syllogism is one of form only. See E. M. Cope: *Introduction to Aristotle's Rhetoric,* London, 1867, p. 103. Enthymemes are discussed in the *Lectures,* pp. 129-31.

[7]*Rhetoric,* 1393 b, trans. Lane Cooper: *Lectures,* pp. 129-31.

information about commonplaces as they were explained by Aristotle, such as the *topoi,* or regions, where they may be found, and the general classification of the kinds of commonplaces to fit particular needs of the speaker.[8]

Discussion of emotional proof in the *Lectures* is basically the same as that found in the *Rhetoric.* In his two lectures on this subject Lawson includes consideration of sources of emotions, the necessity for address to the passions, five rules for the proper use of the pathetic in oratory, the factors that determine the speaker's ability to use the pathetic, its appropriateness and varying effectiveness, and special advice concerning the use of fear, the "most powerful" of all the emotions. The natural condition of mankind is such, Lawson states, that it is necessary not only for the orator to show what is right but also to make use of all his skill "to induce them steadfastly to behold it."[9]

The importance of the speaker's character in his speaking, Lawson accepts from Aristotle, but his emphasis on this point is more like that found in Quintilian's *Institutio Oratoria* than in the *Rhetoric.* "Be what you recommend"[10] is Lawson's admonition to his divinity students. He follows Quintilian in teaching that the speaker's true character is revealed in his speech, and that no one can be an orator—or in Lawson's case a successful preacher—unless he be a man of good character. The first quality requisite in the character of the preacher is virtue, and those who do not possess this qualification are advised to give up the attempt. The *Lectures* are permeated with the ethical teachings of the devout preacher who preaches as much as he lectures, even to the students in his classes.

Lawson's theory of invention includes study of sources of argument and logical, emotional, and ethical proof. He omits consideration of *status* as it applies in the inventive process[11] and he is incomplete, by Aristotelian standards, in his discussion of the enthymeme and

---

[8]*Rhetoric,* II. *Lectures,* pp. 127-28.

[9]*Lectures,* p. 57. Lectures 10, 11, and 21 are concerned with the emotions.

[10]*Lectures,* p. 431.

[11]As, for example, in the *Institutio Oratoria,* III, vi, trans. H. E. Butler. Or in *De Oratore,* II, 24-26, trans. J. S. Watson. Lawson does not mention Cicero's *De Inventione.* Otto A. L. Dieter, in "Stasis," *SM, 17*:345-69, 1950, investigates the origin of this concept.

the example. Proper use of one's inventive genius, according to Lawson, presupposes natural ability, broad educational background, and knowledge of rhetorical method that the speaker may be qualified to recognize all the available means of persuasion.

II. DISPOSITION

The same broad concept of disposition found in Book Seven of Quintilian's *Institutio Oratoria* is apparent in Lawson's *Lectures.*[12] Going far beyond the simple ordering of arguments Lawson, like Quintilian before him, thought of disposition as the selection, arrangement, and adaptation of arguments for a particular speaking situation, involving also the principles relating to the introduction and the conclusion of a speech. Choose arguments which are easily understood, Lawson tells his students, avoiding those that are complex and subtle. Choose arguments which are true, avoiding the false and frivolous. Stress arguments no more than they deserve, and use only enough arguments and no more, avoiding the needless multiplying of arguments. Arguments may be drawn from authority, experience, and from narration. Other arguments present themselves in refuting adversaries and in answering objections.

Arrangement is explained as the proccess of discovering the natural, proper, and most advantageous method of disposing arguments for a particular speaking situation. It is a functional process, the aim of which is to determine the best plan or design for a speech, considering the speaker, subject, audience, time, place, and occasion. Arrangement cannot be taught apart from arguments selected for a *particular* audience at a *known* time, occasion, and place. This is the point of view of Quintilian,[13] restated by Lawson in his *Lectures.* It is a significant part of the doctrine of arrangement, and has implications important to those teaching the theory of speechmaking.

Adaptation of arguments, as discussed by Lawson, is largely that of adapting the sermon to the educational level of the members of the church congregation. The age of the listener, differences is economic status and between the sexes are briefly considered, but the emphasis is upon teaching the young preacher how to speak so as to be under-

---

[12]The discussion of disposition is in Lectures 9, 20, and 21.
[13]*Op. cit.,* VII, Preface 4, and VII, x, 5-12.

stood by illiterate listeners who, Lawson explains, constitute the greater part of church audiences. To his students his advice is, be clear, unadorned, reason correctly, and above all, use good common-sense for "Good Sense is for all Ranks and Understanding."[14] The speaker should imagine himself in the place of the listener and from this position ask himself what he would expect of the speaker. This test should be applied to the selection, adaptation, and ordering of arguments, as well as to considerations of style and delivery.

The short section on the introduction is designed entirely for the sermon. The introduction should be short, practical, and delivered with unaffected natural simplicity. General purposes of the introduction are "to bespeak Attention, conciliate Favour, or excite Curiosity."[15] These appear similar to Quintilian's statement of the functions of the introduction as "making the audience well-disposed, attentive, and ready to receive instruction."[16] The two methods of concluding a speech described in the *Lectures* are, first, a recapitulation of the arguments of the speech and, second, an appeal to the emotions of the listeners.

The theory of disposition in the *Lectures* is firmly grounded in the rhetorics of Aristotle, Cicero, and Quintilian. In the *Rhetoric* of Aristotle Lawson found basic doctrine on the selection and adaptation of arguments. But for the developmental details of these, and for all of the subject of arrangement and that dealing with the functions of the introduction, Lawson acknowledges indebtedness to Quintilian's *Institutio Oratoria,* in which disposition is so aptly described by Wagner as including "selection, elimination, ordering, massing or proportioning, and coloring—all from the point of view of the necessities imposed by circumstances of time, place, speaker, purpose, and audience."[17]

III. STYLE

Aristotle in Book Three of the *Rhetoric,* Quintilian in Book Eight of *Institutio Oratoria,* and Cicero in Book Three of *De Oratore*

---

[14]*Lectures,* p. 394.

[15]*Lectures,* p. 381.

[16]*Op. cit.,* IV, i, 5.

[17]Russell H. Wagner: The Meaning of Dispositio, in *Studies in Speech and Drama,* Ithaca, New York, 1944, p. 290.

develop the subject of rhetorical style far beyond Lawson's comparatively meager attempts. Any one of these might have provided him with his initial emphasis that clarity is the foremost consideration. Aristotle, for example, stated: "We may therefore assume the general observations of the *Poetics,* and regard it as settled that a good style is, first of all, clear."[18] Clearness is attained by a choice of words that "common Use hath made known, and familiar,"[19] and by purity of native idiom—this latter called by Aristotle "the foundation of good style."[20] In addition, words should be ranged in their natural order for clarity. What the "natural order" of words is, Lawson doesn't bother to explain. Lecture Twelve has a section in which he discusses nine causes of obscurity in language, in method and substance so strikingly similar to the treatment of this subject in the *Institutio Oratoria* that it is easy to imagine Lawson writing with Quintilian's Eighth Book open before him.

Lawson was familiar, however, with other works on the subject of style. He knew the treatise attributed to Longinus, but it is doubtful if he found it of direct value. Dionysius' *De compositione verborum* received special praise from Lawson, and he advised his students to read it. In his lecture on composition Lawson very likely drew from this source. He was familiar with the *Ars Poetica* of Horace and from it drew illustrations, but he makes no mention in this section of Demetrius' *On Style.* He was acquainted with what Pope, Swift, and Sir Philip Sidney had written on style and similarities between the treatment of this subject in the *Lectures* and that found in the works of any of these three may easily be traced, but definite relationships or influences are another matter.

Clarity of style is the first consideration but it is ornament that, properly speaking, makes rhetoric an art. Lawson treats the subject of ornament under two general headings, composition and figures. Composition is defined as "The due Arrangement of Words with Regard to Signification and Sound."[21] Major considerations include variation of sentence length, avoiding unpleasant sound combinations,

---

[18]*Rhetoric,* 1404 b.
[19]*Lectures,* p. 187. Style is discussed in Lectures 12, 13, 14, 15, 16, 17, and the first part of Lecture 18.
[20]*Rhetoric,* 1407 a.
[21]*Lectures,* p. 227.

mixing long and short words to eliminate monotony, taking cognizance of the way a sentence closes and the next one begins and the relationship between the two and, in general, avoiding extremes, observing rather the "due Mean."

Lawson can make no claim to originality in his lecture on composition. The theory of composition he advocates, except for some illustrative details, may be found in complete form in Book Three of Cicero's *De Oratore*. But in both method and substance a more convincing similarity on this point exists between the *Lectures* and Book Nine Chapter Four of the *Institutio Oratoria*. Quintilian, whom Lawson terms "a good Judge," is probably the principal source for the discussion of composition.

The study of figures is divided into three parts, the number, kind, and application of figures. An excess of figures obscures clarity, tires the listener, and reduces the readiness of the hearer to believe the speaker. As for the kind of figures it is suggested that those be avoided that "turn meerly on Sound," and that great care be exercised with others, such as repetition of the same word, synonymous words, bold metaphors, hyperboles, antitheses, and climax. Figures wrongly applied, the third consideration, but "amuse and confuse." Metaphors should not be extended too far, they should not be "mixed and inconsistent," and irony should not be used carelessly. Since the works of the poets best illustrate effective use of figures, Lawson presents in Lectures Sixteen and Seventeen a dialogue on the advantages to the orator of reading the poets. Titled "On the Usefulness of Reading the Poets to an Orator" the dialogue actually is a summary of Lawson's account of style including most of what he had discussed in the four lectures just preceding.

Judged by the space assigned to each subject in the *Lectures* the major emphasis is on style. Yet Lawson made very little, if any, contribution to a general theory of style. From Milton, Shakespeare, Swift, and Pope he drew more recent illustrations to support classical rhetorical theory, while at the same time retaining many good examples that had been used for this purpose from the poetry of Homer, Virgil, and Horace, and the orations of Demosthenes and Cicero. Except for scattered references to that kind of style most appropriate to pulpit speaking his discussion consists of restatements of selected parts of the doctrines of Aristotle, Cicero, and Quintilian. Although seven of the twenty-three lectures in Lawson's book are concerned with the subject of style, it is misleading to say that Lawson stresses style more than he does invention. Style remains one of the sources of persuasion. It is an important source and therefore deserves serious study. Disposition and delivery also provide sources of persuasion that the speaker should not overlook. But Lawson does not lose his perspective. Good argument—truth—comes first. As it relates to invention, the function of style is to "dress up and make Truth beautiful."

IV. DELIVERY

The value of Lecture Twenty-two on "Pronunciation," or speech delivery, is not found in the theory presented but in adaptation of theory to pulpit oratory. The division of the general subject into two parts, voice and action, follows closely the same plan stated by Cicero and Quintilian.[22] When Lawson continues in his discussion of voice by further breaking down the subject into two parts, native endowment and the management of the voice, he is clearly following the same dichotomy chosen by Quintilian, who also furnishes him with the plan for his remarks on gesturing. There is no evidence in the *Lectures* that Lawson knew the two seventeenth century treatises that deal exclusively with speech delivery—Robert Robinson's *Art of Pronynciation* (1617) and John Bulwer's *Chirologia . . . and Chironomia* (1644). But it may well be that he knew them and chose purposely to ignore them, first, because as he states, "Too much study of rules may harm more than it helps in improving delivery," and, second, because they were concerned largely with a study of gestures and it was Lawson's opinion that, "Cicero and Quintilian have left scarcely any Thing to be added on this Subject." In any event, he accepts the theory of speech delivery explained by Cicero and Quintilian, and he found the faults with which the Latin writers illustrated their theory present among the pulpit orators of his time.

In Lawson's lecture on speech delivery there are two arguments of particular interest to students of rhetorical theory. The first is his development of the statement that the best delivery is that which

---

[22]*De Oratore,* III, 59; *Institutio Oratoria,* XI, iii, 1.

closely approximates the speech delivery found in "animated conversation"—anticipating what Winans later popularized under the heading of "Conversational Quality."[23] Lawson advises his students to observe conversation in its simplest form between two people. By successive stages he enlarges upon this picture until he is describing the preacher speaking before his congregation.

> Transport in your Imagination this Man, into a Church. Employ him there, in laying before a large Assembly, Truths of the greatest Moment; wherein he is to explain, prove, encourage, exhort, deter, holding forth Rewards and Punishments without End. Manifest it is, that here also, the Manner of Speaking will remain the same. As the Audience is now much enlarged, it is true the Voice must be raised in Proportion; all will be therefore somewhat augmented; more Strength, more Vehemence, more Passion, more Rapidity in Reasoning, more Inflexions of the Voice, and more evident Variety; yet the whole Form of Pronunciation, the Tones, the Changes, and Emphasis are the same. It is still the same Nature that operates thro' all these Graduations; that reigns equally from the placid Sounds of familiar Dialogue, to the highest Strain of adorned Declamation.[24]

If not the same this is at least very close indeed to Winan's conception of "conversational quality." Nor does Lawson appear to be describing "conversational style," a term that, according to Winans, "suggests too strongly that all should speak in one manner." Assuming an artificial mode of delivery, Lawson states, was one of the "principal Errors, daily committed by public Speakers; especially from the Pulpit."

> A Person ascending the Pulpit imagines, that he is not to express himself from thence in any Sort, as he doth in private; but with

---

[23] James A. Winans: *Public Speaking,* New York, 1915, Chapter 2. This similarity between Winan's "conversational quality" and Lawson's explanation in the *Lectures* has been noted by others. By H. F. Harding in his "English Rhetorical Theory, 1750-1800," Ph.D. Dissertation, Cornell University, 1937, p. 40, and by Warren A. Guthrie in "The Development of Rhetorical Theory in America, 1635-1850," Ph.D. Dissertation, Northwestern University, 1940, p. 51. Guthrie, however, apparently overlooked Lawson's lecture on delivery, stating in his study, page 50, that "all the advice Lawson gives on delivery is presented in the two chapters on emotions," obviously referring to Lectures 10 and 11.
[24] *Lectures,* pp. 414-15.

this new Situation assumeth to himself a Character altogether new, a stately, solemn, pompous Gravity. His Language, his Utterance, his Cadences become all affected, and his Voice feigned; which Practice is undoubtedly wrong.[25]

While Lawson's discussion of this point is suggestive of Winans' "conversational quality," it is, however, neither as clear nor as complete as the exposition by Winans. Conversational quality as it is analyzed in detail by Winans is, by Lawson, left too much in the vague "follow nature" category common with the writers of his time.[26]

The second argument of significance to students of rhetorical theory is Lawson's sincere objection to the use of any "systems" for the marking of emphasis, accent, inflection, pause, etc. as an aid to the improvement of speech delivery. In his discussion he refers to "some learned Persons" who "have imagined a Method of rendering Pronunciation easy to all, in a Way which we may name Mechanical."[27] Who the "learned Persons" referred to, is not clear. Blanks[28] suggests that he may have had in mind Walker or Steele. But it would appear more likely that Lawson was aware of the discussions leading up to the publications by Sheridan[29] and Burgh,[30] and in his *Lectures* desired to state his opposition to this departure from classical rhetorical theory. In any event, Lawson remains an advocate of classicism in rhetorical theory, and his *Lectures* voice one of the early objections to the elocutionary philosophy that, according to Sandford,[31] became a separate movement about 1760. Convinced that Cicero and Quintilian—and especially the latter since it was his custom to descend

---

[25]*Ibid.,* p. 416.

[26]An analysis of the "return to nature" philosophy dominant during the period is in Sir Leslie Stephen's *English Thought in the Eighteenth Century,* London, 1876, II, 447-57 in the 1927 reprint.

[27]*Lectures,* p. 423.

[28]Anthony Faulkner Blanks: An Introductory Study in the History of the Teaching of Public Speaking in the United States, Ph.D. Dissertation, Leland Stanford Junior University, 1927, p. 14. However, Blanks does not state whether he is referring to William Walker's *Improvement on the Art of Speaking,* 1717, and Richard Steele's *Grammar of the English Tongue,* 1728, or to Joshua Steele's *Prosodia Rationalis,* 1775, and John Walker's *Elements of Elocution,* 1781.

[29]Thomas Sheridan: *Lectures on Elocution,* London, 1762.

[30]James Burgh: *Art of Speaking,* London, 1762.

[31]W. P. Sandford: *English Theories of Public Address, 1530-1828,* Columbus, Ohio, 1938, p. 138.

"to a very minute Detail"—knew nothing of this mechanical marking of manuscripts, Lawson dismisses such methods, as far as pulpit speaking is concerned, as "altogether chimerical."

Lawson joined with Steele, Addison, and Swift in the first half, and with Goldsmith and Priestley in the second half of the eighteenth century in severely criticizing the cold lifeless, and uncommunicative manner observed in the preacher's delivery of his sermons. Unlike some of these critics, however, Lawson was not "simply a lecturer" who "appeared only in the auditorium, never in the rehearsal hall," as alleged by Haberman.[32] The *Lectures* show that in addition to the more formal lectures before his classes Lawson was present at regular weekly sessions with his students where practice in speech delivery was one of the problems under evaluation.[33]

V. INFLUENCE OF THE *LECTURES*

The *Lectures* never exercised much influence either as a widely used textbook in classes or as a source book for later writers on the subject. Neither the *Lectures* nor their author receives mention in the rhetorics of John Ward, George Campbell, Hugh Blair, or Richard Whately. Although it has been asserted that the *Lectures* were used as a textbook for classes in America,[34] and that the book "was readily available for student use"[35] in this country, no evidence has been uncovered in this investigation that would indicate widespread usage of the *Lectures* either in Europe or America. At the date of this investigation (1950) only eleven copies of the *Lectures* had been located in the United States—two of the 1758 first edition, four of the 1759 second edition, and five of the 1760 or last edition. Collation of these three editions reveals that only minor differences exist be-

---

[32]Frederick W. Haberman: The Elocutionary Movement in England, 1750-1850, Ph.D. Dissertation, Cornell University, 1947, p. 396.

[33]For example, in Lecture 2, p. 23, Lawson explains that "Pronunciation" cannot be taught in a "continued Discourse," but that he is "leaving to our usual weekly Lectures the Care of Pronunciation." The "Weekly Lectures" is in obvious contrast with "continued Discourse" or more formal lecture situation.

[34]Blanks: *op. cit.*, p. 14.

[35]Ota Thomas: The Teaching of Rhetoric in the United States During the Classical Period of Education, in *A History and Criticism of American Public Address*, ed. W. N. Brigance, New York, 1943, I, 202. If the *Lectures* were as available as this implies, it is surprising that so few copies have come down to us.

tween them, and it is suggested that perhaps reprints would have been a more accurate designation than editions.

Addressed to divinity students the *Lectures* probably were read by Lawson to his classes while he was Professor of Oratory and History in Trinity College, Dublin, during the period 1750 to 1759. Since the *Lectures* were first published in November, 1758[36] and Lawson died in January, 1759—only two months later—it is unlikely that the *Lectures* in their published form ever were used by Lawson in his classes. The *Lectures* have been referred to favorably, though in general terms only, by various writers: "His *Lectures* on Oratory are highly commendable . . . a most ingenious treatise."[37] "A course of Lectures on Oratory which display much knowledge of that attractive subject."[38] "This author merits the particular attention of every young clergyman."[39] Lord Chesterfield wrote favorably of the *Lectures* but he was dubious of their success: "I have read them with all the satisfaction that I expected, from my knowledge and esteem of the author. His design is laudable, and his endeavours able, but yet I will not answer for his success . . . make my compliments to Dr. Lawson, and return him my thanks for the flattering mention he has made of me in his excellent work."[40]

VI. SUMMARY

What place do the *Lectures* deserve in the stream of rhetorical

---

[36]Sandford: *op. cit.,* p. 127 states that the *Lectures* were first published in 1752, and Karl R. Wallace in *Francis Bacon on Communication and Rhetoric,* Chapel Hill, North Carolina, 1943, p. 221, probably relying on Sandford, perpetuates this error. For verification of the 1758 date see the following: *Monthly Review,* First Series, *20:*63-79, January 1759; *Gentleman's Magazine, 23:*543, November 1758; *London Magazine, 27:*599, November 1758; *Universal Magazine, 23:*271, November 1758; *Dictionary of National Biography,* XXXII; Robert Watt, *Bibliotheca britannica; or, A general index to British and foreign literature,* Edinburgh, 1824, II, 593 b.

[37]*Notes and Queries,* Third Series, *6:*310, October 1864.

[38]W. B. S. Taylor: *A History of the University of Dublin,* London, 1845, p. 442.

[39]S. A. Allibone: *A Dictionary of British and American Authors,* Philadelphia, 1858.

[40]*The Letters of Philip Dormer Stanhope 4th Earl of Chesterfield,* ed. with an introduction by Bonamy Dobree, New York, 1932, V, 2336. The letter number 2081, is addressed to Alderman Faulkner, the distinguished printer, and is dated January 16, 1759. In Lecture 18 Lawson dedicates a "poetical Essay" called "The Judgment of Plato" to Lord Chesterfield.

tradition? Lawson apparently took little notice of most of the works on rhetoric written during the sixteenth and seventeenth centuries. There is no reference in the *Lectures* to those by Cox, Sherry, Wilson, Taleus, Farnaby, Butler, Bulwer, or Walker. From the *Advancement of Learning,* however, he accepted Bacon's suggestion that the study, collection, and use of commonplaces were a part of classical rhetoric that should no longer be neglected. He rejected the detailed classification of figures found in *De Rhetorica* (1621) of Vossius because "those Writers have multiplied them without Cause." The phrase "those Writers" may perhaps include Sherry's treatment of the subject in his *Figures of Grammer and Rhetoric* (1555), or the discussion of more than one hundred thirty tropes and figures found in John Smith's *Mysterie of Rhetorique Unveiled* (1657) but neither receives any mention in the *Lectures.*

In line with the intellectual trend of his time Lawson attempted to restate some of the classical principles as outlined by Aristotle, Cicero, and Quintilian. His adaptation of classical theory to pulpit oratory, however, does not differ significantly from that attempted by some other writers[41] in the hundred years before his death. Lawson's emphasis on the need for "conversational quality" in preaching does appear to be a unique contribution to the literature of the period. And his criticism of "mechanical systems" for teaching speech delivery places him among the first to raise objections against the elocutionary movement then in its formative stage.

Perhaps the fact that Lawson had been in ill health for months before the *Lectures* were published may account in part for some of the shortcomings present in the *Lectures* in their published form. Some of the lectures should have been more carefully revised for publication. Long digressions, many times bearing little relation to the titled content of the lectures, are tiring for the reader. Organization of some lectures is faulty. The style, although usually clear, is at times redundant, resulting in many long rambling sentences that invite obscurity.

---

[41]Such as that found in Richard Baxter's *Gildas Salvianus,* or *The Reformed Pastor,* 1656, in *The Practical Works of the Late Rev. and Pious Mr. Richard Baxter,* London, 1856, IV; Sir Richard Blackmore: *Accomplished Preacher,* London, 1731; Gilbert Burnet: *A Discourse of the Pastoral Care,* London, 1713; John Wilkins: *Ecclesiastes,* London, 1646; and in Jean Claude: *Traite de la composition d'un sermon,* 1688.

On the other hand, the admittedly eclectic method of the author results in the presentation of classical rhetorical principles seasoned with the good common sense of the practicing preacher who never forgets that in delivering a speech, or a sermon, the audience deserves first consideration.

The appraisal of the *Lectures,* written by William Rose for the *Monthly Review of January,* 1759 is, in general, accurate: "Those who are conversant with such subjects, will find that the doctor has scarce advanced anything new upon them, and that his stile is not always well suited to the dignity of his subject. His language, though clear and strong, is sometimes inelegant; and his periods often harsh and unharmonious. His observations, however, are generally just; his method is easy and natural; and he had displayed no inconsiderable share of learning."

DOMINANT TRENDS IN
ENGLISH RHETORICAL THOUGHT 1750-1800

DOUGLAS EHNINGER

University of Florida

I. INTRODUCTION

THE YEARS between 1750 and 1800 stand forth as a period of unusual productivity in English rhetorical thought. Harding has estimated that during this half century more than two score original treatises on rhetoric came from British presses.[1] Of these, at least half a dozen may be regarded as major landmarks in the history of rhetorical theory. Numerous others, while of lesser stature, have unusual interest and importance, not only for the historian of rhetoric, but for all teachers of the arts of writing and speaking.

The importance of these works grows out of the fact that during the second half of the eighteenth century English rhetorical theory was radically reshaped as a result of impelling pressures exerted upon it by contemporary doctrines of psychology, epistemology, and literary criticism, as well as by altered social conditions and new educational needs. Viewed in sum, these forces freed rhetoric from the degenerate classicism that had been erected upon the ruins left by the Ramean apostasy. Viewed individually, they resulted in four specific movements or trends, each of which contributed in a very material fashion to the development of the modified or adapted classicism which characterizes the majority of our current textbooks.

In this paper I propose to review briefly the nature and etiology

---

[1] Harold F. Harding: English Rhetorical Theory, 1750-1800, Ph.D. Thesis, Cornell University, 1937, 292.

of these movements, and to indicate some of the influences which
each had in forming present-day theories of discourse. The movements with which I shall be concerned are here designated as: Classicism, Psychological-Epistemological Theories of Discourse, Elocutionism, and The Belletristic Rhetoric.

II. CLASSICISM

In the middle decades of the eighteenth century English rhetoric
was in two quite different senses of the word almost exclusively an
"academic" science. Not only did it flourish principally within the
walls of the colleges and academies,[2] but it was, for the most part,
completely unresponsive to contemporary thought and life. Un-
touched by the Lockean revolution in philosophy and uninspired by
the new vistas opening in science and criticism, it was content to do
no more than "abstract . . . adapt [and] synthesize" the doctrines set
forth by the major theorists of antiquity—chiefly those of Quintilian,
Cicero, and Longinus and, to a lesser extent, those of Aristotle.[3]

This dominance of ancient rhetorical thought was the end result
of a trend that had its inception as early as 1660.[4] But after 1700
three separate forces gave added momentum to the development of
a rhetoric strictly classical in nature. These were: 1) the appearance
of numerous editions of the classical tracts, 2) the translation into
English of contemporary Continental works expressing the classical
tradition, and 3) the publication by Englishmen of original treatises
closely modeled upon the ancient analysis.[5]

A tabulation that is suggestive rather than complete reveals that
Latin versions of Quintilian were printed in England in 1715, 1716,

---

[2] Rhetorical instruction in the English universities during the eighteenth century
is well described in Christopher Wordsworth: *Scholae Academicae,* Cambridge,
1877. See especially 87-9, 332, and 350-1.

The best single source on the teaching of rhetoric in the nonconformist academies is H. McLachlan: *English Education Under the Test Acts,* Manchester, 1931.

[3] Harding: 1, 278.

[4] William P. Sandford: *English Theories of Public Address, 1530-1828,* Columbus,
Ohio, 1938, 70.

[5] On "the classical predilection and preoccupation of the English mind" during
the eighteenth century, and its effect on art and letters, see Osbert Sitwell and
Margaret Barton: Taste, *Johnson's England,* ed. A. S. Turberville, 2 vols., Oxford,
1931, II, 1-4 *passim.*

1738, and 1758 with William Guthrie's important translation coming to the public in 1756. Longinus, extremely popular and influential throughout the entire century, was printed in 1710, 1718, 1724, 1730, 1732, 1733, 1743, 1751, 1752-62, and translated in 1712, 1739, 1742, 1752, and in 1757. *De Oratore* appeared in Latin in 1706, 1714, 1716, 1718, 1732, 1745, 1746, 1749, and in English in 1723, 1742, 1755, and 1759. Dates for *Ad Herennium* are 1714, and 1718; for Greek or Latin texts of Aristotle's *Rhetoric,* 1726, 1728, and 1759; for his *Poetics,* 1728, 1731, and 1745, with translations 1705, 1709, and 1714.

Of the contempory Continental work in the classical tradition which were translated into English between 1660 and 1760 probably the three most influential were Bernard Lami's *L'Art de Parler* (1675), English versions of which appeared in 1676, 1696, 1737, 1780, etc.; Charles Rollin's *Traité des Etudes* (1726-8), translated 1742 and 1749;[6] and Fénelon's *Dialogues sur l'Eloquence* (Amsterdam, 1717; Paris 1718), English translations of which were issued in 1722, 1750, and 1760.

British authors who offered treatises falling strictly within the classical framework include John Brightland, *A Grammar of the English Tongue* (1712); John Constable, *Reflections Upon Accuracy of Style* (1734); and John Holmes, *The Art of Rhetoric* (1739). The two last named books are, in fact, little more than paraphrases of parts of Quintilian.

Midway in the century the trend toward classicism culminated in the publication of two works of very considerable importance: John Lawson's *Lectures Concerning Oratory* (1752)[7] and John Ward's *A System of Oratory* (1759). Both are printings of academic lectures, Lawson having been "lecturer on oratory and history on the foundation of Erasmus Smith" at Trinity College, Dublin; and Ward, professor of rhetoric at Gresham College in London. Moreover, both present in great detail, and without any significant modifications, the principles and methods of the classical rhetoric. Ward's *System,* which covers more than eight hundred pages, may be regarded as the most

---

[6]Also published in French at London, 1734. The continued popularity of this work in England during the second half of the eighteenth century is indicated by the fact that translations appeared 1768, 1769, 1770.

[7]Other editions: 1758, 1759, 1760.

complete statement of ancient rhetorical doctrine ever written in English.[8]

Interest in the classical rhetoric continued throughout the century as is evidenced by the publication of Thomas Leland's *A Dissertation on the Principles of Human Eloquence* (London, 1764; Dublin, 1765), Lord Monboddo's *Origin and Progress of Language* (Edinburgh, 1774-92),[9] and a fresh edition of Thomas Gale's *Rhetores Selecti* [1773].[10] However, after Ward and Lawson a new tendency in rhetorical theory began to appear. Advancing beyond the sterile rehearsal of classical doctrine, writers undertook to adapt their works to new and changed conditions; to take into account current philosophical, critical, and aesthetic doctrines; to evolve a rhetoric out of contemporary thought, specifically designed to meet contemporary needs.

As developed principally in the works of George Campbell, Joseph Priestley, and John Ogilvie, this tendency resulted in what have here been called Psychological-Epistemological Theories of Discourse.

III. PSYCHOLOGICAL-EPISTEMOLOGICAL THEORIES OF DISCOURSE

Although the science of psychology as we know it today was not born until the latter decades of the nineteenth century and the term "psychology" did not itself become current until late in the eighteenth,[11] the great speculative thinkers of the Enlightenment, both in England and on the Continent, devoted themselves very largely to a systematic study of the mental nature of man. This concerted effort to examine and describe conscious processes produced three distinct theories of mind which exerted important influences on rhetorical doctrine. The first two—provided we remember that a nineteenth-century term is being appropriated—may most conveniently be called the "psychology of association" and the "psychology of the

---

[8]Douglas Ehninger: John Ward and His Rhetoric, *Speech Monographs, XVIII*: 15, March 1951.

[9]In the sixth and final volume of this monumental work Lord Monboddo presents a discussion of rhetoric that does little more than summarize Aristotle's doctrines.

[10]First published 1676. Contains excerpts from Demetrius Tiberius Rhetor and other ancient theorists.

[11]Gladys Bryson: *Man and Society,* Princeton, 1945, 114, 264.

faculties." The third is usually known as the "common sense phil-osophy."

The psychology of association was primarily an English develop-ment, and its influence is abundantly apparent in the writings of Locke, Berkeley, and Hume. It was, however, at the hands of the physician David Hartley that associationism received its most com-prehensive treatment.[12] Hartley set for himself the task of explain-ing how all psychical phenomena, even the most complex, arise from "simple" sensations. These, in turn, are organized by the mind ac-cording to the "laws" of association—continuity in space, succession in time, and contrast in relation. Secondary associations and affec-tions result in those pleasures and pains which are the more complex components of mental life.

Christian Wolff, a German (1679-1754), is generally regarded as the father of the faculty psychology. In his *psychologia Empirica* (1732) and *Psychologia Rationalis* (1734) he asserted that the mind, though basically unitary, functions "in distinct capacities, now re-membering and then imagining, each being a power (faculty) as well as a process."[13] The primary faculties—and in this later writers generally concurred—he described as knowing and feeling.

In the field of rhetoric, associationism is represented principally by Joseph Priestley's *Course of Lectures on Oratory and Criticism* (1777). Indeed, as Priestley himself suggests in the Preface,[14] the *Course* was given to the public partly for the purpose of illustrating how associational principles might be applied in formulating a coher-ent system of persuasion. Associationism also provided the general theoretical basis for Lord Kames' influential *Elements of Criticism* (1762).

The faculty psychology, on the other hand, was appropriated almost bodily by John Ogilvie for the doctrinal foundation of his *Philosophical and Critical Observations on the Nature, Characters, and Various Species of Composition* (1774);[15] and was also influential

---

[12]Hartley's principal work, *Observations on Man,* was published at London in 1749.

[13]Joseph Jastrow: Psychology, *Encyclopedia of the Social Sciences,* ed. Edwin R. A. Seligman, New York, 1930-4, XII, 590.

[14]Joseph Priestley: *A Course of Lectures on Oratory and Criticism,* London, 1777, i-ii.

[15]Ogilvie recognized four faculties: understanding (or judgment or reason), imagi-nation, penetration (or discernment), and memory.

in shaping the analysis offered by Hugh Blair, author of the well-known *Lectures on Rhetoric and Belles Lettres* (1783). In fact, it is more or less evident in all of the important rhetorical treatises of the period.[16] To it George Campbell owes not only his famous statement of the "conviction-persuasion duality," but also his epoch-making classification of the "ends" of speaking.[17]

The name of Campbell brings us to a consideration of the third of the influences mentioned above—that of the so-called "common sense philosophy." This philosophy is generally associated with the name of the Scottish thinker, Thomas Reid. Reacting against the scepticism of Hume, and in a very real sense anticipating some of the fundamental assumptions of Immanuel Kant, Reid posited the existence of certain "common" presuppositions, or conditions, which underlie all human knowledge; and which, because they are instinctive, are unassailable by doubt. Moreover, he directly challenged the view held by Locke, Berkeley, and Hume that between the knowing mind and the knowable world there intervenes a *tertium quid* in the form of an "idea." Instead, he believed that under certain conditions "immediate" knowledge was possible.[18] This doctrine furnished, as I have shown elsewhere,[19] much of the theoretical groundwork for George Campbell's brilliant *Philosophy of Rhetoric* (1776). In particular, it accounts for his analysis of "evidence."

Taken as a whole, the major works in the psychological-epistemological tradition are of first importance in the history of rhetorical theory. For not only did they help break the hard shell of classicism, but in so doing they laid many of the foundation stones upon which rest our present-day theories of writing and speaking. Thus, for example, our custom of classifying speeches according to the end sought by the speaker rather than according to the circumstances under which they are delivered (deliberative, epideictic, forensic); our distinction between "conviction" as resting upon logical argu-

---

[16]Irving J. Lee: A Study of Emotional Appeal in Rhetorical Theory. With Special Reference to Invention, Arrangement, and Style, Ph.D. Thesis, Northwestern University, 1939, 200.

[17]Sandford: 110-1, 113.

[18]Reid's views are most fully and clearly stated in his *Inquiry into the Human Mind, on the Principles of Common Sense,* Edinburgh, 1764.

[19]Douglas Ehninger: George Campbell and the Revolution in Inventional Theory, *The Southern Speech Journal, XV*:270-6, May 1950.

ment and "persuasion" as resting upon psychological appeal; and our general emphasis upon the importance of the audience as a factor in the total speaking situation may all be directly traced to the doctrines of associationism, the faculty psychology, or the philosophy of common sense.[20]

IV. ELOCUTIONISM

Coincident with the development of the psychological-epistemological rhetoric was another movement which also played a significant role in the creation of modern rhetorical theory. This was elocutionism.

While the elocutionists differed among themselves on finer points of doctrine and employed diverse instructional methods, they all agreed that training in delivery should constitute the core of rhetorical education. With this end in view they concentrated their teaching on such matters as accent and emphasis, pitch and modulation, pause and timing, articulation and pronunciation, and gesture.[21]

A powerful force stimulating the elocutionary movement was the intense criticism of British public address, especially preaching, which had arisen during the early decades of the eighteenth century. Addison, Swift, Hume, and Chesterfield were among those who had raised their voices in protest against the crabbed composition and lifeless delivery of contemporary speakers.[22] In 1771 Anselm Bayly, a sub-deacon of his Majesty's Chapel-Royal, wrote a book titled *A Practical Treatise on Singing and Playing* in which he specifically lamented the fact that training in delivery did not constitute an important part of every youth's education. Nearly twenty years later in his *Alliance of Music, Poetry, and Oratory* (1789) he renewed the criticism. Additional pleas for the teaching of speaking and oral reading were made by Vicesimus Knox in his *Liberal Education* (1781) and by Richard Edgeworth in *Practical Elocution* (1798).

---

[20]See Douglas Ehninger: Selected Theories of *Inventio* in English Rhetoric, 1759-1828, Ph.D. Thesis, The Ohio State University, 1949, 130-220. For a typical evaluation of the audience as a crucial factor in the speaking situation see Donald C. Bryant and Karl R. Wallace: *Fundamentals of Public Speaking,* New York, 1947, 15.

[21]Mary Margaret Robb: *Oral Interpretation of Literature in American Colleges and Universities,* New York, 1941, 46 ff.

[22]A useful summary of this criticism is presented in Lester Thonssen and A. Craig Baird: *Speech Criticism,* New York, 1948, 211-4.

Although the first important elocutionary manuals to appear in England—Robert Dodsley's *Preceptor* and John Mason's *An Essay on Elocution*—were both published in 1748, the movement received its chief impetus some years later from the work of Thomas Sheridan who, through his teaching and lecturing as well as through the publication of four important treatises,[23] fathered what is commonly referred to as "the natural method" of oral reading. The other major pedagogical approach to the teaching of delivery, "the mechanical method," was developed principally by John Walker in his *Elements of Elocution* (1781) and *Rhetorical Grammar* (1785),[24] and by Joshua Steele in his *Prosodia Rationalis* (1775). Gilbert Austin's *Chironomia* (1806) is an extensive discussion of gesture.[25]

Lesser works in the elocutionary movement include James Burgh's *Art of Speaking* [1762 or 1763], while William Enfield's *Exercises in Elocution* (1780), and John Rice's *An Introduction to the Art of Reading with Energy and Propriety* (1765).

One of the important results of elocutionism was to help popularize rhetoric by taking it out of its traditional academic environment. Sheridan and some of the other elocutionists lectured to popular as well as to learned audiences throughout England and Scotland. Their textbooks were directed not only at school boys but also at adult men and women in all walks of life. Moreover, by regarding language as something essentially oral rather than written, they anticipated modern theories of language teaching.[26] Most important of all, however, the elocutionists brought about an increased awareness of the importance of delivery as an element in persuasion, thus effect-

---

[23]*British Education* (1756); *Discourse Being Introductory to a Course of Lectures on Elocution and the English Language* (1759); *Lectures on Elocution* (1763); *Lectures on Reading* (1775).

[24]Other books by Walker are: *Exercises for Improvement in Elocution* (1777); *Hints for Improvement in the Art of Reading* (1783); *The Melody of Speaking Delineated* (1787); *The Teacher's Assistant* (1787).

[25]For a convenient summary of the works of Sheridan, Walker, and Austin see Charles A. Fritz: From Sheridan to Rush: The Beginnings of English Elocution, *The Quarterly Journal of Speech*, *XVI*:75-88, February 1930. A new and challenging interpretation of the mechanists is presented in W. M. Parrish: The Concept of 'Naturalness,' *The Quarterly Journal of Speech*, *XXXVII*:448-54, December 1951.

[26]John William Adamson: An Outline of English Education, 1760-1902, *The Cambridge History of English Literature*, 15 vols., Cambridge, 1907-27, XIV, 398.

ing a new balance among the "parts" of rhetoric—a balance which tends to give delivery a position equal in importance and dignity to those traditionally enjoyed by invention and disposition. Needless to remark, this is a balance which is exhibited in most of our current textbooks.

V. BELLETRISTIC RHETORIC

A fourth trend in English rhetorical thought during the years between 1750 and 1800 was the habit of viewing rhetoric as one facet of the broad field of *belles lettres;* or, stated conversely, the habit of stretching rhetoric "into the Science of Literature, or Literary Theory and Literary Criticism universally, and [making] it treat the principles of Historical Writing, Poetry, and Expository Writing, as well as of Oratory."[27]

The roots of the belletristic rhetoric are deep. In 1658 the Dutch rhetorician Vossius in his *De Philosophia* had placed his discussion of eloquence between the chapter devoted to politics and that given over to literary criticism. Moreover, he had categorically asserted that "eloquence is twofold, oratorical and poetical. . . ."[28] During the later decades of the eighteenth century the rhetoric of *belles lettres* played a role of major importance. Best exemplified, perhaps, in Hugh Blair's previously mentioned *Lectures on Rhetoric and Belles Lettres,* it held that rhetorical theory, literary theory, and the science of criticism may be grouped under a single head. Because they all are, as we might say today, language arts, they have a common foundation in words and are merely more or less specialized developments of the same root.

Such a view naturally tends to blur, although it does not completely obliterate, the Aristotelian distinction between practical and imaginative discourse. In addition, it has the effect of giving style a position of enhanced importance, at the same time reducing the significance of the place held by invention.[89] Both of these altera-

---

[27]*The Collected Writings of Thomas DeQuincey,* ed. David Masson, 14 vols., London, 1896-7, X, 85. Editor's note.

[28]Charles Sears Baldwin: Rhetoric, *A Cyclopedia of Education,* ed. Paul Monroe, New York, 1911-3, V, 177.

[29]The relationship between the belletristic rhetoric and the standard classical analysis is well discussed in George R. Creecraft: Three Scottish Rhetoricians of the Eighteenth Century: Kames, Campbell, and Blair, M. A. Thesis, University of Illinois, 1922.

tions arise from the fact that expression rather than substance is made the focal point in rhetorical theory. Indeed, this evaluation of the part played in discourse by expression may be regarded as the key to the belletristic analysis. The result was, as Baldwin has said, "to detain rhetoric in the field of diction and to consider it in aspects related to poetics."[30]

In the rhetoric of *belles lettres* nearly all specific rules and principles have a double function. On the one hand, they are guides to composing; on the other, standards for judging. Thus they are, at least in theory, equally useful to the writer or speaker and to the critic. In practice, however, it transpired that the second of these functions gradually came to overshadow the first. Therefore, rhetoric, now newly called by the name of "eloquence," became, in the words of Saintsbury, "the Art of Literature, or in other words, Criticism."[31] That is, it largely lost the character of a practical art concerned with composition and became almost exclusively a speculative science concerned with judging.

With rhetoric viewed as a tool for criticism, it required but another step to consider it a part of the general science of aesthetics and place it under a common rubric with inquiries into the nature of beauty and the foundations of taste. Thus it occasions no surprise to find in Lord Kames' *Elements of Criticism* some five hundred pages which may quite properly be regarded as "a combined rhetoric and poetic."[32] In fact, in this and similar treatises rhetorical theory definitely throws off the role assigned it by the ancients and acquires a new scope and function.

Of all the modifications in rhetoric resulting from the influence of the belletristic school, none is perhaps more important, or more familiar, than the abolishment of the line between written and spoken discourse. It is, indeed, because of the basic assumptions of the rhetoric of *belles lettres* about the unity of all language arts that those of us whose freshman days in college date back some twenty or thirty

---

[30]Baldwin: 177.
[31]George Saintsbury: *A History of Criticism and Literary Taste in Europe from the Earliest Texts to the Present Day*, 3 vols., New York, Edinburgh, and London, 1902, II, 471.
[32]Helen Whitcomb Randall: The Critical Theory of Lord Kames, *Smith College Studies in Modern Languages*, *XXII*:23, October 1940-July 1941.

years often studied our grammar and written composition in courses named Rhetoric I and II.[33]

---

[33]While the sixteenth- and seventeenth-century rhetoric of style continued to be expressed in such works as Thomas Gibbon's *Rhetoric* (1767), John Stirling's *System of Rhetoric* (first published 1733, but frequently reissued after 1750), and Peter Peckard's *The Proper Stile of Christian Oratory* (1770), it was hardly influential enough to be called one of the dominant trends in English rhetorical thought between 1750 and 1800.

THOMAS SHERIDAN AND THE NATURAL SCHOOL

DANIEL E. VANDRAEGEN

University of California at Los Angeles

WE HAVE BEEN trained to respect labels. Once a label has been affixed to a thing, be it to a bottle or to a man and his teachings, we frequently are inclined to accept it as proof of the thing itself. Thus, mere inscription usurps description and proposes itself as the nature of content. Sometimes this may be insufficient guarantee. Sometimes it may be misleading.

More specifically, this problem presents itself when considering much that has been written about the eighteenth century British elocutionist Thomas Sheridan. He has been contrarily labeled "natural" by some writers and "mechanical" by others.

Among those calling his philosophy and teachings "natural" are such authorities as William Sandford and Mary Margaret Robb. Sandford writes that "we find in the works of Sheridan a sane and natural approach, with great emphasis upon the conversational manner as the norm of presentation, and with definite opposition to mechanical means of teaching expression."[1] Robb agrees and additionally refers to Sheridan as the "leader" of a "Natural School." A school, she says, which "followed natural laws."[2]

On the other hand, there are those who regard Sheridan's ideas and practice as "mechanical." Wayland Maxfield Parrish observes that

---

[1]William Phillips Sandford: *English Theories of Public Address*, Columbus, Ohio, 1938, pp. 131-132.

[2]Mary Margaret Robb: *Oral Interpretation of Literature in American Colleges and Universities*, New York, 1941, p. 31.

"Sheridan leaned toward the mechanical method, for he adopted a set of marks for denoting the different pauses, emphases, etc."[3] Professor Winans is more emphatic. He insists that Sheridan's method of reading was "thoroughly mechanical."[4] He also declares that he finds no fundamental difference between Sheridan and John Walker whose methods have been universally regarded as being mechanistic and whom Robb regards as the leader of the "Mechanical School."[5]

Another student of the elocutionary movement in eighteenth century England, Frederick W. Haberman, agrees with Winans' criticism of Sheridan and shares his conclusion that Sheridan's "work-a-day philosophy was a mechanistic one."[6] He then goes on to question Robb's statement that "two schools evolved following opposing pedagogical ideas."[7] He expresses his opinion in the following words:

> . . . it would seem that the evidence cited by Robb for the contention held jointly by her and Professor Fritz that the elocutionary movement split into a natural school and a mechanical school does not compel acceptance. On the contrary, there is no external evidence whatsoever to indicate that such schools actually existed; and whatever conclusions are to be drawn from the internal evidence of the work of these early elocutionists lead us to believe that the predominate philosophy of the entire group was a mechanistic one. But, in reality, we have scratched only the surface of this question.[8]

The concluding admission of surface scratching may explain, but will hardly encourage acceptance of, Haberman's pronouncements. Particularly, one is inclined to suspect the labeling of the entire group of elocutionists as "mechanistic." As for "internal evidence" supporting this claim, it depends considerably upon what portions of the material one selects to examine.

In reading the literature of the eighteenth century elocutionists, we become aware of an interesting and curious fact. Both groups, now

---

[3]Wayland Maxfield Parrish: *Reading Aloud,* New York, 1941, p. 33.
[4]James A. Winans: Whateley on Elocution, *QJS, XXI*:2, February 1945.
[5]Robb: *op. cit.,* p. 31.
[6]Fredrick William Haberman: The Elocutionary Movement in England, 1750-1850, Ph.D. Dissertation, Cornell University, 1947, p. 57.
[7]Robb: *op. cit.,* p. 31.
[8]Haberman: *op. cit.,* p. 59.

referred to as the "natural" and the "mechanical," pursue the same prime objective. Both endeavor to teach students to speak and read naturally. Robb's assertion that two separate schools followed "opposing pedagogical ideas" is misleading. Internal evidence reveals that while there are differences of method, both groups completely agree on the central pedagogical objective of directing students to perform in a natural manner.

It is also significant that no term in the eighteenth century has been so diversely interpreted as this one of "natural" or "nature." Professor A. O. Lovejoy calls it "this verbal jack-of-all-trades."[9] In explanation he describes as many as sixty different meanings historically employed for "nature" as an esthetic norm.[10] He then adds the following caution that nothing "is more needful, especially for the student of literature and philosophy of the seventeenth and eighteenth centuries, than a thorough understanding of the diversity of the word."[11]

Certainly it is true that most controversies would soon be concluded if those involved would first precisely define their terms and then afterwards, adhere to their definitions. The difficulty with the term "natural" is that it has been all things to all men. Its protean character has permitted us to slip more or less insensibly from one connotation to another. Consequently, as Lovejoy points out, this has frequently led us "to pass from one ethical or esthetic standard to its very antithesis, while nominally professing the same principles."[12] This confusion of identity has been one of the difficulties in evaluating the contribution of the elocutionists. It is no less true of Sheridan.

Without undertaking a detailed semasiological investigation of the manifold doctrines and interpretations associated with this term "natural,"[13] it seems entirely reasonable to settle upon two prevailing tendencies in the eighteenth century. Two manifestations of the human spirit were esthetically active—the neo-classical and the romantic. Both modes attempted to follow "Nature."

[9]A. O. Lovejoy: Nature as an Aesthetic Norm, *Modern Language Notes, XLVII*: 444, November 1927.

[10]*Ibid.*, 444-450.

[11]*Ibid.*, 444.

[12]*Ibid.*

[13]For a stimulating discussion of the concept of nature during the period under consideration see Basil Willey: *The Eighteenth Century Background. Studies on the Idea of Nature in the Thought of the Period*, London, 1940.

To the neo-classicist, this meant recognizing and expressing that which was typical and customary in nature and human experience. It meant performance governed by rules based upon order, regularity, and patterns of common acceptance. It also meant that these rules were based upon proved models. This, in turn, indicates that imitation was a desirable, if not necessary, concomitant of training.

All of the foregoing is suggestive of the ideas and teachings of the group which, through common agreement, we have come to recognize as constituting a so-called Mechanical School. The followers of this school of thought favored listing types of emotions and moods. They then designed appropriate vocal and gesture patterns each regulated by its particular rule for proper portrayal. Matter, to a large measure, was dominated by form. Typical examples of this method are the instruction manuals of James Burgh and John Walker, universally regarded as being mechanistic.[14]

The mechanical nature of the Burgh and Walker approach to elocution is familiar to us. Burgh lists and analyzes ninety-eight complex "Passions and Humors" and prescribes the "natural" way to express them. For example, according to Burgh, this is the way "nature expresses" the emotion of "Joy:"

> *Joy* . . . expresses itself by *clapping of hands,* and *exultation,* or leaping. The *eyes* are *opened* wide; perhaps filled with *tears;* often raised to *heaven,* especially by devout persons. The countenance is smiling, not composedly, but with features *aggravated.* The voice rises, from time to time, to very *high* notes.[15]

This sample is quite representative of the rest of the material in Burgh's book. It is sterotyped action patterns such as this that the speaker and oral reader are advised to practice assiduously. The hope is that through repetition these patterns of expression will become part of the speaker's and reader's repertoire from which they may be skillfully brought forth and applied when the requisite speaking or reading occasion presents itself.

[14]See James Burgh: *The Art of Speaking,* Danbury, Conn., 1795. (First edition printed in London, England, 1762. By 1767 this edition appeared on the lists of Harvard University Library.) Also see John Walker: *Elements of Elocution,* Boston, Mass., 1810. (First edition printed in London, England, 1781. There were a number of British and American editions of this popular work.)

[15]Burgh: *op. cit.,* p. 21.

In the matter of expressive bodily action Walker faithfully follows Burgh. In addition, he provides a plethora of rules by which the speaker and reader are to examine every type of sentence and govern every phase of vocal modulation, inflection, emphasis, and pause. For example, in his *Elements of Elocution,* which is possibly the best known of his ten books on elocution, Walker uses one hundred and eleven pages and discusses some thirty-one rules governing inflections occurring in every type of sentence. He presents seven rules for the regulation of general vocal modulation. He dictates more rules for the use of emphasis, and he employs some seventy pages elucidating sixteen rules for pauses. This identical mechanical approach is consistently followed in his other works where these same subjects happen to be discussed.

So we see that the mechanical elocutionist "followed nature" by relying upon a system of rules and a stock of predetermined and pre-scribed voice and action patterns. In this manner he achieved expressive patterns of communication which were typical and customary, and thereby, "natural."

To the romanticist, on the other hand, following nature meant performing spontaneously and sincerely out of the fullness and force of heartfelt emotion. It meant recognizing and expressing that which was unique and personal in nature and human experience. It meant recognition of irregularity, an acceptance of deviation from set patterns of performance. It meant a distrust of rules, a suspicion of models, and a questioning of imitation as a discipline of instruction. It meant, above all, a reliance upon the individual's personal response.[16]

The ideas just presented, with modification tempered by the influence of classical rhetorical tradition, appear dominant in the teaching of the eighteenth century elocutionists we have come to recognize as constituting a so-called Natural School. Thomas Sheridan emphatically voices these view points when he advises the oral reader to "forget that he ever learned to read; at least let him wholly forget his reading tones. Let him speak entirely from his feelings; and they will find much truer signs to manifest themselves by, than he could

---

[16]For an eloquent statement by a writer of the middle eighteenth century giving precedence to "natural genius" over the genius formed by art and imitation, see Edward Young: *Conjectures on Original Composition* [1759], ed. Edith J. Morley, London and New York, 1918.

find for them."[17] Furthermore, Sheridan condemns the practice of imitation, expresses distrust of rules, and praises individuality and sincerity of communication when he declares that "he who speaks from his heart, can never fall into any absurdity in his manner; this is what they only are liable to, who adopt the manner of another, or are governed by imperfect, or ill-founded rules of art."[18]

A point will be raised here that Sheridan frequently expresses a desire for rules and standards of delivery together with qualified instructors to teach them. He does.[19] These declarations have further influenced critics to label his methods mechanical. But Sheridan particularly refrains from actually presenting any rules in this connection. He reasons that they would be worthless without the establishment of an organized and comprehensive system of speech education[20] such as, for example, functions today in a substantial number of our universities. Until such a state of affairs "comes to pass," he declares that "nothing would be more easy, than to produce a more comprehensive system of rules, on that head, than any extant." Nevertheless, he rejects doing so on the grounds that they "would be a work of more ostentation than use."[21]

He also rejects the use of prescriptive rules governing tonal modulations, gestures, and patterns of expression. Such behavior, he remarks, is contrary to the native character of Englishmen. In explanation, he states that the English simply are not inclined to use conventionalized vocal and gesticulatory patterns as are the French, Spaniards, and Italians, or as were the ancient Greeks and Romans.[22] He observes that "of all nations in the world, the English seem to have the least use of this language of signs; there being few instituted signs of emotions, either of tones, looks, or gestures, that are adopted into general use."[23] He therefore declares that it is pointless and artificial to employ prescriptive rules of delivery and formalized patterns of presentation because of the relative nonexistence of referable standards based upon

---

[17]Thomas Sheridan: *A Course of Lectures on Elocution,* London, 1762, p. 121.
[18]*Ibid.,* p. 125.
[19]*Ibid.,* p. 123.
[20]*Ibid.,* pp. viii, 17, 123.
[21]*Ibid.,* p. 123.
[22]*Ibid.,* p. 118.
[23]*Ibid.*

common usage.[24] One of Sheridan's comments expressing this point of view reads as follows:

> But in England, where there are scare any traces of a general agreement in the use of such signs, there can be no observations drawn from general practice, no rules laid down that require explanation by example, nor no manner recommended which demands the aid of patterns.[25]

It is neither necessary nor desirable, says Sheridan, to resort to artificial or external forms of expression for the reason that the vital potentials of expressive delivery are contained naturally within one's self. To liberate and utilize these potentials he advises that

> ... it is necessary that each reader should not only understand, but feel the sentiments of the Author; and if he enters into the spirit of the Author's sentiments, as well as into the meaning of his words, he will not fail to deliver the words in properly varied tones.[26]

He also instructs both the speaker and the oral reader to speak purposefully and sincerely from the heart,[27] and to avoid affectation and imitation by developing an individual style. He explains that the person who "forms to himself a manner of his own, will probably acquire such a one, as will be most consonant with his own powers and his own feelings."[28] This romantic pronouncement is obviously at odds with the typical neo-classical view that style rises out of the universal and is opposed to the particular and singular.[29] Sheridan, however, pointedly comments that "Singularity of manner, is so far from giving

---

[24]For an example of a mechanistic opposite of this treatment of Sheridan's see Gilbert Austin: *Chironomia; or a Treatise on Rhetorical Delivery,* London, 1806. Notice Austin's use of symbols indicating voice changes and minutely detailed diagrams of formalized action patterns.

[25]Sheridan: *Lectures on Elocution,* p. 119.

[26]Sheridan: *A Rhetorical Grammar of the English Language,* Philadelphia, 1783, p. 99.

[27]Sheridan: *Lectures on Elocution,* p. 121.

[28]*Ibid.,* p. 119.

[29]For a representative statement of this attitude see Sir Joshua Reynolds: *Fifteen Discourses,* ed. Ernest Rhys, Everyman's Library, London and New York, 1928, p. 106.

us any idea of impropriety, because it is so customary, as to seem conformable to the very genius of the nation."[30]

He places the highest value upon natural ability. This is not only in keeping with the romantic point of view expressed by Edward Young in his *Conjectures on Original Composition* but Cicero and Quintilian, to whom Sheridan repeatedly refers, also profess this preference.[31] As an example of the effectiveness of native ability, Sheridan quotes Cicero's mention of the great honors paid to such speakers "as relied on nature, and had their delivery wholly governed by their emotions."[32] Although in agreement with the classical tradition that perfection in both public speaking and oral reading may be best obtained by the "united endeavors of art and nature,"[33] Sheridan is also of the opinion that it is better to be awkward and untrained yet sincere than to be polished but affected.[34] In support of this viewpoint he practically paraphrases both Cicero and Quintilian.[35] Sheridan writes as follows:

> In elocution, the two great articles are, force, and grace; the one has its foundations chiefly in nature, the other in art. When united, they mutually support each other; when separated, their powers are very different. Nature can do much without art; art but little without nature. Nature, assaults the heart; art, plays upon the fancy. Force of speaking, will produce emotion and conviction; grace, only excites pleasure and admiration. As the one is the primary, and the other but a secondary end of speech, it is evident, that where one or the other, is wholly to take place, the former should have the preference.[36]

Thus we see that although Sheridan stresses the importance of delivery, he subordinates this art to the drive of vital communicative energy arising from inner conviction and feeling. It is this energy or "force" which he regards as the chief constituent in successful communication.

---

[30]Sheridan: *Lectures on Elocution*, p. 125.

[31]Cicero: *De Oratore*, trans. E. W. Sutton, Loeb Classical Library, London and New York, 1923, i. 25. 113-116. Quintilian: *Institutio Oratoria*, trans. H. E. Butler, Loeb Classical Library, London and New York, 1922, xi. 3. 13.

[32]Sheridan: *Lectures on Elocution*, p. 129. Also see Cicero: *op. cit.*, i. 25. 117.

[33]Sheridan: *Lectures on Elocution*, p. 133.

[34]*Ibid.*, p. 121.

[35]See Cicero: *op. cit.*, i. 25. 113-116, and Quintilian: *op. cit.*, ii. 19. 2.3.

[36]Sheridan: *Lectures* on Elocution, p. 121.

He also clearly states that "the main object of all discourse, whether in prose or verse, is to communicate thoughts and sentiments."[37]

Let us now consider Professor Winans' charge that the methods of both Walker and Sheridan are "thoroughly mechanical."[38] In support of his contention Winans presents examples from the work of each. Unquestionably they reveal a surprising similarity. Similar emotions and moods are listed and superficially described; and the same facial expressions and accompanying gestures are prescribed. Professor Winans comments that "some years after Walker published his *Elements* Sheridan published a book in which he also told how to express emotions."[39] Winans then concludes his examination of the curious duplication by posing the question: "Were both copying from the same actor's manual?"[40]

The Sheridan book to which Winans refers is the *Rhetorical Grammar* which was published before, not after, Walker's *Elements of Elocution*.[41] Furthermore, the common source for these two books is not "some actor's manual" but Burgh's *Art of Speaking*.[42] Walker acknowledges the title of his source but fails to mention Burgh's name.[43] No mention of either Burgh or the title of his book occurs in Sheridan's *Rhetorical Grammar*.

In addition to these unusual circumstances, the *Rhetorical Grammar* itself presents a contradiction. The first part of the book enunciates the same naturalistic principles Sheridan introduced eighteen years

---

[37]Sheridan: *Lectures on the Art of Reading,* London, 1781, p. 305.

[38]Winans: *op. cit.,* p. 3.

[39]*Ibid.*

[40]*Ibid.*

[41]See Austin S. Allibone: *A Critical Dictionary of English Literature and British and American Authors . . .,* Philadelphia, 1870, II, p. 2080. Allibone lists the *Rhetorical Grammar* published as a prefix to Sheridan's *General Dictionary . . .* in 1780. This same publication date is confirmed in the *British Museum Catalogue of Printed Books,* old series: see entry under Sheridan.

[42]See Warren Guthrie: The Development of Rhetorical Theory in America, 1635-1850, Ph.D. Dissertation, Northwestern University, 1940, p. 176. Guthrie recognizes the similarity between Burgh's *Art of Speaking* and Sheridan's *Rhetorical Grammar* but he erroneously attributes priority (and originality) to the Sheridan material stating that much of Burgh's "material on action is quoted from Sheridan's *Rhetorical Grammar,* although no acknowledgement is made." This is obviously in error and the respective publication dates render it chronologically impossible. Burgh published in 1762, Sheridan in 1780.

[43]Walker: *op. cit.,* p. 316.

earlier in his *Lectures on Elocution*.[44] And it is important to note that aspects of these same basic viewpoints are consistently repeated, with no deviation at all, in all his books, some fifteen in number. So it is the more remarkable that when we come to the second part of the *Rhetorical Grammar* we discover that the naturalistic beliefs of the first part, and of all his works, are utterly abandoned. It is in this particular section that Sheridan's *Rhetorical Grammar* repeats Burgh verbatim.[45] The entire repertory of the "principal Passions and Humors, Sentiments and Intentions" makes its appearance and specific directions are prescribed for their proper rendition. Unquestionably, the entire content of the last sixty-nine pages of the *Rhetorical Grammar* is unrelievedly mechanical.

When we consider that Sheridan, in his 1762 *Lectures on Elocution*, condemned and rejected mechanistic patterns of expression at the very same time that Burgh was proposing such methods, his apparent slavish copying of Burgh almost two decades later seems startling in its inconsistency. If viewed apart from the body of naturalistic philosophy and practice Sheridan vigorously and consistently followed for over twenty years of teaching, this isolated and adventitious section in the *Rhetorical Grammar* provides ample evidence to support claims that his methods were similar to those of the mechanical elocutionists. And apparently many who have condemned him as being mechanical have limited their inquiry and evaluation to just this brief section. But to understand and appreciate the true nature of Sheridan's method and contribution, we must consider the whole content of his work and not this isolated and totally foreign segment.

Whether the utterly incongruous appearance of mechanical methods in the *Rhetorical Grammar* represents a true change of attitude, or whether it merely indicates an attempt to ride the band wagon of popular taste, or, what is more likely, it is the willful inclusion of some piratical printer or publisher, the fact remains that the entire portion of his own work falls well within the frame of theories and general practices represented by the Natural School. But there is no evidence to support the claim that he was the directing leader of such a school. In a sense, rather than being a leader, Sheridan was a follower. He was

44"See Sheridan's *Rhetorical Grammar*, pp. 1-148.
45*Ibid.*, pp. 149-218, and Burgh: *op. cit.*, pp. 3-60.

a follower of the classical rhetorical tradition guided by such men as Cicero and Quintilian who were an inspirational, even as they were an actual, source of much of his teaching. The extent of his teaching, the quantity of his lectures and publications on the various aspects of speech all demonstrating the basic tenets of the natural group, give him a preeminence which leads us to regard him as one of its outstanding practitioners. Even Whately refers to him as "one of the best writers" on the subject of oral reading and agrees that the two of them have many points in common.[46]

It is true that Sheridan employs technical, and sometimes mechanical, means to achieve his purpose. But he always subordinates the "graces" and polish of delivery to sincerity of communication and naturalness of manner. His methods, by modern standards and terminology, might be called eclectic. Yet it is necessary to recognize that the mechanical techniques occurring in his own teaching are always grounded in fundamental ideas of the Natural School: clearly understand the meaning of what you speak[47] and "be guided in all changes of . . . voice, by the sense only."[48] The only exception to the wealth of sound naturalistic theory and practice he advocates occurs briefly, as we have seen, in the sixty-nine pages of non-original material crammed into the *Rhetorical Grammar*. Therefore, if one is required to label Sheridan as either "mechanical" or "natural," existing evidence justifies identifying him as a member in good standing of the Natural School.

---

[46]Richard Whately: *Elements of Rhetoric,* New York, 1846, pp. 399f.
[47]Sheridan: *Lectures on Elocution,* p. 70.
[48]Sheridan: *Art of Reading,* p. 122.

FROM SHERIDAN TO RUSH:
THE BEGINNINGS OF ENGLISH ELOCUTION

CHARLES A. FRITZ

New York University

T HE ELOCUTION which was taught for so many years in American schools owes its origin to the work of the English writers of the Eighteenth Century. Here was the first attempt to work out a philosophy of the voice or to place elocution upon a scientific basis. Until that time it had been assumed that the graces of delivery were gifts of nature and could not be taught except in some cases by imitation.

The ancients, we know, gave only general advice on delivery. They made no effort to give a scientific treatment of the voice. In general the marks of Greek accent, acute ($\searrow$) and ($\diagup$) grave were understood to indicate sliding movements of the voice. Aristotle spoke of volume, rhythm and pitch, but did not analyse them. Quintilian spoke of the raising and lowering of the voice as tending to move the feelings of the hearers, but gave no suggestions as to method.

Thus the English writers had little data upon which to base their work. The first writer to speak of acuteness or gravity of the voice was an old English grammarian, Charles Butler of Magdalen College, Oxford. He brought out the principle that a question beginning with a verb is to be read not only in a higher tone, but with a different "turn" of the voice from other questions.[1] The next important contribution was that of Sir Joshua Steele who "discovered" that the slide or accent of the Greeks was a necessary accomplishment of every syllable of spoken language.[2] The theories of Steele were not put into their final

---

[1] Murdoch, James: *A Plea for Spoken Language,* New York, Van Antwerp Bragg & Co., 1883, p. 22.
[2] *Ibid.,* p. 23.

form, however, until 1775 when they were published in *The Prosodia
Rationalis;* or an *Essay Towards Establishing the Melody and Measure of Speech, to be Expressed and Perpetuated by Peculiar Symbols.*
This book was an attempt to prove that the English language has
melody of modulations and rhythms of quantity, that it possesses the
slide and quantity which were supposed to belong exclusively to the
classic tongue. Steele held the idea that the tones of the voice in speech
through rhythm and melody could be set down as accurately as could
the notes in song. It is this elaborate system of notation which he
worked out for accent, quantity and emphasis which *The Prosodia
Rationalis* attempted to set forth. Much of the book consists of examples of speech set down with notation.

The most popular work of the time was Sheridan's *Lectures on Elocution* which was published in its first form before the *Prosodia Rationalis* appeared. Thomas Sheridan (1719-1788), the father of Richard Brinsley Sheridan, was an actor who also delivered lectures on
elocution at the universities and who published during his lifetime a
number of works on the English language. The *Lectures on Elocution*
was first published in England in 1763, the first American edition in
1803. James Murdock says that Sheridan was the first writer to call
attention to the power of sound in our language. He made no analysis
of the intonations of the voice. The core of his theory is found in the
following extract from the *Lectures:*

> "A just delivery consists in a distinct articulation of words,
> pronounced in proper tones, suitably varied to the senses, and the
> emotions of the mind; with due observation of accent; of emphasis
> in its several graduations; of rests or pauses of the voice, in proper
> places and well measured degrees of time; and the whole accom-
> panied with looks and significant gesture."[3]

He then proceeded to discuss in the *Lectures* articulation and pronunciation, accent, emphasis, pauses or stops, pitch and management
of the voice, tones and gestures. As to emphasis and pitch he advised
following the tones of private conversation. As Murdoch says, Sheridan
"favored" 'word painting' and a progress of sounds, or melody made
up from following the movements of unpremeditated speech, varied
and impulsive.[4]

---

[3]Sheridan, Thomas: *Lectures on Elocution,* American edition, 1803, p. 13.
[4]Murdoch, James: *A Plea for Spoken Language,* p. 35.

Sheridan further developed his theories in *A Rhetorical Grammar of the English Language,* a book of 218 pages, which was published in Philadelphia in 1788. In the treatment of voice this was much the same as the *Lectures,* but twenty pages were devoted to showing how the different parts of the body contribute to expression. All the principal passions and sentiments were analyzed to show how they are expressed by various attitudes, will serve as an example of these:

> "Modesty or submission, bends the body forward; levels the eyes to the breast, if not to the feet, of the superior character. The voice low; the tone submissive; and words few."[5]

Sheridan, it can be seen, gave only general suggestions in regard to the voice; he set forth no definite rules. He became leader of what was known later as the "follow nature" school and his underlying philosophy was adopted by several later writers.

The first attempt at a scientific treatment of the voice was made by John Walker (1732-1807) whom Murdoch calls the father of the English system of elocution. Walker claimed the honor of having discovered the upward and downward movements of the voice in speech, which he called the rising and falling inflections. Certain turns of the voice, he found, were a combination of rising and falling and these he called circumflexes. This theory of the inflections is set forth in the first part of his *Elements of Elocution,* first published in 1781 in London. In this to indicate the rising and falling of the voice, the author uses a system of notation made of inclined planes, as falling ‾‾\ , rising ___/. These inflections are essental in bringing out emphasis.[6] In this book, too, the author introduces briefly the subject of "harmonic inflection," which we now know as melody.

There is a lengthy description of the various passions such as tranquillity, cheerfulness, mirth, etc., and the manner of expressing each. For example, complaining is described thus:

> Complaining, as when one is under violent bodily pain, distorts the features, almost closes the eye; sometimes raises them wistfully; opens the mouth, gnashes the teeth, draws up the upper lip, draws down the head upon the breast, and contracts the whole

---

[5]Sheridan, Thomas: *A Rhetorical Grammar of the English Language,* Philadelphia, 1788, p. 171.
[6]Walker, John: *Elements of Elocution,* Boston, 1810, p. 166.

body. The arms are violently bent at the elbows, and the fists strongly clinched. The voice is uttered in groans, lamentations, and sometimes violent screams.[7]

There is little treatment of time and force in the book and only a few general suggestions in regard to gestures. In fact, the section on voice is largely a treatment of the author's pet theory of inflections. It "was the first attempt to describe and record the variations of the voice."[8]

These theories were further developed by Walker in *A Rhetorical Grammar, or a Course of Lectures in Elocution,* first published in London in 1785, and dedicated to Samuel Johnson. In the *Introduction,* which is addressed to parents and teachers of elocution, the author advises that in reading the pupil should imitate the teacher as closely as possible. The pupil should be shown how to read every passage. The teacher is advised to mark the pause and inflection and to have the pupil observe these in reading. If the pupils are to be taught in classes, six is enough and the procedure should be as follows:

"The best reader ought to be placed first, the next best second and so on. When they are arranged at some distance, let the teacher give each of these a book of the same kind, then let him read a sentence, and order the first pupil to read the same sentence. When this is done, let the teacher read the next sentence, and order the second pupils to read it likewise; and so let him proceed, in the same manner with the rest, till each pupil has read his sentence after the teacher."[9]

In the body of the book there comes first a discussion of pronunciation, then rules for pausing after various words, particularly parts of speech.

In the treatment of inflection the author goes beyond his earlier work for he gives definite rules for inflections, such, for instance, as that a rising inflection is used at the end of the first direct period of a compact sentence, in words of a series, etc.

In a section on the modulation and management of the voice some general directions are given of which the following are the most important:

[7]Walker, John: *Elements of Elocution,* Boston, 1810, p. 351.
[8]Murdoch, James: *A Plea for Spoken Language,* p. 36.
[9]Walker, John: *A Rhetorical Grammar,* 2nd London Edition. 1787, Introduction.

To strengthen the middle tone, we ought to read and speak in as loud a tone as possible, without raising the voice into a higher key.

If in the course of reading the voice should slide into a higher tone, and this tone should too often recur, care must be taken to throw in a variety, by beginning subsequent sentences in a lower tone, and if the subject will admit it, in a monotone.[10]

As to gesture, there are three pages of general suggestions of which the following is typical:

In speaking extempore we should be sparing of the use of the left hand, which except in strong emotion may hang easily down by the side. The right hand ought to rise extending from the side, that is in a direction from left to right, till it is on a line with the hip; and then be propelled forwards, with the fingers open and easily, and differently curved; the arm should move chiefly from the elbow, the hand should seldom be raised higher than the shoulder, and when it has described its object, or enforced its emphasis, ought to drip lifeless down to the side, ready to commence action afresh.[11]

The last part of the book (pages 219-346) is made up of "A Praxis to the Foregoing Rules on the Art of Reading." The sentences and selections are distributed into several classes according to their structure, as compact sentences, antithetic sentences, etc., and in which the inflections are marked. General directions for reading are given in connection with each kind of sentence.

In the first American edition of the *Rhetorical Grammar,* published in Boston in 1814, the essential theories are the same, but so much of the old material has been omitted and so much new added that it is almost a new work. The Praxis of sentences has been omitted and rules for composition have been supplied from "the best source, Blair's *Lectures* and what was deficient in these has been furnished from Ward's *Lectures on Oratory,* so . . . it is presumed the present work is the most perfect of its kind in the language."[12]

Walker explains that the motive for the new edition was to present his idea of the circumflexes of the voice. The rising and falling

---

[10]*Ibid.,* p. 206.

[11]*Ibid.,* p. 214.

[12]Walker, John: *A Rhetorical Grammar,* 1st American edition, Boston, Cummings and Hilliar, 1814, Preface.

inflections were explained in the two previous works, but the combination of these on a word or syllable had not been worked out. He says, "These appeared so inseparable from the human voice, so new, and of such real utility in teaching to read and speak, that I could scarcely think that I had discharged my duty to my country till I had given these modifications of the speaking voice as clear an explanation as I was able."[13] The author states that he had observed that every word had necessarily an upward or downward turn or continued in a monotone. This had been presented in the *Elements of Elocution,* but little notice had been taken of it until the last three or four years. He states that he had observed about ten years before that "these two turns were sometimes united on the same syllable and formed a compound turn either beginning with the upward and ending with the downward or vice versa." These compound tones he called circumflexes, and says of them, "It is to be the novelty and utility of this distinction that the author claims the distinction of the public."[14]

It is interesting to note here the author's reaction to the lack of public interest in these discoveries. He says in the Preface to the revised edition, "The sanguine expectations I had once entertained that this analysis of the human voice would be received by the learned with avidity and applause are now over. . . . I have had the mortification to find few of my pupils listen to anything but my pronunciation." So difficult did the modification of the voice appear that he "was generally obliged to follow the old method 'read as I read, without any reason for it.' Sooner or later these distinctions of the voice must become the vehicle of instruction in reading and speaking."[15]

In this edition as far as the treatment of pronunciation, emphasis and pausing is concerned, there is little change from the earlier edition. It is naturally in the treatment of inflections that the greatest change is found. Here is added the definition of the circumflex. The kinds of inflections here are indicated by $/$ for the rising, $\setminus$ for the falling, and $\wedge$ for the circumflex. A number of rules are given for the use of inflections on various kinds of phrases and sentences. The following will give an idea of them.

---

[13]Walker, John: *A Rhetorical Grammar,* 1st American ed., 1814, Preface.
[14]*Ibid.,* Introduction.
[15]*Ibid.,* Preface.

1. In a direct period with two conjunctions a long pause with a rising inflection is used at the end of the first principal member.

2. In a direct period with one conjunction a long pause with the rising inflection is used at the end of the first part.[16]

Rules are given for the inflection on various kinds of questions and on words used in contrast and in series. This is very much like our own elocution in the latter part of the Nineteenth Century.

The section "Of Rules for Reading Verse" is more detailed than in the previous edition. Rule V is a good sample:

> In order to form a cadence in a period in rhyming verse, we must adopt the falling inflection with considerable force in the cadence of the last line but one.[17]

The section, "An Explanation of the Figures of Rhetoric, with Directions for the Proper Manner of Pronouncing them," contains many more figures in this edition. The list includes metaphor, allegory, metonymy, synecdoche, hyperbole, catachresis or abuse, irony, exclamation, interrogation, enumeration, graduation, climax, repetition, anticipation, concession, correction, inversion, apostrophe, asyndeton, antithesis, omission, communication, lively description, vision, simile, personification.

The treatment of the modulation and management of the voice is more extensive than in the earlier edition; it contains instructions for acquiring high tones and low tones for the voice and also instructions for vocal management. The rules for gesture are the same.

Thus it can be seen that John Walker was an important figure in the history of early speech training. Not only was he a well-known actor of his time, but a philologist and lexicographer as well. His best known work was *A Critical Pronouncing Dictionary of the English Language,* published in 1791. Among his other works were *Exercises for Improvement in Elocution* (1777), *Hints for Improvement in the Art of Reading* (1783), *The Melody of Speaking Delineated: or Elocution Taught like Music: by Visible Signs Adapted to the Tones, Variations and Inflections of the Voice, in Reading and Speaking* (1787). In this he introduced the interval, the distance between two degrees of pitch at different elevations. Each interval was given a

[16]*Ibid.,* pp. 93, 94.
[17]*Ibid.,* p. 172.

name determined by the number of degrees on the scale which it covered. With the exception of the interval nothing new was added to his theory by the works just mentioned. They elaborated the system and added exercises for practice.

The mechanical theories of Walker coming into conflict with the "follow Nature" ideas of Sheridan gave rise to the two schools of elocution which were destined to exist for so long. The followers of Sheridan attacked Walker's system of inflections as highly artificial. The conflict was carried over to the American colleges and academies. Several American editions were published of the works of both Sheridan and Walker and were used as texts in the schools until well into the Nineteenth Century.

The earliest texts published in America were based upon Sheridan and added nothing to his theory. Two of these, namely, James Burgh's *The Art of Speaking* (1795) and William Scott's *Lessons in Elocution* (1795) were discussed by this writer in a previous article.[18] Two others, *The Orator's Assistant* (1797) by Alexander Thomas and *The Pious Instructor* (1806) by by Daniel Cooledge were also reviewed by this writer in the Old Books section of *The Quarterly Journal of Speech* of June, 1928. Another American book based directly upon Sheridan's theories was William Enfield's *The Speaker* (1799). In this the author states that "Follow nature is the fundamental law of oratory." He adds, however, that the acquisition of this art may be facilitated by rules. These rules are general, such as: 1) Let the articulation be distinct and deliberate; 2) Let pronunciation be bold and forcible; 3) Acquire a compass and variety in the height of the voice; 4) Use proper accent; and 5) Distinguish more significant words by a natural, forcible and varied emphasis. Follow the manner of conversation.[19]

The first important American writer to follow the theories of Walker and the most popular author of the early American period was Ebenezer Porter, president of Andover Theological Seminary. In 1827 he published *An Analysis of the Principles of Rhetorical Delivery*. This was a text for colleges and there is record of its use at Harvard,

---

[18]Fritz, C. A.: *Early American Works on Speech Training*, QJSE, April, 1927.
[19]Enfield, Wm.: *The Speaker*, Philadelphia, W. W. Woodward, 1799, p. 17.

Middlebury, Bowdoin and Andover Theological Seminary. The author states his purpose in writing as follows:

> (To) guard against the tendency of withdrawing attention from emotion and at the same time to accomplish the ends at which Walker aims, in his *Elements of Elocution*, I have much desired to see a manual for students, free both from the obscurity and the extreme particularity of his system.[20]

President Porter's theory of the teaching of elocution is embodied in his directions to teachers:

> (The) student should learn the distinction of inflections . . . and the teacher's voice should set him right whenever he makes a mistake. In the same manner he should go through all the rules successively. . . . After getting the command of the voice, the great point to be kept steadily in view is to apply the principles of emphasis and inflection just as nature and sentiment demand. . . . No description that can be given of inflection, emphasis and tones which accompany emotion can impart this emotion or be a substitute for it.[21]

The book is in two parts. Part I (Pages 13 to 269) is devoted to the discussion of articulation, tones and inflections, accent, emphasis, modulation and action. In the description of inflections the author follows Walker closely, but holds him defective as to the rules for their use. All inflections, he says, cannot be reduced to an exact system, especially in sentiment.[22] The examples for illustration here are chosen from colloquial language because, he thinks, the tones of conversation ought to be the basis of natural speech. In fact, this insistence on a natural or conversational delivery runs through much of the discussion. The rules for inflection are much simpler than those of Walker. The idea of accent is that "the accented syllable of a word is always uttered with a louder note than the rest."[23]

Modulation, Dr. Porter defines as variety in managing the voice. To get this variety the speaker must: 1) learn to emphasize, and 2) to

---

[20]Porter, Ebenezer: *An Analysis of Rhetorical Delivery*, Andover, Mark Newman, 1928, Preface, p. 6.
[21]*Ibid.*, p. 8.
[22]*Ibid.*, p. 45.
[23]*Ibid.*, p. 67.

cultivate a good degree of discrimination as to vocal tones and inflections. The pitch of the voice may be high, middle or low. A system of notation is given to indicate changes from one pitch to another and to indicate changes in time as (o) high, (..) slow, (oo) low and loud.[24]

In action, the author feels that the best course is to follow nature. There are two extremes, he says, in teaching action, 1) that which encumbers a speaker with so much technical regulation of his movements as to make him an automaton, and 2) that which condemns all precepts. There should be some training, but this should be in the form of general principles rather than minute directions. The habits of the student are of prime importance. "Let these habits be well formed and his own, so as to govern his movements spontaneously, and trust the rest to emotion."[25] The chief purpose of training in action, according to this author, should be to eliminate defects and to correct faults, the chief of which are too much motion, absence of any motion, want of appropriateness of gesture, too constant action and mechanical variety.[26]

At the close of this part are given many exercises under articulation, inflection and modulation. The principle is first stated, followed by a number of sentences with the notations giving directions for reading. The notations are given, however, only when the author's judgment is clear as to the reading.

Part II (pages 267 to 402) is a collection of exercises for practice, made up mostly of familiar pieces such as Hamlet's instruction to the players. No notation is applied to these.

In the light of the modern theory of speaking this book impresses one as the most sensible text of the time. While the author follows Walker most closely, he avoids the extremes both of Walker and of those who could have no rules.

Four years later (1831) Dr. Porter published another book intended for academies and high schools, but which we know was used at Wesleyan University.[27] This was *The Rhetorical Reader: Consisting of Instructions for Regulating the Voice, with a Rhetorical Notation, Illustrating Inflection, Emphasis and Modulation, and a Course of*

---

[24]*Ibid.,* p. 121.
[25]*Ibid.,* p. 145.
[26]*Ibid.,* pp. 152-162.
[27]*Wesleyan College Catalogue,* 1846.

Rhetorical Exercises. As this text has been reviewed in this *Journal*[28] it is not necessary to discuss it here. The popularity of the book is shown by the fact, as Professor Ewbank states, that in 1843 it had already passed through three hundred editions. It is on the same plan as the *Analysis,* but is adapted to younger pupils. Something of the author's method is reflected in the following extract from the directions to teachers:

> The best way to overcome bad habits is to go directly into the *analysis of vocal sounds as they occur in conversation.*
>
> The pupil should first study the exercise, then mark with a pencil the inflections, emphasis, etc., then read it rhetorically to his teacher. Then he should commit it perfectly before reciting.[29]

Ebenezer Porter was the latest important writer on elocution who acknowledged the influence of the English writers and carried on their theories. Already had begun a movement which attempted to place elocution on an entirely scientific basis and which was destined to change completely the teaching of speech in America. This movement will be the subject of a later article.

We can hardly leave this discussion of the beginnings of elocution without some mention of gesture as a part of expression. None of the texts so far had said anything about action except for a few general suggestions. In 1806 there was published in London a treatise by Gilbert Austin which was the first detailed philosophy of action and which was destined to influence greatly the teaching of speech delivery in our own country. This was called *Chironomia: or a Treatise on Rhetorical Delivery.* As the title page states this is a "Treatise on Rhetorical Delivery: Comprehending many Precepts, both Ancient and Modern for the Proper Regulation of the Voice, the Countenance, and Gesture. Together with an Investigation of the Elements of Gesture, and a New Method of Notation Thereof: Illustrated by many Figures." Chironomia, it should be said, means here the art of gesture. There are in the book 438 pages, the greater number given to action. The author laments the lack of attention given to gesture and

---

[28]Ewbank, H. L.: *The Rhetorical Reader* by Ebenezer Porter (Reviewed), *QJSE,* November 1927.

[29]Porter, Ebenezer: *The Rhetorical Reader,* New York, Dayton & Newman, 1835, p. 6.

delivery by earlier writers. He proceeds to outline an elaborate system of notation illustrated by numerous engraved figures showing every conceivable position of the hand and attitude of the body. The purpose of this notation, he says, is "to produce a language of symbols so simple and so perfect as to render it possible with facility to represent every action of an orator throughout the speech . . . and to record them for posterity and for repetition and practice, as was all common language recorded . . . and may be esteemed useful. An attempt at such a language is here presented to the public."[30]

He then proceeds to describe the various positions of the hands and feet and to apply to them his symbols of notation. In standing, he says, the body must be supported on either limb, while "the front foot . . . which sustains the principal weight must be so placed that a perpendicular line let fall from the hole of the neck shall pass through the heel of that foot."[31] The other foot is merely to keep the body balanced. The various positions of the feet are then described as the first position right (R. 1.), and second position right (R. 2.), first position left (L. 1.), and so on. The mechanical nature of these directions can be seen in the instructions for the first position right:

"In this position the right foot (advanced before the left about the breadth of the narrowest part of the foot) forms with the left an angle of about 75 degrees. The lines which form this angle passing through the length of each foot, meet its vertex under the heel of the left. The principal weight of the body is sustained by the left foot, the right foot rests lightly but in its whole extent upon the ground."[32]

And again in R. 2. the "right sliding forward about half of the breadth of the foot receives the principal weight of the body, the left heel being raised and the ball of the left foot only lightly touching the ground."[33] R. 1. and R. 2. are the same except that the left foot is forward. In the same way several positions and attitudes are worked out.

To illustrate the positions of the whole arm the body is shown in its relation to a sphere. In some gestures the arm must be toward the

---

[30]Austin, Gilbert: *Chironomia: or a Treatise on Rhetorical Delivery*, London, W. Bulmer and Co., 1806, pp. 274-275.

[31]*Ibid.*, p. 296.

[32]*Ibid.*, p. 298.

[33]*Ibid.*, p. 298.

zenith (Z), in some in the middle plane, and in others in the lower plane.

The various positions of the hand are then described and the symbol for each given, as s -hand supine (palm up), i -hand index (fore-finger extended, other under the thumb), etc.

Several general rules for gestures are given, as:[34]

The stroke of the gesture should come on the accented syllable of the emphatic word.[35]

Each gesture should have a preparation, stroke, transition and finish.[36]

Gestures should be used with moderation, only for illustration and enforcement.[37]

Gestures should have magnificence, boldness, energy, variety, simplicity, grace, propriety and precision.[38]

Grace of gesture is acquired by imitation of the best models.[39]

Each gesture or position of the parts of the body has its own significance, as,

'The head is averted in horror.'
'The eyes are raised in prayer.'
'The hands descent prone in blessing.'[40]

The last chapter is composed of a number of selections for practice with symbols on each line to indicate the gestures to be used in recit-

---

[34]The System of notation can be illustrated by the sentence—

    D   B s e q
    And stands in rapture o'er his hoard:|
                  R2
    D —eyes downwards
    R2—second position right
    B —both hands
    s —surprise
    e —elevated
    q —oblique
    | —pause
    From Austin, Gilbert: *Chironomia,* p. 369.

[35]*Ibid.,* Chap. 16.

[36]*Ibid.,* Chap. 18.

[37]*Ibid.,* Chap. 19.

[38]*Ibid.,* Chap. 20.

[39]*Ibid.,* Chap. 22.

[40]*Ibid.,* Chap. 21, pp. 483-484.

ing it, just as on the line quoted above. At the end is a series of plates showing every position of the body with special reference to the hands and feet, with a key explaining what each gesture or position is used to express.

The *Chironomia* with its mechanical treatment of action exercised an enormous influence upon elocutionary writers for a long time, indeed far beyond the period of the English writers we are now discussing. The discussion of action in Fulton and Trueblood's *Elements of Elocution* (1893) was based directly upon it and some of the plates were there reproduced. The nomenclature given to the positions of the hand in some of our present texts is the same as that first suggested by Austin. Those who followed James Rush at a later period in their treatment of the elements of the voice generally went back to Austin in their consideration of gesture.

This brings us to the close of the period of predominance of the early English writers on elocution. We have seen the work begun by Sheridan and Walker carried to America and the conflict here between their theories. An understanding of these early writers should give us an insight into the reason for the widely differing systems and methods of teaching speech delivery which existed through the whole of the Nineteenth Century and which are found to a slightly lesser extent even at the present time.

HUGH BLAIR'S THEORY OF TASTE

HERMAN COHEN

University of Oregon

Hugh Blair begins his *Lectures on Rhetoric and Belles Lettres* with material which is common to both speaking and writing. These opening lectures concern taste and style. In terms of his announced conception of rhetoric, Blair's examination of taste and style is designed for three groups of readers: those who aspire to proficiency in speaking; those who would improve their literary powers; and those who merely wish to improve their critical judgment of literature and rhetoric.[1] Only when he comes to treat of eloquence and literature as separate disciplines does Blair draw a distinction in terms of the criteria which are to be utilized in evaluating each species of art.

Blair was alone in his time in discussing taste as a part of rhetoric. Campbell ignored the aesthetic aspects of the art, as did Whately. Only Blair, among contemporary British rhetorical theorists, undertook to investigate the manner in which a listener may judge the merits and faults of a discourse. While his theories were not notably unique, Blair's exposition of his concept of taste marked one of the first times in which such a system had been applied to oral discourse. Kames had concerned himself with taste to a greater degree than had Blair, but his treatment was not directed to the art of speechmaking as such. We can say, therefore, that while Hugh Blair's theories are derivative of the philosophies of his time, his *Lectures on Rhetoric and Belles Lettres* was the first British work in which these ideas were applied to oral communication.

The treatment of taste is in direct contrast to much of the later

---

[1] Hugh Blair: *Lectures on Rhetoric and Belles Lettres,* Philadelphia, 1833, p. 11.

material in his work. In the more didactic sections of the *Lectures,*
Blair is largely concerned with the formulation of rules and suggestions.
The lectures on taste, however, represent a speculative inquiry into
the nature of that faculty which "enables men to judge and judge
well." Instead of a series of rules, Blair's theory of taste emerges as
a few rather generalized principles.

It is Blair's hope that an understanding of these principles will
enable his readers to become more competent judges of the speeches
they hear. They are expected to relate the general considerations of
taste to the more specific attributes of rhetoric which are treated in
the later portion of the lectures. An understanding of the principles
of taste will allow the critic to apply them to such factors as style,
organization, and delivery as well as to the speech as a complete work.

Although much of Blair's rhetorical theory is firmly rooted in the
classicists, his theory of taste is essentially that of the eighteenth-century
School of Taste which held that taste was an innate but precisely
improvable talent. The same general point of view as Blair's is presented by such critics and theorists as Francis Hutchison, David
Hartley, William Shenstone, Archibald Allison, and Erasmus Darwin.
In particular Blair's concept of taste seems most closely related to the
writings of his contemporaries Sir Joshua Reynolds and Edmund
Burke and his friends Lord Kames and David Hume. It is not surprising that Kames' influence is particularly pervasive in Blair's remarks on taste. Much that Blair had to say seems to have been derived
from conversations with Kames, at whose instigation he had begun the
lectures.[2]

Blair divides his discussion of taste into five distinct but complementary areas of inquiry. Of their division, he says,

> I shall first explain the Nature of Taste as a power or faculty
> in the human mind. I shall next consider how far it is an improv-
> able faculty. I shall show the sources of its improvement, and the
> Characters of Taste in its most perfect state. I shall then examine
> the various fluctuations to which it is liable, and inquire whether
> there be any standard to which we can bring the different tastes,
> in order to distinguish the corrupted from the true.[3]

[2]Helen Randall: *The Critical Theory of Lord Kames,* Northampton, Massachusetts,
1941, p. 82.
[3]Blair: p. 16.

Blair begins his analysis by defining taste as "the power of receiving pleasure from the beauties of nature and art." It is quite clear that he considers taste to be a receptive or critical power rather than a creative faculty.

This common-sense definition of taste in no way represents a departure from established neo-classical critical thought. In one way or another, the same definition had been propounded by rhetorical and critical writers of the period. Blair's definition in its essentials is particularly close to that presented by Edmund Burke, who defined taste as "that faculty or faculties of the mind, which are affected with, or which form a judgment of, the works of imagination and the elegant arts."[4] The only significant difference between the two definitions is that Blair substitutes "nature" for Burke's "imagination" as the medium for taste.

As in much of his writing on rhetoric, Blair is concerned with the relationship between nature and art in determining the characteristics of taste. In order to discuss taste systematically and formulate any intelligible standard for its use, it is first necessary to decide whether the faculty is to be considered as an internal sense or as an exertion of reason. If one accepts Blair's assumption that reason is "that power of the mind which in speculative matters discovers truth, and in practical matters judges of the fitness of means to an end," the question is not difficult to answer. It is obvious, Blair argues, that the mind does not receive pleasure through the discovery of the understanding or the deduction of an argument. Pleasure will often strike, in the same manner, at persons of varying mental development and abilities. Hence, taste seems more closely allied to a feeling or sense than to a process of the mind. Although he believes that taste is ultimately founded on a certain natural and instinctive sensibility to beauty, Blair is careful to point out that reason is not entirely excluded from its exertions. Reason, while it does not create taste, does assist in its operation and serves to enlarge its power. Blair's postulate in regard to the innate nature of taste is closely related to the concept of Lord Kames, but it differs rather sharply from the more rationalistic attitudes of other contemporary writers, who had assigned a somewhat more significant role to reason than had Blair or Kames. Kames, for

---

[4]Edmund Burke: *On the Sublime and Beautiful,* New York, 1885, p. 5.

example, had written, "Our taste is not accidental, but uniform and universal, making a branch of our nature."[5] David Hume, in contrast, had drawn a clear distinction between the functions of taste and of reason:

> Reason conveys the knowledge of truth and falsehood; taste gives the sentiment of beauty and deformity, vice and virtue. The one discloses objects without addition or diminution; the other has a productive faculty; and gilding or staining all natural objects with the colours, borrowed from the internal sentiment, raises, in a manner a new creation.[4]

Burke had advanced the thesis that taste might well be as rigidly governed by rules as was reason:

> The logic of taste, if I may be allowed the expression, might very possibly be as well digested, and we might come to discuss matters of this nature with as much certainty, as those which seem immediately within the province of mere reason. For if taste has no fixed principles, if the imagination is not affected according to some invariable and certain laws, our labor is like to be employed to very little purpose; as it must be judged an useless if not absurd undertaking to lay down rules for caprice, and to set up for a legislator of whims and fancies.[7]

Sir Joshua Reynolds also argued that taste must be subject to rules and to reason when he wrote:

> It is supposed that their powers are intuitive; that under the name of genius great works are produced, and under the name of taste an exact judgment is given, without our knowing why, and without our being under the least obligation to reason, precepts, or experience. One can scarce state these opinions without exposing their absurdity; yet they are constantly in the mouths of men, and particularly of artists.[8]

Since taste is an innate faculty, Blair reasons, it must be common in some degree to all men. Even among the rudest of civilizations and among the young and unlettered there is some appreciation of the

---

[5]Henry Home, Lord of Kames: *Elements of Criticism,* Edinburgh, 1761, p. 44.
[6]David Hume: *Essays Literary, Moral and Political,* London, 1875, p. 484.
[7]Burke: p. 4.
[8]Sir Joshua Reynolds: *Discourses on Art,* Chicago, 1945, p. 189.

beauties of nature and of art. Therefore, it is reasonable to conclude that it is no less essential to men to have some discernment of beauty than it is to possess the attributes of reason and of speech. In keeping with his conception of the innate nature of taste, Blair feels that there is not an even distribution of the faculty of appreciation. Some men have taste which is coarse, weak, and confused, while others possess a taste which is refined, powerful, and orderly.

Blair seeks out two reasons for the inequalities in taste and in so doing indicates the rational basis of his aesthetic theories. In many cases, inferior or superior taste may be attributed to inherited sensibility. To a much greater extent, however, variations are due to education and culture. Blair's theory thus evolves into the consideration of a faculty which is fundamentally innate but which is subject to great improvement through the operation of environmental factors. In postulating this view of taste as an improvable attribute, Blair's thinking parallels that of other representatives of the School of Taste. Burke had also postulated the innate and improvable character of taste:

> So far, then, as taste belongs to the imagination, its principles is the same in all men; there is no difference in the manner of their being affected, nor in the causes of the affection; but in the *degree* there is a difference, which arises from two causes principally: either a greater degree of natural sensibility, or from a closer and longer attention to the object.[9]

Hume's view was not far removed from that of his contemporaries:

> Strong sense, united to delicate sentiment, improved by practice, perfected by comparison, and cleared of all prejudice can alone entitle critics to this valuable character.[10]

Reynolds in his investigation of taste had discussed the relationship between nature and art in much the same manner as other representatives of the School of Taste:

> To form this just taste is undoubtedly in your own power, but it is to reason and philosophy that you must have recourse; from them you must borrow the balance, by which is to be weighed and

---

[9]Burke: p. 16.
[10]Hume: p. 278.

estimated the value of every pretension that intrudes itself on your power.[11]

Lord Kames had expressed essentially the same idea when he said:

> With respect to the common nature of man in particular, we have a conviction that it is invariable not less than universal. Nor are we deceived: because, giving allowance for the difference of culture and gradual refinement of manners, the fact corresponds on our conviction.[12]

As proof of his assertion, Blair points to the superior taste of civilized nations over barbarous nations and to the superior taste of educated people over the unlettered. The same sort of argument had also been presented by David Hume in his essay *On The Standards of Taste*.

Blair also agrees with Hume and Burke in regard to the means by which innate taste can be improved. Together with these critics he feels that improvement in taste must be predicated on exercise in criticism and reason. Just as in any skill an individual will become more proficient with practice, so he will also become more and more skilled in taste as he exercises that faculty. Blair emphasizes this point of view when he says:

> When one is only beginning his acquaintance with works of genius, the sentiment which attends them is obscure and confused. He cannot point out the several excellencies or blemishes of a performance which he peruses; he is at a loss on what to rest his judgment: all that can be expected is, that he should tell in general whether he be pleased or not. But allow him more experience in works of this kind, and his taste becomes by degrees more exact and enlightened. He begins to perceive not only the character of the whole, but the beauties and defects of each part; and is able to describe the peculiar qualities which he praises or blames. The mist dissipates which seemed formerly to hang over the object; and he can at length pronounce firmly and without hesitation concerning it. Thus in taste, considered as mere sensibility, exercise opens a great source of improvement.[13]

Blair's statement in this matter bears a close resemblance to the idea expressed earlier by Hume who had written:

---

[11]Reynolds: p. 212.
[12]Kames: p. 298.
[13]Blair: p. 19.

But though there be naturally a wide difference in point of delicacy between one person and another, nothing tends farther to increase and improve this talent, than *practice* in a particular art, and the frequent study or contemplation of a particular species of beauty. . . . So advantageous is practice to the discernment of beauty, that, before we can give judgment on any work of importance, it will even be requisite, that every individual performance be more than once perused by us, and be surveyed in different lights with attention and deliberation.[14]

Burke's point of view was similar to that of Blair and Hume:

It is known that the taste (whatever it is) is improved exactly as we improve our judgment, by extending our knowledge, by a steady attention to our object, and by frequent exercise.[15]

Although taste may be founded ultimately on sensibility, it must not be considered as instinctive sensibility alone. Reason and good sense also have an extensive influence on the operations and decisions of taste. Thus, Blair arrives at his final definition of taste: "a thorough good taste may well be considered as a power compounded of natural sensibility to beauty, and of improved understanding." To demonstrate this conclusion, Blair posits the Aristotelian dictum that "the greater part of the productions are no other than imitations of nature; representations of the characters, actions or manners of men." The pleasure which is received from such imitations or representations is founded on mere taste. The judgment, however, of whether such imitations are properly executed is an attribute of the understanding. We are pleased through our own natural sense of beauty, but reason shows us why and upon what grounds we are pleased. A critic whose taste is well developed will not only be able to react favorably or unfavorably but will also be able to recognize when a work is a just representation of nature. Hugh Blair's view of taste, then, is that of a characteristic which is the result of both nature and art. It supposes our natural sense of beauty to be refined by frequent attention to the most beautiful objects, and at the same time be guided and improved by the light of understanding. In proposing this view of taste, Blair again reflects the general attitude of the School of Taste.

---

[14]Hume: pp. 274-275.
[15]Burke: p. 22.

In Blair's judgment, the characteristics of taste, when richly improved, are reducible to two: delicacy and correctness. The former "respects principally the perfection of that natural sensibility on which taste is founded." Delicacy of taste presupposes that a person "feels strongly and feels accurately." Anyone possessing this characteristic is able to see "distinctions and differences where others see none; the most latent beauty does not escape him and he is sensible of the smallest blemish." Correctness, on the other hand, results from the application of understanding to the faculty of taste. Of correctness Blair says:

> A man of correct taste is one who is never imposed on by counterfeit beauties; who carries always in his mind that standard of good sense which he employs in judging of everything. He estimates with propriety the comparative merit of the several beauties which he meets with in any work of genius; refers them to their proper classes; assigns the principles, as far as they can be traced, whence their power of pleasing flows, and is pleased himself precisely in that degree which he ought, and no more.[16]

The two characteristics of taste which Blair proposes reflect the respective roles of nature and art in the theory of taste. Delicacy leans more to feeling and sensibility; correctness, more to reason and judgment. The former is the gift of nature; the latter a product of culture and art. Blair himself confirms this when he says, "The power of delicacy is chiefly seen in discerning the true merit of a work; the power of correctness in rejecting false pretentions to merit." David Hume in formulating his standards of taste had also ascribed delicacy and correctness as two of the essential characteristics of taste:

> Whenever you can ascertain a delicacy of taste, it is sure to meet with approbation; and the best way of ascertaining it is to appeal to those models and principles, which have been established by the uniform consent and experience of nations and ages.[17]

Moreover, a similar division in somewhat different terms had been suggested by Burke, who spoke of "sensibility" and "judgment" rather than delicacy and correctness:

---

[16]Blair: p. 21.
[17]Hume: p. 274.

> Whilst we consider taste merely according to its nature and species, we shall find its principles entirely uniform; but the degree in which these principles prevail, in the several individuals of mankind, is altogether as different as the principles themselves are similar. For sensibility and judgment [sic], which are the qualities that compose what we commonly call a *taste,* vary exceedingly in various people.[18]

This division, however, pre-supposes the existence of a criterion or standard to which critics may appeal in distinguishing between good and bad artistic endeavor. Blair recognizes that there must be a standard or else all taste will be equally good. If no standards of taste are to be formulated by which critical judgment is to be made, the critic will be forced to accept the view that "there is no disputing of taste; but that whatever pleases is right and for that reason it does please." Blair rejects this attitude as one which is demonstrably absurd. He asks rhetorically:

> For is there anyone who will seriously maintain that the taste of a Hottentot or a Laplander is as delicate and as correct as that of a Longinus or an Addison? or, that he can be charged with no defect or incapacity who thinks a common newswriter as excellent an historian as Tacitus?[19]

Since it is fallacious to reason in this manner, Blair is led to the conclusion that there must be some foundation for the preference of one man's taste to that of another; and there must be a good and a bad, a right and a wrong, in taste as in other things. Thus there must be some standard of taste to which the critic can appeal in judging a discourse.

The rejection of the notion that individual tastes could not be disputed was by no means original with Blair. Many eighteenth-century critics had predicated their formulation of standards of taste upon similar arguments. Kames at some length had pointed out:

> The proverb [there is no disputing of taste] will hold true as to the particulars now explained; but when applied in general to every subject of taste, the difficulties to be encountered are insuperable. We need only to mention the difficulty that arises from

---

[18]Burke: pp. 18-19.
[19]Blair: p. 22.

human nature itself. Do we not talk of a good and bad taste?—
of a right and a wrong taste?—and upon that supposition do we
not censure writers, painters, architects and everyone who deals
in the fine arts? Are such criticisms absurd and void of common
sense? Have the foregoing expressions, familiar in all languages
and among all people, no sort of meaning? This can hardly be;
for what is universal, must have a foundation in nature. If we
can reach that foundation, the standard of taste will no longer
be secret.[20]

Reynolds had written in much the same vein:

> The common saying that *tastes are not to be disputed* owes its
> influence, and its general reception to the same error which leads
> us to imagine this faculty of too high an original to submit to the
> authority of an earthly tribunal. It likewise corresponds with the
> notions of those who consider it as a mere phantom of the imag-
> ination, so devoid of substance as to elude all criticism.[21]

Burke's writings reflected the same attitudes as his contemporaries:

> So that when it is said, taste cannot be disputed, it can only mean,
> that no one can strictly answer what pleasure or paint some par-
> ticular man may find from the taste of some particular thing. This
> indeed cannot be disputed; but we may dispute and with sufficient
> clearness too, concerning the things which are naturally pleasing
> or disagreeable to the sense.[22]

In devising the foundations of the standard of taste, Blair carefully
indicates that diversity does not necessarily imply corruption. He says,
"The tastes of men may differ very considerably as to their object,
and yet none of them be wrong." Hence, he points out:

> It is not in matters of taste, as in questions of mere reason, where
> there is but one conclusion that can be true, and all the rest are
> erroneous. Truth, which is the object of reason, is one; Beauty,
> which is object of taste, is manifold. Taste, therefore, admits of
> latitude and diversity of objects, in sufficient consistency with
> goodness or justness of taste.[23]

---

[20]Kames: p. 297.
[21]Reynolds: p. 190.
[22]Burke: p. 8.
[23]Blair: pp. 22-23.

Blair, however, recognizes that there is a distinction between diversity and error. Men may disagree as to the comparative merits of two works but, as the Scottish writer explains,

> Where it is with respect to the same object that men disagree, when one condemns that as ugly which another admires as highly beautiful; then it is no longer diversity, but direct opposition of taste that takes place; and therefore one must be in the right, and another in the wrong, unless that absurd paradox were allowed to hold, that all tastes are equally good and true.[24]

While the allowance for diversity and the distinction between diversity and error was rather universal in Blair's time, the concept had received its strongest enunciation in the writings of Hume, who had argued:

> But though this axiom, by passing into the proverb, seems to have attained the sanction of common sense; there is certainly a species of common sense which opposes it, at least seems to modify and restrain it. Whoever would assert an equality of genius and elegance between Ogilby and Milton, or Bunyan and Addison, would be thought to defend no less an extravagance, than if he had maintained a mole hill to be as high as Teneriffe, or a pond as extensive as the ocean. Though there may be found persons who give the preference to the former authors; no one pays attention to such a taste; and we pronounce without scruple the sentiments of these pretended critics to be absurd and ridiculous. The principle of the natural equality of tastes is then totally forgot, and while we admit it on some occasions, where the objects seem near an equality, it appears an extravagant paradox, or rather a palpable absurdity, where objects so disproportionate are compared together.[25]

The standard to which Blair appeals when there is opposition of taste is clear. A standard properly conceived, "signifies that which is of such undoubted authority as to be the test of other things of the same kind." Blair agrees with the Aristotelian point of view that conformity to nature is a principle which can be applied in formulating a standard of taste. In this regard, Blair is fairly close to the point of view held by Reynolds and Kames, although he assigns a somewhat less significant role to the criteria of nature. He feels that nature is

---

[24]*Ibid.*, p. 23.
[25]Hume: p. 269.

only a partial standard and is not completely adequate. He makes his case as follows:

> There is no doubt, that in all cases where an imitation is intended of some object that exists in nature, as in representing human characters or actions, conformity to nature affords a full and distinct criterion of what is truly beautiful. Reason hath in such cases full scope for exerting its authority; for approving or condemning; by comparing the copy with the original. But there are innumerable cases in which this rule cannot be at all applied; and conformity to nature is an expression frequently used, without any distinct or determinate meaning. We must therefore search for somewhat that can be rendered more clear and precise, to be the standard of taste.[26]

The clearer and more precise standard to which Blair appeals is the taste of men in general. That which men concur the most in admiring must be held to be the most beautiful. That person's taste must be esteemed just and true which coincides with the general sentiments of mankind. On this standard, then, Blair rests his theory. The ultimate criteria in all works of taste must be in the sense of mankind.

It is clear, however, that Blair does not intend that standards of taste should be determined by pure majority vote. To the contrary, he imposes rather severe restrictions on his concept of *men in general.* He does not believe that an individual must collect the voices of others before he forms any judgment for himself of what deserves to be praised. He states:

> By no means; there are principles of reason and sound judgment which can be applied to matters of taste, as well as to the subjects of science and philosophy. He who admires or censures any work of genius, is always ready, if his taste be in any degree improved, to assign some reasons for his decision. He appeals to principles and points out the ground on which he proceeds. Taste is a sort of compound power; in which the light of the understanding always mingles, more or less with the feelings of sentiment.[27]

---

[26]Blair: p. 23.
[27]*Ibid.*, p. 24.

Thus, in determining his standard of taste, Blair gives further consideration to the relative importance of nature and art. Both factors are included in the standard, but primary emphasis is given to nature, or sensibility, rather than to art, or reason. Although reason may be use to validate the criteria, the standards themselves are based on art. The ultimate conclusions to which reasoning leads are based, in the final analysis, on sense and perception. Reasoning may correct the caprice of unenlightened taste and establish principles for judging that which deserves praise; but, at the same time, these reasonings appeal ultimately to feeling. The foundation upon which they rest is what has been found from experience to please mankind universally.

Blair further limits his conception of the universal tastes of man by indicating that the doctrine of universal testimony is valid only if the men involved live in situations which are conducive to the proper exertions of taste. Any notions concerning taste which are entertained by rude and uncivilized people and during periods of ignorance and darkness carry no authority. The doctrine deals largely with "the sentiments of mankind in polished and flourishing nations; when arts are cultivated and manners refined; when works of genius are subject to free discussion, and taste is improved by science and philosophy."[28]

Even among such nations, at such a period of society, Blair admits that accidental causes may occasionally warp the proper operations of taste:

> Sometimes the form of government may for a while pervert; a licentious court may introduce a taste for false ornaments, and dissolute writings. The usage of one admired genius may procure approbation for his faults and even render them fashionable. Sometimes envy may have power to bear down, for a little, productions of great merit; while popular humour, or party spirit, may, at other times, exalt to a high, though shortlived reputation, what little deserves it. But though such casual circumstances give the appearances of caprice to the judgments of taste, that appearance is easily corrected. In the course of time, the genuine taste of human nature never fails to disclose itself and to gain the ascendant over any fantastic and corrupted modes of taste which may

---

[28]*Ibid.*, p. 25.

chance to have been introduced. These may have currency for a while, and mislead superficial judges; but being subject to examination, by degrees they pass away; while that alone remains which is founded on sound reason, and the native feelings of men.[29]

There is nothing particularly novel or startling in Blair's standard of taste. The ultimate appeal to the sentiment and feelings of *man in general* was an extremely pervasive part of eighteenth-century, neo-classical critical thought. McKillop points out that classicism based literature and criticism on the permanent and universal elements in human nature, that is, on man's long-run experiences of his own powers and limitations. In such experience, moderation, self-control, the need to come to terms with other men, clear communication, counted for most.[30] That position set up a central fixed standard, based at once on the uniformity of nature, the workings of the rational mind, and the coherence of organized society. It did not exclude diversity or spontaneity from art or life, but it looked on them as secondary and limited. It preferred the stable, the normal, the continuous, and the predictable to the unstable, the abnormal, the discontinuous, and the unpredictable. It was thus with a firm foundation in eighteenth-century critical thought that Blair formulated his standard of taste. It was a point of view shared by many contemporary writers and was not, by any means, original with Blair.

Similar, though not identical, standards of taste had been posited by other writers of the period and it is quite possible that Blair's standards may have evolved from his contacts with Kames and Hume. Kames had found his standard of taste in the "common nature of man," a concept not far removed from the "nature of universal man":

> With respect to the common nature of man in particular, we have a conviction that is invariable not less than universal. Nor are we deceived: because giving allowance for the difference of culture and gradual refinement of manners, the fact corresponds to our conviction. We are so constituted as to conceive this common nature to be invariable, *perfect* or *right;* and that individuals

[29]*Ibid.*, p. 25.
[30]Alan Dugald McKillop: *English Literature from Dryden to Burns,* New York, 1948, pp. 173-177.

ought to be made conformable to it. Every remarkable deviation from the standards makes an impression on us of imperfection, irregularity, or disorder. It is disagreeable and raises in us a painful emotion. . . . Thus upon a conviction common to the species is erected a standard of taste; which standard, ascertaining what actions are right or wrong, proper or improper has enabled moralists to establish rules for our conduct, from which no person is permitted to swerve. We have the same standard for ascertaining in all the fine arts, what is beautiful or ugly, high or low, proper or improper, proportioned or disproportioned.[31]

David Hume had also based his standard of taste on the universal and generally unvarying nature of man:

The general principles of taste are uniform in human nature: where men vary in their judgments, some defect or perversion in the faculties may commonly be remarked; proceeding either from prejudice, want of practice, or want of delicacy; and there is just reason for approving one taste and condemning another.[32]

Sir Joshua Reynolds had also chosen the universality of mankind as the basis for his standards of taste:

I shall now say something on the part of *taste*, which as I have hinted to you before, does not belong so much to the external form of things, but is addressed to the mind and depends on its original frame, or to use the expression, the organisation of the soul; I mean the imagination and the passions. The principles of these are as invariable as the former, and are to be known and reasoned upon in the same manner, by an appeal to common sense depending upon the common feelings of mankind.[33]

Blair's theory of taste is reducible to several clearly defined propositions. Taste, in Blair's view, is far from being an arbitrary force which is subject to the fancy of every individual and which admits of no criteria for determining whether it is false or true. Its foundation is the same in all human minds. It is built upon sentiments and perceptions which belong to our nature; and which, in general, operate with the same uniformity as our other faculties. When those senti-

---

[31]Kames: pp. 298-299.
[32]Hume: p. 280.
[33]Reynolds: pp. 200-201.

ments are perverted by ignorance and prejudice, they are capable of being rectified by reason. Their sound and natural state is ultimately determined by comparing them with the general taste of mankind. As Blair says, "In every composition, what interests the imagination and touches the heart pleases all ages and all nations. There is a certain string to which, when properly struck, the human heart is made to answer."[34] Blair himself epitomizes his theory of taste when he says, *"Opinium commenta delet dies; naturæ judicia confirmat.* Time overflows the illusions of opinion but establishes the decisions of nature."

Blair does not directly apply his theory of taste to the judgment of specific speeches. The implication of his doctrine is quite clear, however. In order to criticize oratory effectively, the critic must have some criteria to which he can appeal. In this respect the evaluation of speeches does not differ from the criticisms of other works of art. Blair's advice to the critic is to base his standards of judgment partially on conformity to nature; partially on the rules of reason; and partially on the tastes of mankind in general. In addition it is clear that the rhetorical critic will apply the principles and instructions which are presented in the more strictly rhetorical sections of the *Lectures.*

---

[34]Blair: p. 26.

GEORGE CAMPBELL AND THE
CLASSICAL TRADITION

DOUGLAS McDERMOTT

University of California, Davis

IN 1950 THE VIEW was first put forth that the works of Campbell, Blair, and Whately represented a radical substantive break with the tradition of classical rhetoric. Because this view was initially stated in an attempt to correct what was felt to be an established but erroneous one, and because this new thesis has been maintained for some time now with continuing force and consistency, it stands in need of some qualifying comment, particularly with regard to George Campbell.

In his article, "George Campbell and the Revolution in Inventional Theory," Douglas Ehninger characterized Campbell's work as "a revolution which swept away the last remnants of an *inventio* that had constituted the supreme achievement of ancient rhetorical thought."[1] In the same article he described this *inventio* as "merely an organized body of procedures for searching out materials from which the orator *might* select the substance of his address."[2] Such an *inventio* implied, he said, a concentration on the speech itself. Classical *inventio*, he said, was merely a series of "devices calculated to supply an abundance of appropriate and telling speech materials. As such, however, they bore little relation to the speaker, the audience, or the occasion."[3] The revolution in *inventio* for which he thought Campbell

---

[1] Douglas Ehninger: George Campbell and the Revolution in Inventional Theory, *The Southern Speech Journal,* XV:270, May 1950. Hereafter referred to as "Revolution."

[2] *Ibid.,* p. 273.

[3] *Ibid.,* pp. 272-273.

responsible was Campbell's placing the hearer, rather than the speech itself, at the center of the rhetorical situation.

In more recent articles he has slightly modified this position.[4] Adhering to the same description of classical *inventio*,[5] he goes farther than before and argues that Campbell rejects not only invention, but the entire five-part classical canon of invention, arrangement, style, memory, and delivery. This sweeping rejection forms the basis for four of six distinctions which he makes between Campbell's work and that of his classical predecessors.[6]

Previously, Campbell's rejection of classical invention had implied a rejection of the speech itself as the center of rhetoric. Now, however, Campbell's rejection of the entire classical canon implies a rejection of one means of classifying speeches for another. Arguing that Campbell does not "follow the classical practice of classifying speeches in terms of the function of the 'judge' or audience," but classifies them "according to the end or aim which the orator has in speaking," Ehninger states that such a shift is a "refocusing [of] traditional materials toward the new teleology of 'ends.' "[7] The shift which was initially ascribed to Campbell, the shift from speech to hearer, seems to be one of kind. This new shift, from classifying the speech according to the function of the judge to classifying it according to the reaction desired of him, seems to be one of degree. Nevertheless, the Campbellian revolution continues to be characterized as "radical" and "major." Throughout, with all the changes of terminology and mutations of concept, the thesis remains constant: in some way Campbell rejected the categories of classical rhetoric and thus rejected its essential focus for a radically new one of his own. What is most important is that behind this argument lies the assumption that these categories were central to classical rhetoric as treated by the major writers.

Unquestionably, Campbell discards the classical five-part termi-

---

[4]"Campbell, Blair, and Whately: Old Friends in a New Light," *Western Speech, XIX*:263-269, October 1955; and "Campbell, Blair, and Whately Revisited," *Southern Speech Journal, XXVIII*:169-182, Spring 1963. Hereafter referred to as "Revisited."

[5]"The system of rhetorical invention devised by the ancients proceeded very largely by mechanical or 'artificial' means." Ehninger: "Revisited," p. 172.

[6]*Ibid.*, pp. 173-177.

[7]*Ibid.*, p. 174.

nology of invention, arrangement, style, memory, and delivery for a two-part terminology of analysis and synthesis.[8] Nor is there any question that he rejects the classification of speeches according to function for a new classification according to effect. However, there is a question whether or not such semantic shifts imply the substantive shifts that are inferred. I will consider two points in answering this question. The first concerns the nature of classical rhetoric. Ehninger is correct in his summary of what *inventio* was to certain classical writers, but to assume that it, or, for that matter, the entire five-part canon, was central to their thought as cause rather than effect, is to ignore their specific statements to the contrary. The second point is the assumption that Campbell's revolution is the placing of the hearer at the center, or nearer the center, of the rhetorical situation. Such an assumption implies that the classical writers were not concerned with the hearer and did not consider him to be central. In this paper I will examine both points in the light of certain characteristics common to both the principal classical rhetoricians and George Campbell.

The five-part classical canon was a methodological system that was taught in the schools of antiquity, and which was embodied in nearly all classical works on rhetoric. However, there are two distinct traditions of rhetoric in antiquity, each one of which produced its characteristic treatises. There was the pedagogical tradition, which attempted to make the citizen a better speaker, and of which the *Ad Herennium* is typical; and there was the philosophical tradition, which attempted to explain the foundation of rhetoric in human behavior, of which *De Oratore* is typical. Campbell's work falls into the latter category and is not comparable to anything in the former. Significantly, Ehninger seems to have only the pedagogical tradition in mind when speaking of classical rhetoric, yet the writers in the philosophical tradition whose work provides the only relevant comparison to Campbell's are all careful to dissociate themselves from the schools, their teachers, and the rules taught in them. Plato candidly called the rhetoric of Gorgias "flattery," and likened its effect to that of cookery. Plato's great rival, Isocrates, agreed with him in this, accusing the sophists of trying to teach rhetoric as though it were the

---

[8]For a fuller discussion of this point see Wilbur Samuel Howell: The Declaration of Independence and Eighteenth-Century Logic," *William and Mary Quarterly,* *XVIII*:463-484, October 1961.

alphabet.[9] In this same tradition, Aristotle begins his *Rhetoric* by accusing the teachers of "dwelling upon irrelevant matters" with their rules.[10]

Cicero indulges in the most elaborate criticism of the teachers of public speaking. In *De Oratore* he begins by disowning his own text-book, *De Inventione,* as "unfinished and crude,"[11] and then goes on to plead with parents to teach their children "not to believe that they can gain their coveted object by reliance on the rules of teachers or methods of practice employed by everybody."[12] Finally, he carefully extricates Aristotle from any connection with the teachers: "Aristotle . . . wrote not only much better but also much more than all the teachers of rhetoric put together."[13] Although, in this matter of criticizing the teachers, Cicero is the most elaborate, Quintilian is the most explicit. He refuses to make any such rules in his own work.[14] Granted that both Cicero and Quintilian use the terminology of the canon, it always remains a method for using their thought, not the substance of the thought itself.

From Plato to Quintilian, these classical rhetoricians continue to disavow mere methodology, and, thus, if the canon is methodology, to disavow it. In this light it does not seem reasonable to argue that something for which all these writers express their distaste constitutes the central doctrine of their thought. The primary concern of these writers is more fundamental than the rules for effective speechmaking, and the nature of this primary concern can be judged from two characteristics present in almost all of their works: they regard the faculty of speech as the distinctive characteristic of man, and they regard rhetoric, the highest development of this faculty, as essential to human society.

Isocrates explicitly argues that speech is distinctive of man: that

---

[9]"Against the Sophists" 12, in *Isocrates* II, trans. George Norlin, New York, 1929. All references are to this edition.

[10]*Rhetoric,* 1354b, trans. Lane Cooper, New York, 1932. All references are to this edition.

[11]*De Oratore,* ii, 2, 5, trans. E. W. Sutton and H. Rackham, Cambridge, Mass., 1942. All references are to this edition.

[12]*Ibid.,* i, 5, 19.

[13]*Ibid.,* i, 10, 43.

[14]*Institutio Oratoria,* ii, 13, 1, trans. H. E. Butler, New York, 1921. All references are to this edition.

because man is able to persuade and communicate he has "escaped the life of the wild beasts," and has "come together and founded cities and made laws and invented arts."[15] In this same matter, Aristotle is more reserved. He argues that reason is most distinctive of man.[16] However, since this statement occurs in the section where he is listing the uses of rhetoric, it seems reasonable to assume that rhetoric is the means by which man manifests this distinctive characteristic. Cicero echoes Isocrates in arguing that the difference between man and beast is the matter of communication,[17] and Quintilian attributes the faculty of speech to God, who has distinguished man from the beasts in this way.[18]

Not only do the principal classical writers consider speech to be the distinctive characteristic of man, but they regard rhetoric as the highest development of it. As such, rhetoric is essential to man's social endeavors. Each of these writers finds an intimate connection between rhetoric and an important aspect of man's behavior in society. Plato understands that rhetoric is essential to philosophy because the philosopher must convince others of the truth. On the other hand, Isocrates believes that rhetoric does more than convince; it actually helps form a just character in man.[19] Aristotle regards rhetoric as a counterpart of dialectic and a branch of politics,[20] while Cicero restricts it to politics.[21] Quintilian deals primarily with the law courts because he believes that justice, which is essential to rhetoric, is found there.[22]

These considerations seem to point to a classical concept of rhetoric that is opposed to a purely methodological study like that of the *De Inventione* and the *Ad Herennium*. Rhetoric is the highest development of man's most distinctive faculty. As such it is essential to his society and his attempts to operate in that society. Rhetoric is a social instrument for the classical writers, and in so far as society involves men it is an instrument for dealing with, persuading, and understanding

---

[15]"Antidosis," 254, in *Isocrates*, II, trans. George Norlin, New York, 1929. All references are to this edition.
[16]*Rhetoric*, 1355b.
[17]*De Oratore*, i, 7, 32.
[18]*Institutio Oratoria*, ii, 16, 12.
[19]"Against the Sophists," 21.
[20]*Rhetoric*, 1356b.
[21]*De Oratore*, i, 8, 34.
[22]*Institutio Oratoria*, ii, 15, 29.

them. It is a process of communication which is at once necessary to and distinctive of the human mind.[23]

Consequently, for classical writers the heart of rhetoric becomes the study of the human mind, and it is in this respect that Campbell seems to fall within the classical tradition. He shares the classical distaste for rules and handbooks which enable men to practice a science without understanding its principles:

> Indeed, in almost every art, even as used by mere practitioners, there are certain rules . . . which must carefully be followed, and which serve the artist instead of principles. An acquaintance with these is one step, and but one step towards science.[24]

While he does not explicitly consider speech to be distinctive of man, he does acknowledge its pervasiveness and importance. Speech is one of the two arts that are both useful and pleasant. In one or the other of these functions it has been with man from the beginning and it will remain with him until the end of organized society.[25] Finally, he believes that rhetoric is essential to logic and ethics because it indicates how these two arts are to be used:

> . . . if the logical art, and the ethical, be useful, eloquence is useful, as it instructs us how these arts must be applied for the conviction and the persuasion of others. It is indeed the grand art of communication. . . .[26]

Classical rhetoric is primarily concerned with man's mind and his attempts to communicate the contents of his mind to the minds of others. Thus, classical rhetoric is concerned with the minds of both speaker and hearer. Campbell, too, is most explicit about his belief that rhetoric is a science of the mind: ". . . there is no art whatever that hath so close a connexion with all the faculties and powers

---

[23]For a fuller discussion of the prevasiveness of rhetoric in classical culture see George A. Kennedy: *The Art of Persuasion in Greece,* Princeton, N. J., 1963, pp. 3-8; and Werner Jaeger: *Paideia: The Ideals of Greek Culture,* trans. Gilbert Highet, New York, 1939, I, 310-313 and III, 190-196.

[24]George Campbell: *The Philosophy of Rhetoric* [1776], ed. Lloyd F. Bitzer, Carbondale, Ill., 1963, p. xlvi. All references are to this edition.

[25]*Ibid.,* pp. xlvii, xlviii.

[26]*Ibid.,* p. xlix.

of the mind, as eloquence. . . ."[27] Such a connection leads to an understanding of how the mind works:

> . . . it not only traces the operations of the intellect and imagination, but discloses the lurking springs of action in the heart. In this view it is perhaps the surest and the shortest, as well as the pleasantest way of arriving at the science of the human mind.[28]

If, in its general concern, Campbell's philosophy of rhetoric is within the classical tradition, then it is difficult to imagine that he could radically diverge from it. If he is within the classical tradition, then it is ambiguous to imply that the hearer could in some way be more central to him than to the classical writers. Indeed, it would seem that the distinction between classification based on audience function and classification based on audience reaction is purely semantic. If the audience were expected to perform a specific judging function, then classification according to that function indicates that a certain kind of judgment is the desired reaction. Rather than something different, the classification according to function is the classical equivalent of Campbell's classification according to reaction. The difference is one of social context, not rhetorical concept.

To support his contention that classical rhetoric was not concerned with the audience, Ehninger refers to Plato's statement that the rhetorician needs to be a good logician.[29] However, Plato qualifies this statement by observing that a knowledge of logic is not sufficient to persuade. Rhetoric is needed to persuade, and Plato defines rhetoric as "the art of winning the soul by discourse."[30] In order to win the soul, the rhetorician must know that "there are so and so many kinds of souls, of such and such a nature, and hence men severally are of such a sort, and such another."[31] Logic appears to be only half of the rhetorical situation; psychology is the other half.

Like Plato, Aristotle is concerned with psychology. Furthermore, his concern with it parallels Campbell's. This can be seen most clearly by comparing his discussion of proof with Campbell's. Aristotle's

[27]*Ibid.*

[28]*Ibid.,* p. 1.

[29]Ehninger: "Revolution," p. 274.

[30]"Phaedrus," 261A, in *Plato,* trans. Lane Cooper, New York, 1938. All references are to this edition.

[31]*Ibid.,* 271D.

three means of proof are all oriented towards the persuasion of an audience. As he observes, " 'Persuasive' means persuasive to a person."[32] Furthermore, he treats of the same three means of proof that Campbell does, and he treats of them in the same way. The first means of proof is the *ethos* of the speaker. Aristotle says that the speech must be uttered in such a way as to make the speaker worthy of belief.[33] Campbell says, "By this we are to understand . . . that which is obtained reflexively from the opinion entertained of him by the hearers, or the character which he bears with them."[34]

The argument is that Campbell's concept of ethical proof is non-classical, that while his concept is "essentially a social construct," the classical concept reflects the intrinsic "goodness" of the speaker.[35] This, I take it, is an interpretation of Aristotle's statement that "this trust [produced by *ethos*], however, should be created by the speech itself, and not left to depend upon an antecedent impression."[36] However, it is equally possible to interpret this passage as a caution to use ethical proof consciously rather than ignore it or leave it to chance.

Aristotle then discusses pathetic proof, which he defines as "producing a certain attitude in the hearer."[37] This is important because "we give very different decisions under the sway of pain or joy, liking or hatred."[38] This is the same concept of pathetic proof that Campbell has. He observes that if the emotions are not aroused no action will result: "I have no passion for the object. I am indifferent whether I procure it or not"; but, he says, if the passions are aroused, ". . . I am instantly at your command."[39] He then goes on to list the passions most useful to the speaker and the means of appealing to them. This is precisely the same procedure which Aristotle follows.[40]

Finally, Aristotle discusses logical proof, which he defines as the demonstration of real or apparent truth "by such means as inhere in particular cases."[41] He considers this to be the most important

---

[32]*Rhetoric,* 1356b.
[33]*Ibid.,* 1356a.
[34]Campbell: p. 96.
[35]Ehninger: "Revisited," p. 177.
[36]*Rhetoric,* 1356a.
[37]*Ibid.*
[38]*Ibid.,* 1356b.
[39]Campbell: p. 78.
[40]*Rhetoric,* 1377b-1389b.

of the three means of proof because "we entertain the strongest conviction of a thing if we believe that it has been 'demonstrated.' "[42] Although he disapproves of the syllogism as a means of proof, Campbell acknowledges the usefulness of the example, and he stresses the fact that the audience must understand the connection between the desired object and the speaker's proposed plan of action before they will accept it. The primary difference between Aristotle and Campbell in this matter of proof is a difference in emphasis. Aristotle believes logical proof to be the most effective, while Campbell believes that pathetic proof is the most effective; but both regard effectiveness as a matter of influencing the audience.

Ehninger argues for another difference between Campbell and the classical rhetoricians in this matter of proof. He argues that in classical thought each of the modes of proof was regarded as autonomous: "Each was considered as complete in itself, and as entirely capable of effecting conviction without aid from the others."[43] On the other hand, he says, Campbell treats them as "mutually subservient forces, and in the clearest and strongest of language [argued] that in order to achieve persuasion these forces must work in concert."[44] This argument overlooks Aristotle's specific statement that "the speaker must not merely see to it that his speech shall be convincing and persuasive, but he must give the right impression of himself, and get his judge into the right state of mind."[45] Although Aristotle recognizes that in certain situations certain types of proof will be more effective than others, he clearly states that they must all be used because rhetoric is the art of persuasion and all three modes of proof constitute the instruments of persuasion.[46]

Two conclusions can be drawn from this discussion. The first is that the methodology expressed in the five-part canon was not central to the thought of classical rhetoric. Rather it seems that the heart of classical rhetoric was an understanding of man's mind as he operated in society. As Crassus summarizes the classical tradition, "Our im-

---

[41]*Ibid.*, 1356a.
[42]*Ibid.*, 1355a.
[43]Ehninger: "Revisited," p. 172.
[44]*Ibid.*, pp. 174-175.
[45]*Rhetoric*, 1377b.
[46]*Ibid.*, 1356a.

mediate task is not to display any system of speaking, but to hand on to highly educated men certain lessons, as I may call them, learned from our own practice."[47] The second conclusion is that the revolutionary aspect of Campbell's work, and I am well aware that it is a revolution, was not his placing of the hearer at or near to the center of the rhetorical situation, because, this had been implicit in the classical tradition. Rather, he acknowledges the excellence of his classical predecessors for their progress in devising the proper rules of composition, "not only [in] the two sorts of poesy, epic and dramatic, but also in the three sorts of oration which were in most frequent use among them, the deliberative, the judiciary, and the demonstrative," and concludes that "as far as I have been able to discover, there has been little or no improvement in this respect made by the moderns."[48] Consequently, he does not propose to repeat the work of classical rhetoricians, but, instead, to carry it one step farther: ". . . to canvass those principles in our nature to which the various attempts are adapted, and by which, in any instance, their success or want of success may be accounted for."[49] It is in this attempt to link rhetoric with the psychological principles of the human mind that Campbell may, indeed, be said to bring us into a new country.[50]

---

[47]*De Oratore*, ii, 41, 175.

[48]Campbell: p. li.

[49]*Ibid.*, pp. l, li.

[50]For a fuller discussion of Campbell's unique contribution to rhetorical theory see Lloyd F. Bitzer: The Lively Idea: A Study of Hume's Influence on George Campbell's *Philosophy of Rhetoric,* unpublished Ph.D. dissertation, State University of Iowa, 1962.

CAMPBELL, BLAIR, AND WHATELY REVISITED

DOUGLAS EHNINGER

State University of Iowa

I. INTRODUCTION

In an article published in 1955 and entitled "Campbell, Blair, and Whately: Old Friends in a New Light,"[1] I questioned the generally accepted view that after 1625 or 1630, British rhetoric, repudiating the excesses of the stylists and the dichotomizing of the Ramists, began a gradual "reversion" to the five-part doctrine of the ancients; and that this trend, continued to grow in strength and influence, reached its culmination in the late eighteenth and early nineteenth centuries in the works of George Campbell, Hugh Blair, and Richard Whately.[2]

Instead, I suggested that the classical "reversion" attained its zenith about the middle of the century in the compendiums of John Lawson and John Ward, and that following these writers British rhetoric, responding to contemporary developments in epistemology, psychology, and literary criticism, began to move in new and essentially non-classical directions.[3] Specifically, I contended that the treatises of Campbell, Blair, and Whately, rather than marking the high tide of a rejuvenated classicism, are among the pivotal works upon which these new departures turn.

[1] *Western Speech Journal, XIX*:263-269, January 1955.
[2] George Campbell: *The Philosophy of Rhetoric*, London and Edinburgh, 1776; Hugh Blair: *Lectures on Rhetoric and Belles Lettres*, London and Edinburgh, 1783; Richard Whately: *Elements of Rhetoric*, London, 1828.
[3] See also my article, John Ward and His Rhetoric, *Speech Monographs, XVIII*: 1-16, March 1951, and my unpubl. diss., Selected Theories of *Inventio* in English Rhetoric, 1759-1828, Ohio State, 1949.

Although intended as a preliminary statement, during the past eight years this article has received considerable attention, both by way of endorsement and of criticism.[4] Stimulated by the remarks of later writers and drawing upon a continued study of the problem, I here attempt a more comprehensive statement of the proposition originally developed. In addition to the common characteristics of all three works as previously described, I seek additional support for my thesis by a closer examination of certain traits which they exhibit individually. Moreover, as a ground for my argument, I supply some notion of what I understand by the term "classical rhetoric"—an explanation which was missing from the earlier article, and the absence of which has occasioned misunderstanding. Finally, insofar as space allows, I supplement my earlier discussion by suggesting the extent to which the works in question helped shape present-day theories of oral discourse.

II. THE CLASSICAL RHETORIC

During the centuries which separate Corax from Augustine, rhetoric, as a time- and culture-bound art, underwent profound changes. Despite these changes, however, at least eight characteristics remained stable enough to warrant description.

1. Among the ancients, rhetoric was conceived of broadly, as encompassing two quite different questions: (a) What may be said on behalf of a given cause? (b) How may it best be said? The first question was assigned to the *officium* of invention; the second was distributed among the remaining *officia* of disposition, style, memory, and delivery.

---

[4]See, for example, Lloyd Bitzer: The Lively Idea; A Study of Hume's Influence on George Campbell's *Philosophy of Rhetoric,* unpubl. diss., Iowa, 1962; Douglas McDermott: George Campbell and the Classical Tradition, Debut in Rhetoric and Public Address, SAA, New York, 1961; Ross Stafford North: Joseph Priestley on Language, Oratory, and Criticism, unpubl. diss., Florida, 1957; Ronald Reid: The Boylston Professorship of Rhetoric and Oratory, 1806-1904: A Case Study in Changing Concepts of Rhetoric and Pedagogy, *Quarterly Journal of Speech, XLV*:249, October 1959; John Ward's Influence in America: Joseph McKean and the Boylston Lectures on Rhetoric and Oratory, *Speech Monographs, XXVII*: 343, November 1961. Also cf. Clarence W. Edney: Campbell's *Lectures on Pulpit Eloquence, Speech Monographs, XIX*:9, March 1952, with my earlier article, George Campbell and the Revolution in Inventional Theory, *SSJ, XV*:270-276, May 1950.

As organized within the framework of ancient rhetorical systems, these questions were characteristically attacked in order, attention first being paid to the techniques and routines for "discovering" or "discerning" proofs and then to the principles governing their adaptation to a particular audience and their appropriate expression. Moreover, each of these activities—the discovery of proofs no less than their adaptation and expression—was regarded as an indispensable part of rhetoric, and was assigned its own body of precepts and procedures. As a result, rhetoric had a discrete body of rules for organizing and expressing thought—rules which, though similar to the dicta governing these functions in literary discourse, yet were distinct from them. It also had its own inventional system, parallel to but independent of the inventional systems belonging to dialectic or to the various substantive sciences.

2. With few exceptions, the rhetorical treatises of the ancient world were organized according to one or the other of two basic patterns—the Hellenic or the Hellenistic. Under the Hellenic pattern, arrangement was by the five *officia*—invention, disposition, style, memory, and delivery; or, as in the case of Aristotle's *Rhetoric,* invention, style, and disposition, with delivery scanted and memory omitted. Under the Hellenistic pattern, arrangement was by the parts of the speech—proem, narration, confirmation, refutation, and the like—with appropriate advice concerning invention and disposition subsumed under each of these heads, and style and delivery treated independently. A typical example is the *Rhetorica ad Herennium.*

3. In the surviving ancient rhetorical treatises, without major exception, speeches were classified according to the scene or circumstance in which each was habitually delivered—the deliberative address in the legislative chamber, the forensic in the courtroom, and the epideictic on the ceremonial or special occasion. This, of course, is only another way of saying that they were classified in terms of the function assigned to the judge or auditor—whether a decision was to be rendered concerning the justice or injustice of things past, the expediency or inexpediency of things future, or the worth or worthlessness of things present. Speeches were never catalogued as we catalogue them today, according to the speaker's purpose—to inform, to entertain, or to persuade.

4. While the classical rhetoricians fully recognized that in any piece of real-life persuasive discourse the three modes of artistic proof—*ethos, pathos,* and *pistis*—would all undoubtedly be present and inextricably interwoven into the thought fabric of the address, at the same time, so far as the theory as distinguished from the practice of persuasion was concerned, from first to last and without significant exception, these modes were viewed as autonomous. Each was considered as complete in itself, and as entirely capable of effecting conviction without aid from the others. In any given speaking situation, therefore, while some listeners might be persuaded by the totality of the orator's proofs, others might equally well be persuaded by his ethical proofs alone, or his pathetic proofs alone, or his logical proofs alone. It was not thought necessary that the modes operate in concert in order to effect conviction.

5. The system of rhetorical invention devised by the ancients proceeded very largely by mechanical or "artificial" means. That is, it attempted to reduce the inventional process to certain fixed routines which could be applied to any subject, and which because they insured an exhaustive survey of the potentials for persuasion inherent within that subject tended to eliminate individual differences in insight and creativity.

The machinery of this system, as developed in the high classical rhetoric of the period from Hermagoras to Quintilian, consisted, first, of a scheme for cataloguing disputable questions; second, of the *status;* third, of the topics; and, fourth, of a description of the stages through which a dispute passes in approaching resolution.

6. Despite the efforts of Quintilian and a very few of the later theorists to broaden its scope, the classical rhetoric as a whole was primarily oriented toward the single end of persuasion. Rhetoric was almost exclusively the art of influencing belief or action, and did not extend to the considerations involved in informing or entertaining an audience.

Still more specifically, for the ancients, rhetoric as the art of persuasion was first and foremost the art of persuasive forensic address. It was upon the forensic genre that the classical theorists lavished their most detailed attention, and it was this genre that they principally had in mind in the development of such doctrinal elements as the *status* and the six-fold division of the parts of the speech into proem, narration, proposition, confirmation, refutation, and peroration. As Donald Bryant has properly remarked, even the ancient theory of epideictic address was developed within the general framework of persuasion and brought into the system as a whole only at the expense of considerable forcing.[5]

7. In all of their theorizing the ancients were careful to keep as definite and precise as might be the divisions among the five *officia,* and especially that which separated invention from disposition. While the location and contour of the line between these two departments might shift, depending on whether a writer fell within the Hellenic or Hellenistic tradition—making invention extremely narrow in the first case and extremely broad in the second—as to the existence of the line itself and the general division of functions which it signified there never was any doubt. Certain routines were assigned to invention; others to disposition. There was no confusion or uncertainty; no intermingling or overlapping.

8. Just as the ancients were careful to keep distinct the lines separating the *officia,* so also were they careful in theory, if not always in practice, to distinguish between the related fields of rhetoric and poetic, assigning to poetic authority over the realm of imaginative discourse, usually written and designed to elevate the sentiments or to give pleasure, and assigning to rhetoric authority over practical discourse, usually oral and designed to influence belief or action.

III. COMMON TRAITS

Holding in mind the eight characteristics of the classical rhetoric just specified, let us now consider certain traits which the treatises of Campbell, Blair, and Whately exhibit in common.

1. None of the books in question is organized according to either of the standard classical patterns—that which treats the subject in terms of the *officia,* or that which effects arrangement according to the "parts" of the speech.

Campbell, starting from the premise that the "radical principles"

---

[5]Donald C. Bryant: Rhetoric: Its Functions and Its Scope, *Quarterly Journal of Speech, XXXIX*:405, December 1953.

of rhetoric may be explained by an examination of human mental processes, approaches the subject through an abstract analysis of how men think and know, how they are aroused and stirred to action —in short, through a description of the mind of the listener rather than through the traditional series of steps for analyzing and synthesizing the potential subject matter of an address.

Blair, in turn, departs from the classical structure by organizing his *Lectures* in accordance with the belletristic assumption that the various species of discourse—oratory, history, poetry, drama, etc.— are branches of a common trunk; a trunk which itself is rooted in those principles of effective language usage which constitute the lore of "style." Hence, he does not treat public speaking as a self-contained discipline, but as a more or less specialized development within the field of polite letters, and does not even introduce the subject of speechmaking until he has spent twenty-four lectures on such foundation matters as genius and taste, sentence structure, figures of speech, and the kinds of style.

Whately, for his part, begins his *Elements* with a deep-cutting distinction between "the method of inquiry" and "the method of proof," assigning inquiry to the province of the philosopher and reserving only proof as the proper preserve of the rhetorician. By this dichotomy he exercises at the outset a fair half of what the ancients had included within the science of rhetoric, and begins his book where he conceives rhetoric to begin, not with an elaborate description of a set of artificial tools for deriving proofs which may later be evaluated and disposed, but rather with a discussion of how previously derived truth claims may be supported through the use of different types of "arguments" and appeals.

2. Campbell, Blair, and Whately do not follow the classical practice of classifying speeches in terms of the function of the "judge" or audience—that is, according to whether the listener must decide concerning things future or things past or merely has the role of passive critic-appreciator. Instead, influenced by the prevailing psychology of the faculties and by the desire to enhance the usefulness of rhetoric in a world that bore little resemblance to the world of Aristotle and Cicero, they discarded the classical categories. In their place they put the more functional—and also, inci-

dentally, the more pedagogically practical—system of classifying discourses according to the end or aim which the orator has in speaking—to inform, to correct erroneous opinions, to stimulate the imagination, to arouse the passions, or to move the will. In so doing they not only transformed the character of rhetoric by refocusing traditional materials toward the new teleology of "ends," but they also broadened the scope of the science by expanding it beyond the realm of persuasion and making it the organon of informative as well as suasory discourse.

3. Contrary to the classical view that *ethos, pathos,* and *pistis* are independent modes of persuasion, each capable of effecting the speaker's aim without aid from the others, Campbell, Blair, and Whately treat *pathos* and *pistis* as mutually subservient forces, and in the clearest and strongest of language argue that in order to achieve persuasion these forces must work in concert. Therefore, they constructed what the late Irving J. Lee aptly termed the "linear adjunct theory of persuasion"—the theory which holds that in order to win belief or action the speaker must *both* convince the reason and move the passions; and, furthermore, that this double task must be carried out in a prescribed fashion.[6] For Blair this meant beginning with the "conviction" of the reason, and then upon the foundation of acquired intellectual assent, erecting those emotional persuasives which are the final movers of the will. In Campbell's case, as in Whately's, the recommended procedure was reversed, so that the speaker was first to crystallize a wish or emotion and then to "demonstrate" how it may be satisfied. For our present purpose, however, these variations are of little significance. The important point is that all three authors— again profoundly influenced by the psychology of the faculties—departed in a major respect from ancient doctrine, and offered a far more sophisticated analysis of the persuasive process than had been developed in the classical rhetoric, or, indeed, than had been possible within the limited framework of ancient theories of psychology and epistemology.

4. Campbell, Blair, and Whately do not include within rhetoric an inventional system peculiar to that discipline and consisting, for

---

[6]Irving J. Lee: A Study of Emotional Appeal in Rhetorical Theory, with Special Reference to Invention, Arrangement, and Style, unpubl. diss., Northwestern, 1939, 371.

the most part, of purely "artificial" routines. On the contrary, all three authors—Campbell by the strongest of implications and Blair and Whately explicitly—rule investigation as a whole out of the province of rhetorical science and assign it to other substantive or methodological disciplines. Moreover, they either openly attack the machinery designed to effect invention by "artificial" means—the *status,* topics, and the like—or are silent concerning it.

5. As might be expected of churchmen, all three wrote with the problems of the Christian preacher constantly in mind, thus adding to their rhetorics a dimension unknown and unneeded in the classical world. Besides the lectures which Campbell and Blair devote specifically to preaching, their preoccupation with the subject is evident at many points in their works. Whately, for his part, develops in the *Elements* as a whole what Parrish has very correctly described as an "ecclesiastical rhetoric"[7]—one which divides its attention almost equally between arming the pulpit orator for his task of demonstrating the revealed truths of religion to an unlettered congregation and equipping the Christian apologist who is called upon to defend his faith against the attacks of unbelievers.

6. Lastly under this head, and of very great significance to the argument here being developed, is the fact that Campbell, Blair, and Whately ignore the dividing line, which, as I have said, the ancients so carefully erected between the departments of invention and disposition. These two *officia* they fused into a new functional science concerned with "the conduct of a discourse in all of its parts"—a science which, borrowing a term from Blair, we may designate as "management." In this new concept of "management" classical inventional and dispositional processes are so completely intermingled that it is useless to attempt to disentangle them. In fact, when such an attempt is made and the various elements of "management" are forced into one or the other of the traditional categories, they lose much of their meaning and significance.

All we can do, therefore, is accept the new ordering at its face value. We are forced to say that Campbell's discussion of invention lies partly in his attack on syllogism, partly in his analysis of the "oc-

---

[7]Wayland Maxfield Parrish: Abstract of diss., "Richard Whately's *Elements of Rhetoric,* Parts I and II," Cornell, 1929, unpaged.

casion," etc. But nowhere in the *Philosophy* are we able to point to any one place and say, "Here Campbell's discussion of invention (or disposition) begins," or to another and say, "Here it ends." Indeed, Campbell's inventional doctrine is actually as much a spirit and point of view as it is a specific body of rules and methods.

As for Blair, he himself has guided us in the matter by categorically asserting that processes for investigating subject matter cannot be standardized and reduced to a science. Attempts in this direction, he declares, will only produce a childish and trifling study in which the impotence of the process is hidden under a mass of intricate terminology. As a consequence, for Blair rhetoric as an organized discipline finds its natural limits in teaching us how to use most judiciously and to best advantage the materials furnished by extra-rhetorical means, while whatever inventional functions rhetoric does possess lie more in the direction of "judgment" and the "handling" of material than in that of "discovery" or "discernment."

Whately, having arbitrarily excluded investigation from rhetoric, teaches that as a first step the speaker or writer must learn the various kinds of arguments—experience, progressive approach, the calculation of chances, and the like—and also the potential strengths and weaknesses of each. Then upon the basis of this knowledge, he is to acquire skill and judgment in their use—know when and how each type should be employed in order most effectively to establish the matter in question, as that matter is conditioned by where the presumption and burden of proof lie, whether the discourse seeks to confirm or refute, etc. In short, in Whately analysis and synthesis, discovery and selection, discernment and application, methodology and substance—all of which had been carefully distinguished by the ancients—are brought together and welded into one general body of doctrine directed toward teaching how the *a priori* conclusions of the Christian orator or disputant may be impressed upon others.

IV. THE WORKS INDIVIDUALLY

When the authors are considered not as a group but individually, a mass of additional evidence bearing upon our thesis at once becomes apparent.

Departing from the classical view that ethical appeal, even when artifically derived, is at bottom an expression of the speaker's intrinsic "goodness," Campbell equates the Greek word *ethos* with the English word "disposition," and justifies this association on the ground that ethical proof is essentially a social construct—an estimate "obtained reflexively" from the habitual attitudes or actions of the speaker, as these are interpreted or evaluated, not in the abstract, but in the light of the listener's own standards and mores. By this means, he develops a "socialized" conception of "disposition" which represents a considerable departure from the more straightforward and naive treatment of ethical appeal found in the classical writers.

Second, unlike the ancients who regarded the syllogism—embodied, of course, in its rhetorical counterpart, the enthymeme—as the central engine of popular proof, Campbell is at pains to deny syllogism in any of its forms a legitimate place in the science of rhetoric. Syllogistic inference, he argues, is useful neither as a method of inquiry nor as a method of proof. For while in inquiry the mind normally advances from things better known to things less well known or new, syllogism in its progression from universals to particulars follows exactly the opposite path, the properties or traits of a class always being less clear and vivid than the properties or traits of the individuals who compose that class. So far as proof is concerned, the syllogism, says Campbell, has not the "least affinity to moral [or popular] reasoning": first, because in "moral" reasoning, as in inquiry, we habitually proceed from the particular to the general; and, second, because the laws of syllogism, based as they are upon the principle of inclusion and exclusion, make no provision for the contingent.

Two other significant departures from classical doctrine on Campbell's part are direct reflections of the stimulating intellectual environment in which he lived. First, he makes Hume's "lively" or "vivacious" idea the chief effector of persuasion, and conceives the orator's task as primarily one of causing ideas of "imagination" to approach ideas of "experience" in vividness and compulsion. Second, he follows Thomas Reid in regarding confidence in testimony as an "original principle" of human nature—as we might say loosely, an instinct—and on this ground assigns testimony unusual persuasive potency.

Passing now to Blair, it may first be observed that disregarding the classical distinctions between rhetoric and poetic, and between spoken and written discourse, he constructs within the framework of the belletristic analysis, a body of doctrine that cuts across these lines, unifying all four areas into a single science of composition and transmission. Thus his book was entitled *Lectures on Rhetoric and Belles Lettres,* and in addition to advice on public speaking, letter writing, and the construction of essays—the usual subject matter of rhetoric—also includes considerations of epic and lyric poetry, tragedy and comedy, and the like.

Similarly, Blair disregarded the ancient division between rhetoric as an art or science of *production,* and criticism as an art or science of *judgment,* and fused these two functions in such a way that each rule or principle is made to serve a double purpose, providing, on the one hand, a guide to be followed in composing, and on the other, a standard to be applied in judging.

But even on matters not influenced by the belletristic orientation, Blair was decidedly non-classical. No writer of his age—indeed, few writers of any age—leveled so strong an attack against the topics as artificial aids to invention. Believing that topics hamper rather than aid the inventional process, and saying that while they may turn out showy academic declamations, they can never produce persuasive discourses capable of effecting real business, he declares that proofs which are truly "solid and persuasive" must be drawn *ex visceribus causæ,* by long study and profound meditation. For such study and meditation, no "artificial" substitute is possible.

And lastly, as I have shown elsewhere, Blair is non-classical in his marked tendency to take over the rhetorical and critical doctrines of a developing Romanticism.[8] His conception of sublimity as involving strength and grandeur, his emphasis upon "original genius," his proclivity toward "primitivism," and his admiration of Shakespeare are only a few of the tell-tale signs. There are many others—indeed, so many that they constitute an important factor in accounting for the persistent popularity of Blair's *Lectures* as the nineteenth century advanced. For as the influence of Neo-classicism waned

[8]Douglas Ehninger and James Golden: The Intrinsic Sources of Blair's Popularity, *SSJ, XXI*:19-21, Fall 1955.

and that of Romanticism waxed, the *Lectures* continued to be read and studied because, among other things, they were congenial to this developing trend.

What, finally, of Whately? In what more particular respects does his *Elements of Rhetoric* depart from the classical analysis?

First, as Parrish and nearly all subsequent students of Whately have observed, the Archbishop leaves unmentioned the probable or contingent nature of rhetoric, as insisted upon by the ancient theorists.[9] For Whately, rhetoric, using as its central agent of persuasion the syllogism, and employing as premises the revealed truths of religion could, like the analytic of science, arrive at demonstrated conclusions. The possibility of such demonstration he declared by calling rhetoric "the" art rather than "an" art of persuasion.

Second, Whately ignores the three-fold division of discourse into deliberative, epideictic, and forensic, displaying everywhere a greater concern with fact past than with fact present or future, and with a single exception, developing a body of theory devoted exclusively to the confirmation of prior premises.

Third, in line with his conception of rhetoric as "the" art of persuasion, Whately lifts "testimony" out of the province of inartificial proofs, and transfers it into the realm of the artificial, classifying it as a species of "sign." For, as he sees it, "the existence of the testimony" may be taken as a mark or indication of the event referred to.

Fourth, working an equally violent alteration on another of the major concepts of classical rhetoric, Whately denies *ethos* independent status as a mode of persuasion, treating it instead as a subdivision of the *pathos;* his argument here being that "admiration" and "esteem," the qualities which it is the purpose of *ethos* to elicit, are to be numbered among the "affections."

Fifth, as I have shown elsewhere, and can mention only in passing, Whately views rhetoric as an "off-shoot" of dialectic or logic in the sense that its controlling principles are ultimately derived from the laws of formal proof.[10] Thus logic is related to rhetoric as parent to child, rather than as brother or "counterpart."

---

[9]Parrish: *op. cit.*
[10]Whately on *Dispositio, Quarterly Journal of Speech, XL*:439-441, December 1954.

Sixth, let us remember it was Whately who introduced into the corpus of rhetorical theory the concepts of presumption and burden of proof. Although recognized from earliest times as principles governing legal procedure and the law of evidence, these concepts were not a part of classical rhetorical doctrine prior to Whately.

V. INFERENCES AND CONCLUSION

In proportion as the preceding argument is valid—in proportion as the works of Campbell, Blair, and Whately may properly be regarded, not as somewhat modified restatements of the classical rhetoric, but rather as expressing new and essentially non-classical tendencies—to that degree we shall be forced to re-write certain chapters in the history of modern rhetorical thought. For there can be no argument but that the widespread and long-continued use of these works, as well as the impress they made on later writers, adds up to a total influence incomparably greater than that exercised by the strictly classical eighteenth-century rhetorics of Holmes, Lawson, Ward, and Monboddo.[11] Therefore, in the perspective of time it is apparent that the really significant counterpoise against the sixteenth- and seventeenth-century rhetorics of style and of Ramism was not—contrary to the commonly held view—a rejuvenated classicism, but instead the new and basically non-classical views of our three authors. More specifically, it was the new psychology and epistemology of the great British empiricists as expressed by George Campbell, the new critical system of the belletristic school as interpreted and applied by Hugh Blair, and the Coplestonian logico-rhetoric of early nineteenth-century Oxford as developed by Richard Whately that put the rhetoric of style and of Ramism once and for all to rest.

But over and above this service, which was in itself significant, the rhetorics of Campbell, Blair, and Whately stand as the great

---

[11]John Holmes: *The Art of Rhetoric Made Easy*, London, 1739; John Lawson: *Lectures concerning Oratory*, Dublin, 1758; John Ward: *A System of Oratory*, London, 1759; James Burnett [Lord Monboddo]: *Of the Origin and Progress of Language*, Edinburgh, 1774-92, IV.

[12]Joseph Priestley: *A Course of Lectures on Oratory and Criticism*, London, 1777; John Ogilvie: *Philosophical and Critical Observations on the Nature, Characters, and Various Species of Composition*, London, 1774; William Barron: *Lectures on Belles Lettres and Logic*, London, 1806.

watershed that divides earlier from modern rhetorical thought. When we read a work of pre-Campbellian vintage isolated areas of doctrine may strike us as familiar, but on the whole, we somehow feel we are upon foreign ground. On the other hand, most of the treatises that post-date Whately possess an unmistakable air of contemporaneity. Nor is this to be wondered at. Many of the leading terms and concepts of our present-day textbooks—the rhetorical concepts as distinguished from the psychological and epistemological ones—stem directly or indirectly from our three authors. The custom of classifying speeches in terms of the purpose of the speaker rather than the function of the judge stems ultimately from Campbell. The distinction between logical argument and psychological appeal, to which, for better or worse, we still largely adhere in our teaching, is a vestige of the psychology of the faculties as expressed by Campbell and Blair, and by most of their contemporaries. The groundings for the greater part of our contemporary theory of argumentation and debate are to be found in Whately. Hugh Blair, as the first influential expounder, if not the father of the rhetoric of *belles lettres,* is the indirect ancestor of present-day courses in communication skills in which instruction in speaking is correlated with training in writing, reading, and listening.

And so I might go on. But anyone who examines these works with an eye to modern parallels can discover other instances for himself. Here our closing paragraphs may more profitably be devoted to exploring a proposition of broader import. It is this: Chiefly because of the influence of Campbell, Blair, and Whately—and of Joseph Priestley, John Ogilvie, William Barron,[12] and certain other of their contemporaries whom I have not been able to mention here —in many major respects the rhetoric embodied in our courses and textbooks today differs from classical doctrine more than it resembles that body of theory. We do not talk of states and quasi-states, or of universal and particular topics; we do not distinguish between theses and hypotheses, or follow the traditional classification of causes; we do not, as a rule, set off artificial and inartificial proofs; we do not follow the ancient classification of the parts of a speech, or the "levels" of style. On the other hand, we pay a great deal more attention to delivery than did most of the ancient writers, and we extend rhetoric to include informative and entertaining, as well as suasory discourse.

In brief, while it cannot be denied that the ancient theorists set the guide lines that were to give rhetoric its essential direction and determine certain of its groundings for all time, it is decidedly incorrect to assert that our rhetoric today is basically classical. And those individuals who from time to time contend that it is, and that Aristotle's *Rhetoric* or Cicero's *De Oratore* would make the ideal textbook for the modern undergraduate are quite surely misguided. Of all the arts, rhetoric is perhaps the most sensitive to the intellectual and social milieu in which it finds itself, and is constantly changing with the times. Indeed, it would prove advantageous if we stopped talking of "the history of rhetoric" and began to speak of "the history of rhetorics."

Without pretending that the doctrines of Campbell, Blair, and Whately were the only forces influential in shaping the rhetoric found in most of our textbooks and courses today, I would yet maintain that their influence was certainly a major one—major enough, to persist and to set the dominant pattern for nearly two centuries. Only now are the essentials of that pattern beginning to be broken by such present-day theorists as Kenneth Burke and I. A. Richards.[13] Perhaps we are living in the midst of another great period of creative effort in rhetoric. This, of course, remains to be seen. More certain is the fact that the combined efforts of Whately, Campbell, and Blair produced such a period, and that the weight of their contributions was essentially non-classical—the thesis with which we began.

---

[13]Kenneth Burke: *A Rhetoric of Motives*, New York, 1950, etc.; I. A. Richards: *The Philosophy of Rhetoric*, New York, 1936.

WHATELY AND HIS RHETORIC

WAYLAND MAXFIELD PARRISH

University of Pittsburgh

IF ONE ACCEPTS Aristotle's statement that rhetoric is "an off-shoot of Dialectic and of that Ethical science which may fairly be called Politics," then Richard Whately was unusually well qualified by taste, temperament, and training for the composition of a text on rhetoric.

He published in 1826 a textbook on Logic, which he several times revised in the course of its eight later editions, he served as Professor of Political Economy at Oxford from 1829 until his elevation to the Archbishopric, and he founded and endowed in the University of Dublin a chair of Political Economy. The influences surrounding him as student and tutor at Oriel College reacted favorably upon a temperament already strongly disposed to disputation, and his entire life was spent in an atmosphere of theological controversy. Whately's *Rhetoric* is essentially a textbook on argumentation. It was this phase of rhetoric which was of primary interest and importance in his mind, and which received from him the most attention in the five revisions of the work.

A. FORMATIVE INFLUENCES

The Influence of Copleston

Little is known of Whately's undergraduate years at Oxford

---

[1] This is a study of the Introduction and Parts I and II of Whately's *Elements of Rhetoric,* and the statements here made must be understood as applying only to those portions of the work. The two remaining, and perhaps the most valuable and original parts, are on Style and Elocution. Page references are to the seventh edition (1846).

except that he early attracted the favorable notice of his tutor, Edward Copleston, and the two formed a strong attachment which lasted as long as the latter lived. It is easy to imagine that Whately's taste for controversy may have been whetted by familiarity with the satirical and argumentative works which his tutor was at this time publishing. The first of these, *Advice to a Young Reviewer,* appeared in 1807, one year before Whately came up for honors. His *Examiner Examined, or Logic Vindicated* appeared two years later. It is a spirited, and at times brutal, attack upon Kett's *Logic Made Easy.* His furious controversy with the *Edinburgh Review* raged through the years 1811 and 1812. It is inconceivable that the young Whately, who must have known their authorship though they were all published anonymously, should not have been deeply stirred by these glorious battles of his beloved tutor, and it is quite likely that they did much to stimulate his interest in logic and in the technique of controversy. His indebtedness to Copleston for materials in his own treatise on Logic is freely acknowledged, in his dedication and preface to that work, and in various places in his later correspondence with Copleston.[2]

Copleston's views on the nature and province of Rhetoric, particularly in its relation to Logic, are stated in one of the closing paragraphs of his attack on Kett:

> Of the various purposes then which Language may be made to serve, the first in order and in utility is that which Logic regulates. This may be placed at one extremity of the series. At the other extremity is Poetry, where language, as well as thought, is made subservient to the production of a refined pleasure. The several graduations of the scale between these extreme points are occupied by the various branches of Rhetoric, taking Rhetoric in its most extensive signification as the art of good writing. To demonstrate the reason of those principles which conduce to the end of good writing, to shew how they depart, and why they depart, from the rigid laws of Logic, is one of the most grateful services which philosophy can render to polite literature. When we measure these anomalies, as they may be called, by that standard, we better know how to estimate their propriety, their

---

[2]Cf. Whately, E. Jane: *Life and Correspondence of Richard Whately, D. D.,* London, 1866, I, 60, 352; II, 80.

congruity, their relative force, and their utility. The doing of this, I admit, belongs to the province of Rhetoric, but without Logic it cannot be done. *The Examiner Examined,* p. 52.

A fuller account of the place of rhetoric in Whately's education may be found in Copleston's account of the "Course of Studies pursued at Oxford," which forms Chapter IV of his first *Reply to the Calumnies of the Edinburgh Review against Oxford.* In both the preliminary and the final examinations, candidates for honors were examined in logic (p. 140). In the later case:

> The Examination then proceeds to Rhetoric and Ethics. Upon these subjects the celebrated treatises of Aristotle are chiefly used: and whoever is master of them knows what an exercise of the mind it is to acquire a thorough insight into the argument, and what a serious discipline the student must have undergone, who has accomplished this point. The accurate method observed in each treatise renders it not a perplexing, but merely an arduous task: the precision of the language, the close connection of the reasoning, the enlarged philosophical views, and the immense store of principles and maxims which they contain, point them out as the best calculated perhaps of any single works for bringing into play all the energies of the intellect, and for trying, not merely the intelligence of the scholar, but the habit of discrimination he has formed, the general accuracy of his thoughts, and the force and vigor of his mind. If it be at all of use to divide, to distinguish, and to define, to study clear arrangement and order, to discern connection, and to comprehend a plan composed of many widely separated parts, hardly any works can be named, so well adapted to these purposes. To these is often added, at the option of the student, the treatise on Politics, which is in fact a continuation and completion of the Ethical System.
>
> Besides these treatises of Aristotle, Quintilian as belonging to Rhetoric, and the philosophical works of Cicero, especially that De Officiis, as belonging to Ethics, are admitted. And these last, as being of easier attainment, are of course the choice of many candidates. But neither of them are strictly indispensable (pp. 140-1).

This passage shows not only the content of a part of Whately's education, but also something of the aim and method of his tutor in teaching. It should be remembered that this content and this method were in all probability continued in Whately's own teaching during the years when the *Rhetoric* was taking form in his own mind and on paper. It is significant that the relative importance in Copleston's mind of the works here mentioned is almost exactly echoed in the number of references to each in Whately's *Rhetoric*.

The high esteem in which Aristotle's *Rhetoric* was held by Copleston is further shown in that portion of the first *Reply* devoted to a defense of Aristotle:

> The Treatise on Rhetoric is a magazine of intellectual riches. Under an arrangement the most accurate perhaps and the most luminous ever marked out, the diversified elements of thought, of feeling, and of taste, are presented in due order to the reader's mind. Nothing is arbitrary, nothing gratuitous. Long experience with mankind, attentive observation of human nature in public and private life, the political history of past times, and the occurrences of his own age, furnished him with the materials of his great work. In the course of the enquiry, nothing is left untouched, on which Rhetoric, in all its branches, has any bearing. His principles are the result of extensive original induction. He sought them, if every man did seek them, in the living pattern of the human heart. All the recesses and windings of that hidden region he has explored: all its caprices and affections, whatever tends to excite, to ruffle, to amuse, to gratify, or to offend it, have been carefully examined. The reason of these phaenomena is demonstrated, the method of creating them is explained. The third Book contains a body of rules for good writing, traced to these natural principles, out of which they all grow, and illustrated by examples, which his own intimate acquaintance with the best poets and orators of Greece readily supplied. The whole is a textbook of human feeling; a storehouse of taste; an examplar of condensed and accurate, but uniformly clear and candid, reasoning (pp. 26-7).
>
> It would lead me too far, if I were to do justice to my own feelings on this subject (pp. 26-7).

Small wonder then that Whately should have been deeply influenced by Aristotle, and especially by the *Rhetoric*.

Whately's biographer says, "He was perhaps the leader among those who rendered the ethics and rhetoric of the Stagirite for many years the class-book of his University, and who studied to unite them, by comparison and analysis, with all that they esteemed most valuable in modern philosophy. For the enthusiastic and exclusive Aristotelian tendency of Oxford minds, for a whole generation after his introduction to tutorial life, no man was so responsible as Whately."[3]

Of a somewhat later period John Morley wrote, "Whately's common sense had set a new fashion, and Aristotle was studied as the master of those who know how to teach us the right way about the real world."[4]

The Oriel Common Room

A very important formative influence of a later period was the Oriel Common Room. "Oriel College at that time," says a student of the period, "contained some of the most distinguished personages, the most vigorous minds, and the most attractive characters in Oxford. From the provost, Dr. Copleston, to the youngest undergraduate they had been carefully selected, for to get a son into Oriel was a great thing in those days. Keble, Whately, Tyler, and Hawkins were tutors."[5] He continues later (p. 21), "There was something more than a morbid intellectual restlessness in the so-called Oriel School of that day." This was the period "when Copleston and Whately ruled the college and threatened to dominate over the University" (p. 23).

"Copleston, Whately, Keble, Davison, Hawkins, Hampden, and Arnold," says another student,[6] "formed in Oxford what was known as the *Noetic* School, maintaining around them a continuing dialectical and mental ferment. Tommy Short used to say that Davison and Whately habitually crammed for after-dinner talk; and unfortunate outlanders whose digestion of the dinner and enjoyment of the port wine was spoiled by it, complained that Oriel Common Room *stunk* of logic. A country gentleman once, after listening to Whately's talk throughout the evening, thanked him formally for the pains he had

---

[3]*Life*, I, p. 19.
[4]*Life of Gladstone*, I, P. 51.
[5]Mozley, Rev. T.: *Reminiscences, Chiefly of Oriel College and the Oxford Movement*, Boston, 1882, V. I., p. 18.
[6]Tuckwell, W.: *Reminiscences of Oxford*, London, 1907, p. 17.

taken to instruct him. 'Oh, no,' said Whately, 'not instruct; I did not mean to be didactic; but one sometimes likes having an anvil on which to beat out one's thoughts. '"

Bishop Hinds, his pupil and a lifelong friend, wrote that the "Common Room was to him not a mere place of resort for relaxation and recreation, but a school for sharpening his argumentative powers, and for training him to make that use of them in his social intercourse, in Parliament, and in other public assemblies, which was so striking and effective. It is hardly too much to say, that he was not less indebted to Oriel Common Room than to the college lectures in the earlier portion of his life."[7] Mark Pattison said the Noetics "called everything in question; they appealed to first principles, and disallowed authority as a judge in intellectual matters. There was a wholesome intellectual ferment constantly maintained in the Oriel Common-room."[8]

Such an environment would tend to stimulate Whately's natural independence and originality in thinking. He had in addition a blunt uncompromising honesty which, fostered in this circle of brilliant and sympathetic friends, led him to be at times more outspoken and tactless than was good for his own reputation. Mozley says,[9] "It would not be possible now to describe the terror his presence was sure to infuse among all who wished things to remain such as they were in their own lifetime. Instead of being comforted and built up in the good old fashion they were told they were altogether wrong, and must first retrace all their steps and undo all they had been doing. What was worse, the efficacy of the cure which had become necessary consisted in the hearers thinking it out for themselves." His biographer admits[10] that "Whately was never a popular man in the ordinary sense of the word. His opinions clashed too decidedly with those which prevailed in the Oxford society of his day to render him so in general life." The *Edinburgh Review,* in an obituary notice reviewing his *Common-place Book,* and Fitzpatrick's *Memoirs of Richard Whately,* says,[11] "With younger men he had

[7]*Life,* pp. 26-7.
[8]*Memoirs,* London, 1885, p. 79.
[9]*Op. cit.,* p. 20.
[10]*Life,* I, p. 27.
[11]Vol. CXX, Oct. 1864, p. 372.

great influence through the generous and expansive nature of his
political liberalism, and (it must be added) not a little of the
Johnsonian tendency to argue down, trip up, and domineer over,
antagonists in controversy."

Whately's Independence of Mind

No understanding of the *Rhetoric* can be complete which does
not reckon with the vigor and originality of Whately's mind. He
prided himself upon the independence of his thinking, and attempted
to impart the same independence to his pupils. He was a master
of the Socratic dialectic (though strangely indifferent to Plato[12]
and insisted always that his pupils think for themselves. Bishop
Hinds gives an excellent example from his early Oxford days (1813)
of his employment of the Socratic method upon a stranger encountered in a stage coach.[13] "Do not adopt my opinions because
they *are mine*," he said to one of his pupils, "but judge for yourself."[14]
To Lady Osborn he wrote, "And is it getting up a faction for me
you are after? No, I'll have no Whatelyites! . . . I wish people to
believe all the facts which I state on my own knowledge—because I
state none which I have not ascertained to be true; and to listen to
the reasons I give for my conclusions—because I never use any
arguments which do not appear to me sound. And that is all the
conformity I covet. Any one who tries to imitate me, is sure to be
unlike me in the important circumstance of being an imitator;
and no one can think as I do who does not think for himself."[15]

But while urging his pupils to think for themselves he sometimes,
like the Platonic Socrates, insisted that they should reach the same
conclusions as himself. While Newman acknowledges freely that
Whately "opened his mind, and taught him to think and to use his
reason," he adds, "When I was diverging from him in opinion
(which he did not like) I thought of dedicating my first book to
him, in words to the effect that he had not only taught me to think,

---

[12]"With Plato's intellectual peculiarities, on the other hand, he had little sympathy." *Life*, I, p. 19.
[13]*Life*, I, pp. 24-6.
[14]*Life*, I, p. 32.
[15]*Life*, II, p. 47.

but to think for myself."[16] Mozley is probably not far wrong in saying that Newman "would have been ready to love and admire Whately to the end, but for the inexorable condition of friendship imposed by Whately—absolute and implicit agreement in thought, word, and deed."[17]

As a partial consequence perhaps of this intolerance of opposition, he was frequently caught as his biographer observes,[18] "quoting, with much approbation, expressions of this or that follower, which in truth are mere 'Whateleiana,' consciously or unconsciously borrowed from him." It is certainly true that his religious works, as well as the *Rhetoric,* contain frequent appeals to the writings of his lifelong friends and followers: Hinds, Hampden, Senior, and Dickinson. On this point the *Edinburgh Review* observes,[19] " 'What people most readily and cordially approve,' he somewhere says, 'is the echo of their own sentiments'; and he does not seem to have been in the least aware how truly he was characterizing himself."

In this connection should be noted the comment of J. S. Mill that "he was the least equipped with books among any of the great thinkers of his time."[20]

"His favorite authors were few," says his biographer. "Aristotle, Thucydides, Bacon, Bishop Butler, Warburton, Adam Smith; these were, perhaps, his principal intimates among great writers; and it will be easily seen that they are among the most 'suggestive'; among those who could furnish the most ready texts on which his ruminating powers might be expended."[21]

This meagre acquaintance with books was perhaps not so great a handicap in the composition of his *Rhetoric* as in the composition of some of his other works. He was well grounded in the rhetorical works of Aristotle, Cicero, Quintilian, Bacon, and of his immediate predecessors, Blair and Campbell. However, he evidently lacked acquaintance with, or interest in, the orations of Demosthenes, Cicero,

---

[16]*Apologia pro Vita Sua,* London, 1921, p. 11.

[17]*Op. cit.,* p. 29.

Cf. the correspondence on their break in the *Apologia,* pp. 380-7, or in Whately's *Life,* I, pp. 233-40.

[18]*Life,* I, p. 28.

[19]CXX, Oct. 1864, p. 389.

[20]Camb: *Hist. of Lit.,* XII, p. 316.

[21]*Life,* I, p. 10.

and Burke,[22] and when he needs an illustration he turns, not to standard oratory, but to some theological essay of his own, or to the sermon of one of his pupils or friends.

Though Whately was independent and liberal in his religious opinions, so liberal that many questioned the wisdom of his elevation to the archiepiscopacy,[23] and the Commissioner of Stamps refused to exempt his *Thoughts on the Sabbath* from the Pamphlet Duty on the ground that it was not a religious work,[24] yet in fundamental matters he was sound and conservative, and a staunch champion of his church and creed.[25] So in the *Rhetoric*, though he states frankly all the objections that have been raised to the study and practice of rhetoric, and even claims that only second-rate minds can expect high success in oratory (p. 31), yet he takes Aristotle as his master, claiming that his treatise, though the earliest on the subject, is also the best (p. 7), since it is not *an* art of rhetoric, but *the* art of rhetoric (p. 16) and so follows in the main the traditional methods and teachings in the subject.

Guizot, then ambassador to England, who met him in London in 1840, has left an admirable summary of his character:

> *Parmi les prélats anglicans avec lesquels je fis connaissance, l'archevêque de Dublin, M. Whately, correspondant de notre insitut, m'intéressa et me surprit; esprit originel, fécond, inattendu, instruit et ingénieux plutôt que profond dans les sciences philosophiques et sociales, le meilleur des hommes, parfaitement désintéressé, tolérant, libéral, populaire, et, à travers son infatigable activité et son intarissable conversation, étrangement distrait, familier, ahuri, dégiggandé, amiable et attachant, quelque impolitesse qu'il commette et quelque convenance qu'il oublie."[26]*

---

[22]Though he refers twice to "Demosthenes on the Crown" (pp. 140 and 03), and once to "Cicero against Verres" (p. 197).

[23]Cf. *Life, I,* pp. 102-4.

[24]Cf. *Westminister Review,* Vol. XIII, July 1830, p. 183.

[25]Cf. Arnold's letter to Rev. Cornish, Dec. 23, 1831, in Stanley's *Life of Arnold,* Vol. I, p. 275. "Now I am sure that in point of real essential holiness, so far as man can judge of man, there does not live a truer Christian than Whately; and it does grieve me most deeply to hear people speak of him as a dangerous and latitudinarian character, because in him the intellectual part of his nature keeps pace with the spiritual."

[26]Quoted in the *Life,* I, p. 454.

His Method of Composition

Whately's method of working out his ideas is described by his biographer:

> As in the early school and Oxford days, of which we are now writing, so down to his latest times, the daily occupation of his brain was to seize on some notion of what he considered a practical order, belonging to any one of the various subjects with which his mind occupied itself; to follow it out to its minutest ramifications to bring it home with him, turned from the mere germ into the complete production. And this perpetual 'chopping logic with himself' he carried on not less copiously when his usually solitary walks were enlivened with companionship. His talk was rather didactic than controversial; which naturally rendered his company unpopular with some, while it gave him the mastery over other spirits of a different mould. 'His real object, or his original objects,' (sic) writes one of his earliest and ablest friends, 'was to get up clearly and beat out his ideas for his own use. Thus he wrote his books.' *Life,* I, pp. 10-11.

It was thus that he worked out the principal parts of the *Logic* with his friend and tutor, Copleston.[27] And in a similar manner was evolved his early satire, *Historic Doubts Relative to Napoleon Bonaparte.*[28] Fitzpatrick records a letter from Newman in which he says, "It was one of his pecularities at that time to hammer out his thoughts (if I may so speak) by means of other minds, and he conversed so well and so profitably, that it was a pleasure to be so employed by him."[29] Newman is here writing of his part in the composition of Whately's *Logic.* It is regrettable that no such direct testimony is available as to the composition of the *Rhetoric.* But presumably it was "hammered out" in much the same way, the anonymous "young friends" mentioned in the Preface serving as anvils.

[27]"It was in their long walks together in the woods and meadows near Oxford that they discussed and worked out such subjects as form much of the groundwork of the 'Logic'." *Life,* I, p. 14.

[28]Rev. R. N. Boultbee, a former pupil, writes, "I was in the habit of walking out into the country with him two or three times a week, and during these rambles I was made the recipient of many of his most original thoughts, preserved in his Commonplace Book. Well do I remember the shady bank in Bagley Wood, where he first read to me the draft of the 'Historic Doubts'." *Life,* I, p. 38.

[29]Fitzpatrick, W. J.: *Memoirs of Richard Whately,* London, 1864, Vol. I, p. 47.

As early as 1809 Whately began jotting down his thoughts in a Commonplace Book.[30] "He always considered this practice to have been highly beneficial to his own mind,"[31] said his daughter. "It contributed undoubtedly to the clearness and correctness of his style; and by thus working out, correcting, and revising the results of his own reflections and studies, a vast body of materials was prepared for future works." The entries in the Commonplace Book are brief essays of one to ten pages each. It is significant that the notes to his edition of Bacon's Essays (1856) are not textual criticism or exposition, but similar brief essays on thoughts suggested by Bacon. Many of his longer writings, include the *Rhetoric,* as will be shown later, are made up of just brief original essays, connected into a more or less coherent structure by short transitional passages.

His Interest in Political Economy

Whately's interest in Political Economy may well have been derived from the studies of his undergraduate days. Copleston records that the subject was introduced into the lectures on Modern History. To him, as to Whately, it was more a treatment of economy than of politics, though he deplores the fact that the study often narrowed the student's views, and "made him regard every public measure simply in the relation it bears to national wealth.[32] Whately's fondness for puzzles, problems, and "logical traps,"[33] and his unsuitablity for political philosophy of Burkian breadth, would lead one to expect in him a greater interest in speculation over economic problems, than in the application of political principles to a criticism of the British Constitution. It follows that for him Political Economy had little relation to rhetoric. He conceived rhetoric more as an art of theological disputation than as a science of influencing voters, legislators and judges. The *Rhetoric* contains four references to Adam Smith's *Theory of Moral Sentiments,* but none to his *Wealth of Nations.* It contains one reference to Burke *On the Sublime,* but none to his speeches. It has frequent references to the then current theological

[30]*Life,* I, p. 14.
[31]*Miscellaneous Remains from the Commonplace Book of Richard Whately, D. D.,* London, 1864, p. vi.
[32]First *Reply,* p. 172.
[33]Cf. *Edinburgh Review,* Vol. CXX, p. 397.

controversies, but it contains no reference at all to the oratory of Pitt, Fox, Erskine, Canning, Brougham, or O'Connell. Oxford in Whately's day (1805-1831) might well have been a religious cloister, completely insulated from all political ideas. When later Whately sat with the bench of bishops in the House of Lords, he took an active interest in only three political problems: the transportation of criminals, Jewish disabilities, and the Irish poor laws. Lord Holland's remark to Guizot is significant: " 'Je ne suis pas sur', me dit Lord Holland, de bonne raison pour qu'il y ait, à la Chambre des Lords, un banc 'que dans son indiscrète sincérité il ne dise pas qu'il ne sait point des éveques."[34]

Summary

Out of this milieu then was Whately's *Rhetoric* formed. The factors contributing to it may be summarized thus: A natural fondness for dialectic (in the Platonic sense of discussion by dialogue) and disputation, fostered by early training in logic, and in Aristotle's Rhetoric, and by the ferment of the Oriel Common Room; a long experience as a tutor in teaching both logic and rhetoric; a vigorous and independent mind, coupled with a blunt uncompromising honesty; an early acquired habit of using others as an anvil on which to hammer out his own thoughts, which were then recorded in essay form in his Commonplace Book; a tendency to depend too much upon a few congenial friends and a few familiar books; an ability to examine most questions with candid and unprejudiced mind while clinging tenaciously, almost intolerantly, to fundamental premises; a deep interest in political economy coupled with a curious indifference to politics.

B. PROBABLE DATE OF THE COMPOSITION OF THE RHETORIC

Of the exact date of the composition of the Rhetoric it is impossible to speak with accuracy. The finished work was published in 1828, probably early in the year, as it was reviewed in the *Monthly Review* for February of that year. De Quincey's well-known review appeared in the December number of *Blackwood's*.

---

[34]Quoted from Guizot's *Mémories* in Whately's *Life,* I, p. 454.

Of the history of the work prior to its publication we know little
more than is stated in its Preface: "A brief outline of the principal part of the following work was sketched out several years ago
for the private use of some young friends; and from that MS.
chiefly, the Article "Rhetoric" in the Encyclopædia Metropolitana
was afterwards drawn up. I was induced to believe that it might
be more useful if published in a separate form, and I have accordingly, with the assistance of some friends revised the treatise, and
made a few additions and other alterations which suggested themselves; besides dividing it in a manner more convenient for reference."

The identity of the "young friends" is unknown, but they were
doubtless Whately's pupils at Oxford during the period between
1811, when he was elected fellow of Oriel College, and 1822, when
he married and left Oxford to take a pastoral living at Halesworth.

The *Encyclopædia Metropolitana, or Universal Dictionary of
Knowledge, on an Original Plan,* projected by S. T. Coleridge, began to appear in 1817, and continued by "parts" until 1845.
Volume I, containing the *Rhetoric* and *Logic,* seems to have been
published complete for the first time in 1829. Coleridge's Introduction, attempting a methodical organization of the whole field of
knowledge, makes no mention of rhetoric, but Whately's article on
that subject follows immediately after his article on logic. Whately's
two contributions are preceded by Grammar, and followed by
Geometry, Arithmetic, Algebra, etc.—all of which (Rhetoric omitted)
are classified in Coleridge's curious Prospectus as Formal Sciences,
in the general division of Pure Sciences.[35]

The *Quarterly Review* for October, 1817, lists under "New Publications" Volume I, Part I of the new encyclopædia. *Blackwood's* for
May, 1818, notes the publication of Part II. And from then on for
many years there are in various reviews announcements of the publication of successive "parts" of the work. Just what each part contained it seems impossible now to determine. There is, however, a

---

[35]Whately said of Coleridge's dissertation, "I had thought to cut it out and burn
it when I had the volume bound, but I resolved to keep it as a curious specimen
of what trash a very clever man *can* write." *Life,* II, p. 316. He could not have
been pleased at the publication in 1851 of Coleridge's dissertation, together with
his own articles on Logic and Rhetoric under the title, "Encyclopaedia of Mental Science."

hint in the *Gentleman's Magazine* for May, 1818, which notes under works nearly ready for publication, "The Third Part of the *Encyclopædia Metropolitana,* containing the continuation of Grammar, in the Pure Sciences; the conclusion of Hydrodynamics, as including Hydrostatics and Hydraulics in the mixed and applied sciences; sections of the early History of Egypt, Assyria," etc. One may infer from this that the various articles were published piecemeal, and that a part of the *Rhetoric* was composed and published perhaps ten years before the publication of the entire work in 1828. But there is one factor which points to a later date. Cardinal Newman, in a letter to W. J. Fitzpatrick written in 1864,[36] says, "My part in Whately's Logic was small indeed. He wrote it originally in 'Analytical Dialogues', as he called them. In this shape I first saw it in 1822. At the same date he employed me to draw it up in synthetical form; and when he wrote his article for the *Encyclopædia Metropolitana* he made use of this rough draft of mine as a sort of basis for his own work." It is apparent then, if Newman's memory is accurate over this period of 42 years, that the article "Logic" was composed after 1822. And it seems likely that the *Rhetoric* was composed after the *Logic.* It was certainly second in Whately's interest, it follows the *Logic* in the *Metropolitana,* and as a separate work it appeared two years after the *Logic* was published.

It would seem to be a safe assumption, then, that though Whately may have made notes on rhetoric during his first years of teaching, and doubtless did at that time make numerous entries on the subject in his Commonplace Book, yet the finished work as it appeared in the *Metropolitana* was probably not put together until the years of his pastoral service at Halesworth (1822-5), or possibly even after his return to Oxford as Principal of Alban Hall.

C. GROWTH OF THE *RHETORIC*

The *Rhetoric* received a share of Whately's attention during at least twenty years of his life; that is, from its first conception, probably during his tutorial service at Oxford, till its final revision in 1846, after he had served for fifteen years as Archbishop of Dublin. During this period it went through eight editions: its first appearance in the

---

[36] Cf. Fitzpatrick's *Memoirs of Richard Whately,* London, 1864, Vol. I, p. 47.

Metropolitana and seven editions as a separate work. It was five times revised: in the first,[37] third, fifth, sixth, and seventh editions, and in the course of these revisions grew to considerably more than double its original dimensions. It would seem that to Bishop Whately to revise meant to enlarge. It is true that there are frequent changes in wording, aiming generally at increased clarity, but the bulk of the changes are additions, often of single phrases and sentences, but more often of whole paragraphs, or even of longer passages of one to twenty pages.

There are only three important excisions. One was a note to a part of the preface in which he took to task a writer in the *Westminster Review* for some criticism of Oxford. This note appeared in the first two editions, and thereafter was omitted. The second was a part of a note (cf. p. 158) defending himself from some criticism on his *Logic*. It too appeared only in the first two editions. The third was a passage of three long paragraphs (cf. p. 208) in criticism of Bentham's *Book of Fallacies,* which appeared originally in the text of the *Metropolitana* article, was reduced to a footnote in the first two editions, and thereafter omitted. It would seem that at about the time of his elevation to the See of Dublin, Whately made it a settled rule to abstain from personal controversy.

Of the 271 pages in that portion of the *Rhetoric* here under consideration, approximately 109 were in the *Metropolitana* article. A total of about sixteen pages was added in the first edition, thirty-three in the third, ten in the fifth, nineteen in the sixth, and finally eighty-four in the seventh. The figures do not include additions placed in the appendix. Of the total of 162 pages added from first to last, eleven

---

[37] I have been unable to find a first edition, but assume on what seems to be good evidence that the second edition, which I have examined, is a reprinting of the first. It appeared in the same year as the first. When the third edition appeared two years later it carried after the Preface the following Advertisement: "Some considerable additions having been made to the third edition, the Author has directed all of them that are of any material consequence to be printed for the accommodation of the purchasers of the former editions, separately and in such form as to be conveniently appended to the volume." The fourth edition, which is a second printing of the third, contained the same notice under the same heading, viz., "Advertisement to the Third Edition." The fifth, sixth, and seventh editions are all marked on the title page "Revised." No such notice appears in the second edition.

went to form a Preface, twenty-five were added to the Introduction, seventy-eight to Part I, on Conviction, and forty-eight to Part II, on Persuasion. If we exclude from Part II the lecture on "The Intellectual and Moral Influences of the Professions," the additions to this Part total only twenty-two pages. To Part III, on Style, barely six pages were added to the original seventy-five, and to Part IV, on Elocution, a similar amount was added. It is plain that Whately's primary interest was in Conviction, that part of rhetoric which lies closest to logic.

It is obvious from an examination of these changes that twenty years of revision made little alteration in the basic plan of the work. There is not one change in the order in which the items are presented, and there are only a few changes in the location of illustrative material. Neither are any important new topics introduced, if one excepts the discussion in the Introduction of composition exercises and debating societies. The most extensive additions are those on testimony and authority, analogy, and burden of proof and presumption, in Part I, and on the employment of appeals to the feelings and on inconsistency, in Part II. None of these, unless it be the last, is strictly speaking a new topic. The additions are in the main either slight variations on themes discussed in the original publication, or further illustration of such matter.

D. SOURCES OF THE *RHETORIC*

It is time now to inquire as to the sources from which Whately drew his materials. As he was scrupulously honest in acknowledging all his borrowings, this is a relatively easy task. As hinted above, his principal indebtedness is to Aristotle's *Rhetoric,* no less than thirty-nine specific references to that work being made. There are besides several references to the *Poetics, Politics, and Ethics.* It would be difficult to find in Whately (or for that matter in *any* sound work on rhetoric) anything that is not stated or at least suggested in Aristotle, and yet he makes not a single quotation of any length from his acknowledged master. This is especially surprising since he does quote at length from Cicero, from Thucydides, from Campbell, and from others. But Aristotle seems merely to have furnished him with texts on which his own ruminative powers might work.

Whately's Definition of Rhetoric

Whately's definition of rhetoric is unique. He does not follow Aristotle in limiting rhetoric to persuasion. This he thinks is too narrow a province. On the other hand he rejects the conception which he finds current in his day that rhetoric includes all composition in prose. Between these two he intends to steer a middle course, and to treat of rhetoric as "argumentative composition, generally and exclusively" (p. 4). Instead of accepting the traditional or the current definition of the term, he uses "rhetoric" arbitrarily to cover the particular activity in which he is most interested. Then instead of justifying under such a definition the inclusion of a dissertation on persuasion, he remarks at the beginning of his treatment of that subject that "the *Conviction* of the understanding . . . is an essential *part* of Persuasion" (p. 175). He does not deplore appeals to the "passions" as extraneous to rhetoric, but quotes with approval Campbell's defense of such appeals as right and necessary (pp. 176-7), and claims that Aristotle deplored only "the excitement of such feelings as *ought not to influence* the decision of the question in hand" (p. 177). But he makes no attempt to justify his inclusion of rules for persuasion in a treatise which is to consider "argumentative composition exclusively." Indeed, in introducing the subject he says (p. 188) that he intends to give a few rules for "those parts of any Composition which are designed to influence the Will," as if he were treating here of a different kind of composition. His definition applies properly to his Introduction and Part I, but not to his treatment of Persuasion, Style, and Elocution, as he practically concedes in the first two paragraphs of Part I, Chapter II. All of these could have been included under Aristotle's definition.

It should be noted that Whately avoided the confusion of rhetoric with poetic which prevailed generally after Aristotle down to Campbell. Whately was evidently unacquainted with mediæval rhetoric, and was not in this matter of definition influenced by his immediate predecessors, Blair and Campbell. His distaste for poetry was also perhaps an advantage.

The Subdivisions of Rhetoric

Whately's fourfold division of rhetoric into Conviction (the invention of arguments), Persuasion, Style, and Elocution, is distinctly his own. It does not parallel Aristotle's division of all proofs into artificial and inartificial, which Whately definitely rejects,[38] nor to the division of artificial into ethical, pathetic, and logical proofs. Whately, however, includes all these forms of proof, giving them his own arrangement, making ethical proof subsidiary to pathetic (Pt. II, iii). He ignores also Aristotle's division of rhetoric into three species, —deliberative, forensic, and epideiktic. This is to be expected since he had little interest in either legal or legislative procedure, and eulogistic oratory was rare in his day. Neither does he follow the traditional fivefold division of classical rhetoric: *inventio, dispositio, elocutio, pronuntiatio,* and *memoria.* His Part I treats of the "invention" or arguments, and in the same Part, Chapter III, sections 4, 5, 7, and 9, in Chapter IV, and in Part II, Chapter II, section 5, there are discussions of "disposition." The traditional *elocutio* is treated in his Part III, Style; *pronuntiatio* and *memoria,* in Part IV, Elocution. Whately was the first important writer to transfer the term "elocution" from style to delivery.

Sources of Part I

Whately's indebtedness to Aristotle for his treatment of "Conviction," his page heading for this Part, is readily apparent. His division of all arguments into *a priori* and "the other class" (he rejects the term *a posteriori,* p. 52) is derived from Aristotle.[39] Though he departs from Aristotle's subdivision when he classifies arguments from sign not with probabilities, but with example, under what are generally called *a posteriori* arguments. His discussion of probability (p. 47 ff.) borrows from both the *Rhetoric* and *Poetics* of Aristotle, and acknowledges indebtedness also to Campbell. On Testimony his debt to Aristotle is less evident. He borrows from Locke, Paley, and Campbell, and here as throughout the

---

[38]Cf. his note p. 39.
[39]*Rhet.,* I, iii.

Rhetoric makes frequent reference to his *Elements of Logic*.[40] The section on the calculation of chances (pp. 76-81) is typically Whateleian in its presumably original observations based upon common sense and common experience, and in its evidence of a fondness for problems, and skill in inventing examples. The same may be said for the section on the argument from "progressive approach."

The treatment of example and induction (pp. 85-108) owes more to Aristotle, though he again makes frequent reference to his own *Logic*. He draws illustrative material from theology, chemistry, political economy, history, medicine, and common experience. He quotes from or refers to his own works on Logic, on Political Economy, his *Lessons on Reasoning*, his speech on the Jewish Relief Bill, and cites also the Bible, Thucydides, Cicero, Mandeville, Bacon, Adam Smith, Copleston, and the *Edinburgh Review*.

The section distinguishing arguments of confutation from those which aim only to satisfy a candid mind (pp. 108-12), is again largely original, though it borrows paragraphs from Adam Smith and Paley, and refers once to Aristotle's *Ethics*. Whately's ruminative habits are further evident in the long section on Presumption and burden of proof (pp. 112-32). There is no clue as to what caused him to insert this topic in the third edition, and amplify it in subsequent editions. It owes no indebtedness to Aristotle or Campbell, but seems to be characteristically the product of Whately's own mind. The sources of his illustrations are as usual diverse. He cites his own *Logic* and several of his theological works, and draws material from Horace, Shakespeare, Milton, Bacon, Hooker, Johnson, and the Bible, as well as from his experiences with Parliament, and the popularity of his work on Logic.

In treating of arrangement, too (pp. 137-46), he follows in the main his own mind, expressing regret that Aristotle and Cicero did not furnish more precepts on this topic. He returns to Aristotle for a text for his treatment of refutation (146-50), citing his division of refutation into counter-syllogism and objection, and his statement that there is no distinct class of refutatory arguments. Much of the

---

[40]The *Logic* seems to have been based largely upon a work by Aldrich, then in general use at Oxford. Doubtless much of it was original with Whately and Copleston. His indebtedness to others is not as freely or as frequently acknowledged in the *Logic* as in the *Rhetoric*.

discussion of this topic is somewhat technical, being drawn largely from the *Logic,* but it is unusually rich in illustrative material, drawn as usual from a wide range of reading and observation. Chapter IV on Introductions and Conclusions draws again from Aristotle and Cicero, but is characteristically original in treatment and illustration.

Sources of Part II

In his treatment of persuasion Whately again takes his texts in the main from Aristotle and Campbell. The subject invites him to typical brief essays on the prejudice existing against excitement of the feelings, on the necessary indirectness of appeals to the feelings, on the dangers of practicing rhetoric on oneself, etc. Following the teachings of eighteenth century "Moral Philosophy" he conceives of reason and will as existing in separate compartments, and so not to be moved by the same means. He accepts Dugald Stewart's division of the "Active Principles of our nature" into appetites, desires, and affections, to which he adds self-love, and the "Moral-faculty" (Adam Smith's "sense of propriety"), but in the ensuing discussion of the conduct of appeals to the feelings, he makes no use of this division. Such an analysis of the various feelings as Aristotle gives, he does not feel called upon to make.

His brief caution against exhortation (pp. 190-2) seems to be his own, but in discussing the advantages of copious detail he borrows from Cicero, Quintilian, and Campbell. His only reference to Cicero's orations occurs in his treatment of climax (p. 197). Comparison, climax, and amplification are all considered in relation to their effect on the feelings, though Whately recognizes that they are "connected in some degree with style" (p. 199). The modes of heightening an impression, suggested in Aristotle's treatment of style, are by Whately included in this general discussion of the conduct of appeals to the feelings (p. 199). In lieu of Aristotle's analysis of the emotions and description "of the prevailing Characters of men of different ages and situations," Whately inserts at this point (p. 204) a reference to his lecture on the professional dangers to which ministers, physicians, and lawyers are subject.

In introducing the subject of "ethical" persuasion Whately

frequently acknowledges his indebtedness to Aristotle, and quotes twice again from Campbell. He gives the subject an original turn by discussing the speaker's character chiefly in terms of the varying taste and intelligence of his hearers. His remarks on the disadvantages of being thought eloquent (pp. 210-15) are largely original. The basis of this discussion throughout is Aristotle's threefold division of character into intelligence, virtue, and goodwill, and he found Aristotle especially rich in texts for his discussion of "authority derived from experience," "allaying of unfavorable impressions," and "ridicule."

In summary, then, it may be said that Aristotle's *Rhetoric* furnished the bulk of the texts from which Whately developed his thoughts on rhetoric. The whole treatise bears evidence of his preoccupation with logic. He borrows frequently from Campbell, and gets occasional thoughts from Cicero and Bacon. His thinking is colored throughout by his close familiarity with the writings of Butler, Paley, Adam Smith, and Copleston.

Sources of His Illustrations

His illustrations are drawn from a somewhat wider range of reading. Among the ancients he refers frequently to Thucydides, and less often to Horace and Tacitus. He is familiar with Shakespeare. He draws more from eighteenth century literature than from his contemporaries. He refers frequently to the Bible, and very frequently to his own theological writings, and those of his friends, Copleston, Hinds, and Dickinson.

It may be well to tabulate the number of his references to or quotations from his principal sources. They are as follows: Aristotle's *Rhetoric,* 39; *Poetics,* 2; *Ethics,* 4; *Politics,* 1; Whately's *Elements of Logic,* 32; his various volumes of essays on theological subjects, 10; his charges, speeches, sermons, and other works, 15; the Bible, 16; Cicero's *De Oratore,* 8; *De Officiis,* 2; *Oration on Verres,* 1; Campbell's *Rhetoric,* 9; Bacon, 9; Thucydides, 8; Paley, 6; Shakespeare, 5; Adam Smith's *Theory of Moral Sentiments,* 4; the *Edinburgh Review,* 4; *Butler's Analogy,* 4; Dugald Stewart, 3; Horace, 3; Tacitus, 3; Warburton, 2; Burke *On the Sublime,* 1; *Defense of Natural Society,* 1; Milton's *Paradise Lost,* 1; *Tractate of Education,* 1; Swift, 2.

The Lowndes *Bibliographical Manual* lists ninety-seven pub-lished works by Richard Whately. These, so far as I have examined them, contain numerous quotations from and cross references to each other. The *Rhetoric* (i.e. excluding the portions on Style and Elocution) has no fewer than fifty-seven references to his other published works. It is hardly inaccurate to say that Whately's chief source was his own other works. Well might his biographer say, in commenting upon his comparative want of reading, that "he continually stumbled upon the thoughts of others, and reproduced them in perfect honesty as his own. This was one of his charac-teristics through life. It is singular to read one of his earlier critics commenting on his tendency to reproduce the 'commonplace of other writers, not unfrequently, without any apparent conscious-ness of their ever having seen the light before'; while one of his latest, Mr. Stuart Mill, speaking of his philosophical investigations, says that 'of all persons in modern times, entitled to the name of philosophers, the two, probably, whose reading was the scantiest, in proportion to their intellectual capacity, were Archbishop Whately and Dr. Brown. But though indolent readers they were both of them active and fertile thinkers.' "[41]

A word should be added concerning the facility with which Whately found illustrations from common observation of life, and the felicity with which he used them. For instance, in defending the necessity for having names for rhetorical terms, he asks us to consider the inconvenience to a carpenter of "having no names for the several operations of *sawing, planing, boring,* etc." (p. 19). In discussing the selection of subjects for school compositions, he says (p. 23), the student "may freely transplant indeed from other writers such thoughts as will take root in the soil of his own mind; but he must never be tempted to collect *dried specimens.*" He recommends (p. 142) that an unpopular thesis be kept out of sight as much as possible "because men listen with prejudice, if at all, to arguments that are avowedly leading to a conclusion which they are indisposed to admit;" and "if we thus, as it were, mask the battery, they will not be able to shelter themselves from the dis-charge." In recommending moderation in combating deep-rooted

---

[41]*Life,* I, p. 10.

prejudice he says (p. 165), "Laborers who are employed in *driving wedges* into a block of wood, are careful to use blows of no greater force than is just sufficient. If they strike *too hard,* the elasticity of the wood will *throw out the wedge."*

In conclusion it may be said that inasmuch as the field of Rhetoric is somewhat limited, and was completely surveyed by Aristotle, no new principles are to be expected in a modern work on this subject. Whatever claim to originality may be made for Whately, must consist chiefly in his novelty of illustration and of arrangement. As to his point of view it should be noted that throughout his treatment of the subject he looks primarily to the establishment of past fact, rather than to the determination of future policy. Even in his discussion of Persuasion, he seems more concerned with an abstract moving of the will, than with a practical incitement to present action. Rhetoric for him has little to do with the legislature, charged with the determination of a wise future policy. It is rather the instrument of the theologian, bent upon proving the soundness of his doctrines, or the authenticity of his beliefs.

WHATELY ON ELOCUTION

JAMES A. WINANS

Dartmouth College

In Bishop Whately's *Elements of Rhetoric,* which Jebb pronounces "undoubtedly the best modern book on the subject," the part most significant in the history of rhetoric deals with the topic he knew least about. I refer to Part IV which he entitles "Of Elocution." Few of us consider his treatment adequate and many consider it unsound; but by his insistence that delivery should spring from thought and feeling rather than from rules and imitation he exerted a far-reaching and wholesome influence. The idea had been suggested before, but apparently waited for Whately to work it out and make it the core of a method of teaching.

The subject is not without present-day interest; for, as I believe, the majority of teachers of speaking still are Walkerites, though some of them may not know it and though many of this majority pay lip service to Whately's teachings. It may, therefore, be worth-while to clear up one's ideas of what Whately actually taught and what he was warring against.

His strictures on earlier writers lead one to turn to some of them, and especially to Sheridan, Walker, and Blair, whose work were in Whately's mind as he wrote.

Thomas Sheridan was an actor. Perhaps his greatest contribution to the world was fathering Richard Brinsley Sheridan; but he may have considered his greatest contribution to be his *Lectures on Elocution,* first published in book form in 1763. Fritz tells[1] us that this book was "the most popular work of the time."

---

[1]From Sheridan to Rush, *Quarterly Journal of Speech,* XVI, 76, February 1930.

Sheridan laments the low state of English delivery, both in reading and speaking. This low state, he says, cannot be due to any inability in the English people, for if you listen to Englishmen conversing earnestly you will note that they deliver their sentences well. But if you write down their remarks and ask the same men to read their own words, they will do so in an artificial manner.

Sheridan blames the faults of English elocution on faulty teaching and false notions of what good delivery is. The true standard he finds in conversation, the natural standard of men conversing in earnest. So if you have a passage to read, he advises, think how you would say it if you were expressing the same ideas and sentiments in conversation, and say the passage that way. Moreover, "here is the sure standard for force and propriety in public speaking, which is to make use of the same manner" in public speaking as in conversation.

It seems evident that this fundamental rule of Sheridan's will tend to produce conversational style, mode, or manner, but not conversational quality. As I understand him, you are to go on the platform and imitate yourself as you speak in conversation. He does not say speak in public with the same mental action, or in the same spirit as in conversation, or with the same purpose of communication. His thought is always of manner, a manner consciously adopted, which will have the air of genuineness. Perhaps a natural thought for an actor.

There are, to be sure, passages in Sheridan which, read hastily and out of their contexts, might lead one to suppose his doctrine to be quite other than what it really is. Some of these have to do with persuasion, though persuasion receives but slight attention in the *Lectures* as a whole. For example:

> When we reflect that the end of public speaking is persuasion . . . and that in order to persuade others to belief in any point, it must first appear that the person who attempts it is firmly persuaded of the truth of it himself; how can we suppose it possible to affect this unless he delivers himself in the manner which is always used by persons who speak in earnest? How shall his words pass for the words of truth when they bear not the stamp of truth?

These words sound like gospel, but a careful reading reveals that Sheridan calls only for the appearance of sincerity. "The speaker should at least appear himself to believe what he utters . . . but this can never be the case where there is any evident mark of affectation or art." So Sheridan advises the speaker who cannot have an ideal training:

> Let him give up all pretensions to art, for it is certain that it is better to have none than not enough; and no man has enough who has not arrived at such a perfection of art as wholly to conceal his art; a thing not to be compassed but by the united endeavors of the best instruction, perfect patterns, and constant practice.

The passage just quoted reminds one who has studied the lectures as a whole that they are addressed to adults who cannot hope to have proper instruction and to whom he is offering suggestions to enable them to do tolerably well. If they are still awkward and their tones are ill-regulated, well, after all, if they follow Sheridan's suggestions, they will probably do better than most English speakers. But he makes it clear that the ideal training is quite different; only unfortunately there is a lack of skilled masters to give such training. Ideally the masters would be equipped with elaborate rules in which they would train their pupils until the pupils had the art which conceals art; and presumably the masters would be "perfect patterns."

How thoroughly mechanical was Sheridan's method of reading is shown by his repeated lament that there is no established system of symbols by which an author could indicate in print, not only emphases, pauses, and inflections, but also tones and gestures. But still the case is not hopeless. When you are to read in public, either the words of another or your own, Sheridan suggests that you should go over the passage and decide on emphases, pauses, inflections, tones and gestures, marking them in some manner intelligible to yourself; and then you should go on the platform and give your mind wholly—to what? The content? No, to the manner of delivery.

If you speak extempore, continues Sheridan, you cannot, of course, follow this method; but if you will forget all those bad reading tones and the affectations common to English speakers, and try to speak in the same manner as in conversation, you will, let us hope, do pretty well.

Sheridan had done some thinking, and his insistence on "natural manner" probably contributed to the development of Whately's ideas.

Whately refers to him as one of the best writers on the subject, "though he differs from me on the main question—as to the system to be followed with a view to the proposed object."

Contemporary with Sheridan was John Walker, another actor, whose *Elements of Elocution* (1781) has greatly influenced the teaching of delivery. One who takes no account of the temperaments of authors might suppose that Sheridan welcomed this book, for it seems to supply just that system of rules and that basis for the training of masters the lack of which Sheridan had lamented; but, as a matter of fact, Sheridan and Walker came to be looked upon as leaders of two hostile schools of elocution.

Walker's great pride was in his "discovery" of the upward and downward "turns" of the voice, and later of the circumflex. He tells us by definite rules how to use the turns for simple emphasis, double emphasis, and general emphasis. He lays down an appalling number of rules, many loaded with exceptions. For example:

> Direct periods [i.e., periodic sentences] which commence with participles of the present or past tense, consist of two parts; between which must be inserted the long pause and rising inflection.
>
> But when the last word of the first part of these sentences requires a strong emphasis, the falling inflection must be used instead of the rising.

Walker treats of the modulation and management of the voice, of gesture, and of the passions. He tells us how to depict by voice, attitude, and gesture seventy-six different emotions. He thinks it is better when the reader feels the emotion, but since often he cannot feel a given emotion to order, Walker tells him how to show it anyhow.

It is interesting to note that some years after Walker published his *Elements* Sheridan published a book in which he also told how to express emotions. A comparison of the two treatments shows how close these two rivals were in their thinking. For instance, Walker says:

> Modesty bends the body forward, has a placid, downcast countenance, levels the eyes to the breast, if not to the feet, of the superior character; the voice is low, the tone submissive, the words few.

While Sheridan says:

> Modesty, or submission, bends the body forward; levels the
> eyes to the breast, if not to the feet, of the superior character.
> The voice low, the tone submissive; and words few.

Were both copying from the same actors' manual?

I am not here concerned with the correctness of Walker's rules.
I was trained in some of them and they give me nostalgia for college
days. They may have done me some good as a sort of voice training;
but I am sure they did me much more harm. I have brought Walker
in chiefly to say that I find no fundamental difference between him
and Sheridan. Sheridan takes for his standard conversation; Walker
does not say what his standard is. Probably it is the way he, a trained
actor, delivered sentences. The methods of both are thoroughly
mechanical and tend to take the speaker's mind off meaning and
audience.

My second reason for bringing in Walker is that his system is one
of those, perhaps the chief one, that Whately objects to and ridicules.

The Reverend Hugh Blair devoted one discourse of his *Lectures on
Rhetoric* (1783) to Pronunciation or Delivery. In great part his ideas
seem to be derived from Sheridan, with perhaps an admixture from
Walker. While he puts more stress on a "just conception of the force
and spirit of those sentiments which you are to pronounce," the
methods he suggests are as mechanical as theirs. For example, take
these two bits of pure Sheridan doctrine:

> The capital direction is to copy the proper tones for expressing
> every sentiment from those which Nature dictates to us in con-
> versation with others.
>
> In all prepared discourses it would be of great use if they were
> read over and rehearsed in private, with this particular view, to
> search for the proper emphases, before they were pronounced in
> public, marking at the same time the emphatical words in every
> sentence . . . and fixing them well in memory.

It is very difficult to see how Blair gets from such directions as
these to his concluding words:

> When a speaker is engaged in Public Discourse, he should not
> then be employing his attention about his manner, or thinking of
> his tones and his gestures. If he be so employed, study and affecta-
> tion will appear. He ought then to be quite in earnest, wholly oc-

cupied with his subject and his sentiments, leaving nature and previously acquired habits to prompt and suggest his manner of delivery.

Plainly Blair had not thought out clearly a theory of delivery. He is mentioned here only because his concluding words may have had a part in setting to work the more logical mind of Whately.

In his *Elements of Rhetoric,* first published in 1828, Whately writes about Elocution with a fervor which indicates that he does not include the subject merely because it was customary to treat delivery in works on rhetoric. He roundly condemns all the systems of instruction that have been brought forward; and he doubts that they have helped any one to attain a really good delivery.

> But there are many, probably nearly as many as have fully tried the experiment, who have by this means been totally spoiled;—who have fallen irrecoverably into an affected style of *spouting,* worse, in all respects, than their original mode of delivery. Many accordingly have, not unreasonably, conceived a disgust for the subject altogether; considering it hopeless that Elocution should be *taught* by any rules; and acquiescing in the conclusion that it is to be regarded as entirely the gift of nature, or an accidental acquirement of practice. It is to counteract the prejudice which may result from these feelings, that I profess in the outset a dissent from the principles generally adopted, and lay claim to some degree of originality in my own. Novelty affords at least an opening for hope.

Admitting that previous writers have made some valuable remarks on elocution generally, Whately asserts that "there is one principle running through their precepts which . . . must vitiate every system founded upon it. The principle I mean is, that in order to acquire the best style of Delivery it is requisite to study analytically the emphases, tones, pauses, degrees of loudness, &c. which give the proper effect to each passage that is well delivered—to frame rules founded on the observation of these—and then, in practice, deliberately and carefully to conform the utterance to these rules, so as to form a complete artificial system of Elocution."

Before proceeding to argument Whately attempts to forestall some criticisms that are still being made upon his contentions; first by saying

When however I protest against all artificial systems of Elocution, and all *direct* attention to Delivery, *at the time,* it must not
be supposed that a general inattention to that point is recommended . . . though it may safely be affirmed that even this negative plan would succeed far better than a studied modulation. But
it is evident that if any one wishes to . . . deliver a written composition with some degree of the manner and effect of one that
is extemporaneous, he will have a considerable difficulty to sur-
mount; since, though this may be called, in a certain sense, the
Natural Manner, it is by no means what he will naturally, i.e.
spontaneously, fall into. It is by no means natural for any one to
read as if he were *not* reading, but speaking.[2]

Here we can see the difficulties in the term *natural manner,* which
Whately has taken over from Sheridan. It has too many meanings,
requires too much explanation, and leads to the absurdity, as here,
of saying that it is not natural to be natural. Besides, it involves the
fallacy of assuming that whatever is natural is good, an assumption that
might be stretched to cover stammering, mumbling, cleft palates,
thievery, and murder.

Whately also tries to forestall another objection by saying that it
is not enough that the reader should actually understand the
composition to be read, nor that he should be impressed with its force.
He may still read as if he did not understand and were not impressed.
He continues:

The remedy that has been commonly proposed for these defects, is to point out in such a work, for instance, as the Liturgy,
which words ought to be marked as emphatic,—in what places the
voice is to be suspended, raised, lowered, &c. One of the best
writers on the subject, Sheridan, . . . adopts a peculiar set of
marks for denoting the different pauses, emphases, &c. . . . recommending that the habit be formed of regulating the voice by his
marks. . . . To the adoption of any such artificial system there are
three weighty objections. . . .

First, such a system must necessarily be imperfect. No variety of

---

[2] I am keeping in Whately's excess of italics, capitals, and punctuation, for I have
found that taking away these devices from a writer who has depended upon them
may change the significance of a passage. Certainly without his italics the reader
loses something of the tang of Whately's composition.

marks that could be invented,—not even musical notation,— would suffice to indicate the different *tones* which the different emphatic words should be pronounced.

Among other examples Whately uses Macbeth's reply to the witches when they call his name three times: "Had I three ears I'd hear thee." Although emphasizing the right word a reader may give the absurd meaning, "Since I have but two ears I cannot hear you." Probably Walker would have said that with his marks for slides and turns he could indicate the proper reading of Macbeth's sentence; but Whately holds that the infinite possibilities of emphasis, pause, rate, and tone make an adequate system of marks impossible.

2ndly, But were it even possible to bring to the highest perfection the proposed system of marks, it would still be a circuitous road to the desired end. . . . The learner might ask, "but *why* should this tone suit the awful,—this the pathetic,—this the narrative style? . . . The only answer that could be given, is, that these tones, emphases, &c. are a part of the language;—that nature, or custom, which is second nature, suggests spontaneously these different modes of giving expression to the different thoughts, feelings, and designs, which are present to the mind of any one who, without study, is speaking in earnest his own sentiments. Then, if this be the case, why not leave nature to do her own work? Impress but the mind fully with the sentiments, &c. to be uttered; withdraw the attention from the sound, and fix it on the sense; and nature, or habit, will spontaneously suggest the proper Delivery. That this will be the case is not only true, but is the very supposition on which the artificial system proceeds; for it professes to teach the mode of Delivery *naturally* adapted to each occasion.

It is surely, therefore, a circuitous path that is proposed, when the learner is directed, first to consider how each passage ought to be read; i.e. what mode of delivering each part of it would *spontaneously* occur to him, if he were attending exclusively to the matter of it; then to observe all the modulations, &c. of voice; then, to note these down, by established marks, writing; and, lastly, to pronounce according to these marks. This seems like recommending, for the purpose of raising the hand to the mouth, that he should first observe, when performing that action without thought of anything else, what muscles are contracted,—in what

degrees,—and in what order; then, that he should note down
these observations; and lastly, that he should, in conformity with
these notes, contract each muscle in due degree, and in proper
order; to the end that he may be enabled, after all, to—lift his
hand to his mouth; which by supposition, he had already done.

Whately's analogy here is the probable source of Nathan Shepard's
more spicy comparison in his *Before an Audience:* "Finding that when
eating, every time your elbow bends your mouth flies open, therefore
this rule: When your elbow bends, open your mouth."

> 3. Lastly, waving both of the above objections, if a person could
> thus learn to read and speak, as it were, *by note,*—still the desired
> object of a perfectly *natural* as well as correct Elocution, would
> never be in this way attained. The reader's attention being fixed
> on his own voice . . . the inevitable consequence would be that
> he would betray more or less his studied and artificial Delivery.

Whately does not explicitly recognize as a fourth the most serious
objection of all: that thinking how one's voice goes interfers with one's
attention to meaning. But that objection is plainly indicated in later
passages; for example:

> The practical rule then to be adopted . . . is, not only to pay
> no attention to the voice, but studiously to *withdraw* the thoughts
> from it, and to dwell as intently as possible on the Sense; trusting
> to nature to suggest spontaneously the proper emphases and tones.
> This natural manner, i.e. the manner which one naturally falls
> into who is *really speaking*, in earnest, and with a mind *exclusively*
> intent on what he has to say.

Whately will not compromise and agree with many who acknowledge that "it is a great fault for a reader to be *too much* occupied with
thoughts respecting his own voice," and think to steer a middle course
between opposite extremes. "A reader is sure to pay *too much* attention to his voice, not only if he pays *any at all*, but if he does not
strenuously *labor to withdraw* his attention from it altogether."

This does not mean, Whately points out, taking no pains. It is
not easy to keep attention on meaning to the degree he proposes.
One's mind tends to wander to other matters, or to leap forward to
the next sentence. He also points out that his method precludes the
easy way of imitation.

So far Whately has been treating of reading and mostly of reading the words of others, for he, like Sheridan, was particularly interested in improving the reading of the church service. He also takes up the reading of one's own compositions, and his treatment of this topic may be passed with the statement that it is just what one would expect from the foregoing. The aim in such reading is to approach as nearly as may be to extempore style; and while it is impossible to reach extempore style when reading, one may approach indefinitely near. If Whately's ideas are carried out, he says, the reader will not seem, as most do, to be saying as a running commentary, "I do not mean, think, or feel all this; I only mean to recite it with propriety."

Bishop Whately seems to think no difficulties arise in carrying out his ideas when speaking extempore. He ignores the fact that at times it is very difficult to keep one's mind from straying even when extemporizing.

Passing over much in Whately's discussion and also over the criticisms[3] that have been made upon it, I now proceed to some comments of my own upon his doctrine.

1. While Sheridan, Blair, and Whately all agree that thinking and feeling prompt adequate expression in wide-awake conversation and in extempore speechmaking, Whately was the only one of these to state clearly, and to make the statement an article of faith, that the same cause will prompt adequate expression in reading. There should be no rules, no marks for emphasis, pause, inflection, tone, or gesture. One should speak with "a mind exclusively intent on what he has to say" and trust entirely to thought, feeling, and speech habits.

2. Whately pays little attention to voice training and the like. He does say (following Blair in this) that if one has habitually ungraceful gestures, or if in common discourse one has indistinct, hesitating, dialectal, or otherwise faulty speech, he should endeavor to remedy the defect, "not in public speaking only, but in ordinary conversation. It is in these points, principally, that the remarks of an intelligent friend will be beneficial."

If the Bishop should today look over the battlements—presumably

---

[3]A good idea of the controversy that has raged around Whately's teaching can be gained from Corson's *Voice and Spiritual Education,* Curry's *Province of Expression,* and Parrish's *Reading Aloud.*

of heaven—he would be amazed to see the expensive laboratories and the corps of specialists who now take the place of his intelligent friend. It would hardly have occurred to a cultivated Englishman who did his teaching in Oxford that speech defects were problems. Had his teaching been done in one of our city or state universities, with students reared under all sorts of influences, he might have given the topic more than a page. Nevertheless in that page he did open the door for remedial work. I imagine he would say now, "Very well, so long as you keep your training strictly as training and do not cause considerations of phonetics, intonation and the like to become a part of your student's speechmaking consciousness; so long as you do not cause your students to think of these matters when on the platform."

3. While the teachings of Sheridan and Blair would tend to produce conversational *style* or *mode,* through imitation of delivery in conversation, I doubt that Whately's teaching would do even that, or tend to the natural manner they all aim at. Whately says many will object to what they will call a "colloquial style of delivery" and say it is "indecorous and unsuitable to the solemnity of serious and especially of religious discourse." He says also that the natural manner even when most elevated and solemn, will remind the hearers of the *tone* of conversation. All this indicates that he aimed at public delivery which *sounds* like conversation. But I fail to see how he could get that out of his teaching, for he puts all the stress on *exclusive* attention to matter.

Now *exclusive* is a strong word, and Whately uses it over and over and stresses it with italics. But it seems evident that if one gives all his attention to subject matter, he cannot give any to the audience. Think the thought, feel the sentiment, says Whately, and all will be well. But I suppose that is precisely what Hamlet was doing when he exclaimed in solitude, "Oh, what a rogue and peasant slave am I!" and when he gave vehement thought to suicide. Yet surely it would take a dull auditor, listening to a poor actor, to miss the difference between Hamlet's soliloquies and his direct speeches. Whately's teaching misses a half or two-thirds of the truth, and leads straight to soliloquy.

Soliloquy may be a natural manner, and it is natural for some to stand up in public and talk with themselves; but soliloquy is certainly not the kind of speaking Whately is advocating, which is delivery that sounds like conversation. Sheridan might attain conversational style by imitating conversation; but Whately's teaching will not lead even to that. And certainly his teaching will not lead to conversational *quality,* for soliloquy lacks the essential element of conversation, communication with others.

It is surprising that the keen Whately never came through to recognize the other necessary element in delivery, what I like to call "a sense of communication." The idea seems to have been lurking in the back of his mind, and he comes so near to it that at times one feels like crying out, as in the game of button, button, "He's getting warm!" One of his warmest spots is where he says that one not used to the "natural manner may be embarrassed at finding himself, as it were, stripped of the sheltering wall of a conventional delivery— delivering his thoughts as one man *speaking* to other men"; and also that the audience may give greater attention "from their perceiving themselves to be personally *addressed,* and feeling that he is not merely reciting something before them, but saying it to them." Whately is warm here!

But probably because he is intent on combating mechanical methods and enforcing the belief that thinking should prompt delivery, he never quite comes through to say that the feeling of contact with the audience has a definite effect upon delivery, and he never urges that the learner should cultivate this feeling. His nearest approaches to the idea are rather incidental. When he is really telling us how to acquire the "natural manner," his stress is all on exclusive attention to subject matter.

Nevertheless, although Whately missed a trick, we owe him much, even those who do not agree with him in the main. It was wholesome to have his ideas vigorously pressed upon us, for we are all prone to get lost in technicalities.

DE QUINCEY ON
SCIENCE, RHETORIC, AND POETRY

WILBUR SAMUEL HOWELL

Princeton University

D<small>E</small> Q<small>UINCEY</small>'s famous distinction between the literature of knowledge and the literature of power is considered by Charles Sears
Baldwin to confirm the ancient Greek distinction between rhetoric
and poetics.[1] Baldwin expresses this opinion without any attendant
elaboration or analysis; he is merely interested at the moment in
pointing to a few modern examples of the sort of critical thinking
that had been prevalent in antiquity. It doubtless seemed obvious to
him that his casual reference to De Quincey was sufficiently clear
in its context and needed nothing in the way of specific explanation.
At any rate, we have no recourse but to examine that context as best we
can and make it say whatever Baldwin allows it to suggest, if we are
properly to evaluate his statement about De Quincey.

Not long before he mentions De Quincey, Baldwin speaks of
rhetorical theory and poetical theory in ancient Greece as pre-
supposing that "the art of speaking and writing is not throughout its
various phases single and constant, but distinctly twofold;" he says
further that "the ancients discerned and developed an art of daily
communication, especially of public address, τεχνη ρητορικη, *ars oratoria,*
rhetoric; on the other hand, an art of imaginative appeal, τεχνη ποιητικη,
ars poetica, poetic;" and he refers, moreover, to Aristotle's *Rhetoric*
and *Poetics* as the only ancient works to define sharply and elaborate
fully the distinction between these two grand divisions of discourse.[2]

---

[1]Baldwin, C. S.: *Ancient Rhetoric and Poetic,* New York, 1924, p. 4.
[2]*Ibid.,* pp. 1-4. The direct quotations are from p. 1.

Hence, when he goes on almost at once to identify De Quincey's distinction with that of the ancient critics, we must assume—must we not?—that to him De Quincey voiced opinions closely similar to those of Aristotle.

Baldwin is completely right in insisting that the distinction between rhetoric and poetics is a fundamental postulate of Aristotle's literary theory and is so pervasive in Greek and Roman criticism that its latent presence is everywhere discernible. But he ought to have emphasized that the ancient critics considered dialectic and rhetoric, rather than rhetoric alone, to have pre-eminent jurisdiction over the rhetorical, or better, the non-imitative branch of literature. His failure to stress this fact and to explain that in the Aristotelian view dialectic was what we would call today the theory of formal scientific writing, while rhetoric was what we call the theory of popular argumentation, makes his analysis of Aristotle's theory of non-imitative discourse incomplete and to some extent misleading.[3] Somewhat misleading, also, is his account of the ancient theory of poetical or imitative literature. He says that poetry and its companion forms were considered by the ancients to be "primarily imaginative, a progress from image to image determined emotionally."[4] Such language as this he did not borrow from Aristotle's *Poetics* but from much later works. What he does—and this deserves stress—is to superimpose upon his account of ancient poetical theory a terminology in which severe cleavages between intellect and imagination, reason and emotion, are more consciously presupposed than they were by Aristotle. But, despite these two weaknesses in his analysis of ancient rhetorical and poetical theory, his emphasis upon the tendency of Greek criticism to presuppose or even to acknowledge explicitly the existence of two great families of discourse, one different in fundamental ways from the other, is both necessary and significant.

It is my purpose in this paper to inquire into the propriety of Baldwin's remark that De Quincey's distinction between the literature of knowledge and the literature of power supports and strengthens Aristotle's distinction between rhetoric and poetry. What I shall do

---

[3]For a discussion of the relations between dialectic and rhetoric in antiquity, see Howell, W. S.: *The Rhetoric of Alcuin and Charlemagne,* Princeton, 1941, pp. 33-64.

[4]Baldwin: *op. cit.,* p. 3; see also pp. 134-135.

is to examine first of all De Quincey's opinions on rhetoric and eloquence, in an attempt to show that he and Aristotle have little in common so far as these subjects are concerned. Then I shall examine De Quincey's distinction between the literature of knowledge and the literature of power and compare it with Aristotle's conception of the relations between non-imitative and imitative literature. It will, I hope, become obvious as I proceed that De Quincey did not design his theory of the two great classes of discourse as Aristotle designed his. And it will probably be obvious, too, that in my opinion De Quincey's distinction is less satisfactory than Aristotle's as a way of accounting for the major difference between non-poetical and poetical literature.

In the year 1828, De Quincey contributed to *Blackwood's Magazine* a review of Whately's *Elements of Rhetoric,* in which he sought not so much to evaluate the work of his learned contemporary as to set forth at some length his own theory of the difference between rhetoric and eloquence. Nowhere else in his writings does he afford us a better opportunity to understand his own conception of these two subjects or his own knowledge of Aristotelian rhetoric. Therefore, to his review I shall now devote some attention.

At an early stage of his review,[5] De Quincey mentions that Coleridge was "in the habit of drawing the line with much philosophical beauty between Rhetoric and Eloquence." Admitting, however, that he had never been so fortunate as to hear Coleridge explore this topic, he proceeds to distinguish the two terms in his own way. To him, eloquence is "the overflow of powerful feelings upon occasions fitted to excite them," whereas "Rhetoric is the art of aggrandizing and bringing out into strong relief, by means of various and striking thoughts, some aspect of truth which of itself is supported by no spontaneous feelings, and therefore rests upon artificial aids." These, I repeat, are De Quincey's own definitions. Certainly he intended them to limit eloquence to the type of discourse in which an appeal is made to the passions; and to divorce rhetoric, as a theory of composition, from any interest in the methods of conviction and demonstration.

---

[5]The text to which I refer throughout this study is in *The Collected Writings of Thomas De Quincey,* New and Enlarged Edition, ed. by David Masson, 14 vols., Edinburgh, 1889-1890, X, 81-133. The reference to Coleridge and the definitions of eloquence and rhetoric are on page 92. In subsequent notes "De Quincey" will stand for this edition.

This intention is fully clarified when he remarks, as a prelude to these definitions, that "where conviction begins, the field of Rhetoric ends; that is our opinion; and, as to the passions, we contend that they are not within the province of Rhetoric, but of Eloquence."[6]

"In this view of Rhetoric and its functions," De Quincey observes, "we coincide with Aristotle; as indeed originally we took it up on a suggestion derived from him."[7] This avowal by De Quincey of his direct indebtedness to Aristotle's *Rhetoric* led David Masson, the editor of De Quincey's collected writings, to explain in a detailed footnote some of the meanings that the word "rhetoric" had acquired since the time of Aristotle, and to set forth those points in Aristotle's doctrine that De Quincey had imperfectly remembered or wrongly understood. But such explanations need not enter our present discussion. It is for the moment sufficient to emphasize that eloquence designated to De Quincey the sort of discourses which Aristotle would have regarded as the typical products of rhetorical theory, and that rhetoric meant to De Quincey all of the typical products of that narrow, unphilosophical rhetoric which Aristotle did so much to condemn. Perhaps we should add that the conception of rhetoric constructed by De Quincey under the authority of Aristotle is so attenuated, so unreal, so far divorced from actual human experience, so completely devoid of connection with the urgent issues of politics and law, that we can only wonder why De Quincey would think it worth while for Aristotle or any serious-minded person to bother with it in any theoretical or practical way.[8]

The narrowness of De Quincey's idea of rhetoric is apparent throughout his review of Whately's *Elements*. Sketching the history of rhetoric, and accounting for its periods of popularity and oblivion, he has something to say of the rhetorics of Greece, Rome, England, France, Germany, Italy, and Spain. At one point he remarks:

> Rhetoric, in its finest and most absolute burnish, may be called
> an *eloquentia umbratica;* that is, it aims at an elaborate form of

[6]De Quincey: X, 82.

[7]*Ibid.,* p. 83.

[8]For a more favorable view than mine of De Quincey's theory of rhetoric, see Hudson, H. H.: De Quincey on Rhetoric and Public Speaking, *Studies in Rhetoric and Public Speaking in honor of James Albert Winans,* New York, 1925, pp. 133-151.

beauty which shrinks from the strife of business, and could neither arise nor make itself felt in a tumultous assembly.[9]

A moment later, he observes that "all great rhetoricians in selecting their subject have shunned the determinate cases of real life." This remark leads him to speak of rhetoric in Greece. He says:

> We can readily understand, therefore, why the fervid oratory of the Athenian assemblies, and the intense reality of its interest, should stifle the growth of rhetoric: the smoke, tarnish, and demoniac glare of Vesuvius easily eclipse the pallid coruscations of the aurora borealis. And, in fact, amongst the greater orators of Greece there is not a solitary gleam of rhetoric. Isocrates may have a little, being (to say the truth) neither orator nor rhetorician in any eminent sense; Demosthenes has none.[10]

If it seems strange to us that not a solitary gleam of rhetoric is to be found among the great orators and the great orations of Greece, especially when we remember that Aristotle, writing what he conceived to be the theory of what orations are and what orators do, called that theory rhetoric, De Quincey's treatment of the rhetoricians in Rome seems even stranger, even more capricious. He includes among them Livy and Ovid, the two Plinys, Lucan, Petronius, Quintilian; above them all he places the two Senecas.[11] He does not mention Cicero—Cicero, a great speaker, who almost alone among the great speakers of Western Europe interested himself in the theory of his art and wrote treatises on rhetoric which constitute in sum the most enlightened of such works in the Roman period and the best synthesis of Aristotle's *Rhetoric* ever attempted. De Quincey is not interested in the theory that would give an explanation of the orations against Catiline; to him rhetoric grows out of society's sterility and defeat, and out of the rhetorician's preoccupation with language when language is used without reference to the things it symbolizes. In fact, he clearly suggests this view when he says:

> To hang upon one's own thoughts as an object of conscious interest, to play with them, to watch and pursue them through a maze of inversions, evolutions, and harlequin changes, implies

---

[9] De Quincey: X, 93.
[10] *Ibid.,* p. 94.
[11] *Ibid.,* p. 95.

a condition of society either, like that in the monastic ages, forced to introvert its energies from mere defect of books (whence arose the scholastic metaphysics, admirable for its subtlety, but famishing the mind whilst it sharpened its edge in one exclusive direction) ; or, if it implies no absolute starvation of intellect, as in the case of the Roman rhetoric, which arose upon a considerable (though not very various) literature, it proclaims at least a quiescent state of the public mind, unoccupied with daily novelties, and at leisure from the agitations of eternal change.[12]

Small wonder that, in De Quincey's view, "the age of Rhetoric, like that of Chivalry, has passed amongst forgotten things"![13] Even eloquence, he observes, has suffered an eclipse in the modern world. He adds, however:

Eloquence is not banished from the public business of this country as useless, but as difficult, and as not spontaneously arising from topics such as generally furnish the staple of debate. But rhetoric, if attempted on a formal scale, would be summarily exploded as pure foppery and trifling with time.[14]

Inconsistencies in De Quincey's conception of rhetoric begin to show when he names the English authors who qualify as eminent masters of that art. Foremost among these he places Donne. Opposing Dr. Johnson's designation of Donne as a "metaphysical poet," De Quincey remarks that Donne is better described as "rhetorical." "In saying *that*, however," he hastens to add, "we must remind our readers that we revert to the original use of the word *Rhetoric*, as laying the principal stress upon the management of the thoughts, and only a secondary one upon the ornaments of style."[15] Is not De Quincey's reminder perplexing in the extreme? Up to this point he has been treating rhetoric as the art of stylistic ornamentation, or as that kind of composition in which an author eddies about his own thoughts, allows his fancy to move "self-sustained from its own activities," and indulges in a "flux and reflux of thought, half meditative, half capricious;"[16] and he has claimed for this conception

---

[12]*Ibid.*, p. 97.
[13]*Ibid.*, p. 97.
[14]*Ibid.*, p. 100.
[15]*Ibid.*, p. 101.

the authority of Aristotle. Now he emphasizes that rhetoric is something more than mere verbal intricacy—that it is the art of managing thoughts and by extension the art of coming to terms with the objective realities to which thoughts and words ultimately refer. Would Aristotle prefer this latter view to the former? De Quincey does not openly say he would. But the fact that the two views are not identical, and that De Quincey has both in mind, may account for his inclusion of the names of Burton, Milton, Jeremy Taylor, Sir Thomas Browne, Bolingbroke, Canning, and (with some qualifications) Burke among the great English rhetoricians. Hailing Burke as "the supreme writer of his century, the man of the largest and finest understanding," De Quincey adds that he was not the one "to play with his fancy for the purpose of separable ornament," and that only in rare cases did he "indulge himself in a pure rhetorician's use of fancy."[17]

In these remarks, and in others about Burton, Milton, Taylor, and Browne, De Quincey may be said to preserve his conception that rhetoric is the art of dressing thoughts *en grand costume:* but if he had explicitly to alter this view in order to make Donne a respectable rhetorician, we cannot be too sure that he did not implicitly alter it in giving his other authors that same title.

Our survey of De Quincey's opinions on rhetoric and eloquence indicates that the second of these terms, and on rare occasions the first, meant to him what the first meant to such writers as Aristotle and Cicero. As we turn now to De Quincey's discussion of the literature of knowledge and the literature of power, we ought to keep in mind that, if these large classes of discourse are to be regarded as parallel to the rhetorical and the poetical branches of ancient theory, then we would expect to find De Quincey classifying what he called eloquence, and perhaps what he called rhetoric, within the scope of the literature of knowledge. In other words, we would expect that De Quincey's distinction between the one sort of literature and the other would not place the oration and the sermon within the field of poetry. But our expectation is not fulfilled by De Quincey. He visualizes sermons,

---

[16]These phrases appear later in the work under consideration; see De Quincey: X, 121.

[17]For the references to Burke, see De Quincey: X, 114-115. The discussion of English rhetoricians begins on p. 100 and extends to p. 121.

orations, and that curious kind of word-play which he calls rhetoric, as more nearly akin to poetry than to scientific writing. Emphasizing that the literature of power, or literature properly so called, includes works printed in books and works published by other means,—by oral communication, for example,—he remarks that "much literature, scenic forensic, or didactic (as from lecturers and public orators), may never come into books, and much that *does* come into books may connect itself with no literary interest."[18] Somewhat earlier he said:

> The weekly sermons of Christendom, that vast pulpit literature which acts so extensively upon the popular mind—to warn, to uphold, to renew, to comfort, to alarm—does not attain the sanctuary of libraries in the ten-thousandth part of its extent. The Drama again,—as, for instance, the finest of Shakespeare's plays in England, and all leading Athenian plays in the noontide of the Attic stage,—operated as a literature on the public mind, and were (according to the strictest letter of that term) *published* through the audiences that witnessed their representation some time before they were published as things to be read. . . .[19]

If these positive statements are not in themselves sufficient evidence of De Quincey's intention to regard orations and sermons as part of the literature of power, they tend at least in that direction. So also do the remarks that he makes when he describes the actual specimens of the literature of knowledge. To this class he assigns no work that he would call rhetorical or oratorical. To this class, instead, he assigns such books as dictionaries, encyclopedias, grammars, spelling-books, the Court Calendar, and the parliamentary reports, these being the humbler examples, while histories, biographies, travels, and works like Newton's *Principia* and those of Laplace, he specifies as higher examples and warns that they are sometimes confused with true literature by unperceptive critics.[20]

It ought to be remarked at this point that De Quincey's distinction between the literature of knowledge and the literature of power exists in two versions, one of which was published in 1823, when he was 37

---

[18]De Quincey: XI, 54.

[19]*Ibid.*, pp. 53-54.

[20]He mentions in several places the types of works which belong to the literature of knowledge; see especially De Quincey: X, 47, and XI, 57, 59.

years of age, and the second in 1848, when he was 63.[21] The first version appears in a work entitled "Letters to a Young Man whose Education has been Neglected," published in several installments in the *London Magazine*. Advising his readers upon the question of selecting foreign languages for a coherent plan of education, De Quincey remarks that a particular language ought to be chosen after one has decided whether his inclinations lie in the direction of science or in the direction of literature. How can one make this decision? De Quincy's answer, which he credits in its broad outline to many years' conversation with Wordsworth,[22] is given as a distinction between what he calls books of knowledge, or anti-literature, or *literæ didacticæ*, or παιδεια, on the one hand, and literature, or *literæ humaniores*, on the other. The terms "literature of knowledge" and "literature of power," as a way of expressing this distinction, appear in the second version, which was published in the *North British Review* for August, 1848, in connection with De Quincey's critical estimate of Roscoe's edition of the works of Pope.

The first version provides two criteria which the critic may use in determining whether a given work justly belongs to science or to literature. One criterion involves certain realities in the given work itself. If it is a work, says De Quincey, "in which the matter to be communicated is paramount to the manner or form of its communication,"[23] then it belongs to science—it is a book of knowledge. He does not state what the relation of matter and form would have to be in the work of literature. But he is thinking of one class as the logical antithesis of the other, and we may therefore assume that in his view the literary work would be that in which form or manner of communication is paramount to the matter. The second criterion involves the effect of the given work upon the reader. "All that is literature," says he, "seeks to communicate power; all that is not literature, to communicate knowledge."[24] What, then, we ask, is power? De Quincey's answer is explicit. Reduced to its simplest terms,

---

[21]For the text of the first version, see De Quincey: X, 33-52; for that of the second, see De Quincey: XI, 51-97.

[22]De Quincey: X, 48, note. For the terms used by him in this first version, see *ibid.*, pp. 47, 49.

[23]*Ibid.*, p. 47.

[24]*Ibid.*, p. 48.

his idea is that power is a personal possession of the reader of a literary work when that work has so affected him as to make him conscious of unhabitual emotions and of their organization. De Quincey's own definition of power is as follows:

> Now, if it be asked what is meant by communicating power, I, in my turn, would ask by what name a man would designate the case in which I should be made to feel vividly, and with a vital consciousness, emotions which ordinary life rarely or never supplies occasions for exciting, and which had previously lain unwakened, and hardly within the dawn of consciousness—as myriads of modes of feeling are at this moment in every human mind for want of a poet to organize them? I say, when these inert and sleeping forms *are* organized, when these possibilities *are* actualized, is this conscious and living possession of mine *power,* or what is it?[25]

A consciousness of unhabitual emotions and of their organization, their structure—this, then, is the state of mind of the reader of a great poem. De Quincey illustrates this effect by describing with warmth and skill how *King Lear* and *Paradise Lost* affected him. Unfortunately he does not turn then to give a parallel definition of knowledge, conceived as the effect of a good work in science upon the mind of a reader. Remembering, however, as we did a moment ago, that he is thinking of books of knowledge as the logical antithesis of literature, and reminding ourselves that in the old psychology *thought* was regarded as a kind of antithesis of *emotion,* we may assume that to De Quincey *knowledge* is a consciousness of new thoughts and their structure.

Is there not a fundamental inconsistency between the two criteria proposed by De Quincey as a means of determining whether a book is literary or scientific? If a scientific work is such that in his view of the matter to be communicated is paramount to the manner or form of the communication, then the reader of that work must be conscious of matter rather than form. That is to say, the formal aspects of that work, the structure and organization of its parts, will not appear in the reader's consciousness as configurations of his awareness of substance. Yet, if our statement of the effect of that kind of work upon the

---

[25]*Ibid.,* p. 48.

reader is a true antithesis of De Quincey's definition of power, then he himself would declare that the reader of a scientific work would be conscious not only of new thoughts, but also of their organization, their structure. In short, according to De Quincey's second criterion, the reader of a work in science would have that very consciousness of manner or form which the first criterion seeks to deny to him. Would not De Quincey have been wise to discard altogether his first criterion, and to recognize explicitly that scientific works have a system of forms or structures suitable to themselves, and literature has a different system of structures to complement and administer its different procedures?

Another difficulty arises even when we abandon De Quincey's first criterion. His second criterion implies that the literature of power gives us no values except those associated with our consciousness of unhabitual emotions and their organization. Yet it is fair to insist that literature has something to do with our thoughts—that literature may make us aware no less than science of new thoughts and their organization. Once we admit this, we have destroyed much of the validity of De Quincey's second criterion; but we have prepared the way for a distinction between science and literature that will limit neither to an exclusive preoccupation with some one faculty of the mind, conceived as having power to operate more or less independently of other faculties. Perhaps it is because we can no longer believe in the validity of such a conception of the mind that we cannot accept De Quincey's definition of a power as a full account of the happenings within ourselves when we read some great work like *King Lear* or *Paradise Lost*.

Twenty-five years after De Quincey formulated his distinction between science and literature, he stated it again, this time in the form which most scholars and critics associate with his name. Perhaps he felt that some of the inconsistencies in his earlier version should be eliminated; perhaps he had changed his mind on some details; perhaps he had even forgotten exactly what he had previously said. At any rate, his second account differs markedly from the first.

Whereas in the earlier version he had alluded with some contempt to the vulgar antithesis between instruction and pleasure as the determining factor in the distinction between the two kinds of discourse, and had dismissed it with the remark that "this wretched antithesis will be of no service to us,"[26] he now uses a modification of it as the entering wedge for his dichotomy. He observes:

> In that great social organ which, collectively, we call literature, there may be distinguished two separate offices that may blend and often *do* so, but capable, severally, of a severe insulation, and naturally fitted for reciprocal repulsion. There is, first, the literature of *knowledge;* and, secondly, the literature of *power.* The function of the first is—to *teach;* the function of the second is—to *move;* the first is a rudder; the second, an oar or a sail. The first speaks to the *mere* discursive understanding; the second speaks ultimately, it may happen, to the higher understanding or reason, but always *through* affections of pleasure and sympathy.[27]

Involved in these words is one set of terms which may need a bit of explanation. The "mere discursive understanding," to which the literature of knowledge speaks, is probably to be accepted as De Quincey's term for man's intelligence; the "higher understanding or reason," to which speaks the literature of power, is his term for man's intuitive faculty. Something of the force of these terms within the framework of his whole distinction can be gathered from what he himself says a moment later:

> It [that is, the literature of power] is concerned with what is highest in man: for the Scriptures themselves never condescended to deal by suggestion or co-operation with the mere discursive understanding; when speaking of man in his intellectual capacity, the Scriptures speak not of the understanding, but of *"the understanding heart,"*—making the heart, *i.e.,* the great *intuitive* (or non-discursive) organ, to be the interchangeable formula for man in his highest state of capacity for the infinite.[28]

In De Quincey's review of Whately's *Elements,* he has something to say which further clarifies the meaning he assigns to the intuition and the ordinary intelligence. There he observes:

> An *intuition* is any knowledge whatsoever, sensuous or intellectual, which is apprehended *immediately;* a notion, on the other

---

[26]*Ibid.,* p. 47.
[27]*Ibid.,* XI, 54.
[28]*Ibid.,* p. 56.

hand, or product of the discursive faculty, is any knowledge whatsoever which is apprehended *mediately*. All reasoning is carried on discursively; that is, *discurrendo*,—by running about to the right and the left, laying the separate notices together, and thence mediately deriving some third apprehension.[29]

These words, it may be observed, are written by De Quincey in order that he may deliver a reprimand to Milton for degrading the fallen angels in *Paradise Lost* by making them debate with the ordinary instruments of the discursive faculty. Arguing that spiritual beings must share with God the ability to see the whole argument in a flash of intuition, not in a slow development of intermediate propositions, and that Milton had violated this propriety, De Quincey calls the Second Book of *Paradise Lost* a descent from poetry into rhetoric, and suggests that Milton doesn't do any better in his logic than would the House of Commons. Be that as it may. What is of interest to us at this moment is that to De Quincey the process of mediate inference in logic, with its concern for the fully articulated syllogism, is characteristic of man's reasoning faculty, whereas the immediate inference of logic, with its mode of inferring one proposition directly from another without the use of a middle term, is the instrument of man's intuition.

It is now clear that De Quincey's second version of the distinction between the two kinds of literature involves in the last analysis not so much the terms *teaching* and *moving* as the terms *intelligence* and *intuition*. What he has to say about the difference between scientific truth and literary truth illustrates this point. A scientific truth he describes as a truth which a person may be absolutely unconscious of before he learns it. "To be capable of transplantation," he observes, "is the immediate criterion of a truth that ranges on a lower scale."[30] That is to say, a man may not know that a stone is hard; but the knowledge can be given him, either by direct experience with a stone, or by words from somebody who transplants the notion in his consciousness. When man first acquires such notions as these, they are new to him, or at least, as De Quincey says, they are "connected with something of absolute novelty." But literary truth is that of

---

[29]*Ibid.,* X, 103.
[30]*Ibid.,* XI, 55.

which a person is never, at any time in his life, wholly unconscious.
De Quincy says:

> . . . it is the grandeur of all truth which *can* occupy a very high
> place in human interests that it is never absolutely novel to the
> meanest of minds; it exists eternally by way of germ or latent
> principle in the lowest as in the highest, needing to be developed,
> but never to be planted.[31]

This higher truth is connected with man's innate ideas. "Tragedy,
romance, fairy tale, or epogee," declares De Quincey, "all alike restore
to man's mind the ideals of justice, of hope, of truth, of mercy, of
retribution, which else (left to the support of daily life in its realities)
would languish for want of sufficient illustration."[32]

In De Quincey's view, the literature of power not only presents
higher truth but also creates in the reader a deep sympathy for it. Indeed, he finds a parallel between the effect of literature and the effect
of children or of direct experience upon the individual of society.
In one of his most attractive passages he says:

> What is the effect, for instance, upon society, of children? By
> the pity, by the tenderness, and by the peculiar modes of admira-
> tion, which connect themselves with the helplessness, with the
> innocence, and with the simplicity of children, not only are the
> primal affections strengthened and continually renewed, but the
> qualities which are dearest in the sight of heaven,—the frailty,
> for instance, which appeals to forbearance, the innocence which
> symbolizes the heavenly, and the simplicity which is most alien
> from the worldly,—are kept up in perpetual remembrance, and
> their ideals are continually refreshed. A purpose of the same
> nature is answered by the higher literature, viz. the literature of
> power.[33]

And again he speaks to the same purpose:

> Were it not that human sensibilities are ventilated and contin-
> ually called out into exercise by the great phenomena of infancy,
> or of real life as it moves through chance and change, or of liter-
> ature as it recombines these elements in the mimicries of poetry,

[31]*Ibid.,* p. 55.
[32]*Ibid.,* p. 56.
[33]*Ibid.,* p. 55.

romance, etc., it is certain that, like any animal power or muscular energy falling into disuse, all such sensibilities would gradually droop and dwindle.[34]

As he completes his second version of the distinction between science and literature, De Quincey remarks upon the provisional character of the one as contrasted to the permanent character of the other:

> The very highest work that has ever existed in the Literature of Knowledge is but a *provisional* work: a book upon trial and sufferance, and *quamdiu bene se gesserit.* Let its teaching be even partially revised, let it be but expanded—nay, even let its teaching be placed in a better order,—and instantly it is superseded. Whereas the feeblest works in the Literature of Power, surviving at all, survive as finished and unalterable amongst men.[35]

De Quincey provides an illustration of this statement by comparing Newton's *Principia* with such works as the *Iliad* and *Hamlet*. The former survives, he observes, only so far as it can continue to surpass the rival works of Laplace in respect to exact truth and felicity of arrangement; but the *Iliad* and *Hamlet* survive without vying with each other—they survive because each is unique, self-sustained, triumphant for ever.

In this analysis of De Quincey's thinking upon the subject of science, rhetoric, and literature, we have seen that rhetoric, conceived by him to be stylistic virtuosity, lies within the province of literature properly so called, near the subdivision of eloquence, and not far from the subdivision which contains the highest poetry. There can be little or no doubt that he would tend to identify poetry, on the one hand, with oratory and verbal ingenuity, on the other; for poetry, in his view, is directly concerned with an emotional effect, so far, at least, as it operates through affections of pleasure and sympathy, whereas rhetoric aims at an elaborate form of beauty, and eloquence is an overflow of powerful feelings. We have also seen that the literature of knowledge is coextensive in his thinking with all sorts and degrees of scientific writing, and that his theory of the division of discourse into two classes makes one class rather small and narrow and definite, the other being wide and strangely assorted and blurred in its internal groupings. We

[34]*Ibid.,* p. 56.
[35]*Ibid.,* p. 57.

have looked closely at his two versions of this theory. The first as we have indicated, affords two criteria for discerning whether a book belongs to science or to literature. The second criterion, which identifies function with a reader's consciousness of emotion and their organization or of thoughts and their organization, seems to us to contradict the first, in which De Quincey states that matter is paramount in science, form in literature. The second criterion, moreover, because it implies that man's emotions and his thoughts can be, as it were, dissociated, and can respond as separable units of consciousness, without close organic interconnection, seems today to be questionable. What, now, of the second version of De Quincey's theory? That, as has been pointed out, depends upon a third criterion —the difference between man's faculty of intuition and his faculty of reason. If we accept this criterion as a way of establishing a scheme of values for scientific writing and poetry, we may often wonder how far it is allowable for us to exclude intuition from science or reason from literature. We may also wonder why, if De Quincey makes a distinction at one time between two things in terms of emotion and thought, and a later distinction in other terms, it is not incumbent upon him to explain rather than to ignore this change in his basic terms. It would seem, therefore, that De Quincey's two attempts to distinguish between science and literature are not of the highest value, when we judge them in and for themselves. He poses a very important question in criticism; he raises essential issues. But his answer to the question is vitiated by an inconsistency and founded upon a psychological theory that denies the possibility of interconnections between emotional and intellectual experience.[36]

The question whether De Quincey's theory of the divisions of discourse corroborates that of Aristotle need not concern us at great length. The chief resemblance between the two is that each postulates two main families of discourse and seeks to explain the differences between them. But here close resemblance ends. And it may at once be

---

[36] J. H. Fowler, in *De Quincey as Literary Critic,* The English Association, Pamphlet No. 52, July 1922, pp. 4-8, finds DeQuincey's distinction between literature of knowledge and literature of power to be unhelpful, false, harmful. In making this appraisal, Fowler only examines the second version of the distinction, and does not press his analysis of it to the point where he perceives the importance of the issues raised by De Quincey.

anticipated that a correspondence based upon a postulate of this sort need not be extensive or systematic, and would not in itself establish Baldwin's statement that De Quincey's theory confirms Aristotle's.

To Aristotle, the two main families of discourse embrace, on the one hand scientific writing, historical writing, and oratory, and on the other drama, epic poetry, and lyric poetry That is to say, he does not draw the line between the two families in such a way as to place oratory in the class of poetical compositions; rather, he places oratory in the other class, no doubt in the belief that the oral utterance in the law court and the public legislative body has somewhat the same ultimate relation to the realities with which it deals as does the oral or written utterance in the philosophical academy or the historical seminar. Nor does he draw the line between the two families in such a way as to suggest a severe insulation, a reciprocal repulsion, between the mental faculties to which scientific discourse and poetical discourse are sometimes considered respectively to relate. Had he drawn both of these lines, his theory would have anticipated De Quincey's, and De Quincey's would have supported his. But his real distinction is made with other postulates in mind.

The works of Aristotle to which we must refer in determining the main outlines of his whole theory of discourse are the *Topics,* the *Rhetoric,* and the *Poetics.* At least, these are to be regarded as his major contributions to literary speculation. It may be said that each of these works focuses attention upon one of the three chief activities in the field of discourse, and that, taken together, the three works cover the field.

The reader of the *Topics* and the *Rhetoric* does not need to be reminded that these two works are interconnected at many points. Indeed, the *Rhetoric* begins with the statement that "Rhetoric is the counterpart of Dialectic,"[37] dialectic being of course the true subject of the *Topics:* and the cross-references between the former work and the latter are frequent and suggestive. When Aristotle's thinking upon these two subjects has been explored, the conclusion is plain that he intended dialectic to be the theory of the formal scientific utterance,

---

[37]Cooper, Lane: *The Rhetoric of Aristotle, An Expanded Translation,* New York, 1932, p. 1.

in an age when scientific procedures were in the hands of philosophers
and dialecticians, and rhetoric to be the theory of popularizing and
defending truth or good probability. Although rhetoricians might
seem at times to be using verbal deception and fraudulent statements
as a substitute for accurate expression and to be therefore adhering to
a theory that contradicts good procedures in scientific and historical
writing, yet Aristotle, particularly in his analysis of the four uses of
rhetoric, insists upon the superior persuasiveness of true statements
over false,[38] and thus clearly recognizes the correspondence between
truth in scientific writing and persuasiveness in oratory.

In sum, Aristotle's *Topics* and *Rhetoric* offer together a theory of
one of the two main families of discourse. Aristotle gives no name to
this family. But might we not say that his treatises on scientific
writing, or dialectic, and oratorical expression, or rhetoric, constitute
a kind of theory of the literature of statement? That is to say, these
treatises investigate the relations between statements, as verbal phenomena, and the facts to which words refer—these treatises investigate
the degrees and kinds of correspondence that must exist between
verbal descriptions of reality and reality itself, if those descriptions
are to convince people, as in the case of science, or persuade people,
as in the case of oratory.

Looking now at Aristotle's theory of the other main family of discourse, we observe that in the *Poetics* he states very explicitly the
principle which differentiates poetry and science. He says:

> Turning first to the conception of poetry in general, we may
> follow the natural order, and begin with what is fundamental,
> the principle of artistic imitation. Epic Poetry and Tragedy, as
> well as Comedy and Dithyrambic Poetry, and for the most part
> the music of the flute and lyre, in their general nature are forms
> of imitation; that is, they represent, or imitate, something through
> an arrangement of words or notes.[39]

Here then, is the underlying poetic principle—the principle that forms
of poetry are forms of imitation, with words as the medium. Elsewhere

---

[38]*Ibid.*, pp. 5-6. See also Plato's *Phaedrus,* where the same theory of persuasion
is advanced.

[39]Cooper, Lane: *Aristotle on the Art of Poetry, An Amplified Version,* New York,
1913, p. 2.

in the same chapter, Aristotle applies this principle to a case in which scientific writing might be confused with poetry, and shows how the principle operates to preserve the separate identity of these two kinds of discourse. Empedocles had written versified natural science; Homer, too, had written in verse. But should Empedocles and Homer both be called poets, their work poetry? No, says Aristotle. And why not? Because such terminology would be accurate only "if it were not the principle of imitation that characterized the artist"; and he adds, "hence, if it is proper to style Homer a poet, Empedocles must be classed as a natural scientist rather than a poet."[40]

What Aristotle says later about the difference between the historian and poet is an elaboration of the distinction between scientific writing and poetry, history being scientific in the sense that historians seek to state accurately in words the events that once actually transpired. Says Aristotle:

> The essential distinction [between history and poetry] lies in this, that the Historian relates what has happened, and the Poet represents what might happen—what is typical. Poetry, therefore, is something more philosophic and of high seriousness than History; for Poetry tends rather to express what is universal, whereas History relates particular events as such.[41]

The universals expressed in poetry are of course conceptions—conceptions about actual human life and actual human behavior. These conceptions direct the poet in his selection of a story that will reveal them; these conceptions dominate the story, give it unity, mood, purpose. But the story is partly or wholly invented. It is the process of using such stories and episodes to embody the meaning and the purpose of human life as the poet has actually observed it round about him that suggests what Aristotle means by "imitation" or representation." In other words, the poet gathers his conceptions from his own observation of human situations in his experience; but he transmits these conceptions to other men by telling a story or presenting a dramatic action that stands by analogy for his own observation and experience. The historian, however, transmits to other men a consciousness of events that once transpired, by means of words that

[40]*Ibid.*, p. 4.
[41]*Ibid.*, pp. 31-32.

stand directly—not by way of symbol and analogy—for those actual events. Wherever the historian's method is at work—and it is at work in science and in oratory as in history—we may call it the method of statement, and its products, the literature of statement. Wherever the poet's method is at work, we may call it the method of representation, and its products, the literature of representation. At any rate, Aristotle would seem by express statement and by implication to lend support to such a way of describing the differences between the two great families of discourse.

We may conclude, therefore, that Aristotle's distinction would place rhetoric within the province of De Quincey's literature of knowledge, whereas De Quincey himself would place rhetoric within the province of the literature of power. We may also conclude that De Quincey bases his distinction upon an assumption of a sharp separation between the faculties of reason and emotion, or (in his second version) reason and intuition, whereas Aristotle bases his upon the asumption that truth finds it way from one man to another either by words that directly convey it or by words that represent it by means of symbols. Thus Baldwin would appear to have little basis for his statement that De Quincey confirms Aristotle. But what is more important is that if criticism is to provide an accurate description of the difference between rhetoric and poetry, Aristotle would seem to establish a better foundation than would De Quincey.

THE DEVELOPMENT OF RHETORICAL THEORY IN AMERICA: THE GROWTH OF THE CLASSICAL TRADITION, 1730-1785

WARREN GUTHRIE

Western Reserve University

THE PORT ROYAL INFLUENCE

SOME YEARS BEFORE the general interest in rhetoric took anything resembling a classical turn, there was evidence of interest in a fuller and more complete rhetoric than that offered by Ramus and his followers. We have noted some indications of the growth of this wider conception in an earlier study in this series.[1] Early in the eighteenth century there are several signs of use of a very different and, for the time, unusual book, the Port Royal *Art of Speaking*.[2] A copy now in the Harvard library has inscribed in it, "Edward Wigglesworth, 1716." Wigglesworth was graduated by Harvard in 1712. In 1722 a copy of the Port Royal rhetoric was in the library of the *New England Courant*.[3] Samuel Johnson read it in 1722 and wished for a better edition some twenty years later.[4] Johnson commended it for students in 1748,[5] and he recommended it to Franklin

---

[1]Guthrie, Warren: The Development of Rhetorical Theory in America, *Speech Monographs*, XIII:1:14-22, 1946.

[2]Messieurs Du Port Royal: *The Art of Speaking Written in French by Messieurs Du Port Royal: In persuance of a former Treatise, Intitled, The Art of Thinking.* Rendered into English, London, 1696.

[3]Cook, Elizabeth C.: *Literary Influence in Colonial Newspapers*, New York, 1912, p. 21.

[4]Johnson, Samuel: *His Career and Writings*, ed. Herbert and Carol Schneider, New York, 1929, I, 111.

[5]*Ibid.*, II, 317.

for use in his "English School" in Philadelphia.[6]

Although the Port Royal work was dismissed by one student of American rhetorical training as a "pious but singularly persuasive work,"[7] the *Art of Speaking* has large importance, not only because it presages a shift in emphasis that was to revolutionize American rhetoric, but because of its solid worth as a rhetorical document.

The *Art of Speaking* is in reality two books bound into one—an "Art of Speaking" and an "Art of Persuasion." The first section or book treats of rudimentary voice science and style, and the second, in method and in material, is influenced by the classical tradition, especially Cicero. It is the second volume of the work, "Art of Persuasion," that is most interesting to use, for it foreshadows the rapid turn to the classical tradition which is to follow.

> The *Art of Persuasion* consists of five parts. The first is, Invention of Proper Means; the second is, Disposition of the Means; the third is, Elocution; the fourth, Memory; the fifth, Pronunciation.[8]

This division of the parts of rhetoric is far from the Ramean doctrines, and to the students nurtured on Dugard or even Farnaby, the rest of the work offers a clear pointing of the way back to the concept of rhetoric as an active art, concerned with the moving and influencing of men.

There is a fairly detailed treatment of invention, with a consideration of the topics which is taken especially from Cicero.[9] The orator is thought of in the Ciceronian manner, too, for:

> . . . it is of importance that an Auditory has an esteem for the person who speaks. . . . Wherefore in an Orator these four Qualities are especially requisite, Probity, Prudence, Civility, and Modesty.[10]

---

[6]Smith, Albert Henry: *The Writings of Benjamin Franklin,* New York, 1908, III, footnote, p. 29.

[7]Perrin, Porter G.: The Teaching of Rhetoric in American Colleges Before 1750, unpublished Ph.D. dissertation, Department of English, University of Chicago, 1936, p. 86. In fairness to Mr. Perrin it should be pointed out that he spends some time in a later chapter examining similarities between many Harvard theses of the years 1720-1746 and dicta in the Port Royal work; but he does not analyze the rhetorical doctrine in the *Art of Speaking.*

[8]Port Royal: *op. cit.,* The Art of Persuasion, p. 268.

[9]*Ibid.,* pp. 268-281.

[10]*Ibid.,* pp. 283-284.

After some later discussion of methods by which the audience can be made to yield their minds to the orator, the same point is made anew. "The qualities that we have show'd to be necessary in an Orator, ought not to be counterfeit."[11] Thus is *ethos* joined to logical argument as one of the available means of persuasion.

The third chapter on invention adds *pathos* to the treatment, for it deals with the means by which the emotions may be touched in order to secure response. Its stress is constantly that it is not enough to produce good arguments, not enough to deliver them with clearness—the successful orator must be able to secure and hold attention.[12]

Under arrangement, the parts of the speech are listed as the Exordium, Proposition, Narration, Proofs, Refutation, and the Epilogue, and the treatment is in the Roman tradition throughout. Style is dismissed with only a reference to the earlier work bound in the same volume, the "Art of Speaking." Memory is dismissed with the statement: "all the world knows it is a gift of Nature, not to be improved by anything but exercise."[13]

Only two pages of discussion are given to delivery, although there is sharp stress on the importance which it must have to the orator.

> Pronunciation is of such advantage to the Orator, that it deserves to be treated on at large; for there is a Rhetorick in the eye, the motion and air of the Body, that persuades as much as Arguments. . . . Every Passion has its peculiar gesture, its peculiar *miene,* which if good or bad, makes a good or bad Orator . . . and the pains that we take to pronounce things well, will neither be vain nor unprofitable. But in Books or Writing it will be more vain. Rules for Pronunciation cannot be well taught, but by Experience and Practice.[14]

Here was a new concept of rhetoric for the colonial scholar, and we find it a keystone in the bridge between the abbreviated rhetoric of the early period and the full classical approach which was soon to become dominant.[15]

---

[11]*Ibid.,* p. 295.

[12]*Ibid.,* pp. 302-304.

[13]*Ibid.,* p. 323.

[14]*Ibid.,* pp. 323-324.

[15]Perrin: *op. cit.,* pp. 113-114, gives some indication of the impact of the Port Royal work on Harvard students.

THE CLASSICAL RHETORICS DURING THE PERIOD

Aristotle. In spite of the increased influence of the Aristotelian doctrines, there is almost as little evidence of the direct use of Aristotle in this period as in the period just preceding it. This is not unusual, however, in that the newer works filled the place that the *Rhetoric* might otherwise have been expected to hold.

Aristotle's *Opera* were offered for sale by a New York book seller in 1755.[16] The manuscript charging record of the Harvard library shows that the *Opera* were drawn twice in 1762. Of course, this may have been for an examination of any of the Aristotelian writings contained there. Specific reference is found to the *Rhetoric* in 1782, however. The Brown library catalogue of that year, a manuscript thought to be in President Manning's handwriting, records "Aristotles de Arte Rhetorica." Additions to this catalogue, penned in 1784, include "Aristotle upon Rhetoric."

No further evidence of use of Aristotle during the period has been found. Since almost all of the college libraries of a slightly later period contained the work, however, it is to be assumed that the *Rhetoric* was at least easily available in the colonies some time after 1750.

Cicero. Perhaps because of the interest in Cicero as an orator,[17] perhaps because of the increased emphasis on Latin rather than on Greek—whatever the cause, Cicero's *De Oratore* became one of the most popular works on speech in the colonies. The Yale library catalogue of 1743 starred the work as especially useful for upperclassmen, and there were "6 dupl." copies. *The Orator* was listed on almost every charging list of the Harvard library from 1762 on through 1770. A manuscript catalogue of books in the Harvard library in 1765 includes Guthrie's translation of the *De Oratore*. This translation was first published in London in 1742. The translation was also listed in the 1757 catalogue of the Philadelphia Library Company. Student claims were filed for it after the fire of 1763 at Harvard.[18] It was listed in the Brown

[16]*A Catalogue of Books in History, Divinity, Law, Arts and Science, and the several parts of Polite Literature: to be sold by Garrat Noel, Bookseller in Dock Street, New York,* New York, 1755.

[17]The college laws of all of the colonial colleges required the study of Cicero's orations; and other writings of his were frequently listed in the laws.

[18]Seybolt, R. F.: Student Libraries at Harvard, 1763-64, *Publications of the Colonial Society of Massachusetts* (Transactions), *XXVIII*:454, 1920-33.

course of study given by Solomon Browne in 1772.[19] Two copies of
the *De Oratore* were in the library of Col. Wm. Byrd in Virginia, when
a catalogue of that library was prepared about 1777.[20] President Stiles'
Diary lists it in the Yale course of study in 1781.[21] It is listed with Latin
works studied at Harvard in 1787.[22] Directly and indirectly, the rhetorical doctrine of Cicero exerted ever increasing influence on colonial
thought.

Quintilian. There seems to have been fairly wide-spread use of
Quintilian also. Two copies were in the Yale library in 1743. "Select
parts" were studied at the University of Pennsylvania in 1756.[23] It is
listed frequently on the Harvard charging records from 1762 to 1770,
and a translation by Guthrie was listed in a select catalogue of volumes
in frequent use which was published by Harvard in 1773.[24] Selected
parts were also studied at Washington College in Maryland in 1783.[25]

Mention might also be made of the use of John Constable's *Reflections on Accuracy of Style,*[26] which was an attempt to present in English the doctrines of Quintilian. This book was in the Harvard library
by 1765, and was also in the *Selected Catalogue* of 1773.

Thus it can be seen that there was an increased use of the classical
rhetorical works during the late eighteenth century. As we shall find
in following pages, this was accompanied by a great interest in those
rhetorical works written in England which followed the classical
tradition.

IMPORTED RHETORICS IN THE CLASSICAL TRADITION

All of the rhetorics in use in the colonies at this time were imported

---

[19]Bronson, W. C.: *The History of Brown University, 1764-1914,* Providence, 1914,
pp. 102-103.

[20]*The Writings of "Col. Wm. Byrd of Westover in Virginia Esq."* ed. John Spencer Bassett, New York, 1901, Appendix A.

[21]*Letters and Papers of Ezra Stiles,* ed. Isabel M. Calder, New Haven, 1933, p. 48.

[22]Records of Overseers [MSS.], 350-351

[23]Montgomery, T. H.: *A History of the University of Pennsylvania from its foundation to A.D. 1770,* Philadelphia, 1900, pp. 238-239.

[24]*Selected Catalogue of Harvard College,* Boston, 1773. It is interesting to note as
well, that when various libraries were "sequestered" during the Revolution, Quintilian was included in at least two "Harvard College Papers" [MSS.], II, 39-40.

[25]Parker, William: *An Account of Washington College in the State of Maryland,*
Philadelphia, 1784, p. 41.

[26]The copy examined was a London edition of 1781.

and the great majority of those were English in origin. The first work displaying a strong classical influence we have already surveyed, the French *Art of Speaking* or Port Royal Rhetoric.

Brightland. One of the first English rhetorics attempting the full classical doctrine to find circulation in the colonies was that of John Brightland.[27] The first record found of it in the colonies was in the catalogue of the Library Company of Philadelphia which was published in 1721. The Union Library Company (Philadelphia) catalogue also listed the work in 1765. No other evidence of use has been found.

Since the book attempts to cover many fields, as can be seen from its title, the treatment of rhetoric is necessarily brief. In spite of its brevity, however, it is remarkably complete. The preface gives a clear idea of the kind of rhetoric favored by Brightland:

> The General *Rhetorics* of the Schools in *England* meddle only with the Tropes and Figures of Words and Sentences, but neglect the Cultivation of a young Invention. . . . By here using Youth early to a Methodical Invention, Exercise and Time will give a Readiness and Facility in seeing what all Subjects will afford of Use to Persuasion, which a Mind unused to that way of thinking, will not easily find out.[28]

The book does not contribute much to rhetorical theory, but it does indicate the growth of interest in a rhetoric of persuasion in America. Other works presenting a more complete treatment of the classical theories were soon to follow.

Rollin. Another of the early works which contained discussion of rhetoric was that of Charles Rollin.[29] The first evidence of its use in the colonies is its listing in the 1721 catalogue of the Library Com-

---

[27]*A Grammar of the English Tongue, with the Arts of Logic, Rhetoric, Poetry, etc.*, London, 1712. The notes for this discussion were taken from the 9th edition, London, 1759.

[28]*Ibid.*, p. x.

[29]*The Method of Teaching and Studying the Belles Lettres; or, an Introduction to Languages, Poetry, Rhetoric, History, Moral Philosophy, Physics, etc.*, 4 vols., 5th edition, Edinburgh, 1759. Book the Third, Volume II contains the matter on rhetoric. Rollin's work also provides almost two-thirds of the matter contained in the *anonymous Rhetoric: or the Principles of Oratory Delineated*, London, 1736.

pany of Philadelphia. It was read in 1735 by Samuel Johnson.[30] In 1755 it was offered for sale by Garrat Noel in New York,[31] and by William Bradford in Philadelphia.[32] Bradford also listed the work in his catalogues for 1760 and 1769, although this may indicate failure to sell the copy offered in 1755 rather than new copies. On the other hand, popularity of the work over the whole colonies might indicate new copies.

The work seemed to have some currency in the colleges as well as in private libraries. A copy now in the Harvard library was acquired by them in 1766. The book was listed by Joseph Russell (Brown, 1772) as one of those studied by him in 1771.[33] It seems to have been one of the works consulted by the members of the Harvard Speaking Club during the decade from 1770 to 1780.[34] Rollin's work was listed in the catalogue of the library of Colonel William Byrd, prepared about 1777, and was imported for sale by Henry Knox in Boston in 1773. Thus the book was widely circulated and easily available in public or private libraries.

Rollin, although drawing freely from classical sources, does not present a balanced rhetorical work. His own first precept tells his readers that, "The best way to learn Rhetoric would be to imbibe it at the fountain head, I mean, from Aristotle, Dionysius Halicanarssus, Longinus, Cicero, and Quintilian,"[35] but Rollin's emphasis is quite different from theirs. He uses his classical sources, especially Quintilian, to conclude that the reading of authors is the best way to learn rhetoric.[36] Accordingly, some three hundred pages are devoted to the reading and explaining of the literary works of contemporary writers. Few orators or orations are included.

Fénelon. A French work which was primarily critical in its nature and influenced strongly by Longinus as well as by Aristotle, Cicero,

[30]*Op. cit.,* App.

[31]*Op cit.*

[32]*Books just imported from London, and to be sold by Wm. Bradford, at his shop, adjoining the London Coffee-House in Market Street,* Philadelphia, n. d. The Pennsylvania Historical Society lists the catalogue with works printed in 1755.

[33]Van Hoessen, II. B.: *The Brown University Library,* Providence, 1938, pp. 60-61.

[34]Goodhue, Albert: The Reading of Harvard Students, 1770-1781, as shown by the Records of the Speaking Club, *Essex Institute, Historical Collections,* 1937, p. 124.

[35]*Op. cit.,* II, 2.

[36]*Ibid.,* p. 2.

and Quintilian was that of Francois Fénelon.[37] It was read by Samuel Johnson in 1741, and was in each of the society libraries in Philadelphia by 1765. The work was also listed in the Harvard *Selected Catalogue* in 1773. American editions of the work were published in Boston in 1810.

This writer held the same high concept of the place of rhetoric that was held by Aristotle and Longinus. Such comments as "I should be more pleased with a discourse which has more body in it, and less spirit,"[38] are frequent in the work. It is urged that persuasion should not be approached until one has studied the nature of man—truth; and that one must add to this the study of laws and customs—all of the solid parts of philosophy and politics.

> To make a complete orator then, we must find a philosopher who knows both how to demonstrate any truth; and at the same time, to give accurate reasoning all the natural beauty and vehemence of an agreeable, moving discourse . . . the orator not only convinces your judgment, but commands your passions.[39]

Lawson. Another English work found in the colonies was that of John Lawson.[40] The first record we have of its presence in the colonies is the listing in unknown handwriting on the Yale library catalogue of 1755. The Harvard library charging list shows its withdrawal from that library on two occasions in 1767. The *Lectures* are listed in the *Selected Catalogue* published in 1773 by Harvard College, and are included in the Brown library catalogue in 1782.

The lectures were planned for divinity classes, and were probably delivered at Dublin before their publication. Drawing freely from classical sources, Lawson seems to have absorbed his broad objectives for the work from Aristotle, although most of the examples and details are taken from Cicero and Quintilian. Two chapters[41] are devoted

---

[37]*Dialogues Concerning Eloquence*, trans. William Stevenson, London, 1722.

[38]*Ibid.*, p. 8.

[39]*Ibid.*, p. 64.

[40]*Lectures Concerning Oratory*, Dublin, 1760. There seems to be some question as to the date of the first edition. W. P. Sandford asserts that it is 1752 (*English Theories of Public Address, 1530-1828*, Columbus, 1928). H. F. Harding offers 1758 ("English Rhetorical Theory, 1750-1800," unpublished Ph.D. dissertation, Department of Speech and Drama, Cornell University, 1928). The earliest edition found in this study was a 1758 edition.

[41]Lawson: *op. cit.*, Chapters 3, 4.

to an analysis of the classical works, and students are advised to read the originals.[42]

After some consideration of the history and growth of eloquence, there are two chapters devoted to reasoning, two more to the emotions (in which all of the advice that is given on delivery is presented), and the rest of the book treats of elocution or style. The final chapters deal largely with the eloquence of the pulpit.

Although the book did not have wide circulation in the colonies, it has an interest for us because of two unusual sections. One of these attempts to show that there can be no separate appeal to the mind and to the heart, anticipating some modern psychological dicta.[43] The other especially interesting section anticipates by many scores of years the doctrine of conversational quality made prominent by Professor Winans.[44]

Leland. Also available to the colonists was Thomas Leland's *Dissertation on the Principles of Human Eloquence.*[45] The book was listed in the *Selected Catalogue* of Harvard College in 1773, and was charged from the library more often than any other strictly rhetorical work during the decade from 1760 to 1770.

Leland writes in large part a defense of eloquence, combined with detailed discussions of style. The book, which was written primarily for clerical students, does not contribute much else to rhetorical theory. Frequent citations from Plato, Aristotle, Cicero, Quintilian, and Longinus indicate an acquaintanceship with the best in classical rhetoric, but Leland's emphasis is on style, and he is much concerned with literary criticism. One sentence from Chapter IV of the *Dissertation* gives a clue to the tenor of the work:

---

[42]*Ibid.,* p. 44.

[43]*Ibid.,* pp. 153-154. "The Manner in which both Moralists and Rhetoricans have treated of the Operations of the Mind, hath given Occasion to a great Mistake concerning them. Examine closely into the Opinions generally contained about them, you will find that they are looked upon as several independent Principles, distinct Beings, grafted as it were into the Mind, and acting by their own Force. . . . A very little Application to this Study would teach them, that it is the whole Soul which acts in every Case, that judges, imagines, remembers; that all Mode of Apprehension . . . many of which we distinguish by the names of several faculties, are only actions of the Understanding."

[44]*Ibid.,* pp. 413-430.

[45](London, 1764).

Perfect eloquence is, and must be, the expression of truth; if you would persuade and influence, the language must be that of nature; and whatever persuades and influences is the *Eloquence of Nature* and nothing else.[46]

Only once does he seem to conceive of eloquence as the art of persuasion in its complete sense, so as "to prompt and rouse us to action, the final scope and object of eloquence."[47] For the rest, it is a book in the classical manner, although fundamentally concerned with criticism and with style.

Holmes. A peculiar little book which attempted nothing more than a digest of earlier writings was also circulated in the colonies.[48] The preface of the book tells us that here are the precepts of Isocrates, Aristotle, Cicero, Quintilian, Longinus, Vossius, Ramus, Farnaby, and all of the good moderns! The scheme is to divest the ancients of their "copious parts" and thus to make the rhetoric more suitable to boys, meanwhile including some two hundred and fifty of the best tropes, and more examples taken from the classics and the scriptures than "you'll find in all the rhetoricians put together."[49]

Holmes does just about what he sets out to do, and gives his readers what amounts to an annotated source book of classical rhetorical theory. Quintilian is the primary source used, although almost every rhetorician of any note from Aristotle to Farnaby gets some mention. The simplicity of the presentation and the frequent exercises which should have made teaching from the book a relatively simple task probably contributed to the long popularity of the work in England and America. It was offered for sale in America as early as 1769,[50] and seems to have been used as a text at Yale for some ten years or more after that date.[51] The American edition prepared by Professor

---

[46]*Ibid.,* p. 24.

[47]*Ibid.,* p. 48.

[48]Holmes, John: *The Art of Rhetoric Made Easy,* 3rd ed., London, 1766. The first edition of the work was 1755, and other editions were published in 1786, 1806, and 1849. This last was a Philadelphia edition, and was recommended by the Professor of Rhetoric and Oratory at the University of Pennsylvania. The first American edition seems to have been brought out by Hugh Gaines in New York, 1792.

[49]*Ibid.,* Preface.

[50]By William Bradford, Philadelphia, and in 1773 by Henry Knox in Boston.

[51]See especially Montgomery: *op. cit.,* p. 251; and Schwab, John C.: *The Yale College Curriculum, 1701-1901,* New York, 1901, p. 6.

Gettys in 1849 would seem to indicate continued use until the middle of the nineteenth century.

Priestley. Although only one reference has been found which would indicate that Joseph Priestley's *Lectures on Oratory and Criticism*[52] were studied during the colonial period, the work should probably be mentioned in this study. The work was ordered from England by Brown University in 1783.[53] Priestley presents in thirty-five lectures a complete rhetorical doctrine except for his omission of delivery. Five lectures are given to Recollection or invention, five to Method or disposition, and the remaining twenty-five treat of style. He acknowledges freely his debt to Ward, Kames, and Hartley for ideas and organization, and draws on both Locke and Hume. It seems likely that Harding's evaluation of the influence of the *Lectures* is a fair estimate for America at least—it is "unlikely they attracted much attention or gained any wide adoption."[54]

Monboddo. Brown University in 1783 also ordered Lord Monboddo's *Origin and Progress of Language,* which includes a treatment of rhetoric in the sixth volume. The book contributes nothing more than an effort on the part of Monboddo to present Aristotle's doctrines.[55]

Ward. While appearing earlier than some of those listed above, Ward is reserved for last mention because of his great influence in this period.[56] Called the "most complete statement of classical rhetoric written in the English tongue,"[57] Ward's *System* is considered representative of the classical point of view, and exerted important influence on English rhetorical theory for many years after its publication. It was equally important in America.

It is probable that Ward's *System* was brought to the colonies a very short time after it appeared in England, for "Ward's Oratory" has been added by an unknown penman to the 1755 catalogue of the Yale Col-

---

[52](Dublin, 1781). The first edition was printed in London, 1777, and the lectures were given from 1761 to 1767.

[53]"Catalogue of Books ordered from England for the library of Rhode Island College" [MSS.] in Brown University Archives, 1783.

[54]Harding: *op. cit.,* p. 179.

[55]For a more complete discussion of Monboddo's attachment to Aristotelian beliefs see Harding: *op. cit.,* p. 243.

[56]Ward, John: *A System of Oratory,* London, 1759.

[57]Sandford: *op. cit.,* p. 110.

lege library. Ward is also listed in the Harvard catalogue of 1765. Only two years later, in 1767, Ward was a part of the Yale course of study.[58] Four years later it was an integral part of the studies at Brown.[59] The laws of Brown in 1783 mentioned its use, and the importance which the faculty placed on its study is shown by a letter of President Manning to a prospective student in 1783.[60] Two extra copies were given Harvard in 1771, and the book is included in the *Selected Catalogue* of Harvard in 1773, which would seem to indicate its frequent use there as well. A copy is known to have been in the collection of the Library Company in Philadelphia in 1775.[61] Thus Ward commanded the college field before 1780, and was in some general circulation as well. Only the forthcoming works of Campbell and Blair were to destroy its influence.

Ward's *System* is truly a tremendous synthesis of Greek and Roman rhetorical theory, and one of the largest works devoted to rhetoric ever written. Fifty-four lectures which take up more than eight hundred pages make up the two large volumes. All of the parts of ancient rhetoric are treated, with a relative emphasis not too far from that of Aristotle, Cicero, and Quintilian, save that delivery is given more detailed treatment. Since the work was significant in the development of American rhetoric, and since it has been infrequently examined by students of the period, we shall treat its doctrines in some detail.

After an introduction in Latin, the first lecture treats of the rise and progress of oratory. The second lecture, On the Nature of Oratory, presents many of the general dicta which Ward is to follow. "Oratory is the art of speaking well on any subject, in order to persuade." Quintilian and Cicero are quoted in support of this definition.[62] The business of oratory is to teach one to speak well; that is, justly, methodi-

---

[58]Schwab: *op. cit.*, p. 6. "In the study of English the use of John Ward's *System of Oratory* in 1767 indicates that the students were trained in the use of their mother tongue as a part of their training in argumentation."

[59]Bronson: *op. cit.*, pp. 102-103.

[60]*Ibid.*, pp. 103-104. "If Mr. Wood means to enter the Sophimore Class next Fall I advise him to read with great Attention Cicero and the Greek Testat: and make himself Master of the Grammar of each Language; also to study with great Attention Lowth's English Grammar, and Stirling's, or Turner's Rhetoric, as preparatory to Ward's Oratory."

[61]*The Charter, Laws, and Catalog of Books of the Library Company of Philadelphia,* Philadelphia, 1775.

[62]Ward: *op. cit.*, I, 19.

cally, floridly, and copiously.[63] "The subject of oratory is everything."[64]
"The principal end and design of oratory is to persuade."[65]

The third lecture is on the Division of Oratory, and Ward elim-
inates Memory from the usual five, although it had been treated briefly
in the second lecture. His justification of the inclusion of invention and
disposition gives a clear picture of the shift which has taken place in
English rhetorical thought since the days of Dugard and Smith:

> Indeed some have excluded both invention and disposition from
> the art of oratory, supposing they more properly belong to logic;
> but I think, without any just reason. For as was shown in my last
> discourse, two arts may be conversant about the same subject,
> without interfering, provided they have not the same end, and
> their manner of treating it be likewise different. Thus both logic
> and rhetoric teach us to reason from the same principles. . . . But
> besides these, rhetoric directs us to other considerations, more
> peculiarly adapted to conciliate the mind, and affect the passions,
> with which the other art has no concernment. For logic, contents
> itself with such principles of reasoning, which arising from the
> nature of things, and their relations to each other, may suffice to
> discover truth from falsehood, and satisfy thinking and considerate
> persons. Nor does it propose anything more than assent, upon
> a just view of things fairly represented to the mind. But rhetoric
> not only directs to those arguments, which are proper to convince
> the mind; but also considers the various passions and interests
> of mankind, with the bias they receive from temper, education,
> converse, or other circumstances of life; and teaches how to fetch
> such reasons from each of these, as are of the greatest force in
> persuasion. It is plain therefore that rhetoric not only supplies us
> with more heads in *invention* than logic, but that they very much
> differ from each other in the use and design of them; the one
> employing them only as principles of knowledge, but the other
> chiefly as motives to action.
>
> Nor is their manner of treating them less different, which re-
> spects *disposition*. The logician so places the several propositions
> or a syllogism in a certain prescribed method, that the relation
> between terms may be evident, and the conclusion appear to be

---

[63]*Ibid.*, I, 21.
[64]*Ibid.*, I, 25.
[65]*Ibid.*, I, 27.

fairly drawn from the premises. . . . But the orator is not thus tied down to mode and figure; or to perfect syllogisms, which he seldom uses: but reasons in the manner he thinks most convenient; begins with either of the premises, and sometimes with the conclusion itself. . . . Besides, he considers the frame and structure of his whole discourse and as his view is not everywhere the same, he divides it into certain parts, and so disposes each of them, as may best answer his intention. From all of which it appears, that *disposition*, considered as a part of oratory, is widely different from that, which is taught by logic.[66]

Ward is no less direct in his feeling that Style can never be the end of serious rhetoric. Speaking of Elocution or Style he says:

All acknowledge it belongs to this art, tho many seem to mistake the true nature and extent of it. For nothing is more common, than to suppose that only to be oratory, which is delivered in a florid and pompous style. Whereas *Elocution* comprehends all characters of style, and shows how much each of them is to be applied; and directs as well to choice of words, and propriety of expression, as to the ornaments of tropes and figures. Indeed as the florid and sublime characters more especially relate to the orator's province, who has the greatest occasion for them; the name of *Eloquence* has been more peculiarly appropriated to those characters. But to suppose from hence, that the art of oratory is wholly confined to these, or that the orator acts out of his sphere, when he does not use them, is equally to mistake in both cases.[67]

Throughout Ward is careful to stress the position he takes as to the relative importance of each of the divisions, and he attempts to keep a balance between them that is much the same as that of Cicero and Quintilian.[68]

The next fifteen lectures treat of Invention and Disposition, and to review their content would simple be to review the classical rules in their entirety. Under invention, the commonplaces, the use of external topics, the doctrine of status, and the special topics for demonstrative, deliberative, and judicial oratory are discussed. A lecture is given to

---

[66]*Ibid.,* I, 31-33.
[67]*Ibid.,* I, 34.
[68]*Ibid.;* see especially Lecture XX, in which Ward introduces his reader to the subject of Style.

ethical proof, and another to pathetic. Lectures on disposition treat of the parts of the speech, Ward listing the introduction, narration, proposition, confirmation, confutation, and conclusion. Some time is spent on a consideration of the proper topics to use in each division. Ward follows the precedent set by Quintilian and others in combining his discussion of Invention and Arrangement in this manner throughout the work.

Lectures XX to XLVI are devoted to style. The general qualities of style are first discussed, and as might be suspected from the earlier quotation, purity and perspicuity are considered as most fundamental to elegance. There are some ten lectures on tropes and figures. A lecture is devoted to the low style, another to the middle style, and two to the Sublime. "Longinus" is followed very closely in these lectures on the sublime. After a short discussion of wit and humor, there are four lectures dealing with the style and content of History.

After a summary chapter on the style of the orator, five lectures are devoted to delivery. Voice and gesture are treated in some detail, and the general tenor of the entire treatment is contained in the passage: "What fits well upon one, will appear very awkward in another. Everyone, therefore, should first endeavor to know himself, and manage accordingly."[69] A short discussion of imitation concludes the lectures.

Thus Ward has presented to his readers a careful and systematic digest of classical rhetoric. Unduly repetitious, and probably longer than necessary, the *System* nevertheless presents to America in balanced form an active rhetoric whose medium was oratory, and whose end was moving the minds of men. By 1770 the way was prepared for the great English works to follow.

ENGLISH RHETORICS OF STYLE

The importation and use of the English rhetorics in the classical manner, did not mean that the colonists were no longer interested in the rhetorics of style. Indeed, as more and more interest began to be taken in the belles-lettristic side of rhetoric, rhetorics of style in English became almost as popular and as prevalent as their Latin predecessors.

Blackwell. One of the earliest of these to appear in America

[69] *Ibid.,* II, 376.

was that of Anthony Blackwell.[70] The first record of use in America
which has been found is the inclusion of the work in the catalogue
of readings of Samuel Johnson for 1736.[71] The same catalogue notes
that it was re-read by him in 1740 and again in 1756. The work
was listed in the Yale College library catalogue of 1743, and in 1755
was offered for sale in New York by Garrat Noel, book seller.

The whole work is devoted to tropes and figures as the sub-title
would seem to indicate: *An Essay on the Nature of those Emphatical
and Beautiful Figures which give Strength and Ornament to Writing.*
There is not much that is new in the book, although it is worth noting
that the discussion of figures is drawn from classical rather than from
modern sources. Of special interest however are the appreciation
Blackwell had of the eloquence of his own language[72] in a time when
there was still no agreement as to the value of studying English, and
also the stress placed in the work on the oral aspects of rhetoric.[73]
Although Blackwell confines the province of rhetoric to style, he
advises: "Let your Discourse always be founded on Nature and
Sense, supported with strong Reason and Proof; and then add the
Ornaments and Heightening of *Figures*. . . . Figures must not be
over-adorned, nor affectedly labour'd" lest the orator "betray and
expose himself" as a "Trifler and Hypocryt."[74]

Dodsley. Further evidence that the vogue of the rhetoric of style
was not destroyed by the increase in the use of English, is contributed
by the popularity of the *Rhetoric* taken from *The Preceptor*, by
Robert Dodsley.[75] Next to Ward's *Lectures on Oratory*, Dodsley's
treatment seems to have been the most popular in the colonies during
this period. Again the reading list of Samuel Johnson provides the
first record of the work's use in America. Johnson read *The Preceptor*
in 1749.[76] In 1756 it was recommended at the University of Penn-

---

[70]*Introduction to the Classics,* London, 1718. These notes are from the 6th edition,
1746.
[71]*Op. cit.,* App.
[72]Blackwell: *op. cit.,* pp. 135-136.
[73]*Ibid.,* see especially pp. 59-62.
[74]*Ibid.,* pp. 186-188.
[75](London, 1748). Many later editions of *The Preceptor* were published. The
work was in two volumes, and treated of almost all learning. Of the twelve parts,
one was devoted to rhetoric and poetry, and another to reading, speaking, and
writing letters.
[76]*Op. cit.,* App.

sylvania, along with Longinus, Quintilian, and the orations of Cicero and Demosthenes.[77] *The Preceptor* was offered for sale by William Bradford in Philadelphia in 1755, by Henry Knox in Boston in 1773, and was listed in the catalogue of both the Philadelphia Library Company, and the Associated Library Company of Philadelphia in 1770. Its last record of use is at Harvard College, where in 1786 the *College Records* recorded the action of the Board of overseers, "Voted, that the Rhetoric contained in the Preceptor be printed and introduced into the University as a reciting book."[78] Accordingly, an American edition was published, "for the use of the University in Cambridge." Although there is no record of its having been dropped from the course of study, the adoption of Blair in 1788 would seem to indicate that the influence of Dodsley at Harvard was short-lived.

Dodsley presents virtually an encyclopedia, considering rhetoric as only one of twelve fields, and as a separate field from speaking. Thus his treatment is necessarily brief, and is not only brief, but lifted almost verbatim from other authors.[79]

Stirling. Another evidence of the continuance of the rhetoric of trope and figure in English is the peculiar little *System of Rhetoric* by John Stirling.[80] Offered for sale as early as 1753 in Philadelphia,[81] President Manning's letter to a prospective Brown student referred to earlier, shows that it had some currency in grammar school.[82]

Although the book is only some twenty-five or thirty pages in length, it contains a catalogue of ninety-seven tropes and figures in their Greek and Latin names along with English translations, each simply defined and exemplified. These make up the first part. The

---

[77]Montgomery: *op. cit.*, p. 527.

[78]*Harvard College Records*, III, 261.

[79]The material on rhetoric is lifted from Blackwell with only the most minor of changes.

[80](New York, 1845). The first edition was probably in 1733, there were eight by 1772, and other London editions were published in 1786, 1806, 1817, etc. A New York edition was published in 1824.

[81]By William Bradford.

[82]Bronson: *op. cit.*, p. 103. The other work referred to in Manning's letter, Daniel Turner, *Abstract of English Grammar and Rhetoric*, London, 1739, is also an elementary manual of trope and figure, but does not seem to have been as available in America at this time. Manning's reference to it is the only one found in the preparation of this study.

second part is called *Ars Rhetorica* and is no more nor no less than a Latin rendering of the first.

The author's method and procedure can be seen in his treatment of one of the more common figures:

> Hyperbole soars high, or creeps too low; 6
> Exceeds the truth, things wonderful to show.
> > Examples
> > 6.   He runs swifter than the wind, i.e., very swiftly.
> > > Terms Englished
> > 6.   Excess.

Thus the work presented material compactly arranged for memorization, and its very simplicity probably contributed to its popularity.

Gibbon. Another work making the usual attempt to systematize the tropes and figures is that of Thomas Gibbon.[83] The only record of the use of his *Rhetoric* in America is the order placed in England for it by Brown University in 1783.[84] Gibbon feels that the work improves on both Blackwell and Ward, since examples have been selected largely from the scriptures, and since "Tropes and figures are the beauty, the nerves, the life, the soul of Oratory."[85] The organization and treatment offer nothing new, however, and the contribution made by the work must be considered slight.

WORKS ON ELOCUTION

During this period from 1730 to 1785 the first works devoted solely to the delivery of materials began to appear, both in England and in America. One of the first, that of John Mason,[86] gave to this new art of delivery as a separate discipline, the name of "Elocution," and within a very few years the term came to mean, popularly, delivery rather than style. Other works followed in a very short time, and soon the classical division of *pronuntiatio* became almost a separate field for study and practice, now known as "Elocution." The works on elocution became so numerous in America that they require separate treatment in a projected following article.

Three of these works had circulation in the colonies before 1780.

---

[83]*Rhetoric: or, a view of its principal Tropes and Figures,* London, 1767.
[84]"Catalogue of Books . . . of Rhode Island College."
[85]Gibbon: *op. cit.,* Preface.
[86]*Essay on Elocution,* London, 1748. Later editions were printed in 1751 and 1761.

The earliest, both from the point of view of composition and of importation into America, is the *Art of Speaking in Public*.[87] This work, whose authorship is unknown, was read by Samuel Johnson in 1755.[88] By 1755 Mason's *Essay* was offered for sale in New York,[89] and in 1762 it is known to have been in the Harvard Library.[90] Three years later the famous *Lectures on Elocution* by Thomas Sheridan were in the Harvard library catalogue.[91] These works were the vanguard of a tremendous army of works that were soon to follow.

OTHER WORKS

A number of other works of interest to the rhetorical scholar were available in the colonies at this time, and are included in this section either because they received little notice or because they are scarcely rhetorical in the sense in which the term is used in this study. One work in Latin retained some circulation in this period, although instruction had changed to the vernacular. It was *Rhetores Selecti*, a collection of excerpted rhetorical writings from Demetrius, Phalereus, Tiberius Rhetor, and others.[92] There is no specific evidence that the work was even used as a rhetorical text. The references found to it simply indicate that it was in the Yale library in 1743, and the work was listed in the Harvard *Selected Catalogue* of 1773.

Listed in the catalogue of the Philadelphia Library Company for 1757, and recommended as supplementary reading at the University of Pennsylvania in 1756[93] is the work titled *The Arts of Logick and Rhetoric*, by Dominque Bouhours.[94] Bouhours was more critic than rhetorician,[95] and incorporated that emphasis in this work. Disavowing the Port Royal work as too devoted to showing "how to conceive simple ideas,"[96] Bouhours sets out to discuss the thoughts to use in

---

[87](London, 1727).

[88]*Op. cit.*, App.

[89]By Garrat Noel: *op. cit.*

[90]"Charging List" [MS.], 1762.

[91]Manuscript Catalogue in Harvard Archives.

[92]Ed. Thomas Gale, Oxonii, 1676.

[93]Montgomery: *op. cit.*, p. 527.

[94]Translated by J. Oldmixon, London, 1728.

[95]Oldmixon stresses in his dedication that Bouhours is "the most penetrating of the French critics." Bouhours: *op. cit.*, Dedication, p. ix.

[96]*Ibid.*, p. 2.

rhetoric. He considers their justness, their sublimity, their intelligibility, and relates all of his consideration to the *phrasing* of the thought rather than to the *discovery* of the thought. Thus the work is a manual of style, more philosophical than most of the others of the period, and influenced more directly by Longinus.

One work on voice science was brought to the colonies during this period, that of John Herries.[97] An early correction manual and drill book, it is more complete than Holder's work mentioned earlier, but seems to have attracted little attention, either in England or America. Writers of the time were more concerned with composition or delivery than with vocal theory.

Two other works should be mentioned. During this period the first American rhetoric of which we have record was being produced through the lectures of President Witherspoon of Princeton. This work, later published with Witherspoon's collected writings, and separately under the title of *Lectures on Moral Philosophy and Eloquence,* was largely influenced by the classical authors, although there are significant differences. It deserves more complete treatment than can be afforded here, and in one dealing with American rhetoric only. Suffice it to note here, that it seems to have had no immediate influence save at Princeton, where the lectures were delivered.

The second book is the extremely popular work on taste and composition by Henry Home, Lord Kames, *The Elements of Criticism.*[98] Just a year after publication the three volumes comprising the work were shipped to Harvard College,[99] and copies were soon to be found all through the colonies. The work was used as a text book at Brown as early as 1771,[100] and it was still in use there in 1855.[101]

It is difficult to determine whether or not the work should be treated in this study, for it is more nearly a philosophical treatment of taste and criticism than a systematic rhetoric. There is no direct rhetorical instruction of any kind, and the whole application of the

---

[97]*The Elements of Speech,* London, 1773.

[98]The first edition was printed in London, 1762. Seven editions were published before 1790, and the book was used in England and America through most of the ninteenth century. The first American edition was published in 1796.

[99]Harvard College Papers, 1650-1753 [MSS.], I, 206.

[100]Van Hoessen: *op. cit.,* pp. 60-61.

[101]*Catalogue of Brown University,* 1855.

Elements to persuasion is remote. One is inclined to agree with Goldsmith's evaluation of the work which is quoted by Boswell in his *Life of Johnson,*—"It is easier to write that book than to read it."[102]

Home here endeavors to investigate, systematically, the metaphysical principles of the fine arts, and, discarding all of the accepted rules for literary composition which have been derived from authority, he attempts to arrive inductively at new rules based on human nature. The primary influence of the *Elements* seems to have been in the realm of criticism and such reference as we find to it in the works of later rhetoricians are likely to be in connection with drama or poetry.[103] It must be stated, however, that the work probably did give impetus to literary endeavor and study in America.

ENGLISH RHETORICAL THEORY, 1730-1785

We have already noted the influence of English rhetorics of the period in the colonies. It may be well to consider briefly the major trends in English rhetorical theory during the same span of years.

Harding's survey of English rhetoric has this summary of the period:

> It may be said that the first fifty years of the eighteenth century were marked by a study of classical works (which continued throughout the century) and by the criticism of British oratory; that classical doctrines, as interpreted by Lawson, Ward, Campbell, Priestley, Blair, and Whately, held an important place from 1750 to 1828; and finally, that the elocutionary movement originated and developed during the period from ca. 1760, finding its characteristic exposition in the works of Sheridan, Burgh, Walker, and Austin.[104]

Thus all of the works listed by Harding as especially significant are found to be in America and also of interest here.

It may be concluded that the main trends in English and American rhetoric were essentially the same in this period. The principal difference, as might be expected, is in the priority of these developments in England. It was England that was influencing America.

---

[102]Quoted by S. Austin Allibone: *A Critical Dictionary of English Literature and British and American Authors,* Philadelphia, 1891, I, 872.

[103]Blair refers to Kames, for example, in connection with his disapproval of English Comedy: *Lectures on Rhetoric and Belles Lettres,* Philadelphia, 1858, p. 543.

[104]Harding, H. F.: *op. cit.,* pp. 137-138.

RHETORIC IN THE COLLEGES

Some consideration of the training offered during the period in representative colleges will give added detail to this picture of the development of American rhetoric. We have already noted the use of new and more complete texts in rhetoric. During this period rhetoric became more vital and more complete. As might be expected there is a corresponding sharpening of the college requirements in rhetoric as well, and greater student interest in the rhetorical exercises.

Harvard. We are now able to find more specific requirements concerning rhetorical study and practice at Harvard. The Records of the Harvard Overseers note with increasing frequency concern about the performances of the students. On April 24, 1759, it was voted that there should be a regular public exhibition of oratory on each visiting day.[105] During the following year, the requirement of regular declamation was re-stressed, and a fine of three shillings was levied for all violations.[106] Even this did not seem to solve the problem of the students' speech, for on May 4, 1762, the committee of visitation, having heard the students' performance, decided that they needed more practice "to form them to a graceful elocution."[107] Three years later they were well enough pleased to vote praise to the students for their proficiency in "literature and elocution."[108]

The interest of overseers and students continued, and on May 6, 1766, it was voted "That on Friday and Saturday Mornings each class shall be instructed by a distinct Tutor in Elocution, Composition in English, Rhetoric, and the other parts of the Belles Lettres."[109]

The next significant action was taken on October 1, 1777, when the Committee on Exhibitions filed the following report:

> The Committee of the Overseers having had some Agreeable Specimens in the Chapel of the Students, and their proficiency in Elocution and literature—For the encouragement of the young Gentlemen who gave these specimens, desire the Reverend Pres-

[105]Records of Overseers [MSS.], II, 58.

[106]*Ibid.,* II, 74.

[107]*Ibid.,* II, 123.

[108]*Ibid.,* II, 203.

[109]*Ibid.,* II, 258. Note that the change from Latin to English presaged in an earlier period is now almost complete. Students now are not forbidden the use of English; rather they get a special tutor in it!

ident to signify in such way as he shall think proper the Committees approbation of these laudable attempts and their particular acceptance of those Performances. And their hopes that they and the other students will continue to improve in those literary accomplishments which will render them ornaments to the College and Blessings to their Country—and that they will particularly cultivate the are of speaking which will greatly add to the reputation this seat of learning hath already obtained.[110]

During these same years the Speaking Club was organized to "improve in the Art of Speaking," and its discussions became increasingly political and realistic. The laws of the club show the concept of rhetoric as an active, communicative art, for they forbade speaking in Latin without the express consent of the club president.[111]

Yale. A similar increase in emphasis was taking place at Yale, and changes occurred rapidly enough that a Yale graduate of 1714 would write in 1779, "Oratory was but little known, studied, or famed, to what it is now."[112]

English Declamation was introduced at Yale by President Clap in 1751.[113] Its introduction aroused enough current interest that Benjamin Franklin sent a letter to a trustee on December 24, 1751, stating,

> I am glad that you have introduced English declamation into your college. It will be of great service to the youth, especially if care be taken to form their pronunciation on the best models. . . . It is a matter that hath been too much neglected.[114]

Some idea as to the nature and value of these declamations can be seen by the following comment on the manner in which they were being conducted in 1766:

> Twice a week five or six deliver a Declamation memoriter from

---

[110]Manuscript in the Harvard Archives.

[111]Goodhue: *op. cit.,* p. 108. Earlier reference was made to the Spy Club; see p. 30, Ch. I.

[112]Quoted by Dexter, F. B.: *Biographical Sketches of the Graduates of Yale College with Annals,* New York, 1885, I, 115-6.

[113]Dexter, F. B.: *A Selection from Miscellaneous Historical Papers,* New Haven, 1918, p. 184.

[114]Letter of Benjamin Franklin to the Reverend Jared Eliot, quoted by Dexter: *Biographical Sketches,* II, 275-276.

the oratorical Rostrum; the President makes some observations upon the manner of Delivery and sometimes upon the Subject; and sometimes give some small Laurel to him who best acts the Part of an Orator. These declamations are beforehand supervised by their Tutor, who corrects the Orthography and Punctuation.[115]

Pennsylvania. Rhetoric and Oratory probably held a more prominent place at early Pennsylvania than at any other colonial college with the possible exception of Brown. Provost Smith wrote in the *Pennsylvania Gazette* in 1757, "ever since the first Foundation of the College and Academy in this city, the Improvement of the Youth in *Oratory* and *Correct Speaking,* has always been considered an essential Branch of their Education."[116] As early as 1753 Pennsylvania had a Professor of English and Oratory, one Reverend Ebenezer Kinnersley,[117] and in 1768 he was given two assistants to relieve his heavy schedule of teaching the "art of public speaking."[118] Even after Kinnersley had resigned there was no fading of interest on the part of the trustees, for their minutes on February 2, 1773, record that,

> The College suffers greatly since Mr. Kinnersley left it, for want of a person to teach public speaking, so that the present classes have not those opportunities of learning to declaim and speak which have been of so much use to their predecessors, and have contributed greatly to raise the credit of the Institution.[119]

Further evidence of the interest at the Philadelphia school is seen from this account in the *American Magazine* for October, 1758:

> The *Professor* of *English* and *Oratory* stands by to correct whatever may be amiss, either in their *Speech* or *Gesture.* . . . This attention to public speaking, which is begun here, is continued to

---

[115]Clap, Thomas: *The Annals or History of Yale College,* New Haven, 1766, Appendix on the Present State of the College, p. 82. For a more complete study of the practices at Yale, Harvard, and Dartmouth see Thomas, Ota: The Theory and Practice of Disputation at Yale, Harvard and Dartmouth, from 1750 to 1800, unpublished Ph.D. dissertation, University of Iowa, 1941.

[116]Quoted in Wood, George: *Early History of the University of Pennsylvania,* Philadelphia, 1896, p. 243.

[117]*Ibid.,* p. 33.

[118]*Ibid.,* p. 249.

[119]*Ibid.,* p. 251.

the end, and especially in the philosophy schools, where the youth frequently deliver exercises of their own composition at commencements, examinations, and other public occasions.[120]

Columbia (Kings). Similar interest is shown by the announcement of the opening of Kings College which appeared in the *New York Gazette* or *Weekly Post Boy* for June 3, 1754.

> It is further the Design of the College, to instruct and perfect the Youth in the learned languages, and in the Arts of *Reasoning* exactly, of *writing* correctly, and *speaking* eloquently. . . .

Princeton. The presidency of John Witherspoon from 1768 to 1794 would seem to indicate similar interest there, since his later published lectures on eloquence show great concern with correct and effective speaking.[121]

Brown. Interest here, which culminated in the establishment of the second chair of Rhetoric to be endowed in America, is shown by the college laws. The laws of 1774 made special provisions for declamation and for oratory, and those of 1783 stressed that "the two upper classes shall make use of their own composition."[122]

One of the earliest speaking clubs, the Pronouncing Society, was formed at Brown in 1771 for "mutual improvement in the art of speaking," and at least one early graduate became an instructor in rhetoric and Oratory at the University of Pennsylvania.[123]

RHETORICAL THESES

From the theses which were defended at commencement exercises during the period, comes additional evidence as to the development of a rhetoric of persuasion rather than of display. As early as 1720 there was evidence of a turn away from the rhetoric of trope and figure, as shown by such a thesis as "Rhetoric is the art of discovering and putting forth all things having to do with persuasion." (Harvard,

---

[120]*Ibid.,* Appendix E.
[121]For a complete study of the practice in Columbia, Princeton, and Pennsylvania see Paden, Elaine Pagel: Theory & Practice of Disputation at Princeton, Columbia & the University of Pennsylvania from 1750-1800, unpublished Ph.D. dissertation, University of Iowa, 1943.
[122]Bronson: *op. cit.,* pp. 104-105.
[123]*Ibid.,* p. 120.

1721.) With increasing frequency definitions in the theses began to note delivery and persuasion as well as elegance.

The first thesis to contain an explicit statement of more than two parts or divisions of rhetoric was presented by a Harvard student in 1748, listing the parts as invention, disposition, style, and delivery. During each of the next three years at least one thesis treated of invention, and one of disposition. A Yale thesis of 1758 presents the doctrine of four fields to rhetoric: "To find arguments, to arrange the things found, to adorn the things arranged, to deliver and speak the things adorned; these things comprise the whole art of the orator." Similar, though more cogent, was the Pennsylvania thesis of 1761: "Invention, method, style, and delivery are the parts of Rhetoric." And the Brown thesis repeated almost continuously from 1770 to 1790 stated that, "Rhetoric is the art of making clear, with evidence and persuasive force through words and gestures of the body."

From the theses also come evidences of greater interest in criticism, in delivery, in the belles lettres. Note some representative dicta: "The grand style leads to stupor, not persuasion." (Yale, 1753.) "Elocution is the beautifully measured use in speaking of the countenance, the voice, and gesture." (Yale, 1781.) "Rhetoric differs from oratory as theory differs from practice." (Harvard, 1780.) "In the poetic art, images rightly exceed the truth; but in oratory, propriety and truth are required." (Harvard, 1776.) "The critical art consists not more in noting faults than excellencies." (Brown, 1771.) "True sublimity consists more in ideas than in diction." (Brown, 1773.) "The English orators excel present day speakers of all other nationalities in eloquence, force or reasoning, clarity of thought, and elegance of style." (Yale, 1751.)

Thus, by the end of the period, the rhetorical theses were raising more advanced problems in stylistic criticism, propounding questions in delivery to an increasing extent, and what is most important, they give evidence that rhetoric is conceived in terms of persuasion.

SUMMARY

The period from 1730 to 1785 saw a steady growth in the direct influence of the works of Aristotle, Quintilian, and Cicero—a growth presaged by the popularity of the Port Royal *Rhetoric* at the opening of the period. The interest in trope and figure so prominent in earlier American rhetoric (1635-1730) persisted, but was reinterpreted and enlarged in terms of a rhetoric of persuasion and more adequate classical treatments of style. Frequent references are found to matters of taste and literary criticism, thus allying rhetoric to belles-lettres as well as to persuasion. The period saw the growth of interest in rhetoric as an active art in the colleges. In general, rhetorical theory in America followed the pattern of that in England, although a few decades behind the English trend.

THE BOYLSTON CHAIR OF RHETORIC AND ORATORY

PAUL E. RIED

Denison University

Harvard University has for many years enjoyed an aura of tradition and leadership in the world of education. With certain qualifications, the Boylston Chair of Rhetoric and Oratory at Harvard has had a similar significance as a force in speech education. Everett Lee Hunt, when reviewing the *Copeland Reader,* referred to the Boylston Chair in these terms: "The men who have occupied this Chair, the books they have written, and the educational influence they have wielded have made it easily the most distinguished chair of rhetoric and oratory in America."[1] This evaluation is representative of similar ones made by other speech educators.

To date no concentrated effort has been made to analyze critically the total development of the educational philosophy of the Boylston Chair. Detailed research has been done on only two of the individuals who have occupied the Chair; Horace Rahskopf wrote on John Quincy Adams and Dorothy Anderson on Edward Tyrrel Channing.[2] Too, Warren Guthrie touched on the Boylston Professors, but from an oblique rather than with a direct approach; and scattered comments concerning the Boylston Chair are found in *A History of Speech Education in America* and *A History and Criticism of American Public*

---

[1] Everett L. Hunt: The Copeland Reader, *QJS, XIII*:202, April 1927.

[2] Horace Rahskopf: John Quincy Adams: Speaker and Rhetorician, *QJS, XXXII*: 435, Dec. 1946; Dorothy Anderson: Edward T. Channing's Definition of Rhetoric, *SM, XIV*:81, 1947, and Edward T. Channing's Teaching of Rhetoric, *SM, XVI*:69, 1949.

Address.[3] Donald Goodfellow's article represents the only purely historical study of John Quincy Adams' connection with the Boylston Chair and gives essential information concerning its origin.[4] Yet in research little has been done to clarify the movements and cross currents that have marked the development of the Chair at Harvard. Our purpose in his study is to trace the development of the philosophy of speech education in the Boylston Chair of Rhetoric and Oratory at Harvard University from 1806 to the present.

The Chair was established through the generosity of Nicholas Boylston, a Boston merchant whose family was prominent in Colonial New England. An endowment of 1500 pounds sterling in "lawful money" was paid to Harvard in 1772 for the purpose of a chair of rhetoric and oratory.[5] The original grant plus interest was put to use in 1806, and the rules and directions were drawn up in April of 1804 by a committee for the Corporation and the Board of Overseers. These rules were evidently written for the committee by Eliphalet Pearson, who was then Hancock Professor of Hebrew and other Oriental Languages at Harvard (until 1810 English Grammar and Composition were taught by the professor of Hebrew at Harvard).[6] In 1810, however, the teaching of English Composition became a part of the duties of the Boylston Professor. The rules gave a broad interpretation to the meaning of rhetoric, allowing for both written and oral exercises in English. The rules for lectures and course content were spelled out in terms of the classical canons of rhetoric and oratory. Joseph McKean, the second Boylston Professor, stated that Pearson, when he drew up the rules, based them on John Ward's *System of Oratory*.[7] The philosophy of speech education of the Boylston Chair is not a neat, easy one to trace because the policy governing the philosophy and the methods used by those who held the Chair was characterized by a lack of consistency. This resulted from the fact that, despite the intent of the founder of the Chair and the original

[3] Warren Guthrie: The Development of Rhetorical Theory in America, *SM, XVI*: 98, 1949.

[4] Donald M. Goodfellow: The First Boylston Professor of Rhetoric and Oratory, *New England Quarterly, XIX*:372, Sept. 1946.

[5] Manuscript extract of the will of Nicholas Boylston, Harvard Library.

[6] Manuscript drafts of the "Rules, Directions and Statutes of the Boylston Professorship of Rhetoric and Oratory in Harvard College," Harvard Library.

[7] London, 1759, 2 Vols.

rules laid down for it, the men who occupied the Chair each individually determined policy. It is necessary then to study the development of the Boylston Chair in terms of the men who were responsible
for and administered the duties of the office.

The first Boylston professor, John Quincy Adams, who was serving
at the time in Congress as Senator from Massachusetts, was inaugurated
in June of 1806. When he accepted the position, Adams adhered to
the spirit of the rules set down by the Harvard Overseers. His *Lectures*
to "young sophisters" were an application of classical rhetoric to
modern oratory.[8] As Adams developed his lectures, he called upon
the "giant shadows" of the past—Aristotle, Cicero, and Quintilian.
Adams might well be called the Suarez, the Fénelon, or the Ward of
the United States in that he kept alive and revamped classical rhetoric
for contemporary use. His lectures resemble those of Ward in general
organization and were built around the five classical canons as prescribed in the rules and directions of his office. Rahskopf summarized
the work of Adams when he said, "His [Adams'] *Lectures* though
confused in some matters of detail, were an admirably organized summary of classical rhetoric . . . probably the best such summary ever
made by an American."[9]

After Adams' resignation, the Board of Overseers voted to keep a
"full time" man in residence to administer the duties of the Boylston
professorship. They appointed the Reverend Joseph McKean, who
held the chair from 1809 to 1818. In his lectures McKean followed
the rules of his office even more closely than did Adams.[10] McKean
lectured on almost every individual point covered in the directions for
the professorship. In "Lecture No. 3, The Rise and Progress of
Oratory among the Ancients," his point of view was made especially
clear.

> This rhetoric is one of the subjects of human attention in which
> the moderns have been contented to follow in the steps marked out
> by their illustrious predecessors of Greece and Rome. So judged
> those who prescribed this course of lectures which is on the exact
> plan of the system of Professor Ward, who candidly avows his

---

[8]John Quincy Adams: *Lectures on Rhetoric and Oratory,* Cambridge, 1810.
[9]Horace Rahskopf: John Quincy Adams' Theory and Practice of Public Speaking,
    unpublished Ph.D. dissertation, U. of Iowa, 1935, p. 40.
[10]Manuscript Lectures of Joseph McKean, Harvard Library.

full concurrence with the amiable and eloquent Fenelon, that to combine portions of Aristotle and Longinus with Cicero and Quintilian and to confirm their maxims by references to the purist authors of antiquity, would even now form the best system of oratory.[11]

McKean's lectures were not unique, but were in essence a condensed view of what he considered important from past works dealing with rhetoric. They were perhaps of greatest value for the criticisms which he gave of contemporary British rhetoricians and for his brief commentaries on the oratory of his time. The only American rhetorician to whom he referred was John Quincy Adams. In general, McKean relied on the classics as a source for his lectures and in so doing continued the tradition for which Adams had set the precedent.

Edward Tyrrel Channing was appointed to the Chair in 1819 and remained until 1851. In his *Lectures on Rhetoric and Oratory* Channing made no reference to his predecessors—evidently Adams and McKean had little effect on him.[12] The first half of Channing's lectures was unified by a series of comparisons between classical rhetoric and his own concept of contemporaneous rhetoric. He fulfilled the regulations of the office by basing part of his lectures on classical rhetoric, but he did not adhere to the spirit of the regulations in that he negated by implication the modern application of classical theory. In accord with his background in journalism, Channing defined rhetoric to include written communication. The second half of the lectures dealt with the habits and faculties of the writer. In a sense, he was the forerunner of the present-day advocate of the "communications" course and he gave most of his efforts to the written work of his students. Because of this emphasis on the writing, teachers of elocution were appointed in 1826 to give substantial criticism to the delivery of the students. Jonathan Barbour was among those hired for this purpose. During Channing's tenure in the Chair, the gradual shift of emphasis from the oral to the written word was probably due to a composite of factors: first, New England was moving into the Golden Age of American literature; second, educators were stressing the need for student exercises in written communi-

---

[11]*Ibid.*, Lecture III, 37.
[12]Edward T. Channing: *Lectures on Rhetoric and Oratory*, Boston, 1856.

cation; third, elocution was coming more and more to be synonymous with speech; fourth, Channing was undoubtedly influenced by his work as editor of the *North American Review;* and, finally, Adams had done such a complete job of summarizing classical rhetoric that his work fulfilled that need. Perhaps Channing felt that he could not improve on the treatment which Adams had given to classical rhetoricians and so he could direct his efforts toward other objectives. In short, Channing's own bent and the circumstances of the times worked together to produce the inclusion of both written and oral communication under the general heading of rhetoric.

Precedent was set! When Francis J. Child assumed the duties of the office in 1851, the movement in the Boylston Chair toward written communication and away from oral communication had crystalized. Child was trained in Germany in philology. While in the Chair he taught composition and later published an edition of English and Scottish ballads. He had no enthusiasm for either the art of oratory or the chore of grading themes. "One bitter note in his [Child's] sweet cheeriness was sometimes aroused by the remembrance of the great proportion of his life that had been spent on theme-correction."[13] In 1876 a Chair of English was created for Child, and he became the founder of the school which Kittredge later made famous.

Adams Sherman Hill, a classmate of Charles Eliot, occupied the Chair from 1876 to 1904. He published several books under the title of "rhetoric," with a definition of rhetoric based on grammar. His books were grounded in the assumption that rhetoric was defined as the set of principles behind the skills of writing. In his book, *The Principles of Rhetoric,* Hill included sections on grammatical purity, violations of good use, choice of words, number of words, written narration, exposition, argumentation, and persuasion.[14] He referred twice to Adams' *Lectures*—once in regard to verbosity in narration and, again, to the arrangement of words. Hill was the chief force and guiding power behind the phenomenal growth of the area of English at Harvard. His effectiveness in influencing education is emphasized by the fact that his books are still very much in use. The difference between the philosophies of Hill and Adams was all pervading. Their

---

[13]Samuel E. Morison: *The Development of Harvard University 1869-1929,* Cambridge, 1930, p. 66.

[14]Adams S. Hill: *The Principles of Rhetoric,* New York, 1898, p. 431.

theories of rhetoric differed in definition, subject matter, emphasis, and technique. In 1904 Hill retired and was replaced by one of his assistants, Le Baron Russell Briggs, beloved Dean of Harvard and President of Radcliffe. Briggs continued to administer the Chair in the tradition established in part by Child and completed by Hill.

Charles Townsend Copeland succeeded Briggs as Boylston Professor in 1925. Copeland's trademark, *The Copeland Reader,* was an anthology of prose and poetry which he had read aloud in his classes.[15] Everett Lee Hunt evaluated the *Reader* and Copeland's philosophy when he wrote that "it will have a nation-wide influence in raising the level of courses in interpretative reading and in humanizing the teaching of literature."[16]

The last three men to occupy the Chair have been poets: Robert S. Hillyer (1937-1944), Theodore Spencer (1946-1949), and Archibald MacLeish, the present incumbent, an authority in poetics. During an interview with MacLeish, he indicated that, in his opinion, the function of the Boylston Chair was encompassed in his article, "Why Do We Teach Poetry?" "Poetry" as he saw it, "ought to be taught as a most essential form of human expression. . . . To be ignorant of poetry is to be ignorant therefore of the one means of reaching the world of our experience."[17] When asked about the relationship of classical rhetoric to the Boylston Chair, he stated that his one attempt to teach classical rhetoric in a class in expository writing was "untimely."[18]

Briefly, then, the Boylston Chair has passed through the respective stages of classical rhetoric, philology, English grammar, oral reading, and finally, poetics, all under the guise of "Rhetoric." Classical rhetoric was represented by Adams and McKean; communications by Channing; philology by Child; grammar by Hill and Briggs; oral interpretation by Copeland; and poetics by Hillyer, Spencer, and MacLeish. The spectrum of speech philosophies is represented here in almost all of its varied shades and tints. Emphasis has shifted from speech to writing, invention to grammar and style, classical rhetoric to

---

[15]New York, 1926.
[16]Hunt: *op.* cit., 206.
[17]*The Atlantic Monthly, 197*:48 and 53, March 1956.
[18]Interview with Archibald MacLeish, November, 1958.

modern poetics, and, finally, to the attitude that speech is not a part of rhetoric, or if it is, that it is of secondary importance.

What actually have been the influences of the Boylston Chair on speech education in the United States? The effect of John Quincy Adams on speech education was important but indirect in nature. The direct effect of his rhetoric was negligible. He is quoted largely with emphasis on the effect which his name produced rather than for his contributions to rhetorical theory. Authorities in speech have gone directly to the sources from which Adams drew rather than working from or through his *Lectures*. Indirectly, when the name of Adams and the prestige of Harvard were combined, initial impetus was given to consider speech as a separate academic discipline. "Previously" stated Thomas, "the subject speech had been taught by some tutor who also instructed in numerous other fields and was frequently not specifically prepared for teaching speech. But after Adams began his duties other colleges established similar professorships. From this meagre beginning have sprung the speech departments of the present day."[19] From these beginnings speech education spread into the mid-West via missionaries from Yale and other Eastern schools, however, it seems that the philosophy of Adams and McKean have had little apparent effect. The Boylston Chair as a symbol of rhetoric at Harvard has represented at best a neutral effect rather than a positive aid to the development of speech education. Hunt was correct when he stated that the Boylston Chair of Rhetoric was perhaps the most distinguished and influential chair of rhetoric in America—but the definition of the term rhetoric, as this paper has pointed out, is in need of severe qualification.

---

[19]Ota Thomas: The Teaching of Rhetoric in the United States during the Classical Period of Education, in *A History and Criticism of American Public Address*, ed. W. N. Brigance, New York, 1943, I, 196.

JOHN QUINCY ADAMS:
SPEAKER AND RHETORICIAN*

HORACE G. RAHSKOPF

University of Washington

JOHN QUINCY ADAMS is barely mentioned in our books on the history and criticism of public address. Of the late nineteenth century writers, Sears,[1] Hardwicke,[2] and Mathews[3] do not mention him at all. Of more recent writers, Shaw merely names Adams as an important speaker, but makes no comment on either his speeches or rhetorical theories.[4] Platz refers in passing to one or two phases of Adams' speaking and mentions the excessive verbiage in his *Lectures on Rhetoric and Oratory*.[5] Our sixth President is not among the twenty-nine distinguished speakers in the recently published *History and Criticism of American Public Address;* and, indeed, his work as rhetorician is mentioned only in a footnote.[6] Some of the anthologies,

---

*This paper is in part based on the author's earlier study, "John Quincy Adams' Theory and Practice of Public Speaking," *Archives of Speech,* Vol. I, September 1936.

[1]Lorenzo Sears: *The History of Oratory,* Chicago, 1896.
[2]Henry Hardwicke: *History of Oratory and Orators,* 1896.
[3]William Mathews: *Oratory and Orators,* 12th ed., Chicago, 1896.
[4]Warren Choate Shaw: *History of American Oratory,* Indianapolis, 1928. See pp. 173, 174, 191.
[5]Mabel Platz: *The History of Public Speaking,* 1935. See pp. 219, 241, 254.
[6]*A History and Criticism of American Public Address,* ed. W. N. Brigance, 2 vols., 1943. See Ota Thomas' essay, "The Teaching of Rhetoric in the United States," in Vol. I, especially p. 205 and fn. 2. We find some difficulty understanding why the rhetorics of Witherspoon, Channing, and Porter should be given some lines of comment, while J. Q. Adams' *Lectures on Rhetoric and Oratory* are relegated to a footnote.

such as those compiled by Platz[7] and Brewer,[8] include two or three of Adams' better known demonstrative addresses; but the texts of his most important speeches remain buried in the *Congressional Globe* or in pamphlets long out of print.[9] In the main we must agree with the judgment pronounced by such neglect. The diplomatic and political achievements of John Quincy Adams have all but pushed into oblivion his rhetorical as well as his scientific and literary contributions to American life.

Nevertheless, his speaking on the platform, at the bar, and in the Congress played an important part in the first sixty years of our national life, from the founding of government under the Constitution until his death scarcely more than a dozen years before the Civil War. The texts of his speeches fill hundreds of pages of the records of Congress and many pamphlets. Two of the most important of his biographers have given major emphasis to his speaking,[10] and one of these has characterized him as the "Old Man Eloquent." The second Adams moreover, was a student of rhetoric as well as an orator, a theorist and systematizer as well as a practitioner. In fact he is one of the few speakers of modern times who formulated a systematic rhetorical theory. His career is of some interest to students of public address, not only because of its dramatic qualities and historic values, but especially because it brings forward the problem of the relation between theory and practice in public speaking. To what extent were Adams' theory and practice consistent with or divergent from each other? We propose to review quickly the facts of his speaking career, to summarize his rhetorical theory, and then to lay the principles and practice side by side for comparison.

J. Q. Adams' career as a speaker began at his graduation from Harvard College in 1787. His commencement oration, "The Necessity of Public Faith to the Well-being of the Community," was a bold pronouncement against repudiation of public debts, and because of

---

[7]*Anthology of Public Speeches,* ed. Mabel Platz, 1940.

[8]*World's Best Orations,* ed. D. J. Brewer, St. Louis, 1899.

[9]For a list of these pamphlets and of other works by and about J. Q. Adams, see John W. Cronin and W. Harley Wise: *A Bibliography of John Adams and John Quincy Adams,* Washington, D. C., 1935.

[10]John T. Morse, Jr.: *John Quincy Adams,* 1898; and Bennett Champ Clark: *John Quincy Adams: Old Man Eloquent,* Boston, 1932.

the financial difficulties of the new Federal Government it attracted considerable public interest.[11] During the next twenty years Adams made notable speeches on commenorative occasions, before the United States Supreme Court, and in the Senate of the United States where he represented Massachusetts from 1803 to 1808. His well known "Oration at Plymouth"[12] and most of his arguments at the bar[13] were spoken during this early period. In his Senate career he is remembered chiefly as the New England Federalist who defied party control to support Jefferson's purchase of Louisiana Territory and the embargo on foreign shipping. Some of his speeches on other subjects, however, especially that advocating expulsion of Senator John Smith of Ohio,[14] are more important for the student of speaking.

After 1809 Adams occupied diplomatic and executive positions in the Federal Government almost continuously until he retired from the Presidency in 1829, and his speaking was limited to a few addresses of the demonstrative type. Of these, the "Address at Washington," July 4, 1821, attracted greatest attention because of its scathing criticism of England, even at a time when, as Van Buren said, prejudice against England seemed to be a national sentiment in the United States.[15] Adams, it will be recalled, was Secretary of State, and his remarks were severely criticized in the press and even caused some comment on the part of foreign diplomats.[16]

The final and greatest period of J. Q. Adams' career as a speaker

---

[11]This speech was printed in the *Columbian Magazine, I*:625-628, September 1787. See comments in J. Q. Adams' *Memoirs,* ed. C. F. Adams, Philadelphia, 1874-1877, I, 22; VI, 77; and in his *Writings,* ed. W. C. Ford, New York, 1913, I, 34-36; VII, 319-320.

[12]Delivered December 22, 1802.

[13]The most important cases in which Adams appeared were Head and Armory *vs.* Providence Insurance Co. (1804), Church *vs.* Hubbart (1804), Fletcher *vs.* Peck (1809), Hope Insurance Co. *vs.* Boardman (1809), and United States *vs.* Cinque and others (1841). Summaries of the arguments are in *United States Supreme Court Reports,* 2 Cranch 127, 2 Cranch 187, 6 Cranch 87, 5 Cranch 57, 13 Peters 518, for the respective cases in the order named.

[14]*Annals of Congress,* XVII, 228 ff.

[15]*Autobiography.* Report of the American Historical Association, 1918, Washington, 1920, II, p. 494.

[16]See, for example, the anonymous, "Remarks of Servius Sulphitius on an Address by John Quincy Adams," reprinted from the *Alexandria Gazette* by John Shaw, Jr., Alexandria, 1822; W. J. Spooner's: Review of the Address Delivered by Hon. John Quincy Adams at Washington, on 4th of July, 1821, Boston, 1821.

began in 1831 when he was elected to Congress. There until his death in 1848 he wielded the power of the spoken word in support of nationalism, in opposition to slavery, and in defense of constitutional rights, especially the right of petition. His biographers, John T. Morse and Bennett Champ Clark, have extolled adequately the courage and effectiveness of his efforts during those years.[17] He favored internal improvements, supported Jackson in the French controversy of 1832 to 1836, opposed the Compromise Act of 1833 and the whole doctrine of nullification, warned his countrymen of the impending struggle over slavery, and defeated almost single-handed the attempts of the powerful slavery bloc in the House of Representatives to censure and expel him. His most noteworthy speeches were probably the arguments by which he defeated resolutions of censure in 1837[18] and again in 1842,[19] and his speech "On Indian Hostilities"[20] in 1836 in which he enunciated the doctrine of emancipation under martial law used by Abraham Lincoln in freeing the slaves twenty-seven years later.[21]

During this final period of his life Adams did little campaign speaking; yet some of his addresses, such as those to his constituents at Braintree, Massachusetts, on September 17, 1842,[22] and October 30, 1844,[23] were significant statements of his political views as well as red-hot blasts against his political enemies. The platform and occasional orations of this period, though numerous, have been neglected almost entirely by the biographers and critics. The published versions of most of these speeches are long and verbose, yet they constitute an open book of Adams' political and social philosophy and his intellectual interests. He spoke, for example, on astronomy, education, religion, temperance, the social compact, and the Con-

---

[17]*Op. cit.*

[18]Right of Slaves to Petition. *Appendix to the Congressional Globe,* Twenty-fourth Congress, Second Session, Vol. IV, Part 2, pp. 260-263.

[19]Defense Against Censure. *Ibid.,* Twenty-seventh Congress, Second Session, Vol. XI, pp. 975-983; and *Congressional Globe,* XI, 205-208.

[20]*Appendix to Congressional Globe,* Twenty-fourth Congress, First Session, III, 447-451.

[21]See C. F. Adams' "John Quincy Adams and Emancipation under Martial Law," Massachusetts Historical Society, *Proceedings,* Second Series, XV, 436-478.

[22]Printed in *Niles Register,* LXIII, 135-140, 171-175, 189-191.

[23]*Ibid.,* LXXII, 155-159.

stitution. The most important of these demonstrative addresses were probably "The Jubilee of the Constitution,"[24] "The Social Compact,"[25] and the address at Cincinnati,[26] in addition to the well-known "Oration on Lafayette."[27]

John Quincy Adams cannot be placed in the select company of our greatest speakers, but as Justice Brewer said of him, "his orations and public speeches will be found to stand for a tradition of painstaking, scholastic finish hardly to be found elsewhere in American orations. . . . His speeches are important, historically, because they define political tendencies as a result of which the Whig party took the place of the Federalist."[28]

Near the close of the first period of his career as a speaker and while he was a member of the United States Senate, Adams was appointed Boylston Professor of Rhetoric and Oratory at Harvard University. Between sessions of the Senate from 1806 to 1809 he lectured on rhetoric once each week and presided over the student speaking exercises in Cambridge. His published *Lectures on Rhetoric and Oratory*[29] constitute one of the earliest and most systematic American contributions to the theory of speaking. Adams himself said that he "should never, unless by some special favor of Heaven, accomplish any work of higher elevation or more extensive compass."[30] Edward Everett, who as a student listened to the lectures, said that they "formed an era in the University."[31]

The material which Adams presented was primarily classical both in content and arrangement.[32] He drew his principles of speaking

[24]Delivered before the New York Historical Society on April 30, 1839, the fiftieth anniversary of the inauguration of George Washington as President of the United States.

[25]Delivered before the Franklin lyceum at Providence, Rhode Island, on November 25, 1842.

[26]"An Oration Delivered before the Cincinnati Astronomical Association," November 10, 1843.

[27]Delivered before the Congress of the United States on December 31, 1834.

[28]Brewer: *op. cit.*, I, 64-65.

[29]2 vols., Cambridge, 1810.

[30]*Memoirs*, II, 148.

[31]*Eulogy on the Life and Character of John Quincy Adams*, Boston, 1848.

[32]Rules of the Boylston Professorship required the lecturer to follow a prescribed classical pattern. Adams frequently mentioned this requirement. See the *Lectures on Rhetoric and Oratory*, I, 171, 178, 229, 397; and II, 139, 142; and Adams' *Writings*, III, 123-126; 148-149.

largely from three ancient writers—Aristotle, Cicero, and Quintilian. Of the entire course of 36 lectures, seven were introductory, nine dealt with invention, eight with disposition, ten with style, one with memory and the final lecture with delivery. Adams' theory of invention was based on Aristotle's modes of proof—logical, ethical, and pathetic; and included some of Cicero's ideas on the topics or sources of material, and some of Quintilian's ideas on speech purposes. The concept of disposition or speech organization was in substance a repetition of Cicero's divisions of a speech—exordium, narration, proposition, proof, refutation, and conclusion. The treatment of style was based on Cicero's definition, "the application of proper words and sentences to the materials of invention," and included many precepts which were derived from ancient languages, and which, by Adams' own admission, were inapplicable to spoken English. Most of the remarks on delivery were culled from Quintilian.

Along with this classical foundation, however, the *Lectures on Rhetoric and Oratory* contained some independent developments and showed some influences of the period in which they were given. Adams developed his own ideas about purity of style, figurative language, and pulpit speaking; and based his doctrines of court room speaking on his analysis of American law and judicial procedure. He ignored the work of the English elocutionists, Sheridan, Steele, and Walker; and often disagreed with the English rhetoricians, Lawson, Campbell, and Blair. Moreover, Adams' emphases on deliberative and judicial eloquence and on speaking as an instrument of public service were in harmony with the growing spirit of democracy in America and with the new educational ideals of the time which emphasized preparation for citizenship rather than for the ministry and a few other professions.

After these brief surveys of John Quincy Adams' work as a speaker and of his rhetorical theory, we may ask what relation existed between the theory and practice. Unfortunately we cannot assert that either was primarily influenced by the other. Adams so clearly based his lectures at Harvard on his reading of classical rhetoricians that we cannot say his principles grew directly out of his experience as a speaker. Nor can we assert that Adams deliberately applied to his speaking the principles discussed in his lectures. He may have done so, but there are few, if any, references in any of his speeches or in his *Memoirs* which reveal conscious use of his own rhetorical precepts.

We must recognize that in some respects there is not even a correspondence between Adams' theory and practice of speaking. For example, in congressional debate he showed himself a master of such special methods of refutation as exposing inconsistencies, *reductio ad absurdum,* turning the tables, and analyzing the meaning of terms.[33] Nowhere in his *Lectures on Rhetoric and Oratory* do we find a reference to these methods. Again, we find Adams using chronological, logical, and topical methods of organization in his speeches; but no evidence has yet appeared that he ever theorized about these methods of speech organization. Furthermore, Adams used in his speeches such elements of style as restatement, negation, literary reference, ridicule, invective, and sarcasm. These were not mentioned in the *Lectures.* In fact, Adams discussed "elocution" or style more from the standpoint of the writer than the speaker, and recognized that only a few of his teachings on that subject were applicable to the speaker's task. Again, in some of his more bitter congressional debates, Adams appealed to anger and fear. His rhetorical theory opposed appeal to such emotions. In most of his demonstrative and occasional addresses Adams used appeals to religious sentiments. His rhetoric did not even mention them as means of proof. In Cambridge Adams appears to have been a theorist summarizing classical doctrines; in Congress and on the public platform he was a practical speaker seeking by every legitimate means to achieve his purpose.

Yet in broad outline as well as in the larger part of his detailed principles, Adams' theory and practice of speaking harmonized. As a young lecturer on rhetoric he had assigned to eloquence in a free country the high function of public service. His whole career, especially in the House of Representatives, was a thorough exemplification of that doctrine.

He told his students that moral principle was the "all-surrounding

---

[33]This and all following statements about Adams' speech practice are based on specific analysis of speeches in the writer's earlier study, "John Quincy Adams' Theory and Practice of Public Speaking."

orb" in the make-up of a speaker. In his own speeches his character was probably the greatest source of power, for his courage won respect and his veracity and breadth of knowledge won confidence. To be convinced of this one has but to study the growth of his influence in the United States Senate, or to compare the records of attempts to censure him in the House of Representatives in 1837 and 1842 with the respectful attention and the ovations he received there in his declining years. Adams said that a speaker should have benevolence, modesty, confidence, self-command, and power to overcome obstacles. Benevolence he had, although it was often submerged beneath a cold and crusty surface. Modesty, too, was in his life, although as James Truslow Adams has acknowledged, it was overshadowed by a persistent integrity of self and lack of ability to think in terms of "we."[34] There can be little doubt that Adams' character possessed confidence, self-command, and the power of overcoming obstacles. His biographer, Bennett Champ Clark, has expressed doubt that "any other American then living would have had the ability, the self-abnegation, and the courage to make single handed the long, wearisome, and hazardous fight for the right of petition" which Adams made between 1836 and 1844.[35] He deliberately applied to his speeches his own precept that morals were more important for the orator than intellect or emotion. He said: "The merits of whatever compositions I have given to the world, either as a literary man or a politician, consist in the incessant reference . . . of all . . . argument to the standard of right and wrong."[36] Adams recognized the value of specific devices of ethical proof when he said that a speaker might explain his motives, profess his own virtues, recall his good deeds, disprove charges against himself, and praise his audience or express confidence in them. All of these methods he himself used, with one exception—in argumentative speeches he more often defied and challenged than conciliated or praised. Every fact of John Quincy Adams' career as a speaker indicates utter carelessness of personal and political advantage. He spoke boldly what he thought, and therein lay one of the secrets of his strength.

---

[34]*The Adams Family,* Boston, 1930, pp. 40, 95.
[35]*Op. cit.,* p. 292.
[36]*Writings of John Quincy Adams,* II, 202. See also Adams' *Lectures on Rhetoric and Oratory,* I, 355-357.

In the use of logical proof Adams adhered to his own doctrine that deduction was the most conclusive form of reasoning. The basic logic of most of his argumentative speeches was deduction from principles, either moral, legal, or constitutional. To support these principles he often used the two forms of induction (generalization and analogy) which his rhetorical theory had defined, as well as the two traditional methods of refutation he discussed—denying the facts and denying the conclusion.

For pathetic proof Adams appealed to deeply-rooted emotional attitudes such as honor, friendship, love of home, prosperity, and patriotism. These he had discussed with his students at Harvard. Throughout all his speeches the most frequent appeal was to patriotism.

Again, Adams taught that every word a speaker uttered should be aimed at a clearly defined purpose, which he called "state of the controversy." His own speeches seldom digressed from that principle, although they often involved complex purposes which grew out of complex problems and situations. He summarized for his students the ancient rhetoricians' topics or commonplaces of argument with the remark that they "cannot give but they may assist invention"; and in his own speeches he relied largely for his materials on three of those sources—precedents, documents, and testimony. He repeated the familiar precepts that the beginning of a speech should aim to secure good will toward the speaker, attention to his subject, or sympathy for his cause; and in his own speaking he used all three methods, most often drawing attention to the subject. He taught that a conclusion should "reap the harvest of the seed sown in the introduction," and at the close of his own speeches always returned to the fundamental theme, sometimes by summary or reply to opponents but most often by means of emotional appeal.

Adams' oral style, moreover, as far as it can be judged from the printed records, vindicated his theory. Except in some of the demonstrative speeches of his earlier years, the vocabulary was simple and direct. In demonstrative addresses his sentences often expressed emotion by means of inverted order and periodicity; whereas in lectures, court room arguments, and congressional speeches in which appeal was primarily to the understanding, regular sentence order and loose construction were the rule. The figurative language, except in some early speeches and a very few instances in later speeches, was congruous, appropriate, and effective. The general methods of development (climax, comparison and contrast, and accumulation), which Adams discussed in his *Lectures on Rhetoric and Oratory,* were the basis of his own oral style throughout his career.

In keeping with his rhetorical teaching, Adams always prepared his demonstrative addresses in writing, but seldom if ever wrote any of his forensic or deliberative speeches. These were prepared by careful study of evidence and by years of practice as a debater and of experience in public affairs. In early life our sixth President felt keenly his deficiency as an extempore speaker, and made three rules which reveal something about his manner of speech preparation. He resolved, first, to take part in debate only at its late stages, to make notes of the strongest points advanced by his opponents, and to organize these before attempting to reply; second, to observe how the best speakers overcame the difficulties of extemporization; third, to understand every subject upon which he was to speak.[37] The records of his congressional arguments show that, although he always considered himself lacking in talent for extempore speaking,[38] he nevertheless became a ready and effective debater.

In the matter of delivery, John Quincy Adams' theory was not indicative of his practice. The *Lectures on Rhetoric and Oratory* recommended a slow rate of speech, variety of tone, and sufficient loudness to reach the auditor; they briefly summarized Quintilian's

---

[37]*Memoirs,* I, 332.

[38]*Ibid.,* X, 33-34; XI, 364; XII, 99.

[39]Typical comments on Adams' manner of speaking are to be found in the following sources: John Bigelow: *Retrospections of an Active Life,* 1909, I, 53; William Greene: *Oration on John Quincy Adams,* Cincinnati, 1848, 21; Philip Hone: *Diary,* 1927, I, 392; II, 526; Charles King: *Eulogy of John Quincy Adams,* Elizabethtown, New Jersey, 1848; S. Lane-Pool, *Life of Stratford Canning,* London, 1888, I, 308; W. Plumer: *Memorandum of Proceedings in the United States Senate, 1803-1807,* 1923, pp. 445, 643; Ben Poore: *Reminiscences,* Philadelphia, 1886, I, 294; W. H. Seward: *Life and Public Services of John Quincy Adams,* Auburn, New York, 1849, pp. 219, 286; R. W. Thompson: *Recollections of Sixteen Presidents,* Indianapolis, 1896, pp. 153, 159; Martin Van Buren: *Autobiography,* Washington, 1920, pp. 271, 272; G. Waterston: Letters from Washington, *Writings of John Quincy Adams,* VI, 519-520; J. Wentworth: *Congressional Reminiscences,* Chicago, 1882, pp. 12-13; *Niles Weekly Register,* XXVIII, 19-20; *National Intelligencer,* February 15, 1842; June 11, 1842; December 29, 1842.

precepts on gesture. No instructions were given for training the voice; oral practice was scarcely mentioned. Such evidence as we have from Adams' contemporaries indicates that, though his manner was animated and his articulation distinct, he did not always speak slowly nor with sufficient loudness and that his voice was shrill.[39] His most frequent gesture was a striking together of the hands. His appearance, though dignified, was stiff and awkward. Indeed his demeanor was described by some of his friends as cold and lacking "that nameless charm which . . . leads the soul captive." Nevertheless these limitations must have been overshadowed by his enthusiasm and dignity and by the factual basis of his arguments and his moral courage, for Adams' whole career as occasional speaker and lecturer was a succession of triumphs. In his later years especially he was deluged with requests to speak. The delivery of his more controversial speeches was characterized by unquenchable fire and enthusiasm, and with the passing years he won the highest respect for courage and sincerity.

We have reviewed sketchily some of the leading features of John Quincy Adams' rhetorical theory and career as a speaker; and have pointed out that although his theory and practice differed from each other in some respects they harmonized with each other in the main. To resort now to a popular phrase we might ask, "So what?" In answer, three things: First, Adams contributed to American public speaking an organized summary and adaptation of classical rhetoric which, though overshadowed by the elocutionary tradition, holds a significant place in the history of American speech education. Second, Adams' oratory, contrary to the impression created by some of his early occasional addresses, exemplified an eloquence, not of ornate style and polished delivery, but of information and moral courage dedicated to the public service. His speeches were significant because they opposed the philosophies of states' rights and Jacksonian democracy, defended constitutional rights, and served to bring the slavery issue into focus in national affairs. The "Old Man Eloquent" wrote at least an interesting and instructive chapter, if not a great chapter, in the history of American public speaking.

LECTURES ON RHETORIC AND PUBLIC SPEAKING
BY CHAUNCEY ALLEN GOODRICH

Edited with an INTRODUCTION by JOHN P. HOSHOR

University of Washington

O<small>NE OF THE MOST</small> imposing figures in American rhetoric is Chauncey Allen Goodrich, professor of rhetoric at Yale University from 1817 to 1839. His chief published work, *Select British Eloquence,*[1] is one of the few great monuments of rhetorical criticism.

Although he lectured with great success on public speaking and elocution for at least twenty years at Yale,[2] none of his lectures found their way into print and none have hitherto been known to exist in manuscript.[3] The student of American rhetoric interested in Goodrich has therefore been compelled to derive his theory from his critical remarks in *Selected British Eloquence.*

Recently, however, a considerable number of the Goodrich lectures on rhetoric have been found, in his handwriting, and are here published for the first time.

---

[1]Goodrich, Chauncey Allen: *Select British Eloquence,* New York, 1852.

[2]Woolsey, T. D.: *Address Commemorative of Chauncey Allen Goodrich,* New Haven, 1860, pp. 9-10.

[3]In the Yale University Library there is a small pamphlet entitled "Exercises in Elocution" by Chauncey Allen Goodrich. It consists of rules and exercises for improving in oral reading taken directly, apparently, from the works of Sheridan, Walker, and Rush. The pamphlet was printed at the college, but not published.

The Cornell University Library has a manuscript entitled "Lectures on Rhetoric and Oratory, by Chauncey A. Goodrich." It contains about twenty-five hundred words. An examination of it reveals that it is not in Goodrich's hand, and adds nothing to the lectures here printed. It appears to be a précis of some of these lectures, and was probably written by one of Goodrich's students.

Chauncey Allen Goodrich combined, in his career, the work of speaker, teacher, and writer. He was born in New Haven, Connecticut, of a distinguished New England ancestry, on October 23rd, 1790. He entered Yale College in 1806 and was graduated with honors in 1810. He was immediately chosen Rector of the Hopkins Grammar School, where he remained until 1812, when he became tutor in the college. During his tutorship, which lasted for two years, he studied theology with Dr. Timothy Dwight, and found time also for the preparation of a Greek grammar. After resigning his tutorship, Mr. Goodrich preached for some months as a candidate in several pulpits, and held three calls at one time from leading New England churches. In 1817, he was called to fill the newly created chair of Professor of Rhetoric, which position he filled until 1839, when he resigned to accept the position of Professor of the Pastoral Charge in the Yale Divinity School. This latter position, which occupied his time until his death in 1860, included lecturing on expository preaching and sacred eloquence.[4]

Although comparatively unknown for his theory and teaching of rhetoric, Goodrich has been widely acknowledged as a rhetorical critic and lexicographer. Brigance, in his study of rhetorical research, says:

> I think we should recognize that critics of prose literature and biographies have failed, almost without exception, to understand this distinctive purpose and scope of rhetorical literature. England has produced but four or five rhetorical critics who have not so failed—notably Lecky, Trevelyan, Bryce, and Morley. America, since Chauncey Allen Goodrich wrote in 1852, has produced none to my knowledge.[5]

And Wichelns, in his article, "The Literary Criticism of Oratory," speaking of collections of oratory in general, says:

> With a single exception, the collections of eloquence have no critical significance. The exception is *Select British Eloquence,* by Chauncey Allen Goodrich, who prefaced the works of each of his orators with a sketch partly biographical and partly critical.

---

[4]Kingsley, Wm. L.: *Yale College,* New York, 1879, pp. 47-49.
[5]Brigance, William N.: Whither Research?, *QJS, XIX*:557, 1933.

Comparing Goodrich's work with that of Charles Sears Baldwin, Wichelns adds:

> The criticism of Goodrich . . . at his best . . . reveals a more powerful grasp and a more comprehensive view of his subject as a speaker. Baldwin at times takes the view of the printed page; Goodrich consistently thinks of the speeches he discusses as intended for oral delivery.[6]

Although none of Goodrich's rhetorical lectures were published, we do have good contemporary evidence to support the supposition that they must have been substantial and highly regarded at the time. T. D. Woolsey, president of Yale at the time of Goodrich's death, gives us in his commemorative address a good picture of the scope of the work of this teacher of rhetoric, and also indicates the esteem in which he was held by his contemporaries:

> His routine of duties was something like the following. The Sophomores were instructed by him, through the summer term, in Jamieson's Rhetoric. The Senior Classes were taught out of a text-book in higher Rhetoric and Criticism, and read Compositions before him which were afterwards criticized in private . . . The importance of his instruction to the Seniors meanwhile was increased by the study of Demosthenes on the Crown, as the chef d'oeuvre of ancient eloquence, and by a very interesting course of lectures on English oratory. . . .
>
> The tone and tendency of the teaching of Dr. Goodrich was not so much aesthetical as rhetorical, and this harmonized with the practical end which he had in view. His aim was to form vigorous, effective writers, men who by their eloquence should be able to move and lead their fellow-men. . . .[7]

In the light of these facts, then, why is Goodrich comparatively unknown as a lecturer and writer on rhetoric? The reasons are twofold: first, the fact that during the last thirty years of his life Goodrich was engaged in extremely active editorial duties which, together with his teaching, left him no time to organize and publish his rhetorical lectures; and secondly, the fact that after his death, the

[6]Wichelns, H. A.: The Literary Criticism of Oratory, in *Studies in Rhetoric and Public Speaking*, New York, 1925, p. 205.
[7]Woolsey: *op. cit.*, pp. 9-10.

lectures and notes dealing with rhetoric were kept in the family rather than given to Yale Library, and were subsequently lost—so that until now no one has had the opportunity to examine them.

These two facts require a brief elaboration. From 1828 to 1839, Goodrich edited the *Quarterly Christian Spectator,* a magazine devoted to theological and literary discussion and criticism. Besides editing this publication, he contributed at least fifteen articles to its pages, and was actively engaged in the defense of what at that time was called the "New Haven Theology."[8] In addition to these strenuous editorial duties, Goodrich published numerous pamphlets and articles in the thirty year period from 1830 to 1860.[9] But the work upon which he expended the greatest amount of labor was the revision of the *Dictionary of the English Language,* which had been compiled by his father-in-law, Dr. Noah Webster. In 1828, Goodrich and Dr. Joseph E. Worcester prepared, with the consent and to the satisfaction of Dr. Webster, an abridged edition in octavo of the original quarto in two volumes. Then, in 1846 and 1847, Goodrich undertook the monumental task of revising both editions of the unabridged and abridged dictionaries of Noah Webster; and, in 1856, the University edition of the same work.[10] To the 1847 revision and enlargement he prefixed an admirable memoir of Noah Webster; and to the 1859 revision he added an exhaustive treatise on the principles of pronunciation. The Yale historian, Kingsley, states that "the sound judgment and the exhibition of scholarly culture which he displayed did much to maintain the extensive popularity which Dr. Webster's dictionary has so long enjoyed."[11] And Dexter, in his biography of Goodrich, states that "his work on Webster's Dictionary was largely original, though nominally only editorial."[12] When we add to these labors the *Select British Eloquence,* it is not hard to understand why Goodrich did not find time to organize and publish his rhetorical lectures;

---

[8]For representative examples see the following: Review of Wilson's Lectures on the Evidences of Christianity, *Quarterly Christian Spectator,* II:647, 1830; or Jeremiah Day on The Will, *Quarterly Christian Spectator,* X:175, 1838.

[9]For representative examples see the following: *What Does Dr. Bushnell Mean?* Hartford, 1849, or *Can I Conscientiously Vote For Henry Clay?* New Haven, 1844.

[10]Kingsley: *op. cit.,* p. 50.

[11]*Ibid.,* p. 51.

particularly in view of the fact, as Dexter points out, that the latter part of his life was shadowed by ill health.

When the editor began a search for the rhetorical papers of Goodrich, it was early apparent that practically none were known to exist. Consequently, an attempt to trace them was undertaken. This effort was eventually successful in discovering a miscellaneous collection of his original lectures and notes which had passed down through the family without being identified. The chief credit for tracing the material belongs to the Reverend Chauncey W. Goodrich, of Brunswick, Maine, a grandson of Chauncey Allen Goodrich. This gentleman cooperated with the editor in conducting an exhaustive search for these lectures through the descendants of the Yale rhetorician. The inquiry was brought to a successful conclusion with the discovery by Mrs. Chauncey S. Goodrich, widow of the rhetorician's great-grandson, of a box of miscellaneous lectures, papers, and notes by Chauncey Allen Goodrich, which had been stored away in the attic of her Pasadena, California home, along with numerous other family heirlooms. Mrs. Goodrich, in December, 1941, shipped the entire collection to the Yale University Library, through whose cooperation they were made available to this writer.

From these miscellaneous notes and lectures, sections have been selected dealing with rhetoric and elocution which seem to contain the principal elements of Goodrich's theory.[13] Since none of this material was in an organized or chronological form, and most of it represents original lecture notes with transitions and examples often omitted, or merely suggested, it has been necessary to edit the material slightly. This editing, however, has been limited to the combining of lectures dealing with the same topic, the providing of transitions where their omission makes the sense hard to follow,[14] the addition

---

[12]Dexter, F. B.: *Yale Biographies and Annals* (Sixth Series), p. 332.

[13]Among the Goodrich lectures discovered were included also several brief lectures on "The Nature of Missions" and related theological topics. In addition to omitting these, the selection process also involves the omission of approximately ten pages which are clearly a repetition of some of the included material, and approximately five pages which are so fragmentary or sketchy as to be incomprehensible.

[14]All material added by the editor has been enclosed in brackets. These lectures are all in Goodrich's own handwriting, and occasionally it is impossible to decipher a word. In these cases, the editor has conjectured what the word probably was and enclosed it in brackets.

of explanatory footnotes, and the prefacing of each lecture with title and brief summary.

Except for one section, it is not possible to determine the exact date of these lectures. The section dealing with elocution is headed by the notation, in Goodrich's handwriting: "Divinity School, Yale College 1840." On the other hand, in the lecture on refutation there appears a reference to page 499 of *Select British Eloquence.* Since this reference appears as an integral part of the text, and is apparently not a subsequent addition, we must assume that this part of the lectures was composed after 1852, the publication date of *Select British Eloquence.* In the Yale Library are several pages of assorted notes on Goodrich's lectures taken by various students. These bear dates ranging from 1838 to 1843. It would seem, then, that most of the lectures here presented were written during the period from 1838 to 1860.

Chauncey Allen Goodrich was professor of rhetoric at Yale College from 1817 to 1839; and professor of the pastoral charge thereafter until his death in 1860. Since the lectures and the student notes bear dates falling in both of these periods, it is probable that at least some of these lectures were delivered in Yale College, and that all or most were delivered in the Yale Divinity School.

LECTURES ON RHETORIC AND PUBLIC SPEAKING
CHAUNCEY ALLEN GOODRICH

I. The Nature and Importance of Public Speaking

[These lectures discuss first the function and importance of public speaking in a well-ordered society. The true end of public speaking is to "address just and pertinent remarks on the subject under contemplation." For this purpose "genius is not indispensable; the necessary qualities being simply sound sense, thorough knowledge, good style, clear arrangement, and a certain degree of vivacity."

[Oratory is next considered as an art—the art of adapting means to an end on the immutable principles of human nature. The object of oratory, Goodrich says, is rapidly to impress our own strong emotions on the minds of others. Using Demosthenes as his chief example, he proceeds to discuss seven specific techniques for achieving this object.

[Finally, brief distinctions are drawn between eloquence and poetry; and between a debater and an orator.]

I prefer to use the term Public Speaking rather than oratory, because it expresses exactly what I would now present for your consideration. Oratory is of a high order—it supposes eloquence in the true sense of the term. Rhetoric originally meant public speaking, as its etymology shows. Eloquence—Oratory—the true art of public speaking, is the subject which I am now commending.

All agree that in no country is the power of impressing thought on others through the medium of language so controlling in its influence as here. All our institutions and our government are suspended on the contest of mind going on around us.

Each of you as he comes forward will find that it is chiefly by the tongue and the pen he must win his way to influence and distinction. The conflict of opinion incessantly goes on around us—and from the town meeting to the halls of Congress a thousand theatres of debate are opened for the display of talent in public speaking. Men of strong minds and of sound principles must here support their natural superiority by sharing in the contest, or must leave their own interests and the interest of the public to the weak or ambitious. The bar is a great theatre of argument. The pulpit must continually hold forth the divine truth, or all our interests be sacrificed.

It is highly important, therefore, to form a just conception of the true end of public speaking—and of the most effectual means of attaining that end. Whatever experience can suggest or art confirm or meditation contribute is of the highest importance here. It is not speculative merely, but inwrought into all the habits of the mind, as the spontaneous fountain of all our own practice in addressing others.

The end of public speaking is *not* to be eloquent. I say this because an error on this subject has had great influence in corrupting eloquence —peculiarly in this country, because men are here peculiarly dependent on public speaking. It has produced a tendency to speak for the sake of delivery, of attracting the attention of constituents, of establishing a reputation for eloquence. But this attitude always defeats its object, produces unnatural language, strained sentiments, etc.

The true end is to address just and pertinent remarks on the subject

under contemplation. To this genius is not indispensable—sound sense
and thorough knowledge, with good style and clear arrangement are
sufficient. But one more quality is necessary—a certain degree of
vivacity without which men will not listen. Such was Mr. Pitkin,[1]
Washington, Wm. Lowndes,[2] and Franklin.

Eloquence is now less called for than formerly in public affairs:

1. Because society is differently situated and less dependent on the
power of strong impression in public meeting. (Constitutions in the
larger states—no danger from without—more stable principles of
reasoning in the assemblies.)

2. Because the subjects under discussion do not admit of eloquence
to nearly as great an extent—political economy, community affairs.
It is sufficient to speak in a manner adapted to *attain* the *end* for
which we speak, which is Dr. Blair's definition of eloquence.[3]

Still eloquence is a most commanding quality; it gives Oratory and
Preaching a vital power. Definition: Power of rapidly impressing on
to others the strong emotions which agitate our own mind, with a
view to convince or persuade.

The foundation of eloquence, in the mind of the speaker, is deep
and absorbing emotion. There is no eloquence without this. Give
this to Paley[4] and you change him into Fox—the same simplicity.
Take it from Fox and you make him Paley. Dr. Blair has spoken of
passion but only as essential to the foundation, and not of eloquence
but only of *high* elegance. But he turns off immediately to consider it
as giving force to the powers of memory, judgment, reason, etc. They
are totally different things, though an important truth in respect to
the feeling of the Orator. Observe I do not say that mere feeling is in
itself eloquence; the power of our feelings must be *expressed* in full
vent for transferring our feelings into the hearts of others. But mere
feeling is not sufficient. Place Mirabeau in the British Senate—he
wants the medium of communication. The medium of convincing the

---

[1]Pitkin, Timothy (1766-1847; American stateman, historian, economist; U. S. Congress 1805-1819): *Dictionary of American Biography,* New York, 1930, XIV, 639.

[2]Lowndes, William (1782-1822; Congressman from South Carolina 1810-1822; widely admired as a speaker): *DAB, XI,* 473.

[3]Blair, Hugh: *Lectures on Rhetoric and Belles Lettres,* Philadelphia, 1862, p. 261.

[4]Paley, William (1743-1805; instructor of morals and metaphysics at Cambridge University): *Principles of Moral and Political Philosophy,* New York, 1824.

feelings must be *perfectly* possessive: understanding and conception [must be] strong, just, and true.

But all these may act with effect without producing eloquence. You may read Paley till you feel strongly the wisdom of God in creation. But it is by a *process*. Eloquence is not a process; its impression must be rapid. John Foster,[5] for example, had many elements of great eloquence, but in this case it was a process. Hence analysis is not favorable to eloquence. A highly excited state of feeling produces a mode of transmitting thought as described by Grattan. The flashings of his mind, like those of his eye were felt but could not be followed. Preliminary remark: Eloquence is not a quality of a whole oration, but only of splendid parts like sublimity in poetry.

If I could direct my thought upon expression in the calmer parts of public address, this rapidity is not demanded. But when the subject awakens the feelings, the problem is changed. Now this struggling for rapidity makes highly important certain things which are valuable for other things but peculiarly necessary in the demand for rapidity:

1. There must be a perfect command of language, synonyms, slightest threads of thought, memory ready to suggest a single word which often gives the exact idea. Look out for instances.

2. Metaphors to color and tinge the medium with the same hue with that of the mind.

3. Construction of sentences [must be]direct, simple.

4. Preparation of all facts, arguments etc., to take away impediments. Here is the great art—and it is unobserved by others. So natural that we do not see how it could be otherwise. But [the orator must] make the attempt. Demosthenes here admirable.

5. Utmost brevity consistent with clearness and impression.

    a. Throw away redundent phraseology.

    b. Description and narration are different in fiction and oratory. Some writers of Antiquity have been perfect in these respects, but not adapted to oratory. The reason is that their sole object is to please. In oratory this is subservient to the ultimate end. The mind pants to get over them. Demosthenes' description of Philip is admirable.

    c. Reasoning should be brief.

---

[5]Foster, John (1770-1843; English preacher and writer): *Essay on Decision of Character*, Burlington, 1830.

d. Omit all circumstance and painting not absolutely indispensable. Great forbearance is necessary here. There must be
a severe process of selecting as to the ultimate consideration.
Brougham remarks that the Great Orator shows as much by
what he does not say as by what he does.[6]

Interpose nothing to break the force of the descending blow. Thus
everything should be shaped with reference to a definite end. This
constitutes an art.

Every work of art is a *system,* a combination of various subordinate
parts, which combine to produce one harmonious *whole.* Each distinct
part therefore is nothing in itself—its value is *relative.* Its excellence
is to be estimated by its adaption [sic] to promote the general end.
In the case of a watch, gold is in its proper place, but a wheel, or
spring of gold would but poorly answer the object in view. Now
it is for want of understanding this fundamental principle, that many
persons are unable to discover the eloquence of Demosthenes.

They open his orations and find no profound reflections, no large
and comprehensive principles of general policy which may instruct
mankind, no depth of philosophical remark, very few ornaments of
style, few splendid passages which stand out prominent from the
rest, no wit, no humor. Where then does this perfection lie? We only
see a perfect man of business, dealing out his facts and arguments
with his whole soul totally regardless of everything else but the one
subject before him. And what else should he do? His speech must be
judged of as a *whole,*—any single part is no more a criterion for
judging than the brick of a barn. The difference is [that] according
to the modern taste *immediate effect* is aimed at—the effect of each
part taken by itself; according to Demosthenes the general effect—to
carry his audience with him and gain his cause. Every thing is
sacrificed to this perfect entireness and harmony of the result. You
feel yourself to be embarked on a mighty stream. Every thing is
bearing you towards one great result; all is involved with deep feeling.

Now it is our conception of this result which will control the
structure of the oration. Take the definition—object is rapidly to
impress our own strong emotions on the minds of others. Now in

[6]Brougham, Lord Henry: Dissertation on the Eloquence of the Ancients, in
Speeches of Henry Lord Brougham, Edinburgh, 1838, IV, 445.

doing this, the whole course will be modified by the word rapidly—and depth of feeling.

1. In an oration [the orator] should spring from his feelings on the commanding object at once—only one commanding object in the mind of the hearer can be made interesting.

2. Settling the status controversy, deciding where the whole current of thought and feeling must be directed. Bringing all to bear on this point—all the systems of thought; join issues as to subordinate topics. Necessary from the oneness of the impression aimed at—oneness of feeling to be produced. Take some commanding status.

3. Reducing the considerations to [be] urged down to their ultimate turning points—few. You converse with a friend, and after an hour's discussion find your difference can be stated in three sentences. This sifting, throwing away everything not absolutely essential is the most admirable. To a prolific mind ten thousand thoughts first rise—to sift—to reject. To some men every argument appears of equal value, they must go back to demonstrate the fundamental principle of every truth to be used. Like bringing in the discovery of America on every occasion. The oration is overlooked, the feelings flag, nor force of genius can give life and animation to so great a mass.

This is the secret of that simplicity and almost nakedness which so distinguished Demosthenes—[he was] perpetually endeavoring to escape from minor topics—throw them in to parentheses. Demosthenes' oration for the crown [lasted only] about three hours, [yet in spite of having to relate the] events of twenty years—crushed under the weight of misfortune, his country ruined, all his measures unsuccessful, accused of not respecting the first peace— [he managed] to reply to all the arguments [and employ his own] invective also in three hours—[the length of time] occupied in many of our courts in arguing a question involving not twenty dollars. Strong emotion makes all inferior topics disgusting—hurry forward to great and striking points. This is possible when the topics to be urged are selected and arranged.

4. Preparation of the mind to receive them easily and naturally—shaping their statement so that they shall almost seem to prove themselves. Two kinds of truths, those which carry their own evidence with them. Lord Chatham—very little reasoning or argument, so

arranged as to avoid all obstructions—one sentence grows out of another—one thought prepares the way for another. All seems perfectly without art, and seems hardly to need being proved. *Objections* not formally refuted—but the mind led to a point when as if by accident we have laid the foundation for a complete answer, and then point out the fact—the objection is refuted in its very statement. All this is peculiarly necessary because the progress of passion must not be obstructed, must not cool.

5. In all this the speaker must carry his audience along with him. A mere didactic orator has the stage entirely to himself—the hearer is almost passive. But the audience must be a part in the drama, they must be constantly appealed—we are arguing with them, not merely before them. This makes all the difference in the world and constitutes one of the great defeats in most sermons. But the very idea of moving the mind requires this constant communion of his soul with theirs. Nothing is more preposterous than a train of abstract and metaphysical reasoning and then a vivid and powerful appeal in conclusion. Now in this carrying the audience with you you must feel on a level with them—not fear them—feel you can sway them. [This is] one of the greatest difficulties in parliamentary eloquence— Lawyer better situated. Demosthenes feels his way at every step, never ventures when he is not sure of their following—or even going before him; these accompanying emotions are the support and the life of the orator.

6. Nothing *abstract*—the terms are not clearly understood, depend upon exact meaning being preserved. Like Algebra is must be translated into actual objects.

7. Compact—pressing as possible. Not concise by rejecting any necessary thought, or by any hardness of expressing. [Achieve] this, [rather], from the feeling and rapidity.

Distinction between Eloquence and Poetry.

Poetry "conforms the show of things to the desires of the mind," instead of subjecting the soul to external things or reason. Eloquence conforms the state of things to the reality. To gratify the desires and feeling of the mind by a vivid impression of them is the object of poetry. To impress *literal* truth is the object of Eloquence.

In poetry, then, we depart from strict reality:

1. By its very language, which is commonly rhythmical if not strictly numbers. As Milton says:

> Thoughts that voluntary move
> Harmonious numbers.[7]

2. It represents things, not exactly as they are in themselves, but as they appear to the imagination. In this sense of the term (the true one) imagination is a complex power, passive in union with the association of resemblance or the picturization faculty. Present an object to the sense when under the influence of fear or agitation, and we magnify it and collect around it other ideas which serve to heighten the idea. Thus each feeling sets off its object: joy, in L'Allegro; melancholy, in Il Pensoroso. Beautifully to imagine a thing to sympathize with your feelings is the real meaning of Imagination.

> The flame of the tapes
> Bows toward her and would under her lids peek
> To see the inclosed lights. . . .[8]

A mere facsimile picture, then, is not poetry. The lame reality is left out; the most expressive circumstances are brought forward.

Distinction between a Debater and An Orator. The English distinguish between an Orator and a debater. Promptitude of thought, sagacity in discerning the weak and strong points of our antagonist's cause, dexterity in evading difficulties, quickness in anticipating objections, and sturdiness in refuting them, the power of retort—these are the qualities of a debater.

The adaptation of his matter to the temper of his audience is one of the great arts of a public speaker. Readiness in applying general principles to particular occasions, copiousness and felicity in illustration, earnestness in enforcing, vehemence in refuting, plainness of language without vulgarity and grandeur without bombast are the constituents of the orator. Also in this respect should be mentioned unclouded perspicuity of statement, undisturbed regularity of reasoning, correctness, fertility, and originality of conception.

---

[7]Milton, John: Paradise Lost, in *The Works of John Milton*, New York, 1931, Vol. II, Book III, line 37.

[8]The editor is unable to locate this passage. Presumably it was not written by Milton.

In the application of sound solemn saintly morality to political subjects in a variety of allusions, in richness of imagery, in copiousness and magnificence of diction, and in all those higher graces which invention itself, the highest faculty of the human mind, can bestow on human composition, the eloquence of Mr. Burke never has been nor I believe, ever will be excelled. But he wandered too suddenly and too often from his subject, went beyond the bounds of decorum in his reproaches and of probability in his descriptions, was too regardless of the feelings of his audience, sympathized too little with the prejudices and humors of his hearers, and soared too high and too long above the track of their ordinary conceptions, and hence was an unsuccessful debater.

II. Invention

[These lectures begin by discussing deep emotion as the foundation of eloquence. Goodrich stresses the importance of making emotional appeals through the intellectual powers, thus rejecting the conviction-persuasion dichotomy. The discussion of pathos concludes by stressing the importance of controlling and regulating the emotions in speaking.

[Principles of refutation in public speaking and debate are next discussed by Goodrich. He first deals with the modes of detecting the errors of an adversary; and then takes up the problem of refuting the arguments of an opponent.

[These lectures conclude with an examination of argumentation and the forms of reasoning.]

We shall now dwell for a few moments on the nature of that deep emotion which lays the foundation of eloquence. To secure high eloquence: 1. It must be intense and permanent. If the emotion is considerable, but not intense, we have an animated, not an eloquent speaker. To this a large portion of men aspire. But it is not sufficient that the emotion should be intense; it must be *permanent,* must take full and durable possession of the mind, and for the time being absorb completely all its powers. In some persons feelings burst out quickly into a flame, and soon dies away. Others may seem at first to feel much less, because their feelings are regulated, reduced to a permanent state of existence. The one is like the flame of some light combustible substance, the latter like burning lava. This permanency is connected with a strong sense of the reasons for feeling and great energy of will. It is a deep-seated unconquerable determination of the soul or will, and energy of feeling. Hence, virility of character and feeling are characteristic of eloquence; fancy, flashing, brilliant character and feeling are commonly not. Humor and wit commonly do not connect with eloquence. The serious feelings, sarcasm, irony, and retort, are natural to eloquence.

This deep feeling must spring out of the subject itself. The eloquence is in the man, the subject, the occasion. Here lies the error of many. A speaker may have very deep emotions when he arises to speak, but they may spring chiefly from some other source. For instance, he may have a deep sense of the magnitude of the question to be decided, and of the *interests* dependent on the appeal he is about to make. 2. He may have strong sympathies with the individuals for whom he speaks, or the situation of those whom he addresses. 3. There may be the excitement created by the presence of a great assmbly or the sublimity of the scene. 4. He may glow with the desire to please— to appear eloquent; and under the influence of this desire may do so. The feeling almost gives him life to speak with the power of a true orator. But if this is all, he must fail. If the subject is not one which developed on the true relations adapted to produce deep emotion, if his own emotion is not owing to such a development of the subject before his own mind, he must fail. He must be absorbed in his subject to carry his field. Here great self-denial is requisite; perfect forgetfulness of self.

Here, then, we have the answer to a question which is often put: is this deep emotion from which eloquence must spring, capable of being cultivated, and what are the means? The reply must be: There is great original difference among men in warmth of feeling; and a man who is constitutionally cold cannot be eloquent. But we see that a vast number of men even in the common walks of life do occasionally express themselves with great power on particular subjects which deeply interest their feelings. Emotion, thus, is suppressed.

The two great means of cultivating this fundamental quality: (a). Not to repress it in early life. (Nations differ. e.g., the Scotch and Irish; New England is too much repressed, some folly may be allowed. But we should not be ashamed to carry out warm feeling.

In College we are too much repressed for fear of making a mistake.)
(b). Second Means. So far as this part of the subject is concerned,
we must fill our minds with the subject; become perfectly familiar
with it in all its parts and remoter bearings, so that in speaking we
shall seem to have been elevated to a height and to come down upon
as perfectly at our command, not to be continually starting upward
in the endeavor to grasp it in its true greatness. The effect of this
perfect familiarity is to dilate the subject in the mind which contemplates, and then if it has any sense of the sublime, any feelings
of enthusiasm, they will be called forth—vivid images and bold turns
will result. This deep interest in the subject is the great correction of
vanity, or imitation, or the desire to please. It produces what the
French call the *abandon de soi meme,* the forgetfulness of self, which
is so essential to true eloquence. It gives indubitable evidence of deep
sincerity and creates that native air which characterizes all great
speakers. Let me repeat, then, the deep emotion from which eloquence
springs in a given case, must be the honest emotion created by the
subject itself. You must have full feeling in your cause and principles.
Exaggeration here is good.

Must this feeling be really founded in truth, must the cause of the
speaker be always a *just* one in order to admit of eloquence? In deciding this question we must consider, that it is chiefly through
sympathy that we share in the strong emotions of the speaker. Nor if
his cause is most obviously bad, if the facts most clearly and plainly
are against him, and our hearts tell him he has no right to feel as he
does, however strongly he may feel, we cannot sympathize with him.
It would be doing violence to our understanding; we would despise
ourselves for doing it. He has deep feeling but not the power of
transferring it into our minds because it revolts our understanding.
So you will occasionally see persons of a very peculiar temperament,
who have deep feelings, in which others cannot share, joys and
sorrows which do not seem to the rest of the world to be at all
connected with the reality of things. Strong expressions of feeling in
such cases seem to us more like raving than eloquence. It would
be eloquence if it were not all fanciful and false.

There are cases then in which we cannot sympathize; but when
the cause is good, when the feelings are perfectly conformative to

the truth of things, the sympathy if the speaker feels strongly is more likely to be awakened. Still it is not necessary to eloquence to be called forth by *exact truth*. Most subjects admit of evidence on both sides. Now there must always be *probability* in the ground taken by the speaker before we can call the strong language in which he express his feeling eloquence. We must say, *if* the premises are so, if the facts are as he conceives, he is justified in his feeling—and we feel with him. His emotions are all true to nature, if the state of the case is as he conceives. And, during the delivery of an able speech, we naturally surrender ourselves to the speaker's train of thought; we admit his premises and sympathize with him in his feeling—when cool reflection may afterwards convince us that he is wrong. Do we then in reading the speech say, it is not eloquent, etc.? At least, not generally. There is so much plausibility in the ground taken by the speaker, that we admit it was natural to sympathize with him in the view presented. This may explain why the same speech to different persons of equal and great ability, may seem very different as an exhibition of eloquence. One sees clearly from the first that the whole is grounded in error—he calls it rant. Another agrees in the principles and therefore sympathizes in the feeling.

Here, then, we see how confidence in the speaker's judgment, a character for probity, prepares for the impression. Demosthenes says truly: "Man's eloquence depends on the manner in which the audience regards him."

Moral character of the deep emotion. Quintilian says none but a virtuous man can be an orator. On his principles none but virtuous sentiments lay the foundation of eloquence in the speaker; and none but virtuous emotions can rouse the soul to true eloquence. Now even in our praise of virtue we must not violate truth. A man's character may be bad, and yet his cause a good one, so that we can justly feel with him in the strong emotions which he feels. By virtue in the proper sense of the term we mean a governing principle of supreme love to our maker, and an impartial love to our fellow beings. Virtue is certainly not *necessary* to eloquence—though it is favorable to its most perfect exercise. On the other hand eloquence can never be founded on a positively bad feeling. We cannot sympathize with pure selfishness, arraying itself without disguise against the interests of society. The strongest exhibition of malignity, revenge, or envy would only shock the soul—we should not call it eloquence but the raving of manic passion. In poetry we dwell on such exhibitions of passion with a kind of horror and delight, firm in our love of strong excitement, because we know it to be fiction. But the moment we bring such feelings into the region of truth we contemplate them with disgust. Eloquence, then, may spring from the strong, generous natural sensibilities which are not in themselves virtue in the true acceptation of the word, and which often exists in every high degree in men whose lives are far from the strictness of real virtue. Mr. Fox, for instance, had a deep sense of the baseness of injustice and oppression, warm sympathy with the unfortunate, indignant contempt of everything mean, great love of frank, open, manly conduct, magnanimity, generosity, love of freedom.

Now when this feeling dictates severity, then there must be seen to be good reason. Anger is a justifiable feeling when directed against crime. Resentment, contempt, sarcasm, irony, are not inconsistent with virtuous feeling, and when they exist it adds to the impression.

Such, then, are the general views which I would offer respecting the nature of that deep emotion which in the breast of the speaker is the foundation of his eloquence—strong and permanent, awakened by the subject, heightened by virtue, operating through sympathy.

We now turn to the connection between eloquence and the intellectual powers as the instrument of impressing our own emotions on the minds of others. It is obvious that however deep and just our own feeling may be, it is only by presenting thought to the minds of others that we can transfer our emotions into their breasts. Now in doing this different speakers rely on different parts of our intellectual powers for success:

1. Imagination. (The word is very indefinite; it involves the association of resemblance.) Many rely greatly on the power of painting a scene strongly to the eye: Curran[9] in his picture of Orr in prison, Rowan[10] with uncovered head soliciting charity for his

---

[9]Curran, John Philpot (1750-1817; Irish orator and lawyer): see his speech in behalf of Peter Pinnerty, in Goodrich, Chauncey Allen: *Select British Eloquence,* New York, 1870, p. 810.

[10]See Curran's speech in behalf of Rowan, in Goodrich, *op. cit.,* p. 804.

starving countrymen; Wirt[11] in his picture of Burr and Blinchefelt, the enchanted island, etc. Brief pictures are very effective but the principal reliance cannot be placed here. The impression dies away with the scene.

2. The sense of sublimity. (Rational and Moral.) This feeling belongs to highly gifted minds whose conceptions, by enlisting the subject almost instantly, dilate in sublime associations and relations The most striking instance perhaps in any age and country is the late Robert Hall.[12] In him it became almost oppression. We do not so much sympathize with him as stand in breathless astonishment at the grandeur of his conceptions. Sir James McIntosh[13] had this quality in a less degree, and it gave admirable power to his eloquence (moral sublimity).

3. Pathos. The power of awakening the gentler feelings, and melting the audience into tears. Many think this the highest triumph of the orator, but it may sometimes be done with but little permanent impression. A clergyman who could paint with wonderful power, said, "I must change my style of preaching." Pathos owes much of its power to our estimate of the man.

4. A powerful understanding appealing to the sense of truth is the chief instrument to be relied on. The rest should all be subsidiary to this. It is then to the understanding of men that eloquence should be chiefly addressed. (Readiness in applying general principles to particular occasions.) But not as Dr. Blair has said, first set aside a part to convince and then to persuade. But address their understanding through their passion. When satisfaction, entire surrender to sympathy, permanence of impression is achieved in all the highest efforts of genius—in drama, poetry, and even painting—it is not fancy but truth in the hearts of men which has been addressed. Those who terrify, persuade, soften, and impel by charming the judgment while appealing to the natural sensibilities are the most eloquent men. It

[11]Wirt, William (1772-1834; attorney-general of the U. S.): *Life of Patrick Henry,* New York, 1831.

[12]Hall, Robert (1754-1831; famous English preacher; Lord Brougham remarked of him: "In the eloquence of the pulpit, Robert Hall comes nearer to Massillon than either Cicero or Aeschines to Demosthenes."): Allibone, S. Austin: *A Critical Dictionary of English Literature,* Philadelphia, 1874, I, 644.

[13]McIntosh, Sir James (1765-1832; English orator, member of Parliament, and lecturer): *Dissertation on the Progress of Ethical Philosophy,* London, 1829.

has ever been and ever will be true, that those who have exercised the greatest mastery over the passions of others are those who have most satisfied the reason. It was so with Homer, Sophocles, Demosthenes. The startling truth conveyed in some of the greatest bursts of eloquence constitutes the great secret of their power. "I know," said Mirabeau, at a moment when from being the idol of the people, he had suddenly become the object of denunciations which threatened his life that very day. "I know that there is but one step from the Capital to the Rock." "What matters it," said Demosthenes, "whether Philip be alive or dead. When heaven shall have delivered you from him you yourselves will be another Philip." It is this striking condensation of *truth* in such passages, which constitutes the sublime eloquence.

Refutation. This may be introduced either in a speech on the subject—or in a reply. Of the former only observe that the nature of the case must decide whether to dwell much here. If there are supposed to be strong arguments against your cause, you must in that case meet them, or you will be considered as unable. All your arguments will be listened to with distrust. It may, therefore, in such a case be advisable to bring forward one principal objection and answer it early. But if it can be avoided, the best way is after opening the subject, to take a brief notice of what may be objected; give some pointed answer, and then promise to consider them at the close. Having thus gained the confidence of the hearers, state your arguments in all their force, and then refute towards the conclusion with the advantage just gained.

Mode of detecting the errors of an adversary—if not formal may be implied.

1. Watch his definitions with great care.

2. Watch for ambiguity in the use of terms or phrases. A large part of metaphysical and philosophical controversy arise from the ambiguity of language, and your antagonist's argument may be all founded on this. The word *motive,* sometimes object of desire, or a desire itself. *Labor* sometimes the *act* of laboring, sometimes the result. McCulloch[14] considers the growth of a tree, and the improve-

---

[14]McCulloch, John (M.D., 1773-1835; Scotch physician and geologist): *Remarks on the Art of Making Wine,* London, 1816.

ment of wine by age, as labor. The phrase, *own* happiness, gave rise to a controversy: Sometimes it means simply what belongs to any one, and sometimes what belongs to one person in *opposition* to others.

3. Watch whether he is consistent with himself in the use of his own leading terms on which the argument rests. Nothing more common than for an able speaker to use a term in very different senses in different parts of his argument. Thus he may begin to use it in the same sense with yourself, and then when laboring to establish some point in the progress of the argument, may artfully or ignorantly take it in another sense, draw a just conclusion from it when used in that sense, and then apply it for a thing proved to original statement, when the meaning is different, and when of course, the principle does not hold.

4. Watch for inconsistent statements or principles in different parts of his argument. Powerful minds are very apt to err here especially on philosophical subjects. A divine for example is bent upon establishing our entire dependence on God. In doing this he is often led to lay propositions which properly and naturally understood trench on the fact of man's perfect freedom and moral accountability. And then in a different view on the subject, he states this latter truth perhaps so strongly as in fact to set aside the other.

5. Look closely at his proposition. See whether it does not fairly involve more than he thinks.

6. Watch to see whether he does not artfully or perhaps ignorantly beg the question, *i.e.,* take for granted somewhere in carrying out his reasoning (proving his premises); the very point to be proved. This commonly done by *assuming* some principle which rests on the thing. Hume[15] argument against miracles. We have experiences that individuals falsify—but have no experience of a miracle. The laws of nature do not change. Hence no evidence can prove a miracle. But whose experience proves that the laws of nature never change? All minds? Certainly not; the apostles say their was different. They testify to this fact at the stake. If he does not mean this he would mean that nothing contrary to each individual's experience could be believed. King of . . .[16] never saw ice, therefore rationally concluded

---

[15]Hume, David (1711-1776; English philosopher, historian, and political economist): *An Enquiry Concerning Human Understanding,* London, 1777.

[16]King of . . . ?, this name is unreadable on the lecture notes.

to reject all testimony. We never have experienced dying though [that is] no proof that we shall never die. This would be too pointless, and of course he did beg the question. Reasoning in a circle is of this nature, no more obvious.

7. See whether he does not take up false theories or hypotheses which are not capable of proof. For some centuries it was assumed that the Hebrew text of the Bible was immaculate—that the Masonites had a mode of procuring accuracy which could not fail. The hypotheses that if the balance of trade is against a country, the trade is bad.

8. See whether the maxims on which he founds his reasoning are not erroneous. They may be false, and only supported by the authority of names; they may be selfish and unworthy of a generous mind.

9. Examine whether his argument does not prove too much. By this we mean if it proves what he says it must likewise prove other things of which he is not aware and does not admit. Therefore proves nothing.

10. See whether he does not add something to the case and mistake incidentals for essentials. Mr. Webster on the question of metallic currency.

11. See whether his argument does not really prove something different from what he thinks.

12. Watch for mistakes as to the true cause of a given result— noncomitancy for cause—

13. Scrutinize all his statements of facts; see whether if there is not falsehood there is not a suppressed vice.

14. Arguing from one order of things to another.

15. Hasty generalization.

Reply when Attacked. 1. Distinguish in your mind between apology and defense. Never if possible place yourself in the attitude of excusing yourself, of apologizing for your conduct or principles, but assume the high ground of conscious integrity and reason.

2. Endeavor immediately to put your antagonist in the wrong; seize hold of something in his spirit, mode of discussing, attempting to shift the ground, mistake as to facts, wandering from the subject, mistaking incidentals for essentials—show what has been artfully brought in to blind the judgment, detect some sophistry, [protest]

against such attempts to mislead the audience, do it with a sense of injury as done to them and you, detect motives, show how different from what professed.

3. May now be useful to restate the question on the ground you took, with some one clear short decisive argument to support your ground, and then compare it with the representation of your opponent, showing beyond all question that he either misrepresents you intentionally or ignorantly misunderstands your meaning.

4. It is often an excellent effect in reply first to take your antagonist on his own ground, and show that his conclusions do not follow, and then show that his premises themselves are false. Mr. Binney[17] on the deposit. One reason for removing them is that the Bank has sought political power. Admit this, but show it has failed. The letter of the secretary shows it. What then is the character of the act of removal? Is it punitive or vindictive? Plainly vindictive. And is this a motive on which a government should act? But the Bank has not sought political power. Her publications went only to defend herself.

5. Show not only that your antagonist has blundered in answering either as to act or argument, but show how he came to do so by overlooking this distinction, or by confounding these terms, by a total misconception of the case or of your statements, though you had clearly defined your meaning.

6. In stating his objections, it is policy to state them strongly, especially if you have a decisive answer. Mr. Fox was remarkable for stating the argument of antagonists with a force and clearness which his opponent could not himself reach and then seizing on some principle which shows its fallacy, and then tearing it to pieces.

7. It has an excellent effect when you have triumphantly answered your antagonist on any point to bring forward some sweeping condemnation which he has passed upon you, some contemptuous expression, and close that part of the subject with a brief comment. Fox, British Eloquence, 499.[18]

8. It was a maxim of a great parliamentary orator. Answer ridicule or taunt seriously. Show that it was misplaced by alluding

---

[17]Binney, Horace (1780-1875; Philadelphia lawyer and director of the first United States Bank: *DAB, II,* 281-282.

[18]Goodrich: *op. cit.,* p. 499.

to the magnitude of the subject, make it recoil. Mr. Webster answered Mr. Hayne kindly when asked why he had turned from Mr. Benton to him. (Mr. Hayne.) Was the gentleman afraid of finding himself overmatched by the gentleman from Missouri?

"Matches and overmatches, Sir, the gentleman seems to forget where and what we are. This, sir, is a senate of equals, men of individual honor and personal character and of absolute independence. This is a hall of mutual discussion and not an arena of gladiators. I offer myself as a match to no man. I throw the challenge of [debate] at no man's feet. But I tell the gentleman that holding myself to be the humblest of the members here, I see nothing on the arm of his friend from Missouri either alone or when aided by the arm of *his* friend from S. C. that need deter even me from espousing any opinion I may choose to espouse, from debating whenever I choose to debate, from speaking whatever I may see fit to say on the floor of the Senate."

9. So on the other hand when the argument of your antagonist is strained, then answer it with ridicule, carry it out, but as a general fact and seriously as more becoming your character and the respect due the assembly.

10. Always round off each part, show that you have answered this fairly close each part by bringing the mind clearly back to question. Some leave it obscure.

11. Wrestling arguments or allusions out of your opponent's hand. Mr. Wirt, Mr. Webster.

12. It adds much to the severity of a reply or attack to compare the conduct or principles of someone who has acted under the same circumstances should here he come to different conclusions and then turn to the conclusions or conduct of the man whom we condemn.

Spoke at the last meeting of the principal means of enforcing truth upon the mind.

1. Direct appeals to common sense which carry their evidence in their very statement.

2. Arguments or proof by which we establish our conclusions.

In the first case the evidence is intuitive; in the other we introduce intermediate truths which lead forward the mind from intuitive knowledge to the position which we wish to establish. Shall now attend to the latter. Useful in respect to debate, in societies and in future life.

In every such case, we suppose your opinion to be formed, your ground to be taken. The process by which you thus reach a conclusion is one of great interest, and will be considered hereafter. The art of investigation—of analyzing a subject and ascertaining what is true— is the highest value to every one who writes or speaks. But as it depends to a great extent on some of the modes of reasoning now to be considered, I shall reserve it for future examination.

In collecting arguments, the first thing to be done is to state with great distinctness to your own mind the point to be proved. In doing this reduce your views to a proposition or verbal statement. Adopt the same course under each head or branch of the proof. This will guard you against the error of [treating] on a *term,* or general subject, instead of providing the proposition. Thus a man treats of the love of country, and the term would involve great numbers of distinct compositions; e.g., that it springs from a certain source—that it is cherished by such and such principles and modes of development— that it is productive of such and such beneficial results. Thus an essay or popular oration, is made up of numerous propositions, some of which are too obvious to need proof, while others become the object of argument. But in every process of reasoning, whether it relates to the main point or those of a subordinate character, it is highly important to state to yourselves the proposition of doing this.

1. State it in different forms.

2. Examine each [of] the terms to detect any ambiguity or source of mistake.

3. State negatively what it does not include, rejecting those things which may seem to be true which may seem to be inclined under it. Thus you avoid a fruitful source of error.

4. Be careful not to cover more ground than your cause demands; evils; 1. You may overload the subject. 2. May introduce what is unnecessary and what may give rise to objection or doubt from the addition. 3. May leave an opportunity to your antagonist to attack you on this excess in your statement.

Kinds of Arguments. These may be considered either as related to their subject matter or the form in which they are made to bear on the mind of the hearer. As my object is not to be strictly logical in this statement, but to lay it before you in various light I shall dwell on both these, though at the expense of repetition.

I. Reasoning from cause to effect. This kind of reasoning may be used to great effect in showing the results of proposed measures in many cases. Particularly in showing that a certain cause accounts for a given result, and that the result arose from that cause. Considerations of great moment here.

1. It must be a real cause and not a mere antecedent. Prolific sources of error: to confound a mere sign (δημετον) [sic] with a cause. The existence of ice is a certain sign the mercury is below 30 degrees of Fahrenheit, but ice is not the cause of the descent of the mercury. The sinking of the mercury in the barometer is a very common sign of rain, but not the cause of it. The error of mistaking the necessary conditions or attendant of a thing for a cause is illustrated by Burke, Works 1.97.[19] If a man killed another it is a necessary condition that he should have been alive and able to do it, but not the cause of it. This confusion is very common when a thing is a necessary condition of the result. Define necessary condition sine qua non. Locke[20] in respect to space supposes the cause of this idea to lie in matter, the idea to be from sensation. So time or duration [results] from a succession [of sensations]. Thus the condition or occasion of a thing may be mistaken for its cause. Ambiguity of language adds to the difficulty. The word *reason* covers both.

2. It must be fully adequate to produce the effect.

3. That no impediments intervene to defeat the operations of the assigned cause, or change the nature of the influence.

Reasoning from causes takes place as mentioned above:

1. When we wish to predict what the natural or necessary results or effects of a proposed measure [will be].

2. When we wish to settle the source or origin of a human event. For example, an act of murder. We point out a sufficient cause is the malice of a particular individual, motive of self-interest added— exclude all other causes as far as possible.

This argument from causes may be absolute demonstration. Only one cause can be possible and that may be necessary and irresistible.

---

[19]Burke, Edmund: A Philosophical Enquiry into the Origin of our Ideas of the Sublime and Beautiful, in *The Works of The Right Honourable Edmund Burke,* London, 1826, I, 97.

[20]Locke, John (1632-1704; English philosopher): *An Essay Concerning Humane Understanding,* London, 1690.

In other cases it may afford slighter degrees of evidence, so the argument becomes merely probability, plausible, of the least possible value.

The sources of error are: 1. May be more causes than one—combined operation different from what is imagined. 2. Opposing causes may obstruct the natural operation of the cause assigned.

II. *Tendency.* This belongs to the first head and I mentioned it separately from the manner in which it is urged. It takes a given measure and considers it as a cause. It then argues in favor or against it by tracing out its tendency on the general principle of causation.

1. May be counteracting tendencies in the measure itself.

2. May be counteracting tendencies in the existing state of things which prevent the result.

III. From effect to cause. Here we reverse the process, take a given state of things, and endeavor to decide that they have sprung from a given cause. Difficulties here like those above:

1. Mistakes of causa pro causa—a mere antecedent for cause.

2. Perverting influence of what is really a cause.

IV. Argument from the nature of the case or of the thing in question. By nature, we mean the constitution of a thing, the fundamental law of its existence. Wide application of this argument. In determining what the nature of a thing is, we may go back to structure and resolve it into its constituent parts by definition; or See what are the ends or effects which it is designed to arouse.

Thus the true nature of the thing becomes a decisive *criterion* to be applied in examining measures. When properly settled and applied [this] is of great weight.

Great difficulty here will be to settle the true nature and end of the thing in question. Accidental qualities mistaken for essential—force of association in connecting things which do not necessarily go together.

V. *Sign* or Attendant circumstances. Though it is an error to confound this with a cause, yet this argument is often of great force. If the attendant circumstances is a necessary condition, then the argument is demonstrative. This may be in two ways:

1. Positively. If the event does always take place when this condition or circumstance occurs, then it is positive proof that the event

will happen. Existence of ice always proves the mercury to be below 30.

2. Negatively. If it is a sine qua non—then we can argue with certainty that the event will not occur since it is absent, though it may not follow if the sign be present that it will certainly occur, for the cause may not be in operation. Health may be a sine qua non of long continued mental power, but cannot infer from health that a man is a good reasoner. This argument from attendant circumstances, as signs or evidence of the true character of a measure is very wide in its scope and powerful in its application.

VI. From necessary consequence logically considered. Peculiarly adapted to put down the antagonist. Take his principle and run it out into positions which everyone sees to be absurd and ridiculous. Peculiarly applicable to position taken upon [principles] in [which] men trust, or tradition. In practical concerns it is necessary that their consequences must be intuitively certain.

VII. Exhaustion. Enumerating all the possible propositions, examining each, and showing by proper evidence that it is not true, except the one you maintained. Highly satisfactory if the enumeration is complete. Great danger if errors appear. Dilemma is on this principle.

VIII. Evils or absurdity of the contrary measures or principles. One of the most fertile things for painting, exhibiting the evils of the contrary force—or absurdity or inconsistency of contrary principle. May be used in defending a course pursued or proposed.

IX. Ex concessio. We appeal to the acknowledged principles of a man. Put down an antagonist. Ad hominem.

X. A position from what is admitted to something stronger which is involved in that admission.

XI. Induction. We here point out something belonging to an individual and then infer that it belongs to the whole class.
Example
Experience
Analogy. Greatly used at the bar where a vast number of cases arise not exactly provided for in the laws. Take the nearest case, show that the principle applies.

XII. Documents, Laws, Interpretations.

III. Language and Style

[These lectures take up, first, the questions of the origin, nature,

and function of language in the human race, and then proceed to
a more detailed treatment of the problem of acquiring a ready and
accurate use of language. As a first step in this process, Goodrich
proposes to treat three aspects of composition: Words and Forms
of Construction, the Structure of Sentences, and Figures of
Speech. Of these three, however, only the first is covered by these
lectures.]

Language is the medium by which thoughts are communicated
from one mind to another. Elevated as we are above the inferior orders
of creation, we owe our distinction almost entirely to the use of
language. Our race presents the singular spectacle of an order of
beings, at once the most weak and the most powerful, among the
inhabitants of Earth. In our infancy, we are more helpless and dependent, than the young of any, and are trained to a hardy existence
by the hand of nature. We are, for a long time, scarcely sustained
in being by the watchfulness of parental affection. As we rise from
this feeble state to the dominion of the world around us, we drag all
our strength from a *union with each other.* And this union results,
from the power of *communicating our thoughts by language.* In the
possession of this power, we are no longer like the inferior animals
insulated individuals, each dependent on his own sagacity and strength.
Our force is combined under the guidance of reason and experience.
Our wants, and enjoyments, and discoveries are made known to
others; and each in a thousand secret ways, ministers to the security
and happiness of those around him. Thus have the human race, by
the simple principle of uniting their strength, risen by degrees not
only to a dominion over the inferior orders of creation, but to a
wide command over the great powers of nature itself. Thus have
sprung into being government, subordination, arts, sciences, order,
happiness and virtue—all in short that which makes the world a
theatre of wonders around us and opens a nobler world to our view
as the reward of virtue.

While we are thus indebted to language for the power of *making*
these attainments we are enabled by the same means to *transmit them*
to future generations. All the accumulated stores of reason and observation, are preserved by language; and we come into life, not to toil
our way into the attainments of a single generation, but to enter, at

once, on the rich inheritance of past ages—the long line of intellectual labor through successive centuries.

Indebted as we thus are to language as our bond of union for almost all the attainments of our race, we cannot but feel a deep interest in examining its structure, its progressive improvement, and the power which it gives us over the minds of others. In this inquiry we go back to the earliest stages of society. We find language, like every other art, in its rudest state, and we are often compelled to smile at the expedients resorted to in the infancy of language for the expression of ideas. Our inquiries present us with a map of the human intellect, in its slow progress from ignorance and weakness to knowledge and power; for every step of the progress is impressed upon the language, by the invention of new words and new forms of expression to convey and record the new discoveries.

While the progress of language is thus a subject of rational curiosity, the study of our own language, in its present improved state is of the highest importance to success and usefulness in life. In a republic like ours, the great end of education is to train the mind to vigorous and manly action. Few, comparatively, can hope to pass their lives in the enjoyment of patrimonial wealth or literary ease. It is by the tongue and the pen that you are enabled to win your way to influence, property, and usefulness. Eloquence, therefore, should be the object to which all your efforts are ultimately aimed. And fortunately, the rewards of Eloquence are probably greater in this country, than any spot on earth. A *wider field* is here opened for the exercise of talent. Our popular assemblies are far more numerous, as the people decide themselves of the measures which respect their immediate interests. The standard is not yet so high that that most men are able, animated by enthusiasm and persevering effort, to reap the reward of their labors.

If then we consider public speaking as the great end to which your mental discipline should be directed, the high importance of those studies on which you are now entering will be obvious. Language is the instrument of your success in life—the instrument by which you are to act, on the understanding and feelings of others; and surely if the common instruments of music—the organ or the flute, are placed at our command only by long and habitual practice; what degree of labor should we not bestow on an instrument, so various, so comprehensive, so commanding, which if skillfully managed gives almost unlimited power over the minds of others, and opens to its possessor the enjoyment of wealth, influence, and fame.

To a writer and public speaker, there are two objects of pursuit:

1. The power of originating just, forcible, and elegant *trains of thought*.

2. The power of *expressing* these thoughts in *rich, appropriate,* and *beautiful* language, and thus carrying home to the bosoms of others the warm emotions with which his own heart is inspired.

These two objects can not indeed be entirely separated. We can never employ language without conveying thought of some kind. Still we may pursue these objects by themselves in part; and it is highly desirable to gain at an early period of life a ready command of language as the medium of thought—to understand perfectly the principles of composition—the exact meaning of the words we use—the line which separates the elegant from the low and vulgar—the rules of syntax—the proper distribution of the clauses which compose a sentence—the correct use of figurative language and especially that easy precision and gracefulness of style which throw a charm over the writing of Addison and Goldsmith. When we have thus acquired a ready command of language, we shall originate thought with greater ease and clearness, we shall not be embarrassed and distracted with two efforts of the mind at the same time—the effort to invent thoughts and to invent language to express them. The language will flow forth of itself as the ideas are in the mind, and we shall pour out our feeling with greater warmth and richness, as there is nothing to impede their progress.

For this reason *Composition* is placed among the earliest of your exercises and studies; commencing with translations, an exercise so highly recommended by Cicero, and practiced with so much assiduity during his whole life by that accomplished orator for the purpose of preserving the richness, strength and copiousness of his style. The practice of translation has this peculiar advantage that our attention is directed *solely to the style*. As we have not the labor of *thinking,* to originate the ideas, we may compose in this way within a given period more than is possible, if we express only our own thoughts;

while the improvement in our style, is still the same. For this reason I would recommend to you all the continuance of this practice during the whole of your collegiate life: It cannot be too strongly enforced, that nothing will enable you to write well, but great *frequency* in composition—a frequency tenfold greater than is demanded in the established cource of collegiate exercises. Writing is in a great measure a mechanical business—far more so than you are now disposed to believe. An easy and perspicuous style may be acquired by any one who will make the proper effort and all who have clearness of intellect and warmth of feeling, may add to this attainment, the higher excellence of energy of thought and richness of imagination.

Nor does the study of language serve merely to improve our style. It disciplines the understanding and prepares us to think with greater accuracy. The habit of distinguishing the exact meaning of words, and expressing neither more nor less than the precise idea before our mind gives a high degree of acuteness to the intellect. The mind may thus receive the same kind of discipline which it derives from the study of Geometry or Algebra. It ought likewise to be remembered that we think *chiefly in words* that the accuracy of our reasoning depends in a great measure, on a perfect acquaintance with the terms we use. So true indeed is this, that the immortal Locke in composing his Treatise on the human understanding, found himself compelled to go back to the nature of language, when his work was nearly half completed to illustrate the operations of the human mind. As we acquire an exact knowledge of words, we gain at the same time an acquaintance with the ideas they represent. We thus store the mind with the materials of knowledge, and prepare ourselves to combine our ideas into new forms and relations as occasion may require. A knowledge of words alone will not indeed make anyone a deep thinker; but no man can think with clearness or strength, who has not bestowed much attention on the distinctive meanings of words.

But dismissing this part of the subject, there is a charm in language alone, aside from the leading train of thought conveyed, which all admire and all most earnestly covet. Your observation has taught you that truth alone has comparatively little power over the mind. It is the manner of exhibiting the truth—of making it press with irresistible force on the understanding and the conscience which constitutes the Orator. The most powerful appeals of Demosthenes may be translated into other language retaining every truth which they exhibit and yet stripped of every particle of their eloquence. Your own feeling, will teach you far better than I am able to express that value of that attainment, which enables the Orator simply by a different collocation of thought and language, and the infusion of a glowing enthusiasm, to shake distant thrones, and make the extremities of the earth to tremble. In the inferior classes of literature it is the same commanding power of arrangement and language which can even render thought of but little value, delightful for the elegance and ease with which they are expressed; which has given an indescribable charm to the so often trite and feeble sentiments of Goldsmith—which has made Junius with all his malignity, imperishable as the language which records his vileness—which has constituted Hume, partial and inaccurate as he frequently is, the great Historian of England, while the laborious correctness of Rapin[21] and Henry[22] are thrown aside with disgust.

IV. Voice and Delivery

[These lectures begin by examining the place of rhetorical training in the total educational picture. The specific advantages to be gained from a proficiency in elocution are discussed, and the importance of conversational ability is stressed.

[Problems of voice and articulation are considered next. Goodrich believed that vocal quality is largely determined by nature and is not susceptible to any appreciable modification. However, he believed that everyone could acquire a definite and pleasing articulation. He examines the nature of the articulatory process in some detail and lays down principles for the improvement of articulation.]

Whatever then may be your employment in future life, though you may never be called to the pulpit or to the bar, it is a sacred duty which you owe to yourselves and your friends, to cultivate those graces and accomplishments of our nature—those elegances of taste and imagina-

---

[21]Rapin, Rene (1621-1687; French writer and theologian): *Reflexions sur l'usage de l'eloquence de ce temps,* Oxford, 1672.
[22]Henry, Robert (1718-1790; British historian): *The History of Great Britian,* London, 1771.

tion; of language and of address, which, in every profession, give the crowning ornament to intellectual superiority.

In speaking of those pursuits which belong particularly to the department under my care, I shall first call your attention for a few lectures to the subject of *elocution*. There are two reasons for which I do this. First because I wish to lay before you briefly the great principles which have guided me in my attempts to aid you in the practice of speaking—principles which you may find of use in that future course of discipline which now devolves upon yourselves. And secondly because many of you will hereafter be instructors and will therefore feel an additional interest, in understanding the principles of an art which you may soon be called to teach.

All will admit that an elocution, at once distinct and easy, forcible and varied, is of high importance at least to a public man. It is your great medium of intercourse with those around us; and the remark of Johnson is founded on wisdom, that "what we are called upon to do frequently, we should qualify ourselves to do well."[23] At your entrance into life, especially—a period so often decisive of our future character and success—the *first* exhibition of talent which you can make, in promiscuous society—the standard by which you will first be tried—is by your ability in *conversation*. And it is here in a peculiar degree that elegance of address, triumphs over strength of intellect. If you are here found to be confused, indistinct and ungraceful, the tones harsh and monotonous, the manner abrupt, timid or hesitating, the clearest indications of intelligence or moral worth can scarcely prevent the impression from being painful or disgusting. An easy self-possession on the contrary, dignified without stiffness, and familiar without obtrusion, united to rich and expressive intonations which exhibit the feelings in all their variety of light and shade, gives a new grace to every sentiment which is uttered. When you consider how large a portion of our enjoyment and even of our influence is derived from social intercourse, you cannot but agree with me in this opinion. Those qualities are indeed worthy of assiduous cultivation, which give a charm to their possessor and light up a feeling of joy in every circle which he enters; and the want of which on the contrary, will leave a

---

[23]The editor is unable to locate this quotation.

man of the soundest intellect and the purest principles, to be dreaded as a cold and repulsive companion.

To a mind of sensibility the consciousness of a deficiency in Elocution, will often prove an insuperable barrier to success in the higher qualities of conversation. Many whose intellect and taste would have rendered them ornaments of the social circle, have been self-banished from society, by early habits of speaking acquired in early life, and neglected, unhappily, until they could not be subdued. Such a one I well remember of the soundest understanding and the most fervid genius, with an imagination bold and luxuriant, a taste of the highest elegance and refinement, the pride of his class and the ornament of his College, who stung with shame, at deficiencies in elocution, which he had too long neglected, retired on leaving College to his father's house, and has never from that period been seen by the nearest neighbors, except as he sometimes wanders, the victim of disappointment, along a stream which skirts his father's grounds.

If such be the value of a graceful elocution as an accomplishment of the social circle, how much higher is the estimate which it deserves from those who are to make it the instrument of success in their professional pursuits. Intellectual ability, however commanding, can never obtain the palm of eloquence. Your observation has taught you that *truth alone* has comparatively little power over the mind. It is the manner of *exhibiting* that truth—of making it press with irresistible force on the understanding, and the feelings, and the conscience, which constitutes the Orator. The most powerful appeals of "the old man eloquent of Greece" may be translated into other languages, retaining every truth which they exhibit, and yet stripped of every particle of eloquence—your own feelings have taught you far better than I am able to express, the value of that attainment which enables the Orator simply by a different collocation of thought and language, and the expression of a glowing enthusiasm to shake distant thrones and make the extremities of the earth to tremble. In the inferior classes of literature it is the same commanding power of arrangement and language, which can render thoughts of but little value, delightful for the elegance or force with which they are expressed, which has given an indescribable charm so often to the trite and feeble sentiments of Goldsmith—which has made Junius with all his malignity imperishable as the language which records his violences—which has made Hume, superficial and inaccurate as he frequently is, the great historian of England, while the laborious correctness of Rapin or Henry are thrown aside with disgust.

But while you are filled with admiration at the power of language as an instrument of impression, and are willing to dedicate your days and nights to the attainment of so commanding a talent, permit me to ask if there be in the delivery of language, a power exactly similar to this which we have been considering in its *arrangement*. If there be a combination of emphasis, tone, inflection and gesture which arrays a sentence in ten-fold strength and beauty—which carries the appeal home to the soul with a depth of sentiment never before experienced, and which thus gives a command over the minds of others never before attained. I ask is not this talent of the same value to the Orator, whose instrument is the voice, as the command of language which you admire so greatly in the Author whose medium is the press? Why, then, let me urge the question, do you consider years of labor as well bestowed in acquiring an elegant and forcible style of writing when few of you expect ever to address the public through the press— and at the same time employ not one-tenth or one-hundredth part as much exertion in cultivating a similar talent which would cloathe you with greater power as a public speaker, the employment to which most of you are destined. Nothing, I am confident, could save you from the conviction of a serious violation of duty in this respect but the general inattention to speaking at the present day which has lowered the standard of attainment in this art. Among the great body of our public speakers how few will you find, who are not marked by some offensive peculiarities, which continually force themselves on the view, and which you are compelled to forget and pardon for the value of the sentiments, which are thus debarred in the delivery. Negative excellence therefore, freedom from gross faults is regarded as a high attainment; while those more elevated qualities on which the true force of speaking lies, are left in a great measure uncultivated and forgotten.

A large part of mankind, at the present day, are, I believe, totally unconscious of the real power of the voice and manner, in producing impressions on the mind. They have never witnessed its exhibition and are therefore ignorant of its prodigious energy. That high order of speaking, in which the strongest appeals are made to the feelings, is unhappily confined almost entirely to the Stage; and here is in too many instances degraded by rant, affectation and grimace. Players are, in most cases, men of uncultivated minds, ignorant of philosophical principles, destitute of an elegant taste in composition, generally of degraded moral principles, and barred by the nature of their employment from the higher ranks of society. It is not therefore surprising that they adopt a false standard of taste, and depart from the simplicity of nature, especially when we consider how prone men are to monotony or affectation in delivering the sentiments of others. But with all these disadvantages, the command which they sometimes gain over the feelings of the most enlightened mind is astonishing. And when a man of this profession, like Garrick, has the benefit of a better education, of purer principles and more honorable associates— when nature seeks through such a man in all her simplicity and force to the genuine sentiments of the heart, the effect is overwhelming, you feel that a new power is added to our race, and that man is elevated in the scale of existence.

Suppose for example a man like Garrick, fitted with the power of swaying the emotions by delivering the sentiments of others, suppose that such a man could cast off his borrowed character and come down to you with the energy of real earnestness, and could add to a highly cultivated intellect, a rich imagination and genuine enthusiasm of feeling, qualities possessed by so many actors—could add, I say, that high talent of blending with these powers, that prodigious energy which he inspires into his imaginary characters—how powerful an ally would you not feel yourself to have gained could you enlist such a man in the cause of truth and virtue? Now it was to this object, that the just and fervid genius of the Ancients directed the Orator, not that sense should be sacrificed to sound, but that the noblest effusion of the intellect and of fancy should be sustained and enforced by correspondent energy of diction. Their triumph was complete and you are no more astonished, that the Oration of Cicero for Marcellus, from which you are left with a feeble impression on your mind, should in the delivery have melted the inflexible soul of Caesar on the tribunal of justice, till every feeling of resentment, of consistency of character, and his repeated declarations, is forgotten and the sentence of condemnation falls from his hand. With such examples before them, we shall cease to wonder at the high importance attached by the Ancients to *delivery* as the instrument and organ of impassioned eloquence—and that every attempt at oratory, without high attainments in this art, were considered by them as negatory [nugatory?] and vain.

The great error on this subject has arisen from an impression that words alone are adequate to communicate all that passes in our minds. But the passions and the imagination, have a language of their own independent of words—they speak the emotions of the heart which have other and more powerful means of being addressed. Words are arbitrary signs suggesting intellectual ideas indirectly with reading; and, to a limited extent associated with the feelings. But tones and inflexions are established by the Creator as the great exciting causes of emotion with the deepest sensibilities of our nature. They are associated not by the arbitrary inventions of man, but by the original principles of our constitution. Their power over the coolest and best disciplined minds, is often astonishing. Hence you may perhaps have experienced that a pathetic story like that of Le Fevre[24] or Le Roche[25] when perceived with eye, has awakened but little emotion; but when you have attempted to read to yourself aloud in simple and pathetic tones, you have found yourself unconsciously melted into tears. Even in trains of reasoning, when words alone are adequate to call up all the ideas intended, we shall sympathize with the apparent feelings of the speaker. If delivery be negligent and feeble we instinctively feel that he has no interest in his argument, and therefore have no interest ourselves; if on the contrary his tones and manner betray the earnestness of strong emotion, a deep feeling for the success of his causes, we merge our sympathies with his—our attention is at once fixed—and our conviction has double strength, because we feel it deserves to be convinced.

But when we rise from the region of reasoning into that of the imagination and the passions, if we neglect those outward indica-

---

[24]Probably refers to Pierre-Francois-Alexandre Le Fevre (1741-1813; French dramatist and tragedian): *Don Carlos,* Paris, 1821.
[25]Probably refers to Le Roche du Maine (1740-1792; French soldier of fortune and writer): *Dissertation on Jean of Arc,* London, 1776.

tions of feeling which nature has stamped on our constitution, the effect will be far from negative—the contrast is, in many cases, so striking as to produce emotions directly the reverse of those intended—and the most striking passages have a painful or ludicrous impression. It ought never to be forgotten that the habits of *delivery* which we form, exert a powerful influence throughout our life on our style of writing and extemporaneous speaking. He who is conscious of his inability to deliver glowing conceptions and pathetic emotions in correspondent and appropriate tones, will be deterred from an attempt which might end in his own confusion. When such conceptions rise to his mind in the fervour of address he rejects them with a sigh that he is chained down by his habits of delivery to a lower range of Oratory. A perpetual restraint is thus imposed on the excursions of his genius and the finest trait of his mind may be sacrificed to an early neglect of delivery.

I have opened the subject with these remarks on the power of delivery in giving impressiveness to thought and language not because there is an individual present who is not convinced of the value of this attainment; or whose own mind has not at times borne witness to its overwhelming influence. But as to any practical benefit to yourselves, a cool conviction is nothing. Nor is this an attainment which can be forced upon you in the regular routine of education, like that discipline of mind which springs from the study of language and the mathematics. A few gross errors may indeed be corrected. But composition of every kind whether it be the arrangement of language to convey thought, or the adjustment of tones, inflections and emphasis to awaken feelings—must be the spontaneous effusion of deep interest. A glowing enthusiasm to enkindle in the hearts of others the emotions which enflame and agitate our own. It is not the passive reception of knowledge to which the most sluggish mind may submit—but a creative act to which all knowledge should be subservient, requiring the stimulus of motives the most powerful and constant: a deep sense of duty; a lively perception of high advantage to be gained; a generous emulation to excel; an increasing delight in that active and vigorous state of mind created by those intellectual habits.

In speaking to you on this subject for the last time I can only cast myself upon your feelings—your sense of duty—your interest in the honor and success of this Institution, in your own honor and your desire for success in the active scene of life which are already beginning to open before you. Take then the sober convictions of your understanding on this subject, the testimony of your own observation and of all enlightened men as to the value of this attainment, and ask is it not your *duty* to become able and accomplished speakers? Is there not an amount of moral power placed within your reach, which you cannot throw away without trampling upon your own interests and violating a sacred duty which you owe to your friends and to your country, and, above all, to that being who has intrusted us with talents for his service and will soon call in to account for their improvement? To make the case more particular let me select a single individual who is destined to the pulpit: and I say to him, cultivate all your *other powers* assiduously up to a given point, and enter upon life in the neglect of this qualification, your sphere of usefulness will always be much more limited. The whole collected energy of those other powers which you cultivate must throughout life, be hemmed in by a narrower sphere of action—*Add* to them the powers of a commanding elocution, through which all your intellectual force is to be poured on the minds of others, and it is my sober conviction you may in many instances double throughout life the extent of your usefulness. Larger congregations will solicit your labors; taste and feeling will be enlisted on your side; a deeper solemnity and a more penetrating influence will attend the truths you deliver; and, in short, every intellectual exertion you make in the service of God and your fellow-men, will be diffused over double the number of human beings. Let no one plead that he is exempted, by *natural* defects, from the obligation to be a powerful speaker, until he has faithfully and perseveringly made the attempt. The two great Orators of Antiquity, I need not remind you, had peculiar natural impediments to encounter. The original structure of the voice you cannot indeed change—and if unharmonious it must in a great degree remain so still. But industry and enthusiasm, will do almost all the rest. It is remarkable that some of the most distinguished speakers of the present age, had uncommonly bad voices —harsh, dissonant, and unsubdued. Thus I am told was the case with Cook,[26] Kean,[27] Kemble,[28] and Dr. Mason.[29] The most

---

[26]Probably Russell S. Cook (1811-1864; Massachusetts clergyman and speaker): *DAB, IV,* 378.

melodious voice badly managed is disgusting—and a harsh voice, if animated with just inflections, tones, and emphases has a commanding power.

In the course of discipline which I am to recommend to you in these Lectures, designed not merely to direct your practice, while members of College but during your professional studies and in some degree the whole course of your lives as public speakers, I would remind you that it is not merely theoretical knowledge of principles, nor a few inactive wishes, or occasional emotions that will avail. Every valuable attainment must cost you labor, and nothing certainly but close and persevering application can give the command which you ought to have over that powerful instrument the voice. It is an application, however, which need not greatly interfere with other pursuits. By a regular distribution and by carrying practice in this art into your hours of exercise and amusement much may be accomplished.

The ease with which a good speaker controls his voice, deceives us into the belief that this command was a *natural* gift and required but little labor. A large portion of the difficulty no doubt arises from bad habits to be subdued, habits which in some individuals have less force than in others. But rarely did any man speak impressively without much secret labor. I have made this an object of enquiry, as to a number of individuals most distinguished for their excellence in this respect—and have learned with surprise the unwearied secret exertions which it cost them to acquire that spontaneous flow of delivery which seemed the suggestion of the moment. To speak according to the dictates of nature is indeed the great principle of excellence. But it is not nature cramped and debased as observed in the habits of most of us, whose whole course of education from childhood has been hostile to freedom and force in speaking. Nor will you find a spotless exhibition of nature even in the greatest of Orators of our age. Your conception

---

[27]Probably Charles John Kean (1811-1868; eminent actor of the period): see Carson, William G. B.: *Letters of Mr. and Mrs. Charles Kean Relating to Their American Tours*, St. Louis, 1945.

[28]Probably Gouverneur Kemble (1786-1875; U. S. Congressman 1837-1841): *DAB, X,* 316.

[29]Probably John Mitchell Mason (1770-1829, clergyman and educator): see *A Plea for Sacramental Communion on Catholick Principles,* New York, 1816.

of it must be formed like the Venus of the Ancient sculptor, by collecting the scattered elements of beauty and strength around you, into one finished picture of unattained and unattainable perfection. He who with such an image of excellence before him, aims with inflexible determination at high attainments will not lose his reward.

If then there is an individual who does not design utterly to abandon himself to the powers of evil habits, let him not lose one moment in resisting its sway. The organs of speech lose their flexibility as we advance in years—the power of habit is gaining force, and what may not be successfully corrected may soon be beyond your power.

The first thing to be guarded against is the *mechanical* and monotonous manner of speaking which we are so apt to acquire in early life by delivering the compositions of others. I would urge from this time never to declaim, but to *converse*—with a dignity and strength more sustained as the subject rises in importance. Colloquial tones, inflexions, and emphases are the basis of all good speaking; and your first endeavor therefore should be to acquire such a command over your *mental habits* (for the fault lies partly here) as well as over the bodily organs that you can read or speak as you converse.

But this is not sufficient. As the occasion, the subject, and the style rise in dignity and force, a correspondent elevation is necessary in the manner of delivery. And here lies the difficulty. We attempt to be easy, and instantly become too familiar and feeble for the occasion. We aim at dignity and strength and at once swell into declamation. To unite dignity with ease—variety with strength—feeling with simplicity—is the great art of elocution. It is not true therefore that the mode of delivering a sentence which spontaneously suggests itself, even when the feelings are most excited is of course the best. Such a mode is generally a good one—i.e., usually free from gross faults. But to infuse into the delivery all the force of which the sentence is capable, requires study, and experiment with various modes till the best is discovered. Hence the great Orators of Antiquity scarcely ever trusted themselves to speak in public until they had composed their productions with unwearied labor, and prepared for their delivery by numerous repetitions. More force certainly can be thus infused into eloquence provided we guard against the stiffness and want of feeling which are apt to spring up in retried composition. Habitual practice, however, as in every other art will give in most cases the power of instantaneous decision and this power is necessary in extemporaneous speaking. In written composition some hours should be spent before hand in adapting the expression to sentiment.

The rehearsal of players affords a strong confirmation of these remarks. They are required to deliver written language like spoken— adapting the manner to that degree of dignity which the occasion and the sentiment demand. Now in doing this, it is not the first nor the second, nor the twelfth experiment which enables them to fit on the exact manner in which the words are to be uttered. Yet when ultimately delivered, they strike you as so perfectly natural that they must have flowed without labor from the spontaneous suggestion of the moment. It is indeed the suggestion of the moment but not the first suggestion—perfectly correspondent indeed with the existing trace of feeling, but a rapid *copy* of that which was originally produced with labor and art. Nothing indeed will show more forcibly the necessity of study, than attempting to read a comedy aloud, in which although there are no tones to which you are not accustomed, and which you do not instantly recognize as natural when uttered by others, you are entirely unable to command or even to conceive at the first perusal.

This arises from our early habits of reading acquired at school. The use of voice is there not laid according to the relative proportion of thought, but to a measured tune applied to every sentence. Hence in reading the habit is never formed of indicating those delicate relations, correspondences and oppositions of thought, by those organs which nature has provided for their expression. Children do it considerably in conversation—and would be utterly astonished to hear another child talk as he reads. But as they advance in life and of course read more, the pernicious habits of the school gain on the natural tones of conversation. If a man's conversation were taken down on paper, and he were required to read the same words as he had just pronounced, scarcely an individual can be found who is not so much the slave of habit, that the paper before him would not change his mode of delivery. These habits not only injure our reading and speaking but they weaken our capacity for doing it. We love that variety of tone, that wide command of the voice which nature has given us. When an accomplished speaker throws in a sentence a variety ten times greater than we had ever thought of, and thus points out numerous relations of ideas which we had never attempted to express in delivery—we admire the talent. We instantly feel the beauty and truth to nature. But when we seek to imitate, the organs of speech do not second our desires. Their flexibility is gone—they move only in the beaten track of habit.

To guard against these dangers I shall attempt in our next meeting, to analyze that measured and declamatory tone so generally prevalent in public speech, and to point out the best means of correcting these errors: and shall then proceed in the progress of this course, to consider the several qualities of good speaking: melody, compass and strength of voice, distinctiveness of articulation, propriety of pauses, correctness and variety of inflections and the principles of Emphasis.

*   *   *

As our last meeting, we examined the structure of those organs on which the original sound of the human voice depends; and to whose perfect action we are indebted for the melody and richness of our tones, the extent and variety of their combinations, and the impressiveness and ease with which they are thrown upon the ear. Some suggestions were added, on the best means within our power of cultivating and improving these organs.

Although much may be accomplished by persevering industry in subduing the vocal organs to our will, in supplying deficiencies and correcting error—still there is an original character impressed by the hand of nature on these organs, which can never be changed. There is a melody, a boldness and strength in some voices, which arising from the primary structures of the vocal organ can never be transferred to others less highly gifted by nature.

In this, however, as in most of the original diversities of our constitution, the superiority enjoyed by the favored few, is an instrument rather of gratification, than of substantial utility—a source of rich enjoyment, indeed, to the taste, but of little effect in the serious concerns of life. It is to the *second* class of organs (of which I am now to speak) that we are indebted for the incalculable benefits of social intercourse; and the power of impressing our sentiments, with distinctness and force, on the minds of others. The organs of *speech*, unlike those of the *voice* have, with very few exceptions, *no* original difference of structure. It is their cultivation or their neglect alone, which gives rise to the wide diversity which we observe in the speech of men as distinguished from their voice. Melody of tone, like a rich imagination may be the prerogative of but few; but distinctness of articulation, variety and east of transition, justness of emphasis, compass of inflection—*all,* in short, that there is of *mind* in vocal language, may be possessed in almost equal degrees, by those who aspire to the attainment with enthusiasm and perseverance.

As the object of speaking is not merely to convey sound to the ear, but to stamp each portion of sound with a distinctive character, as the representative of thought, the *fundamental* quality of elocution (without which no other can have existence) is a clear articulation. To the musician it is of very little importance whether the *words* which he utters are understood or not: he relies for success not on the ideas conveyed to the *understanding,* but on the rich combinations of sound impressed upon the *ear.* But he who speaks, has accomplished nothing, until each combination of sound awakens its appropriate *idea* in the mind. He may *then* point out their relations by pauses and inflections, or deepen their impression by emphasis and tone: But, until this *primary* object is attained, by distinct articulation, the highest graces of delivery, are of no more value than if expressed in an unknown tongue.

Nor is it sufficient barely to convey the idea; there is great beauty in doing it with perfect distinctness and openness of voice; preserving a happy medium between that confused and hurried manner, so generally prevalent in our speakers, on the one hand, and the air of labor and measured precision, which we are in danger of acquiring, on the other, from our anxious endeavors to correct the opposite fault. An articulation thus clear and well-proportioned has not merely negative *excellence* or freedom from defects: It has, like perspicuity of style, a high degree of *positive beauty;* and awakens the same pleasure that we feel in receiving thought through the clear medium of Addison or Goldsmith or contemplating the Landscape, in a pure atmosphere and under a serene sky.

The structure of our language lays us under peculiar difficulties, in acquiring a just and easy articulation. We have indeed nearly the same elementary sounds with the finest languages of antiquity and of modern times. But in combining these sounds into syllables and words, very little regard has been paid, to the harmony of their union or the ease of transition from one sound to another. The Ancients on the contrary adjusted these combinations and transitions, with the strictest attention to ease and gracefulness of delivery; and to this *single* principle may be referred almost all the irregularities which occur in the inflection of their nouns and verbs. In *our* language we have not only a larger proportion of consonant sounds, but unfortunately those which are most difficult to pronounce, are in numerous instances, brought into immediate contact; making the transition so rapid and so entire, in passing from one of these discordant sounds to another, as greatly to impair the ease and distinctness of our enunciation.

This difficulty is greatly enhanced by our principles of accent. We lay a peculiar stress on *one* syllable of a word and pass lightly and rapidly over the rest. The *tendency* of our language is to place the accent near the beginning of a word; and hence in some instances, two, three, or even four syllables which follow are pronounced with great rapidity and but little stress of voice. This produces, too often, a confusion and negligence in the articulation of these syllables, which if it does not *obscure* the sense destroys all measure and proportion, and consequently all *harmony* of delivery. From this cause, likewise, unaccented syllables are in numerous instances entirely omitted; in others the finest and most open sounds of our language sink into the worst; and in others, still, part of the consonant sounds are either entirely lost or transformed into others to which they bear a resemblance. There is from these causes, in the sound of our unaccented syllables (which of course bear a large proportion to the whole body of the language) an indefiniteness of pronunciation, which occasions the greatest perplexity to foreigners, and not infrequently to ourselves, when called upon to read in a deliberate and distinct manner. Some of these will be more particularly stated in a subsequent part of the Lecture.

The difficulties to which I have now adverted, have induced all experienced Teachers of Elocution to unite in the opinion that to remedy a defective articulation or attain any high degree of excellence in this respect, it is necessary to analyze the sound of our language; to commence as in singing with a course of practice on the most short and easy combinations, to rise gradually to the more complicated. In such a course of exercises, after practising on single words for a time, the most harmonious sentences should next be chosen; the articulation of which is, of course, most easy. When the clearness and melody of tone natural to such compositions have become habitual, we should gradually select the more discordant combinations which occasion the greatest difficulty; and pronounce them in the same clear and open manner. In the commencement of the course, therefore, the best exercises would be in Poetry, were it not for the danger of acquiring a tone, from the regular succession of its numbers. The Greek and Latin languages having a larger proportion of vowel sounds than our own, are peculiarly adapted to this purpose; and have likewise the additional advantage that as we have never used them in the rapidity of conversation, we can more easily pronounce them with great deliberation and distinctness. This course of discipline, though it may produce, at first, a laborious and unnatural precision of sound, may gradually be softened in ease and gracefulness, while a clear and mellow articulation are still preserved. He who has thus acquired a perfect command over the organs of speech will learn how to estimate the comparative excellence of each elementary sound; and to decide instantaneously where to prolong and where to curtail them, in a manner best adapted to give melody and strength to his delivery. He will recognize certain combinations on which the voice may dwell with peculiar satisfaction; and by their means spread a beauty and openness of sound over all his delivery. There are others over which his sole object will be to pass with ease and lightness; and to conceal their faults, by mingling them in the flow of those which are more harmonious. But to an undisciplined reader or speaker, all sounds come [become?] alike indifferent. Instead of aiming to render them harmonious, he clusters them together; curtails the finest of their due length; gives too great prominence to those which are harsh; runs, not infrequently, one sound into another, so that none is heard distinctly; and reduces nearly all of them to mutes or aspirates.

The office of the Enunciative organs, as I intimated at our last meeting, is two-fold:

1. To break off the stream of voice into small distinct portions.

2. To stamp on each of these portions a distinctive impression, thus making it an element of speech.

The inquiry has often been made, in what does the latter process consist: how is voice as it proceeds from the Larnyx, converted into *speech,* or a succession of elementary sounds—what is articulation in this sense of the term? Simple as the question may appear, it is not easy to answer. Indeed a very able writer in one of the leading Reviews of the present day, has pronounced it to be a question which never was satisfactorily answered, and probably never will be. For my own part, though I would speak with hesitation on the subject, the most natural solution appears to be this. In the act of *whispering,* the enunciative organs alone are employed; and the sound is produced by the vibration of the lips, tongue or other portions of the mouth, which are brought into near approach or contact. There then we have *articulation,* and in this manner without the aid of voice, all the elementary sounds of the language may be formed by the mere action of the breath, on the organs of enunciation, in certain position. If while the sound is thus going on, another sound from the Larnyx, to wit voice, is added, the articulation or elementary sound is still produced as *before,* solely by the vibration of the Enunciative organs. The sound which is *added,* merely mingles itself with the original elementary sound, and gives strength and sonorousness to the whole without changing its character. Thus the letter *f* is formed by the vibration of the lips, and the letter *s* by the vibration of the teeth, while air is passing rapidly from the mouth; and notice that eight of our consonant sounds are thus mere articulation formed by the enunciative organs without any *voice* or action of the larnyx. And what is remarkable we have eight other letters, which are exactly the same articulations, with a small portion of voice or vibration from the larynx added to them. *F,* for example, becomes *v,* when voice is added to it; *s,* becomes *z; t,* becomes *d; p* becomes *b.* These second eight therefore are not new articulations, but merely the former eight sustained and strengthened by one quality common to them all—a vibration of the larynx. Their distinctive character as letters therefore lies not in this latter vibration, but in the original vibration of the Enunciative organs, which produced the sound of *f, s,* and *t. Articula-*

tion, therefore, is solely that vibration—the vibration of the larynx merely strengthens and sustains it.

Leaving this inquiry, however, as rather curious than useful, it is important to remark that the distinct portions of sound, broken off by the Enunciative organs, are not, in most speakers, sufficiently long. [1.?] Time should be allowed for each letter to impress itself upon the ear with perfect distinctness, and for the organs to pass without difficulty or confusion to the subsequent position. Rapidity of speaking as we have already remarked is unquestionably one of the great sources of a bad articulation. But when this is not the case, when by a vigorous action of the organs, every sound *is* made to reach the ear with distinctness, a rapid delivery is destructive to all dignity and force of impression. In many cases indeed there is a beauty in passing lightly, over connecting words and clauses; but on important members of a sentence, especially in forcible and pathetic speaking, there *must* be a certain degree of prolongation or there can be no dignity and strength. A command of the voice in this respect, is likewise of peculiar value, in its influence upon emphasis. Occasionally to emphasize by prolonging a word, gives not only more variety, but frequently much greater force, than mere stress of voice. 2. In stamping upon each portion of sound its specific character, all distinctness depends on applying the Enunciative organs to each other, in their several points of approach or contact, with firmness and tension; on suffering no sound to escape till the proper moment has arrived; and then, with equal promptitude, on giving to it a complete and energetic expression. This depends chiefly on the consonants, which separate the flowing sounds of the vowels by strong boundaries obvious to the ear; adding force and expression; and furnishing useful varieties and pleasing contrasts. Thence you may observe that in singing, the voice dwells chiefly on the vowel sounds: the consonants are felt to be an impediment, and are passed over as lightly as possible, while the vowels are prolonged and blended. In *speaking* on the contrary, there is no distinctness, unless the limits of each vowel are marked and ascertained by a firm enunciation of the intervening consonants.

General rules however are of no value, on a subject of this kind, unless applied to specific cases. As my object is entirely practical, I shall therefore, as intimated on a former occasion, descend to a minute statement of some of the difficulties which impede the articulation of our language, together with their causes and the faults to which they lead. I do it the rather, because there is not work within my knowledge, which touches, to any extent, on this subject; and I have thought, the results of some years of observation and experience, would not be without their use in your future course of discipline, and particularly in the office of instructors to which some of you will soon be called. I shall therefore mention them so deliberately as to allow any who choose, to take them down.

Consonants. I. *Drawing consonants together, and omitting the intermediate vowel sounds.* We have certain consonants, which from the position of the organs, in forming them, combine more naturally without the intervention of a vowel; as for example the mute and liquids, *br, fr, tr.* We are apt, therefore, in syllables not under the accent, to omit a vowel between these consonants, and to draw them together; of which I will mention quite a number of instances, the more fully to convey my meaning.

Between T and R. Histry, for history; litral, for literal; litrature, for literature; pastral for pastoral; victry for victory; votry for votary; natral for natural, etc.

P and R. Corp'rate for corporate; corp'ral for corporal.

B and R. Neighb'ring; lab'ring; lib'ral.

D and R. Wond'ring; wond'rous.

C and R. Acc'rate; acc'racy.

V and R. Fav'rable; av'rice.

F and R. Suff'rable; pref'rable.

G and R. Stagg'ring; dang'rous.

Also N and R, M and R, S and R.

When the participial form *ing* is added to R under these circumstances, this difficulty always takes place—as flattering.

When the formative *er*, denoting the agent, is added, the same omission is apt to take place, murdrer, hindrer.

The two last classes of words (viz. participles in *ing* and nouns in *er* denoting the agent) being quite numerous, the fault now mentioned occurs very frequently.

When the letter L follows a vowel and a mute the same remark applies to it as to the letter R, b'lieve, abs'lute.

There are, however, words in which the omission at the *end* of a word has become so common as to be sanctioned by good use.

When N is in the same circumstance, d, n, ord'nary, card'nal, ord'nal, tend'ncy.

t, n, obst'nate, etc.

s, n, cons'nant.

So strong is this tendency to coalescence in the case of the letter N that we have yielded to it in most words of more than one syllable which end in *on* or *en;* as beacon; heaven; even; garden. In a few words of this kind, however, the coalescence does not take place, as in sudden, fatten, chicken, and it is peculiarly important to commit these words to memory. At a future period, if any are disposed, I will designate these exceptions and trace the general principles of English pronunciation. Enough has been said, however, to show that a coalescence of the consonants by the omission of an intermediate vowel is a fault which prevails to a great extent and to be carefully avoided.

II. *Omitting consonants which should be sounded.* 1. Dropping the letter R when it occurs between S and T.

This is so vulgar that I should hardly think it worthy of being mentioned, were it not too common even here. *Fust* for first, *wust* for worst, *bust* for burst, *cust* for curst.

2. Dropping the aspirate H: child'ood, man'ood. This is very frequent in the verb *to have* and pronouns *him, her:* "Where've you been." "I saw 'em." The same omission is very common in the case of *wh: wile, wen,* for while, when. *Th* is frequently omitted in the word them: I told 'em.

3. The great difficulty in this respect, however, arises from the letters *d* and *t,* which being mutes, arrest the passage of the sound. Hence when preceded by another consonant, it is often difficult to sound both letters with distinctness—fact, exact, mind. For this reason the copulative *and* creates a great difficulty. Perhaps in the majority of instances, it is not fully sounded, men *an'* money, question *an'* answer. This embarrassment with the letters *d* and *t* is greatly increased when they are followed as well as preceded by a consonant, mil'ly for mildly, kin'ness for kindness, lan'scape, frien'ship, col'ly. It is still greater when *t* is preceded by *c*—as enactment, directly distinctness.

In these cases it is almost impossible to retain the sound fully. Words of this class become very numerous by the addition of the letter S to form the plural of nouns, and the 3rd singular of verbs: He finds, relents; products, pretexts, exacts. Hence new letters are sometimes formed by dropping the *t* or *d:* "The *ax* of parliament." In like manner *th* when followed by *s,* is suffered to sink in to *s* or *z;* months-monse, breathes-breeze, truths-truce, clothes-cloze. This last has become so common as even to be partially admitted by Walker from its prevalence; though condemned as vulgar. In the same manner *d* is often changed into *g:* adjourned-ajourn, adjudicate-ajudicate.

III. *Interchanging Letters.* One great fault of this occurs in the termination *ing,* which in some parts of our country is always pronounced like *n:* writin, walkin, speakin. This is a vulgarity which ought to be most carefully avoided. The sound of the *ing* should be heard in these instances with entire fulness. The only case in which this omission is justified by Walker[30] is when the *ng* is immediately preceded by another *ng* as in ringing, singing. In these instances however, I should prefer to give the second *ng* distinctly, though with less force than the first.

Another case of this interchange occurs in what we call lisping, which consists merely in using the letter *th* for *s;* or in some instances the *s* for *th.* It is therefore perfectly easy to cure this offensive habit, though many persons are so unthinking as to imagine it to result from some natural deficiency or impediment.

This error as to natural impediments is very common. More than one case has fallen under my notice of persons, who had never pronounced the letter R and imagined they could not; but uniformly employed the letter L in its room. I need hardly add that the error was corrected in a moment by pointing out the proper position of the organs, and a little practice was sufficient to correct the habit.

There is one more case of interchanging sounds which is worthy of notice: I mean the rough and the smooth sound of the letter R. In the commencement of a word R has always a rough and jarring sound, as Rome. In all other instances the rough sound is withheld from the R. Most of the nations of Europe, however, together with

---

[30]Walker, John: *A Critical Pronouncing Dictionary and Expositor of the English Language,* New York, 1819, p. 47.

the inhabitants of Ireland, give the rough sound to R in all parts of a word; and we therefore instantly distinguish a foreigner or an Irishman by this sound of the R in the middle or end of words, Sir, sorrow.

IV. It is difficult frequently to repeat the *same letter;* or letters which are similar. Hence, the labor we experience in pronouncing such words as Cacheny. For this reason the words "Smith's Thucydides" presents a combination of sound so difficult that few persons can pronounce them without stumbling. The indefinite article *an,* often subjects us to serious inconvenience in this respect. "In an inelegant manner," "In an innocent animal." Such combinations should be avoided in compositions at almost any expense, though we shall sometimes find it difficult.

Having illustrated a part of the causes which lead to harshness, confusion, and negligence in the consonant sounds, I shall turn your attention for a moment to the vowel sounds.

Vowels. To these we are principally indebted for the beauty of language. One of the highest qualifications of a good speaker is an open and full pronunciation of these sounds. The finest of our vowel sounds are the three sounds of *a* in *fall, far,* and *fame;* the sound of *o* in *noble;* the sound *u* in *muse;* and the diphthongal sound *oi* as in *join:* and it is from the judicious prolongation of these sounds, as Walker justly remarks, that our pronounciation derives one of its greatest beauties. When these sounds are under the accent, they are pronounced by most persons with a considerable degree of fulness. But in syllables which are unaccented the finest vowels are too often sunk into an obscure sound like that of *e* or *u.*

O. upinion, for opinion; cathulic, for catholic; memury, for memory; in all these cases *o* should have the same full sound as in the word *open.*

U. monement, edycation, argument, volum.

E. uvent, for event; socity, for society.

From this strong tendency to obscure sounds, Sheridan[31] recommends that all the unaccented syllables be, at first, pronounced with greater stress and fulness than we design ultimately to give them. The language of Walker is so strong that I give it entire: "There is

---

[31]Sheridan, Thomas: *Lectures on the Art of Reading,* London, 1781, p. 106.

scarcely anything," he remarks, "which more distinguishes a person of mean from one of good education, than the pronounciation of the unaccented vowels. When vowels are under the accent, the prince and the lowest of the people, pronounce them in the same manner. But, the unaccented syllables, in the mouth of the former have a distinct, open, and specific sound; while the latter, often totally sink them, or change them into other sounds. Those therefore who wish to pronounce well will be particularly attentive to the unaccented syllables; and will select them, for a time, as the objects of peculiar practice."[32] I have already stated that the principal sounds which deserve attention are those of *o* as in opinion; of *au* as in authority, of *u* as in singular; of *e* as in event, and of *i* (to which Walker gives the sound of *e*) in sentiment.

In addition to the instances enumerated above, I would particularly direct your attention:

1. To terminations in *ment,* judgment
2. To terminations in *ent,* consistent, commencement
3. To terminations in *ence,* existence
4. To terminations in *ible,* terrible
6. To terminations in *ow,* vulgarly sunk into *or* as in fellow, pillow
7. The diphthong *oi* vulgarly shortened into *i,* as join, appoint, disjoint
8. The *aw* at the end of a word or syllable is vulgarly changed into *or:* lor for law, sor for saw. This is very common in some parts of our country.

In adverting to so many cases where the unaccented vowel ought to retain its own sound, full and open; the question may occur: is this *always* the case? Is the unaccented syllable never to sink into an obscure sound?

It *is* in many instances, e.g., village, etc. All therefore who would speak with correctness should investigate the principles of English pronunciation in this, as well as in other respects. By ascertaining these principles, they will learn to pronounce with confidence and force; to give the obscure, and the open sound, in their proper places.

In considering the difficulties to which I have partially adverted in the Lecture, and the extent to which a bad articulation prevails, you

[32]Walker: *op. cit.,* p. 30.

will be less surprised at the earnestness with which all Teachers of Elocution recommend a short course of practice on the elementary sounds, and their easiest combinations. The following remarks of a highly distinguished Instructor in the Metropolis of Great Britain, will strike your mind as just. "Having learned to speak fast before we had acquired a correct utterance of the separate sounds, we must now return to these; and when we are assured that our fundamental errors are corrected, we may proceed by degrees to acquire facility, reading slowly at first, dwelling on all the consonants and making every one tell on the ear. At length the organs will become more expert in their office; will start into different positions with perfect ease; and make a ready and smooth transition without marring or confounding them. Thus will be gained a distinct and nervous articulation; free at the same time from any appearance of restraint or labor."[33] To this I would only add the suggestion that while our enunciation is improved by these exercises, we are likewise gaining a deeper insight into those principles on which the *harmony* of our language depends; and are thus acquiring a delicacy of taste in this respect, which will enable us to add the charm of gracefulness and ease to our own compositions.

---

[33]The editor is unable to locate the source of this quotation. In his pamphlet, *Exercises in Elocution* (Yale Library), Goodrich mentions the following persons as teachers of elocution: Knowles, Jones, Perry, Sheridan, Walker, Cummings, Jamieson, Fulton, and Knight.

DR. JAMES RUSH
PSYCHOLOGIST AND VOICE SCIENTIST

LESTER L. HALE

University of Florida

DR. JAMES RUSH made important contributions to the body of knowledge of our era; his work deserves accurate evaluation and reasonable recognition. Most advanced students of speech have heard his name, but many associate it only with his treatise, *The Philosophy of the Human Voice*[1] and are not aware of the true significance of his life's labor.[2] Few appreciate (1) the approach underlying his philosophy of voice, (2) his primary and basic postulates, (3) his major contributions to the field of speech. This article attempts to state these points, and to point out his important position as an early American investigator in the science of voice.

---

[1]James Rush: *The Philosophy of the Human Voice: Embracing Its Physiological History; Together With a System of Principles, by Which Criticism in the Art of Elocution May Be Rendered Intelligible, and Instruction, Definite and Comprehensive. To Which is Added a Brief Analysis of Song and Recitative*, Philadelphia, 1827. Cited hereafter as the *Philosophy*.

[2]For the reader's convenience, the publications of Rush are listed below in chronological order:

1827, *The Philosophy of the Human Voice*, 1st edition.
1833, *Philosophy*, 2nd edition (a revision).
1834, *Hamlet, A Dramatic Prelude in Five Acts* (a play).
1845, *Philosophy*, 3rd edition (a revision).
1855, *Philosophy*, 4th edition (a revision).
1859, *Philosophy*, 5th edition (a revision).
1865, *A Brief Outline of an Analysis of the Human Intellect* (begun in 1818).
1867, *Philosophy*, 6th edition (a minor revision).
1869, *Rhymes of Contrast on Wisdom and Folly*.
1879, *Philosophy*, 7th edition (a reprint).

In the first place, it should be remembered that Dr. James Rush was not a teacher of speech. He was a *physician,* and the son of a physician. In fact, his father, Dr. Benjamin Rush, a signer of the Declaration of Independence and one-time Surgeon General of Washington's army, was the famous physician for whom the Rush Medical School in Chicago was named.[3] His father endowed him with an honest, scientific curiosity, and apparently encouraged him in his study of medicine. James became a reputable physician, a fact which is borne out in many personal letters of testimony.[4]

During James Rush's practice of medicine he became especially interested in the controlling powers of *mind* and began making specific observations and investigations of the phenomenon of thought. In 1813 he lectured on *mind* to his father's classes at the medical school at the University of Pennsylvania. The essence of his early teaching was that "reasoning is only a train of physical perception," and that "mind in its outline consisted only of perception and memory; . . . this view seemed to be the basis of the general phenomena of thinking."[5] These observations, with modifications, were put in unpublished notation under date of 1818.[6]

By 1823, however, Rush stopped writing on *mind* and it was not until 1865 that he published *An Analysis of the Human Intellect.*[7] This delay was occasioned by at least five circumstances. The first of these was his desire to acquire "further knowledge of the various

---

[3]Biographers differ on the date of James Rush's birth; some say March 1, and others March 15, of 1786. However, the family tree and tombstone give March 15 as the date of James' birth; his brother, John, was born on March 1.

[4]Lester L. Hale: A Re-Evaluation of the Vocal Philosophy of Dr. James Rush as Based on a Study of His Sources, unpublished doctoral dissertation, Louisiana State University, 1942. Dr. James Rush willed the major portion of his sizeable estate to the Library Company of Philadelphia for the creation of the Ridgeway Branch, named for his deceased wife, Anne Ridgeway. In it is housed his own personal collection of books, manuscripts, and correspondence as well as that of his father. Much of the continuing research on Rush being done by this investigator is based on a study of this material.

[5]James Rush: *A Brief Outline of the Analysis of the Human Intellect,* Philadelphia, 1865, 2, 436. Cited hereafter as *Human Intellect.*

[6]Rush made notations in what he called his 'Common Book of Medicine' between the years 1818 and 1822. Reference to this unpublished work as well as excerpts from it may be found in *Human Intellect,* 2, 435 ff.

[7]*Human Intellect,* 2 vols.

departments of nature, science, art and life."[8] In order to make more objective observations on *mind* he sensed a need to acquaint himself in greater detail with areas in which it functioned. In further study of this phenomenon he found it involved not only perception and memory, but the manner in which mind was capable of expression.

Secondly, then, this led him to the realization that one of the outstanding agents of expression was the voice. In order to observe the function of *mind* it became necessary to record vocal behavior carefully. As will be later seen, this constituted the main reason for his detailed concern with voice and the organization of his observations into *The Philosophy of the Human Voice*.

His third reason for delaying publication of his investigations on *mind* was his hesitancy to encroach upon the realm of research dominated at that time by the "privileged order of metaphysicians."[9] In that day the popular approach to any study of *mind* was by way of metaphysical speculation. It was generally believed that *mind* was the *spirit,* and the *spirit* was an entity separated from matter and under the control of occult powers. To depart from this general approach, as did Rush, and undertake to describe the function of *mind* as a physiological phenomenon was heresy. Indeed, there was some belief that Rush was an atheistic crackpot because of such contemplations. But Rush believed in a "First Cause" capable of creating life and its organization in relation to matter. The departure from a position acceptable to his contemporary society was explained by his belief that even though an Almighty Power created initially all life together with an organization of minerals, that "laws of a full and perfect structure of vegetable and animal life"[10] would in turn yield themselves to human scientific investigation and classification. One of his earliest inventories of *mind* was made in terms of tangible descriptions of functional details; he attempted to show some of the physical ways in which mind controls thought and behavior; he sought to break down the governing agent of human life into discernible parts; and, he was persistent in his acknowledgment that an

---

[8]*Ibid.,* 471.
[9]*Ibid.,* 472.
[10]*Human Intellect,* 1.37.

Almighty God had created all existence and that our scientific investigation of the elements merely aided us in understanding His instruments of life. Rush had pried open the door of scientific investigation of *mind* at a time when public and religious reaction to such an inquiry was intense.

Of lesser significance, but constituting another reason for laying aside his treatise on the human intellect, was his desire to write in the field of medicine itself. He hoped to write a book that would be of a most practical nature and not one which confused fact and fiction. He proposed to call this book "Novus Ordo Medicinæ."

The detour in reaching his objective, a rationale of *mind,* was finally occasioned by his effort to court social approval of his authority. He reasoned that neither a text in medicine nor a professional dissertation on *mind* would be accepted by the hostile public until he had received acclaim through the medium of other publications more readily understandable and easily appreciated. This sensitivity no doubt intensified his determination first to complete the *Philosophy.*

When the *Philosophy of the Human Voice* was published in 1827, it was heralded by several teachers such as Jonathan Barber as an unprecedented triumph. The association and friendship which developed between Rush and Barber became a source of encouragement to Rush and contributed to his feeling that the *Philosophy* would be most popular.[11] Rush even anticipated its becoming a monumental work. The publication in 1834 of *Hamlet, A Dramatic Prelude in Five Acts,*[12] was a further attempt to receive favor through the writing of fiction. He hoped that by showing his ability to produce non-factual material he could command greater respect for his scientific reporting.

Only after examination of these reasons for the later publication (in 1865) of Rush's efforts to fathom the function of *mind* can one discern the underlying approach this physician made to a treatise in the field of speech.

---

[11] Jonathan Barber wrote in 1823, *Exercises in Reading and Recitation* (Baltimore). He and Rush were drawn to each other because of their identical points of view. Barber had migrated from England to Philadelphia where he taught elocution. He was the first to read and understand Rush's text, and three weeks after its publication gave public lectures in Musical Fund Hall of Philadelphia to illustrate the nature and uses of the work. Rush considered Jonathan Barber the maker of the early fortune of the *Philosophy.*

[12] James Rush: *Hamlet, A Dramatic Prelude in Five Acts,* Philadelphia, 1834.

The hybrid process of reasoning and experimentation made the investigations of Rush an interesting cross between the armchair psychology of his contemporaries and the experimental psychology which followed almost half a century later. It should be remembered that his 1818 recorded notations were contemporary with Bessel's report of the Greenwich observatory incident which called attention to individual differences and ushered in a new era in psychology. Thus, his primary postulates on mind and voice become historically significant in the field of psychology as well as speech.

Rush's first concern, then was with the *functioning of mind,* and his first major contention was that mind should be regarded as a physiological function as orderly as sensation itself and as tangible as muscle movement. His two volumes on the subject of the human intellect are too involved and cumbersome to be reported upon in detail, but it can be seen that he started from a premise of sound physiologic reality.

> All that man perceives, thinks, pronounces, and performs is respectively through his senses, his brain, and his muscles. From these physical and directive agencies proceed his science and his art; and from their proper or improper use severally arise his good and his evil, his error and his truth.[13]

He proceeds to break the function of mind into five "constituents." These are:

> First, primary perceptions of things before the senses. Second, memorial perceptions after their removal. Third, joint perceptions; by which primary are compared with primary, or memorial with memorials which are called unmixed; and mixed, when these two different forms are compared with each other. Fourth, conclusive perceptions, or those by which we come finally to a knowledge of the relationships of two or more of the primary and memorial to each other; from their agreement or identity to classify the things of nature; affirm their laws; and apply them to the purpose of science, of art, and of our physical, moral and intellectual selves. Fifth, verbal perceptions, or vocal and written signs of all the other four different forms; without which allotted and manageable signs; or in common phrase, without language of sound, or of

---

[13] *Human Intellect,* 1.9.

symbol, for thought, and passion; the human mind would be as limited as that of the brute.[14]

What Rush was saying simply meant that the complicated and mysterious functioning of mind was really an orderly sequence of sensation, memory, association, conclusive perception, and muscular and verbal performance responses.

> All its [mind's] intellectual functions and products, whether of thought, or passion, properly so distinguished; or of passion carried into nervous, muscular, or vocal action, are the effects, the whole effects, and nothing but the effects of these.[15]

His effort as a physician-scientist to understand mind as a physiological phenomenon—a function of tangible matter and human material—was one of the earliest beginnings of modern classifications in psychology. It was no doubt a forerunner of physiological psychology.

Secondly, he insisted that the function of mind was not complete until it had evidenced itself in some form of expression.

> The mind as we only can know it; is an indivisible compound of Thought and Speech or other sign. Which first begins, if they are not co-eval, is a point for Metaphysicians. We know that without mind, there would be no significant indication of it; and without speech or other sign of the mind, there would be no knowledge of its existence: or if known as a germ, it could not without language, be capable of self growth or expansion. With a joint agency, however, they give to man, all his power, beyond that of the brute, of greater muscular strength than his own. To describe the mind, therefore, it is necessary to show the inseparable connection between thought and the voice; with their influences on each other: for they cannot, separately, be fully known.[16]

Rush spent nearly forty years developing his concept of the verbal

---

[14]*Ibid.,* 195 (Beginning with the fourth edition, 1855, of the *Philosophy,* Rush attempted to introduce the double comma as a punctuation mark to be of value between a single comma and a semi-colon).

[15]*Ibid.,* 189.

[16]*Ibid.,* 4.

expression, verbal sign (the fifth constituent of mind), before completing his general study of mind.[17]

In pointing out the interdependence of thought and speech, and in demonstrating the functions of mind to be a physiological phenomenon, the third basic postulate becomes evident—that speech is part and parcel of a total mental and physical response. Although in both his books he stops the moving wheel to count its spokes, he remains constantly aware of man's dynamic nature, his integration, his existence as a unit, and his whole personality. "Wisdom, folly, virtue, and vice, with all their forms and effects are enacted by the mind,"[18] he says, and what a person is, and what he will be, is determined by the cultivated use of sensation, memory, association, and the verbal resultant. Mental processes, then, are one and the same with physical sensation and expression; and, speech cannot be isolated or disassociated from the physical being, or whole personality, for it is actually the fifth constituent of mind itself. These tenets of Rush remind one of current opinion in psychology and speech. In fact, the major philosophy of Charles Henry Woolbert, whose writings and teachings continue to influence our modern methodology was not unlike this point of view. In the preface to the first edition of his *Fundamentals of Speech,* Woolbert says:

> With this end in view it [his textbook] aims to offer speech-training for the whole man: body, voice, and mental mechanism. It is frankly psychological in foundation, and of psychologies is outspokenly behavioristic—that is to say, it insists that speech is a matter of the whole man, the cooperative activity of the entire organism; that it is a revelation of personality, but that the true definition of personality gives a picture compounded of thinking apparatus, emotional machinery, muscular activity, and body-wide participating parts—voice, brain, muscles, trunk, and limbs.[19]

Fourthly, in recording his *Philosophy of the Human Voice,* Rush endeavored to furnish "physiological data to Rhetoricians."[20] It was

---

[17]In a footnote Rush says that the *Philosophy of the Human Voice* would have been more properly called, the *Philosophy of the Verbal Sign of the Intellect. Human Intellect,* 1, 190.

[18]*Human Intellect,* 2.1.

[19]Charles Henry Woolbert: *The Fundamentals of Speech,* New York, 1920, i-ii.

[20]Rush's marginal notation in his personal copy of John Walker: *Elements of Elocution,* Boston, 1810, 244.

not his concern to create a system of rules, but to observe nature that he might give a physiological foundation to expressive art.

> Although I have gone deeply into the philosophical analysis of speech, and have spared no pains or detail in illustrating whatever might otherwise be obscure from its novelty; I have not pretended to make specific application of the principles of intonation, to all styles of reading and speaking voice. This assumption of the discipline and practice of the habitual teacher, is beyond my design.[21]

The anatomy of the speech mechanism had already been described by science, but the physiology or function of the mechanism had not been detailed beyond discernment of the parts of the system that produced the sound. Rhetoricians, on the other hand, had noted the elements of voice—force, pitch, quality, etc.,—but had not identified them with the functions of the anatomy. In publishing a vocal philosophy which gave a physiological foundation and explanation to vocal theory, Rush gave an entirely new and different emphasis to the study and teaching of speech.[22]

His last postulate has to do with the application he believed could be made of his organized arrangement and description of the vocal elements. Rush insisted that the natural phenomena of vocal expression were describable, and further, that only from such a description could students be guided in making their own analysis of nature. He believed that an actor's or speaker's first obligation was to nature, that to be natural in all expression was the prime prerequisite, but that a student must have the cues to recognition of nature's unfoldment which a study of the *Philosophy* should give him. Furthermore, when the dictates of nature inspire a performer he must have at his command the skill of a voice potential which will serve his creative instinct. That potential can be cultivated by exercise of the voice, unrelated to any specific performance effort. He reasoned that as a violinist must learn finger dexterity and tonal control through exercise, so should a vocalist, speaker, or singer, achieve vocal capacity that would serve him satisfactorily in moments of creative expression.

Having explained how Dr. Rush came to write in the field of

------

hy, 1827, 25.
Philadelphia, 1845, 123.

speech and what major premises formed the foundation of his various writings, we are now in position to examine the original contributions he made specifically in the field of speech.

The greater part of the *Philosophy of the Human Voice* consists of adaptation of principles found in other books by Rush's contemporaries and predecessors. It was his adaptation and treatment of these that was new. He acknowledged that most of the elements he treated were universally known, and in some cases already were deleveoped carefully. But there were several outstanding contributions in his book that apparently were products of his own thinking.

This report does not propose to show the influence of these contributions upon the work of later scholars, but there are notable points of comparison between his writings and modern thought. Many ideas usually attributed by recent writers to Rush are not among those regarded by this writer as original with him. For example: *eight qualities of voice* are attributed to Rush by Tressider.

> Most discussions of quality include the classifications of the various types of quality, usually eight, according to the list first made out by Dr. James Rush, an early pioneer in speech work. Deliberate application of those types: *aspirate, guttural, pectoral, nasal, oral, falsetto, normal,* and *orotund,* was of considerably more use to the old student of elocution than it is to modern students of the "natural" methods.[23]

Actually, Rush described only four: normal, falsetto, whisper, nasal, and even these were previously mentioned by Cooke, Hastings, Cockin, Mason, and others. Rush claimed no originality here except as to functional details of description. On the other hand, his points of greatest originality are not found as references in modern textbooks. This may be due to the fact that his individual approach and his original view-point were more that of a scientist, in an era when emphasis in teaching was upon oral and dramatic performance. By the time experimental phonetics commanded attention, Rush's pedagogical reputation had already been established and his profound purpose and important contributions forgotten.

---

[23]Argus Tressider: *Reading to Others,* New York, 1940, 200. A similar quotation can be found in Sarett and Foster: *Basic Principles of Speech,* New York, 1936, 215.

There are five major and original contributions of Rush to the field of speech. In the first place, he made a bold gesture at clarifying speech nomenclature. Such confusion had resulted from earlier writers using terms so freely and interchangeably that their concepts themselves were often obscured. Rush attempted to give rhyme and reason to the terms currently being used. For example, he drew together the "elements." He classified voice under five general heads: quality, force, time, abruptness, and pitch.[24] Discussion of pitch became more perspicuous under his terminology because he used terms with parallel reference in music. Many other useful gains were achieved in his reordering nomenclature. No doubt the nomenclature described and used in the *Philosophy* was a great influence in developing the speech terminology in use today.

The second, and without doubt the most important original, contribution was his concept of a *radical* and *vanishing* movement in the production of phonetic units. A greater part of his text is based upon this concept. Much of his work on pitch and stress appears to be more original with him than it actually was because of his use of *radical* and *vanish* to explain them. *Radical* is the beginning or *root* of each sound unit from which the *vanish* can develop all manner of movement to complete the unit. This *vanishing* movement has usually a fading effect, although in some cases the *radical* fades into a *stressed vanish*. The simplest illustration of *radical* and *vanish* is the diphthong or receding glide. In vowel movements of the word *day,* Rush refers to the [e] as the *Radical* and the [I] or [j] as the *vanish*. In the approaching glide [j] as in the word *yes,* the *radical* is the [j] and the [ɛ] the *stressed vanish*. There is no definite division of movement into two parts; rather these terms are "general reference to the two extremes of the movement."[25]

He further points out that when the voice moves through the *radical* and *vanish* in a smooth manner with no effort to prolong either the attack or the release of the sound, the *equable concrete* movement is formed. If the first part of the sound is prolonged and the *vanish* is terminated rapidly, the *protracted radical* is created. Likewise, the *protracted vanish* occurs when the *radical* is slighted greater stress and duration is given the *vanish*.

---

v, 1827, 29.

Rush's whole approach to vocal analysis through this principle of the *radical* and *vanishing* movement has a very modern flavor. Indeed, present day advocates of dynamic phonetics should find themselves quite at home with this concept.

Much can be explained by *radical* and *vanish*. Differences in stress and loudness occur always between the *radical* and *vanishing* movement. Between the *radical* and *vanish* there must be a difference in pitch. Song is distinguished from speech in that song is characteristically a *monotone*. The pitch differences in song are of melodic nature, but a word or syllable sung on a single melody note is a *monotone*. Rush says there can be no such thing as a *monotone* in speech for there must be a change in pitch sometime during the *radical-vanishing* movement to each syllable. This can certainly be observed when a person speaks in a so-called *monotone,* for the monotonous effect comes from a predominant pitch or pitch pattern, while there are still present the slight pitch changes during each *radical-vanishing* movement. The uses to which this principle can be put in voice training and speech correction are legion. Space will not permit a discussion of these applications here, but a lengthy discourse might be written on Rush's *radical* and *vanish* concept.

The third phase of his original work on voice was his explanation of the phonetic elements upon the function of *radical* and *vanish*. He not only reclassified them to avoid the inconsistencies of spelling, but also to observe the intonation of speech. He recognized thirty-five phonetic elements which he divided into three groups: the *tonics,* *subtonics,* and *atonics.* The *tonics* are capable of complete *radical* and *vanish* movements (vowels, glides); the *subtonics* can embrace this movement within themselves less perfectly, depending usually upon an adjacent tonic for completion (voiced consonants); and the *atonics* are incapable of employing the movement, but serve in the capacity of initiators or terminators (unvoiced consonants). The *tonics* serve best as vehicles of flexibility in intonation, the *subtonics* next best, and the *atonics* are of least value in that respect. He also described the sounds as to aspiration, abruptness and other phonetic characteristics. His was the clearest and most reasonable phonetic analysis of his day and one which is worthy of current consideration.

The fourth vocal principle he projected was his doctrine of syllabication. This again was based upon the *radical* and *vanishing* movement. A syllable depends upon the completion of the *radical* and *vanish*. When that movement has been terminated any new sound produced will of necessity initiate another syllable. The presence of a final *atonic* means that another syllable will be of necessity be initiated if it is followed by a *subtonic* or *tonic* which has the capacity to begin a new *radical* and *vanish* movement. Two adjacent *atonics* prolong the syllable, but once the *vanish* is completed by an *atonic* a new movement cannot be begun without a second syllable resulting. This concept of the continuing capacity of *subtonics* is in use today in the dynamic phonetic approach some choral directors use to instruct their people to "sing" voiced consonants. The whole concept of syllabication as based on the *radical* and *vanish* movement can be exceedingly useful in many phases of vocal instruction.

The fifth point of originality in Rush's vocal theory was his detailed description of the specific interval of inflection. He described the emotional and intellectual impressions created by the use of certain intervals of pitch-change in the spoken word. These vary from semi-tone changes in plaintive expression, when the change in pitch is so slight between the *radical* and *vanishing* movement that only the trained ear will recognize it as a varying pitch, to the octave inflection of interrogation and emphasis. He describes the effect of these intervals as they occur in both rising or falling *slides,* in the *circumflex* and in the *step* forms. These variations are so rapid and in some cases so minute that it is difficult to recognize their existence as an important discriminating factor between speech and song. They are responsible, however, for much of the emotion and shades of meaning in speech.

These five phases of his vocal philosophy can be regarded as the most significant and original contributions within his speech text.

The Philosophy of the Human Voice was so exhaustive for the time in which it appeared, that it served as a textbook in speech and made Rush an authoritative reference. Unfortunately, while it was widely employed by his immediate followers, the basic philosophy under which he labored became distorted. The *descriptive* analysis resulting from his philosophy and primary postulates came soon to be regarded by his students as a *prescriptive* system easily adapted to the needs of their various methods of vocal instruction, and Dr. James Rush became identified with the elocutionary systems and artifices which predominated the early American teaching in the field of speech.

How succeeding generations drew further and further away from his precepts cannot be told here, but to correct the mistaken identity we must judge Rush on the basis of his entire program of research and not alone upon a superficial view of his work on voice as recorded in the *Philosophy*.

It is easy to pass too hastily over the *title* of his book: *The Philosophy of the Human Voice.* The word *philosophy* was no random choice![26] It embodied the key to his purpose. Rush did not plan a prescriptive system of elocution. His purpose was to show speech to be a part of nature's orderly design; his classification of vocal phenomena which grew out of his classification of mind was a descriptive analysis of the voice potential. He is deserving of greater acclaim than simple identification with an outmoded system of histrionics. Perhaps he should be named in the textbooks of today as one of the important early contributors to the modern concept of speech as the index to total personality. He was a speech psychologist, and probably America's first voice scientist.

---

[26]The word *Philosophy* in Rush's day signified analysis and scientific investigation of facts and principles of reality and human nature. (Until the late 19th Century *physics* was *natural philosophy*.) Modern tools of science were unknown in his time, and he used the only available instrument of observation of the vocal phenomenon—the human ear. Rather than passing judgment on his descriptions, it would be exceedingly interesting to submit them to modern research to discern how much truth there was in them.

EDWARD A. PHILLIPS
MODERN PIONEER IN PUBLIC SPEAKING

RAYMOND G. SMITH

University of Wisconsin

THOUGH HIS TEXTBOOKS found wide acceptance throughout the country during the last four decades, relatively little is known of Arthur Edward Phillips, one of the modern founders of our profession. He deserves a place among the great American teachers and practitioners whose contributions secured for speech its present favorable academic standing.

Born in England January 31, 1867, at Sheerness-on-sea, he was brought to Toronto, Ontario as a child of four when the Phillips family emigrated. As one of four children he lived the life of a normal boy. He was educated in the public schools of Toronto where he was known as a brilliant and original pupil. That he had a keen,versatile mind was early evidenced not only by his being an honor pupil in school, but also by his frequent victories in chess when playing against adult members of the Toronto chess club. In describing Phillips' early life, his brother wrote:

> His early interests were Reading and Dramatics and everything pertaining to the stage. His reciting of The Chariot Race from *Ben Hur*, The Charge of the Light Brigade, and the impersonation of many Shakesperean characters made him unusually popular at the age of sixteen and attracted considerable attention until he was twenty, when he assembled a company of local talent and formed a dramatic company, producing Shakesperean plays and light comedies in Toronto and nearby towns. He was an unusual Shakesperean scholar. His early ambition was to portray Shakes-

[542]

perean characters and adopt the stage as his vocation. He had impersonated Hamlet, Richard III, Merchant of Venice and many others.[1]

With this career in dramatics he combined a career in business. Upon graduation from the Toronto Public Schools he took a position with the Canadian Steamship Railway Company, largest transportation company in Canada, and at the age of twenty-one was secretary to the company president.

In 1888 he married his boyhood sweetheart and leading lady, Maud Billings of Toronto, who died two years later leaving him a daughter less than a year old.

In 1892 the entire Phillips family moved to Chicago. Arthur promptly took out papers, becoming a United States citizen some five years later. In 1894, after nearly a decade of public lecturing, acting, and reading, he founded the Century School of Expression in Chicago which became the Phillips School of Oratory in 1900 and remained operative as such until 1932.

Phillips married Miss Abbie Birdsall of Rockford, Illinois, one of the instructors in his school, in 1896. The year before he had been appointed Head of the Department of Public Speaking of the Lutheran Theological Seminary of Chicago, a position which he held for the following thirty-seven years.

In addition to his teaching in the two schools, Phillips managed a consulting and tutoring service for business and professional persons. Here lawyers, ministers, and interpreters from many parts of the country came for his assistance.

He frequently lectured in and around Chicago. His pedagogical lectures covered various aspects of his specialties, current social problems, and the classics. Titles included: Mrichchakati, Sakuntala, Hamlet, Macbeth, Milton, and Dante. Titles of his popular lectures indicate concern for the individual listener's problems—Doubling Your Power, for instance. He also wrote a series of articles for New York magazines on public questions and was in popular demand as critic judge for intercollegiate debates.

Physically Phillips was small. Persons meeting him for the first

---

[1]Letter from Albert E. Phillips, a brother, to Mrs. Arthur Edward Phillips, February 26, 1944.

time estimated his height at about five feet five inches when actually he missed that figure by a full three inches. This mistaken impression arose from a great shock of hair—snow white before he was fifty— that spread over his head almost like a wig. He had fine, clear cut, well-proportioned features, florid complexion, and rather large ears. Despite a full mustache and a determined chin his face radiated friendliness and intelligence. Although short, he was rather stockily built and was an impressive figure.

Upon coming into his presence for the first time, students felt the compelling, almost indefinable power of his personality. This power apparently rested in an unusually complete knowledge of human nature. His students, perhaps the best of all judges, attribute much of his greatness as a teacher to his sympathetic understanding of their personalities and needs.

Phillips had an unusually fine voice. It was characterized by power, mellowness, richness, and an extremely wide range. A student and friend[2] writes that, so complete was his mastery over his vocal mechanism, he could conceal extreme fatigue and even illness from his best friends. This becomes significant in view of the fact that Phillips was a life-long sufferer from heart disease. The final ten years of his life were spent in constant ill health.

The story of Phillips' life would be incomplete without mention of his deep friendship and close association with Professor S. H. Clark of the University of Chicago. He often visited Clark's classes at the university and acted as a guest instructor in public speaking and interpretation, and was a favorite speaker at convocation exercises. He declined a teaching appointment in the university on the grounds that it would limit his many other activities.

Against the advice of physician and friends, Phillips maintained his high level of activity in teaching, lecturing, and creative writing up to the time of his death in 1932. He was ever willing to give time and counsel to all who came to him and he continued to do so in spite of frequent warnings against the inevitable consequences of overwork.[3]

Perhaps the best picture of Phillips, the man, condensed to a few words, is found in the following quotation:

[2]Personal letter from Benjamin F. J. Odell, May 15, 1946.
[3]Personal letter from Mrs. Arthur Edward Phillips, May 27, 1946.

He was particularly fitted for his life work by his rare inspirational power, sympathetic understanding of the student's needs, and extreme enthusiasm for his work. He was a man of indomitable will and self-discipline, of fine Christian character, high purposes, and genial kindly disposition.[4]

Phillips' philosophy of life was expressed in the philosophical dialogue, *The Life Magnificent*, which was published posthumously. This book contains a definition of the quality of life which he advocated and lived: "A life founded upon justice, and maintained by the exercise of a highly developed intelligence, guided by character and ennobled by love."[5]

The first record of Phillips' activity as a member of the National Association of Elocutionists appears in 1895. With the exception of two years he was present at every meeting of the association from then until 1915 when it was replaced by the National Association of Academic Teachers of Public Speaking, at which time, because of poor health, he dropped active membership.

As a member of the Association of Elocutionists, Phillips was a leader in the movement to substitute the word *speech* for the term *elocution*. Teachers of elocution were in ill repute with their doctrines of artificiality and their exaggerated emphasis upon delivery. A few of the more discerning members recognized the undesirable connotations in the term elocution itself, and advocated, as a necessary first-step in any reform, the discontinuance of its use.

According to the minutes of the fourth meeting of the National Association (Boston 1895), association secretary Thomas C. Trueblood[6] read a paper by A. E. Phillips on Speech, its Origin, Present Usage, and History. Following a careful etymological and historical linguistic analysis Phillips defined speech as: "Intelligible human utterance exclusive of singing."[7] However, it was not until 1906 that the Phillips faction succeeded in changing the name to The National

---

[4] *The National Cyclopaedia of American Biography*, 23, 402.

[5] *The Life Magnificent*, Chicago, 1934.

[6] In a personal letter dated June 16, 1946, Professor Trueblood wrote in answer to my inquiry: 'I never read any one's paper before the association but my own.' Someone must have neglected to correct the minutes!

[7] Reports of the 4th Annual Meeting of the National Association of Elocutionists, Boston, 1895.

Association for the Advancement of Speech Arts. During the eleven
year interim the minutes of the annual meetings carried repercussions
of the controversy aroused by the Phillips paper.

After starting his school of oratory and taking over the direction
of public speaking at the seminary, Phillips fully realized the need
for a new approach to the teaching of public speaking and interpretation. This, of course, was quite in line with his dislike for the term
elocution and all it connoted. With a dissatisfaction both for current
text-books and for current pedagogical practices as a point of departure, he spent more than half of his time and effort for the next
fifteen years in an attempt to analyze the need and supply a remedy.

His study was both thorough and systematic. In Canada he had
made acquaintance with the Rush system, where *The Philosophy of
the Human Voice* was used as a textbook. He now made an analysis
of the philosophies of Murdoch and Russell. This was followed by a
thorough study of W. D. Whitney, the lexicographer; Ellis, author
of *Early English Pronunciation;* Joshua Steele, Walker, Sheridan,
Shoemaker, and Alexander Melville Bell. Among the rhetoricians
studied were Aristotle, Quintilian, Cicero, Lord Kames, Day, Blair,
Whately, Hill, and Genung. He next made a study of the epics, novels,
and dramas of such authors as Shakespeare, Milton, Homer, Hugo,
and Dante. For help in making his analysis Phillips turned to the
then rapidly developing science of psychology. In Bautain's *Psychologie
expérimentale,* 1839; in William James' *The Principle of Psychology,*
1890; and in Ladd's *Psychology: Descriptive, Explanatory,* 1903, he
found material of inestimable value in helping him to formulate his
criteria objectively. He then made a systematic examination of the
master speeches of all ages, attempting to extract and state their
universal rhetorical principles. He also analyzed contemporary speakers, good and poor, including those heard at the national speech
association meetings. During the course of this research he accumulated
a personal library of some 1500 volumes.

His method, in brief, was as follows: He first listed all elements
found in great literature and in successful oratory. In a parallel
manner he listed the elements of mediocre speeches. Then, by an almost
mechanical process of elimination he determined the elements universally present in the great art and absent in the mediocre. Psychology
furnished him with a functional terminology in which to synthesize

the resultant principles. His success in thus determining and stating the universals in usable and unequivocal language may be to some extent judged from the following quotations. Karl R. Wallace in reviewing the revision of *Effective Speaking* wrote in 1938:

> Those familiar with the first edition (1908) of *Effective Speaking* will recall that Phillips offered a logical, practical, beautifully clear theory of speech composition. He distinguished five kinds of oratorical prose as determined by their general ends. Two cardinal means to each end were designated as the principle of reference to experience and the principle of cumulation. Each end was promoted, furthermore, by four forms of support or amplification: restatement, general illustration, specific instance, and testimony. These forms of support and cardinal principles, as well as simple yet adequate precepts of speech organization and style, Phillips applied copiously to persuasive discourse.[8]

Robert West said in 1943:

> I studied the book as a text at Milton College. I don't believe that there has ever been a book as superior to its predecessors as this book was to its predecessors. This book was a star in the firmament when there were no other stars. The outstanding things in the book are its classifications, the impelling motives, and the fundamental purposes of the kinds of speeches. His ideas lived and had a profound influence upon every textbook that followed his.[9]

The termination of the elocutionary period and the beginning of the present era in the teaching of speech can be dated from the modernization of classical rhetorical theory and the application of individual and group psychology to functional speech needs. Phillips' contribution and Trueblood's success in securing speech course credit at the University of Michigan[10] were milestones in this transition.

The Tone System was published in 1899, *Effective Speaking* in 1908, and *Natural Drills in Expression With Selections* in 1909. These were books, which, although strictly speech textbooks, could be shown to school administrators with full confidence in the academic respectability of their content. *Effective Speaking* received commenda-

---

[8]Karl R. Wallace: *QJS*, 24:510, 1938.
[9]Robert West: personal interview, August 4, 1943.
[10]Thomas A. Trueblood: *QJS*, 27:503, 1941.

tions from over two hundred teachers of public speaking in American colleges and universities, was widely adopted, and sold over 75,000 copies. A modern pioneer had made his contribution.

THE EVOLUTION OF PUBLIC SPEAKING
BY JAMES A. WINANS

LIONEL CROCKER

Denison University

IN 1922, I was giving a commencement address in a small consolidated high school outside Adrian, Michigan. Before the address, I was looking over the books in the library in the superintendent's office and I noticed Professor Winans' book. This discovery symbolized for me the widespread use of this book which has so greatly influenced the teaching and practice of public speaking in the United States during the twentieth century. At about this time the book was earning its heaviest royalties. Undoubtedly this text on public speaking has earned more for its author than any other similar work.

Lester Thonssen in the bibliography of his *Readings in Rhetoric and Public Speaking* listed only one text on public speaking published in this century. That book is the one under consideration. Historians in this field will agree with Thonssen that this book will take its place in the tradition alongside Blair, Campbell and Whately.

My interest in this topic goes back ten years ago to a bookstore in Chicago where I ran across Winan's *Notes on Public Speaking*, published in 1911. This is a thin volume of 126 pages. Like hundreds of other teachers of public speaking, I had used the edition of *Public Speaking* put out by The Century Company. Later in a second hand book store in Columbus, Ohio, I stumbled on to a copy of the 1915 edition of *Public Speaking* published privately by Mr. Winans. In spare moments I found myself comparing these with the 1916 edition and making notes. In Detroit in 1942, I had the pleasure of cornering Mr. Winans in the lobby of the Statler Hotel for a couple of hours.

He reminisced about his teaching career and about the origins of his text. I could not remember all that he said, so I begged him to write me a letter. He sent me a letter of five pages single-spaced. I also had a letter from him written in 1929 when I was beginning my study of Henry Ward Beecher. In addition to these materials, Mr. Winans sent me a copy of *The Public Speaking Review* of 1914 which has an article on "Persuasion" by him. It is from these sources that I am writing the following.

In 1893, Winans enrolled at Hamilton College. There he had a close drill in Frink's adaptation of Austin Phelps' *English Style in Public Discourse*. But the most important training the students got in actual public speaking was in their noon chapels. The professor's description of these periods is so vivid that I am going to quote from his letter.

> The most important training we got was in our "noon chapels." On Wednesdays at 12 the three lower classes (there were only about 140 students in the college at that time) met in chapel for declamations. And ripsnorting declamations were in favor. But this was toned by the fact that sophomores "shook up" the frosh, and the frosh retaliated. This shaking up, or razzing, at times became pretty violent, derisive applause, catcalls, and even missiles unless the professor in charge was a strong man. Smith wasn't, and by the end of my senior year even grave and reverend seniors were shaken up. I was the last man in my class to be up (or *on*, as the idiom was) in chapel with a senior oration, and my own class shook me up; but by that time one was either completely cowed or thoroughly hardened. Apparently though I have never been a brave spirit and have suffered as much as most from stage fright, I seem to have been hardened; for I quite enjoyed myself that day. The loud and frequent applause, which had no relation to what I said, only enabled me to cover up the fact that I was ill prepared. I doubt if I could take it now.

In addition to this training, the entire college assembled on Saturday noons for freshmen and sophomore essays, junior debates and senior orations. The debating at Hamilton was largely impromptu. Little or no preparation was made. There was no assembling of material, no analysis. Wise cracks were the order of the day. Winans said he once brought down the house when he cried out in a debate on some

Near-Eastern question, when the Kurds had been committing their usual atrocities, "But what about the blood-curdling Kurds?" But when his colleagues discovered that he had thought of this smart remark the night before, they turned away in disgust.

For two years after graduation, Winans taught in a small high school in New York State. In 1899, he was recommended to Duncan Campbell Lee of Cornell University as an assistant in public speaking. He was to take the place of Edwin DuBois Shurter who left his part-time teaching and practice of law in Ithaca to go to Texas. It is interesting that the man who recommended Winans was Professor Oren Root of the Department of Mathematics at Hamilton College, a brother of Elihu Root. Professor Oren Root had an interest in public speaking and did all he could to promote it at Hamilton College.

Duncan Campbell Lee had gone over completely to the "think the thought school" and Winans was introduced to this, which was in a sense a radical change from the mechanical training in elocution he had received up to this point. But he was prepared for the change. In one of his declamations at Hamilton College, he felt the thrill that comes from having an audience listen. He was reciting a declamation from Chauncey DePew on some current problem, and he was saying it in a way which challenged the attention of his fellow students. The idea of conversing with an audience as a norm of public speaking was planted in the mind of Winans through this experience. Duncan Campbell Lee was probably influenced by the teachings of Emerson and S. S. Curry, both of Boston. Later Winans studied with Curry. A book which influenced Lee's teaching was Kirby's *Public Speaking and Reading*. This book is referred to several times by Winans in the course of his text. Lee wrote a leaflet called "How to Study a Declamation" which is drawn upon by Winans in his section on studying selections. What Professor Winans says of his colleague is interesting:

> Lee was an excellent teacher and could get a class going. I listened to him a great deal for the next two years, and watched his teaching. Since we worked in the same sections it was up to me to fall in line. But while he was good, I doubt if he ever worked out ideas very fully. He carried the idea of visualization to an extreme, insisting on an image for every word. He knew little of psychology. Of course, I am speaking of his work on delivery. He had no unusual rhetorical theories; but did inspire (and help)

his students to write very good college orations. And he was a good debate coach, and got excellent work in briefing. He was a master hand in working up occasions, and could fill a considerable theatre downtown for a debate. We had one a year—with Penn.

Two thoughts in this quotation are worth noting. Professor Winans points to Lee's lack of knowledge of psychology and to his insistence on briefing. I'll return to these matters shortly.

After three years teaching at Cornell, Winans had an offer from the University of California. He went there for a year, but did not like it, and he returned to Cornell to teach and study law. In 1914 he was made a full professor of public speaking with his own department. In a way this smashed the tradition that there had never been a full professor of the subject at Cornell University. In 1907, by working summers, Winans managed to get his law degree. If his health had not been wrecked in the process of teaching and studying, he might have gone into the practice of law. Instead, he stuck to teaching. In 1920 Dartmouth doubled his salary and took him away from Cornell. At the age of seventy, he will retire this year.

The book as we know it today had its beginnings in 1908 when he had printed for his classes two chapters on "Conversing with an Audience," and "Further Study of Delivery." In 1911, he published his *Notes on Public Speaking,* which included the following topics: Introduction, Problem of Delivery, Conversing with an Audience, Attention, Development of Attention, Imagination and Feeling, Attention of the Audience, A Chapter of Fragments, Gesture, Study and Delivery of Selections, Conclusion.

In 1914, there was an article in *The Public Speaking Review* on "Persuasion" by Winans. This article quotes liberally from Professor James. The *Notes on Public Speaking* had long extracts from the prominent psychologists of the day. In the article in *The Public Speaking Review,* he puts into italics this statement: "We thus find that we reach the heart of our inquiry into volition when we ask by what process it is that the thought of any given action comes to prevail stably in the mind." (This quotation from William James is used on the model card in the 1916 edition drawn up to show the student how to use index cards in accumulating material.) He queries toward the end of the article, "Tact, sincerity of the speaker, reference to experience, precedent, and the other elements of persuasion—do they not all fit into the theory? Do they not all serve to induce the audience to look straight at your proposal? Now can we not go a step, a big step, further, and say that to make a man *believe* a proposition is to lead him to give attention to one set of reasons and to banish another set from the mind?"

The period from 1911 to 1915, Winans describes as his best four years. They were the years that saw the book into its final shape. Let me quote from his letter:

> Then began my four best years. Always too busy with classes and the individual work I have always insisted upon, the running of the department, I managed to get in some thinking and in the next three years I blocked out *Public Speaking,* but when in the early fall of '15 I set the presses running much was still unfinished, which explains some things about the book. But some of the parts done under the pressure of the call for copy are best. Working summers and vacation and when I could, I got the book out just before January 1, 1916. I published it myself because the bookmen had ideas that did not suit me. And there I was, teacher, author, publisher, salesman, ad-writer, wrapper and general utility man. Too much; and in the spring I sold out, at a much better rate than I could have had before I proved the market. Then as I had no plates and as my 5000 edition threatened to be used up by fall, I was told to revise at once if I wished to at all. I was teaching in the University of California that summer, and was also president of the N.A.T.S.

From the time of its publication in 1916 by The Century Company until it was superseded by *Speech-Making,* it was one of the leading textbooks in its field. Dana Ferrin of The Century Company has written me that *Public Speaking* has gone through twenty-four printings or about an average of one each year.

Winans took his *Notes* of 1911 and, using it as a base, added eight more chapters for the edition which he printed privately. He left the treatment, which has been described in a previous paragraph as it was, and added chapters on Attention, The Expository Speech, Influencing Conduct, Persuasion and Belief, Selecting the Subject, Finding Material and Extemporaneous or Written. When he revised the book for The Century Company, he took the material on voice and delivery from the middle of the book and shifted it to the back. This shift is significant in that it symbolizes Winans' determination to play down action and play up materials and organizations, persuasion and belief. Throughout all his writings on public speaking we detect Winans' reaction against elocution. One sees also in his writings a distaste for dogmatism in the teaching of public speaking. He believes, for example, that a great debt is due to A. E. Phillips for his stress on speech composition but he does not like the attempt to boil down to one page the theory of public speaking.

The concepts of the book that make it a distinct contribution to the teaching of public speaking in the twentieth century are those of communication with an audience, the idea of attention and persuasion, and the idea of interest. In his letter of 1929 to me he says, "I suppose my ideas of attention and persuasion are as near to originality as I get." Of his treatment of conversation, he said, "I do not mean that I have discovered some new thing but I thought I had crystallized it and put in a more tangible form."

As I have pointed out Winans made the observation that Lee did not know much psychology. The subject must have fascinated Winans. In the course of the *Notes* and the editions of 1915 and 1916, I find the following texts referred to. Winans was more than a dabbler in the subject. He quoted from the following imposing list: Angell, Bain, Baldwin, Betts, Bos, Colvin and Bagley, Creighton, DeGarmo, Dewey, Halleck, Hollingsworth, James, Judd, Knowleton, Ladd, LeBon, McDougall, O'Shea, Pillsbury, Pyle, Ross, Royce, Scott, Sidis, Squires, Titchener, and Thorndike. The two psychologists to whom he is most indebted are James and Titchener.

In the twentieth century, there has been no book on public speaking that has drawn so heavily upon the accumulated store of writings on rhetoric and public speaking as has Winans' *Public Speaking*. His book is a mosaic of quotations from the following authors overlaid with his own interpretations. Most of these books are familiar to the teacher of public speaking. Aristotle, Bacon, Baker, Baldwin, Beecher, Brooks, Clark, Cooper, Curry, Emerson, Essenwein, Foster, Frink, Gardiner, Genung, Fulton and Trueblood, Hart, Hill, Jellife, Kirby, Ketcham, Lamont, Matthews, Marsh, Newcomer, Perry, Phelps, Phillips, Plato, Quintilian, Sears, Shepard, Shurter, Smith,

Spencer, Barrett, Wendell, and Whately. The rhetoricians who interested him most seem to be Genung, Baker, Curry, and Phillips.

As I have said, I believe that *Public Speaking* by James A. Winans will be regarded by historians as *the* textbook of the first half of the twentieth century. It might conceivably be the subject for a Ph.D. thesis in the year of 2011, a hundred years after the *Notes* were published.

KENNETH BURKE AND THE "NEW RHETORIC"

MARIE HOCHMUTH

University of Illinois

"W E DO NOT flatter ourselves that any one book can contribute much to counteract the torrents of ill will into which so many of our contemporaries have so avidly and sanctimoniously plunged," observes Kenneth Burke in introducing his latest book, *A Rhetoric of Motives,* but "the more strident our journalists, politicians, and alas! even many of our churchmen become, the more convinced we are that books should be written for tolerance and contemplation."[1] Burke has offered all his writings to these ends.

Burke's first work, *Counter-Statement,* published in 1931, was hailed as a work of "revolutionary importance," presenting "in essence, a new view of rhetoric."[2] Since that time, he has written a succession of books either centrally or peripherally concerned with rhetoric: *Permanence and Change,* 1935; *Attitudes toward History,* 1937; *The Philosophy of Literary Form,* 1941; *A Grammar of Motives,* 1945; and his latest, *A Rhetoric of Motives,* 1950. An unfinished work entitled *A Symbolic of Motives* further indicates his concern with the problem of language.

Sometimes thought to be "one of the few truly speculative thinkers of our time,"[3] and "unquestionably the most brilliant and suggestive

---

[1] Kenneth Burke: *A Rhetoric of Motives,* New York, Prentice-Hall, Inc., 1950, p. xv. Reprinted by permission.

[2] Isidor Schneider: A New View of Rhetoric, *New York Herald Tribune Books, VIII*:4, December 13, 1931.

[3] Malcolm Cowley: Prolegomena to Kenneth Burke, *The New Republic, CXXII*: 18, 19, June 5, 1950.

critic now writing in America,"[4] Burke deserves to be related to the great tradition of rhetoric.

Although we propose to examine particularly *A Rhetoric of Motives* we shall range freely over all his works in order to discover his principles. We propose to find first the point of departure and orientation from which he approaches rhetoric; next to examine his general concept of rhetoric; then to seek his method for the analysis of motivation; and finally, to discover his application of principles to specific literary works.

In 1931, in *Counter-Statement,* Burke noted, "The reader of modern prose is ever on guard against 'rhetoric,' yet the word, by lexicographer's definition, refers but to 'the use of language in such a way as to produce a desired impression upon the reader or hearer.' "[5] Hence, accepting the lexicographer's definition, he concluded that "effective literature could be nothing else but rhetoric."[6] In truth, "Eloquence is simply the end of art, and is thus its essence."[7]

As a literary critic, representing a minority view, Burke has persisted in his concern with rhetoric, believing that "rhetorical analysis throws light on literary texts and human relations generally."[8] Although Burke is primarily concerned with literature "as art,"[9] he gives no narrow interpretation to the conception of literature. He means simply works "designed for the express purpose of arousing emotions,"[10] going so far as to say, "But sometimes literature so designed fails to arouse emotions—and words said purely by way of explanation may have an unintended emotional effect of considerable magnitude."[11] Thus a discussion of "effectiveness" in literature "should be able to include unintended effects as well as intended ones."[12] "By literature we mean written or spoken words."[13]

As has been observed, the breadth of Burke's concepts results "in a

---

[4]W. H. Auden: A Grammar of Assent, *The New Republic, CV:*59, July 14, 1941.
[5]*Counter-Statement,* New York, 1931, p. 265.
[6]*Ibid.,* p. 265.
[7]*Ibid.,* p. 53.
[8]*A Rhetoric of Motives,* pp. xiv, xv.
[9]*Counter-Statement,* p. 156.
[10]*Ibid.*
[11]*Ibid.*
[12]*Ibid.*
[13]*Ibid.*

similar embracing of trash of every description. . . . For purposes of analysis or illustration Burke draws as readily on a popular movie, a radio quiz program, a *Herald Tribune* news item about the National Association of Manufacturers, or a Carter Glass speech on gold as on Sophocles or Shakespeare. Those things are a kind of poetry too, full of symbolic and rhetorical ingredients, and if they are bad poetry, it is a bad poetry of vital significance in our lives."[14]

Sometimes calling himself a pragmatist, sometimes a sociological critic, Burke believes that literature is designed to "do something"[15] for the writer and the reader or hearer. "Art is a means of communication. As such it is certainly designed to elicit a 'response' of some sort."[16] The most relevant observations are to be made about literature when it is considered as the embodiment of an "act,"[17] or as "symbolic action."[18] Words must be thought of as "acts upon a scene,"[19] and a "symbolic act" is the *"dancing of an attitude,"*[20] or incipient action. Critical and imaginative works are "answers to questions posed by the situation in which they arose." Not merely "answers," they are *"strategic* answers," or *"stylized* answers."[21] Hence, a literary work is essentially a *"strategy for encompassing a situation."*[22] And, as Burke observes, another name for strategies might be *"attitudes."*[23] The United States Constitution, e.g., must be thought of as the *"answer"* or *"rejoinder"* to "assertions current in the situation in which it arose."[24]

Although Burke distinguishes between literature "for the express purpose of arousing emotions" and "literature for use," the distinction is flexible enough to permit him to see even in such a poem as Milton's *Samson Agonistes,* "moralistic prophecy" and thus to class it as "also a kind of 'literature for use,' use at one remove. . . ."[25]

---

[14]Stanley Edgar Hyman: *The Armed Vision,* New York, 1948, pp. 386, 387.
[15]*The Philosophy of Literary Form,* Louisiana, 1941, p. 89.
[16]*Ibid.,* pp. 235, 236.
[17]*Ibid.,* p. 89.
[18]*Ibid.,* p. 8.
[19]*Ibid.,* p. vii.
[20]*Ibid.,* p. 9.
[21]*Ibid.,* p. 1.
[22]*Ibid.,* p. 109.
[23]*Ibid.,* p. 297.
[24]*Ibid.,* p. 109.
[25]*A Rhetoric of Motives,* p. 5.

In further support of his comprehensive notion of art is his conception that since "pure art makes for acceptance," it tends to "become a social menace in so far as it assists us in tolerating the intolerable."[26] Therefore, "under conditions of competitive capitalism there must necessarily be a large *corrective* or *propaganda* element in art."[27] Art must have a "horatory function, an element of suasion or inducement of the educational variety; it must be partially *forensic.*"[28]

Burke thus approaches the subject of rhetoric through a comprehensive view of art in general. And it is this indirect approach that enables him to present what he believes to be a "New Rhetoric."[29] In part, he has as his object only to "rediscover rhetorical elements that had become obscured when rhetoric as a term fell into disuse, and other specialized disciplines such as esthetics, anthropology, psychoanalysis, and sociology came to the fore (so that esthetics sought to outlaw rhetoric, while the other sciences . . . took over, each in its own terms, the rich rhetorical elements that esthetics would ban)."[30]

Sometimes though to be "intuitive" and "idiosyncratic"[31] in his general theories, Burke might be expected to be so in his theory of rhetoric. "Strongly influenced by anthropological inquiries,"[32] and finding Freud "suggestive almost to the point of bewilderment,"[33] Burke, essentially a classicist in his theory of rhetoric, has given the subject its most searching analysis in modern times.

According to Burke, "Rhetoric [comprises] both the *use* of persuasive resources *(rhetorica utens,* as with the philippics of Demosthenes) and the *study* of them *(rhetorica docens,* as with Aristotle's treatise on the 'art' of Rhetoric)."[34] The "basic function of rhetoric" is the "use of words by human agents to form attitudes or to induce

---

[26]*The Philosophy of Literary Form,* p. 321.
[27]*Ibid.*
[28]*Ibid.*
[29]*A Rhetoric of Motives,* p. 40.
[30]*Ibid.,* pp. xiii, 40.
[31]*The Philosophy of Literary Form,* p. 68.
[32]*A Rhetoric of Motives,* p. 40.
[33]*The Philosophy of Literary Form,* p. 258.
[34]*A Rhetoric of Motives,* p. 36.

actions in other human agents. . . ."[35] It is *"rooted in an essential function of language itself, a function that is wholly realistic, and is continually born anew; the use of language as a symbolic means of inducing cooperation in beings that by nature respond to symbols."*[36] The basis of rhetoric lies in "generic divisiveness which, being common to all men, is a universal fact about them, prior to any divisiveness caused by social classes." "Out of this emerge the motives for linguistic persuasion. Then, *secondarily,* we get the motives peculiar to particular economic situations. In parturition begins the centrality of the nervous system. The different nervous systems, through language and the ways of production, erect various communities of interests and insights, social communities varying in nature and scope. And out of the division and the community arises the 'universal' rhetorical situation."[37]

Burke devotes 131 pages to a discussion of traditional principles of rhetoric, reviewing Aristotle, Cicero, Quintilian, St. Augustine, the Mediaevalists, and such more recent writers as De Quincey, De Gourmont, Bentham, Marx, Veblen, Freud, Mannheim, Mead, Richards, and others,[38] noting the "wide range of meanings already associated with rhetoric, in ancient texts. . . ."[39] Thus he comes upon the concept of rhetoric as "persuasion;" the nature of rhetoric as "addressed" to an audience for a particular purpose; rhetoric as the art of "proving opposites;" rhetoric as an "appeal to emotions and prejudices;" rhetoric as "agonistic;" rhetoric as an art of gaining "advantage;" rhetoric as "demonstration;" rhetoric as the verbal "counterpart" of dialectic; rhetoric, in the Stoic usage, as opposed to dialectic; rhetoric in the Marxist sense of persuasion "grounded in dialectic." Whereas he finds that these meanings are "often not consistent with one another, or even flatly at odds,"[40] he believes that they can all be derived from "persuasion" as the "Edenic" term, from which they have all "Babylonically" split, while persuasion, in turn "involves communication by the signs of consubstantiality, the appeal

---

[35]*Ibid.,* p. 41.
[36]*Ibid.,* p. 43.
[37]*Ibid.,* p. 146.
[38]*Ibid.,* pp. 49-180.
[39]*Ibid.,* p. 61.
[40]*Ibid.,* pp. 61, 62.

of *identification.*"[41] As the "simplest case of persuasion," he notes that "You persuade a man only insofar as you can talk his language by speech, gesture, tonality, order, image, attitude, idea, *identifying* your ways with his."[42]

In using *identification* as his key term, Burke notes, "Traditionally, the key term for rhetoric is not 'identification,' but 'persuasion.' . . . Our treatment, in terms of identification, is decidedly not meant as a substitute for the sound traditional approach. Rather, . . . it is but an accessory to the standard lore."[43] He had noted that "when we come upon such aspects of persuasion as are found in 'mystification,' courtship, and the 'magic' of class relationships, the reader will see why the classical notion of clear persuasive intent is not an accurate fit, for describing the ways in which the members of a group promote social cohesion by acting rhetorically upon themselves and one another."[44] Burke is completely aware that he is not introducing a totally new concept, observing that Aristotle had long ago commented, "It is not hard . . . to praise Athenians among Athenians,"[45] and that one persuades by "identifying" one's ways with those of his audience.[46] In an observation of W. C. Blum, Burke found additional support for his emphasis on *identification* as a key concept. "In identification lies the source of dedications and enslavements, in fact of cooperation."[47] As for the precise relationship between identification and persuasion as ends of rhetoric, Burke concludes, "we might well keep it in mind that a speaker persuades an audience by the use of stylistic identifications; his act of persuasion may be for the purpose of causing the audience to identify itself with the speaker's interests; and the speaker draws on identification of interests to establish rapport between himself and his audience. So, there is no chance of our keeping apart the meanings of persuasion, identification ('consubstantiality') and communication (the nature of rhetoric as 'addressed'). But, in given instances, one or another of these elements

---

[41] *Ibid.*, p. 62.
[42] *Ibid.*, p. 55.
[43] *Ibid.*, p. xiv.
[44] *Ibid.*
[45] *Ibid.*, p. 55.
[46] *Ibid.*
[47] *Ibid.*, p. xiv.

may serve best for extending a line of analysis in some particular direction."[48] "All told, persuasion ranges from the bluntest quest of advantage, as in sales promotion or propaganda, through courtship, social etiquette, education, and the sermon, to a 'pure' form that delights in the process of appeal for itself alone, without ulterior purpose. And identification ranges from the politician who, addressing an audience of farmers, says, 'I was a farm boy myself,' through the mysteries of social status, to the mystic's devout identification with the source of all being."[49] The difference between the "old" rhetoric and the "new" rhetoric may be summed up in this manner: whereas the key term for the "old" rhetoric was *persuasion* and its stress was upon deliberate design, the key term for the "new" rhetoric is *identification* and this may include partially "unconscious" factors in its appeal. Identification, at its simplest level, may be a deliberate device, or a means, as when a speaker identifies his interests with those of his audience. But *identification* can also be an "end," as "when people earnestly yearn to identify themselves with some group or other." They are thus not necessarily acted upon by a conscious external agent, but may act upon themselves to this end. Identification "includes the realm of transcendence."[50]

Burke affirms the significance of *identification* as a key concept because men are at odds with one another, or because there is "division." Identification is compensatory to division. If men were not apart from one another, there would be no need for the rhetorician to proclaim their unity. If men were wholly and truly of one substance, absolute communication would be of man's very essence."[51] In pure identification there would be no strife. Likewise, there would be no strife in absolute separateness, since opponents can join battle only through a mediatory ground that makes their communication possible, thus providing the first condition necessary for their interchange of blows. But put identification and division ambiguously together . . . and you have the characteristic invitation to rhetoric.

---

[48]*Ibid.,* p. 46.
[49]*Ibid.,* p. xiv.
[50]Kenneth Burke: Rhetoric—Old and New, *The Journal of General Education,* V:203, April 1951.
[51]*A Rhetoric of Motives,* p. 22.

Here is a major reason why rhetoric, according to Aristotle, 'proves opposites.' "[52]

As a philosopher and metaphysician Burke is impelled to give a philosophic treatment to the concept of unity or identity by an analysis of the nature of *substance* in general. In this respect he makes his most basic contribution to a philosophy of rhetoric. "Metaphysically, a thing is identified by its *properties*,"[53] he observes. "To call a man a friend or brother is to proclaim him consubstantial with oneself, one's values or purposes. To call a man a bastard is to attack him by attacking his whole line, his 'authorship,' his 'principle' or 'motive' (as expressed in terms of the familial). An epithet assigns substance doubly, for in stating the character of the object it . . . contains an implicit program of action with regard to the object, thus serving as motive."[54]

According to Burke, language of all things "is most public, most collective, in its substance."[55] Aware that modern thinkers have been skeptical about the utility of a doctrine of substance,[56] he nevertheless recalls that "substance, in the old philosophies, was an *act;* and a way of life is an *acting-together;* and in acting together, men have common sensations, concepts, images, ideas, attitudes that make them *consubstantial*."[57] "A doctrine of *consubstantiality* . . . may be necessary to any way of life."[58] Like Kant, Burke regards substance as a "necessary form of the mind." Instead of trying to exclude a doctrine of substance, he restores it to a central position and throws critical light upon it.

In so far as rhetoric is concerned, the "ambiguity of substance" affords a major resource. "What handier linguistic resource could a

---

[52]*Ibid.*, p. 25.

[53]*Ibid.*, p. 23.

[54]*A Grammar of Motives,* New York, 1945, p. 57. For discussion of *substance* as a concept, see, *Ibid.*, pp. 21-58; Aristotle: *Categoriae,* tr. by E. M. Edghill, *The Works of Aristotle,* ed. by W. D. Ross, I, Ch. 5; Aristotle: *Metaphysics,* tr. by W. D. Ross, Book Δ, 8, 1017b, 10; Spinoza: *The Ethics,* in *The Chief Works of Benedict De Spinoza,* tr. by R. H. M. Elwes, London, 1901, Rev. ed., II, 45 ff; John Locke: *An Essay Concerning Human Understanding,* London, 1760, 15th ed., I, Bk. II, Chs. XXIII, XXIV.

[55]*The Philosophy of Literary Form,* p. 44.

[56]*A Rhetoric of Motives,* p. 21.

[57]*Ibid.*

[58]*Ibid.*

rhetorician want than an ambiguity whereby he can say 'The state of affairs is substantial such-and-such,' instead of having to say 'The state of affairs *is* and/or *is not* such-and-such?'"[59]

The "commonplaces" or "topics" of Aristotle's *Rhetoric* are a "quick survey of opinion" of "things that people generally consider persuasive." As such, they are means of proclaiming *substantial* unity with an audience and are clearly instances of identification.[60] In truth, *identification* is "hardly other than a name for the function of sociality."[61] Likewise, the many tropes and figures, and rhetorical form in the large as treated by the ancients are to be considered as modes of identification.[62] They are the "signs" by which the speaker identifies himself with the reader or hearer. "In its simplest manifestation, style is ingratiation."[63] It is an attempt to "gain favor by the hypnotic or suggestive process of 'saying the right thing.' "[64] Burke discusses form in general as "the psychology of the *audience*,"[65] the "arousing and fulfillment of desires."[66] The exordium of a Greek oration is an instance of "conventional"[67] form, a form which is expected by the audience and therefore satisfies it. Other recognizable types of form are "syllogistic progression," "repetitive" form, and "minor or incidental" forms which include such devices as the metaphor, apostrophe, series, reversal, etc.[68] The proliferation and the variety of formal devices make a work eloquent.[69]

Reviewing *A Rhetoric of Motives,* Thomas W. Copeland observed, "It gradually appears that there is no form of action of men upon each other (or of individuals on themselvs) which is really outside of rhetoric. But if so, we should certainly ask whether rhetoric *as a term* has any defining value."[70] The observation is probably not fair,

---

[59]*A Grammar of Motives,* pp. 51, 52.
[60]*A Rhetoric of Motives,* pp. 56, 57.
[61]*Attitudes toward History,* New York, 1937, II, 144.
[62]*A Rhetoric of Motives,* p. 59.
[63]*Permanence and Change,* New York, 1935, p. 71.
[64]*Ibid.*
[65]*Counter-Statement,* pp. 38-57.
[66]*Ibid.,* p. 157.
[67]*Ibid.,* p. 159.
[68]*Ibid.,* pp. 157-161.
[69]*Ibid.,* pp. 209-211.
[70]Thomas W. Copeland: Critics at Work, *The Yale Review,* XL:167-169, Autumn 1950.

for Burke does give rhetoric a defining value in terms of persuasion, identification, and address or communication to an audience of some sort, despite his observation, "Wherever there is persuasion, there is rhetoric. And wherever there is 'meaning' there is 'persuasion.' "[71]

It is true that in his effort to show "how a rhetorical motive is often present where it is not usually recognized, or thought to belong,"[72] Burke either points out linkages which have not been commonly stressed, or widens the scope of rhetoric. A twentieth-century orientation in social-psychological theory thus enables him to note that we may with "more accuracy speak of persuasion 'to attitude,' rather than persuasion to out-and-out action." For persuasion "involves choice, will; it is directed to a man only insofar as he is *free*." In so far as men "*must* do something, rhetoric is unnecessary, its work being done by the nature of things, though often these necessities are not of natural origin, but come from necessities imposed by man-made conditions,"[73] such as dictatorships or near-dictatorships. His notion of persuasion to "attitude" does not alter his generally classical view of rhetoric, for as he points out, in "Cicero and Augustine there is a shift between the words 'move' *(movere)* and 'bend' *(flectere)* to name the ultimate function of rhetoric." And he merely finds that this shift "corresponds to a distinction between act and attitude (attitude being an incipient act, a leaning or inclination)."[74] His notion of persuasion to "attitude" enables him to point out a linkage with poetry: "Thus the notion of persuasion to *attitude* would permit the application of rhetorical terms to purely *poetic* structures; the study of lyrical devices might be classed under the head of rhetoric, when these devices are considered for their power to induce or communicate states of mind to readers, even though the kinds of assent evoked have no overt, practical outcome."[75]

In his reading of classical texts, he had noted a stress "upon *teaching* as an 'office' of rhetoric." Such an observation enables him to link the fields of rhetoric and semantics. He concludes that "once you treat instruction as an aim of rhetoric you introduce a principle that

---

[71]*A Rhetoric of Motives*, p. 172.
[72]*Ibid.*, p. xiii.
[73]*Ibid.*, p. 50.
[74]*Ibid.*
[75]*Ibid.*

can widen the scope of rhetoric beyond persuasion. It is on the way to include also works on the theory and practice of exposition, description, *communication* in general. Thus, finally, out of this principle, you can derive contemporary 'semantics' as an aspect of rhetoric."[76]

As he persists in "tracking down" the function of the term *rhetoric*, Burke notes an ingredient of rhetoric "lurking in such anthropologist's terms as 'magic' and 'witchcraft.' "[77] and concludes that one "comes closer to the true state of affairs if one treats the socializing aspects of magic as a 'primitive rhetoric' than if one sees modern rhetoric simply as a 'survival of primitive magic.' "[78] Whereas he does not believe that the term *rhetoric* is a "substitute" for such terms as *magic, witchcraft, socialization,* or *communication,* the term *rhetoric* "designates a *function* . . . present in the areas variously covered by those other terms."[79] Thus, one can place within the scope of rhetoric "all those statements by anthropologists, ethnologists, individual and social psychologists, and the like, that bear upon the *persuasive* aspects of language, the function of language as *addressed,* as direct or round-about appeal to real or ideal audiences, without or within."[80] All these disciplines have made "good contributions to the New Rhetoric."[81]

In "individual psychology," particularly the Freudian concern with the neuroses of individual patients, "there is a strongly rhetorical ingredient."[82] Burke asks the question, "Indeed, what could be more profoundly rhetorical than Freud's notion of a dream that attains expression by stylistic subterfuges designed to evade the inhibitions of a moralistic censor? What is this but the exact analogue of the rhetorical devices of literature under political or theocratic censorship? The *ego* with its *id* confronts the *super-ego* much as an orator would confront a somewhat alien audience, whose susceptibilities he must flatter as a necessary step towards persuasion. The Freudian psyche

---

[76]*Ibid.*, p. 77.
[77]*Ibid.*, p. 44.
[78]*Ibid.*, p. 43.
[79]*Ibid.*, p. 44.
[80]*Ibid.*, pp. 43-44.
[81]*Ibid.*, p. 40.
[82]*Ibid.*, p. 37.

is quite a parliament, with conflicting interests expressed in ways variously designed to take the claims of rival factions into account."[83]

By considering the individual self as "audience" Burke brings morals and ethics into the realm of rhetoric. He notes that "a modern 'post-Christian' rhetoric must also concern itself with the thought that, under the heading of appeal to audiences, would also be included any ideas or images privately addressed to the individual self for moralistic or incantatory purposes. For you become your own audience, in some respects a very lax one, in some respects very exacting, when you become involved in psychologically stylistic subterfuges for presenting your own case to yourself in sympathetic terms (and even terms that seem harsh can often be found on closer scrutiny to be flattering, as with neurotics who visit sufferings upon themselves in the name of very high-powered motives which, whatever their discomfiture, feed pride." Therefore, the "individual person, striving to form himself in accordance with the communicative norms that match the cooperative ways of his society, is by the same token concerned with the rhetoric of identification."[84]

By considering style as essentially a mode of "ingratiation" or as a technique by which one gives the signs of identification and consubstantiality, Burke finds a rhetorical motive in clothes, pastoral, courtship, and the like.[85]

Burke links dialectics with rhetoric through a definition of dialectics in "its most general sense" as "linguistic transformation"[86] and through an analysis of three different levels of language, or linguistic terminology.[87] Grammatically, he discusses the subject from the point of view of linguistic merger and division, polarity, and transcendence, being aware that there are "other definitions of dialectics:"[88] "reasoning from opinion;" "the discovery of truth by the give and take of converse and redefinition;" "the art of disputation;" "the processes of 'interaction' between the verbal and the non-verbal;" "the competition of coöperation or the coöperation of competition;"

[83]*Ibid.*, pp. 37, 38.
[84]*Ibid.*, pp. 38, 39.
[85]*Ibid.*, pp. 115-127; see, also, p. xiv.
[86]*A Grammar of Motives*, p. 402.
[87]*A Rhetoric of Motives*, p. 183.
[88]*A Grammar of Motives*, p. 402, 403.

"the spinning of terms out of terms;" "the internal dialogue of thought;" "any development . . . got by the interplay of various factors that mutually modify one another, and may be thought of as voices in a dialogue or roles in a play, with each voice or role in its partiality contributing to the development of the whole;" "the placement of one thought or thing in terms of its opposite;" "the progressive or successive development and reconciliation of opposites;" and "so putting questions to nature that nature can give unequivocal answer."[89] He considers all of these definitions as "variants or special applications of the functions"[90] of linguistic transformation conceived in terms of "Merger and division," "The three Major Pairs: action-passion, mind-body, being-nothing," and "Transcendence."[91]

Burke devotes 150 pages to the treatment of the dialectics of persuasion in the *Rhetoric*,[92] in addition to extensive treatment of it on the grammatical level.[93] Linguistic terminology is considered variously persuasive in its Positive, Dialectical, and Ultimate levels or orders.[94] "A positive term is most unambiguously itself when it names a visible and tangible thing which can be located in time and place."[95] Dialectical terms "have no such strict location."[96] Thus terms like "Elizabethanism" or "capitalism" having no positive referent may be called "dialectical."[97] Often called "polar" terms,[98] they require an "opposite"[99] to define them and are on the level of "action," "principles," "ideas."[100] In an "ultimate order" of terminology, there is a "guiding idea" or "unitary principle."[101]

From the point of view of rhetoric, Burke believes that the "difference between a merely 'dialectic' confronting of parliamentary conflict and an 'ultimate' treatment of it would reside in this: The

---

[89]*Ibid.*, p. 403.
[90]*Ibid.*
[91]*Ibid.*, p. 402.
[92]*A Rhetoric of Motives*, pp. 183-333.
[93]*A Grammar of Motives*, pp. 323-443.
[94]*A Rhetoric of Motives*, p. 183.
[95]*Ibid.*
[96]*Ibid.*, p. 184.
[97]*Ibid.*
[98]*Ibid.*
[99]*The Philosophy of Literary Form*, n. 26, p. 109.
[100]*A Rhetoric of Motives*, p. 184.
[101]*Ibid.*, p. 187.

'dialectical' order would leave the competing voices in a jangling relation with one another (a conflict solved *faute de mieux* by 'horse-trading'); but the 'ultimate' order would place these competing voices themselves in a *hierarchy,* or *sequence,* or *evaluative series,* so that, in some way, we went by a fixed and reasoned progression from one of these to another, the members of the entire group being arranged *developmentally* with relation to one another."[102] To Burke "much of the *rhetorical* strength in the Marxist dialectic comes from the fact that it is 'ultimate' in its order,"[103] for a "spokesman for the proletariat can think of himself as representing not only the interests of that class alone, but the grand design of the entire historical sequence. . . ."[104]

In his concept of a "pure persuasion," Burke seems to be extending the area of rhetoric beyond its usual scope. As a metaphysician he attempts to carry the process of rhetorical appeal to its ultimate limits. He admits that what he means by "pure persuasion" in the "absolute sense" exists nowhere, but believes that it can be present as a motivational ingredient in any rhetoric, no matter how "advantage-seeking such a rhetoric may be."[105] "Pure persuasion involves the saying of something, not for an extraverbal advantage to be got by the saying, but because of a satisfaction intrinsic to the saying. It summons because it likes the feel of a summons. It would be nonplused if the summons were answered. It attacks because it revels in the sheer syllables of vituperation. It would be horrified if, each time it finds a way of saying, 'Be damned,' it really did send a soul to rot in hell. It intuitively says, 'This is so,' purely and simply because this is so."[106] With such a concept Burke finds himself at the "borders of meta-physics, or perhaps better 'meta-rhetoric'. . . ."[107]

Of great significance to the rhetorician is Burke's consideration of the general problem of motivation. Concerned with the problem of motivation in literary strategy,[108] he nevertheless intends that his

---

[102]*Ibid.*
[103]*Ibid.,* p. 190.
[104]*Ibid.,* pp. 190, 191.
[105]*Ibid.,* p. 269.
[106]*Ibid.*
[107]*Ibid.,* p. 267.
[108]*The Philosophy of Literary Form,* p. 78.

observations be considered pertinent to the social sphere in general.[109]
He had observed that people's conduct has been explained by an
"endless variety of theories: ethnological, geographical, sociological,
physiological, historical, endocrinological, economic, anatomical, mystical, pathological, and so on."[110] The assigning of motives, he concludes, is a "matter of *appeal*,"[111] and this depends upon one's general
orientation. "A motive is not some fixed thing, like a table, which one
can go to and look at. It is a term of interpretation, and being such
it will naturally take its place within the framework of our *Weltan-
schauung* as a whole."[112] "To explain one's conduct by the vocabulary
of motives current among one's group is about as self-deceptive as
giving the area of a field in the accepted terms of measurement. One
is simply interpreting with the only vocabulary he knows. One is
stating his orientation, which involves a vocabulary of ought and
ought-not, with attendant vocabulary of praiseworthy and blame-
worthy."[113] "We discern situational patterns by means of the particular vocabulary of the cultural group into which we are born."[114]
Motives are "distinctly linguistic products."[115]

To Burke, the subject of motivation is a "philosophic one, not
ultimately to be solved in terms of empirical science."[116] A motive
is a "shorthand" term for "situation."[117] One may discuss motives on
three levels, rhetorical, symbolic, and grammatical.[118] One is on the
"grammatical" level when he concerns himself with the problem of
the "intrinsic," or the problem of "substance."[119] "Men's conception
of motive . . . is integrally related to their conception of substance.
Hence, to deal with problems of motive is to deal with problems of
substance."[120]

---

[109]*Ibid.*, p. 105.
[110]*Permanence and Change*, p. 47.
[111]*Ibid.*, p. 38.
[112]*Ibid.*
[113]*Ibid.*, p. 33.
[114]*Ibid.*, p. 52.
[115]*Ibid.*
[116]*A Grammar of Motives*, p. xxiii.
[117]*Permanence and Change*, p. 44.
[118]*A Grammar of Motives*, p. 465.
[119]*Ibid.*
[120]*Ibid.*, p. 337.

On the "grammatical" level Burke gives his most profound treatment of the problem of motivation. Strongly allied with the classicists throughout all his works in both his ideas and his methodology, Burke shows indebtedness to Aristotle for his treatment of motivation. Taking a clue from Aristotle's consideration of the "circumstances" of an action,[121] Burke concludes that "In a rounded statement about motives, you must have some word that names the *act* (names what took place, in thought or deed), and another that names the *scene* (the background of the act, the situation in which it occurred); also, you must indicate what person or kind of person *(agent)* performed the act, what means or instruments he used *(agency)*, and the *purpose.*"[122] Act, Scene, Agent, Agency, Purpose become the "pentad" for pondering the problem of human motivation.[123] Among these various terms grammatical "ratios" prevail which have rhetorical implications. One might illustrate by saying that, for instance, between *scene* and *act* a logic prevails which indicates that a certain quality of scene calls for an analogous quality of act. Hence, if a situation is said to be of a certain nature, a corresponding attitude toward it is implied. Burke explains by pointing to such an instance as that employed by a speaker who, in discussing Roosevelt's war-time power exhorted that Roosevelt should be granted "unusual powers" because the country was in an "unusual international situation." The scene-act "ratio" may be applied in two ways. "It can be applied deterministically in statements that a certain policy *had* to be adopted in a certain situation, or it may be applied in hortatory statements to the effect that a certain policy *should be* adopted in conformity with the situation."[124] These ratios are "principles of determination."[125] The pentad would allow for ten such ratios: scene-act, scene-agent, scene-agency, scene-purpose, act-purpose, act-agent, act-agency, agent-purpose, agent-agency, and agency-purpose.[126] Political commentators now generally use *situation* as their synonym for *scene*, "though often

[121]*Ethica Nicomachea*, tr. by W. D. Ross, III, i, 16.
[122]*A Grammar of Motives*, p. xv.
[123]*Ibid.*
[124]*Ibid.*, p. 13.
[125]*Ibid.*, p. 15.
[126]*Ibid.*

without any clear concept of its function as a statement about motives."[127]

Burke draws his key terms for the study of motivation from the analysis of drama. Being developed from the analysis of drama, his pentad "treats language and thought primarily as modes of action."[128] His method for handling motivation is designed to contrast with the methodology of the physical sciences which considers the subject of motivation in mechanistic terms of "flat cause-and-effect or stimulus-and-response."[129] Physicalist terminologies are proper to non-verbalizing entities, but man as species should be approached through his specific trait, his use of symbols. Burke opposes the reduction of the human realm to terms that lack sufficient "coordinates;" he does not, however, question the fitness of physicalist terminologies for treating the physical realm. According to Burke, "Philsophy, like common sense, must think of human motivation dramatistically, in terms of action and its ends."[130] "Language being essentially human, we should view human relations in terms of the linguistic instrument."[131] His "vocabulary" or "set of coordinates" serves "for the integration of all phenomena studied by the *social* sciences."[132] It also serves as a "perspective for the analysis of history which is a 'dramatic' process. . . ."[133]

One may wonder with Charles Morris whether "an analysis of man through his language provides us with a full account of human motives."[134] One strongly feels the absence of insights into motivation deriving from the psychologists and scientists.

Burke is not only philosopher and theorist; he has applied his critical principles practically to a great number of literary works. Of these, three are of particular interest to the rhetorician. In two instances, Burke attempts to explain the communicative relationship between the writer and his audience. Taking the speech of Antony

[127]*Ibid.,* p. 13.
[128]*Ibid.,* p. xxii.
[129]*The Philosophy of Literary Forms,* pp. 103, 106.
[130]*A Grammar of Motives,* pp. 55, 56.
[131]*Ibid.,* p. 317.
[132]*The Philosophy of Literary Form,* p. 105.
[133]*Ibid.,* p. 317.
[134]Charles Morris: The Strategy of Kenneth Burke, *The Nation, CLXIII*:106, July 27, 1946.

from Shakespeare's *Julius Cæsar*,[135] Burke examines the speech from
"the standpoint of the rhetorician, who is concerned with a work's
processes of appeal."[136] A similar operation is performed on a scene
from *Twelfth Night*.[137]

Undoubtedly one of his most straightforward attempts at analysis
of a work of "literature for use," occurs in an essay on "The Rhetoric
of Hitler's 'Baale.' "[138] "The main ideal of criticism, as I conceive it,"
Burke has observed, "is to use all that there is to use."[139] "If there
is any slogan that should reign among critical precepts, it is that 'circumstances alter occasions.' "[140] Considering *Mein Kampf* as "the well
of Nazi magic,"[141] Burke brings his knowledge of sociology and
anthropology to bear in order to "discover what kind of 'medicine'
this medicine-man has concocted, that we may know, with greater
accuracy, exactly what to guard against, if we are to forestall the
concocting of similar medicine in America."[142] He considers Hitler's
"centralizing hub of *ideas*"[143] and his selection of Munich as a "mecca
geographically located"[144] as methods of recruiting followers "from
among many discordant and divergent bands. . . ."[145] He examines
the symbol of the "international Jew"[146] as that "of a *common
enemy*,"[147] the " 'medicinal' appeal of the Jew as scapegoat. . . ."[148]

His knowledge of psychoanalysis is useful in the analysis of the
"sexual symbolism" that runs through the book: "Germany in
dispersion is the 'dehorned Siegfried.' The masses are 'feminine.' As
such, they desire to be led by a dominating male. This male, as
orator, woos them—and, when he has won them, he commands them.
The rival male, the villainous Jew, would on the contrary 'seduce'

---

[135]Antony in Behalf of the Play, *Philosophy of Literary Form*, pp. 329-343.
[136]*Ibid.*, p. 330.
[137]Trial Translation (from *Twelfth Night*), *Ibid.*, pp. 344-349.
[138]*Ibid.*, pp. 191-220.
[139]*Ibid.*, p. 23.
[140]*Ibid.*
[141]*Ibid.*, p. 192.
[142]*Ibid.*, p. 191.
[143]*Ibid.*, p. 192.
[144]*Ibid.*
[145]*Ibid.*
[146]*Ibid.*, p. 194.
[147]*Ibid.*, p. 193.
[148]*Ibid.*, p. 195.

them. If he succeeds, he poisons their blood by intermingling with them. Whereupon, by purely associative connections of ideas, we are moved into attacks upon syphilis, prostitution, incest, and other similar misfortunes, which are introduced as a kind of 'musical' argument when he is on the subject of 'blood poisoning' by inter-marriage or, in its 'spiritual' equivalent, by the infection of 'Jewish' ideas. . . ."[149]

His knowledge of history and religion is employed to show that the "*materialization* of a religious pattern" is "one terrifically effective weapon . . . in a period where religion has been progressively weakened by many centuries of capitalist materialism."[150]

Conventional rhetorical knowledge leads him to call attention to the "power of endless repetition;"[151] the appeal of a sense of "community;"[152] the appeal of security resulting from "a world view" for a people who had previously seen the world only "piecemeal;"[153] and the appeal of Hitler's "inner voice"[154] which served as a technique of leader-people "identification."[155]

Burke's analysis is comprehensive and penetrating. It stands as a superb example of the fruitfulness of a method of comprehensive rhetorical analysis which goes far beyond conventional patterns.

CONCLUSION

Burke is difficult and often confusing. He cannot be understood by casual reading of his various volumes. In part the difficulty arises from numerous vocabularies he employs. His words in isolation are usually simple enough, but he often uses them in new contexts. To read one of his volumes independently, without regard to the chronology of publication, makes the problem of comprehension even more difficult because of the specialized meanings attaching to various words and phrases.

Burke is often criticized for "obscurity" in his writings. The charge may be justified. However, some of the difficulty of comprehension

---

[149]*Ibid.*
[150]*Ibid.*, p. 194.
[151]*Ibid.*, p. 217.
[152]*Ibid.*
[153]*Ibid.*, p. 218.
[154]*Ibid.*, p. 207.
[155]*Ibid.*

arises from the compactness of his writing, the uniqueness of his organizational patterns, the penetration of his thought, and the breadth of his endeavor. "In books like the *Grammar* and the *Rhetoric*," observed Malcolm Cowley, "we begin to see the outlines of a philosophical system on the grand scale. . . Already it has its own methodology (called 'dramatism'), its own esthetics (based on the principle that works of art are symbolic actions), its logic and dialectics, its ethics (or picture of the good life) and even its metaphysics, which Burke prefers to describe as a meta-rhetoric."[156]

One cannot possibly compress the whole of Burke's thought into an article. The most that one can achieve is to signify his importance as a theorist and critic and to suggest the broad outlines of his work. Years of study and contemplation of the general idea of effectiveness in language have equipped him to deal competently with the subject of rhetoric from its beginning as a specialized discipline to the present time. To his thorough knowledge of classical tradition he has added rich insights gained from serious study of anthropology, sociology, history, psychology, philosophy, and the whole body of humane letters. With such equipment, he has become the most profound student of rhetoric now writing in America.

---

[156]Malcolm Cowley: Prolegomena to Kenneth Burke, *The New Republic, CXXII*: 18, 19, June 5, 1950.

I. A. RICHARDS AND THE "NEW RHETORIC"

MARIE HOCHMUTH

University of Illinois

"NO ONE, I imagine, migrates from Literature to Education for fun," wrote I. A. Richards in 1955, "but through a feeling as to what will happen if we do not develop improved teaching soon enough."[1] To approach Richards merely as a literary man concerned with literary problems is to lose sight of the sense of urgency that runs through all his writings. *As a literary man he found himself dealing with a verbal medium,* and he became profoundly concerned with the influence of the medium upon thought in all its forms. Conceiving of the language medium as the "instrument of all distinctively human development,"[2] he became persistent in a search for a sounder theoretical approach to language, a method for comprehending it in its various forms and multifarious uses, and the efficiency of language as an instrument. His twin interests have produced a stream of books that begins in 1922 and continues undiminished. Problems once comprehended under the ancient trivium—logic, grammar, and rhetoric—have reappeared under many titles, *The Foundations of Aesthetics* (with C. K. Ogden and James Wood, 1922), *The Meaning of Meaning* (with C. K. Ogden, 1923), *Principles of Literary Criticism* (1924), *Science and Poetry* (1926), *Practical Criticism* (1929), *Mencius on the Mind* (1932), *Basic Rules of Reason* (1933), *Coleridge on the Imagination* (1934), *Philosophy of Rhetoric* (1936), *Interpretation in Teaching* (1938), *How to Read a Page* (1942),

---

[1] I. A. Richards: *Speculative Instruments,* Chicago, 1955, p. xi.
[2] *The Philosophy of Rhetoric,* New York, 1936, p. 131.

Speculative Instruments (1955), and other works dealing with Basic English.

In 1936, Richards opened his *Philosophy of Rhetoric* with the remark: "These lectures are an attempt to revive an old subject. I need spend no time, I think, in describing the present state of Rhetoric. . . . So low has Rhetoric sunk that we would do better just to dismiss it to Limbo than to trouble ourselves with it—unless we can find reason for believing that it can become a study that will minister successfully to important needs."[3]

Even if Richards had never written a book under the caption of *The Philosophy of Rhetoric,* his other works would have considerable relevance for the student of rhetoric. His lifelong concern has been with the working of words in their many functions, and none of his works leaves any doubt that he is aware of a rhetorical function.

My purpose is primarily to examine Richards' attempt to revive an old subject. Although a central concern will be with his *Philosophy of Rhetoric,* I shall range freely over all his writings in order to determine his guiding principles. I shall be concerned with his conception of language, his theory of communication in general, his attempt to reorient rhetoric, his critical principles. I shall also be concerned with his place in the great tradition of rhetoric.

In 1923, when Richards' first important book, *The Meaning of Meaning,* was published with C. K. Ogden as collaborator, the authors voiced their conviction of an urgency which existed for a stricter examination of language from a point of view then not receiving attention.[4] Their timing was based upon two considerations: (1) the "readiness amongst psychologists to admit the importance of the problem" of language; and (2) the "realization that men of learning and sincerity are lamentably at the mercy of forms of speech."[5] Thus, in the preface, they suggested a psychological approach to the problems of language and trusted that dividends from such an approach might be seen in the lives of men of the work-a-day world.

As the authors turned to the matter of the fundamental nature of language, they concluded that "though often spoken of as a medium

---

[3] *Ibid.,* p. 3.
[4] *The Meaning of Meaning,* New impression, New York, 1953, p. x.
[5] *Ibid.,* pp. x, xi.

of communication," it is "best regarded as an instrument; and all instruments are extensions, or refinements, of our sense-organs."[6] Although language is to be considered a "system of signs,"[7] it is "no mere signalling system"[8] or "code;"[9] it is an "organ—the supreme organ of the mind's self-ordering growth."[10] It is an "instrument for controlling our becoming."[11]

What, precisely, a sign is, and how language might be thought to be a member of the family of signs have long been problems to psychologists and students of language. In attempting to definitize the concept of sign, the authors concluded that anything which can be experienced or enjoyed and is understood to refer to something else is to be regarded as a sign.[12] Sign experience comes about as the result of the recurrence of experiences in partial uniformity.[13] Signs function by virtue of previous membership in a context or configuration that once affected us as a whole.[14] Even when part of the context reappears, that part affects us as though the whole context were present. Thus, that part of the context may be said to have sign or referential function. For instance, dark skies, thunder, lightning, and rain may once have constituted for us a configuration or context. Thereafter, if thunder or any of the other constituents of the configuration are noted, they affect us as though the rest of the context were present, and we take them as a sign of rain necessitating appropriate adaptive responses. A sign is "always a stimulus similar to some part of an original stimulus and sufficient to call up" an engram or residual trace left by the preceding experience.[15]

Words in language share the referential nature and work by the same mechanism as do all signs. However, since those signs that are used for purposes of communication and as instruments of thought occupy a peculiar place in the family of signs, and, according to

---

[6]*Ibid.,* p. 98.
[7]*Ibid.,* p. vii.
[8]*The Philosophy of Rhetoric,* p. 131.
[9]*Speculative Instruments,* p. 9.
[10]*Ibid.,* p. 9.
[11]*Ibid.,* p. 9.
[12]*The Meaning of Meaning,* Note, p. 21; see also, p. 50.
[13]*Principles of Literary Criticism,* 13th impression, New York, 1952, p. 90.
[14]*The Meaning of Meaning,* p. 55.
[15]*Ibid.,* p. 53.

Richards, in human experience generally, they may, for convenience, be referred to as *symbols*. Words, arrangments of words, images, gestures, drawings, and mimetic sounds are all to be considered instruments of thought and communication. These devices are all used to direct and organize, record and communicate; consequently they are to be referred to as symbols.[16]

In stating what symbols direct and organize, or what they record and communicate, Richards distinguishes between Thoughts and Things. It is Thought, or as Richards says, *reference* which is directed and organized; it is also Thought which is recorded and communicated. Language may trick us into believing that things are recorded and communicated; however, it is really thought about things or reference to things which is symbolized. Although we say that "the gardener mows the lawn when we know that it is the lawn-mower which actually does the cutting, so, though we know that the direct relation of symbols is with thought, we also say that symbols record events and communicate facts."[17]

When language is used to make a statement, three factors are involved: (1) the symbol; (2) thought or reference; and (3) the object of thought, or referent. Between the thought and a symbol, "causal relations hold." When we speak, we employ symbolism caused partly by reference and partly by social and psychological factors, including the purpose for which we make the reference, an intended effect upon other persons, and our attitude. When we listen, the symbols that we hear cause us to perform acts of reference and to assume attitudes which will be more or less similar to the act and attitude of the speaker.[18]

Richards' famous triangle showing the relations among symbols, reference, and referent has become a useful tool among psychologists. In addition to revealing a causal relation between a symbol and reference, it reveals that between thought and referent there is also a relation, "more or less direct," as when we think about or attend to a painting which we see, or "indirect," as when we think of or refer to Hitler. Between the symbol and the referent, there is no

---

[16]*Ibid.*, pp. 23, 9.
[17]*Ibid.*, p. 9.
[18]*Ibid.*, pp. 10, 11.

really relevant relation other than an indirect one resulting from its being used by someone to stand for some referent.[19]

Thus, one notes that, according to Richards' analysis of language, "thinking or reference is reducible to causal relations." When one speaks of a reference, he is, in fact, speaking of external and psychological contexts by which a sign is linked to its referent. The mental events that take place in an act of reference to produce the symbol, Richards calls "psychological context." "All thinking, all reference," he maintains, "is adaptation due to psychological contexts which link together elements in external contexts." The contextual thory of reference covers all "beliefs, ideas, conceptions and 'thinkings of' " which relate the symbol to the referent. It asserts the recurrence of mental events in their main features with partial uniformity.[20]

Let us take the following three sets of symbols to illustrate Richards' analysis of language and the classification of its uses:

1. Winston Churchill is eighty-three years old.
2. The grand old man who occupied 10 Downing Street during the Second World War is eighty-three years old.
3. Four-score and three he counts his years, proud England's mighty son.

The first sentence Richards would identify as a purely referential statement, and, therefore, a *scientific* use of language. The context out of which the symbol grew would include recurrent experiences with the process of explicit naming and counting. The referent is the person bearing the name and having those years.

The second sentence represents a change in symbolization. The references, or psychological context, out of which the symbols were composed might include an affectionate attitude on the part of the composer of the symbol, a remembering of the events of the war, a recollection of others who had occupied the house at 10 Downing Street, in addition to a strict reference to the number of years of life. The referent is still to a person. The symbol, however, has not been produced for merely referential uses. Attitudes, reminiscences, and perhaps other factors have exerted strong influence. This use of language Richards, labels "emotive" or "mixed," hence, "rhetorical."[21]

---

[19]*Ibid.*, p. 11.
[20]*Ibid.*, pp. 73, 68, 200, 57.
[21]*Ibid.*, p. 234.

The third set of symbols represents still further change in symbolization. The purely referential function of language has almost completely vanished. Who is being talked about is no longer definite. The psychological context out of which this symbolization grew might contain feelings about age and England and some queries about relations, sonship, fatherhood. It might even include feelings about Lincoln at Gettysburg. This use of language represents almost completely the "emotive" function of language and would be regarded as poetry, good or bad.

When Richards and his collaborator published *The Meaning of Meaning,* they claimed among their peculiar contributions the following: "An account of interpretation in causal terms by which the treatment of language as a system of signs becomes capable of results," and second, "A division of the functions of language into two groups, the symbolic and the emotive." The symbolic use of words is *"statement;* the recording, the support, the organization and the communication of references." The emotive use of words is the "use of words to express or excite feelings and attitudes."[22] There are, in other words, "two totally distinct uses of language."[23]

Communication, according to Richards, starts from the "natural isolation and severance of minds." The experience of any two people can be but similar.[24] There can be no such thing as transference of experience or participation in identical experience.[25] By the use of symbols one may provoke experience in another. A "language transaction or a communication" may be defined as "a use of symbols in such a way that acts of reference occur in a hearer which are similar in all relevant respects to those which are symbolized by them in the speaker."[26] Accordingly, communication takes place "when one mind so acts upon its environment that another mind is influenced, and in that other mind an experience occurs which is like the experience in the first mind, and is caused in part by that experience." This is a

---

[22]*Ibid.,* pp. vii, viii, 149.

[23]*Principles of Literary Criticism,* p. 261; see, T. C. Pollock: A Critique of I. A. Richards' Theory of Language and Literature, in *A Theory of Meaning Analyzed,* Chicago, 1942, pp. 1-25.

[24]*Principles of Literary Criticism,* p. 177.

[25]*Ibid.,* p. 176.

[26]*The Meaning of Meaning,* pp. 205, 206.

complicated process and capable of degrees in at least two respects. In the first place, two experiences may be more or less similar, and in the second, one experience may be more or less dependent upon the other. All that occurs is that "under certain conditions, separate minds have closely similar experiences."[27]

Richards recognizes certain favorable conditions for communication. Courage or audacity, freedom from pride and conceit, honesty, humaneness, humility, humor, tolerance, good health—the Confucian characteristics of the "superior man"—all these favor communication.[28]

In the absence of special communicative gifts, there is needed a fund of common experience, long and varied acquaintanceship, close familiarity. Even when one possesses special communicative ability, the success of communication in difficult circumstances depends upon the extent to which one may make use of past similarities in experience. Often in difficult circumstances the speaker must supply and control a large part of the causes of the listener's experiences, and correspondingly, the listener must try to block out intrusive, irrelevant elements from his past experiences.[29]

Richards' division of the functions of language yields two types of communication, that which he calls *scientific* and that which he calls *emotive*. Into the first type of communication go those language transactions concerned with strict attention to the symbolization of references. Outside the sciences this form of communication is rare.

In all discussions one finds that what is said is only in part determined by reference, Richards remarks.[30] Preoccupations with things other than referencing often determine the use of words, and unless one is aware of preoccupations, purposes, and interests of the moment, one will not really know what another may be talking about.[31] "When we speak, the symbolism . . . is caused partly by the reference we are making and partly by social and psychological factors—the purpose for which we are making the reference, the proposed effect of our

---

[27]*Principles of Literary Criticism,* pp. 177, 176.
[28]*Ibid.,* p. 180.
[29]*Ibid.,* p. 178.
[30]*The Meaning of Meaning,* p. 126.
[31]*Ibid.,* p. 126.

symbols on other persons, and our own attitude."[32] Presumably to a much greater extent than we realize, we communicate through "offerings of Choices," not through presentation of fact.[33]

Communication may be classified on the basis of the degree to which emotive elements of language usage enters, ranging from strict referential use to poetic use, where the referential purpose is absent altogether or occupies a clearly subordinate position. Poetry, says Richards, affords the clearest examples of the "subordination of reference to attitude. It is the supreme form of *emotive* language."[34] The statements used in poetic discourse are "pseudo-statements." These statements are not justified by their truth or falsity as are the scientific statements; they are justified by their "effect in releasing or organizing our impulses and attitudes."[35] The difference between "emotive beliefs and scientific beliefs" is "not one of degree, but of kind." Thus, there is a truth of "reference" and a truth of "acceptability" of attitude.[36]

In considering the arrangements of words in various kinds of discourse Richards points out that in scientific uses of language not only must the references be correct for success, but the relations of references to one another must be logical. In emotive communications, logical arrangements are not necessary and may actually be an obstacle. Attitudes have their own proper organization, their own emotional interconnection which must be respected.[37]

Since, in the main, Richards is not concerned with specific ends and practices in discourse, his theory of communication presents no theoretical basis for the classification and differentiation of "mixed" uses of language in communication, as, for instance, the sermon, the advertisement, the political speech, the poem. One should note, however, that he has no objection to classifications that serve useful purposes. He does not deny that older classifications of expository communication or persuasive communication, the machinery of epideictic, deliberative, or forensic communications, or lyric and epic

[32]*Ibid.,* pp. 10, 11.
[33]*Speculative Instruments,* p. 139.
[34]*Principles of Literary Criticism,* p. 273.
[35]*Science and Poetry,* New York, 1926, pp. 70, 71.
[36]*Principles of Literary Criticism,* pp. 278, 268, 269.
[37]*Ibid.,* p. 268.

poetry have their uses.[38] He simply denies that such classifications are useful where theoretical considerations of language are uppermost. Language has as many jobs as we find "convenient to distinguish for a purpose,"[39] he observes. Linguistic conveniences, so long as they are not taken to be a description of reality or to "apply directly to the make-up of the mind," are "useful, indispensable for their special purposes."[40]

The student of rhetoric may avoid confusion by remembering that according to Richards, communication which is partly emotive and partly referential, that is, communication which is classed as "mixed," is rhetorical communication. Into the class would go historical writing, most philosophical writing, some poetry, speeches, and discourse of any kind.

When Richards turns explicitly to the subject of Rhetoric, he does so with considerable complaint and suspicion, finding one of the general themes of the old Rhetoric especially pertinent to his discussion. "The old Rhetoric was an offspring of dispute," he remarks; "it developed as the rationale of pleadings and persuadings; it was the theory of the battle of words and has always been itself dominated by the combative impulse. Perhaps what it has most to teach us is the narrowing and blinding influence of that preoccupation, that debater's interest."[41]

Thus, in effect, does Richards in Olympian fashion seem to dispose of the theory underlying the practice of a Pericles, a St. Augustine, a Fenélon, a Burke, a Churchill, a Roosevelt. Nor does he stop there. Outside of some reading in educational theory which leans on psychology, he can find no more disheartening reading than "the dreary pages of those masters of Rhetoric who thought themselves perfectly acquainted wth the subject when they had learnt only to name some of its tools."[42] Thus, seemingly, is dismissed any theory of rhetoric from Aristotle to Whately which had concern with "observing in any given case the available means of persuasion,"[43] or "influencing

---

[38]*How to Read a Page,* New York, 1942, p. 100.

[39]*Ibid.,* p. 100.

[40]*Ibid.,* p. 100; see, also, *The Meaning of Meaning,* p. 95.

[41]*The Philosophy of Rhetoric,* p. 24.

[42]*Interpretation in Teaching,* New York, 1938, p. 11.

[43]Rhetorica, tr. W. Rhys Roberts, *The Works of Aristotle,* ed. W. D. Ross, Oxford, 1924, XI, Bk. I, 2, 1355b.

the *Will*."[44] What sorts of persuasions are there? and to what ends may we reasonably employ them? he asks in derision. "This is a question we all hope to dodge."[45] "Persuasion is only one among the aims of discourse. It poaches on the others—especially on that of *exposition,* which is concerned to state a view, not to persuade people to agree or to do anything more than examine it."[46]

Richards roundly condemns most of the theory and the practices of the past. From the time of the *Gorgias* onwards the literature of rhetoric has been "sales-talk selling sales-talk;" for good reason, we should today be more interested in defensives against eloquent persuasion, not in aids to it.[47]

Although he finds the art of controlled interrogation man's best hope, it becomes man's worst bane when it turns, as it so often does, into a "technique of purblind disputation."[48] Logic-chopping at Cambridge had not convinced him that discussion was very profitable. Finding the traditional vogue of the disputation to be immense, he feels impelled to assert his opposition. "No verbal institution," he remarks, "has done more than disputation to frustrate man, to prevent the referential and emotive functions coming to terms, and to warp the conduct of language—in its highest self-administrating activities most of all." He would take a stand against the "puppy war with words" which has been fought ever since Plato's time. Since immediate specific purpose controls the disputant's interpretations, the disputant is usually too busy making his points to see what the points are.[49] A controversy, says Richards, is "normally an exploitation of a systematic set of misunderstandings for war-like purposes."[50]

According to Richards, the old Rhetoric begins with Aristotle and "may perhaps be said to end with Archbishop Whately." Not chiefly Aristotle, but Whately becomes representative of the old mode of dealing with rhetorical matters, and thus becomes Richards' chief target. Whately, who, according to Richards, begins by urging that

---

[44]Richard Whately: *Elements of Rhetoric,* reprinted from the 7th ed., London, 1866, p. 113.

[45]*Speculative Instruments,* p. 159.

[46]*The Philosophy of Rhetoric,* p. 24.

[47]*Speculative Instruments,* p. 166.

[48]*Ibid.,* p. 131.

[49]*Ibid.,* p. 52.

[50]*The Philosophy of Rhetoric,* p. 39.

"Rhetoric must go deep," ends with merely a "collection of prudential Rules about the best sorts of things to say in various argumentative situations, the order in which to bring out your propositions and proofs and examples, at what point it will be most effective to disparage your opponent, how to recommend oneself to the audience, and like matters." As to all of this, Richards concludes, "no one ever learned about them from a treatise who did not know about them already; at the best, the treatise may be an occasion for realizing that there is skill to be developed in discourse, but it does not and cannot teach the skill." So far as Whately treats style, Richards complains, it is no better. No philosophic inquiry into how words work in discourse emerges; there is nothing more than the "usual postcard's worth of crude common sense" about being clear, being vivacious, not being dry, using metaphors, avoiding ambiguity, etc. The ancients, Richards remarks, merely "play with generalizations" about the effects of words. Such generalizations he finds unimportant unless one goes more deeply and, more particularly, "by another route."[51]

Thus, Richards dismisses the old theory of rhetoric considered as the rationale of persuasive discourse and suggests an approach by another route. A "macroscopic" approach yields neither theoretical nor practical value unless it is supplemented by "an intimate or microscopic inquiry which endeavours to look into the structure of the meanings with which discourse is composed not merely into the effects of various large-scale disposals of these meanings." He admits that there may be much in the old Rhetoric that the new Rhetoric will find useful and advantageous, at least "until man changes his nature, debates and disputes, incites, tricks, bullies and cajoles his fellows less."[52]

Richards appears not to have labored long over the old rhetorical doctrines, particularly the *Inventio* and *Dispositio* phases of ancient doctrine. One does not always find his complaints convincing. To equate *invention* with "finding matters for speech or writing," he remarks, oversimplifies and "narrows interpretation unduly."[53] "It is a

---

[51]*Ibid.*, pp. 5, 7, 8, 9.
[52]*Ibid.*, pp. 9, 24.
[53]*Speculative Instruments,* p. 157.

very frequent meaning, without doubt," he continues, "but neither the only meaning nor the most active meaning in Tarquin's cry, 'O what excuse can my invention make?' "[54] He finds that the "senses of devising, fabricating, discovering, and originating were all current in Shakespeare's time."[55] He complains of Dryden's equating of imagination with Invention, as one of the "humdrum senses of imagination."[56] He presumably is unaware of the adaptations to poetic theory of the classical conception of Invention in the Renaissance. According to Marvin Herrick, "The sixteenth-century commentators and critics, by combining . . . [the] Aristotelian imitation with theories found in Plato, Cicero, Horace, and Quintilian, arrived at a concept of imitation that closely corresponded to the traditional invention of logic and rhetoric. In fact, by the middle of the century, *imitatio, inventio, fictio,* and *fabula* were corollary terms, often used as synonyms."[57] Richards' complaint that the standard classical conception of Invention "narrows interpretation unduly" may well be the case; but such a judgment could appropriately be made only after full awareness of the inclusiveness of the meaning of the ancient canon.

Richards' misinterpretation follows naturally from his conception of the classical rhetoric. "Rhetorical theory," he observes, "in its entire scope is after all no more than a somewhat chaotic collection of observations made on the ways of lively, venturesome speech and writing."[58] Sections in the old rhetorics which dealt with audiences or with "Hearers as Men, in General," Richards remarks facetiously, "should favour mercy."[59] His cavalier handling of ancient doctrines causes R. S. Crane to reprimand him for dismissing "rival" doctrines and substituting others "prior to any inquiry;"[60] and H. M. McLuhan

---

[54]*Ibid.,* p. 157; see, Shakespeare: *The Rape of Lucrece,* Line 225.

[55]*Ibid.,* p. 157.

[56]*Coleridge on the Imagination,* New York, 1950, p. 27.

[57]Marvin T. Herrick: The Place of Rhetoric in Poetic Theory, *The Quarterly Journal of Speech, XXXIV:*13, February 1948.

[58]*Speculative Instruments,* p. 158.

[59]*Interpretation in Teaching,* p. 13; see, George Campbell: *The Philosophy of Rhetoric,* 7th ed., London, 1823, Bk. I, Ch. vii, p. 87.

[60]R. S. Crane: I. A. Richards on the Art of Interpretation, *Critics and Criticism,* ed. R. S. Crane, Chicago, Illinois, University of Chicago Press, 1952, p. 44.

ascribes too quickly, no doubt, the label "true nominalist son of . . . Agricola, and Ramus."[61]

In Richards, what was first proposed as a supplement becomes the entire rationale for his philosophy of rhetoric. The new rhetoric which arises is a rhetoric concerned, not with persuasion as a specific end, but with the meanings of statements in any type of discourse. The new rhetoric, Richards urges, "should be a study of misunderstanding and its remedies." It should concern itself with "How much and in how many ways may good communication differ from bad?"[62]

"Rhetoric I take to be 'the art by which discourse is adapted to its end,' " says Richards, echoing the well-known definition of George Campbell's eighteenth-century *The Philosophy of Rhetoric*.[63] What should be among its topics may be seen from the contents of Campbell's book, he says, "a book which deserves more attention than it is likely ever again to receive."[64] He does not believe that Campbell fulfilled his promise, but had he done so, he would have given us "all we need to know."[65]

As Richards turns to the general task of a new rhetoric, he is concerned both with the task and with the mode of presentation of principles. One should teach rhetoric, "not by dogmatic formula but *by exercises in comparison.*" Such exercises should give an understanding of the different modes of speech, their changing forms, and their disguises. The chief divisions of the field for comparison may be "statement, full and explicit, or condensed (by abstraction, ambiguity or implication, the hint, the aposiopesis); statement literal or direct, and indirect (by metaphor, simile, comparison, parallel etc.); suasion, open (from appeal to cajolery) or concealed (either as mere statement or as mere ornament) and so on." The more particular problems of rhetoric he believes to be problems concerning the Figures of Speech, about which present practice is deceiving and out of date.[66]

The art of rhetoric, says Richards, should be a "philosophic

---

[61]H. M. McLuhan: Poetic vs. Rhetorical Exegesis, *Sewanee Review*, 52:266-276, Winter 1944.

[62]*The Philosophy of Rhetoric*, p. 3.

[63]*Interpretation in Teaching*, p. 12; Cf. Campbell, Bk. I, Ch. 1, p. 13.

[64]*Interpretation in Teaching*, p. 12.

[65]*Ibid.*, p. 13.

[66]*Ibid.*, pp. 14, 15.

discipline aiming at a mastery of the fundamental laws of the use of language, not just a set of dodges that will be found to work sometimes."[67] Philosophy he takes to be a critique of assumptions; hence, a philosophy of rhetoric would have as its concern assumptions about the nature of language.

"To account for understanding and misunderstanding, to study the efficiency of language and its conditions," which he believes to be the role of the new rhetoric, is to face squarely the fact that meanings do not reside in words, but in responders to words, that ambiguity, instead of being a fault of language, is its inevitable condition, that metaphor, instead of being a "happy extra trick," is the constitutive nature of language, thought itself being metaphoric. Richards urges that we renounce the view "that words just have their meanings and that what a discourse does is to be explained as a composition of these meanings—as a wall can be represented as a composition of its bricks." The focus of analysis, he argues, should be shifted in order to attempt a more minute grasp of the structures of the smallest discussable units of meaning, and the ways in which these units vary when they are put with other units.[68]

Richards' contextual theory of meaning, thus, paves the way for his conception of the new rhetoric and suggests its role as being that of separating the referential function of language from the other language functions.[69]

After pondering the question, What is the relationship of rhetoric, grammar, and logic? Richards concludes that these three ways to intelligence cannot be separated without frustration. "By Definition things arise," giving us "things-to-be-thought-of." When things are thought of, those things are determined both by references and by other psychological factors. This intermingling of language functions makes for inconstancy. Richards urges a frank recognition of the fact that how any word is used is a matter of choice and consent and not a matter of regimentation or compulsion. Meanings are to be determined by how words are used in a sentence and not by any discrete senses they are imagined to possess.[70] Logic must be the

---

[67]*The Philosophy of Rhetoric*, p. 7.
[68]*Ibid.*, pp. 9, 10, 90, 93.
[69]*Interpretation in Teaching*, p. 395.
[70]*Ibid.*, pp. 3, 393, 395.

systematizer. Logic, which has been "preoccupied either with judgments which are psychological, or with 'propositions,' which were treated as objects of thought, distinct from symbols and not psychological," should be concerned with "the systematization of symbols."[71] "All thought is sorting."[72] Logic is the "Art or discipline of managing our sortings." It is the "ethics of thinking."[73]

The relationship of grammar to rhetoric and logic is that grammar is pervasive. Since words do not have proper meanings, but meanings only in relation to a context, grammar is the *"study of the co-operation of words with one another in their contexts."*[74]

Richards conception of the relation of rhetoric to logic and grammar may be revealed by his formulary statement: "The Optative view of Definition (which is the central problem of Logic) makes the creation of the things-to-be-thought-of, that is, the demarcation of Sense from the other language functions (which is the central problem of Rhetoric) a matter of our choice—subject, however, always to the exigencies of communication, that is the provision of sufficiently stable inter-verbal action (which is the central problem of Grammar)."[75]

This, then, is the new Rhetoric. It is concerned with the differentiation of referential and emotive language functions in order to produce understanding or to explain misunderstanding in any type of discourse. It assumes that if one understands the language functions, appropriate uses of language may be chosen for whatever end one may want to advance, be it to state a view clearly, to establish a right relationship with an audience, a right relationship with a subject, win an election, or record one's feelings about things in poetry. It is a study of language behavior and reveals how discourse in being adapted to its end reflects the referential and emotive language functions, the many manoeuverings of which language guided by purpose is capable. It is concerned with the smallest structural units of discourse and not with the large-scale ordonnance of arguments.

The theoretical position of Richards with reference to rhetoric and

---

[71]*The Meaning of Meaning,* p. 87.
[72]*Interpretation in Teaching,* p. 359.
[73]*Ibid.,* p. 16.
[74]*Ibid.,* p. 16.
[75]*Ibid.,* p. 395.

communication has been strongly felt in the field of criticism. With care and precision equal to that manifested in his articulation of a theory of communication and meaning, Richards has articulated a critical theory that has given him significance in modern times.

John Crowe Ransom, long-time editor of the *Kenyon Review,* has remarked that "Discussion of the new criticism must start with Mr. Richards. The new criticism very nearly began with him."[76] With this statement few would disagree. Whereas one may find difficulty in defining the precise nature of the New Criticism, he would find the direction of the critical movement clear enough. Criticism simply shifted from a poet-poem or speaker-speech relationship to a poem-audience or speech-audience relationship. Finding metaphysical concern with such questions as What is poetry? or What is a poet? unfruitful, Richards turned to explore what the reader or listener gets from discourse. Poetry became for him an instrument by which experience of some kind is communicated to a reader or listener. To a generation accustomed to contemplating the beauties of poetry as aesthetic object, he asserted in somewhat lowly fashion, "But poetry itself is a mode of communication."[77] What it communicates and how it does so and the worth of what is communicated form the subject-matter of criticism. It follows that criticism . . . is very largely, though not wholly, an exercise in navigation."[78] Thus was paved the introduction of a psychological approach to criticism to oppose metaphysical approaches.

We are not concerned with the influence of Richards on the new critical movement, although with Cleanth Brooks we may agree that he may be regarded as the critic "through whose mediation psychology was to make its greatest impact upon literary criticism."[79] We are concerned with the relevance of Richards to the student of rhetoric, for whatever else rhetoric may be, its concern is with communication. Since Richards does not view literature as a private haven for aesthetes, his remarks may be generalized. In truth, he generalizes

[76]John Crowe Ransom: *The New Criticism,* Norfolk, Connecticut, 1941, p. 3.

[77]*Practical Criticism,* New Impression, New York, 1954, p. 11.

[78]*Ibid.,* p. 11.

[79]William K. Wimsatt, Jr. & Cleanth Brooks: *Literary Criticism,* New York, 1957, p. 613; see also, Stanley Hyman: I. A. Richards and the Criticism of Interpretation, *The Armed Vision,* New York, 1948, p. 308.

them himself. "The world of poetry," he remarks, "has in no sense any different reality from the rest of the world and it has no special laws and no other-worldly peculiarities. It is made up of experiences of exactly the same kinds as those that come to us in other ways."[80]

The chief weakness of our best criticism today, Richards remarks, "is the pretense that fundamental matters can be profitably discussed without prolonged and technical thinking." Accordingly, "Most evaluative criticism is not statement or even attempted statement. It is either suasion, which is politics, or it is social communion."[81] Critics and even theorists in criticism currently assume, he remarks, "that their first duty is to be moving, to excite in the mind emotions appropriate to their august subject-matter."[82] Nor will case-history studies of utterances as socio-economic-political products solve current critical problems. Although we should encourage them, since they "feed the scholars who make them," these critical studies, which may tell us "*why* something was said," do not in their present form tell "*what it was*" that was said.[83] Critics, he believes, have hardly begun to ask the question what they are doing and under what conditions they are working.[84]

As Richards understands it, criticism is "the endeavour to discriminate between experiences and to evaluate them." This cannot be done, he believes, without an understanding of the nature of experience, or without theories of value and communication. The principles which apply to criticism must be taken from more fundamental studies. So far as he can see, "critical remarks are merely a branch of psychological remarks."[85]

On the foundation of his theory of language and communication Richards raises his critical structure. Criticism is the "science of . . . meanings and the meanings which larger groups of words may carry." It is not a mere account of what men have written or how they have written, with answers to such questions being determined by borrowed

---

[80]*Principles of Literary Criticism*, p. 78.
[81]*Coleridge on the Imagination*, pp. 5, xiii.
[82]*Principles of Literary Criticism*, p. 3.
[83]*Speculative Instruments*, p. 82.
[84]*Principles of Literary Criticism*, p. 227.
[85]*Ibid.*, pp. 2, 23.

standards, often applied without reference to the nature of the mind or to our growing outlook on the world.[86]

To Richards the critic must have three qualifications. He must be first "an adept at experiencing, without eccentricities, the state of mind relevant to the work of art he is judging. Secondly, he must be able to distinguish experiences from one another as regards their less superficial features. Thirdly, he must be a sound judge of values."[87]

Criticism has only one goal. All critical endeavor, all interpretation, appreciation, exhortation, praise, or abuse has as its goal "improvement in communication." Although he is aware that such a conception may appear to be an exaggeration, nevertheless he asserts that in practice this is true. Critical rules and principles are but means to the end of attaining more precise and more discriminating communication. There is, he admits, "a valuation side of criticism," but he asserts that "When we have solved, completely, the communication problem, when we have got, perfectly, the experience, *the mental condition* relevant," the problem of worth "nearly always settles itself; or rather, our own inmost nature and the nature of the world in which we live decide it for us." Value, he believes, cannot be demonstrated except through the communication of what is valuable.[88]

As Richards begins his critical theory he announces that there are two pillars upon which a theory of criticism must rest. These are an account of value and an account of communication.[89] The judgment "that a passage is good is an act of living. The examination and description of its merits is an act of theory."[90] A full critical statement, accordingly, consists of two parts. The part which describes the value of the experience Richards refers to as the *critical* part. The part dealing with a description of the object arousing the experience he refers to as the *technical* part.[91]

His critical system presents the theory underlying the judgment of both sides of the coin. His first concern is with the question, What kind of experiences are good? "What is good or valuable," he re-

---

[86]*Coleridge on the Imagination,* pp. 231, 232.
[87]*Principles of Literary Criticism,* p. 114.
[88]*Practical Criticism,* pp. 11, 12.
[89]*Principles of Literary Criticism,* p. 25.
[90]*Coleridge on the Imagination,* p. 140.
[91]*Principles of Literary Criticism,* p. 23.

marks, "is the exercise of impulses and the satisfaction of their appetencies." An impulse, he defines as the "process in the course of which a mental event may occur, a process . . . beginning in a stimulus and ending in an act." An appetency is a "seeking after." He admits that the word *desire* might serve as well as appetency, were it not for the fact that one cannot easily avoid the implication of accompanying conscious beliefs with reference to what is sought and a further restriction to felt and recognized longings. For him, the term *want* has similar disadvantages. "Appetencies may be, and for the most part are, unconscious, and to leave out those which we cannot discover by introspection would involve extensive errors." For the same reason it is wiser not to start from *feeling.* He extends his conception of what is good or valuable by concluding, "Anything is valuable which will satisfy an appetency without involving the frustration of some equal or *more important* appetency; in other words, the only reason which can be given for not satisfying a desire is that more important desires will thereby be thwarted." The most valuable states of mind are those "which involve the widest and most comprehensive co-ordination of activities and the least curtailment, conflict, starvation, and restriction." The most valuable effects of communicative activity are those to be described in terms of *attitudes,* "the resolution, interinanimation, and balancing of impulses." In a well-developed person imaginal action and incipient action, that is, action which does not go so far as actual movement, is more important than overt action.[92]

As Richards turns to the matter of communication, he remarks that the important fact for the study of literature or any mode of communication is that several kinds of meaning are to be differentiated. Either in speaking and writing or in reading and listening, the "Total Meaning we are engaged with is, almost always, a blend, a combination of several contributory meanings of different types." A critic, therefore, concerned with the matter of discrimination, must first discern what meanings are being communicated, and thereafter, how successfully these are being communicated.[93]

Most human utterance and nearly all articulate speech, he believes, can be profitably regarded from four points of view. The four aspects

---

[92]*Ibid.,* pp. 58, 86, 47, 48, 59, 113, 111.
[93]*Practical Criticism,* p. 180.

which are distinguishable he calls Sense, Feeling, Tone, and Intention. "We speak to say something," he remarks, "and when we listen we expect something to be said. We use words to direct our hearers' attention upon some state of affairs, to present to them some items for consideration and to excite in them some thoughts about these items." This is what Richards means by *Sense,* and, as may be readily recognized, it pertains to the matter of making references. Secondly, we have some "feelings *about these items.*" We have attitudes, biases, and interests with respect to these items, and we use language to reflect these attitudes, interests, and feelings. Thus, *Feeling,* or attitude towards referents, becomes another dimension of meaning. Thirdly, the speaker ordinarily has *"an attitude to his listener."* His word choice and arrangement is largely governed by audience variation in automatic or deliberate "recognition of his relation to them." This is the *Tone* dimension of meaning, in terms of which Richards believes many of the secrets of style could be shown to reside. Finally, speakers have intentions or aims, conscious or unconscious; they desire to secure effects. Purpose modifies one's speech. An understanding of this dimension of meaning, purpose or intention, is "part of the whole business of apprehending . . . meaning." According to Richards, unless we know what a speaker is trying to do, we are unable to estimate the measure of success. Sometimes, Richards notes, a speaker will "purpose no more than to state his thoughts (1), or to express his feelings about what he is thinking of, e.g., Hurrah! Damn! (2), or to express his attitude to his listener (3)." "Frequently his intention operates through and satisfies itself in a combination of the other functions. Yet it has effects not reducible to their effects. It may govern the stress laid upon points in an argument for example, shape the arrangement, and even call attention to itself in such phrases as 'for contrast's sake' or 'lest it be supposed.' " Nevertheless, it "controls the 'plot' in the largest sense of the word, and is at work whenever the author [or speaker] is 'hiding his hand.' "[94]

The difference between better or worse utterances, says Richards, is in "design." Poor speech and poor writing is poor "either because it is not attempting anything worth trying or because it is inefficient."[95]

---

[94]*Ibid.,* pp. 181, 182, 207, 182, 183.
[95]*Speculative Instruments,* p. 122.

Critics often demonstrate unmistakable confusion between value and communicative efficacy.[96] A complete critical statement would be a statement about the value of experience and also a statement about communicative efficacy through which the experience is revealed Thus, Richards' critical theory and practice represent an attempt tc be microscopic in approach, just as does his rhetorical theory and practice.

CONCLUSION

"We struggle all our days with misunderstandings," remarks Richards as he contemplates the process of reviving an old subject, and "no apology is required for any study which can prevent or remove them."[97] That rhetoric as a term has been equivocal throughout its lifetime can scarcely be gainsaid. It has been a term of abuse as well as a virtue word, a term referring to the whole rationale of persuasive discourse, and a term referring to means. Has Richards clarified or confused the concept?

When *The Meaning of Meaning* emerged from the press in 1923, Richards and his collaborator announced a new "science of symbolism." By making the "beginning of a division between what cannot be intelligibly talked of and what can" the authors believed the new science to be in a position to "provide a new basis for Physics,"[98] to solve the most important problems of the theory of knowledge, to dispose of the problem of Truth, and to provide a definitive basis for scientific aesthetics.[99] These were considerably pretentious claims which, of course, have not completely yielded the harvest expected. That the few topics discussed in *The Philosophy of Rhetoric* are to be regarded as solving the problem of understanding and misunderstanding is doubtful. One feels considerable sympathy with the remark of F. R. Leavis, "had the ambition been less the profit might very well have been greater." The "largeness of promise and an impressiveness of operation [are] quite disproportionate to anything that emerges."[100]

---

[96]*Principles of Literary Criticism,* p. 255.

[97]*The Philosophy of Rhetoric,* p. 3.

[98]*The Meaning of Meaning,* pp. vii, 85.

[99]See Max Black: Some Objections to Ogden and Richards' Theory of Interpretation, *The Journal of Philosophy, XXXIX*:281, May 21, 1942.

[100]F. R. Leavis: Review of *The Philosophy of Rhetoric, Scrutiny, VI*:212, September 1937.

As has sometimes been remarked, the importance of Richards' work on communication has been obscured for many people by their annoyance at a too frequent outcropping of the "amateur spirit." A romantic inflation about the significance of the topic, dark hints about the extent of our ignorance, the cataclysm that awaits us unless we accept his new theories, the ready dismissal of all who have gone before him—all these intrude upon the reader to make him suspicious of the performance. "No matter what a man's standing, and no matter how impressive the substance of his views, you can still regard him from an unassailable vantage-ground if only you happen to observe that he isn't capable of understanding what is said to him."[101]

Nevertheless, that Richards is a thoughtful man no one can doubt. Nor can one doubt that he has been a profound student of communication and rhetoric. R. S. Crane has posed a problem which may be seriously regarded by all students of rhetoric: "For what is the force of an appeal to the nature of things against rival doctrines of language or discourse when that nature itself has been determined by a decision, prior to any inquiry, to identify reality only with what can be signified in a particular fixed relationship among three equivocal words. And what is there to compel an abandonment of the distinctions of traditional grammar or logic in an argument which derives all its negative cogency from a metaphor so admirably adapted to the end of destroying such distinctions as that upon which Richards' system is based?"[102]

It would be easy to answer Crane's question with a resounding protest to the effect that there is nothing to compel an abandonment of traditional distinctions. The answer, I think, would not really be a response to Richards' theory. B. F. Skinner has reminded us that classical rhetoric might have been the forerunner of a science of verbal behavior. It began as an objective discipline, closer, perhaps, to a science than either the logic or grammar of the same period. Hundreds of technical terms were developed to describe linguistic features. As rhetoric came to be used for purposes of ornamentation and persuasion, it died as a pure science. "What is wanted is *an account of the events which occur when a man speaks or responds to speech.*"[103]

---

[101]D. W. Harding: I. A. Richards, *Scrutiny*, *I*:336, March 1933.

[102]R. S. Crane: p. 44.

[103]B. F. Skinner: *Verbal Behavior* (William James Lectures), Harvard University, 1948, pp. 4, 5.

No one doubts that there is a rhetoric of practice and persuasion. Richards does not doubt this either. Indeed, without much casuistry, one could argue that Richards does not believe language communications are anything other than instances of persuasion, for he remarks that he "regards all discourse—outside the technicalities of science—as over-determined," that is, as having "multiplicity of meaning" due to the co-presence of referential and other functions of language.[104] Contemporary literary men have found Richards' theory distasteful on this point, that is, that he is willing to place his emphasis in poetry on external relations with an audience rather than on integrated structure to be contemplated for pleasure.[105]

Richards leans heavily upon George Campbell's conception of rhetoric, as the "adaptation of discourse to its ends," and Campbell has long been considered an eighteenth-century interpreter of the classical tradition in rhetoric. Furthermore, Richards has noted the disregard by contemporary scholars of their classical forbears. When, says he, "not long ago some of the very same concerns revived which had originally prompted the *Topica* and the *Rhetoric,* not many of those who set out, behind 'anti-metaphysical' or 'non-Aristotelian' banners, to teach us all how we should talk, evinced much curiosity about the ancient highways leading into their well-advertised new territory."[106]

One cannot easily make an anticlassicist out of Richards. One can far more easily make his work a vast subdivision of the classical tradition. When he opens his *Interpretation in Teaching,* he remarks: "Rhetoric, Grammar, and Logic—the first three liberal Arts, the three ways to intelligence and a command of the mind that met in the Trivium, meet here again." Neither "the general problem nor the plan of attack can be new."[107] "How to *make* minds clear as well as

---

[104]*The Philosophy of Rhetoric,* p. 39.
[105]See H. M. McLuhan: Poetic vs. Rhetorical Exegesis, *op. cit.,* pp. 266-276; also, Charles I. Glicksberg: I. A. Richards and the Science of Criticism, *Sewanee Review, XLVI*:520-533, Oct.-Dec. 1938; also, John Crowe Ransom: A Psychologist Looks at Poetry, in *The World's Body,* New York, 1938, pp. 143-165; also, Christopher Isherwood: *Lions and Shadows,* London, 1933, pp. 121, 122.
[106]*Speculative Instruments,* pp. 164, 165.
[107]*Interpretation in Teaching,* p. 3.

keep them clear," he says, "is . . . for us, as it was for Socrates, the key question."[108]

Allying the wisdom of the past with insights from all times, Richards has presented a "microscopic" supplement to ancient patterns, a gigantic supplement. His desire was to make language theory yield to experimental procedure, to refine and make precise that which has sometimes been cloudy or mystical. Significant scientists of language, including Charles Morris, have paid tribute to his "pioneer" work in the field of semeiotic, and a large segment of rhetorical scientists at work today testify to the helpfulness of the pioneering.[109]

Rhetoric and poetic severely separated in the nineteenth century meet again in the twentieth century through Richards in the ancient trivium, Rhetoric, Grammar, and Logic. This writer suspects that the future is in the direction of Richards. As understanding increases, a mere falling back upon tradition will not work. Sheer ecstasy and cults of the obscure will give way to ordered procedures and uses of the best tools for analysis that are available, whatever the field from which they come.

---

[108]*Speculative Instruments,* p. 71.
[109]Charles Morris: *Signs, Language and Behavior,* New York, 1946, pp. vii, 265.